*The Protestant Ethic
and Modernization*

THE

Edited by

S. N. Eisenstadt

BASIC BOOKS, INC.,

PROTESTANT ETHIC AND MODERNIZATION

A Comparative View

Publishers, New York, London

To the Memory of Yonina Talmon

PREFACE

This collection of essays illustrates the development of scientific discussion and controversy around one of the most provocative theses in the social sciences: Max Weber's famous Protestant ethic thesis.

In the beginning this controversy was centered on the European and, to some extent, the American scene. Lately it has been taken up in the wider context of studies of modernization and development, thus bringing it back to the broad framework of comparative studies as Weber first conceived it.

The fascination which this thesis has exerted was due not only to its specific details but, as attested by the essays collected here, to its broader analytical implications in general and to its importance for the study of modernity in particular.

The essays presented here can be divided into three parts. First, essays dealing with the exposition of Weber's thesis within the context of his general sociological analyses. Second, essays which deal with various specific aspects of his thesis in the context of Europe and America. Third, essays which deal with attempts to test the applicability of the thesis or of its derivatives, or which apply a similar approach, to non-European settings.

I would like to thank Mrs. R. Shaco for her help in preparing the book for print.

S. N. Eisenstadt

The Hebrew University, Jerusalem
November 1967

CONTENTS

I

THE PROTESTANT ETHIC THESIS IN THE FRAMEWORK OF SOCIOLOGICAL THEORY AND OF WEBER'S WORK

1

THE PROTESTANT ETHIC
THESIS IN AN ANALYTICAL AND
COMPARATIVE FRAMEWORK

S. N. Eisenstadt

I

Weber's famous "Protestant Ethic" thesis,[1] which attributed the rise of modern, as distinct from premodern, types of capitalism[2] to the influence of Protestantism and especially of Calvinism, has provided, probably more than any other single *specific thesis* in the social sciences, a continuous focus of scientific controversy. In each decade this controversy has erupted anew, each generation of scholars seeing in it a continuing challenge. Although in each generation there were some, like Robertson in the twenties, Fanfani in the thirties, and Samuelsson in the fifties,[3] who denied it any validity, yet somehow even such denials had to be stressed again and again. Each generation had to grapple with the fact that so many still attributed to Weber's thesis some central importance in social sciences in general and in the understanding of modernity in particular. During the last fifteen years or so, with the expansion of economic development and modernization in non-Western countries, interest in Weber's thesis has stirred once more. Many seek in the Protestant ethic or some equivalent the key to an understanding of why some non-Western countries have achieved modernization while others have not.

In order to be able to understand what it is in this thesis that may be of such critical importance, it would be worth while to survey very briefly some of the major stages of the controversy that has grown up around it. It is, of course, impossible to present a complete history of the controversy.

A shorter version of this essay was read before the Israel Academy of Humanities and Sciences.

We may very broadly distinguish between two types of arguments with regard to the Weberian thesis. They correspond to some extent with the chronological stages in the argument's development.

The first stage of this controversy, best summarized in Fischoff's article and in Beerling's book,[4] has mostly, although not entirely, dealt with the analysis of the alleged direct causal connection between the Protestant-Calvinist ethic on the one hand and the development of capitalism on the other. At this stage, the Weberian thesis was attacked at almost all the quotients of the assumed equation. Some have stressed that most of the initial Calvinist communities—be it Calvin's Geneva itself or the earlier Calvinist communities in the Netherlands, Scotland, or the Palatinate—did not favor the development of new, more autonomous economic orientations or organizations, that in their manifest attitudes to economic activity they did not go far beyond the more severe medieval Catholic orientation, and that in some respects they were even more conservative and restrictive with regard to such activity. The Calvinists' predilection for extreme, all-encompassing religious regulation of all aspects of life, the argument runs, made them take all these matters more seriously than Catholics of the late Middle Ages.

On the other side, it was often stressed that the first great upsurges of capitalism occurred in pre-Reformation Catholic Europe—in Italy, Belgium, Germany—and that capitalism was more "developed" there than in the first Protestant or Calvinist countries. On the contrary, very often in many of these latter communities, as for instance in Calvin's Geneva, economic retrogression or retardation set in—to no small degree because of the restrictive orientation of the Protestants.

Others have cast doubt on the specific "mechanism" by which, according to Weber, Calvinist belief became transformed into, or linked to, motivation for worldly economic activity—namely, the psychological derivatives of the idea of predestination. The great anxiety which this idea created among believers supposedly urged them to undertake, in a compulsive way, worldly activity to prove that they were among the elect.

Whereas some doubted the relevance of any aspect of the Calvinist religion for the development of modern economic structures and activities, others such as Hudson and lately the Georges[5] pointed to different aspects of the Calvinist *Weltanschauung* that might have facilitated capitalistic development.[6] They mention, for example, the emphasis on individual responsibility, on "this world" as against the "otherworldly" orientation of many other religions, as well as the general shattering of the traditional *Weltanschauung*.

Still others who admitted the "disposition" of Protestantism to various aspects of the "modern" world—be they economic, scientific, or political—tended to attribute this disposition to the exigencies of the wars of religion and of the Counter Reformation. In the countries in which these movements took place, Protestantism was in a minority position. Some also attributed Protestantism's congruity with the modern world to its indirect impact on the over-all institutional structure of these countries in the direction of pluralism and tolerance. It has often been stressed that the tendency of many Protestant groups—Huguenots in France or in exile, Protestant sects in Holland and England—to participate more actively than their Catholic or even Lutheran neighbors in modern capitalistic enterprises, usually developed later, in the seventeenth and eighteenth centuries. This very often had little to do with the tenets of Calvinism itself. Rather it could be explained by the fact that Protestant groups had been persecuted, forced to emigrate, and denied participation in political and cultural activities.

Still others believed that the tendency of Protestants to participate in capitalistic activities was a later development. Such activity was not necessarily typical of the main stream of Calvinism or Protestantism, but was perhaps symptomatic of its adjustment to a more pluralistic, tolerant, semisecularized world and of the decline of its own strong religious commitments. For these writers it was often the *weakening* of the original "totalistic" religious impulses of the Puritans that provided the basic link between Protestants and modernity.

Tawney's classic study,[7] intended as a sympathetic defense of Weber against many of his earlier critics, did not, however, address itself to the kernel of this theme. It is basically a detailed analysis of exactly such processes of motivational change among Puritan groups in the direction of secularization and of the growing emphasis on economic motives and activities within a society which was becoming more and more "tolerant" and secular.

Thus in almost all the criticisms of this stage of the controversy we find an ambivalent attitude toward Weber's thesis. On the one hand, we find a critique of the alleged direct causal relationship between the rise of Protestantism and the development of economic activities which Weber described in their concrete European and American settings. On the other hand, most of these critics, with the exception of the extreme negativists, such as Robertson, Fanfani, and Samuelsson, admitted that despite everything there was "something" in the Weberian thesis. In one way or another they acknowledged that there was a kernel of truth in Weber's thesis without, however, defining exactly what this kernel of truth might be, except in very broad, general terms such as those outlined above.

II

In order to understand this "kernel" more fully it is necessary to proceed to the second phase of the controversy. The second type of argument occurs first in the earlier works of Troeltsch and Holl.[8] Although these two scholars were in seemingly opposing camps—Troeltsch supporting

Weber's thesis and Holl at least partially denying it—they did have something in common. Neither Troeltsch nor Holl was mainly concerned with analyzing the mechanisms by which the alleged causal relationship between Protestantism and capitalist activity was effected. Troeltsch fully acknowledged that the initial impetus of Calvinism was what would nowadays be called a totalistic one—that is, an attempt to establish a new civilization totally regulated by religious precepts.

But for him—and, according to him, also for Weber—the major problem was not whether this initial orientation promoted or even facilitated various types of modern activities but rather what was Protestantism's influence once it failed to carry out its first totalistic impulses.

Holl's main polemics against both Weber and Troeltsch have been mostly in defense of Lutheranism—which has often been depicted as the more conservative force in the Reformation, with few transformative powers, as compared with the more dynamic, revolutionary Calvinism. In opposition to this view of Lutheranism, Holl claimed that, from a broad comparative standpoint (one which in his work includes an analysis of the Eastern Church), Lutheranism did contain a dynamic, transformative tendency of its own. This, he held, while differing from that of Calvinism —being more centered on the individual and less on the *religious community*—could yet, given appropriate conditions, contribute a great influence on the forms of modern life and culture.[9]

But this type of approach to Weber's thesis was largely neglected since the thirties and has only recently been taken up again—often without reference to the earlier studies—by various scholars. Of these a brief discussion of the work of Trevor-Roper, Lüthy, and Walzer[10] will best serve for purposes of analysis.

Lüthy—and to some extent Trevor-Roper—denies the correctness of Weber's thesis in the economic field proper. They claim that economic development in Europe was independent of the impact of Protestantism. They show, for instance, as others did before them, that the first impact of Protestantism on economic life was, as Calvin's Geneva shows, a restrictive one. But they admit—indeed stress—that especially England, the Netherlands, and to some extent the Scandinavian countries were more successful, after the Counter Reformation, in developing viable, continuous, flexible modern institutions—economic, political, and scientific—than most Catholic countries, like Spain, Italy, or even France, in which many modern institutional frameworks first arose.

On one level of argument it seems as if to Lüthy and Trevor-Roper, as to some of their precursors, this was mostly due to the exigencies of the victory of Protestantism and not necessarily to anything inherent in the Protestant religion in general or in Calvinism and Puritanism in particular. However, on another level the picture is somewhat different. Thus, for instance, Lüthy transposes Weber's theory almost entirely to the political field. For him the major impact of Protestantism on European history has been in politics. This was effected, according to him, through direct reference to the Bible as a source for new bases of legitimation of authority as well as through the new impetus to the development of pluralistic settings which developed as an outcome of the Counter Reformation and the Wars of Religion.

In principle the type of criticism that Lüthy levels against Weber could be easily leveled against his own thesis. It is easy to show that the original political impulse of both Lutheranism and Calvinism was not in a "liberal" or democratic direction but rather in a more totalistic one. Whatever the correctness of such a criticism of details, it would be largely misdirected. Lüthy's analyses deal, not with the direct economic or political "results" of the activities of certain religious groups, but rather, as was the case in the works of Troeltsch and Holl, with their transformative effects.

From this point of view Lüthy's more specific work on the Protestant Bank is very significant.[11] In this he shows how the ultimate difference between Catholic "finance" and Protestant "banks" lay in the extent to which the latter was not tied to a given political order but was conceived as an autonomous sphere of organized activity, supported by the legitimation of an autonomous economic calculus. This legitimation could have been derived from the Calvinist ethic but developed in Geneva largely after the downfall of the initial totalistic-religious regime there. In France the monarchs came to rely on the (mostly foreign) Protestant banks only after the Huguenots had been expelled and the royal (traditional, Catholic) finances were bankrupt.

Parallel indications have been discussed even more fully by Walzer in his independent analysis of the two groups instrumental in the shaping of Puritanism in England—the intelligentsia (ministers, students, and lay intellectuals) and the gentry. Walzer shows that originally the impulses of Calvinism were directed, not to the economic arena, but to the political one and that in this field they were also initially mostly totalistic.[12] He goes on to show, in great detail, how, after the initial failure of these totalistic impulses, in which the Puritans became a persecuted minority—and especially an *exiled* minority of "intellectuals"—there took place a transformation of their orientations and energies in the direction of constructing new rules, organizations, new patterns of human connections, and a new society and polity.

III

Thus Lüthy's work on the bank and Walzer's analysis of the Puritan intelligentsia contain very important indications for a full re-examination of the Weberian thesis in its broadest analytical and comparative applications. What is required for this re-examination is a shift of attention from the allegedly direct, causal relationship between Protestantism and capitalism (or other aspects of the modern world) to the internal transformative capacities of Protestantism and to their impact on the transformation of the modern world.

It is true, of course, that the Reformation was originally not a "modernizing" movement but one whose initial aim was the establishment of a new, purer, sociopolitical religious order. Originally Protestantism was a religious movement aimed at the religious restructuring of the world. It was just because of its strong "this-worldly" religious impulses that from the very beginning Protestantism was caught up in the midst of sociopolitical, economic, and cultural changes that European (especially western and central European) society was undergoing from the end of the seventeenth century on. Such new major trends were the development of capitalism, the rise of Renaissance states, absolutism and the consequent "general" crisis of the seventeenth century (that is, the crisis between "state" and "society"), the development of a secular outlook, and progress in science.[13]

The Reformation did not directly bring about any of these developments, although it did contribute indirectly to the weakening of the traditional framework of European society. Many of these developments stemmed from the same broad roots as did the Reformation—namely, the crisis of Catholic civilization in general and of the Catholic Church in particular. But the groups that fostered them—for example, the humanists such as Erasmus and the new international merchants such as the Fuggers—on the whole differed from the religious reformers, although they sometimes overlapped and often served as important mutual reference groups.

The significance of Protestantism is to be found, not in any direct effect it had on economic, political, or scientific activity, but in the contribution it made toward the restructuring of European society in general. This restructuring came about as a result of all these new developments but in the post-Counter Reformation period came to fuller fruition in the Protestant than in the Catholic countries. This was because of the transformative potential of Protestanism as it developed in certain settings. The crucial impact of Protestantism in the direction of modernity came after it could not fully realize its initial totalistic socioreligious aims. Thus the special importance of Protestantism, from a broad comparative point of view, was that, for a variety of reasons—to be shortly examined—it contained within itself the seeds of such a transformation and that in certain settings these seeds could bear fruit generously to influence the course of European civilization.

IV

Much additional research has attested to the great *transformative* capacity of Protestantism in societies whose structures do not permit the full realization of their initial total religious orientation. For instance, various studies of the later genesis and influence of Protestant conversion in Catholic countries, as in the case of mystical or Protestant sects in Brazil or Italy, indicate a pattern of development not dissimilar from that which describes some of the Puritan groups in England—even if we take into account that the latter developed *within* a Protestant country.[14] Even more significant are the social, political, and economic attitudes and activities of Protestants in a setting in which they were from the very beginning in a minority, even if not a persecuted minority. The researches of Willems and others indicate clearly that in such cases the Protestant groups tended to participate much more actively than the Catholic groups in more differentiated, modern, economic, political, and community activities.[15]

Perhaps even more striking from the standpoint of our analysis is the comparison between the pioneering activities of Catholic and Protestant settlers in the New World. Moog's perceptive, if impressionistic, analysis shows how the difference between the "bandeirantes" or "piratic" settlements in Brazil and the more economically expansive and democratic settlements in the American colonies can be largely attributed to differences in religious outlook among the Catholic and Puritan settlers.[16]

V

This shift of focus from an analysis of the direct causal links between Protestantism and capitalism (or other types of modern institutions) to an analysis of the broader transformative tendencies of Puritanism gives our discussion a broader perspective of the totality of Weber's work. As Mommsen has recently put it so succinctly: "To Max Weber the exemplar among such religious movements that 'change the world' was the Puritans. Although he investigated other variants of Christianity and other great world religions from the standpoint of the social consequences of their teaching, none in his opinion had influenced the course of human development in quite such a revolutionary manner as had Puritanical religiosity."[17] The shift also gives the discussion a broader general comparative and analytical perspective.

The major emphasis in Weber's work on the sociology of religion in general and on the Protestant ethic in particular is not on direct religious injunctions about different types of economic behavior but on the more general *Wirtschaftsethik* of each religion—that is, on those broader attitudes inherent in the ethos of each which influence and direct economic motives and activities. The shift to an analysis of the transformative capacities of different religions contains an additional element—namely, the possibility that, under certain conditions, a given religion may foster new types of activities which go beyond its original *Wirtschaftsethik* (economic ethic). That is, there may take place a transformation of the original religious impulses which may in its turn lead to the transformation of social reality.[18]

It is necessary to reformulate the problem for the general purposes of analysis and particularly for the consequent re-examination of the Weberian thesis—albeit within the context of Weber's over-all work. In addition to identifying and examining the *Wirtschaftsethik* of different religions, or the religious orientations of different social groups (a central aspect of Weber's work which is fully analyzed by Andreski[19]), it is necessary to follow him further and to analyze the *transformative* capacities of different religions (or, for that matter, of secular ideologies). By transformative capacity is meant the capacity to legitimize, in religious or ideological terms, the development of new motivations, activities, and institutions which were not encompassed by their original impulses and views.

Here several problems stand out. The first is: What is it within any given religion (or ideology) that creates or may account for the existence of such transformative capacities? The second problem is: In what directions may such transformative capacities develop? Finally: What are the conditions in the society within which such religious or ideological groups develop which facilitate or impede the institutionalization of such transformative capacities? Only preliminary and very tentative answers can be given to these questions. But even such preliminary answers may indicate some of the latent possibilities of such an analytic and comparative approach.

VI

With regard to the first question—what it is in the nature of a given religion that creates such a transformative potential—the answer has been given by many scholars with reference to Protestantism. The answer probably needs further elaboration and systematization. All the scholars who have dealt with the matter seem to agree that the transformative potential seems not to be connected to a single tenet of the Protestant faith but rather may be inferred from several aspects of its basic religious and ethical outlook. The most important of these are its strong combination of "this-worldliness" and transcendentalism. Such a combination orients individuals toward activities *of* this world but at the same time does not ritually sanctify them—either through a mystic union or ritual activity—as final proofs of religious consummation or worthiness. Second is the strong emphasis on individual activism and responsibility. Third is the direct relationship of the individual to the sacred and to the sacred tradition. This relationship, while strongly emphasizing the importance and

relevance of the sacred tradition, yet minimizes the extent to which individual commitment is mediated by any institution, organization, or tex-
tual exegesis.[20] Hence it opens up the possibility of continuous redefinition and reformulation of the nature and scope of such a tradition, a
possibility which is further enhanced by the strong transcendental emphasis that minimizes the sacredness of any "here and now." [21]

These Protestant and especially Calvinist tendencies were not, however,
confined to the realm of the sacred. They were closely related to and manifest in the conception most Protestant groups had of the social world and
of their own place in it—that is, in what may be called their status images
and orientations. Most Protestant groups developed a combination of two
such orientations. First was their "openness" toward the wider social
structure. This was rooted in their "this-worldly" orientation which was
not limited to the economic sphere but which also, as we shall see, encompassed other social fields. Second, they were characterized by a certain
autonomy and self-sufficiency. They evinced but little dependence—in
crystallizing their own status symbols and identities—on existing political
and religious centers.

VII

With regard to the second question, in what directions such transformative capacities can be effective, the picture is much more complicated—
certainly more so than as Weber presented it. The first institutional aspect
—and probably the one not dealt with by Weber—which Protestantism
tended to transform was the central symbols, identities, and institutions
of the political sphere. Because of the nature of the totalistic reformatory impulses of the Protestants, these institutions constituted natural
focuses of their interest and activities. The basic theological tenets of Luther, Zwingli, and Calvin themselves—however marked were the differences in their attitudes toward political institutions—contained some
very strong reformulations of the relationships between state and "society," between rulers and ruled, and of the scope and nature of the political community.

The initial failure of their totalistic attempts did not abate or nullify
these impulses. On the contrary, the structural roots of the various crises
of European society in the sixteenth and seventeenth centuries, and especially of the crisis of the "state versus society" as well as the political
exigencies of the Protestant communities in various European states, have
facilitated and even reinforced this continuous orientation toward the
political sphere.

And indeed the Protestant Reformation did have a great initial impact
on the central political institutions and symbols. This effect was not necessarily intended by the rulers who adopted Protestantism. Yet their
adoption of the reform did have important structural effects which greatly

facilitated the further development of a more flexible and dynamic social system. Two factors are relevant here. The first was the need of the Protestant rulers to find new sources of legitimation. The second was their need to forge new symbols of national identity. On both levels there developed, initially through the religious impact of the major Protestant groups and then through their transformation, the possibility of a reformation of relations between rulers and ruled, of patterns of political participation, and of the scope and nature of the political community.[22]

The activities of the Protestant rulers also led to a restructuring of central legal institutions. This restructuring was based on the idea of covenant and contract and on the reformulation of many concepts of natural law. Its results were a more differentiated view of the law and the freeing of voluntary and business corporations from the more restricted view of the political sphere inherent in the traditional understanding of natural law.[23] And, indeed, both in the first Protestant societies (in England, Scandinavia, and the Netherlands) and later in the United States, there occurred, through the incorporation of Protestant thought into law, a transformation of the basic interrelationship between the political and social spheres. The change took place perhaps even before new economic motivations and scientific activities fully evolved. It has not only reinforced the relative autonomy of these spheres but created new, more flexible political symbols, new bases of political obligation, and more flexible political institutions.

Here a comparison with Catholic countries, especially during and after the Counter Reformation, is extremely instructive. The seeds for almost all the changes—new bases of legitimation, new national symbols, and autonomy of religious institutions (as evident, for instance, in the Gallican Church)—existed in most of these countries on the eve of the Reformation and even to some extent throughout the Counter Reformation. And yet in the Catholic countries—in Spain, France, and even earlier in the Italian states of the Renaissance in which modern statecraft first developed—these potentially diversifying tendencies were stifled. Here at least two factors played a part. First were various external exigencies, such as the warfare among the small Italian principalities and the deflection of trade routes from them. Second was the fact that the older Catholic symbols of legitimation were maintained, as were the traditional relations between Church and state. Both were viewed as natural or preordained mediators between the individual and the larger community on the one hand and the sacred and natural orders on the other.[24]

VIII

The transformative effects of Protestantism were not limited to central institutions and symbols but were seen in other modern institutions. They were evident particularly in the development of new types of roles, role structures, and role sets and in the motivations required for the adoption and performance of such roles. The core of Weber's Protestant ethic thesis, as distinct from his discussion of the wider effects of Protestantism, is contained in his analysis of the development of the role of economic entrepreneur and of the new type of labor and of the specific setting in which this role could become institutionalized.

Again it is obvious that many of the elements necessary for this development existed before and even after the Counter Reformation to some extent in Catholic countries. But it is also true that in the period after the Counter Reformation these elements—no matter how similar quantitatively to factors that favored economic growth in the Protestant countries —could not be freed, as Lüthy's work on the bank shows, from their dependence, in terms both of goal orientation and legitimation, on the political center. It was largely in Protestant countries or in Protestant (Calvinist) communities that the economic entrepreneur acquired a new type of autonomy which in turn fostered the development of relatively independent and more differentiated economic organization. It was also largely in the Protestant communities that another crucial change took place—namely, the development of intense motivation for undertaking the new roles and goals and for identifying with them.

Thus the transformative potential of Protestantism had at least three specific economic effects in terms of role development. First was the definition of new economic roles and new economic goals and collectivities not tied to existing economic or political frameworks. Second was the provision of broader institutional, organizational, and legal normative settings which gave the new roles both legitimacy and the necessary resources and frameworks with which their continuous operation was facilitated. Last was the development of new types of motivation for the understanding of such roles and for identifying with them.[25] Although these three aspects of the development of new roles and role complexes are very closely interwoven (and were perhaps not fully distinguished by Weber), yet they must be kept distinct, because to some extent at least they may develop to different degrees.

Whatever the exact nature of these new developments, however, it must be emphasized that they occurred not only in the economic sphere but in a great variety of institutional spheres. New roles in fact evolved in the political sphere proper, giving rise to new types of active political participation and organizations, in the form of parties, community organizations, and public services (in Scotland, The Netherlands, and France).[26] They also evolved in the cultural, and especially the scientific and educational, realm.[27] In the economic sphere itself they could develop in other ways distinct from capitalist-mercantile or industrial entrepreneurship. The transformation of the economic activities of the gentry is a case in point.[28] In all these spheres the beginnings of such new roles existed before Protestantism, but in the Protestant countries the roles achieved more autonomy in terms of goals, organizational structure, and legitimation than in the Catholic countries.

IX

We may now pass very briefly to the third question—namely, to the conditions under which the transformative capacities of Protestantism (or of other religions) could become "absorbed" or institutionalized. In very broad terms it would seem that the possibility of such institutionalization is greater the stronger are the seeds within any society for autonomy in the social, cultural, and political orders. The existence of autonomy in the cultural realm facilitated the development of new symbols which could support and legitimize the building of new central institutions. The existence of autonomy in the sphere of social organization facilitated the development of some viable new institutions without disrupting the whole fabric of the pre-existing order and thus enabled the new order to build to some extent on elements of the old.

It was the European, and especially the western European Christian, countries whose cultural, political, and social institutions had the strongest tradition of autonomy; and it was those countries that had the greatest impetus to modernization. The course of modernization was not, of course, even, continuous, or the same in all countries, including those of western and central Europe. The specific transformative potentials of Protestantism are seen in the way in which the new religion took up the elements of autonomy and pluralism and helped recrystallize them in a more differentiated setting. In Catholic countries such as Spain and France the potentially pluralistic impact of various modern trends, including Protestantism itself, was inhibited by the formation of the Catholic state during the Counter Reformation.

Even within the Protestant countries, however, there was great variation. The transformative tendency of Protestantism did not necessarily develop fully or in the same direction among all Protestant groups in all countries, though to some minimal extent it probably existed in most of them. The concrete development and institutionalization of such tendencies depended to no small extent on the interaction between the attitudes and influence of the major Protestant groups on the one hand and, on the other, the pre-existing social structure, especially on the potential openness or flexibility of political and cultural centers and of the broader groups and strata, and on their initial reaction to religious innovation. The exact scope of such institutionalization varied greatly in accordance with the nature of the groups (that is, whether aristocracy, urban patriciate, various "middle" groups, urban proletariate, or peasantry) who were the bearers of Protestantism as well as their placement within the broader social structure, with particular regard to the political and cultural center.

The transformative capacities of the Protestant groups were smallest in those cases in which they attained full powers (as, for instance, as Loubser's analysis in this book shows, in the extreme case of South Africa)—when their more totalistic and therefore restrictive impulses became dominant—and in situations in which they became downtrodden minorities.[29] Conversely, the scope of the new activities and the extent to which they were successful in transforming society were most far-reaching in those cases in which the various Protestant groups were in a position of what may be called very broadly "secondary" elites, close to, but not identified with, the central elites. They were also successful insofar as they became integrated into wider national communities which developed on the basis of the prior autonomy of the estates without becoming the only bearers of such new political or national identity.[30]

Interaction between various transformative potentialities and existing structures might lead to paradoxically similar—or divergent—results. For example, the influence of Lutheranism—allegedly more conservative than Calvinism—was felt in a variety of ways. In the German principalities Lutheranism had a very restrictive effect, because the existing political framework was appropriate for the development of a new national identity and community or for the development of more autonomous and flexible status orientations among the broader strata.[31] The "traditional" or autocratic rulers of the small principalities adopted the new religious beliefs, and in this context the more conservative of these religious orientations became predominant and often restricted further institutional development. In the Scandinavian countries the new religious beliefs were integrated into wider national communities and developed on the basis of the prior autonomy of the Estates. While they certainly did not impede the development of an absolutist state in Sweden, they did help make possible their subsequent political development in a more pluralistic direction.[32]

Similarly paradoxical results, also demonstrating the significance of restrictive prior situations, are evident in the institutionalization of Calvinism. Of special importance is the Prussian case; the institutionalization of Calvinist attitudes by the absolutist, autocratic Hohenzollerns *did not* facilitate the development of a flexible, pluralistic political framework, though it did support the development of more activist collective political goals.[33]

The juxtaposition of the transformative capacities of the various Protestant groups in different institutional settings accounts for the great variety of new symbols, activities, and institutions among the Protestant countries and communities. Only a full comparative analysis of the development of European society during the sixteenth and seventeenth centuries—obviously beyond the scope of the present chapter—could do full justice to this topic and enable us to test more systematically the various indications presented above.

X

Whatever may be the validity of the hypotheses concerning the transformative capacities of Protestantism presented in the preceding sections, they point in the direction of their wider comparative application. The main upsurge of a broader interest came, as was mentioned above, in conjunction with studies of modernization and development in non-Western countries.[34] It is true that the direction of social change in general and of religious change in particular differed in these countries greatly from the initial processes of modernization in Europe. All these countries were latecomers to modernization, in many cases being at the outset on the periphery of the modern European political and cultural centers, or their provinces. The process of modernization developed in them at first largely under the impact of external forces and only to a smaller degree through internal initiative. In each of them the institutional centers which were developed in the first stage were almost always incapable of coping with the growing problems of more intensive social mobilization. As a result, some of the major problems these societies faced arose because of the necessity for developing almost entirely new centers under the impact of relatively intensive social mobilization of broader strata. The new centers evolved very often without a concomitant change in internal regulative mechanisms or in values among the groups caught up in these processes.

Because of the central need in these societies to set up new centers, there developed in all of them a relative primacy of political and power considerations during the entire process of modernization. Similarly, because of their relative "traditionalism" and the relative weakness of the internal modernizing impulses of the broader strata, the policies undertaken by the centers both for fostering and for regulating social mobilization were of special importance in the structuring of the process of modernization. Within this context the problem of finding some continuous "dialogue" between tradition and modernity has been of focal importance, and in this regard developments in the religious field may become very significant.

The initial situation in the religious sphere in these societies also differed from that of late medieval Europe. It is true that in all these societies the process of modernization undermined the older religious systems—including those of the great world religions such as Eastern Christianity, Islam, Buddhism, Hinduism, and Confucianism as well as some of the small tribal religions abounding in Africa—and gave rise to widespread movements of religious reform on the one hand and of religious revivalism on the other. But whatever reformative tendencies developed within these religions, they had from the very beginning to fight, as it were, on two fronts. They had first to effect changes within their own fold and second to maintain some continuity of identity in the face of modernization and Westernization. In particular they had to defend themselves against secular ideologies such as nationalism, liberalism, and socialism, which claimed to have the panacea for all the problems created by modernization. Moreover, the changes in the religious sphere, connected as they were in all these societies with the erosion of traditional patterns of culture, gave rise—to a much greater degree than in either pre-Reformation or Reformation Europe—to new aspirations, some of which became entirely disconnected from broader commitments.

Because of the nature of all these processes, most of the religious—and to some extent the ideological—movements were set in potentially transformative settings. In only a few cases could they fully implement a new social order in terms of their own tenets. Rather they had the difficult choice of either adjusting to the new order or of finding within themselves some forces which, while perhaps necessitating some change in their initial orientation, could transform the new order.

It is because of all these characteristics of non-Western modernization that the problem of the transformative capacities of these religious ideologies (and of secular ideologies which became predominant within them) becomes even more critical. Their success or failure in developing such transformative potential may provide the key to the difference between purely structural or demographic change on the one hand and the ability to force new institutions capable of absorbing continuous, sustained change on the other.[35] Thus the broader application of the Weberian thesis to an analysis of the transformative capacities of these religions and of their impact on institutional development in these countries becomes even more salient.

XI

The search for equivalents of the Protestant ethic in non-Western countries has led in several directions. The relationships that have been studied are to some extent parallel, but not identical, with factors pertaining to the Protestant ethic thesis proper.[36] The first step was to re-examine various religious beliefs and practices in terms of the degree to which they facilitate or sanction the undertaking of continuous "systematic" economic activities. Two aspects of non-Western religions were usually given prominence. One was the extent to which any religious system focuses on "a multitude of very concretely defined and only loosely ordered sacred entities" which emphasize discrete ritual or magical activities that could become involved in an independent, segmented, and immediate "manner" with almost any sort of actual event.[37] Such a system would preclude any sustained effort on the part of its adherents that encouraged, as it were, a continuous dissipation of energies and resources in such immediate situations.

The other, more "rationalized" religious beliefs are not so thoroughly intertwined with the concrete details of ordinary life. They are "apart," "above," or "outside" them; and the relationship of the system of "ritual" and belief in which they are embodied to secular society is not intimate and unexamined but distant and problematic. They are logically coherent, more abstract, and more generally "phased." [38]

It has been claimed that the more "magical" or "discrete" a religious system is, the less it is likely to facilitate the development of more continuous secular activities. The multitude of dispersed religious rituals found in most "primitive" religions were shown to inhibit the development of such sustained effort. But it has also been shown that such nonrationalized religious emphasis is found not only in so-called "primitive" or "simple" religions but also to some extent in many of the peripheral areas of the "higher" religions—Buddhism, Hinduism, Islam, and Eastern Christianity. There have also been numerous illustrations of the ways in which many of the customs of such otherworldly higher religions as Moslem Ramadan are inimical to sustained economic efforts. Of these two factors the first—the extent of the "rationality" of a given religion—seems to be more crucial from the point of view of its potential influence on the "encouragement" of economic or other secular activities.[39]

Religions which have in principle a positive orientation to worldly activities may yet, insofar as discrete, magical rituals are important in them, give little support to more continuous systematic efforts in any field of activity. On the other hand, religions whose main stress is otherworldly may yet exhibit a positive attitude to certain types of secular activities. Such an attitude may be demonstrated in two ways. Certain religions enjoin their adherents to perform their "secular" duties. Second, insofar as such religions have developed a certain level of "rationality" they may also encourage some continuous systematic effort in various secular spheres. The extent to which these religions encourage such activities depends not so much on their *general* this-worldly or otherworldly emphasis but more, as Weber's classical analysis of the great religions showed, on their differential evaluation of various sacred and secular spheres in terms of their more generalized and "rationalized" orientations.[40] However, although such rationalization constitutes a basic prerequisite for the encouragement of more sustained activity in various secular fields, it does not in itself reveal the extent to which there may also develop within these religions more varied transformative orientations to secular spheres of life. As Pieris shows, the existence of some broad, generalized support for economic or other secular activity does not in itself demonstrate the extent to which these religions give *religious legitimation* and sanction for continuous secular activities. It does not tell us the extent to which they endow various activities in the secular world with direct religious meaning or the extent to which such activities become the focus of religiosity.[41]

Religious legitimation of secular activities is a relatively rare phenomenon in the major world religions, whatever their concrete attitudes to this world, so long as they arose within relatively "traditional" settings. This does not necessarily preclude the possibility that, once they are set in the less "congenial" environment in which modernization is taking place, there may develop from within them some transformative tendencies. Such tendencies are not necessarily always positively related to an initial worldly outlook or negatively related to an initial otherworldly outlook. Overtly otherworldly religions may contain within themselves transformative potentials for a growing religious legitimation of worldly activities and for making these activities an active focus of their religiosity. There are necessarily great differences between the various religions as well as between the ability of the settings in which they operate to absorb such transformative potentials. Ames's analysis of some recent religious movements in Buddhist Ceylon and Geertz's of potential "internal conversion" in Bali, as well as several developments in Islamic Indonesia, are cases in point.[42]

Because of the special circumstances in which modernity was thrust upon most of the great non-Western European religions, an additional aspect of their reactions to modernity becomes very important, namely, the extent of their permissiveness. By this we mean the extent to which they do not oppose the new goals, institutions, and activities which modernity brings with it but rather show receptiveness to them. Hinduism on the one hand and the Japanese religious congeries or system on the other are probably the most far-reaching examples of such permissiveness.

Permissiveness need not, however, go hand in hand with a transformative capacity. It seems quite possible that to some degree the two may be opposed to each other. While the permissiveness may indeed facilitate the acceptance of new goals and organization, it cannot provide the new institutional settings with religious legitimation and therefore it cannot effect far-reaching transformation on the institutional or motivational levels. Paradoxical as it may sound, it seems probably true that the more nonpermissive religions may, under certain conditions, develop greater transformative capacities. In the following paragraphs we shall focus most of our analysis on the conditions that may facilitate such permissive and transformative capacities of the major religions.

It will be possible here to give only very preliminary indications concerning the conditions which may influence the effectiveness of the potentials of various religions at the various levels of social organization. Hopefully these indications will serve as guides for future research.

XII

Let us start very briefly with the analysis of those conditions that are related to permissiveness of any religion. Permissiveness is probably related to some aspects of the religious belief; for example, to some degree of rationalization of the religious orientation; to some combination of ritual emphasis with lack of closed intellectual dogma coupled with a relatively small degree of development of a special religious hierarchy.

While some such characteristics may probably be found in all great religions, they seem to be more developed in some than in others. As has been indicated above, such permissiveness need not always be conducive to the development of transformative capacities within the religions.

Following the preceding analysis of Protestantism, we propose that the transformative potential of a given religion is greater the stronger is the emphasis in it on transcendentalism, on individual responsibility and activism, on an "open" unmediated relationship between the individual and the sacred tradition with the concomitant possibility of its continuous redefinition and reformulation, and on a high degree of social openness among the religiously active groups. Of special importance, from the point of view of such social openness and its relationship to innovative potential, are the differences in those aspects of the social organization of a given religion which bear on the relations between sectarian and "central" religious institutions on the one hand and the direction of religious "purity" and transformation on the other. In the case of Protestantism, the development of its innovative potential was very closely related to a specific situation in which the sects held to the "purer," more "rationalized," "unmediated," yet worldly beliefs as against the more ritualized religions and institutional conservatism of the centers.

In Catholicism, and even more in Eastern Christianity, the situation was different.[43] Many of the sects were ritualistic and/or more withdrawn from active participation in the secular world; and even when they did participate in secular life their aim was the conservative one of accommodation to the existing order, not change or transformation. Such combinations of characteristics are even more striking in some parts of Islam, as Gellner's analysis of North African movements shows.[44] A double tendency is discernible in Islam. Some orders, whether emphasizing ritualism or spiritualism, have been mostly conservative, antimodernistic, and closely related to the existing religious establishment; whereas others, such as those in Indonesia and Malaya, have placed greater emphasis on both religious purity and reform.[45]

The very fact that such a variety of constellations may exist, even within one religion, indicates that the several elements which constitute the preconditions for transformative potential in any religion or ideology —transcendentalism, individual responsibility, openness to the sacred tradition, and social openness—do not always go together. Therefore the transformative impacts of different religions vary greatly in intensity and may indeed go in different directions. Hence the impact of a given religion must be analyzed according to the different aspects of social behavior or organization in which, as our preceding analysis indicates, it may become manifest. These aspects are motivation; the development of new roles, organizations, and institutions; and the transformation of central symbols and spheres in society. It is necessary to point to the conditions under which the possibilities of the transformative potential of a given religion may be realized with regard to each of these aspects. In a way, all such conditions constitute variants of the core characteristics of transformative potentials which were pointed out above. However, beyond the common core some differences do exist with regard to these various aspects of personality and social organization.

In the following paragraphs we shall attempt, first, to present a series of general, rather formal hypotheses about such conditions[46] and, second, to illustrate them through an analysis of the processes of modernization in the major Asian civilizations. We shall start with an analysis of conditions conducive to the effective development of transformative potentials on the motivational level and that of central symbols and spheres in society, and proceed to an analysis of conditions conducive to the development of new roles and organizations.

XIII

The effects of the transformative capacities of religious or ideological movements on the motivational level—in the direction of the development of strong motivations to undertake new types of nonreligious roles—seem to be greater the stronger are their transcendental and worldly orientations and the more they evince ideological autonomy with regard to a given social or communal order. Conversely, such transformative effects are smaller the stronger is the immanent orientation, whether in this world or the other, of the religions in question and the more they are intertwined in the existing political and/or social order that is, the more these orders constitute a basic referent of the given religion and/or the greater their negative or apathetic attitude toward these orders.[47] In turn, the transformation of new central symbols and frameworks depends largely on the extent to which the religious (or ideological) systems evince a relatively high level of ideological and organizational autonomy while at the same time they remain oriented to participation in the sociopolitical order.

The more autonomous the religious organizations are and the less they are identified with the existing political order, the more they can develop new types of central political and cultural symbols. Conversely, the smaller is the extent of their distinct organization and the more they are identified with institutions and organs of the state, the smaller is their ability to develop new symbols.

Similarly, the greater the extent to which a given polity and state constituted a basic referent for religious activity, the smaller is the extent to which there could develop from within a given religion movements and systems of reform oriented to the redefinition of the central spheres of the society. Contrariwise, the stronger are the universalistic and transcendental elements within a religion, the greater are the possibilities of such redefinition.

Finally, the more otherworldly are the activist tendencies within a religious value system, the smaller is the extent to which, whatever reformatory movements may have developed within them, they tend to orient themselves to a recrystallization of the central spheres of the society. On the other hand, the greater the extent to which these systems emphasize involvement in the secular world and the stronger their specific ideological formulations, the greater usually is the possibility that such transformations will be effected.

XIV

The extent to which the transformative potentials of a given religion become manifest in institution building, in the development and legitimation of new roles and institutional frameworks, seems to be related to other, somewhat different, although related, aspects of religious organization and attitudes.

The transformative effects of religious and ideological movements tend to be greater insofar as they foster among their adherents orientation of "openness" toward the wider social structure and minimize dependence on existing political centers for legitimation of their status. Similarly, such reformative tendencies are likely to be greater the more they are promoted by relatively cohesive elites with a strong sense of self-identity. Especially important are the secondary elites which, while somewhat distant from the central ruling elite, yet maintain a positive orientation of solidarity to the center and are not entirely alienated from the pre-existing elites or from some of the broader groups in society. Conversely, the reformative potentials of religious and ideological movements tend to be smaller insofar as they are promoted by elites which are relatively noncohesive, are alienated from other elites and from the broader groups and strata of society, and are either quite distant from the existing center or succeed in totally monopolizing it, to the exclusion of other groups and elites.

The transformative effects of religions in the field of institution building and secular role development are greater the more the religiously active groups and elites develop simultaneous orientations to collective ideological transformation and to concrete tasks and problems in different "practical" fields. They are also greater insofar as these groups perceive their own legitimation in terms of such wider changes and not only in terms of providing immediate benefits to different social groups, or in the maintenance of a given status group. Contrariwise, the effectiveness of the reformative potentials of religious or ideological systems at the level of institution building and secular role development is smaller if they are promoted by elites which develop "closure" in their social and status perception. Closure is to be understood as a ritual emphasis on certain specific and very limited types of status orientations.

It is at this point, in the development of new roles and organizations, more than is the case of motivational development—which can be effective in relatively restricted social settings—that characteristics of the broader institutional setting of the societies in which these movements take place may be of great importance in facilitating or impeding the institutionalization of their transformative potentials.

The effects of the transformative potentials of religious and ideological movements will be greater, as indicated above, insofar as the existing social structure is characterized, in its totality or in those of its parts within which these religious and ideological movements are intensive, by some autonomy from the social, cultural, and political orders, and by a relatively strong cohesiveness of the more active broader strata. Autonomy of the religion in the sphere of social organization may facilitate the development and crystallization of some viable new media and institutions without disrupting the whole fabric of the pre-existing order. In this way the new order might build on at least some forces of the old. Similarly, the existence, within broader social strata and family groups, of relatively strong internal cohesion, and of some status autonomy and flexibility together with openness toward the center, may greatly facilitate the internal transformation of these groups. They may develop a positive orientation to the new centers and a willingness to provide these centers with the support and resources they need. Conversely, if the wider social groups have only a small amount of autonomy but are relatively self-contained, they can easily, through the withdrawal of resources and through the development of intensive unregulated demands on the center, undermine the very functioning of the new institutions.

The importance of the preceding institutional setting is evident not only in the extent to which in a general way it facilitates or impedes the "absorption" or institutionalization of the transformative potentials of various religious or ideological groups but also in the concrete features of such institutionalization.

In Europe, the innovative religious groups were very closely related to fairly strong, autonomous middle classes, which played an important role as secondary elites and directly impinged on the central institutions of the society. But, as has been rightly stressed by Wertheim,[48] in most of the non-European (or non-Western European) countries, the initial social setting is not one in which the "middle classes" are strong, autonomous, or predominant. Whatever middle classes exist are much more fragmented, less cohesive, and too dependent on the center to be able by themselves to build new institutions or to impinge directly on the center.

Hence, first of all, the concrete institutional features which tend to develop in these countries differ from the very beginning from the "classical" European pattern; they are much more centralized and bureaucratized.[49] Second, whether the transformative potentials of active groups and elites are effective in a broader setting depends greatly on the extent to which such groups can develop an alliance with more "established" groups located within these centralized, bureaucratized settings.[50]

Needless to say, there is a great variety of possibilities,[51] only two of which will be mentioned here as illustrations.

In some cases in which the development of new motivations is limited to small groups, they may be successful in some specific economic or religious endeavors but may not be able to impinge on the broader social structure. Moreover, in some cases these motivations may themselves be limited to specific spheres (religious, economic) and contain no tendency or need to relate themselves to wider settings. This is especially so if these groups fail to evince an over-all status flexibility and active orientation toward the political and cultural spheres, or if such flexibility and the new orientations are not legitimized by the central institutions and symbols of the society. That was what happened, for instance, in the case of preimperial and imperial Germany. On the other hand, insofar as the innovating orientations are promoted by relatively traditional central elites, and not by broader groups which have undergone internal value transformations—as was, for instance, the case in Japan[52]—motivations for differentiated activities in the economic sphere will develop. However, these motivations will become connected with strong normative centralized regulation in the political-national spheres, without at the same time giving rise to significant individual ideological or religious changes in the definition of the over-all national community.

XV

We shall now proceed to a very preliminary analysis of the processes of modernization and transformation in the major Asian civilizations. In this analysis we shall attempt to illustrate and test in more concrete terms some of the general hypotheses presented above. We shall in each case analyze the basic sociocultural nature of these civilizations and of the major religions and religious movements within them which have effected their initial modernization.[53]

China

In China, among the historic imperial civilizations, we find the closest interweaving, almost an identity, of the cultural and political centers. Although in principle many universalistic ethical elements in the dominant Confucian ideology transcended any given territory or community, in actuality this ideology was very closely tied to the specific political framework of the Chinese empire. The empire was legitimized by the Confucian symbols, but the Confucian symbols and the Confucian ethical orientation found their "natural" place and framework, their major referent, within the empire—although there did indeed often develop tensions between the "pure" and "state" Confucianism.[54]

This, of course, was also related to the fact that no church or cultural organization in China existed independently of the state. The Confucian elite was a relatively cohesive group, sharing a cultural background which was enhanced by the examination system and by adherence to Confucian rituals and classics. But its organization was almost identical with that of the state bureaucracy, and except for some schools and academies it had no organization of its own. Moreover, political activity within the imperial-bureaucratic framework was a basic referent of the Confucian ethical orientation and system—a system which was strongly particularistic and confined to the existing cultural-political setting.[55]

The relationship between the Chinese political and cultural orders parallels the relationship between the political system and social stratification. The most interesting fact here is that the total societal system of stratification was entirely focused on the political center. The imperial center, with its strong Confucian orientation and legitimation, was the sole distributor of prestige and honor. No social groups or strata developed autonomous, independent status orientations, except on the purely local level. The major, almost the only, wider orientations were bound to this monolithic political-religious center. Of crucial importance is the structure of the major stratum linking the imperial center to the broader society—namely, the literati. This stratum was a source of recruitment for the bureaucracy and also maintained close relations with the gentry. Their double status orientation enabled the literati to fulfill certain critical integrative functions in the imperial system.[56] Their special position enabled them to influence the political activities of the rulers and of the leading strata of the population. But they exerted this influence by upholding the ideal of a hierarchical social-political-cultural order binding on the rulers and on these strata. The very existence of the literati as an elite group was contingent on the persistence of the ideal of a unified empire.

These characteristics of the literati were among the most important stabilizing mechanisms in the imperial system, helping it to regulate and absorb changes throughout its long history. But these same characteristics have also severely inhibited any movement for reform within China's culturally and politically most articulate groups.

The lack of capacity for reform within the broader groups of Chinese society is also related to the source of their internal cohesion and self-identity: namely, "familism." Familism has often been designated as one cause of China's relative failure to achieve modernization. But as Levy has shown in his later analysis, it was not familism as such that was important, but rather the nature of the internal cohesion in the family and its links with other institutional spheres.[57] The family was a relatively autonomous, self-contained group, which had few broader criteria or orientations. Beyond a commitment to the bureaucracy, the primary duty of individuals was to increase family strength and resources, not to represent the worthiness of the family according to some external goals and commitments.

In combination, these various aspects of the Chinese social structure go far toward explaining the ineffectiveness of the initial stages of China's modernization. The very close identity of the cultural and political orders and the specific characteristics of the literati tended to maintain the dominance of a stagnative neotraditionalism that continuously reinforced the nontransformative orientations of Chinese culture.

Under the first impact of modernization, Chinese intellectuals and bureaucrats faced certain problems stemming from the fact that their basic cultural symbols were embedded in the existing political structure. A political revolution or reformation in China would necessarily have entailed rejection or destruction of the cultural order. Similarly, the strong ideological emphasis on upholding the social-political status quo permitted few centers to arise which would crystallize new symbols for legitimizing new social institutions which were relatively independent of the preceding order.[58] Hence little capacity developed for viable, flexible institution building, especially in the legal, legislative, or administrative fields. Many such institutions were formally initiated, but they lacked both "precontractual" bases of legitimation and the broader societal conditions and resources for effective functioning.[59]

The ineffectiveness of initial reforms and revolutionary movements in imperial and postimperial China resulted only partly from the ideological identity between the cultural and political orders. No less important were the relations between political institutions and the system of social stratification. In the social sphere as in the ideological or cultural sphere, most groups had few points of internal strength, cohesion, or self-identity on which to found new institutional frameworks or from which to support institutional changes.

This weakness was reinforced by the limited reformative capacities of the Chinese family system. When the empire crumbled and processes of change swept over it, disorganizing and dislocating the traditional structure, and especially the major links to the center—the literati and the bureaucracy—family groups were largely dissociated from the center but lacked the strength to create new autonomous links. These family groups tended also to develop neotraditional orientations, but because they were "closed" groups they could not regulate their demands effectively. This process tended to sap the resources available for internal redistribution. In the modern setting, family groups became highly politicized, making demands on the new, and for them not fully legitimate, center and thus further undermining the functioning of new institutional frameworks.

XVI

Islam

Throughout its history Islam has emphasized the identity between the religious and political communities, seeking to fuse these two institutional spheres in a manner almost unique in the history of the great universalistic religions.[60] The identity between the political and religious communities represents a very important similarity between the Chinese and Islamic societies, though the religious or ideological bases for this identity are very different.

In Islam the unity between the political and religious communities produced some specific ideological and structural characteristics. Within the Caliphate there developed, on the one hand, a very strong universalistic-missionary orientation and a strong emphasis on the state as the framework of the religious community but subordinate to it. On the other hand, no religious functionaries or groups developed an over-all, independent, cohesive organization. These two factors in combination limited political participation mostly to court cliques and to the bureaucracy. They also gave rise to extreme sectarian movements, some seeking to destroy the existing regime and to establish a new, religiously pure one, others remaining politically passive. Thus, in distinction from the Confucian pattern, strong reform movements based on universalistic and transcendental orientations did develop within Islam.[61] It is, however, very significant that these movements were successful only insofar as they were not politically oriented and did not have to establish new central political institutions within the framework of Islamic tradition (as in India, Southeast Asia, and parts of Africa).

Moslem reform movements were more successful in colonial situations, as in Indonesia and in Malaysia, where they were active minorities or where their political objective was to attain independence, and in cultural, educational, and economic activities than they were in the independent Moslem states where they had to try to establish a new Islamic polity. Islamic reform movements in India in the early twentieth century, for instance, evinced a relatively strong emphasis on educational and cultural innovation. Subsequently these movements were transformed into more popular, political ones during the immediate prepartition period and especially in Pakistan after the attainment of independence.[62] Similar indications may be found perhaps in contemporary Africa.

The close identity of the political and religious communities inhibited Islamic reform movements in a way somewhat similar to the way in which such movements were inhibited in China. This made it difficult to build modern institutions and at the same time to forge a national identity based on Islamic premises.

In the Islamic states, as in China, the identity between the cultural and political institutions severely limited the possibilities for innovation necessary to develop viable modern legislative and juridical institutions.[63] Similarly the Islamic prescriptions for appropriate political behavior did not facilitate legal innovations.

No less important was the difficulty of forging new national identities. Any attempt to base a modern nation-state on an Islamic base encountered tremendous obstacles. The Islamic tradition was challenged by various new secular-national symbols, while the quest to legitimize national identities in terms of Islamic tradition intensified the conflicts between various units.[64] The history of the effort to establish an Islamic polity in Pakistan,[65] for example, and similar experiences in various Middle Eastern countries illustrate some of these difficulties.[66] Among the older Moslem states, only Tunisia—through a variety of circumstances which cannot be dealt with here—seems to have succeeded, to some extent at least, in overcoming them.[67] In Turkey—the very core of the older Ottoman empire—new institution building was attempted through the complete negation of the Islamic tradition at the central political and symbolic level.[68]

In the relationship between political institutions and social stratification, Islamic patterns are not so similar to the Chinese. The system of stratification in many Islamic societies was not based to the same extent on the state, although in some extreme cases, as at the core of the Ottoman empire, similar tendencies did develop. On the whole, however, various social and cultural groups—for example, the religious groups, the different orders, the ulemas—manifested a higher degree of organizational and social autonomy. It is true that these very groups often became centers of reaction and traditionalism, but their autonomy did create the possibility for intellectual ferment and social change.

Moreover, within many Islamic societies there was a tradition of local, especially urban, community autonomy, even if it was latent. Although this tradition was, on the whole, weakened under martial Ottoman rule, it did persist at the peripheries of the empire, enhancing receptivity to modern intellectual and organizational movements and the concomitant development of various professional, entrepreneurial, administrative, and intellectual groups.[69] The major weakness of these groups was their inability to develop new, more effective links with the center or to develop adequate self-regulative mechanisms, which gave rise once again to a relatively high degree of politicization. Nevertheless, the major potential for reform and modernization must be sought within these groups.

XVII

Japan

The Japanese case can be compared to the Chinese case on a different plane: here the importance of structural differences exceeds that of ideological or value orientations. On the purely ideological level one may, at first sight, perceive a strong similarity between the Japanese and Chinese experiences. Indeed, an even more closed, particularistic orientation and collective identity did develop in Japan. A very strong emphasis on the Confucian ethic (mixed with Buddhist and Shinto elements) created an even stronger identification with the particular polity than in China. This was especially so because the identity between the cultural and political orders was even closer in Japan, and universalistic elements beyond the existing political and national framework were weaker.[70] Paradoxically enough, these elements did not greatly impede the internal transformation and modernization of Japanese society, although they influenced the direction and limits of modernization.

At the level of value orientation as well as that of the structural location of the central symbols of the society, several points of flexibility developed. First, the structure of the center in the Tokugawa period differed in several crucial and important respects from that of the Chinese and other centralized imperial systems. Japanese centralization existed under a special form of feudalism, and although the different autonomous feudal traditions were weakened or frozen they did not lose their entire vitality and autonomy.[71] Even more important, the arrangement of Tokugawa political institutions was such that the center was less monolithic than the strong ideological identity between the cultural and political orders might have suggested.

The dissociation between the symbolic center, represented by the politically ineffective emperor and the politically effective center of the Shogunate, obviated several of the potential consequences of a close identity between the polity and the cultural order.[72] In some ways this organizational duality constituted a partial—but only a partial—equivalent to a dissociation, on the substantive level, between the cultural and the political order. This has facilitated the political revolution anchored in the ancient imperial political symbolism and has created an almost uniquely successful[73] initial modernization based on neotraditional orientations and symbols.[74]

The revival of the older symbolic center in Japan greatly facilitated and supported the overthrow, by an oligarchic revolution, of the political center of the Shogunate. The continuity of the imperial tradition was not purely "decorative" but constituted the main focus and content of the new major value orientation and of the new national identity, and it greatly helped to mobilize the loyalties of the broader strata.[75] Such a transformation could not be so easily attained in China or in the Islamic states, where either the overthrow of the political center undermined the cultural order or the mobilization of older traditional loyalties weakened the possibilities for crystallizing a new, modern, effective center. In Japan these possibilities were reinforced by several aspects of the content of the religious orientation. First, the syncretic nature and the relative lack of rigid orthodoxy of the Japanese cultural-religious orientation facilitated the absorption of new contents. Second, some strong tendencies to emphasize individual responsibility—manifested in various ways in certain Buddhist and Confucian circles—which became more pronounced, as Bellah has shown, in the late Tokugawa period also facilitated the development, by different groups or individuals, of an independent standard of formulation of the correct, legitimate, collective goals,[76] even if these were often in opposition to the official policies. Moreover, the combination of the religious syncretism and the transcendental emphasis facilitated both the redefinition of the collective goals according to the more modern orientation of the Meiji oligarchs and the mobilization of wider loyalties for the implementation of the new goals.

Of no small importance either were some aspects of the system of stratification and of the internal cohesion of broader groups and strata. Both were closely related to some of the basic characteristics of Japanese feudalism, even in its "frozen" Tokugawa form. Many of the various hierarchically interlocked groups,[77] which constituted the core of this system, had strong commitments to collective obligations. From the point of view of criteria of status and self-identity, these groups evinced a relatively high degree of autonomy—but were not, as in the case of Chinese groups, self-contained—and this identity and the mutual obligations it entailed were not entirely dependent on the political center.

In Japan the very composition of the major strata was much more variegated than in China. There did not exist in Japan a homogeneous monolithic upper political-cultural group, such as the literati in China, which monopolized the central political and status and cultural positions and combined all these in one organizational framework. Instead there were more dispersed and heterogeneous clusters of feudal landlords, merchants, and intellectual groups, each with some autonomy. Unlike the case in most Islamic societies, these groups had many structural links among themselves and to the center, which facilitated their self-transformation or a high level of adaptability to changes from the center. This structural aspect of the status system was reinforced by the strong commitment to collective values. The combination of the structural and value elements made possible the transmission of loyalties from any particular hierarchy —in this case the old feudal Shogunate—to the new center.[78]

Some aspects of Japanese family structure are pertinent here.[79] Although as in China the family constituted a basic unit of solidarity and loyalty, yet the place and standing of the family were to a large extent measured by its ability to serve different centers, to do its share toward a collective goal, and to further the interests of the collectivity. Hence the family units could develop important semiautonomous mechanisms by which to regulate their own activities and problems. This minimized the initial demands they made on the center and enabled the center to mobilize the loyalties and resources of the family groups and major strata of the population.[80]

Some of the more specific structural characteristics of Japanese modernization can be related to specific points of flexibility in the Tokugawa period. The most important has been the specific combination of universalistic and particularistic criteria in the regulation and channeling of the process of social mobility and mobilization. The universalistic criteria became most operative in the educational system, from the point of entrance to schools and universities to full *occupational* levels, but especially at the various points of examination which greatly influenced, though did not determine, the differential entry into the occupational and labor market. Beyond these points there tended to crystallize, on almost all levels of the social and occupational structure, a series of varied particularistic units, such as school cliques, company and bureaucratic cliques and groups, small labor groups, and so on. Within them many traditional forms and attitudes persisted, and between them there was little mobility. At the same time, however, the amount of overlapping among such different particularistic units was relatively small, and—most important—there were few ecological crystallizations of such overlapping. In this way such particularistic developments did not impede—they may even have facilitated —status flexibility and the recrystallization of various social groups.

Several weaknesses in the process of Japanese modernization stand out in relation to those aspects of the Japanese social and cultural structure just analyzed. The first weak point was the nature of the symbolic transformation of the center. The new, organizationally flexible center which was established by the Meiji oligarchs did not undergo any internal value transformation concomitant with its organizational flexibility. The new national identity was expressed mostly in terms of particularistic loyalty to the emperor, rather than in terms of his representation of wider (transcendental) or universalistic orientations. While on the one hand this imperial symbolism was flexible enough to absorb many new political orientations, the basic legitimation of the new political community and action did not transcend this particularistic collective symbolism. Hence there did not develop new value orientations through which the various social forces could be legitimized and impinge on the center in autonomous terms and through which support for various autonomous regulative mechanisms and frameworks could be provided.[81]

Similarly, although there developed in Japan, at a relatively early stage of modernization, a rather high degree of status flexibility among the more central groups, this flexibility was not bolstered by a concomitant autonomous legitimation and self-perception on the part of these groups. This was to no small degree related to the heavy neotraditionalism of the center, which did not foster the development of autonomous value orientations and hence set many limitations on the ability of various social groups to develop institutions which were able to mediate among the interests of various groups and to evolve a broad base of consensus.[82]

XVIII

Hinduism

The most salient feature of Indian civilization, from the point of view of our discussion, is that it is probably the only complex, highly differentiated civilization which throughout history has maintained its cultural identity without being tied to a given political framework.[83] This was true not only during the last centuries of Moslem and later English rule but even before that. Although there did develop in India states and imperial centers small and large, there did not develop a single state with which the cultural tradition became identified. Classical Indian religious thought did, of course, encompass problems of policy, regarding the behavior of princes and the duties and rights of subjects.[84] But to a much greater degree than in many other historical imperial civilizations politics were conceived of in secular terms. The basic religious and cultural orientations, and the specific cultural identity of Indian civilization, were not necessarily tied to a particular political or imperial framework. Whatever partial identity existed during the period before Moslem domination became greatly weakened afterward. In a way, the strength and survival of Indian civilization under alien rule was rooted in this very fact: that it did not identify itself with any political framework.

This basic characteristic of Indian civilization had a very important influence on the structure and orientation of the initial processes of modernization in India which started under the aegis of the British and was then promoted by the national movement. Because of the relative dissociation between the cultural and political order, the process of modernization could get under way in India without being hampered by too specific traditional-cultural orientation toward the political sphere. The modern center was established first of all in terms of Western symbols and was to some extent disconnected from the great Indian cultural tradition.[85] Only during the Gandhian phase of the Indian national movement did its political aspirations become expressed to some extent in traditional symbols or were they at least legitimized by some reinterpretation of such symbols.[86]

This dissociation could be at least partially legitimized in terms of traditional ideological orientations. Some of the symbols and values of the new center which were couched in Western terms—such as political and social justice—could be legitimized in terms of classical Indian political thought. This could be reinforced by the internal reformist tendencies which developed among the upper layers of Hindu society from the second half of the nineteenth century on.

Significantly enough, the new political-ideological center was to a large extent, especially in the pre-Gandhian era but even later, developed and promoted by people from those groups or strata—particularly the Brahmanic groups—who were bearers of the great historical tradition in its nonpolitical aspects and emphases.[87]

The second feature of Indian society which is of great importance for our analysis is closely related to the place of the political system in the system of stratification and to the internal cohesion of broader social groups and strata. The most important fact here is the very high degree of autonomy evinced by these groups in terms of their internal identity and their relation to the political order. Not only were the cultural traditions relatively independent of the political center but the whole complex of castes and villages and the various networks of cultural communication were also to a very high degree autonomous and self-regulating in terms of their own cultural and social identity, with only limited recourse to the political center or centers.[88] This had several important repercussions on the process of modernization. First, the new modern political center could develop without too strong and immediate an impingement of intensive demands on it. Second, the broader strata could absorb through their own mechanisms some of the problems of modernization without either becoming immediately disorganized or creating excessive demands on the political center.

These processes also greatly influenced the concrete structural features of modernization among the broader strata of Indian society. The most important among them have been the continuous process of recrystallization of the traditional frameworks, and especially of the various complexes of caste relations. We find the transformation of the concrete configuration of castes in the assumption by them of new tasks and in their very high adaptability to new economic and political frameworks.[89]

Of special interest is the fact that the caste groups changed both in the more traditional direction and into new, more differentiated, modern groups. Thus on the one hand existing subcaste groups tended to develop many traditional patterns of caste mobility. They assumed some limited new, economic, political, or ritual tasks, more or less within the range of traditional culture, and they attempted to claim for themselves better standing within the old, traditional, ritual order. At the same time the older types of caste groups gave way to new, broader, more differentiated, and more flexible networks of caste associations. These new groups focused their energies mainly on new types of economic, professional, and political activities, which assumed a great variety of new organizational patterns and often, though not always, created new cutting links between the political, social, and economic hierarchies of status.[90]

These various developments contained two weak points. The major weakness in India's attempt at modernization lies in the failure of Hinduism to develop motivational orientations and commitments to the undertaking and performance of new secular roles. On the one hand, Hinduism constitutes perhaps the purest case of a complex otherworldly religious system which yet, because of its high level of rationality, especially at its center (that is, especially among the upper, central castes), rather sustained activity in the secular field. Because of this, as well as its relative openness to a reinterpretation of its sacred traditions, it developed, as we have seen, from within itself various reform movements and was highly adaptable to new circumstances, to the development of new organizations and institutions. At the same time, however, because of the relative weakness of transcendental elements within Hinduism and because of its strong (although not absolute) tendency to embedment in the given social setting, there were few "conversions" from among its adherents to new motivations to perform new secular roles and few tendencies among the "converts" to such secular activities with religious meaning and to make them into focuses of their religiosity.

The various reform movements, as well as the more secular-ideological movements which developed from within Hinduism, were much more articulate on the ideological and symbolical level than on the motivational one and did not facilitate a linkage between the new personal identity and the new collective symbols which developed at the center. It was easier, paradoxically enough, for minority Hindu groups—mainly abroad —to form such a linkage than it was within India herself.[91]

All these factors had several repercussions on the problems of modernization in India. Thus the center, while institutionally and organizationally strong and flexible, did not develop strong common symbols in which elements of both the new and the older cultural traditions could be combined and which could create relatively strong commitments and identity. There arose the question of the extent to which the reforming tendencies of the center could provide not only new symbols of collective identity which might serve as focuses of rebellion against the colonial rulers and to provide legitimation for a new civil order, but also some flexible guidelines for institution building.[92] This becomes extremely important when the center extends, through universal suffrage, the scope of its activities and of its dependence on the broader groups. Then the lack of relationship between the cultural traditions and political framework which was a point of strength in the beginning may become a point of weakness.

Two major problems stand out. One is the extent to which the center will be able to forge new binding symbols of identity which will be able to overcome the more "parochial"—mostly linguistic—symbols of the different regions and states and to develop some feeling of political community. This problem is especially acute as these parochial symbols tend also to become more crystallized and articulated with the growing modernization and politicization of the periphery. The explosive potentiality of the linguistic question in India is highly indicative of this problem.

The second problem is to what extent there will develop within the broad Indian cultural tradition and within its reformative tendencies a permissiveness which would not only facilitate the setting up of new institutional frameworks under external influence and the continuous recrystallization and adaptation of the traditional groups to such new frameworks, but which would also develop new innovative forces, new common integrative frameworks to support continuous institution building.[93]

XIX

Buddhism

We shall touch briefly on some aspects of these problems in Buddhist societies such as Burma, Ceylon, and other states of Southeast Asia. The type of Buddhism prevalent in these societies has some very paradoxical features. From the purely "theological" point of view, it evinces at the level of its "highest" central culture the greatest dissociation from an existing social or political order of any Asian religion. It also harbors within itself very strong universalistic and transcendental elements. Similarly on the organizational level it probably has been the most autonomous and self-contained of the great Asian religions, organized as it was in a congeries of autonomous communities, monasteries, and orders. Yet on the level of solid social reality these characteristics of Buddhism were not the most outstanding or operative in its concrete relations with the (traditional, precolonial) state. There developed within the Buddhist priesthood in most of these countries a very strong tendency toward co-operation with the powers that be, toward interweaving the religious hierarchy into the political one,[94] and toward a full mutual legitimation of the religious and political sphere. Moreover, because of the strong otherworldly orientation of Buddhism, whatever tendency to activism or autonomy developed, it will usually directed not toward active, autonomous participation in the political sphere but toward flight into the segregated life of the exemplary monastic community.

However, these activist orientations were largely confined to the monks, the uppermost—segregated—levels of the religious organization. At the more concrete, popular levels of the system the more rationalized, universalistic elements of the religious orientation were very weak. The linkage between these levels and the "higher culture" of the religion was often spurious.[95]

These characteristics of Buddhist religious organization have greatly influenced their varied responses to the possibility of transformation in situations of modernization. The main stream of such reactions was in the direction of a new traditionalism. It represented at most an attempt to "adapt" to the new secular state, to attain within it the best possible positions, and to impose on it many traditional demands and orientations. The orientation to change and the transformative power were negligible. As for central spheres, societal symbols, and institution building, the major trend was in the direction of strengthening the traditional frameworks, perhaps at most using modern organizational techniques.

The major ideological developments in the sphere of central symbols were toward some syncretism between secular (especially "socialist") and traditional-Buddhist symbols. However, none of them effected a far-reaching transformation or reformulation of the symbols of collective identity nor did they create effective links between those symbols and those of personal identity.[96]

At the same time, however, within the more peripheral parts of Buddhism in these countries there developed, as Ames has shown, by virtue of the more universalistic, autonomous, and potentially transcendental orientation of the religion, some tendency to "internal conversion." This took place in terms of a growing rationalization, religious reformation, and religious commitment to activities in the secular world.[97]

The first impact of such "conversion" was, it seems, mainly on the level of motivation. It only gradually extended to broader spheres of institutions and organizations. But the degree to which such extension became possible greatly depended on the placement of these groups in the over-all social sphere.

XX

The preceding discussion brings out, if only in a preliminary way, the impact of different social forces and movements on the contours of the new institutional frameworks which tended to develop in the Asian countries with the onset of modernization. It also emphasizes the potential importance of the transformative orientations and powers of religious—and possibly also ideological—movements in creating viable modern institutional frameworks. It is not the mere development of structural differentiation and the establishment of such frameworks—which can be found in all Western and non-Western countries alike—which constitute the crucial test of modernization. Rather it is the extent to which within them there tend indeed to develop various transformative forces which may be of crucial importance from the point of view of the establishment of viable modern institutions. The previous discussion also stresses, with Bellah,[98] that it is not the mere development of some transformative orientations or new motivations within any group that is of importance but, beyond this, their possible impact on wider institutional settings and on the central spheres of a society.

All these considerations apply, as mentioned above, not only to religious but also to secular-ideological movements which purport to bring about the complete revolution of modernization. The mere development of such movements does not necessarily assure that they will be successful in attaining these aims. Very often they may evolve along with a general trend to secularization but may only undermine existing patterns of organized behavior and give rise to new aspirations without establishing new norms and sanctions.[99] The extent to which secular-ideological movements are successful may also greatly depend on the degree to which they are able to develop from within themselves transformative orientations, on different levels of individual behavior, and new roles and organizational frameworks similar to those of religious movements.

Until recently very little systematic research has been undertaken with regard to these problems as related to secular ideologies. Only two aspects of the problem have been approached. One line of research, as exemplified in the work of D. C. McClelland, has been the importance of ideological commitments for the development of motivation for (mainly economic) achievement.[100] The other tack has been to analyze different secular elites and groups, especially the "modernizing" intelligentsias and intellectual groups.

While the importance of such groups has been great in almost all the countries studied, they differed greatly in terms of their effectiveness in helping to establish and maintain a growth-sustaining modern institutional structure. These differences may be to some extent related to the variables noted above.[101]

Broadly speaking, we may distinguish between two types of intellectual elites. The first is found in those countries such as Burma and Indonesia where the intellectuals constituted the only initially available modern elite. They had but few internal social or ideological contacts (even if ambivalent ones) either with the adherents to pre-existing traditions or with the wider groups of the society. They did not evince a great ability to establish a strong internal cohesiveness and strong ideological and value identifications with other, potentially modernized groups and strata.[102]

There have been other types of modernizing elites, such as those in Meiji Japan and Kemalist Turkey. They were not usually composed only of intellectual groups alienated from the pre-existing elites and from the broader strata of the society. Rather they had a place in the pre-existing structure as secondary elites and had some positive orientations to the center and to other, broader social groups and strata.

In many ways it is these characteristics of the modernizing elites in general and of intellectual elites in particular that might prove to be the crucial elements in facilitating—or impeding—the crystallization, in situations of continuous social differentiation and mobilization, of those structural conditions conducive to the development of a flexible institutional structure. They may therefore greatly influence the extent of the continuity of modernization or of its breakdown.

However, these are as yet only preliminary indications.

As in the case of our examination of the differential impact of Protestantism in various European and American settings, only a full analysis of the interrelations between these broader forces, the various social strata caught in the process of modernization, and the more dynamic religious or ideological groups can provide a picture of the different concrete institutional contours developing in these countries, the extent to which they are able to deal with problems of continuous change, and the extent to which they are growth-sustaining or tend to stagnate and break down.

NOTES

1. Originally published as "Die protestantische Ethik und der Geist des Kapitalismus" in *Archiv für Sozialwissenschaft und Sozialpolitik*, XX (1901–1902), and reprinted in his *Gesammelte Aufsätze zur Religionssoziologie*, 3 vols. (Tübingen, (1920–1921); English translation: *The Protestant Ethic and the Spirit of Capitalism*, tr. Talcott Parsons, Foreword by T. H. Tawney (New York, 1930).

2. For Weber's distinction between premodern and modern capitalism, see his *General Economic History* (New York, 1961), Part IV.

3. M. Robertson, *Aspects of the Rise of Economic Individualism* (Cambridge, Eng., 1933); Amintore Fanfani, *Catholicism, Protestantism and Capitalism* (London, 1935); Kurt Samuelsson, *Religion and Economic Action*, tr. E. G. French (London, 1961).

4. See E. Fischoff, "The Protestant Ethic and the Spirit of Capitalism," *Social Research*, XI (1944), 54–77; R. F. Beerling, *Protestantisme en Kapitalisme, Max Weber in de Critiek* (Groningen and Batavia, 1946); and R. H. Tawney, "Religion and Economic Life," *The Times Literary Supplement*, 1956.

5. W. S. Hudson, "Puritanism and the Spirit of Capitalism," *Church History*, XVIII (1949), 3–16, and "The Weber Thesis Re-examined," *Church History*, XXX (1961), 88–89; C. H. and Katherine George, *The Protestant Mind and the English Reformation, 1570–1640* (Princeton, N.J., 1961). For a preliminary view, see C. and K. George, Ch. 7 below.

6. In this vein see also the older works of Henri Hauser, reprinted in *La modernité du XVIe siècle*, Cahiers des Annales, No. 21 (Paris, 1963). Several of the relevant studies may be found in R. W. Green (ed.), *Protestantism and Capitalism* (Boston, 1959).

7. R. H. Tawney, *Religion and the Rise of Capitalism* (London and New York, 1926).

8. Ernst Troeltsch, *The Social Teaching of the Christian Churches*, 2 vols. (New York, 1931; new edition, 1956), and *Protestantism and Progress* (Boston, 1958); Karl

Holl, *Gesammelte Aufsätze zur Kirchengeschichte* (Tübingen, 1927), especially Vols. I and II, and *The Cultural Significance of the Reformation* (New York, 1959).

9. On these differentiations between Lutheranism and Calvinism, as seen also from the point of view of Weber's strong emphasis on Calvinism, see Benjamin Nelson, "Max Weber's Sociology of Religion," *American Sociological Review*, XXX, No. 4 (August 1965), 595–601.

See also Alfred Müller-Armack, *Religion und Wirtshaft* (Stuttgart, 1959). More recently a similar thesis with regard to Lutheranism has been propounded by Gerhard Ritter in "Das 16. Jahrhundert als weltgeschichtliche Epoche," *Archiv für Reformationsgeschichte*, Vol. XXXV (1938), and *Die Neugestaltung Europas im 16. Jahrhundert* (Berlin, 1950), especially Ch. 3.

10. H. R. Trevor-Roper, *Religion, the Reformation and Social Change*, Historical Studies IV (London, 1965), pp. 18–45; Herbert Lüthy, Ch. 4 below, reprinted in his *Le passé présent* (Monaco and Paris, 1965), pp. 13–25, in which parts of Lüthy's work on the Protestant Bank (see next note) most relevant to a *general* discussion of the Protestant ethic thesis have been reprinted as "Puritanisme et société industrielle," pp. 58–71, and "Le prêt à intérêt sur la compétence de la théologie en matière économique," pp. 71–99; see also the discussion on Lüthy which took place in various 1964 issues of *Encounter* and *Preuves*; Michael Walzer, Ch. 5 below, and *The Revolution of the Saints* (Cambridge, Mass., 1965).

11. Herbert Lüthy, *La banque protestante en France de la révocation de l'Édit de Nantes à la Révolution*, 2 vols. (Paris, 1959–1961), especially II, 786 ff.

12. Michael Walzer, *The Revolution of the Saints*. A similar emphasis on the political activities of some Protestants, especially French and Scottish, is found in S. A. Burrell, Ch. 6 below; and H. R. Trevor-Roper, "Scotland and the Puritan Revolution," in H. E. Bell and R. L. Ollard (eds.), *Historical Essays, 1660–1750, Presented to David Ogg* (London, 1963), pp. 78–130.

The transformative potentials, in the political field, of the Puritan idea of the covenant have been explored by many people. See, among others, Hudson, articles already cited, and J. G. Breuer, "Puritan Mysticism and the Development of Liberalism," *Church History*, XIX (1950), 80–81.

13. H. R. Trevor-Roper, "The General Crisis of the Seventeenth Century" and "General Crisis: A Symposium," in Trevor Aston (ed.), *Crisis in Europe 1560–1660* (London and New York, 1965), pp. 59–97 and 97–117.

14. See, for instance, Hélène Cassin, "Quelques facteurs historiques et sociaux de la diffusion du protestantisme en Italie méridionale," *Archives de Sociologie des Religions*, II (1956), 55–72.

15. Emilio Willems, Ch. 9 below.

16. C. V. Moog, *Bandeirantes and Pioneers* (New York, 1964). A more enthusiastic analysis of the Bandeirantes is given in Cassian Ricardo, *Marcha para Oeste*, 2 vols. (Rio de Janeiro, 1942); it does not, however, greatly differ from Moog in its analysis and description of the activities of the Bandeirantes. For a general collection on the Bandeirantes, see R. M. Morse (ed.), *The Bandeirantes* (New York, 1965).

17. Wolfgang Mommsen, "Max Weber's Political Sociology," *International Social Science Journal*, XVII, No. 1 (1965), 31.

18. One of the most interesting analyses which deal explicitly with such transformative capacities of religious movements after their initial failure is that of G. Scholem on the Sabbatian movement in the seventeenth century. See Gershom Scholem, *Major Trends in Jewish Mysticism* (New York, 1946, 1956) and *Shabbetai Tzvi*, 2 vols. (Tel Aviv, 1958).

19. Stanislav Andreski, Ch. 2 below. See also C. K. Yang's Introduction in Max

Weber, *The Religion of China* (New York, 1964); and O. B. van der Sprenkel, "Max Weber on China," *Theory and History*, III (1964), 348–370.

20. This point has been analyzed with great skill with regard to the Arminians in The Netherlands and their potentially more open and revolutionary orientation by L. Kolakowski, "La genèse et la structure dans l'étude des idéologies religieuses," in M. de Gaudillac, L. Goldmann, and J. Piaget (eds.), *Entretiens sur les notions de genèse et de structure* (The Hague and Paris, 1965), pp. 307–323.

21. William Pauck, *The Heritage of the Reformation* (Glencoe, Ill., 1961), and also H. Richard Niebuhr, *The Social Sources of Denominationalism* (New York, 1959).

22. One of the earlier expositions of this view is found in A. D. Lindsay, *The Modern Democratic State* (Oxford, 1943).

23. David Little, *The New Order in Old England* (New York: Harpers, 1967).

24. See, for instance, Americo Castro, *The Structure of Spanish History* (Princeton, N.J., 1954); and also, for a very interesting analysis from the Catholic point of view, Henri Daniel-Rops, *The Protestant Reformation* (New York, 1961) and *The Catholic Reformation* (New York, 1961).

25. On the importance of the relations between the motivational and the organizational aspects of role development, see R. N. Bellah, Ch. 11 below.

26. See Burrell, Ch. 6 below.

27. The influence of Protestantism on science constitutes another focus of continued research and controversy growing out of the Protestant ethic thesis; see, for instance, R. K. Merton, "Science, Technology, and Society in Seventeeth Century England," *Osiris*, Vol. IV, No. 2 (1938); L. S. Feuer, *The Scientific Intellectual* (New York and London, 1963); R. Hooykaas, Ch. 10 below; H. van Gelder, *The Two Reformations in the Sixteenth Century* (The Hague, 1961); T. K. Rabb, "Puritanism and the Rise of Experimental Science in England," *Journal of World History*, VII (1962), 46–67; H. F. Kearney, "Puritanism, Capitalism and the Scientific Revolution," *Past and Present*, No. 28 (1964), pp. 81–101, and the other articles in this issue; and Joseph Ben-David, "The Scientific Role: The Conditions of Its Establishment in Europe," *Minerva*, IV, No. 1 (1965), 15–34.

28. Lawrence Stone, review of C. Hill's *Intellectual Origins of the English Revolution*, in *The New York Review of Books*, August 26, 1965, p. 10; and also R. Stone, *The Crisis of Aristocracy* (Oxford, 1965), especially Ch. 13.

29. On their situations as minorities, see, among others, W. C. Scoville, "The Huguenots and the Diffusion of Technology," *Journal of Political Economy*, LX (1952), 294–311; and E. Wayne-Nafziger, *The Mennonite Ethic in the Weberian Framework*, Explorations in Entrepreneurial History, second series, II, No. 3 (1965).

30. Of special interest in this respect are the developments in The Netherlands, specifically the relationship between Protestantism and the development of the Dutch nation. See Pieter Geyl, *The Netherlands in the Seventeenth Century*, 2nd ed. (London, 1961–1965), and *Noord en Zuid* (Utrecht and Antwerp, 1960), especially pp. 150–173; I. Schöffer, "De Nederlandse revolutie," in Z. R. Dittrich *et al.*, *Zeven Revoluties* (Amsterdam, 1964), pp. 9–29, and "Protestantism in Flux during the Revolt of the Netherlands," in J. S. Bromley and E. H. Kossmann (eds.), *Britain and the Netherlands* (Groningen, 1964), II, 67–84; and D. J. Roorda, "The Ruling Classes in Holland in the Seventeenth Century," in Bromley and Kossmann, *op. cit.*, pp. 109–133.

31. See, for instance, A. L. Drummond, *German Protestantism since Luther* (London, 1951); T. McNeill, *The History and Character of Calvinism* (New York, 1954); Ritter, "Das 16. Jahrhundert . . ." and *Die Neugestaltung*, Ch. 3, especially pp. 133–170; and Alfred Adam, "Die nationale Kirche bei Luther," *Archiv für Reformationgeschichte*, XXXV (1938), 30–62.

32. Hjalmar Holmquist, "Kirche und Staat im evangelischen Schweden," *Festgabe für Karl Müller* (Tübingen, 1922), pp. 209–277; Heinz-Horst Schrey, "Geistliches und weltliches Regiment in der schwedischen Reformation," *Archiv für Reformationgeschichte,* XLII (1951), 146–159; Georg Schweiger, *Die Reformation in den nordischen Ländern* (Munich, 1962); and Ritter, *Die Neugestaltung.*

33. Christine R. Kayser, "Calvinism and German Political Life," unpublished Ph.D. dissertation, Radcliffe College, 1961.

34. See, for instance, in fuller detail, S. N. Eisenstadt, *Modernization, Protest, and Change* (New York, 1966), especially Ch. 5.

35. On this problem see Eisenstadt, *op. cit.,* and *Modernization, Growth, and Diversity* (Bloomington, Ind., 1963). On the central religious situation in these countries, see R. N. Bellah (ed.), *Religion and Progress in Modern Asia* (Glencoe, Ill., 1965), especially the editor's Epilogue.

36. For a survey of some of these attempts, see Bellah, Ch. 11 below.

37. Clifford Geertz, " 'Internal Conversion' in Contemporary Bali," in J. Bastian and Roelof Roolvink (eds.), *Malayan and Indonesian Studies* (London, 1964), pp. 289–332.

38. *Ibid.*

39. See, for instance, H. S. Alatas, "The Weber Thesis and South East Asia," *Archives de Sociologie des Religions,* VIII, No. 15 (1963), 21–35.

40. Max Weber, *Gesammelte Aufsätze zur Religionssoziologie;* see also Andreski, Ch. 2 below; and Reinhard Bendix, "Max Webers Religionssoziologie," in R. Konig and J. Winckelman (eds.), "Max Weber zum Gedächtnis," *Kölner Zeitschrift für Soziologie und Sozialpsychologie Sonderheft,* VII (1963), 273–294.

41. Ralph Pieris, Ch. 12 below.

42. Michael Ames, Ch. 14 below; Geertz, *The Religion of Java* (Glencoe, Ill., 1960) and Ch. 16 below.

43. D. Svaramis, "Max Webers Beitrag zum besseren Verständnis der ostkirchlichen und 'ausserweltlichen' Askese," in R. Konig and J. Winckelman (eds.), "Max Weber zum Gedächtnis," *Kölner Zeitschrift für Soziologie und Sozialpsychologie Sonderheft,* VII (1963), 334–358.

44. Ernest Gellner, Ch. 15 below; and W. F. Wertheim, "Religious Reform Movements in South and South East Asia," *Archives de Sociologie des Religions,* XII (1961).

45. See, for instance, A. K. Bador, "Reformisme islamique et politique en Malaisie," *Archives de Sociologie des Religions,* XVII (1964), 68–85; and Geertz, *The Religion of Java.*

46. These hypotheses, as well as the following analysis, are preliminary steps to a wider comparative work which is being undertaken by the author.

47. The relationship between political innovation and religious movements in the premodern centralized empires was analyzed in S. N. Eisenstadt, "Religious Organization and Political Processes in Centralized Empires," *Journal of Asian Studies,* XXI, No. 3 (1962), 279–295.

48. See Wertheim, Ch. 13 below.

49. See *ibid.* and R. P. Dore, "Middle Classes (Non-European)," in *International Encyclopedia of the Social Sciences* (forthcoming).

50. See also Edward Shils, "The Concentration and Dispersion of Charisma: Their Bearing on Economic Policy in Underdeveloped Countries," *World Politics,* XI (1958), 1–19.

51. In this context various broad cultural symbolic patterns may be of great importance, especially in the comparative field, and may influence susceptibility to acceptance of choice and furtherance of intellectual and scientific activities. We will not, however, be able to deal with them at this stage of our analysis.

52. See R. N. Bellah, *Togukawa Religion* (Glencoe, Ill., 1957).

53. This follows partially S. N. Eisenstadt, "Transformation of Social, Political, and Cultural Orders in Modernization," *American Sociological Review*, XXX, No. 5 (October 1965), 659–673.

54. See Eisenstadt, "Religious Organizations and Political Processes," and Étienne Balazs, *Chinese Civilization and Bureaucracy* (New Haven, Conn., 1964).

55. Balazs, *op. cit.*

56. *Ibid.*

57. For the first analysis of Chinese familism from the point of view of modernization, see M. J. Levy, Jr., *The Family Revolution in Modern China* (Cambridge, Mass., 1952). Levy has elaborated and to some extent modified his point of view in "Contrasting Factors in the Modernization of China and Japan," in Simon Kuznets, W. E. Moore, and J. J. Spengler (eds.), *Economic Growth: Brazil, India, Japan* (Durham, N.C., 1955), pp. 496–537.

58. J. R. Levenson, *Confucian China and Its Modern Fate*, 3 vols. (Berkeley, Calif., 1958–1965), and Ssu-Yu Teng and J. K. Fairbanks, *China's Response to the West* (New York, 1963).

59. For the institutional development of modern pre-Communist China, see G. M. Beckman, *The Modernization of China and Japan* (New York, 1962), especially Chs. 23 and 24; and W. L. Tung, *The Political Institutions of Modern China* (The Hague, 1964). For some of the problems of legal reform, see Franz Michael, "The Role of Law in Traditional, Nationalist and Communist China," *The China Quarterly*, IX (1962), 124–148.

60. Claude Cahen, "The Body Politic," in G. E. von Grunebaum (ed.), *Unity and Variety in Muslim Civilization* (Chicago, 1955), pp. 132–163.

61. The first over-all exposition of modernization in Islam is probably H. A. R. Gibb, *Modern Trends in Islam* (Chicago, 1947). For further elaboration, see Muhsin-Mahdi, "Modernity and Islam," in J. M. Kitagawa (ed.), *Modern Trends in World Religions* (La Salle, Ill., 1959); and M. G. S. Hodgson, "Modernity and the Islamic Heritage," Islamic Studies, I (Karachi, 1962).

62. Justus van der Kroef, "Recent Trends in Indonesian Islam," *The Muslim World*, III (1962), and "The Role of Islam in Indonesian Nationalism and Politics," *Western Political Quarterly*, XI (1958), 33–54; Jan Prins, "Some Notes about Islam and Politics in Indonesia," *The World of Islam*, VI (1959), 124–126; C. Geertz, "Modernization in a Muslim Society: The Indonesian Case," in Bellah (ed.), *Religion and Progress in Modern Asia*; C. A. O. van Nieuwenhuize, *Aspects of Islam in Post-Colonial Indonesia* (The Hague, 1958), especially Ch. 1, 2, and 5.

63. On problems of legal reform in modern Islam, see J. N. D. Anderson, *Islamic Law in the Modern World* (New York and London, 1959); Joseph Schacht, "Problems of Modern Islamic Legislation," in R. H. Nolte (ed.), *The Modern Middle East* (New York, 1963), pp. 172–201; N. J. Coulson, *A History of Islamic Law* (Edinburgh, 1964).

64. See F. Rahman, "Muslim Modernism in the Indo-Pakistan Subcontinent," *Bulletin of the School of Oriental and African Studies*, XXI (1958), 82–99; Louis Dumont, "Nationalism and Communism," *Contributions to Indian Sociology*, VII (1964), 30–70; Hafez Malik, *Moslem Nationalism in India and Pakistan* (Washington, D.C., 1963).

65. Leonard Binder, *Religion and Politics in Pakistan* (Berkeley, Calif., 1961) and "Problems of Islamic Political Thought in the Light of Recent Developments in Pakistan," *Journal of Politics*, XX (1958), 675–685.

66. See Leonard Binder, *The Ideological Revolution in the Middle East* (New York, 1964); and Nadav Safran, *Egypt in Search of Political Community* (Cambridge, Mass., 1961).

67. See C. H. Moore, "The Neo-Destour Party in Tunisia: A Structure for Democracy?," *World Politics*, XIV (1962), 461–482; C. A. Micaud, L. C. Brown, and C. H. Moore, *Tunisia: The Politics of Modernization* (New York, 1964); Gabriel Ardant, *La Tunisie d'aujourdhui et de demain* (Paris, 1961).

68. Bernard Lewis, *The Emergence of Modern Turkey* (London, 1961).

69. Claude Cahen, "L'histoire économique et sociale de l'Orient musulman médiéval," *Studia Islamica*, CXI (1955), 93–116, and "Les facteurs économiques et sociaux dans l'ankylose culturelle de l'Islam," in R. Brunschwig and G. E. von Grunebaum (eds.), *Actes du symposium international d'histoire de la civilisation musulmane* (Paris, 1957), pp. 195–217.

70. Bellah, *Tokugawa Religion* and "Values and Social Change in Modern Japan," *Asian Cultural Studies*, III (1962), 13–56; D. M. Earl, *Emperor and Nation in Japan—Political Themes of the Tokugawa Period* (Seattle, 1964).

71. See M. B. Jansen, *Sakamoto Ryoma and the Meiji Restoration* (Princeton, N.J., 1961); and A. M. Craig, *Choshu in the Meiji Restoration* (Cambridge, Mass., 1961).

72. R. P. Dore, *Education in Tokugawa Japan* (Berkeley, Calif., 1964).

73. Some of the traditional kingdoms such as Morocco, Buganda, and Ethiopia may also attempt to modernize in this way; however, they face the very great difficulty that within them there did not exist a dissociation between the traditional symbolic and the effective centers. A partial parallel may perhaps be found in northern Nigeria, where its very incorporation in the federal framework may have provided some equivalent to such a dissociation.

74. See on this, among others, M. B. Jansen, "Changing Japanese Attitudes toward Modernization," in M. B. Jansen (ed.), *Changing Japanese Attitudes toward Modernization* (Princeton, N.J., 1965); R. N. Bellah, "Values and Social Change in Modern Japan," and the Epilogue to his *Religion and Progress in Modern Asia;* Herbert Passin, "Modernization and the Japanese Intellectual: Some Comparative Observations," in Jansen (ed.), *op. cit.*

75. R. P. Dore, "The Legacy of Tokugawa Education," in Jansen (ed.), *op. cit.*

76. Bellah, *Tokugawa Religion;* and Dore, *Education in Tokugawa Japan.*

77. Herbert Norman, *Japan's Emergence as a Modern State* (New York, 1940); Levy, "Contrasting Factors . . ."; Craig, *Choshu in the Meiji Restoration.*

78. Dore, "The Legacy of Tokugawa Education" and *Education in Tokugawa Japan.*

79. Levy, "Contrasting Factors . . . ," *op. cit.*

80. *Ibid.*

81. Masao Maruyama, "Patterns of Individuation and the Case of Japan: A Conceptual Scheme," in Jansen (ed.), *op. cit.*, pp. 489–533; Bellah, *Religion and Progress in Modern Asia*, Epilogue, and "Values and Social Change in Modern Japan"; Herbert Passin, "Stratigraphy of Protest in Japan," in Morton Kaplan (ed.), *The Revolution in World Politics* (New York, 1963), pp. 92–110.

82. Dore, *Education in Tokugawa Japan* and "The Legacy of Tokugawa Education," Passin, *op. cit.*

83. See Percival Spear, *India: A Modern History* (Ann Arbor, Mich., 1961); Louis Renou, Jean Filliozat, *et al.*, *L'Inde classique,* 2 vols. (Paris, 1947, 1953); H. N. Sinha, *The Development of Indian Polity* (Bombay, 1963).

84. This aspect of Indian political thought is elaborated from different points of view in V. P. Varma, *Studies in Hindu Political Thought and Its Metaphysical Background* (Benares, 1954); Louis Dumont, *La civilisation indienne et nous* (Paris, 1964) and "The Conception of Kingship in Ancient India," *Contributions to Indian Sociology,* VI (1962), 46–76; and Charles Drekmeier, *Kingship and Community in Early India* (Stanford, 1962). The best-known classical text is the Arthashastra; see Rudrapatna

Shammasastry (ed.), *Kautilya's Arthashastra*, 5th ed. (Mysore, 1960). Some additional texts are found in W. T. de Bary, S. N. Hay, Rayal Weiler, and Andrew Yarrow, *Sources of Indian Tradition* (New York, 1958), pp. 236–258.

85. See, for instance, L. L. Rai, "The Remedy for Revolution," Jawaharlal Nehru, "Satyagrapha," and M. K. Gandhi, "Face to Face with Ahimsa," all in D. M. Brown (ed.), *Indian Political Thought from Ranade to Bhave* (Berkeley, Calif., 1961); and S. A. Wolfert, *Tilak and Gohale in Revolution and Reform in the Making of Modern India* (Berkeley, Calif., 1962).

86. See the first chapter of the forthcoming work by Gopal Krishna, *The Development of the Organization of the Indian National Congress, 1918–1932* (mimeographed). On the reforming potential of Hinduism, see J. W. Elder, "Industrialism in Hindu Society: A Case Study in Social Change," *The Journal of Asian Studies*, XXV (May 1966), 413–431; and Milton Singer *et al.*, "India's Cultural Values and Economic Development: A Discussion," *Economic Development and Cultural Change*, VII (1958), 1–12.

87. See Milton Singer (ed.), *Traditional India: Structure and Change* (Philadelphia, 1959); and Myron Weiner, "India's Two Political Cultures," in his *Political Change in South Asia* (Calcutta, 1965), pp. 115–153. On the development of the "modern" center, see Rajni Kothari, "The Congress System in India," *Asian Survey*, IV (1964), 1161–1174.

88. The best-known analysis of these developments is M. N. Srinivas, *Caste in Modern India* (Bombay, 1962), especially Chs. 1, 2, and 4.

89. See André Beteille, *Closed and Open Social Stratification in India* (New Delhi, 1965); and Rajni Kothari and A. Maru, "Caste and Secularism in India—A Case Study of a Caste Federation," *Journal of Asian Studies*, XXV (1965), 33–51.

90. See Kothari, "The Congress System in India," and Weiner, *op. cit.*

91. See, for instance, Ch. Jayawardena, "Religious Belief and Social Change: Aspects of the Development of Hinduism in British Guiana," *Comparative Studies in Society and History*, VIII, No. 2 (1966), 211–241.

92. On these different possibilities, see L. I. Rudolph and Susanne H. Rudolph, "The Political Role of India's Caste Associations," *Pacific Affairs*, XXXIII (1960), 5–22; Beteille, *op. cit.*; and Srinivas, *op. cit.*

93. See S. S. Harrison, *India: The Most Dangerous Decades* (Princeton, N.J., 1960); Paul Friedrich, "Language and Politics in India," *Daedalus*, XCI (1962), 543–559.

94. See Michael Ames, "Magical Animism and Buddhism: A Structural Analysis of the Sinhalese Religious System," *Journal of Asian Studies*, XXII (1964), 21–53.

On the close association between the religious and political orders in Southeast Asia (especially Burmese, Ceylonese, and Thai) Buddhism, see the works of P. Mus, especially his *Barabadur esquisse d'une histoire du buddhisme* (Hanoi, 1935).

95. G. Obeyesekere, "The Great Tradition and the Little in the Perspective of Sinhalese Buddhism," *Journal of Asian Studies*, XXII (1963), 139–155.

96. Manning Nash, *The Golden Road to Modernity: Village Life in Contemporary Burma* (New York, 1965); and R. P. Dore, "Le réveil politiqe et la politique," *Archives de Sociologie des Religions*, No. 17 (1964), pp. 45–53; Mendelsohn, *Buddhism and the Burmese Establishment*, pp. 85–97; W. L. King, *A Thousand Lives Away: Buddhism in Contemporary Burma* (Cambridge, Mass., 1964); D. E. Smith, *Religion and Politics in Burma* (Princeton, N.J., 1965); F. R. von der Mehden, *Religion and Nationalism in South East Asia* (Madison, Wisc., 1963).

97. See Ames, Ch. 14 below.

98. See Bellah, Ch. 11 below.

99. Gino Germani, Ch. 17 below.

100. See D. C. McClelland, *The Achieving Society* (New York, 1961) and "National

Character and Economic Growth in Turkey and Iran," in Lucian Pye (ed.), *Communications and Political Development* (Princeton, N.J., 1963), pp. 152–188.

101. See Eisenstadt, *Modernization, Protest, and Change;* and Shils, *op. cit.*

102. See H. Benda, "Political Elites in Colonial South East Asia: A Historical Analysis," *Comparative Studies in History and Society*, VII (1965), 233–252, and "Non-Western Intelligentsia as Political Elites," in J. H. Kautsky (ed.), *Political Change in Underdeveloped Countries* (New York, 1962), pp. 235–251.

2

METHOD AND SUBSTANTIVE THEORY IN MAX WEBER

Stanislav Andreski

PHILOSOPHICAL FOUNDATIONS

The way in which most textbooks on the history of sociology classify Max Weber provides a good example of how people tend to affix labels by seizing on trifles: the pigeonhole assigned to him bears the label "understanding sociology" (*verstehende Soziologie*). If we take the word *understanding* at its usual connotation, we arrive at the conclusion that Max Weber had a monopoly on understanding society. This seems to be a slight exaggeration, although many sociological publications (including those which invoke Weber's name in vain) could very well be classified as "nonunderstanding sociology." Weber's distinction (not very clearly formulated) between "understanding" and "explaining" refers to something that has been known to philosophers for a very long time: namely, that we interpret actions of other human beings by attributing to them the feelings and thoughts which we should have if we carried out such actions. As Fichte showed, the validity of this procedure can never be proved; but neither can it be disproved, and nobody can utter its denial without contradicting himself, for the mere intent to communicate presupposes it. This analogy from subjective experience is not nowadays used in interpreting the behavior of objects other than the higher animals. Its continuous application does distinguish the study of man and society from other branches of learning, but it in no way distinguishes the thought of Max Weber. In fact, dustmen, historians, detectives, pimps, philosophers, all have to rely on their subjective experiences in order to be able to explain and predict the actions of others. Even the most astringent behaviorists, who avoid the humans and concentrate on rats, speak of organisms seeking and escaping.

Reprinted from The British Journal of Sociology, *XV, No. 1 (March 1964), 1–18.*

Weber, naturally, never claimed that he invented the procedure of *verstehen* or that it was in any way peculiar to his way of thinking. It was the commentators who committed this folly. Moreover, when dealing with definite sociological problems as distinguished from the discussion of the method of sociology—Weber (as far as I can recall) never refers to the distinction in question. In *Wirtschaft und Gesellschaft* there are only a few phrases on this matter. Naturally, he devotes more space to it in his methodological writings, but I do not think that there is anything in that discussion which has not been said better and earlier by some philosopher. I must confess that in spite of my great admiration for Weber, I find his formulations of philosophical problems to be rather mediocre: he labored under the baneful influence of the main current of German philosophy, with its habits of ponderous and elusive verbosity. (This was not so when it came to inductive theorizing, based on concrete data.) Notwithstanding this weakness, some of his thoughts on the methodology are of fundamental importance.

Three ideas constitute the essence of Weber's contribution to the methodology of the social sciences: firstly, the paradigm of reducibility of sociological concepts to actions of individuals; secondly, the paradigm of ethical neutrality; thirdly, the concept of the ideal type. The paradigm of reducibility amounts to a prophylactic rule. The practice of explaining the meaning of words denoting social conditions and positions in terms of the actions of individuals is as old as analytical thought. If we look in a dictionary for the meaning of "unemployment," we find it defined as "a condition when large numbers of workers have no jobs." "Ruler" is given as "one who rules," and so on. Yet, abstract terms, which refer to phenomena which cannot be directly observed in their totality, tend to be bandied about without the least concern for their meaning. Millions of people (including many professional sociologists) talk about "socialism," "democracy," "imperialism," "nationalization," "social integration," and what not without ever stopping to consider what these words mean in terms of concrete actions of real persons. Formulating his paradigm, Weber simply erected into a methodological canon what always was the practice of all sound thinkers; but it was an important step forward because it makes a great difference whether a procedure is intuitive or reasoned out, and there is great merit in having said something that ought to have been obvious but was not, and still is not to most people. A further merit of Weber was that he stuck to methodology, and steered clear of the futile ontological problem, to which many of his contemporaries devoted their energies, which sidetracked even Durkheim, and which to this day haunts the precincts of some methodological seminars, namely the question of whether it is the society or the individuals that really exist. I cannot recall any statements of Weber on this point, but I feel sure by inference that he took it for granted that the parts existed just as "really" as the wholes. Weber, however, was not unique in this respect, for Auguste Comte and Herbert Spencer had perfectly clear ideas on this matter, and the reification of social processes by the Durkheimians was a retrograde step.

The requirement of *Wertfreiheit*—which has been translated as value-freedom or ethical neutrality, but which I propose to call the paradigm of nonvaluation—has often been misunderstood. Some people interpreted it as enjoining upon the sociologist an olympian indifference to the ills of mankind. Even apart from anything that Weber wrote, his passionate advocacy of various causes shows that this was not what he had in mind. His paradigm of nonhortation can best be regarded as a methodological and semantic rule for classifying propositions, in accordance with which we include in sociology only nonvaluative propositions. Naturally, in view of the emotional loading of all the words which describe human relations, the strict adherence to this ideal would silence us forever. But this is no argument against trying to approach it, because the same is true of ideals such as logical consistency or clarity, which are universally upheld, though only intermittently attained. The validity of a methodological precept is not a matter of truth, but of heuristic utility, and by definition a precept cannot be *wertfrei*. We must, then, examine the claim of this paradigm on the assumption that knowledge of social phenomena is valuable.

The first argument in its favor is that, when dealing with matters which arouse our emotions, we must discipline our reasoning, so as to avoid wishful or "hate-inspired" thinking. The adherence to the canon of nonvaluation—that is, careful separation of judgments of value from judgments of fact—is useful for this purpose. Secondly, the paradigm in question can be recommended on the grounds of semantic expediency. People differ considerably in their valuations, and it is often difficult to infer from the words of praise or denigration what features the objects exhibit, other than the capacity to please or displease the utterer. This difficulty might be obviated if all publications carried as preamble a full exposition of the author's values, but, plainly, the acceptance of the paradigm of nonvaluation provides a far more economical solution. The third reason for recommending this paradigm is that by excluding numerous controversial issues, it enables people who disagree on many values, but share the wish to advance the knowledge of social phenomena, to collaborate in the furtherance of this end. In short, nonvaluation in analyzing social phenomena commends itself for the sake of objectivity. Objectivity, incidentally, can be defined as the freedom of reasoning from the influence of the desires, other than the desire to know the truth. Only in this sense can objectivity be approached, if not attained, for obviously no reasoning can be independent of the concepts with which it operates or of the knowledge on the basis of which it proceeds. Arguments for or against the admission of any given proposition into the body of accepted sociological knowledge cannot, of course, be free from judgments of value: they presuppose positive valuation of truth, consistency, and other ideals of scientific thought. They belong, however, not to sociology itself but to its metalanguage, to use the expression current among comtempory philosophers.

IDEAL TYPES

The concept of ideal type is rather difficult. In the first place, it might be said that to talk about an ideal type is like talking about wet water, for any type, being an abstraction, is ideal and not real in the sense that a given material object is real: there exists this horse and that, but not a horse in general. The difference between an ideal type and a type pure and simple lies not in the abstractness of connotation but in the definiteness of denotation: whereas the types established by biological systematics have referents which fall under them, and nowhere else, this is not the case with ideal types. No horse in general ever lived, but there are many horses which satisfy perfectly the specifications of "horsiness," while nothing like a perfectly rational organization has ever been observed. The idea behind the concept of ideal type is that social phenomena, in virtue of their manifold and fluid nature, can be analyzed solely in terms of the extreme forms of their characteristics, which can never be observed in their purity. This idea is perfectly sound, but was presented in a manner somewhat lacking in clarity. It might be even argued that Pareto's treatment of the problem of conceptualization in sociology was less open to criticism. Pareto pointed out that all concepts of physical sciences are idealizations: that no movement without resistance of the medium has ever been observed (but only surmised in the case of celestial bodies), that nothing perfectly straight has ever been found, that vectorial analysis assumes movements which never take place, and that social sciences must proceed likewise. As far as social sciences are concerned, the most useful idealizations can be found in the most mature of them, which is not surprising: the concepts of economic theory, such as perfect competition or static equilibrium, provide the best examples of ideal types. On the other hand, there is nothing very "ideal" about Weber's own typologies. When he talks about bureaucracy or feudalism or capitalism, he moves on the level of abstraction which is not very far removed from observable reality. Moreover, these concepts are taken at their current meaning. Altogether, there is nothing methodologically new in Weber's handling of typologies: he is doing exactly the same as did all the other good thinkers, beginning with Aristotle. The originality lay not in methodological novelty, but in substantive implications of the features, which on several occasions he singled out for consideration. For example, his distinction between producing and consuming towns—*Produzentenstadt* and *Konsumentenstadt* —is of fundamental importance to the problem of the conditions which permitted the rise of capitalism, but there is nothing logically distinctive about these concepts. The master's touch reveals itself in the way he uses them as the tools of analysis. On some occasions his typologies are less illuminating, or even useless: this is the case, I think, with his classification of the forms of rationality, as well as with that of the types of action. On these points common-sense notions seem to be better.

COMPARATIVE METHOD

What I have said so far may have sounded almost as a denigration. This is far from being my intention. I regard Max Weber's contribution as the most monumental there has been to sociology, but I feel that the relatively less valuable parts of it have attracted the greater share of attention. To say that other parts of his works are more impressive is not to claim that the methodological writings are without importance. On the contrary, I am convinced that merely for formulating the methodological ideas discussed above Weber merits a place in the history of sociology. His supremacy, however, is due to his unsurpassed ability for making or suggesting inductive generalizations. This kind of work requires, in addition to a gift for theorizing, a profound knowledge of a wide range of factual data; and in this respect Weber was unrivaled. Nobody who glances through any of his major works can fail to be impressed by the astounding array of detailed information. True, the same can be said about writers like Frazer, Ratzel, Westermarck, Spengler, and Toynbee, but there is a great difference between them and Weber. In the first place, they had nothing useful to say in the way of theoretical generalization. Frazer and Westermarck were interested in establishing a sequence of evolutionary stages, and Ratzel in showing the influence of geographical environment. Actually their works constitute useful encyclopedias of customs, beliefs, and institutions. Toynbee has a theory but it is vague, tautological, and unverifiable; it could be propounded only by somebody unacquainted with the work of generations of thinkers who devoted their lives to the study of society. The *Study of History* has considerable value, but only as a source book of recondite pieces of information. Whilst Frazer and Westermarck catalogued customs, and Spengler and Toynbee filled their books with spurious analogies between superficial features of mostly fictitious entities, Weber compared social structures and their functioning, noting differences as carefully as resemblances and trying to relate isolated features to their structural contexts. When information on the structure of the society in which he was interested was lacking, he made truly herculean efforts to extract it from the sources. Each volume of his *Religionssoziologie* would merit praise even if it were the single product of lifelong work. In spite of many serious errors, the parts devoted to China and India still stand unrivaled as "holistic" (or, if you like, functionalist) analyses of these societies, revealing their inner springs and showing the mutual dependence of culture and society. His original insights into the functioning of these societies are too numerous to be discussed here in detail, so one example must suffice: Weber was first to raise the problem of the distinctive features of the Chinese towns and of how these were related to the structure of the state and of the economy. After fifty years there is still nothing better of this kind. Étienne Balazs—the sinologist who has done more than anybody else to fill this gap—recognizes Weber as the source of his inspiration. To appreciate the magnitude of Weber's achievement, it must be remembered that when he prepared his *Religionssoziologie* next to nothing was known about the social and economic history of China. He extracted his information on the structure of the Chinese society and its development from translated dynastic chronicles, reports of travelers, and the pages of the *Peking Gazette*. The amount of effort and perspicacity necessary for this task must have been prodigious. The same is true of his treatment of India. In the case of Ancient Israel his task was somewhat lighter because the subject has been better studied; and so the factual mistakes appear to be fewer. The history of the economic and political institutions of the ancient Mediterranean had been studied intensively even before Weber was born, and his contemporary Eduard Meyer attempted a synthesis in a remarkable essay on "Economic Development in Antiquity." During the sixty years since the appearance of "Agraverhältnisse in Altertum," many excellent works appeared in this field, the most comprehensive being those of Rostovtzeff and Heichelheim. Nevertheless Weber's sociological history, concealed under the modest title, remains unique. For it is neither an economic history, nor a social history (as it is commonly understood), nor a political nor a military, but a truly structural history, which shows how the economic changes influenced religion, how the innovations in tactics brought about the transformations of social stratification, how the distribution of political power impeded the growth of capitalism, and so on. All the time he tries to trace dynamic relations between various aspects of social life. His treatment of historical data is just as much functionalist as were Malinowski's analyses of the Trobriand society; and in its light, the dispute between the functionalist and the historical schools of anthropology, which raged in the twenties and thirties, appears puerile.

Max Weber was a great historian, but, at least in his later years, he studied history mainly in order to make comparisons. His case studies are strewn with references to other situations and with generalizations or hints at possible generalizations. When writing about the prophets of Ancient Israel, he presents a theory about relations between peasants and town traders and usurers, about the destruction of tribal solidarity by the monetary economy and the bureaucratic state, and about how social protest of the peasants tends to be connected with movements for religious reform. At the end of his analysis of the causes of the fall of the Roman

Empire he draws a comparison with the modern Occident and throws in a prediction that "as in the antiquity, the bureaucracy will become the master of capitalism in the modern world . . . for capitalism is now the chief agent of bureaucratization." This was written before the end of the last century.

Weber was not the first to resort to comparisons in order to arrive at generalizations. Indeed, all the thinkers that have left their mark on the history of sociology did precisely that. Aristotle, ibn-Khaldun, Bodin, Machiavelli, Montesquieu, Buckle, Spencer, Roscher, Mosca, and many others—they all used comparative method. The moral of this, incidentally, is that the aspirants to Weber's mantle should postpone their attempts to produce another *Economy and Society* until they acquire a comparable range of factual information. Weber's achievement shows, moreover, that the knowledge of other societies, and the consequent ability to compare, aids enormously the analysis of any given society, and particularly the discovery of causal relationships. His superiority over his most distinguishted predecessors was largely due to the progress of historiography. Montesquieu could not have used similar data because they just were not available. Today it is possible to correct Weber on a number of points because during the forty years which have elapsed since his death relevant information has accumulated. His greatness can be measured by the profusion of extremely interesting hypotheses which can be found in his works. For instance: is it true, as he suggests in connection with his analysis of the Chinese intellectuals, that bureaucratic connections breed formalism in philosophy?

As is well known, all Weber's works are focused, in one way or another, on the problem of the conditions which permitted the rise of capitalism. Almost needless to say, there was nothing original in this preoccupation; it stems directly from Marx and was shared by many scholars, particularly in Germany. Marxists as well as the economists of the "historical school" discussed it continuously, and the first edition of Werner Sombart's *Der moderne Kapitalismus* appeared before Weber's articles in *Archiv für Sozialwissenschaft* (which were later incorporated into the volumes of *Religionssoziologie*). The originality of Weber's approach consisted, in the first place, in something very simple. In order to discover the causes of the rise of capitalism, other scholars studied in great detail the process of its growth, thus confining their attention to western Europe. He, on the other hand, conceived the brilliant idea of throwing light on this problem by concentrating on cases where capitalism failed to develop. This idea, it is true, would not amount to very much if he were not capable of carrying it out, but coupled with masterly execution, it gave to his works a stamp of uniqueness. The comparative point of view, moreover, saved him from pitfalls into which many others fell: unlike Sombart, for instance, he knew that neither the desire for pecuniary gain nor vast accumulations of liquid wealth were in any way peculiar to the countries where capitalism developed and could not, therefore, be regarded as crucial factors.

The countroversy over Weber's thesis has been centered around his assertions about the role which the Protestant ethics played in the development of capitalism in Europe, while the conjunction of his views on the impact of religions and economic life failed to attract a similar amount of attention. In what follows, some comments on this wider issue are offered, but in the first place let us look at the economic impact of Protestantism within the setting of the European civilization.

CATHOLICISM AND PROTESTANTISM

Nothing contributed more to Weber's fame than his essay on the Protestant ethics and the rise of capitalism, although it contains no structural analysis, so characteristic of the bulk of his works. Whereas in his treatment of Hinduism, Judaism, and the Chinese religions he tries to relate religious beliefs to social institutions, viewing culture and society as an integrated whole, The Protestant Ethic and the Spirit of Capitalism contains only rather disjointed references to the social circumstances. He nowhere claimed that the Calvinist ethic was the cause of the rise of capitalism, but treated in isolation from his other works the essay gives some justification to the reproach that he overstated his case.

There are two kinds of argument in favor of Weber's thesis: one of them can be described as the argument from harmony; the other as the argument from covariation. Let us look at them in turn. The argument from harmony consists in showing that capitalism can be developed only by people endowed with certain traits of character and that a given creed inculcates such traits.

It can be admitted as self-evident that capitalism cannot grow unless there are people who accumulate capital—that is to say, who do not spend everything they earn. The argument here is that Protestantism, and especially its Calvinist variety, taught thrift, whereas Catholicism did not. No religion, of course, has ever eradicated cupidity, but the disdain for material goods professed by the Catholic Church may have encouraged spending. Cupidity, after all, is something that comes naturally, whereas thrift is not. Thrift alone, however, is not enough.

An economic system whose propelling force is private accumulation of capital will not develop very fast if people are inclined to stop working as soon as they reach a certain level of affluence. Progress of such a system requires that those who have already enough for their needs should go on working and accumulating. The connection with Protestantism, particularly in its Calvinist variety, is that it taught people to regard work as a form of prayer and the growth of possessions as the evidence of the state of grace. Another important influence of Protestantism was its insistence on work as the only legitimate road to riches. Other religions, of course, also prohibit robbery and theft, but Protestant puritanism is unique in condemning gambling. The religious ideals of work, thrift, and enrichment without enjoyment and by means of work only constitute what Weber calls "worldly asceticism." It is extremely plausible that a creed which preached such asceticism did in fact stimulate the growth of capitalism.

The argument that the Reformation first opened up possibilities of investment, by legitimizing interest on loans, carries less force because in reality interest taking was very common during the late Middle Ages and by no means limited to parasitic usury. Nevertheless, it might be claimed that by removing the need for subterfuges, the Reformation helped to direct investment into productive channels, for clandestine gains are more readily linked with parasitically exploitative than with productive employment of capital. We can debate how much weight should be assigned to this factor, but the direction of its influence is beyond dispute.

The weakest point in the argument from harmony is the assertion linking the doctrines of predestination with the acquisitive drive. It is difficult to see how an earnest belief that one's fate is determined by something absolutely beyond one's control could stimulate anybody to exert himself. Fatalism (that is to say, belief in predestination) is generally considered to be one of the greatest obstacles to economic development of the oriental lands—an attitude which saps entrepreneurial energies as well as the spirit of workmanship. What seems to have happened is that Protestants took as little to heart the doctrine of predestination as they did the old injunction to expose the other cheek to an assailant. It appears therefore that this tenet of Calvin's doctrine provided neither stimulus nor obstacle to the growth of capitalism.

The general conclusion which emerges from the foregoing analysis is that, although the doctrine of predestination constituted a neutral influence, the worldly asceticism ought to have stimulated the growth of capitalism. In order to obtain further light on this thesis, let us look at the argument from covariation.

The data included in Weber's essay as well as those supplied by later investigators show clearly that in countries and regions where the Protestants and the Catholics live intermingled, the former occupy prominent positions in business in disproportionate numbers. In France, for instance, the influence of the Protestants in business is astonishing in view of the paucity of their numbers. In this case the explanation that their enthusiasm for business is due to being excluded from other fields of activity cannot be sustained because we would have to go right back to the "ancient regime" to find bars against the entry of Protestants into official posts. There remains a possibility that the mere fact of being in a minority had a bracing effect upon them, but the predominance of the Protestants over the Catholics in the economic life of a country like Germany, with a more or less evenly balanced population, cannot be accounted for in this way. Only in the cases of Ireland and Prussian Poland can the economic inferiority of the Catholics be possibly explained by the fetters imposed upon them by their Protestant rulers. For this reason, these cases lend no support to Weber's thesis, but they do not contradict it either. It could be said that the predominance of the Protestants in American business is due to the fact that they descend mainly from the old-established population, whereas the Catholics came more recently as poor immigrants, but for Canada and Holland this explanation plainly does not hold. The case of Holland is particularly significant because there the Catholics were a minority relegated to a politically subordinate position but with ample opportunities for business activities. Their position resembled in some ways that of the Protestants in France after the end of legal discrimination. Nevertheless, they furnished far fewer successful businessmen than either the Protestants or the Jews. Thus, even if we allow for the influence of other factors, the data unambiguously suggest that Protestantism is more conducive to business activity than Catholicism.

We can adduce another argument from covariation in support of Weber's thesis, using as our units of comparison states, instead of sections of populations located within the boundaries of one state, and pointing out that capitalism developed furthest and fastest in predominantly Protestant countries. In the world of today only the first part of this statement is true: the economies of the English-speaking countries, dominated by the Protestants, continue to represent the furthest stage in the evolution of capitalism, but their rates of growth are exceeded by those of France, Italy, and West Germany. The latter fact, however, does not invalidate the thesis of Weber, but only demands that we make explicit what is implicit: namely, that this thesis applies in full only to the situation where accumulation by private individuals constitutes the driving force of economic development. Once the giant concerns and trusts enter upon the scene and the "plowing back" of their undistributed profits becomes (jointly with the financing by the state) the chief form of investment, worldly asceticism loses its importance because most of the saving becomes then in a sense "forced." It must be remembered, moreover, that Weber's analysis referred to an epoch when the margin of affluence was very much smaller than it is in the industrial countries of today, and as saving is more difficult for the less opulent, worldly asceticism sanctioned by religion was necessary for rapid accumulation and productive investment of the capital. The important point here is that capitalist enterprise of a nonpredatory kind was developed by persons who did not have very much. There have always been large accumulations of liquid and real wealth in the hands of economically parasitic persons and corporations, but they contributed little to industrial growth, at least in its early stages.

With the proviso, then, that it refers without qualifications only to economies consisting of small firms, the arguments from approximative covariation support Weber's thesis. Nevertheless, owing to the bewildering complexity of this problem, these comparative data lend themselves to other
interpretations as well.

In his *Materialistische Geschichtsauffassung* (perhaps the greatest work
of Marxist historiography) Karl Kautsky attempted to invert Weber's argument in accordance with the Marxist view that religion is a mere epiphenomenon without any causal efficacity—a view which is contradicted
by Marx's statement that religion is the opium of the masses, for one
cannot deny the power of opium. Narrating the spread of various heresies
during the later Middle Ages, Kautsky shows how the class of artisans and
petty businessmen provided a fertile ground for the conception and dis-
semination of ideas which found their final embodiment in Calvinism.
For artisans and petty traders, fairly safe behind their walls from the dep-
redations of feudal lords, hard work and saving were unique means of
improving or even merely maintaining their positions. These conditions
generated, according to Kautsky, the mentality which found its final sanction in Calvinism. This argument has considerable force: the evidence
adduced by Kautsky and other writers does show that Calvinism struck
roots above all in the cities where commerce and handicrafts prospered.
The recent investigations show that the protagonists of Calvinism in German cities belonged to circles connected with business. Notwithstanding
these new data, the thesis on the epiphenomenal character of Calvinism
cannot be sustained because it fails to account for its spread among the
Hungarian nobility and, above all, for the conversion of Scotland. At the
time of John Knox, the Scotsmen, who later came to dominate the English
finance, were semitribal rustics renowned for their dissolute ways. Knox
and his followers made them into the most perfect examples of worldly
asceticism. Here then the causation appears to have worked in the direct
opposite to that suggested by Kautsky.

In Scotland, Calvinism came to prevail without capitalism; in Italy,
capitalism failed to bring about religious schism of any kind. The case of
Italy is particularly interesting because it contradicts not only Kautsky's
thesis but the extreme formulations of Weber's thesis as well: in Italy capitalism was born and prospered without any aid from the Protestant ethics
and, in fact, the Papal See was one of the greatest centers of banking
operations in the world. The Italians invented techniques so essential to
capitalism as bill of exchange and double-entry bookkeeping and controlled banking in northern Europe until the seventeenth century: the
main street of the district in London where headquarters of banks are
located still bears the name of Lombard Street. At the times of Calvin and
John Knox capitalism was vastly more developed in Florence and Venice
than in Geneva or Edinburgh. Presumably one of the reasons why Protes-

tantism had so little appeal to the Italian bourgeoisie was the close connection of the Italian bankers with the tributary machinery of the Church
—the fact which might have had something to do with the external manifestations of piety for which Florence (the seat of high finance) was renowned. The second reason might have been the disinclination of the
Italians to fight for their religious convictions: Machiavelli maintained
that the nearer a place was to Rome the less truly pious were its inhabitants. Be that as it may, the fact remains that the example of Italy shows
that neither Protestantism in general nor Calvinism in particular can be
regarded as mere epiphenomena of capitalism.

The thesis of Weber is affected only in the extreme formulations of
some of its interpreters, for although the case of Italy proves that Calvinism could not have been a necessary condition of the emergence of capitalism, it does not rule out the possibility that Calvinism, had it been able
to strike roots, could have given to the Italian capitalism greater impetus.
Indeed, the evidence from Italy supports the less extreme interpretation of this thesis because the Italian capitalism ceased to grow after the
end of the sixteenth century and began to decline thereafter. The causation of this withering of the economic impetus is very difficult to unravel:
there were a number of factors involved such as the loss of the importance
of the Mediterranean as the trade route, foreign invasions, wars between
the Italian states, and so on. The spirit of enterprise had waned, but as at
no time did it have a religious backing, there is little reason to attribute
this to the changes in religious outlook—religion may have had something
to do with it but in an indirect way.

When we look at the geographical distribution of the Catholic and
Protestant populations, it seems so arbitrary that it is difficult to imagine
that it could be the product of any such constant trend as the development of capitalism. A closer inspection of the process of the Reformation
confirms this impression: a single battle often decided whether a country
or a region were to remain Catholic or to become Protestant—and as is
well known outcomes of battles often depend on accidents. The power of
the princes to impose a creed of their choice upon their subjects—proclaimed in the sinister principle of "cuius regio eius religio"—enlarged
the scope of chance, because actions of single individuals exhibit less regularity than joint actions of large numbers.

Although in his writings on oriental religions Weber takes into account
indirect effects of religious beliefs, the explicit stress throughout his *Religionssoziologie* is on what he calls "economic ethics," that is to say, on the
influence upon the attitudes toward business of the code of behavior prescribed by religion. But it might be argued that of greater consequence
for the development of the economy was the influence of the ecclesiastical
organization upon the distribution of power. Some writers have argued
that the most far-reaching impact of the Reformation consisted in re-

placing an autocratic ecclesiastic organization by a looser one, thus weakening the conservative forces of society. Moreover, the Reformation has furthered the growth of capitalism by bringing about the confiscation of the gold in the possession of the churches and monasteries and putting it into circulation, thus eliminating the greatest source of thesaurization, which must have acted as a brake upon productive investment.

There is another way in which Protestantism may have stimulated the growth of capitalism. A perfectly capitalist society is not viable: when the sole motive of individual actions is unbridled pursuit of gain, the administration of the state becomes disorderly and corrupt and the growth of capitalism is impeded thereby. This is not a purely deductive argument because we can see that the countries where capitalism developed furthest and fastest are blessed with more than average share of civic virtues. In the United States the great captains of capitalism may have been utterly ruthless and even dishonest, but on the whole the civic communal spirit is very strong there even today and was much stronger at the time when capitalism began to develop. England, Holland, and lately Sweden have for long been renowned as examples (relative, of course) of orderliness and civic virtues and for the adherence to the principle that honesty is the best policy. The same can be said about the Germans, in spite of their authoritarian proclivities. Japan also exemplifies the usefulness of civic virtues to capitalism, but this case is irrelevant to the comparison of Catholicism with Protestantism. It must be noted, on the other hand, that all the so-called underdeveloped countries are conspicuous for the lack of public spirit.

Accepting as valid the assumption that capitalism requires a good measure of civic virtues if it is to prosper, we face the questions of whether this has anything to do with Protestantism and of whether it is not entirely a matter of circular causation; for it might be argued that widespread poverty undermines civic virtues, and the lack of them makes poverty difficult to eliminate. It is a fact, however, that if we compare the Protestant with the Catholic lands, the difference in the prevalence of civic virtues is striking. Without going into the intricacies of possible causations, we must note the possibility that Protestantism might have stimulated the growth of capitalism indirectly by fostering the civic virtues required for the smooth functioning of the state.

The contention that Protestanism stimulated the growth of capitalism in indirect ways which cannot be subsumed under Weber's concept of economic ethics, far from disproving Weber's thesis merely amplifies it.

Some weight must be assigned to the complete lack of arguments in favor of the contrary thesis that Catholicism is or was more propitious than Protestantism to the development of capitalism. At most it might be argued that under certain circumstances Calvinism fails to produce much spirit of capitalist enterprise. Among the examples which might be cited to this point, the most conspicuous are those of the Calvinist Hungarian nobility and of the Boers of South Africa—although the Boers do show somewhat more inclination toward "worldly asceticism" and business activity than the people who are in economically analogous positions in the Catholic lands. On the whole, then, if we bear in mind that Weber regarded Protestantism as a factor which fostered the development of capitalism, and not as *the* cause thereof, we can accept his thesis as valid.

JUDAISM

The volume of *Religionssoziologie* devoted to Judaism is unquestioningly a great work, full of illuminating insights and brilliant suggestions; nevertheless, its central theme sheds little light on the relation between religion and the rise of capitalism simply because as an economic force Judaism was negligible during its formative period and long afterward. The Jews were a very small nation, leading a precarious interstitial existence, oppressed and pushed around by mighty nations and empires, and finding consolation in religious contemplation. As far as the evolution of ancient capitalism was concerned, the nature of their religion was of no consequence: no matter how conducive to capitalist activity it might have been, the shaping of the economy (even of their own little country) was not in their hands.

During the earlier parts of the Middle Ages the primitive condition of society ruled out any development of capitalist enterprise, regardless of whether the tenets of religion fostered "the spirit of capitalism" or not. As soon as it became materially possible, the Jews began to play a prominent role in commerce and banking but, being restricted in residence and not allowed to own land, they were not in a position to take part in developing industry.

As soon as the restrictions imposed upon them ceased to be crippling, the Jews proved to be at least as successful in business as the Calvinists, and as the successful Jewish businessmen were as a rule just as pious as their Calvinist counterparts, there is no reason to think that the economic ethics of Judaism is in any way less propitious to capitalist activity than that of Calvinism. Indeed, it would be strange if it were so, because the teachings of Protestantism (particularly of its puritanical varieties) consisted mainly of precepts of ancient Judaism.

The so-called "double ethics" of the Jews (that is to say, the principle that it is sinful to cheat a coreligionist but not a Gentile), in which Weber saw a major obstacle to development of "rational" business enterprise, does not belong to the core of Judaism and is perfectly explicable as a response to persecution and disdain. Where the Jews were not harassed and achieved opulence, they usually conducted business just as respectably as anybody else.

In his famous book *The Jews and Modern Capitalism* Werner Sombart argued that the Jews were the true creators of capitalism. He based his contention on a number of instances in which an arrival of Jews in substantial numbers was followed by an efflorescence of business activity and a rapid growth of wealth. This was the case with Holland, Venice, the city of Frankfurt, and many others. Contrariwise, expulsions of the Jews were in several instances followed by an economic decline of the city or even a whole country, as was the case with Spain. However, Sombart does not take into account the data which do not fit his thesis, such as the fact that in England the foundations of capitalism were laid during the period between the expulsion of the Jews and their return. It could even be argued that the presence of a very large number of Jews is fatal to development of capitalism on the ground that the Jews were much more numerous in the economically backward eastern Europe than in the countries of developed capitalism. The causation here is extremely involved.

Originally it was the economic backwardness which was the cause of the influx of the Jews into eastern Europe: objects of animosity from their Gentile competitors in more highly urbanized lands in western Europe, they were welcomed in the countries without a native trading class. However, their presence in large numbers acted subsequently as a brake upon commercial development because as soon as trade came to be monopolized by the Jews it became a depressed occupation. Being isolated from the surrounding population, the Jews were in a much weaker position than a bourgeoisie integrated with the rest of the society, and therefore they were unable to resist the encroachments of the nobility, which was the reason why the Polish and Hungarian nobles preferred them.

In spite of the startling achievements of its adherents in the field of business, Judaism could never become a decisive factor in the development of capitalism because it was a religion of a minority of strangers which could never mold the character of any European nation. The Jews neither wished nor had the chance to convert to their faith the Christian majority; and it was out of the question that they should attain a truly dominating position in any country of the diaspora. In consequence, the Jews could use their aptitude for capitalist enterprise when the circumstances were propitious, but were powerless to create them.

Weber was partly right: Judaism was not a crucial factor in the rise of capitalism; but he was wrong in imputing this to its economic ethics. This ethic was extremely favorable to capitalism but its influence was always severely limited by the non-proselytic character of Judaism.

CONFUCIANISM

Weber's volume on China constitutes an even greater contribution to sociology than his volume on Judaism, but nevertheless its general thesis seems to be wrong. True, everything influences everything in social life, and there can be little doubt that by contributing in some way to the maintenance of the structure of the traditional Chinese society, Confucianism somehow acted as an indirect brake upon the development of capitalism; but as far as the direct influence via the economic ethics is concerned, it does not appear that Confucianism in any way impeded capitalist activity. Analyzing this problem along the lines similar to the foregoing treatment of Protestantism, let us first examine the argument from harmony—or rather disharmony.

In spite of what Weber says, I think that it is difficult to find among the tenets of Confucianism anything directly opposed to capitalist activity. Filial piety, patriarchalism, and family solidarity do not hamper business very much and were by no means absent from the European civilization at the time of the rise of capitalism. Ritualism (which is the factor which Weber stresses) was, it is true, very marked in traditional China, but it concerned personal relations—not economic activities. The general outlook of Confucianism was practical and rationalist. I think that Weber was wrong in maintaining that Christianity contributed to "demagicalization" (*Entzauberung*) of the view of the world.

The assignation of the low status to the merchants by the Confucianist literature cannot be regarded as an important factor for two reasons: firstly, because it was not uncommon in the ideological literature of the countries where capitalism was rising; and secondly, because it was an effect rather than a determinant of the existing distribution of power, as can be seen from the fact that the equally low status assigned to the soldiers in the Confucianist writings did not prevent them from attaining very high positions, and at times dominating the society.

Although many of its preconditions—such as well-developed transport and currency, wide area of peaceful commerce, and very high level of handicrafts—existed in China, capitalist industry could not develop there because of the fetters imposed upon business enterprise by the bureaucratic state. The officials always regarded the businessmen with resentment and employed many means to keep them down. Fiscal extortion prevented, if not accumulation of profits, at least their regular investment in productive establishments, which was in any case difficult owing to official regulation of location and methods of production. That these factors, and not the economic ethics, were responsible for the arrest of capitalism in traditional China is demonstrated by the performance of the Chinese emigrants to the British and Dutch colonies, most of whom continued to adhere strictly to their traditional religion: within the institutional framework of these colonies, their religion constituted no impediment to capitalist enterprise, in which the Chinese immigrants were phenomenally successful.

Confucianism, then, did constitute a serious obstacle to the development of capitalism, but it did so not through the influence of its economic ethics upon the behavior of those engaged in commerce and industry but in virtue of its fitness to serve as a political formula cementing the omnipotent bureaucratic state.

HINDUISM

The central theme of Weber's volume on Hinduism—which like its companions could alone constitute a worthy achievement of lifelong work—is less open to criticism. In reality, Hinduism did constitute a formidable obstacle to the rise of capitalism, owing to its numerous taboos prohibiting utilization of resources and impeding collaboration in production by enjoining avoidance between persons of different castes. Although usury flourished in India since times immemorial, and large-scale financial operations were by no means unknown, the capitalist mode of production together with large-scale trade was first forcibly implanted by the British and began to strike roots as a native growth only when the hold of Hinduism became less astringent, owing to the spread of laicism.

The esoteric mysticism of the Brahmans had, no doubt, something to do with the withering of the early buds of Hindu science, but as far as the shaping of the economy was concerned, more important was the support which Hinduism lent to social parasitism by making the toiling masses listless and utterly servile. As Weber rightly pointed out, with its promise of reincarnation into a higher caste as the reward for keeping dutifully to one's station in life, Hinduism functioned as the most powerful "opium of the people" ever invented. Other factors, too, fortified parasitism in India: frequent conquests, the instability of political order, ruthless fiscal extortion, diverted energies and wealth from productive purposes.

Notwithstanding these qualifications, Weber's central thesis stands: not only indirectly via its influence on the structure of power, but also directly via its economic ethics, Hinduism was effective in preventing the rise of capitalism in India.

Weber's *Religionssoziologie* illustrates how a work can be truly great and nevertheless mistaken in some of its assertions; which only goes to show that science proceeds by successive approximations. Given the novelty, magnitude, and complexity of the problems, insistence on more conclusive verification, and logically more rigorous formulation, would in all likelihood have prevented Weber from producing his works: the first outline had to be rough. It is not our merit but merely luck to be able to see certain points better by standing on his shoulders.

Even if, in some cases, Weber overestimated the efficacity of religious beliefs in directly determining behavior in economic matters, the fact that he considers both directions of influence proves that it is completely unjust to accuse him of unilateralist interpretation. As mentioned above, he explains the stultification and decay of capitalism in the ancient world in terms of structures of power, without bringing in the "economic ethics" as an independent factor. In order to obtain a balanced view of Weber's thought, we must realize that "Agrarian Relations in Antiquity" is in no way less important than "Sociology of Religions" and constitutes its necessary complement.

In passing judgment on Max Weber as a thinker we must remember that he died before completing his main works. The final synthetic conclusions are mostly lacking. Even so, he is the towering figure of sociology. We shall never know what he would have achieved had he lived another twenty years.

II

THE APPLICATION OF
THE PROTESTANT ETHIC
THESIS IN EUROPE
AND THE AMERICAS

3

THE PROTESTANT ETHIC AND THE SPIRIT OF CAPITALISM: THE HISTORY OF A CONTROVERSY

Ephraim Fischoff

I

The whole question of the effects of the Reformation upon subsequent economic development, and particularly of the intimate relation held to subsist between Protestantism, especially in its Calvinistic forms, and the rise of modern capitalism, has evoked a great literature of controversy ever since the publication at the beginning of this century of Max Weber's provocative essay on Protestantism. This continues to be the versatile German pundit's best-known work, perhaps the more so because its intent was largely misunderstood. For over a quarter of a century it has occasioned much debate among social and economic historians on what has been termed the most interesting single question in the field of economic history.[1]

"Die protestantische Ethik und der Geist des Kapitalismus" first appeared in the *Archiv für Sozialwissenschaft und Sozialpolitik*[2] and now stands at the head of Weber's collected essays on the sociology of religion.[3] In the reprint it is essentially unchanged, but contains numerous new footnotes, occasionally very detailed, which serve to give more adequate documentation from the sources and to answer various critics, such as Sombart and Brentano. This edition was translated into English in 1930, under the title *The Protestant Ethic and the Spirit of Capitalism*, by Talcott Parsons, who has probably done most in this country to interpret Weber's work. In the German edition, "Die protestantische Ethik

Reprinted from Social Research, *XI, (1944), 54–77.*

und der Geist des Kapitalismus" is followed by a supplementary essay, "Die protestantische Sekten und der Geist des Kapitalismus," emphasizing the distinctive contributions of the various Protestant sects. The latter essay, which Weber frequently adduces as important for the complete formulation of his thesis, was unfortunately not included by Parsons in his translation. Weber's replies in the *Archiv*[4] to the criticisms of Fischer and Rachfahl are also very important for the clarification of his views, as Troeltsch recognized by his numerous references to them.[5] It is therefore regrettable that these replies have remained buried in the *Archiv* and have not been made available in book form, except for the few extracts from them included in the revised footnotes to the second edition of *Die protestantische Ethik*. Much of the fallacious criticism of Weber would have been obviated by a familiarity with them, for they gather up and crystallize the essential ideas of his whole approach.[6] It is important to emphasize that because of certain special circumstances connected with the composition of the essay these supplementary statements must be read with the original, as a unit. Weber had originally intended to extend the considerations to other areas and then to investigate the reverse aspect of the relationship between religion and the other aspects of culture, notably economic attitudes, practices, and institutions. But for a number of reasons, to be discussed later, he never returned to this task.

Many scholars were intrigued by Weber's ideas, and even those who took issue with him on minor or even major points frequently accepted his main conclusions. In general, his views concerning the relation of Puritanism and capitalism were contested by historians and warmly welcomed by theologians. His essay on Protestantism has become one of the basic works in the sociology of religion and in *Kultursoziologie* generally.

Perhaps the most important influence of the essay was on Troeltsch, who, starting from different premises, produced for the whole past development of Christianity that historical treatment which Weber had originally projected as his own work. Troeltsch, who ranks with Weber as one of the founders of the sociology of religion in Germany, accepted Weber's theory as to the relation of Protestantism to capitalism and indeed did a great deal to develop and popularize it, so that it is not infrequently termed the Weber-Troeltsch theory. Of all the scholars participating in the controversy, he perhaps best understood Weber's intention. He felt that Weber's thesis was of fundamental importance and avowed that in his own works on the nature of Protestantism and its significance for civilization[7] he had taken over Weber's views in general. He had particular praise for Weber's effort to treat the problem in the great setting of the history of civilization and for his illumination of its inner aspect and its bearing on the social-economic dimension.[8] He saw clearly that Weber's intention was the investigation of the affinity between Calvinism and capitalism, the provision by the former of "an inner support or an intellectual-moral vertebra" which made possible the vigorous development of the latter. He accepted Weber's differentiation between the spirit and the economic system of capitalism; his view that these entities need not coexist; and his conclusion that the domination of the capitalistic system over the minds of men does not occur until a historical accident effects a juncture between these two disparate elements.[9]

Weber's thesis was likewise accepted for the most part by church historians like H. von Schubert, F. von Funk, H. Hermelink; by the historian of religion C. H. Becker, whose *Islamstudien* is an exemplary work on the sociology of religion in the spirit of Weber's *Religionssoziologie;* and to a certain degree by the economic historians Werner Sombart and R. H. Tawney. Sombart's general position is related to Weber's but differs in method and conclusion. It was his thesis on the spirit of capitalism that had stimulated Weber's approach to the whole field, but his own treatment was in turn affected by Weber's essay on Protestantism. Sombart's attribution of capitalism to the Jews was sharply challenged by Weber on the basis of an examination of the religious psychology and the sociological setting of Judaism. Tawney recognized the value of Weber's work but suggested certain modifications: he criticized Weber's apparent identification of the "capitalistic spirit" with Calvinism and English Puritanism; he also distinguished between earlier and later Puritanism, suggesting that, in order for the spirit of capitalism to develop, pristine Puritanism had to be largely overcome; and in general he emphasized the economic and political conditions of England during the sixteenth and seventeenth centuries rather than any specifically religious components in accounting for the newer economic practices and attitudes. These modifications have been strengthened in his subsequent writings, for example in his foreword to the English translation of *The Protestant Ethic*. The influence of Tawney's moderate acceptance of the Weberian thesis is apparent in several studies influenced by him: the works of Margaret James, Isabel Grubb, W. J. Warner, T. S. Ashton, and Richard Schlatter.

But if Weber's thesis met with approval in many quarters and exerted considerable influence, it also provoked the opposition of numerous critics, ranging from those who picked minor flaws in his argument but upheld his main thesis as sound, including, apart from Sombart and Tawney, E. Knodt, J. Kulischer, W. Gunsteren, and P. Koch, to those who rejected his entire approach as not only erroneous in detail but inadequate and sterile in essence. These included, among the early writers, H. K. Fischer, F. Rachfahl (particularly elaborate in his strictures), L. Brentano, G. von Below, H. Sée, and H. Pirenne, and more recently H. M. Robertson and P. C. Gordon Walker.

Most of this academic criticism, as well as a large popular literature both positive and negative, interpreted Weber's essay as setting up a causal hypothesis deriving capitalism from Calvinism—in short, as supplanting the materialistic hypothesis with a spiritual one. This is true even of more recent statements, such as those by H. Richard Niebuhr in his *Social Sources of Denominationalism* (1929), which is really on its theoretical side a lucid introduction to the sociology of Christianity, based largely on Weber's sociology of religion. He speaks of "Weber's well-known thesis to the effect that Calvinism was one of the major sources of modern capitalism" (p. 97) and even more strongly in another passage "the theory of Weber, which Tawney criticizes but in part follows, that Calvinism is the parent of capitalism . . ." (p. 288, note 9). More recent examples of this misinterpretation of Weber's intention may be found in J. M. Mecklin, *The Passing of the Saint* (1941), p. 189; Miriam Beard, *A History of the Business Man* (1938), pp. 349, 377; E. Fromm, *Escape from Freedom* (1941), p. 296; and E. Taeusch, "The Concept of Usury," *Journal of the History of Ideas*, III (1942), 291–318. At the opposite pole are those who accuse Weber of being a Marxist and therefore of misunderstanding the nature and function of religion. This is the notion of Catholic writers generally, for example A. Dempf, "Religionssoziologie," *Hochland*, XVIII (1921), 747.

Unfortunately the whole Weberian thesis has been bedeviled by various extrascientific valuations and frequently has been the victim of partisan contention depending on the economic orientation and religious affiliation of the writers in question. Thus most of the critics of Weber adjudged the influence of Protestantism on capitalism in the light of their attitude to capitalism. If they were admirers, they claimed that their particular religion had fathered it; if they were hostile to capitalism, they disallowed all connection between it and their religion. Political bias is also met with in the controversy; for example, Weber's thesis has been construed in the interests of Anglophobia.[10] The bias characteristic of most reactions to Weber's thesis is seen perhaps most clearly in many of the Catholic references to it, culminating in A. Fanfani's attribution of both capitalism and Protestantism to the triumph of "brachycephalic" over "dolichocephalic" rulers.[11] No wonder that Schlatter describes the present status of the problem of the connection between capitalism and Protestantism as mere "rattling of dry bones."[12]

The following review of the controversy around Weber's subtle essay will endeavor to demonstrate that the essay was widely misunderstood by friends and enemies alike; that Weber's cautious and avowedly incomplete research was misconstrued and his critical admonitions for the understanding of his thesis ignored. It will not be the intention of this review to repristinate or justify either Weber's method or his conclusions. The position taken here is only that, apart from its merits as an essay of notable acuteness and impressive learning, Weber's first contribution to a systematic sociology of religion was sound in intention. Moreover, attention will be directed to the fact that his massive later work[13] on the general theme of the sociology of religion, which in many respects constitutes a supplement and correction of the earlier work, was almost universally disregarded. *Habent sua fata libelli.*

Weber continued to engage in the controversy over this essay almost to the end of his life, replying to criticism, adducing new data, and protesting against various misunderstandings. In the meantime, his system had expanded and the whole question had been set in a new perspective of world history. This had the effect of correcting many of the dubious positions of the Protestant essay by giving due attention to the *Realfaktoren* which, in the earlier work, had been not so much ignored as taken for granted. It is indeed remarkable that many famous scholars continued to criticize Weber for earlier views long after they had been set in a proper framework by the later essays of his developing *Religionssoziologie* and by the appropriate sections on the sociology of religion in *Wirtschaft und Gesellschaft* and in *General Economic History*. Among the writers whose published animadversions upon Weber continued to refer only to the Protestant essay, long after Weber had composed his later works and even after his death, are von Below, Brodnitz, Tawney, Knight, H. M. Robertson, Walker, Kraus, M. Beard, Nussbaum, and Taeusch. Indeed, this tendency continues even to the present. An instance of it will serve to illustrate how little Weber's subsequent work is known. F. H. Knight, who translated Weber's *General Economic History,* remarks in "Historical and Theoretical Issues in the Problem of Modern Capitalism" (*Journal of Economic and Business History,* I [1928], 134) that the whole question of the origin of modern capitalism would gain by being stated in negative form: why did capitalism not develop in other times and places than modern western Europe? He then adds that Weber does discuss these questions and cites the *General Economic History.* Surely Professor Knight must have known the other essays in the *Gesammelte Aufsätze zur Religionssoziologie* and the *Wirtschaft und Gesellschaft,* but they are not mentioned. Also G. Brodnitz's summary in the *Economic History Review* (I [1927], 341) of work in German economic history between 1900 and 1927 refers only to the first volume of Weber's *Religionssoziologie.*

That each generation must reinterpret the past in terms of its own experience has become almost axiomatic in historiography and the cultural sciences generally. Since Weber's essay was a conscious reaction to the Marxian hypothesis, it is perhaps natural that it should overstress the consistency and efficacy of ideal factors. It was part of the revolt against the mechanization of man and the increasing dominance of the economic factor which was common to such vastly different figures as Marx and Nietzsche in the generation before Weber and to Freud, Rathenau, and Toennies in his own. Weber's essay in functional historical sociology took the form of emphasizing the crucial importance of religious beliefs in the emergence of a morale favorable to capitalism; this was in line with his emphasis on the importance of sympathetic intuition in the social sciences and his view that history is the *Nacherleben* of the past and sociology a discipline of the inner understanding.

II

Weber's original intention in *The Protestant Ethic* must be seen against the background of his time. An heir of the historical school (he regarded himself as one of the epigoni of Schmoller[14]) and of the Marxist tradition, both of which had combated the isolative treatment of the economic process and the *homo economicus* by abstract classical economics, he probed the history of culture to determine the decisive interconnections of economics with the totality of culture. The whole historical work of Weber has ultimately one primary object: the understanding of contemporary European culture, especially modern capitalism.[15] It presses forward to the underlying morale (*Geist*) of capitalism and its pervasive attitudes to life; and beyond this to modern occidental rationalism as such, which he came to regard as the crucial characteristic of the modern world.

The discussion of problems raised by Marx, who gave the subject of capitalism its large importance in modern social theory, resulted in a great literature on this theme. Certain German scholars had already begun to assimilate Marx's theoretical work into the conceptual framework developed by the German historical school, among them some of the *Kathedersozialisten,* principally Toennies and Sombart. These bourgeois economists and social theorists were much concerned with the problem of the psychological foundations of capitalism and suggested certain corrections of the Marxist hypotheses under the general rubric of "the spirit of capitalism." Weber paid the highest tribute to Marx's genius and recognized the enormous usefulness of the materialistic method as a heuristic device,[16] but he resisted all efforts to absolutize it into the sole method of social science, much less into a *Weltanschauung.* The truth value of this method, as indeed of all intellectual schemata, he regarded as only "ideal-typical." As against the Marxian doctrine of the economic determinism of social change, Weber propounded a pluralistic interactional theory.

It is necessary to be clear as to the limited character of Weber's goal and the cautious manner of his procedure in this essay. In this first work inquiring into the influence of religious doctrines on economic behavior, he had not the slightest intention of producing a complete theory of capitalism, a social theory of religion, or even a complete treatment of the relation between religion and the rise of capitalism. The essay was intended as a tentative effort at understanding one of the basic and distinctive aspects of the modern ethos: its professional, specialized character and its sense of calling or vocation. Already he was impressed by the dominantly rational character of modern life, and he was concerned to demonstrate that there were various types of rationalization, a fact generally overlooked by technological theories of history.

Defining capitalism from his historistic view as a unique system[17] characterized by the general trends of antitraditionalism, dynamism, rationalism, and calculated long-range industrial production, he was principally concerned to analyze and trace the genesis of the character structure adequate to and congruent with it. In his view, modern capitalism was not the automatic product of technological development but of many objective factors, including climate—which influences the conduct of life and labor costs—and many social-political factors, such as the character of the medieval inland city and its citizenry. But he insisted that there was one factor which could not be ignored: the emergence of a rational, antitraditional spirit in the human agents involved. The two main aspects of this are the evolution of modern science and its comparatively modern relationship to economics, and the growth of the modern organization of individual life (Lebensführung), particularly in its practical consequences for economic activity.[18] Weber's limited thesis was merely that in the formation of this pattern of rationally ordered life, with its energetic and unremitting pursuit of a goal and eschewal of all magical escapes, the religious component must be considered as an important factor.[19] How important he was unable to say, and indeed he felt that in historical imputation such quantification is impossible.[20] Consequently his view was that no one can tell how the capitalist economic system would have evolved had the specifically modern elements of the capitalistic spirit been lacking.[21]

In tracing the affinity between the bourgeois life pattern and certain components of the religious stylization of life, as shown most consistently by ascetic Protestantism, Weber emphasized the gradual genesis of a psychological habit which enabled men to meet the requirements of early modern capitalism. That is, instead of the entrepreneur feeling that his gaining of wealth was at best tolerated by God, or that his usuraria pravitas had to be atoned for (as did the native Hindu trader), he went about his business with sturdy confidence that Providence purposely enabled him to prosper for God's glory, that this success was construable as a visible sign of God and, when achieved by legal means, as a measure of his value before God as well as man. On the other hand, the hand worker or laborer, with his willingness to work, derived his sense of a religious state of grace from his conscientiousness in his calling. Finally, because of the abomination of the generic sin of idolatry or apotheosis of created things (Kreaturvergötterung), as manifested in hoarding possessions, indulgence, and frivolous consumption, the money accumulated in the exercise of a calling was turned back into the business enterprise, or saved.

Weber strongly emphasized the importance to bourgeois accumulation of planned this-worldly asceticism (*innerweltliche Askese*), as distinguished from otherworldly asceticism, and of the emotional type of pietism. He insisted that Protestant sects, especially the Quakers and Baptists, engendered a methodical regulation of life, in striking contrast to Catholicism, Lutheranism, and Anglicanism. His crucial point was that ascetic Protestantism[22] created for capitalism the appropriate spirit, so that the vocational man (*Berufsmenschen*) in his acquisition of wealth no longer suffered from the deep inner lesions characteristic of the more earnest individuals of an earlier day, no matter what their apparent solidity and exemplary power. One example of this inner uncertainty regarding economic activity was the practice of restoring at death goods obtained by usury; another was the establishment of religious institutions to atone for financial success. There were innumerable theoretical and practical compromises between conscience and economic activity, between the ideal of *Deo placere non potest,* accepted even by Luther, and the acquisitive careers entered into by many earnest Catholics. In Weber's view the noteworthy degree of congruence or affinity between the modern capitalistic system and the set of attitudes toward it made for a high inner integration, which was of great importance for the subsequent development of capitalism. It was this integration which was the central concern of his essay (*Archiv,* XXX, 200).

Weber made it clear that it was his intention to analyze just one component of the generic *Lebensstil* of our rationalized civilization, among the many which stood at the cradle of modern capitalism, and to trace its changes and its ultimate disappearance. He warned against exclusive concentration on the religious factor, as exerted through the inner psychological motivations and the powerful educational force and discipline provided by the Protestant sects. It was, he insisted, only one factor, and he rejected all attempts to identify it with the spirit of capitalism or to derive capitalism from it.[23] Taking the religious ethic of Protestantism as a constant, and assuming temporarily that it was predominantly a religious product, he proposed to trace the congruence between it and the characterological type requisite for capitalism. It was his intention, however, to return to the problem and investigate the nonreligious components of the religious ethic.

As to the insistence by some of his critics, such as Fischer[24] and Rachfahl,[25] that the problem required a statistical-historical approach, Weber recognized the need of research on the development of particular areas in order to determine the numbers and strength of the various religious groups involved and the importance of the vocational ethics in comparison with other factors.[26] But he insisted that his was a study in the sociology of cultures, investigating the convergence of religious and economic factors in the production of modern "rational" man, and that for his type of study the statistical method was not indicated. His concern was to ascertain the specific direction in which a given religion might operate, the diverse effects of a specific system of religious ethics on the style of life. This problem, he felt, could be approached only by the "understanding" method of motivational analysis which he employed. In this first essay, therefore, he concentrated on tracing the complex ramifications leading from articles of faith to practical conduct, in an acute and learned examination of the psychological motivations issuing out of Reformed Protestantism and leading to methodical rationalization of activity and the consequent encouragement of capitalist behavior and attitudes.[27] This thesis is carried through all the varieties of Reformed Christianity with a subtle and insightful *dogmengeschichtliche* analysis.

The Protestant essay was not regarded by Weber as a final or dogmatic formulation of a theory of the genesis or evolution of the Reformation, but as a preliminary investigation of the influence of certain religious ideas on the development of an economic spirit or the ethos of an economic system. He was not producing an idealistic (or as he preferred to term it, a spiritual) interpretation of capitalism, deriving it from religious factors. Much nonsense has been written on this point because of his alleged rejection of Marxism.[28] Actually, he was an admirer of the Marxian hypothesis, only objecting that it should not be made absolute and universal, a summary philosophy; but then he rejected all absolutes and all monisms. Hence he rejected at least as forcibly any idealistic monism,[29] and in the essay and its supplements he explicitly disavowed the foolish attribution to him of any spiritualistic hypothesis.[30]

He sought no "psychological determination of economic events," [31] but rather emphasized the "fundamental importance of the economic factor." [32] He recognized clearly that economic changes arise in response to economic needs and are conditioned by a wide variety of factors, including the demagogic, geographic, technological, and monetary.[33] He recognized that capitalism would have arisen without Protestantism—in fact that it had done so in many culture complexes—and that it would not and did not come about where the objective conditions were not ripe for it. He admitted that several other systems of religious ethics had developed approaches to the religious ethic of Reformed Protestantism, but he insisted that the psychological motivations involved were necessarily different; what was decisive was the ethos engendered, not preachments or theological compendia, and this, he argued, was unique in Reformed Protestantism for a variety of reasons. He recognized that there are constant functional interactions between the realms of religion and economics, but in this study he concentrated on the influences emanating from the side of religion. He not only indicated his awareness of the other side but demonstrated how by an irony of fate the very fulfillment of religious injunctions had induced changes in the economic structure, which in turn engendered the massive irreligion of a capitalist order. He admitted that the religious ethic itself is not determined exclusively by religion, and he clearly urged the necessity of investigating the influence of the social milieu, especially economic conditions, upon the character and development of religious attitudes.[34]

Yet he held that the religious revelation of the founder of a sect is an autonomous experience and not a mere reflection of accommodation to economic or other needs. It was his feeling that it is no solution to the problem of the distinctiveness of the Calvinist religious form to say that it is an adjustment to capitalistic practices already in existence; the question then arises as to why Catholicism did not show the same results after making the accommodation. But when a religious revelation has become a social phenomenon and has given rise to a community, a process of social selection sets in and class stratification supervenes in the originally homogeneous religious group, causing the formation of distinctive, socially determined differences within the religion.[35] Weber was going to study this side of the problem, but he never returned to the task. In *The Protestant Ethic* he concentrated on the religious factor alone, considering it as though it were exclusively a religious entity. He was, however, well aware of the tentative nature of his contribution, and he sketched the mammoth and indeed unrealizable program of studies necessary before the project could be regarded as complete.

III

By no means all the criticisms leveled against Weber were due to bias or failure to heed his cautions regarding the intention of his essay. First, there is the indubitable fact that as the essay stands it has certain elementary defects of structure, particularly because of the incompleteness which exposes it to misunderstandings by a careless reader, although Weber protested that an academic critic should never be guilty of such malfeasance. Writing in the *Archiv* in 1908, Weber explained again the reasons for the noncompletion of the essay—partly personal factors, partly the pressure of other work, and partly the fact that Troeltsch had begun to treat in the "most felicitous manner a whole series of problems that lay on Weber's route," which the latter was loath to duplicate; and he expressed the hope that in the coming year he might work on the essay and issue it separately. He admitted that critics had a right to charge that the original essay was incomplete, and he recognized the danger that the hasty reader might overlook this fact, but he insisted that it could scarcely be construed as an idealistic construction of history.

Replying to Fischer's criticism,[36] Weber insisted that in the Protestant essay he had expressed himself with utter clarity on the relationship between religion and economics generally, but he admitted nonetheless that misunderstanding might possibly have arisen from certain turns of phrase. Accordingly he promised to remove in a future reissue all expressions which seemed to suggest the derivation of institutions from religious motives; and he expressed his intention of clarifying the fact that it was the spirit of a "methodical" *Lebensführung* which he was deriving from Protestant asceticism and which is related to economic forms only through congruence (*Adäquanz*). In a later anticritical article,[37] adverting with regret to the incompleteness of the essay, Weber suggests ironically that had he completed it as promised by tracing the influence of economic conditions on the formation of Reformed Protestantism, he would probably have been accused of having capitulated to historical materialism, even as he was now charged with an overemphasis on the religious or ideological factor.[38] Hence, he insisted, his essay should properly be regarded only as a fraction of an investigation into the history of the development of the idea of vocation and its infusion into certain callings.

Apart from its incompleteness, this essay betrays the other faults so characteristic of most of Weber's writing—a great carelessness of the reader's requirements, evinced in the plethora of detail in the text and above all in the ocean of footnotes, inundating the reader and frequently sweeping him far from the mainland. His wife speaks of "die montströse Form dieser Abhandlung," [39] which was aggravated in the second edition when the "Fussnotengeschwulst" increased enormously. She sought, however, to justify this flood by pointing out that since Weber was using "careful causal imputation of intuitively apprehended connections," he wished to provide all possible proof in this extensive scholarly apparatus and "to guard himself against any misunderstanding of his cautious relativizations."

The essay may be justly criticized for various errors of fact and interpretation. Weber himself later corrected some erroneous statements appearing in the original essay, as by indicating that when he had said that Calvinism shows the juxtaposition of intensive piety and capitalism, wherever found, he had meant only diaspora Calvinism.[40]

Another justifiable line of attack on Weber's thesis is based on concrete researches into the economic history of the Continent, principally Holland and the Rhineland. Both Weber and Troeltsch had based their work on inadequate study of sources and had quoted Anglo-Saxon writers to demonstrate the effect of German and Netherland Calvinists on the economic development of the Rhineland. On the basis of investigations into the history of Holland—and it must be recalled that this republic was probably the first country in which capitalism developed on a large scale—recent Netherland historians like DeJong, Knappert, and de Pater[41] find no proof to sustain such a theory of a connection between Calvinism and capitalism among the Netherlanders. Further, Beins's researches into the economic ethic of the Calvinist church in the Netherlands between 1565 and 1650[42] lead him to raise serious objections to Weber's thesis. A similar view is expressed in the important economic history of the Netherlands by Baasch, who stresses the secular factors in the evolution of capitalism in Holland which made the Netherlanders the chief bankers of the seventeenth century and by the end of the eighteenth made the colony of Jews in Amsterdam the largest in Europe.[43] The same adverse conclusion is reached by Koch's investigation of the economic development of the lower Rhine area[44] and Andrew Sayous' study of the Genevans; Hashagen's essay on the relation between Calvinism and capitalism in the German Rhineland comes to similar conclusions.[45] Evidence has also accumulated that Calvinism did not have any necessary effect on the rise of capitalism in Hungary, Scotland, or France.

These researches militate against Weber's hypothesis that the Calvinist belief buttressed capitalism or even favored its emergence. But this line of criticism readily degenerates into the oversimplification referred to above: that Weber was intent on establishing the causal primacy of the Protestant ethic in the genesis of capitalism and the necessary determination of the latter by the former wherever it appeared. The tendency toward such an oversimplification vitiates most of the arguments of Robertson and of Hyma, who closely follows him. Insofar as all these writers, among whom may be included Brentano, Sée, Pirenne, Brodnitz, and von Schulze-Gävernitz, construe Weber's thesis as implying a necessary causal influence exerted by Calvinism on the evolution of capitalism, they have misread Weber.

Most animadversions on his thesis, even in works composed during the last decade, spring from a misunderstanding or oversimplification of his theory, for which he is only slightly to blame. Surely Weber, one of the foremost historians of jurisprudence and economics in his generation, needed no reminder that the origins of capitalism are complex and diverse and are due to changes in economic process as well as in spiritual outlook.[46] By and large most of his critics have simply not perceived the direction of his interest, the moderation of his purpose, and the caution of his procedure.

Only a very few of his critics rose to the level of his argument and recognized that his errors or shortcomings were inherent in his particular method. And the handful who did attack Weber's method, such as Sée, Robertson, Walker, and Borkenau, did so in ignorance of his writings on the nature of social science and the method appropriate to it. Weber's shortcomings were not due to ignorance, naïveté, or partisanship; on the contrary, he had a considered and subtle approach. An acquaintance with Weber's views as to the nature and goal of the social sciences—his view of theory as only ideal-typical, and his peculiar method of historical research committed to the interpretative understanding of historical atoms, of particular emergents chosen on the basis of their cultural significance and understood by means of a controlled intuitive method—might have clarified the reason for a whole range of errors or inadequacies in his *Protes-*

tant Ethic. Certainly no validation of his method is here projected: clearly it has shortcomings; its usefulness has very plain limitations; and its employment is fraught with particular occupational hazards. But any essay avowedly composed under that method should be evaluated on its own terms, as an essay in interpretative understanding. From this view not a few of the strictures here listed would lose their point or would at least appear in their proper perspective as the inevitable consequences of Weber's atomistic method.

His employment of the ideal-type method leads to various distortions, as in his overemphasis of the concepts of vocation[47] and predestination. Here a bias in the choice of the historical atom to be interpreted and in the definition of its character and influence makes itself strongly felt. The oversimplification induced by the method also extends to his construction of the Protestant ethic as a component of Calvinism, Puritanism, Pietism, Methodism, and the Anabaptist sects[48] and to his treatment of Puritanism.[49] Another instance is his definition of modern capitalism, accentuating its novelty, rationality, and ascetic character. Once he had so defined it he did not have much difficulty in discovering elements of congruity with the schematic construction of the Protestant ethic slanted in the same direction. To the empirical historian, the whole procedure necessarily appears suffused by a tendency to idealization, with a comparative neglect of secular factors, economic, political, and technological.

Weber's method of atomistic isolation[50] necessarily leads to oversimplification of a complex historical entity through the accentuation and isolation of a particular component factor regarded as significant from a certain point of view, its tracing of alleged influences on the further course of historical evolution, and its tendency toward reifying the particular component factors of a given historical entity. In the nature of the case this method cannot serve for the illumination of a total historical problem or the interpretation of a whole epoch or movement.

His pluralistic agnosticism, manifested in his refusal to pledge allegiance to any exclusive viewpoint lest it do injustice to the unique individuality of historical entities and the perpetual shift of cultural horizons, was laudable in intention. It seemed to be pointing the way to the functionalization of research and interpretation in the social sciences. Actually, however, Weber's isolative treatment led to inevitable distortions. His method entailed the breakdown of any complex phenomenon into its components and then, choosing each one seriatim as a constant, tracing its effects on the other variables. At the end of the process, he indicated, there would have to be a return to assess the varying force of each component in the actual historical composite and to determine how closely the empirical phenomena approached the ideal types he had formulated. This he had planned to do for his problem of the relationship between the Protestant ethic and the spirit of capitalism, but he must have felt the infinite and impossible nature of the task. Moreover, his approach offers no method for determining the interrelation of factors, the degree of influence pertaining to each, or their temporal variations, thereby leaving room for the play of personal evaluation in the choice and characterization of the particular historical atoms.

For the historian concerned with determining the causes of a particular historical datum, the problem of timing historical phenomena and tracing temporal variations is one of the crucial difficulties arising out of the impossibility, inherent in Weber's method, of determining the degree of influence to be assigned to the various factors involved. The ideal-type method neglects the time coefficient, or at any rate impairs the possibility of establishing time sequences, because it involves a telescoping of data. Granted, for instance, that Weber's interpretation of Calvinist theology is correct and that it was of the type that would result in activism, dynamism, industry, and so on, the question still remains whether these influences did not begin to exert a significant effect only after capitalism had already reached a dominant position.

Consequently, while there is readiness enough to accept the congruity between Calvinism and capitalism, it has been suggested that a consideration of the crucial question of timing will show that Calvinism emerged later than capitalism where the latter became decisively powerful. Hence the conclusion that Calvinism could not have causally influenced capitalism and that its subsequent favorable disposition to capitalist practice and ethics is rather to be construed as an adaptation.[51]

The development of the Weberian thesis by Troeltsch and his American disciple Reinhold Niebuhr meets this criticism by tracing the modifications induced in later Calvinism by the various social factors impinging upon it after the first appearance of the original doctrine, such as religious wars, political pressures, and the exigencies of acquisitive life. His rich analysis reveals how the social ethic was the net result of the particular religious and ethical peculiarities of Calvinism, which showed a marked individuality in its doctrine of predestination, its activism, and its ethic, aiming at achieving what was possible and practical. On the other hand, Troeltsch emphasizes the importance in the evolution of the ethic of the republican tendency in politics, the capitalistic tendency in economics, and the diplomatic and militaristic tendencies in international affairs. All these tendencies radiated from Geneva, at first in a very limited way; then they united with similar elements within the Calvinist religion and ethic, and in this union they became stronger and stronger, until in connection with the political, social, and ecclesiastical history of individual countries they received that particular character of the religious morality of the middle classes (or bourgeois world) which differs from the early Calvinism of Geneva and France.[52]

In the light of all this, Weber's thesis must be construed not according to the usual interpretation, as an effort to trace the causative influence of the Protestant ethic upon the emergence of capitalism, but as an exposition of the rich congruency of such diverse aspects of a culture as religion and economics. The essay should be considered as a stimulating project of hermeneutics, a demonstration of interesting correlations between diverse cultural factors. Although at the time of the republication of the essay Weber insisted that he had not changed his views on this matter at all, the whole intent of his later work does show an implicit shift of view, or at any rate of emphasis. No longer laying the basic stress on the causal factors in the economic ethic of radical Protestantism as related to the capitalist spirit, his later researches, culminating in the systematic sociology of religion, accepted rather the congruency of these diverse aspects of our culture and their subsumption under the comprehensive process of rationalization. It is important to emphasize that some of the distortions involved in Weber's ideal-type method are neutralized in his later sociological studies of the non-Christian religions, to which all too little attention has been paid. In these mighty studies, which are cultural sociologies of the *Weltreligionen,* Weber traces the influence of material, geographic, and economic circumstances on the religious and ethical ideas of different cultures. Yet though he treated religious norms, institutions, and practices with cold detachment, he never denied the historical reality and power of the religious complex. His general view remained that human affairs are infinitely complicated, with numerous elements interacting; and it was his unshakable conviction that to attribute causal primacy is to be guilty of oversimplification.

In view of Weber's limited intention and the cautious demarcation of his task (including the frequently expressed indication of its incompleteness), his idiosyncratic method which would not permit statistical proof or disproof, and his later supplementation of the original effort by systematic studies in the sociology of religion, it must be concluded that his task was justified by its results. Although the discussion of his problem has not in itself promoted our knowledge of past economic life in proportion to the considerable effort it has evoked, it has greatly sharpened our appreciation of Catholic and Protestant doctrinal history; and it has also paved the way for the formulation of an adequate social theory of religion. Weber's essay on *The Protestant Ethic* is also in a peculiar sense an introduction to his massive system of sociology and his philosophy of history and exemplifies in striking fashion the anfractuosities of his intellect and temper. As an illuminating tentative[53] approach to a great problem, as an introduction to the domain of the sociology of religion which it served to stake out, as the stimulus to a generation of researchers in this new discipline, and finally, as the precursor of functional analysis in culture history, Weber's essay deserves a better fate than it has thus far enjoyed.

NOTES

1. F. L. Nussbaum, "The Economic History of Renaissance Europe," *Journal of Modern History*, XIII (1941), 537.

2. Vols. XX–XXI (1904–1905).

3. Max Weber, *Gesammelte Aufsätze zur Religionssoziologie*, 3 vols. (Tübingen, 1920–1921).

4. *Archiv für Sozialwissenschaft und Sozialpolitik*, Vols. XXV, XXVI, XXX, XXXI. Hereafter referred to as *Archiv*.

5. Ernst Troeltsch, *The Social Teaching of the Christian Churches*, 2 vols. (New York, 1931): for example, p. 816.

6. See especially the "Antikritisches Schlusswortzum Geist des Kapitalismus," *Archiv*, XXXI (1910), 554–599.

7. For example, his *Die Bedeutung des Protestantismus für die Entstehung der modernen Welt* (Munich, 1911) (English translation, *Protestantism and Progress* [London, 1912]).

8. *The Social Teaching of the Christian Churches*, p. 911.

9. *Ibid.*, pp. 916 ff. Troeltsch adopted various other interpretations of Weber's; for example, the latter's definition of church and sect (pp. 815, 960, 988 ff.) and numerous concrete details (pp. 687, 912, 918, and *passim*). He made, however, some corrections in the general Weberian theory, among which may be mentioned his accentuation of the differences between later and earlier Calvinism and between Lutheranism and Calvinism. Moreover, he felt that he was inclined to emphasize more than Weber did certain nonreligious factors in the development of later Calvinism, such as its exclusion from the various perquisites of the feudal world, which influenced its favorable attitude toward business enterprise. In addition he felt that he had clarified Weber's view on the sect, especially its relation to mysticism, and that his own demonstration of sectarian elements in primitive Calvinism had made more intelligible its subsequent fusion with the sectarian type (p. 989).

10. An illustration of this is the misinterpretation of Weber's position in the article "Puritanism" in *Sachwörterbuch der Deutschkunde*, II (1930), 96 ff. Other expressions of this view will be found in the writings of W. Dibelins; O. Baumgarten, *Religiöses und kirchliches Leben in England* (Leipzig, 1922); L. Schücking, *Die Familie im Puritanismus* (Leipzig, 1929); G. von Schulze-Gävernitz, *Britischer Imperialismus und englischer Freihandel* (Munich, 1906). See also the contumacious perversion of Weber's thesis in Peter Aldag, *Juden in England* (Berlin, 1940): Vol. I, *Juden erobern England;* Vol. II, *Juden beherrschen England.*

11. In his *Cattolicismo e protestantismo nella formazione storica del capitalismo* (English translation, *Catholicism, Protestantism, and Capitalism* [London, 1935]). In an earlier book he considered the origin of the spirit of capitalism from the viewpoint of Catholic doctrine (*Le origini del spirito capitalistico in Italia* [Milan, 1932], now in English translation) and reviewed the whole subject with a wealth of bibliographical detail. He attempts to deflect from Catholicism the accusation of responsibility for capitalism. Accepting Weber's views on Protestantism, he proceeds to vindicate Catholicism and ultimately Italian Fascism, interpreted as a return to virtue after the aberrations of capitalism. But his treatment of the relationship of Catholicism to capitalism and his analysis of Protestantism are biased and unfair. See Ronald Bainton, "Changing Ideas in the Sixteenth Century," *Modern History*, VIII (1936), 439.

Generally speaking, the reaction of Catholic writers to the Weber-Troeltsch thesis regarding the connection of Protestantism and capitalism has been to make propaganda for Catholicism. The Catholic students of this problem approach it with a distinctive bias, seeking on the one hand to find in Catholic ethics the honorific attitudes that might culminate in the industrious, inner-worldly ascetic conduct attributed by Weber to the Puritan; and on the other hand to defend Catholicism from any blame for capitalism, or more correctly for the spiritually dysgenic effects of capitalistic activity. The general conclusion then drawn is that since modern capitalism is an outgrowth of Protestantism, all the evils of modern capitalism are due to Protestantism, and hence the only cure for the ills of our economic life is to be found in Catholicism. Thus F. J. Schmidt's comment on the Weberian thesis was that Calvinism had caused a second fall ("Kapitalismus und Protestantismus," *Preussisches Jahrbuch* [1905]). More recently G. O'Brien has contrasted the unhappy fruits of Calvinism, economic individualism, and all its consequences with the allegedly quite different products of Catholicism (*An Essay on the Economic Effects of the Reformation*, New York, 1923). This whole argument has been clearly analyzed from the point of view of a Protestant theologian who follows the Weber-Troeltsch position in Wünsch's essay on "Protestantischer Kapitalismus und katholische Propaganda," *Christliche Welt*, XXXIX (1925), 350–358.

12. Richard Schlatter, *The Social Ideas of Religious Leaders, 1660–1688* (London, 1940) p. vi.

13. In Weber's later work the question of the evolution of modern capitalism and its distinctive morale becomes subordinate to an analysis of the enormous historical differences between the Orient and the Occident. The whole drift of his later work in the sociology of religion suggests indubitably that for the emergence of a "spirit of modern capitalism" all the factors which produced the modern Occident must be operative. This later position is in essence an admission of the force of Rachfahl's early criticism of Weber's general approach.

14. See the address delivered by Weber on the anniversary of Schmoller's achievement, cited in C. Brinkmann, *Gustav Schmoller und die Volkswirtschaftslehre* (Stuttgart, 1937), pp. 8 ff. See also *Gesammelte Aufsätze zur Wissenschaftslehre* (Tübingen, 1922), p. 208, where he avows his membership in the historical school, though noting his deviation in the direction of a Kantian view of science.

15. In Weber's essay on assuming the editorship of the *Archiv* in 1904, he set forth the leading principle that social-science research must be oriented to the understanding of the modern world and declared that because of its crucial importance the unbiased investigation of capitalism was an imperative task for the social sciences ("Die Objektivität der sozialwissenschaftlichen und sozialpolitischen Erkenntnis," now in *Gesammelte Aufsätze zur Wissenschaftslehre*, pp. 170, 162 ff). See Marianne Weber, *Max Weber* (Tübingen, 1926), p. 290.

16. In "Die Objektivität . . ." Weber indicated an interest in re-establishing the value of the method of historical materialism, but only in the functional sense. Yet he adds significantly that to derive capitalism from religious ideas would be quite inadequate (*ibid.*, p. 169).

17. It was Weber's contention that in the economic history of the world there was a whole scale of capitalisms, adventurous, piratical, usurious, speculative, financial, and so on, and that modern rational industrial capitalism, idiosyncratic of our occidental culture complex, was distinctively different from these earlier forms. The nub of Weber's argument is that for the emergence of our type of capitalism there was required a combination of factors: the full development of certain economic tendencies, the beginnings of which had been apparent in the culture area but had been impeded for various historical reasons; and the emergence of a "capitalistic spirit," a morale or set of attitudes growing out of the various great historical forces which crystallized our distinctive *Lebensform*.

18. *Archiv*, XXXI, 598–599.

19. See *ibid.*, XXVI, 277, 281, for a clear statement that his intention was only to trace the characterological effects of different types of piety, not to discover any predominant factors in the historical occurrences of any particular epoch or any general or universal dynamic forces in the historical process; for him there were no such "ghosts" in history.

20. "Antikritisches Schlusswort," p. 598.

21. *Ibid.*, p. 597.

22. *Archiv*, XXXI, 583, note 18, and 593. Weber firmly rejected (*ibid.*, XXVI, 271) the contention of Fischer that the spirit of the methodical conduct of life had appeared before Puritanism. Weber insisted that this *Lebensmethodik*, which became an influential component of the modern ethic of calling, was altogether different from that of the Japanese samurai, the *cortigiano*, the knightly concept of honor in the Middle Ages, the Stoa, the "objective treatment" of life in the views of the Renaissance (in the Burckhardt sense), the Counter Reformation, or even some of the ideas of Bacon (in this respect close to Puritanism), who stood midway between the influence of the Renaissance and the Reformation. All these had their distinctive regimens, some of the components of which have entered the *Lebensstil* of the leading modern nations; but they were life rationalizations in quite another sense and direction. These ideas Weber believed he had already expressed in the original essay (*ibid.*, p. 278, note 2).

23. *Archiv*, XXX, 197, 202.

24. *Ibid.*, XXVI, 273.

25. *Ibid.*, XXXI, 592, 595.

26. His acceptance of empirical research of the quantitative type in the social sciences was, however, rather limited. In his essay on Roscher (*Gesammelte Aufsätze zur Wissenschaftslehre*, p. 37), written before *The Protestant Ethic*, he appears to affirm Roscher's attitude that only limited use should be made of figures by the healthy sense of the empirical investigator who wishes to understand reality, not dissipate it. Indeed, he thought it nonsensical to expect a statistical study of ultimate value attitudes (see *Archiv*, XXVIII, 263; XXIX, 529; XXX, 191).

27. The decisive matter for him was the unbroken unity of the vocation with the inner ethical core of the personality. He admitted that there were numerous approaches to practical vocational ethics of this sort in the Middle Ages, but insisted that the spiritual bond was lacking. In the same way, this bond is lacking today, as appears clearly in all our talk about life and experience as a specific value, which implies a devaluation of vocational man. Modern capitalism, against whose works this recent attitude is directed, partly on reformist grounds and partly because of its connection with this type of man, no longer needs this support. To be sure, traces of the former importance of religious value for capitalistic development are still to be found (*Archiv*, XXXI, 593–594), but by and large modern capitalism has become emancipated from such influences.

28. Even his wife overemphasizes this point. See Marianne Weber, *op. cit.*, p. 350.

29. See his vitriolic attack on R. Stammler for the latter's alleged theoretical victory over the Marxist method, "R. Stammler's 'Überwindung' des Marxismus," in *Gesammelte Aufsätze zur Wissenschaftslehre;* also the various economic essays of the period 1903–1908.

30. "Die protestantische Ethik und der Geist des Kapitalismus," *Gesammelte Aufsätze zur Religionssoziologie*, 3 vols. (Tübingen, 1920), I, 54, 110; *Archiv*, XXV, 244 ff., and XXX, 192.

31. H. M. Robertson, *Aspects of the Rise of Economic Individualism* (Cambridge, Eng., 1933), p. xii.

32. "Die protestantische Ethik," p. 12.

33. *Ibid.*, pp. 12, 38–39; *General Economic History* (New York, 1961), p. 354; *Wirtschaft und Gesellschaft* (Tübingen, 1922), p. 808.

34. *The Protestant Ethic and the Spirit of Capitalism,* tr. Talcott Parsons (London, 1930), p. 183.

35. R. Michels, *Probleme der Sozialphilosophie* (Leipzig, 1913) p. 192.

36. *Archiv,* XXV, 246 ff.

37. *Ibid.,* XXX, 196 ff.

38. See also *ibid.,* XXVI, 280, note 5.

39. Marianne Weber, *op. cit.,* pp. 351 ff.

40. *Archiv,* XXV, 245, note 5.

41. J. C. H. de Pater, "Die tachtigjarige vorlog," *Geschiedenis von Nederland,* ed. H. Brugmans (Amsterdam, 1936), IV, 98–99.

42. E. Beins, "Die Wirtschaftsethik der Calvinistischen Kirche der Niederlande, 1565–1650," *Nederlandsch Archief voor Kerkegeschiedenis,* new series, XXIV (1931), 81–156.

43. E. Baasch, *Holländische Wirtschaftsgeschichte* (Jena, 1927), pp. 7–8. These studies are summarized in Albert Hyma, *Christianity, Capitalism, and Communism* (Ann Arbor, 1937), Ch. 6; also "Calvinism and Capitalism, 1555–1700," *Journal of Modern History* (1938), 321–343. See also G. Brodnitz, *Englische Wirtschaftsgeschichte* (Jena, 1918), I, 283, note 3.

44. P. Koch, *Der Einfluss des Calvinismus und des Mennonitentums auf die Niederrheinische Textilindustrie* (Krefeld, 1928).

45. Justus Hashagen, "Kalvinismus und Kapitalismus am Rhein," *Schmollers Jahrbuch,* XLVII (1924), 49–72.

46. Thus, in accounting for the nonappearance of a positive dynamic attitude toward capitalism in antiquity, despite the presence of "capitalist" activities, Weber remarks that the causes are essentially political, the requirements of *Staatsräson* and the autarchy of the polis. He held that the bias of ancient political theory against the gaining of wealth was not primarily ethical, or at least was far less so than that of the medieval church, which was antipathetic to purely commercial relations because of their impersonal character. But he insisted that one could not leave out of consideration the psychological factor of the antipathy to work and productive activity in general, including business, which was the dominant attitude of the ruling class. There was no ethical idealization of vocational activity (*Erwerbsarbeit*); and only among the cynics and Hellenistic-oriental petty bourgeoisie are there even slight traces of such activity. Thus the "economic man" of antiquity lacked the support for the rationalization of economic life which his counterpart found at the beginning of the modern period in the vocational ethic, largely a product of religious motivation. The lack of integration in men's attitudes to economic activity must therefore be accounted as one of the reasons for the nonappearance in antiquity of the modern type of capitalism. See "Agrarverhältnisse im Altertum," *Handwörterbuch der Staatswissenschaften,* 3rd ed. (1909), I, 66 ff.; *Archiv,* XXXI, 593, note 25.

47. On the overemphasis of the importance of vocation in Protestantism, see Hyma, *Christianity, Capitalism, and Communism,* pp. 4, 125, and Fanfani, *Catholicism, Protestantism, and Capitalism,* p. 204. See also H. M. Robertson, *op. cit.,* pp. 6, 8, 28, 202.

48. See T. C. Hall, *The Religious Background of American Culture* (Boston, 1930), p. 210.

49. See the Foreword by R. H. Tawney to the English translation of *The Protestant Ethic,* pp. 6–11.

50. His method is dubbed "isolierend-kausal" by F. Borkenau in *Der Übergang vom feudalen zum bürgerlichen Weltbild* (Paris, 1934). Henri Sée characterizes it as "simpliste" in "Dans quelle mesure Puritains et Juifs ont-ils contribué aux progrès du capitalisme moderne?", *Revue Historique,* CLV (1927), 63.

51. This is the view of R. H. Tawney, H. M. Robertson, and Laski, *The Rise of European Liberalism* (New York and London, 1936), p. 34. Hyma says, "Weber and his disciples have committed a grave anachronism in their eagerness to prove a theory" (*Christianity, Capitalism, and Communism*, pp. 126, 161).

52. Troeltsch, *The Social Teaching of the Christian Churches*, II, 519, 645, 818, 894, 911.

53. A poignant expression of Weber's feeling concerning the tentativeness of science and the fateful transiency of the achievements of the scientist, who must nonetheless accept this tragic fact as his destiny and persevere in his calling, is his eloquent essay, "Wissenschaft als Beruf," now in *Gesammelte Aufsätze zur Wissenschaftslehre*.

4

ONCE AGAIN: CALVINISM
AND CAPITALISM

Herbert Lüthy

Max Weber's famous thesis *The Protestant Ethic and the Spirit of Capitalism* appeared in 1904 and has remained the crowning glory of the historical and philosophical school of German sociology. The controversy provoked by this thesis has died down from time to time, but only to be rekindled again and again as the new theses and supplementary subtleties are added to enrich the polemic. Throughout the last fifty years, most of the great scholars of the age have added either a comment or a book: Sombart, Troeltsch, and Brentano in Germany, Tawney and Robertson in England, Hauser and Sée in France, Amintore Fanfani (recently Prime Minister of his country) in Italy, Talcott Parsons in America, and Kurt Samuelsson in Sweden. The commemoration of the 450th anniversary of Calvin's birth has brought a new series of studies, and outstanding among them is a book by a Genevan theologian and national economist. This book [1] confronts the various theses of this debate with the original texts of Calvin's massive teachings. Few historical arguments have produced a greater wealth of intellectually fertile, subtle, and often deeply disturbing *aperçus* and raised deeper passions hidden under the calm surface of scholarship. Few arguments have borne a richer crop of basic misunderstandings; few a more meager harvest of definite, tenable, unambiguous results (I mean results of which we can say not only there's something in it but that's the way it is). The whole subject is lit by the flickering light of the illuminating, frequently obvious, but equivocal relationship between categories of concepts that are remote from one another

Reprinted from Encounter, *XXII, No. 1 (January 1964), 26–38. This essay is a shortened version of the author's "Calvinisme et capitalisme: après soixante ans de débats,"* Cahiers Vilfredo Pareto, *No. 2 (December 1963), which was reprinted in the author's* Le passé présent *(Monaco and Paris, 1965).*

and, furthermore, are themselves essentially vague: the *ethic* of a religious belief and the *spirit* of an economic system, the cure of souls and the balancing of accounts. The establishment of relationships between remote concepts is among the favorite games of the human mind and perhaps one of its most fruitful, for it reveals surprising links and opens new perspectives—but also one of the most dangerous and seductively misleading ones.

In a short paper it is not possible to refer individually even to the most important matters in dispute which the polemic has aroused, not even in the broadest outlines: the result would be a pure chaos of ideas. Here, as elsewhere, the trouble begins with the terminology: what the problem is actually about is subject, on both sides of the equation, to misunderstanding and confusion. The explosive power of Weber's thesis derived from the correlation of two concepts, Protestantism and capitalism. Yet when Weber comes to develop the thesis, it appears that the "Protestantism" referred to in his title is almost exclusively limited to a single one of its many manifestations, Calvinism; and Calvinism itself is examined principally in certain key texts which are only characteristic of certain specific periods and particular forms of Puritanism, such as the Westminster Confession of 1645 (a religious Civil War manifesto), or the utilitarian moral tracts of that Man of the Enlightenment, Benjamin Franklin (his advice "how to become rich"), which reflect an entirely secular theory of virtue, but which can hardly be said to express a religious attitude. It is significant that fifty years elapsed after Weber's thesis before André Biéler set about examining the ensuing polemic in the light of what Calvin himself actually taught—and on this basis rejected most of what had been said on the subject. Perhaps even more deceptive and chameleonlike is the concept on the other side of the equation: capitalism. In the century since Marx this word has been worked to death: it has been applied to every conceivable practice, epoch, and economic system; it has been degraded to a fashionable phrase and to a term of abuse, with the result that it is scarcely viable any more as a historical idea. There are as many definitions of capitalism as there have been economists and sociologists writing about it. The word as commonly used in European journalism is always available in order to express in an apparently concise term any passing feeling of uneasiness with existing society. That Weber spoke not of capitalism but of the *spirit* of capitalism—just as he wrote not about Protestantism as a theological doctrine but about the Protestant *ethic*—was a warning that has been invariably ignored. The word was there, malleable as putty, and the very next man to pick up Weber's thesis, namely Sombart, already made something entirely different of it.

For only in the whole context of his monumental, labyrinthine, and tormented work does Max Weber's thesis achieve its complete and subtle meaning. His great and questioning mind was never particularly interested in the facts of history, nor even in social and economic systems, but rather in the detection of the ultimate impulses behind man's attitudes and behavior. What he analyzed were not the hybrid and wretched forms of a historically realized society (in which such ultimate impulses are never embodied in their purity), but rather the abstract and chemically pure "ideal types" which should provide the essences of a civilization stripped of all the adulterations and accidents of actual history. His religiosociological studies, and also his economic and social-historical works, whether he is writing the agrarian history of the Ancient World or dissecting the Indian caste structure, are in fact always concerned with the one problem posed by the historically unique nature of modern Western civilization. And in this context the words *capitalism* or *spirit of capitalism* are used in a very particular sense: they mean no less than the entire inner structure governing Western society's attitudes—not only its economy but also its legal system, its political structure, its institutionalized sciences and technology, its mathematically based music and architecture. Its economic modes of operation, works discipline, and accountancy methods are all regarded by him as the mere *pars per toto* of a whole civilization type for which Weber's final word is rationality (*Rationalität*)—a rationality which permeates all fields of social behavior, the organization of labor and management as well as the creative sciences, law and order, philosophy and the arts, the state and politics, and the dominant forms of private life. This rationality, driven by its own internal dynamic, has overthrown (or tamed) every form of resistance offered by prerational human nature, magic and tradition, instinct and spontaneity. Finally, with the Reformation, it has forced its way into the innermost temple wherein the motives behind human behavior are generated, into the very heart of religious belief, there to destroy all the dark, magical, mysterious tabernacles—image, cult, and tradition—for which it substitutes the Bible as the authentic truth, supposedly unshakable, accessible to critical examination, and susceptible of proof.

This is what the Reformation means for Weber, and this is the knot with which he linked economic theory and religious doctrine. Weber rightly insists upon the historically well-nigh monstrous uniqueness of this civilization, which cannot be explained in terms of its material bases alone. Those material and technical preconditions on which Europe started to build her civilization after the late Middle Ages existed equally or even more richly in other high cultures, in Hellenism, in ancient Rome, in India, China, and the Arab Caliphate; yet in no other case did they cause a similar leap from the merely static to the irresistibly dynamic. We know today how right Weber was to insist on the precedence of inner spiritual and cultural preconditions over all external and economic forms. He was right against almost all his contemporaries, liberals and Marxists alike, who accepted the availability of capital and of labor force

as adequate preconditions for economic progress and thus believed that a
Western-type civilization could be transplanted or imposed virtually anywhere. And how right he was, too, to be tormented with worry about the
future prospects of a fully and finally rationalized civilization in which
the impulses inherited from its prerational past should have died once
and for all. The fact that he thought he could summarize the nature of
this civilization in the ambiguous term *capitalism* (the catchword for a
purely materialistic dynamic) demonstrates the tension in his thought, a
tension close to breaking point between highest admiration and utter rejection of the achievements of Western civilization at the time of its greatest *hubris.*

A similar inner tension marks his attitude toward Protestantism. He
respected what he called its ethical and moral "values"—an expression
which itself reveals the problematic nature of his attitude—while regarding its religious roots as desiccated and doomed. Having first broken
through the paganism of image, rite, cult, and tradition to find a sure
source of nourishment in the Holy Scriptures, Protestant rationalism (he
thought) must eventually hollow and empty these too. It is this inner
ambivalence toward them both that enabled Weber to draw his connection between the Protestant ethic and the spirit of capitalism and to
create the paradox of his functional equation. It is both the greatness and
the tragedy of Weber—a positivist and a skeptic, a universal spirit and an
ardent German nationalist, who died in 1920 when his world lay in ruins
—that he had attempted to pursue the insoluble contradictions both
within his being and his age in all directions down to their deepest roots,
without ever finding the answer. And it is the obverse of his greatness that
his powerful and fragmentary life's work did not lay the foundations of "a
science of society," but rather has become an inexhaustible mine for glit-
tering esoteric formulas and slogans, many of which have been more misleading and harmful than the one here under discussion.

All this is only a preliminary remark to our subject, yet it has to be
stated in order that the complex starting point of the polemic becomes
comprehensible: and it allows me to anticipate my conclusion. In the debate that Weber began no one else has employed the term *capitalism* as
he did; that is, to denote a whole pattern of civilization. The argument
was immediately transferred to the lower plane of economic management,
accumulation of capital, or even of the simple profit motive. And precisely because of this misunderstanding, the isolated essay on "Capitalism
and Protestantism" (which is the one fragment of Weber's work known
by hearsay at least to all educated persons) has produced its powerful and
irritating effect. If Weber had not so willfully substituted one single feature for the totality, if he had given his work a title that expressed his
actual purpose in common language (such as *Protestantism and Modern
Society* or *The Reformation and the Spirit of Western Civilization*), he

would, in a new form and tone, have only been stating what no one has ever questioned, and it would have caused no such excitement—that the Reformation marks a profound spiritual breach between the Middle Ages and the modern world, bringing a ferment into Western history which has changed its course irreversibly, far beyond the domain of the Protestant churches and communities, to imprint its mark upon the whole Western world; that without Calvin we could not imagine Cromwell, or Rousseau, or the Founding Fathers; that the modern industrial society, as well as creative science, the rule of law, constitutionalism, in brief the free society, first appeared (and have flourished best) in those countries which were molded by Calvinism; and that an indissoluble internal bond links all these aspects of our Western society.

Had this provided the substance of the polemic, it could be terminated here and now without further ado. This development in its factual manifestations is the content of our history during these last four hundred years, and it provides an inexhausible subject for research and speculation; but that it is so no one can doubt. And also that this was not the whole story: that the Reformation was not alone and in itself the turning point, but merely one of its elements intimately linked with others of the age which *together* altered the whole spiritual and material picture of the world—humanism, the Copernican revolution, the mastery of the seas and the discovery of new continents, the sudden emergence of global powers and global trade, all the splendor and chaos, worldly triumph and metaphysical despair engendered in a world that would be henceforth boundless but that had lost all security and all familiarity. And we also know that all this was not a totally new start from the void. The closed world of the Middle Ages had been burst asunder by powerful forces created within that very world—forces that led from the Crusades to the Spanish-Portuguese *Conquista,* from the scholastic universities to humanism, from the medieval schisms and heresies to the Reformation. In a certain sense, Martin Luther's revolt against the worldliness of Renaissance Rome was the revolt of a medieval spirit against the modern world, and not the obverse.

However, the key word *capitalism* had been inserted, and the debate became limited to this one aspect of the relationship between the teachings of the Reformation and economic behavior, and this not as one among many interconnecting links supporting a civilization's entire history but as a direct and causative relation between religious doctrine and economic practice. It was as though the essential thread had suddenly been discovered which would lead dialectically from the nailing of Luther's ninety-five theses on the Wittenberg church door to the assembly lines of Detroit and the ramifications of Standard Oil. It is hardly necessary to add that this entire debate took place beneath the long shadow of Karl Marx, whose challenge no historian and no social scientist of the past hundred years has been able to ignore. Weber's thesis stressing the decisive influence of the spiritual fundamentals upon economic behavior, rather than vice versa, is itself only comprehensible in the context of his intensive debate with historical materialism. The whole ensuing polemic on the primacy of the spiritual or the economic motivations has an odd chicken-and-egg quality: did the Reformation produce the spirit of capitalism, or did the spirit of capitalism produce the Reformation? Only the second thesis, which makes Protestantism the "subjective superstructure," or "the ideology" of capitalism, accords with historical materialism—and in the hands of many a bourgeois historian, historical materialism has become far more vulgar than ever it was in Marx's own version. Thus did the Reformation acquire its place in a very categorical picture of the historical process, considered as "a history of class struggles." In all these versions of modern history, satisfactorily reconstructed on the great lines of the rise to power of the bourgeoisie and the decline of feudalism, the Reformation takes its place as "the first bourgeois revolution." By analyzing the English Puritan Revolution of the seventeenth century as the second bourgeois revolution, Tawney skillfully constructed a bridge to the third and greatest, the French Revolution at the end of the eighteenth century.

So it is that the second catchword was inserted, a twin to the concept of capitalism, equally iridescent and equally ambiguous: *the bourgeoisie.* And with it comes its opposite, the counterconcept of "Feudalism," and even more hopelessly worked to death, if that be possible. In an interpretation of history which reduces acting and thinking historical human beings to the simple function of conscious or unconscious instruments and exponents of class forces, the leaders of the Reformation become spokesmen for the aspiring bourgeoisie, the class that bred capitalism. So self-evident has this interpretation become to a whole generation of historians that we must start all over again if we are to rescue the history of the Reformation and of its endlessly complex effects from the preconceived schemata now deeply embedded in popular history and school textbooks.

For this interpretation, quite simply, is not true.

A DIVIDED MIND

Let us return once more to the starting point of the whole polemic. At the back of Weber's thesis there is one established and supporting set of facts, and this set of facts, be it noted, dates not from the period of the Reformation but from the turn of the twentieth century. Weber's starting point was a statistical survey carried out in 1900 by the German sociologist Max Offenbacher into "the economic condition of Catholics and Protestants" in the religiously mixed (60 per cent Catholic) Grand Duchy of Baden. Offenbacher established that the Protestant citizens of the Grand Duchy owned a disproportionately large percentage of capital assets and occupied more than their share of leading positions, of educational qualifications, academic positions, and skilled-labor jobs. This was the sort of research then being carried out in the very early days of German sociology. At about this time Offenbacher and others had established that the Jews played a disproportionately large role in the commercial and liberal professions. A few years earlier Max Weber himself had carried out research into the Polish "infiltration" (*Unterwanderung*) in the East Prussian territories; and the whole complexity of Weber's personality is evident in the fact that his anticapitalist anger was first aroused by East Prussian agrarian capitalism which, he said, was de-Germanizing the East German territories by recruiting cheap Polish laborers instead of more expensive Germans. These researches were carried out with true German thoroughness, propriety, and scholarliness; and yet, in retrospect, we cannot but feel uneasy about the spirit in which they were conducted—a spirit which finally brought disaster to Europe.

Be that as it may, here was the problem, and now the historian set about discovering the causes. Where was he more likely to find the reason for the economic success of Baden's Protestant minority than in the Protestant doctrine itself? Offenbacher's researches in the Grand Duchy of Baden were directed explicitly and exclusively at the economic status of the members of the two Churches; but they nevertheless established not merely a Protestant predominance in "capitalist activity" but a generally higher degree of ambition and achievement in all fields such as science, academic life, the professions, the civil service, as well as in business. Now this exclusive interest in the Protestants' economic condition, which is implicit in the formulation of the questions in this statistical inquiry, becomes in Weber's interpretation the essence of the whole much larger problem, to the extent that he totally neglects the evidence of Protestant successes in all other fields except as capitalists or entrepreneurs. Acting in all good faith, yet with consequences that were to weigh heavily throughout the whole polemic, Weber thus distorted from the start the entire premise upon which the problem rested.

Similar statistics could obviously have been established for all areas with religiously mixed populations, and quite independently of the economic system or the level of industrialization would have produced similar results. My own country, Switzerland, would provide one excellent field for such research, thanks to its preservation of medieval geopolitical autonomies and its mixture of adjoining religious self-governing communities. The dividing boundaries between highly developed and (in modern parlance) underdeveloped areas of this country correspond almost exactly to the old boundaries between the two religious communities, the adherents of the new and the old faith. This is striking evidence; but these boundaries were already practically the same *before* the Reformation and thus show us the extreme complexity of establishing cause and effect. Even more striking is the case of a country such as France, where since the eighteenth century a tiny Protestant minority has played a leading part grotesquely out of proportion to its numerical strength, not only in industry and finance, but equally in political and intellectual life. Nor are these spectacular achievements limited to the modernized or "capitalist" parts of France. In the poor peasant lands of the south, which since the sixteenth century have been the center of resistance for politically defeated French Calvinism, the Protestant peasants remain to this day a nobility and an elite. And, in spite of entirely different power relationships throughout history, and in spite of the more recent reversal of this power relationship, the same statement applies to agricultural, Catholic, clerical Ireland where the small Protestant minority was and has remained the active elite.

But here I wish to warn against the drawing of hasty conclusions. There can be no doubt of the ethical, intellectual, *and* economic role played by dissenting minorities as an elite (and a "yeast"), but this fact seems to be quite unconnected with the actual form of their dissent. To quote the Church Father: *Opportet haereses esse!* Let us recall the Jews of central and eastern Europe, the religious minorities of the Near East and of India, groups whose achievements obviously have nothing whatever to do with the Protestant ethic and which yet have certain features in common with those of the Protestants in other parts of the world. In each case these are the response to a challenge imposed by legal or social discrimination which produces or evokes a higher level of activity and of discipline whenever the subjective conditions for such a response exist. The fact that Protestant doctrine, in its Calvinist variety, was more suited to the production of such endeavor and self-discipline than was Catholic doctrine is shown to be true by the comparison between the Catholic minority in England and the Protestant minority in France: the general situation and conditions of life were almost identical through four centuries, and yet the English Catholics, unlike the French Protestants, have never acted as "the yeast" within their society. The Protestants' teaching that the believer's behavior as an individual is subject to no sanction by any external spiritual authority but only to the inner sanctions of his own conscience has undoubtedly armed and equipped them better for life in a "hostile" environment, without the paternal protection of established church authority, and it strengthened those virtues of responsibility, self-control, and spiritual independence which even the bitterest enemies of the Reformation have recognized in the Protestant minorities. Another equally important factor of spiritual as well as economic history is that for centuries the Protestant minorities living in Catholic countries, regardless of class, were a Bible-reading people, a "people of the book," like the Jews, and thus constituted a literate minority amidst illiterate masses. Yet we need not depend exclusively on such microsociological comparisons between different religious groups living within one and the same country. Much more striking is (and was already for Weber) the global evidence furnished by the comparison of whole countries and continents. Consider the case of the two parts of the old Low Countries, Belgium and Holland, once a single nation, but the development of which has diverged radically since 1600; no natural or historical preconditions except their different fate in the Reformation can explain why these two sections of one country, living side by side, should have diverged as obviously and to the extent they have. Similarly, on a continental scale, there is the image and counterimage of Anglo-Saxon and Latin America, the sociologist's textbook example of developments and underdevelopment. . . .

And here another question arises, which strangely enough has scarcely ever been mentioned in all this polemic. The Reformation took place at the very height of a period of almost breathtaking growth in Europe, of development in all the fields of the mind, of technology, of the liberation of human personality, of economic and imperial expansion. In no single one of these fields is there a scrap of evidence to show that the Reformation was a fresh start or that it gave birth to anything fundamentally new. All the evidence advanced in favor of Weber's thesis is taken from the eighteenth and nineteeth centuries—that is to say, from a period so remote in time from the age of religious division as to make direct and unambiguous connection with the Reformation quite impossible of proof, and all such examples are but further developments of what in fact started in all Europe toward the end of the Middle Ages.

One can go further: specifically in the field of capitalist organization, Catholic Europe in the fifteenth and early sixteenth centuries (the age of the Fuggers) reached a level of structural and organizational development which was not to be achieved again for a further two centuries. Precisely in this domain a startling decadence and stagnation began in the middle of the sixteenth century. So does the Reformation represent a breakthrough from which a fresh progress can be dated? Or was it not rather the Counter Reformation, as an authoritarian and total reaction against all manifestations of the free heretical spirit, which stopped all further progress and which, after the spiritual and material catastrophes of the Wars of Religion, prevented a resumption of such progress wherever it had been triumphant?

Before the Counter Reformation this progress had not only been common to all Europe but had had as its matrix those very parts of Europe which had now fallen to the Counter Reformation and which now subsided into a sleep of death both economically and (even more) intellectually, and where only the arts continued to flourish in the service of throne and altar. Think of the powerful *translatio imperii* of the sciences from

Italy to England in the seventeenth century, or the astonishing absence of
Catholic Germany from the rebirth of German philosophy and literature
that followed the Thirty Years' War.

And the exception which proves the rule is the confusing special position occupied by France. There the Catholic state church had long been
subordinated to the French crown and served as an instrument of the
absolute monarchy which needed no reformation to establish a national
church sovereignty. It refused to accept the Counter Reformation, the
Tridentine Council, the Inquisition, and clerical control of all intellectual life. During the decisive struggles of the seventeenth century His
Most Christian Majesty of France was invariably allied to the Protestant
states against Catholic Spain, and despite Louis XIV and the persecution
of the Huguenots, Calvinism's imprint remained far stronger in France
than its external history reveals.

It is probably the most absurd failure of this whole discussion concerning the historical role of Protestantism, a discussion carried on in a sort of
intellectual incest behind closed windows, that it has quite simply ignored the other side of its problem: the historical part played by the
Counter Reformation (which was itself a reformation and which in its
own way marked the end of Catholicism as a universal church), as if the
sudden breaking of an ascendant curve of development did not constitute
a far greater problem than its continuance. In the period of the Reformation all the bases of the modern world—capital, wealth, the highest technological and artistic level of development, global power, world trade—
all these were almost exclusively present in countries that were and remained Catholic. Italy was the uncontested center of material and intellectual culture. Spain and Portugal enjoyed the monopoly of colonizing
and exploiting both the Indies, the most important field of enterprise and
the greatest source of wealth in the opening years of the modern age. It
was *here,* and not among the poor and half-barbarian Protestant states on
the fringe of northern and northwestern Europe, that all the material and
technical preconditions for the creation of modern economy and modern
society were to be found.

One century later all this was petrifaction and decay. Catholic historians have shown us what an appalling break the Counter Reformation
was in the cultural history of Europe and how deadly was the shadow cast
by Inquisition and heresy trials across the lands where this reaction had
triumphed. It was as if a spell had been laid upon this half of the continent from which it was not to awake until two centuries had passed,
under the spur of enlightened, anticlerical absolutism (or, even later, as a
sequel to the Revolutionary Wars). During these centuries, in *one* half of
Europe, an intellectual ferment, general and active throughout the *whole*
continent on the eve of the Reformation, was extinguished and destroyed.
The existential minimum of a free society, without which neither intel-

lectual nor industrial pioneers, neither scientific research nor economic progress, are possible, was there totally uprooted. This is a crossroad of history which becomes caricature when we reduce it to a mere economic phenomenon.

Yet even in this narrow perspective we should raise the question *why* the Reformation permitted the free northern Netherlands to preserve and develop the great heritage of industrial and mercantile achievement while in the Spanish Netherlands it was destroyed—instead of reversing the terms of the problem and trying to discover *why* the Reformation produced achievements for which it was not, in fact, responsible. For the splendor and glory of Amsterdam flowed from the same factors that had made the splendor and glory of Antwerp in an earlier age. Amsterdam did not so much invent new commercial and financial devices as inherit what the Spanish wrath destroyed in Antwerp and attract those who fled the Inquisition (Jews, heretics, and others). It is certainly legitimate to single out in the complex course of history *one* line of development (the development of the modern market and of a competitive economy in northwest Europe) as a subject of specialized research. But to believe that this will reveal the essence of the Reformation and of its effects, to wave a bank-account book or a balance sheet and to cry: "Here is the quintessence of Calvinism!"—this is nonsense. And it is as much the duty of the economic historian as of the theologian to protest against such nonsense.

THE PROPHETIC TRADITION

It is scarcely a matter of reproach to the sociologists and social historians who conducted this debate that they were not theologians. It is bad enough that they had little knowledge of the doctrines of the Reformation and apparently none at all of the Counter Reformation; that they seem to have been unaware how similarly, for example, the question of predestination—the theological formulation of the insoluble problem of fate and free will—was posed in Protestant and Catholic theology, and that they jumped with a sort of dilettante enthusiasm into a psychoanalytical interpretation of the Calvinist doctrine of predestination as a theory of justification through success. Even more fatal, perhaps, was the careless and uncritical manner in which the materials provided by social and economic historical research were shoveled together in support of this theory (though in mitigation we must remember that the economic and social history of modern times has only recently emerged from the kindergarten stage). A good proportion of the clever theses produced are of no value because their authors—and unfortunately the names of Tawney and Sombart cannot here be excluded—lacked accurate knowledge of Canonical Law as it affected economic activity, of the basic mechanism of banking in those days, and of the methods of exchange and payment then current.

An example of this is the assumption that the activity of bankers in the seventeenth and eighteenth centuries consisted in lending money on interest, which led to the apparently obvious conclusion that Calvin, when he permitted the charging of interest, opened the locks for the rise of capitalism. . . . This is not the place to delve into the history of banking, which would lead us deep into the weird complexity of the financial economy of that time. Suffice it to say that the Protestant bankers, whose key position in the late eighteenth century has excited the fantasy of so many historians, were in no wise moneylenders. They were specialized operators of the international (and even local) mechanism of exchange and payment, and their techniques and ways of business in no wise differed from those of their Catholic colleagues. The canonical prohibition of usury had not the slightest relevance in this field, since it had never been applied to the foreign exchange dealings. The fact that since the end of the seventeenth century Dutch, English, and above all the highly successful French Huguenot bankers became more important than the old Italian and South German banking houses which had previously been supreme was not due to any new banking techniques, but to the fact that the great trading centers of the Continent were shifting steadily toward the northwest. And so far as the Huguenots were concerned, Calvin's doctrine had far less to do with their successes as bankers than had their destiny as a dispersed minority group scattered all over the world in small communities of religious refugees who were "predestined" to carry on an "international correspondence" among themselves; and international correspondence *was* the basis of all banking activity in those days. This does not constitute a chapter in the history of religious belief, but belongs to the science of historical "group sociology." "Protestant high finance" (the very phrase is an example of historical dilettantism at its worst) only existed as a sociological problem in Catholic countries, and specifically in France; it was the scandal of a successful minority exciting the attention and jealousy of the majority.

Yet these bankers too are invalid and anachronistic witnesses to an untenable hypothesis. The Reformation as the ideology of the emergent capitalism? Let us ask our schoolboys for the names of the great capitalists involved in trade, manufacture, and banking at the time of the Reformation. They all know them: the Medici and the Fuggers. The Medici, who started as bankers to the Roman Curia, rose to be popes themselves, and the pope whom Luther defied was the son of Lorenzo the Magnificent. Or Jakob Fugger, the stanchest ally of emperor and pope in their fight against the reformers, who was the Curia's banker for all central, northern, and eastern Europe, who dealt in bishoprics and abbeys, in the phrase of a Venetian ambassador, as a lesser man might "deal in pepper and melons," and who sovereignly conferred on his nephews and associates the bishoprics of Germany, Poland, and Hungary that were important to his business. The financial affairs of the Church (the collection of tithes, annates, Crusaders' and Peter's pence) and the business side of eternal salvation, together with silver and copper mines and mints, all this Fugger controlled with the most up-to-date techniques of a contemporary world-wide business concern; in the end he was converting for his own purposes indulgences into an infinitely inflatable paper currency based upon a metaphysical gold reserve, the Saints' Treasury of Merit. The most immediate motive of Luther's rebellion against the Roman Church is established beyond dispute and cannot now be "interpreted" away: it was a revolt against the corruption of the Church and simultaneously an outcry against the great capitalist organizations of the time which had found their strongest support and their richest grazing in and about the Holy See of Peter. The Reformation, insofar as it was concerned with the affairs of *this* world, was *also* and very explicitly a protest against the worship of the Golden Calf. To use modern jargon, it was the outbreak of an anticapitalist movement that had long been coming to a head at all levels of society. At that same Diet of Worms where Luther made his spectacular appearance, the second most important subject of debate was the general desire for imperial legislation to curb the trade monopolies, business cartels, pre-emption and usury practices that characterized the Fugger trading and banking house. And this would have produced the first antitrust act in modern history, if it had not been vetoed by Emperor Charles V, whom Jakob Fugger reminded in sharp terms that his election was due to the bribe money lent him by the House of Fugger and not yet repaid. Recall Luther's and Hutten's searing speeches against the monopolies and the capitalized companies and against the money-changers who had set up their tables in the temple and the usurers who were consuming the substance of widows. This was the first occasion in the history of Western Christendom that the spirit and the speech of the Old Testament prophets was heard again, for whom the divine command of justice applied not only in the beyond but here and now, on earth.

This re-emergence of the Old Testament's prophetic tradition, which in the Roman Church had lain completely buried for more than a millennium beneath the Roman imperial and gentile heritage, had an all-embracing effect upon the Christian conscience of the age of the Reformation and upon western Europe's spiritual and intellectual history.

It has affected every aspect of our private and public life and is still to be found even in the deepest undertones of our daily speech. For centuries the English and German languages have drawn their basic tone from the vernacular Bible, and this tone also impregnated the French language in the sixteenth and seventeenth centuries until the authoritarian linguistic regulations of Louis XIV's age rooted it out. It remains, however, so totally foreign to the Romance and Slav languages that no translator's skill can convey to the people who speak those tongues the true flavor of a

Shakespeare or a Milton. We know that the French Huguenots and the English and Scottish Puritans of the period of struggle felt closer to, and derived their inspiration more directly from, the Old Testament than the New. We see this in the strange old Jewish names with which they christened their sons and daughters, in the phrases and quotations from the Psalms and the Prophets that flow through their letters, sermons, and manifestos like heady wine, in the way they take for granted the interpretation of their own age in terms of the passionate figures of Israel's past, anathematizing their foes with the Prophets' curses, calling the pope a priest of Baal or a Nebuchadnezzar, identifying the French queen of St. Bartholomew's night with Jezebel and King Charles I with Rehoboam, the accursed of God, weeping in persecution and defeat beside the waters of Babylon, or celebrating a victory, as did Cromwell after Marston Moor, by striking up a thanksgiving psalm of David's.

"I hate, I despise your feastdays, and I will not smell your holy days. Take away from me the noise of thy songs; for I will not hear the melody of thy viols. But let justice run down as waters, and righteousness as a mighty stream." This outburst of fury on the part of the prophet Amos summarizes the entire spirit of the Reformation. And it was by no means mere literary allegory. It was meant with a deadly, burning seriousness. The social teachings of Zwingli and Calvin, as well as the revolutionary stance of the Huguenots, the Dutch, and the Puritans, are permeated through and through with the spirit of the Old Testament. They found their models in the books of Israel, in the simple people and the shepherds who spoke and argued with God face to face, in the judges, prophets, and leaders of their people who rose against unjust princes and false prophets and who believed that the children of God should be concerned not only with holiness but also with justice and sanctification *here on earth.*

There is no need of subtle interpretations of Calvinist predestination or psychoanalysis of Protestant loneliness—as Max Weber's successors have attempted so repeatedly—to understand why the Calvinist Puritans were conscious of themselves as the Chosen People. This sprang spontaneously from their self-identification with the historical People of God as stated in those ancient books that were their daily reading and their spiritual nourishment. And it was this identification, far more than any theological doctrinal difference, that really made Calvinism into a form of Christianity quite other than that of Rome. With this identification there appeared in the modern world a fragment of that ancient Jewish prophetic spirit which is directed not toward the next world nor to the inner soul, but outward to righteousness and justice in this world. This provided the yeast that fermented their political desires, formed their political behavior, and has left its mark on all the struggles that have convulsed the modern world to create states based upon constitution and upon law.

THE INTELLECTUAL REVOLUTION

Nor is it true that this revolution was a bourgeois or urban-class movement. The Reformation movement in Germany, as in France, affected in large measure all strata of the people, including the urban burghers and officials; but it also produced a much wider and more direct effect upon the peasantry; and, what was far more important politically, it was embraced by the nobility. When the violent struggle for power ended with the victory of one side, the nobility in general conformed to the religion of the prince—whatever it was—and the illiterate and oppressed peasantry, deprived of teachers, ministers, and freedom to worship, sooner or later had to follow the seigneurs. Only the bourgeoisie had the social independence necessary to stick to its faith even as a minority. This is the way French Protestantism became bourgeois: not at the start, but in the end, after centuries, by elimination. This is not a question of doctrine, but of social history—and of a very violent social history. And every single case would have to be discussed here in terms of what actually happened.

In recent years there has taken place in England a thorough, indeed a passionate, re-examination of the Puritan Revolution, which has seriously questioned the historical interpretation of R. H. Tawney and his school, according to which the Cromwellian Commonwealth marked the crest of a bourgeois revolutionary wave. In this titanic struggle for individual freedom, for the independence of the law courts, and for parliamentary control, the urban bourgeoisie of merchants and traders played an almost negligible part and failed to produce a single dominant personality. Tawney's whole analysis of the "social revolution," which ascribes to the English landed gentry of the Cromwellian period a "bourgeois capitalist mentality" which is said to contrast with the spirit prevailing among the court nobility, may simply be a very personal handling of sociological categories. But an approach of this sort can be used with or without almost any sort of historical data to "prove" whatever is desirable of proof, and the contrary as well.

We should in any case hesitate before we assert so casually that the Reformation was this or that—a bourgeois, feudal, proletarian, nationalist, or national-ecclesiastical revolution, according to whichever suits our book. It was all that and more, for it marked a change of epoch that affected everything. What the Reformation was and wished to be cannot be discovered *backward,* by examining what became of the individual reformed churches and sects. These are *the outcome of its failure.*

Originally a spiritual movement embracing all Western Christendom, it tried and failed to reform the one ecumenical Christian Church in its unity and to re-establish it anew according to the Word in all its purity. On the eve of the Reformation an overwhelming majority of the intellectual and moral elite, clerical as well as temporal, of all nations and all classes were in agreement that such a reform was both necessary and urgent, even though they might disagree about the form it should take. The fact that in the fearful struggle between the Reformation and the Counter Reformation this attempt to reform the One Church resulted in a multiplicity of individual churches and sects and in the wreckage of the unity of Western Christendom was a scandal which for two centuries was equally intolerable to all the partisans of both camps. Even the violence of the Wars of Religion and the mutual persecutions bear witness to this stubborn refusal to accept the division of Christianity as definite and final. In this drama of intended reform in unity and the actual splitting of the Church that resulted therefrom, many threads of history converge and separate again.

There is a first and basic distinction which must be made if we would understand the Reformation in its reality as a historical event: on the one hand there is the *religious* aspect, which was concerned with the reform of dogma and of church administration, but which also embraces all the battles for reform and all the heretical movements of the Middle Ages as well as the struggle between the authority of the councils and that of the popes. And on the other hand there is the ecclesiasticopolitical aspect, in which equally ancient lines of development can be traced, but ones that follow quite another direction: the struggle between temporal princely power and spiritual clerical power which had its climaxes in the struggle between emperor and pope, in the triumph of the French monarchy over the papal power in the time of Philippe le Bel, and in the Great Schism of the fourteenth and fifteenth centuries, and which continues in all Catholic countries to this day. And it was in that second aspect that the different reformation movements actually parted their ways.

The grandiose religious impulse of Lutheranism was internally broken by its subordination to the state-church policy of the reigning sovereigns, establishing themselves as the princes of the Church. Ecclesiastically, politically, and also economically, the Reformation in northern Germany, in Scandinavia, and initially in Henry VIII's England began as a campaign of plunder waged by the princes and the nobility against the estates and riches of the Church. In Scandinavia this actually preceded the movement for *religious* reform, which only got under way when the ruling powers felt the need of justification for their confiscation of Church wealth and authority. And it is scarcely necessary to insist that this confiscation was carried out by and to the profit of the crown and the nobility, not by the bourgeoisie. It was only the following waves, the struggles of the Scottish and Puritan revolutionaries against the Anglican Church and the crown, which transformed the merely political nationalization of the Church into a religious reformation.

The significance of Calvinism in world history lies in the fact that it failed to win political power and thereby remained almost free of political-opportunistic considerations and princely usurpations, and so allowed the revolutionary impulse to religious reform to flower free and uncontaminated. It was left to the Calvinists to implement the Reformation not merely by the substitution of new princes of the church and new clerics for old, but by proclaiming that henceforth their communities would recognize "no Lord other than Christ."

Calvin was the only systematizer among the reformers. He belonged to the second generation, already steeled in the battle, the contemporary and counterpart of Ignatius Loyola when the Counter Reformation was in process of organization. He was the political and spiritual leader of all the reformed minorities in Europe who were fighting against the power of the state, from Hungary and Poland to Scotland. He was the revolutionary among the reformers, and it is in him that the Old Testament prophetic passion to conform word and deed, doctrine and daily life, faith and practical politics, breaks forth in its total and elementary force. He forged the Calvinist-Puritan type of man, answerable only to God and to his conscience, that is to say, free and responsible, and he created the Calvinist community that bows to no human authority and for which the separation from the state is always axiomatic unless the state and the community be one (as in old Geneva or in the Puritan settlements of New England). From Geneva, the Zion of the new People of God, a revolution in the truest sense set forth. What made the Calvinists, hard-working and useful subjects though they were, so intolerable to French absolutism was not their religion, for France's rulers had small loyalty toward Rome, but rather what the French intendants and governors rightly describe as "their incurably republican spirit."

And these free men, responsible to themselves and their own conscience and—unlike the inner-directed Lutherans—active in the world, spread their effect far beyond the realm even of the Calvinist diaspora and far beyond the time of the initial intensity of belief, to become a yeast in the Western world, the most active agents of the development toward a modern Western society in which "capitalism" (as defined in the polemic here under discussion) is but one strand among many. The dangers and aberrations of this freedom are known to us, as is the fall of self-responsibility into that self-righteousness and hardheartedness and awful aridity which Protestant societies so often display. In the great polemic which Weber inaugurated, much Protestant self-criticism has come to light and indeed may be said to have provided the keynote of that whole debate carried on over a half-century that was full of despair for the future of the free society and the free individual. Yet no matter how we may evaluate the dangers inherent in this liberation of the self-responsible individual which proceeds so essentially from the Calvinist Reformation—whether we regard it as a blessing or (as did the Romantic under the shadow of the French Revolution) as a curse—here, in the liberation of man from spirit-

ual submission and fear of man, lies the true and deep connection between Calvinism and the modern industrial society. It is the same connection that links rational Calvinist religiosity with positive science, and the
Calvinist community with modern democracy. All else is but by-products.
And that all this hangs inseparably together is at least far better known to
us today than it was to the social critics of the early part of this century,
who so easily took the political and spiritual prerequisites of the modern
society for granted.

All these facts are so old and so well known that my remarks may seem
to resemble a Puritan gunpowder sermon rather than a contribution to a
discussion concerning matters of economic and social history. Yet precisely
what was so well known to everyone was in danger of being forgotten. For
half a century historians in Europe at least regarded it as old-fashioned or
childish to take seriously banalities such as these: that the Reformation
sprang from the scandals of the Church, or that the reformers were preoccupied with the Word of God. It was more up to date to know more about
the motives and views of historical figures than these men had known
themselves. They might have thought that they fought for truth or justice
or freedom, as they understood them; the sociologist had no hesitation in
putting them right and pointing out that they consciously or unconsciously represented class interests, no matter what they themselves may
have said or done. Ignatius Loyola was the exponent of feudalism, Calvin
of the bourgeoisie.

The problem now is not one of returning to a point of view that antedates historical materialism, nor of giving up the investigation of the material history of man which has been so efficiently initiated by Marx and
his followers. Rather it is a question of sorting out the intolerable confusion of categories that has been created by the coarse schematism of the
primitive class concept, and above all of learning once again what the
allegedly naïve liberal historians of a hundred years ago knew because it
is apparent to the naked eye: namely, that the great drama of history is,
when all is said and done, more than the mere clash of economic interests
and groups.

Only when we have achieved once again such a general perspective will
the discussion concerning "Calvinism and Capitalism" have reverted to
its proper place, which is important but secondary, and only then will it
be possible to evaluate its importance in relation to the facts. In the opening and closing pages of my study *La Banque Protestante en France* I
dissected in some detail various particular theses thrown up in the course
of this polemic. I do not intend to repeat those remarks which only apply
in connection with a factual analysis. There is, however, one relevant
point that I should like to make briefly and summarily.

What has been called Calvin's social doctrine is not to be found in any
coherent body of his teaching but is only to be discovered and deduced

from fragments widely scattered among his sermons and his glosses and is in fact in no case anything other than biblical commentary. But this biblical commentary is always made with an eye on the existential needs and the moral problems of the scattered Calvinist communities and of his beleaguered city of Geneva whose responsible leader and counselor he was. In this respect, as well as in others, it was always by referring to Holy Writ that he carried on his radical and critical re-examination of the scholastic Church tradition. It was not Luther nor even Zwingli, statesman and politician though he was, who completed the great breach with the medieval social doctrine of the Catholic Church, but the revolutionary, systematic thinker Calvin, trained in the juristic and humanistic disciplines.

The Catholic schoolmen had based their economic and social doctrine, in a rigidly literal exegesis, on the authority of Aristotle; the very word *economy,* in this tradition, meant the natural economy, which was the only "natural" and therefore the only God-given form of economy, the patriarchal, autarchic, landowner's and householder's economy in opposition to the economy of the market and of exchange, which Aristotle defined as chrematistic, that is, an economy of money and of profit, which he condemned. The whole discussion about Calvinism and capitalism means (and always meant) little else than this: the word *capitalism* is our modern substitute for chrematistics, and the unmentioned, idealized counter-image is the patriarchal, "natural" land economy with its "natural" hierarchical order of master and servant, landlord and serf, monarch and subject—in sum, the image of medieval society—the relationship of which is not defined in terms of money, or of give-and-take, but in terms of personal subordination. The schoolmen's economic and social doctrine, together with the Canonical Law that derived therefrom, had since the High Middle Ages proved incapable of adapting itself to economic change; the doctors of the school and of Canonical Law were never able to incorporate organically into their doctrine the facts of trade, of an urban economy based on industry and market, of finance and exchange—in brief, of all the elements created by a new, nonfeudal development. The result was the decaying Late Scholasticism that lingered on into the eighteenth century, where none of the terms it employed preserved a true meaning and hairsplitting subtlety competed with pedantic ignorance.

The evangelical injunction to charity, *mutuum date nihil inde sperantes*—give and hope not for a return—was interpreted as a law of economic behavior which condemned not only usury but every form of profitable activity, and it was unflinchingly applied in doctrine to market and bargaining, price and wages, overseas trade and capital investment. In practical terms this meant, quite simply, that the whole of economic life as lived in nonagrarian societies was a life of sin, and as the injunction to charity could not be enforced as a market regulation, the market economy was thus abandoned to wallow in its sinfulness. This act of abandonment had in fact taken place long ago. For centuries before the Reformation, the treatises of the schoolmen on such subjects as trade, the laws of exchange, or value and payment, had become mere casuistry, a doctrine consisting solely of exceptions without a rule. And the result of this was a state of intellectual, moral, and legal chaos, in which everything was permitted precisely because all was sinful, and in which all the blasphemies of the *Banco dello Spirito Santo* and of the Fuggers' inflation of bills of indulgence drawn on the Saints' Treasury of Merit could flourish unchecked. Yet for a theologian to recognize the unsuitability of the injunction to charity as a guiding rule for economic life, as a tariff regulation or stock-exchange law, meant no less than a second fall of man. Here Luther, too, was still a schoolman.

Calvin's breach with the body of ecclesiastical doctrine was in the first instance a painful act of intellectual honesty and clarity, in accord with the deep impulse of the Reformation age to establish a more truthful conformity between doctrine and life, between word and deed. How painful this step was is shown by the fact that Calvin was so fearful of what the results might be, should he publish his thoughts on interest and credit, that he only dared utter them in his confidential correspondence. Yet eight years after his death, the Genevan city fathers could claim his authority when the French refugees poured into the city after the Eve of St. Bartholomew. Robbed of all their possessions, they nevertheless remained proud and energetic men who would not beg for alms. They asked for loans, repayable with interest and compound interest, wherewith to rebuild their shattered careers. The tragic circumstance of the age had thus produced the classic example that justified productive credits both on economic and on ethical grounds and which also quite clearly established the difference between interest recovered from a profitable venture and usury extorted from the helpless poor.

As the confusion of these terms haunts this polemic, it is necessary to state here quite bluntly that throughout the centuries the Catholic Church had tolerated usury, not in silence but openly and explicitly. It was not Calvin who permitted the usurers to set up their businesses in Geneva, but the ruling prince bishop, Adhemar Fabri who, a century and a half before Calvin, in his famous *Privileges for the Genevan Trade Fairs,* announced that any person attending the fair, man or woman, cleric or lay, was entitled to practice usury without restriction and was further promised episcopal protection against any complaints or interference on this account. It was not Calvin who introduced usury into Geneva; it was he who abolished it by drawing a clear distinction between interest from capital productively invested (which he declared legitimate under strict regulations and within narrow limits) and usury parasitically derived from the misfortunes of others (which was pitilessly forbidden and prosecuted). The result is known to every economic historian. In the centuries before the French Revolution finally broke the spell of Canonical Law in Catholic Europe too, the difference between the Protestant and the Catholic countries was not that in the one money was lent on interest and in the other interest-free, but that in Protestant lands the cheapness of recognized, openly regulated and precisely defined interest-bearing capital investment provided an important factor in economic development, while in the lands where Canonical Law still obtained, the usurious interest charge for capital loans was one of the principal barriers to economic progress.

The full importance, not only economic but also and perhaps primarily intellectual, of the breach with the scholastic tradition would be a subject not for one essay but for a full-length study. Only when a rational legitimation of capital and interest accounts permitted the introduction of the time coefficient into economic calculations did rational economic thought first become possible at all. But to say that more simply in Calvinist terms: only the clear (if painful) distinction between the realm of private voluntary charity toward other human beings in want, which is dictated by human conscience and to which the Sermon on the Mount applies, and on the other hand the realm of acquisitive economic activity, where the worldly precepts, anchored in positive rights and laws, of probity, legality, and fairness apply—la loi d'équité in Calvin's phrase—only the drawing of this distinction permitted the redemption of the human condition, the material, existential needs and worries of mankind, from the general and indiscriminate curse of sinfulness which simply abandoned everything this side of the grave to sin. In place of this curse it substituted, in this world in which men have to live and act, the simple demand that law and human honesty, so far as this is obtainable, be realized here on earth.

In the Protestant work ethic the breach with the schoolmen's image of the world and of society was even wider. The schoolmen had seen misery and pauperism as an eternal evil, willed by God upon a sinful world. Against humanity's mass misery, the Middle Ages knew no gesture save that of the beggar resignedly holding out his hand and that of the rich man with equal resignation dropping his alms into it. The followers of Calvin had to learn to live their lives in a new, cold, clear light, not in the radiant glow cast by the sanctity of the beggar's profession, nor in the humble acquiescence in misery as the wages of sin, but in the hard school of discipline and work as free and proud men who demanded not pity and grace but work and the right to live their own lives in responsibility toward themselves. And certainly we will not fail also to notice the shadow on the man's image, the social morality of success and utilitarianism which has marked so many puritan societies in which the Father's house had no longer many mansions but had become a single workhouse.

We may perhaps judge more mildly when we realize that only by such drudgery was it possible finally to overcome pauperism and that the harshness of social discipline both toward oneself and toward others was the school in which the free society had to be educated. Yet it is beyond doubt that the shudder we feel even now in the face of this inner hardness when we study the Calvinist Reformation has provided the basic tone of most of the theses concerning "Calvinism and Capitalism." The apparently factual research into problems of economic and social history has often been an expression of our uneasiness in modern society, and to some of the scholars engaged in this controversy Calvinism has provided a fascinating scapegoat for the evils of progress.

NOTE

1. The fullest review is to be found in André Biéler's *La pensée économique et sociale de Calvin* (Geneva, 1959). The polemic was opened by Max Offenbacher, with his *Konfession und soziale Schichtung: Eine Studie über die wirtschaftliche Lage der Katholiken und Protestanten in Baden* (Tübingen, 1900). For an examination of the Puritan Revolution in England, see J. H. Hexter, "Storm over the Gentry" (published in *Encounter* [May, 1958] and commented on in the magazine's correspondence columns in subsequent issues); it has been reprinted in *Reappraisals in History*. Invaluable is Cicely V. Wedgwood's *History of the Puritan Rebellion* in two volumes, of which the first appeared in 1955. As for "economics," "chrematistics," and the problem of usury, see the final pages of my own *Banque protestante en France* (Paris, 1961), Vol. II.

5

PURITANISM AS A REVOLUTIONARY IDEOLOGY

Michael Walzer

I

Puritanism has twice been assigned a unique and creative role in Western history. Neither of these assignments was made by a Marxist historian; it was rather the Whigs and the Weberians who found modernity in the mind of the saints. But in a curious fashion, Marxists have been driven to adopt the insights of both these groups of writers, since both have defended and elaborated the historical connection which the Marxists themselves have so persistently sought to establish—that is, the connection of Puritanism with capitalism and liberalism.

Whig historians of the nineteenth and twentieth centuries saw in Protestantism in general, but more particularly in English Calvinism, the seedbed of liberal politics. The purely individualistic relationship of the saint to his God, the emphasis upon voluntary association and mutual consent to Church government among the saints themselves, the extraordinary reliance upon the printed word, with each man his own interpreter —all this, we have been told, trained and prepared the liberal mind.[1] And then the natural alliance of Puritans and parliamentarians created the liberal society. It is a clear implication of this view, though one not often expressed by Whig writers, that Puritanism *is* liberalism in theological garb, that is, in a primitive and somewhat confused form.[2]

Max Weber credited Puritanism with a rather different character and a different but related contribution to Western development. Writing in a more modern vein and free, up to a point, from Whig prejudices, he suggested that Calvin's ideas—again, especially in England—played a deci-

Reprinted from History and Theory, *III (1964), 61–68, 73–90. Copyright* © *1964 by* History and Theory.

sive part in the creation of the "spirit of capitalism." His views are so familiar that they need not be described in any detail here. But it should be said that they involve two rather distinct arguments, which will be considered separately below. Weber thought that Puritanism had sponsored a significant rationalization in behavior, especially in work: it had trained men to work in a sustained, systematic fashion, to pay attention to detail, to watch the clock. In this sense, the Calvinist ethic is related to that long-term process which culminates, but does not end, in a rational-legal (bureaucratic) society. Weber argued in addition to this that Puritanism had produced an extraordinary and apparently *irrational* impulse toward acquisition, which is more directly connected with the rise of a capitalist economy. The source of both impulses, toward rationalization and endless gain, lay in the anxiety induced by the theory of predestination; but the two are not the same, and it is at least plausible to imagine the first without the second.[3]

A Marxist historian would obviously deny the views of historical causation expressed or implied by both Whigs and Weberians, but he would defend ardently the close connection of Puritanism with the liberal and capitalist worlds. So ardently, indeed, would he do so, that he would probably concede, for the sake of the connection, a kind of "interaction" between economics, politics, and religion and thus open the way for an eclectic amalgamation of the three different points of view. Thus, contemporary Marxist writers tend still to describe Puritanism as the reflection of a rising bourgeoisie, though not necessarily its direct reflection (and this point—suggested, for example, by Tawney's notion of a "magic mirror"—is none too clear). But they then go on to argue that the reflection reacts somehow upon the original subject, reinforcing latent, perhaps underdeveloped, class characteristics, meeting psychic needs, and generally accelerating the progressive evolution.[4] This second argument is made in terms with which Whigs and Weberians would hardly disagree—especially since it constitutes a Marxist appropriation of their own insights. Such an eclecticism may incidentally make more sophisticated the history of all who adopt it; but it does not necessarily do so, for it provides no new insights and often involves the suspension of criticism for the sake of coherence. Giving up the hapless debate over whether Puritanism or capitalism came first would be, perhaps, no such loss. However, it would be a great loss indeed if no one called the union itself into question and sought to work out in a new way the historical experience of the saints.

The resemblance between the Calvinist covenant and the capitalist contract, often invoked and elaborated by Marxist writers, will serve to suggest the kind of questions which need to be raised. The voluntarism of both covenant and contract clearly distinguishes them from earlier traditionalistic relationships; but they are also distinguished from each other by two facts which the Marxists have surely underrated. First, they are based upon very different—indeed, precisely opposite—views of human nature. The contract assumes trust, a mutual recognition of economic rationality and even of good will. The covenant, as will be argued below, institutionalizes suspicion and mutual surveillance. If it is true that sober-minded capitalists preferred to do business with members of the Puritan brotherhood, this may well have been because they knew that the brethren were being watched. Secondly, the two forms of association serve very different human purposes. Puritan godliness and capitalist gain have, perhaps, something to do with each other, though they have little enough in common. The suggestion that they are *really the same thing,* or one the mere reflex, in thought or in action, of the other, has long distorted our understanding of the saints and their English enterprise. In order to grasp the precise nature of this distortion, it is necessary not only to point out the basic incompatibility of Puritanism with both liberalism and capitalism but also to discuss the various methods by which their similarity has been discovered and to attack the attitude toward historical experience which these methods imply.

A number of recent writers have gone so far as to describe the Puritan saints as traditionalists in both politics and economics, a description which has the virtue of standing the older theorists neatly on their heads, but which also makes the revolution incomprehensible.[5] This is not the view which will be argued here; it describes at best only the cautious conformity of Puritan preachers in dealing with such conventional topics as monarchy, rebellion, usury, and charity. On the other hand, it is not difficult to detect the sharply antitraditionalist ideology of these same men working itself out in their attacks upon hierarchy, their new views of ecclesiastical organization, their treatises on family government, their almost Manichean warfare against Sàtan and his worldly allies, their nervous lust for systematic repression and control. The last two of these are obviously not compatible with liberal thinking (or with entrepreneurial activity). They point directly to the revolution, when the struggle against Antichrist would be acted out and, for a brief moment, the repressive Holy Commonwealth established. In the years before the actual revolution, the nature of Puritanism was best revealed in the endless discussions of church government and in the practices of such Puritan congregations as already existed. These practices can by no means be called liberal, even though they were founded upon consent. Precisely because of this foundation, however, they cannot be called traditionalist either. The experience of the saints suggests something very different.

II

It was, perhaps, not without a certain malice that the early Puritans were called "disciplinarians." But malice has its insights, and this one is worth pursuing. The association of the brethren was voluntary, indeed, but it gave rise to a collectivist discipline marked above all by a tense mutual "watchfulness." Puritan individualism never led to a respect for privacy. Tender conscience had its rights, but it was protected only against the interference of worldlings and not against "brotherly admonition." And the admonitions of the brethren were anxious, insistent, continuous. They felt themselves to be living in an age of chaos and crime and sought to train conscience to be permanently on guard against sin. The extent to which they would have carried the moral discipline can be seen in the following list of offenses which merited excommunication in one seventeenth-century congregation:

—for unfaithfulness in his master's service.
—for admitting cardplaying in his house . . .
—for sloth in business.
—for being overtaken in beer.
—for borrowing a pillion and not returning it.
—for jumping for wagers . . .
—for dancing and other vanities.[6]

Had the saints been successful in establishing their Holy Commonwealth, the enforcement of this discipline would have constituted the Puritan terror. In the congregation there was already a kind of local terrorism, maintained by the godly elders as the national discipline would have been by an elite of the saints. Thus, Richard Baxter reported that in his Kidderminster parish the enforcement of the new moral order was made possible "by the zeal and diligence of the godly people of the place who thirsted after the salvation of their neighbours and were in private my assistants." [7]

It was for this moral discipline that the saints fought most persistently, and it was over this issue that Baxter and his colleagues left the Established Church in 1662. Their failure to win from Charles II's bishops the congregational rights of admonition and excommunication finally forced them—as the political Restoration had not done—to acknowledge the failure of their revolutionary effort to turn "all England into a land of the saints." By that time, however, the effort had had a certain prosaic success—not at all of the sort which Puritan preachers once imagined.

The crucial feature of the Puritan discipline was its tendency to transform repression into self-control: worldlings might be forced to be godly, but saints voluntarily gave themselves to godliness. Liberalism also required such voluntary subjection and self-control, but, in sharp contrast to Puritanism, its political and social theory was marked by an extraordinary confidence in the possibility both of a firm sense of human reasonableness and of the ease with which order might be attained. Liberal confidence made repression and the endless struggle against sin unnecessary; it also tended to make self-control invisible, to forget its painful history and naïvely assume its existence. The result was that liberalism did not create

the self-control it required. The Lockian state was not a disciplinary institution, as was the Calvinist Holy Commonwealth, but rather rested on
the assumed political virtue—the "natural political virtue" [8]—of its citizens. It is one of the central arguments of this essay that Puritan repression has its place in the practical history, so to speak, of that strange assumption.

It is not possible, of course, to judge the effectiveness of this repression
or the extent of the social need for it. For the moment it can only be said
that Puritans knew about human sinfulness and that Locke did not need
to know. This probably reflects not only different temperaments but also
different experiences. The very existence and spread of Puritanism in the
years before the Revolution surely argue the presence in English society of
an acute fear of disorder and "wickedness." The anxious tone of Tudor
legislation, which Puritan leaders like William Perkins often vigorously
seconded, is itself a parallel argument. On the other hand, the triumph of
Lockian ideas suggests the overcoming of that anxiety and fear, the appearance of men for whom sin is no longer a problem. In a sense, it might
be said that liberalism is dependent upon the existence of "saints"—that
is, of men whose good behavior can be relied upon. At the same time, the
secular and genteel character of liberalism is determined by the fact that
these are men whose goodness (sociability, self-discipline, moral decency,
or mere respectability) is self-assured and relaxed, entirely free from the
nervousness and fanaticism of Calvinist godliness.

This, then, is the relationship of Puritanism to the liberal world: it is
perhaps one of historical preparation, but not at all of theoretical contribution. Indeed, there was much to be forgotten and much to be surren-
dered before the saint could become a liberal bourgeois. During the great
creative period of English Puritanism, the faith of the saints and the tolerant reasonableness of the liberals had very little in common.

Roughly the same things can be said about the putative connection of
Calvinism and capitalism. The moral discipline of the saints can be interpreted as the historical conditioning of the capitalist man; but the discipline was not itself capitalist. It can be argued that the faith of the brethren, with its emphasis upon methodical endeavor and self-control, was an
admirable preparation for systematic work in shops, offices, and factories.
It trained men for the minute-to-minute attentiveness required in a modern economic system; it taught them to forgo their afternoon naps—as
they had but recently forgone their saints'-day holidays—and to devote
spare hours to bookkeeping and moral introspection. It somehow made
the deprivation and repression inevitable in sustained labor bearable and
even desirable for the saints. And by teaching self-control, it provided the
basis for impersonal, contractual relationships among men, allowing
workmanlike co-operation but not involving any exchange of affection or
any of the risks of intimacy. All this, Calvinism did or helped to do

Whether it did so in a creative fashion or as the ideological reflection of new economic processes is not immediately relevant. The saints learned, as Weber has suggested, a kind of rational and worldly asceticism, and this was probably something more than the economic routine required. They sought in work itself what mere work can never give: a sense of vocation and discipline which would free them from sinfulness and the fear of disorder.[9]

But Weber has said more than this; he has argued that systematic acquisition as well as asceticism has a Calvinist origin. The psychological tension induced by the theory of predestination, working itself out in worldly activity, presumably drove men to seek success as a sign of salvation. The sheer willfulness of an inscrutable God produced in its turn, if Weber is correct, the willfulness of an anxious man and set off the entrepreneurial pursuit of better business techniques and more and more profit. At this point his argument breaks down. If there is in fact a peculiar and irrational quality to the capitalists' lust for gain, its sources must be sought elsewhere than among the saints. For Puritanism was hardly an ideology which encouraged continuous or unrestrained accumulation. Instead, the saints tended to be narrow and conservative in their economic views, urging men to seek no more wealth than they needed for a modest life, or, alternatively, to use up their surplus in charitable giving. The anxiety of the Puritans led to a fearful demand for economic restriction (and political control) rather than to entrepreneurial activity as Weber has described it. Unremitting and relatively unremunerative work was the greatest help toward saintliness and virtue.[10]

The ideas of Puritan writers are here very close to those of such proto-Jacobins as Mably and Morelli in eighteenth-century France, who also watched the development of capitalist enterprise with unfriendly eyes, dreaming of a Spartan republic where bankers and great merchants would be unwelcome.[11] The collective discipline of the Puritans—their Christian Sparta—was equally incompatible with purely acquisitive activity. Virtue would almost certainly require economic regulation. This would be very different from the regulation of medieval corporatism, and perhaps it was the first sense of that difference which received the name *freedom*. It was accompanied by a keen economic realism: thus the Calvinist acknowledgment of the lawfulness of usury. But Calvinist realism was in the service of effective control and not of free activity or self-expression. Who can doubt that, had the Holy Commonwealth ever been firmly established, godly self-discipline and mutual surveillance would have been far more repressive than the corporate system? Once again, in the absence of a Puritan state the discipline was enforced through the congregation. The minutes of a seventeenth-century consistory provide a routine example: "The church was satisfied with Mrs. Carlton," they read, "as to the weight of her butter." Did Mrs. Carlton tremble, awaiting that verdict? Surely if the brethren were unwilling to grant liberty to the local butter seller, they would hardly have granted it to the new capitalist. The ministerial literature, at least, is full of denunciations of enclosers, usurers, monopolists, and projectors—and occasionally even of wily merchants. Puritan casuistry, perhaps, left such men sufficient room in which to range, but it hardly offered them what Weber considers so essential—a good conscience. Only a sustained endeavor in hypocrisy, so crude as to astonish even the Marxist epigone, could have earned them that. The final judgment of the saints with regard to the pursuit of money is that of Bunyan's pilgrim, angry and ill at ease in the town of Vanity, disdainful of such companions as Mr. Money-love and Mr. Save-all.

The converse is equally true: to the triumphant bourgeois, sainthood, with all its attendant enthusiasm and asceticism, would appear atavistic. And this is perhaps the clearest argument of all against the casual acceptance of the Whig or Weberian views of Puritanism. It suggests forcefully that the two views (and the Marxist also, for surprisingly similar reasons) are founded upon anachronism. Even if it is correct to argue that Calvinist faith and discipline played a part in that transformation of character which created the bourgeois—and too little is known about the historical development of character to say this without qualification—the anachronism remains. The historical present is hopelessly distorted unless the tension and repression so essential to the life of the saint are described and accounted for. Even more important, the effort to establish a Holy Commonwealth (to universalize the tension and repression) is rendered inexplicable once liberalism and capitalism are, so to speak, read into the Puritan experience. For then Puritanism is turned into a grand paradox: its radical voluntarism culminates in a rigid discipline; its saints watch their neighbors with brotherly love and suspicion; its ethic teaches sustained and systematic work but warns men against the lust for acquisition and gain. In fact, of course, these seeming contrasts are not paradoxical. The saints experienced a unity, common enough among men, of willfulness and repression, of fanatical *self-control*. Latter-day historians do the Puritans little honor when they search among the elements of the Puritan faith for something more liberal in its political implications or more economically rational. Indeed, the methods of that search invite in their turn the most searching criticism.

· · ·

III

. . . To make Christian a petty bourgeois is to ignore the fact that he was . . . Christian, a pilgrim bound for the heavenly city, and that many of the readers of *Pilgrim's Progress* were in some sense his colleagues.[12] Indeed, the Marxists are no more committed than are Whigs or Weberians to the world of experience which this pilgrimage represents. They are as disinclined to encounter the saints in history; but in their case the disinclination has a methodological reason. They tend to treat such an experience as Christian's journey as an epiphenomenon of objective existence, of what Marx called "real life." This is not to say that the pilgrimage was not actually made. Rather, it involves the assertion that it can only be understood by putting aside Christian's ideology—his perceptions, feelings, thoughts, aspirations—and confronting directly those economic and social processes which somehow underlie and cause the actual journey. But the distinctions presupposed by this kind of explanation are hopelessly precise. Many critics have pointed out that ideas play a vital role in what Marxists call the objective world: no economic relationship is conceivable, for example, which does not involve some shared notions of profit and loss, of security, trust, love, or interest.[13] Ideas are intrinsic to any relationship among men, as they are to any perceived sequence of events. It is simply not possible to treat them as reflections or epiphenomena because one cannot imagine or satisfactorily construct "reality" without them.

Thus there is, so to speak, no journey, but *only* a pilgrimage. One cannot separate the physical motion from the sense of destination and describe the one as an example of increased social mobility and the other as an illusion, a piece of religious confusion, the result of Bunyan's failure to understand social change.

In sharp contrasts to the pilgrim Christian, Defoe's Moll Flanders is something of a Marxist heroine, an economic woman; despite her ideology, she is never confused. Defoe at least suggests that ideas and "real life" can easily be distinguished. But this is only true when ideas have become conventional—like Moll's moralizing—and even then it is not entirely true. For ideology is a way of perceiving and responding to the experienced world, so it is always itself an aspect of experience. In relatively peaceful or stable times (when no one is a pilgrim), perceptions may be widely shared, even inherited, and responses predictable. For ordinary men, ideology may indeed become a reflex, automatic and inescapable, and then the way be opened for all sorts of evasion, hypocrisy, and platitudinizing. Writing about such periods, Marxists have had their greatest success: thus have they struck off the bourgeois ideology. They have done much less well in confronting sharp discontinuities of perception and response. For all his concern with revolution, Marx was himself the product of the same world which produced the great social novels, those elaborate, many-volumed studies of manners, status, and class relationships in which the fundamental stability of the society as a whole and of character (what would today be called "identity") within the society was always assumed.[14] And Marx never questions the second of these assumptions: bourgeois and proletarian appear in his work as *formed characters,* free at least from psychological instability even while their struggle with one another tears apart the social order. But in a time like that of the Puritans, Christian's colleagues, there is an enormous range in perception and response, and—more important—an enormous range in the clarity of perception (even if it be the clarity of madness) and in the intensity of response. Ideology cannot be consistently linked with class experiences because those experiences no longer take place in a regular and predictable order. Hence character is not stable; its very formation, so to speak, is problematic.

It is obvious that Bunyan's pilgrim would hardly set out on his strange journey in such a stable bourgeois society as that of nineteenth-century England. Nor, since Christian is everyman and no medieval saint, would he set out from a stable feudal society. He "corresponds" to what can roughly be called a time of transition. But the time of transition, a time of instability and chronic danger, is only the *condition* of his journey—its cause is ideological. And it is the journey in its ideological setting, complete with purpose and meaning, which constitutes the experience and needs to be explained.

In order to get at the world of experience, it may well be necessary to construct some highly abstract model of economic processes and social change. But this construct is not "real life." It is only an intellectual approach to reality and only one among several possible approaches. The Marxist historian seeks to reconstitute the world which is perceived, while at the same time detaching himself from the particular perceptions of historical men. But it ought to be those very perceptions which direct his work. Reality is too complex, too detailed, too formless: he can never reproduce it. He must seek, instead, to reproduce only those aspects of historical existence which were, so to speak, absorbed into the experience of particular men. And if he is to avoid anachronistic reconstructions, his guide must be the men themselves. It would be absurd to assume a priori that what is of central importance in late sixteenth- and early seventeenth-century history is, for example, the growth of the coal industry. One must look first to see what impact such a phenomenon had upon the lives of men. It is not, of course, only a question of whether they talked about it, but of whether they *felt* it, directly or indirectly, consciously or unconsciously. If they did not, then its significance must be sought in the future.

Marxists become the victims of the very alienation they claim to understand so well when they reverse this procedure and make experience dependent upon what is originally only a creation of the mind. When Tawney writes that Puritanism is the "magic mirror" in which the middle-class man saw himself ennobled and enhanced, he is in no sense enlightening us as to the historical process by which Puritanism developed and spread. For the Puritan is a real man, who can be encountered in history. But the middle-class man is made up, and it is sheer anachronism to describe him as a historical figure, articulate, already in search of an enhanced image. It has been suggested above that Puritanism is a part of the process (the long succession of perceptions and responses) by which men *become* middle class. But to know the particular perceptions upon which it is based or the responses it prescribes, it is necessary to know the Puritan. There is, in fact, no magic mirror; sainthood is no mere enhancement of an already established (even if worrisome) identity. It is a far more active thing than that; it is indeed what Weber suggests: a way of forming an identity.[15]

What must be studied, then, is a mind, or a group of minds, coping with problems and not passively reflecting them. For the mind mediates between the "objective" situation and the human act, and if the act is to be understood, the mind must first be known. The problems it faces are posed by an environment which can of course by analyzed in some objective fashion—for example, statistically. But different aspects of this environment are experienced by different men with different results in consciousness and behavior. Hence the "objective" construct is of no independent value and has no prior significance in explanation. The first task of the historian is to establish his familiarity with the experience of particular men, with their difficulties, aspirations, and achievements, and with the styles in which all these are expressed. This is not to suggest that the historical record should be taken at face value, or the assumption casually made that men always mean what they say. There are, for example, false piety and evasion among the saints which the historian must expose. There are caution and conformity which he must respect, but not too much. For hindsight is also insight into the concealments of respectability and of "Aesopian" prose; and it is often insight as well into purposes half-understood and patterns of thought not yet fully worked out. Hence the methods of the historian must be skeptical, devious, and experimental, even while his general approach is open and sympathetic. But ultimately his sympathy is the key to all else: the best judgment of face value will be made by men with some intuitive understanding of other levels of thinking and feeling.

The problem of the Puritan belief in witchcraft and demonology has already been suggested and may profitably be developed at greater length as an illustration of the argument above. One sees in the mirror (that is, in experience and thought) images which have no easy or readily explained connection with the supposed subject, middle-class man. Witchcraft indeed suggests a world altogether apart from the Marxist universe of interest. In his book *Navaho Witchcraft*, Clyde Kluckhohn has analyzed the psychological basis of the belief in terms of the concepts of hostility and anxiety and has sought to give these concepts some precision. He has discussed the possible ways in which historical events or particular social structures may generate those anxious or hostile feelings which presumably lead to the perception of witches (or of oneself as a witch) and to the responses of persecution and cruelty.[16] Now, the history of the persecution of witches in England (also the history of the practice of witchcraft) directly parallels the career of the Puritans. The first enactments were produced by the returning Marian exiles; the persecution reached its height during the revolutionary period and in the centers of Puritan sentiment; interest in and fear of witches declined after the Restoration.[17] Perhaps Marxists have paid so little attention to witchcraft precisely because it had no future; it was neglected in that final process of selection which constituted the bourgeois world. The point here is that this piece of knowledge about Puritan feeling and behavior suggests certain possibilities in the "objective" environment to which Marxists have been singularly blind.

Anxiety seems to appear in acute form only among men who have experienced some great disorder or are caught up in a process of rapid, incomprehensible change: the breakdown of some habitual system of conventions and routines, a departure to an unaccustomed world, the aftermath of epidemic or war. Events of this sort leave men without customary restraints upon their behavior and no longer responsible to revered authorities. The result often is that extraordinary panic which Erich Fromm has somewhat misleadingly called a "fear of freedom." [18] In human experience, this is more likely a dread of chaos, and one of its aspects is a sharp, if often delusory, perception of danger and of dangerous men.

If Puritanism is studied with these ideas in mind, a new light is thrown on sixteenth- and seventeenth-century history. One searches more deeply in the life experience of the saints for those feelings of fearfulness which parallel the belief in witches—and for the sources of such fear. One searches for sudden changes in environment, habits, authorities. The result is a hypothesis which is in striking contradiction to that of the Marxists: Puritanism appears to be a response to disorder and fear, a way of organizing men to overcome the acute sense of chaos. With this hypothesis it becomes possible to understand, for example, the as yet fragmentary evidence which suggests that the Calvinist faith, especially in its more radical forms, appealed most of all to men newly come to London and not, as Marxists have always assumed, to experienced city dwellers.[19] For coming to the city was an event in a man's life which might well sharpen his sense of danger and even lead him to seek that discipline which has been described above as central to Puritan association. Thus, the sudden increase in London's population between roughly 1580 and 1625 takes on new significance: it may well be that London did not so much prepare men to become "saints" as that sainthood helped them, through the hard transition period, to become Londoners. Once they had become *urbane,* they were in fact unlikely to remain faithful to the original Calvinist creed; they became revisionists. Similarly, it is somewhat less of a paradox than Marxists might suppose that witchcraft should range more widely in the southeast of England, where economic development was most advanced.

For it may be—and this, perhaps, can be investigated—that witchcraft helped solve, in the minds of the people, some of the problems raised by that very development and by its impact upon traditional ways of doing things. (This is, of course, only speculation, but it is speculation which begins at the right place: with a concern for the concerns of the Puritans themselves.)

It seems likely that certain modes of perception and response parallel certain basic historical experiences; if so, comparison is possible, and one might arrive at general propositions. But the relationship between, for example, urbanization and some ideological response to urbanization (once again, it must be said that these are not distinct "spheres") must be understood in dynamic terms. Perhaps it would be best to figure to oneself an energetic man continually struggling to understand and cope with the surrounding world. Undoubtedly, energy and struggle are not universal in history: ways of thinking quickly become habitual, as does experience itself. But it is the creative moments which require explanation, and at such moments ideology is never a mere habit or reflex, but a willful activity. For perhaps a hundred years after the original creative achievement of Calvin, the spread of Puritanism can still be described in the active tense: men, with their own problems and aspirations, continually rediscovered for themselves, with all the enthusiasm which must have attended the first discovery, the truths of the new faith. The historian who begins with these ideology-producing men may then work outward, so to speak, re-experiencing their world and only after this subjecting that world to such further analysis as will improve his own understanding of it.

The Puritan saints are such men, making their ideology and making themselves. The sources and nature of this creativity must next be considered.

IV

The study of the Puritans is best begun with the idea of discipline and all the tension and strain that underlie it, both in their writing and in what can be known of their experience. It is strange that theorists have had so little to say on this topic, especially since the rebellion against Puritan repression, or rather against its ugly remnants—devoid, as Weber's capitalism is, of theological reason—is still a part of our own experience. The persecution of witches, of course, was not a vital aspect of Puritan endeavor, but the active, fearful struggle against wickedness was. And the saints imagined wickedness as a creative and omnipresent demonic force, that is, as a continuous threat. Like Hobbes, they saw disorder and war as the natural state of fallen men, out of which they had been drawn by God's command and by the painful efforts of their own regenerate wills. But they lived always on the very brink of chaos, maintaining their position only through a constant vigilance and, indeed, a constant warfare against their own natural inclinations and against the devil and his worldlings.

The goal of this warfare was repression, and its apparent cause was an extraordinary anxiety. It is by no means necessary to argue that these two constitute the "essence" of Puritanism, only that their full significance has not been realized. In Calvin's own work anxiety is presented as central to the experience of fallen man: this is anxiety of a special sort; it is not the fear of death and damnation, but rather the fear of sudden and violent death. Hobbes would recognize it as the dominant passion of man in his natural state. Thus Calvin:

> Now, whithersoever you turn, all the objects around you are not only unworthy of your confidence, but almost openly menace you, and seem to threaten immediate death. Embark in a ship; there is but a single step between you and death. Mount a horse; the slipping of one foot endangers your life. Walk through the streets of a city; you are liable to as many dangers as there are tiles on the roofs. If there be a sharp weapon in your hand, or that of your friend, the mischief is manifest. All the ferocious animals you see are armed for your destruction. If you endeavor to shut yourself in a garden surrounded with a good fence, and exhibiting nothing but what is delightful, even there sometimes lurks a serpent. Your house, perpetually liable to fire, menaces you by day with poverty, and by night with falling on your head. Your land, exposed to hail, frost, drought and various tempests, threatens you with sterility, and with its attendant, famine. I omit poison, treachery, robbery and open violence, which partly beset us at home and partly pursue us abroad. . . . You will say that these things happen seldom, or certainly not always, nor to every man, [and] never all at once. I grant it; but we are admonished by the examples of others, that it is possible for them to happen to us. . . .[20]

Among the saints such terrible fearfulness was overcome, and that was the great benefit of sainthood: it did not so much promise future ecstasy as present "tranquillity." "When the light of Divine Providence," wrote Calvin, "has once shined on a pious man, he is relieved and delivered not only from the extreme anxiety and dread with which he was previously oppressed, but also from all care." [21] But relief was not rest in the Calvinist world; it was rather that security of mind which might well manifest itself as self-righteousness—or as fanaticism.

In Puritan literature this same fearfulness is made specific in social terms. Once again, it is a fear which Hobbes would understand: the fear of disorder in society. It is apparent in the nervous hostility with which Puritan writers regarded carousal, vagabondage, idleness, all forms of individualistic extravagance (especially in clothing), country dances and urban crowds, the theater with its gay (undisciplined) audiences, gossip, witty talk, love play, dawdling in taverns—the list could be extended.[22] The shrewdest among their contemporaries sensed that this pervasive hostility was a key to Puritanism—though they could hardly help but regard it as hypocritical. Ben Jonson's Zeal-of-the-land Busy is a caricature based, like all good caricatures, on a kernel of truth. Zeal-of-the-land is, for all his comical hypocrisy, insistently and anxiously concerned about the world he lives in, and the aim of his concern is supervision and repression.[23]

At times, Puritan preachers sounded very much like Hobbes: ". . . take sovereignty from the face of the earth," proclaimed Robert Bolton, "and you turn it into a cockpit. Men would become cut-throats and cannibals. . . . Murder, adulteries, incests, rapes, robberies, perjuries, witchcrafts, blasphemies, all kinds of villainies, outrages and savage cruelty would overflow all countries." [24] But secular sovereignty was not their usual appeal. They looked rather to congregational discipline, as has been argued above. Thus Thomas Cartwright promised that the new discipline would restrain stealing, adultery, and murder. Even more, it would "correct" sins "which the magistrate doth not commonly punish" —he listed lying, jesting, choleric speeches.[25] It need hardly be said that John Locke, a century later, was not terribly worried about such sins. Walsingham's spies reported in the 1580's and 1590's that Puritan agitators were promising "that if discipline were planted, there should be no more vagabonds nor beggars." John Penry foresaw the "amendment" of idleness and hence, he thought, of poverty.[26] Now none of these concerns was unusual in Tudor or early Stuart England, but the intensity and extent of Puritan worry and the novelty of the proposed solution have no parallel among statesmen or traditional moralists. These latter groups also watched with apprehension the growth of London, the increasing geographic and social mobility, and the new forms of individualistic experimentation. It must be said, however, that the tone of their writings rarely reached a pitch of anxiety and fearfulness comparable to, for example, the diary of the Puritan minister Richard Rogers, endlessly worried about his own "unsettledness." Nostalgia was a more common theme, satire and mockery a more frequent defense among moralists like Thomas Dekker.[27] And the world they would have substituted for Renaissance England was an already romanticized version of medieval England. Not so the Puritans. Their discipline would have established dramatically new forms of association: the anxiety of the minister Rogers led him to join with his brethren in a solemn covenant—and these brethren were neither his immediate neighbors nor his kinfolk.[28]

What Rogers sought from his covenant was a bolstering of his faith, a steeling of his character. "The sixth of this month [December, 1587] we fasted betwixt ourselves," he reported in his diary, ". . . to the stirring up of ourselves to greater godliness." The need for this "stirring up" is so pervasive among the Puritans that one might well imagine that what they feared so greatly was rather in themselves than in the society about them. In fact, what they feared was the image in themselves of the "unsettledness" of their world. Puritan fearfulness is best explained in terms of the actual experiences of exile, alienation, and social mobility about which the saints so often and insistently wrote.[29] Discipline and repression are responses to these experiences, responses which do not aim at a return to some former security, but rather at a vigorous control and a narrowing of energies—a bold effort to shape a personality amidst "chaos." Thus might be explained the extraordinarily regimented life recorded in Margaret Hoby's diary. Mrs. Hoby was a merchant's daughter, married to a gentleman (the son of the Elizabethan ambassador Sir Thomas Hoby, translator of Castiglione) and carried off to a country estate in Yorkshire where all her neighbors were Catholic and, in her eyes, rowdy and sinful men. There she spent her time in earnest conversations with her minister, reading and listening to sermons and laboriously copying them out in her notebook, adhering to a strict routine of public and private prayer, assiduous in her daily self-recrimination: "I talked of some things not so as I ought when I had considered of them, but I find what is in a man if the Lord's spirit do never so little hide itself . . . but this is my comfort, that my heart is settled to be more watchful hereafter. . . ." [30] How many men have settled since for the same "comfort"!

Undoubtedly, Margaret Hoby's behavior might be differently explained, but not so as to account so well for the similar behavior of her brethren. These people felt themselves exceptionally open to the dangers about them, and this must have been, in part, because they were cut off, as were the men who succumbed to chaos—beggars and vagabonds—from the old forms of order and routine. It is this sense of being cut off, alien, that is expressed in the endless descriptions of the saint as a stranger and pilgrim which are so important in Puritan writing.[31] Pilgrimage is, perhaps, one of the major themes in all Christian literature, but it achieves among the Puritans a unique power, a forcefulness and intensity in its popular expression which culminates finally in Bunyan's classic. Over and over again, with the detail which only experience or, perhaps, a continually engaged imagination can give, Puritans describe life as a journey (or, in the image which Hobbes later made famous, as a race) through alien country. And yet, at the same time, they write of the vagabond with venomous hatred: he is a dangerous man because he has not disciplined and prepared himself for his journey. "Wandering beggars and rogues," wrote William Perkins, "that pass from place to place, being under no certain magistracy or ministry, nor joining themselves to any set society in church or commonwealth, are plagues and banes of both, and are to be taken as main enemies of [the] ordinance of God. . . ." [32] The bitterness of this

passage suggests the self-hatred of the Puritan pilgrim, pitying and worry-
ing about his own "unsettledness." When the famous preacher Richard
Greenham told a Puritan audience, "Paradise is our native country,"
some of his listeners surely must have winced to think: *not England*. "We
dwell here as in Meshech and as in the tents of Kedar, and therefore we
be glad to be at home." It was painful, but inevitable, that the saints
should live in tents. Perkins himself wrote in the same vein, for all his
hatred of the wanderer: "Alas, poor souls, we are no better than passen-
gers in this world, our way it is in the middle of the sea." [33] For many
Puritans, if not for Perkins himself, who grew old in Cambridge, these
words must have had a meaning both literal and poignant. Since the days
of Mary, exile had been a common experience for the saints. And a generation after Perkins wrote, the "middle of the sea" would become a path
for tens of thousands.

The fanatical self-righteousness of that first Puritan John Knox, a Scottish peasant's son, set loose in Europe by war and revolution, is surely in
some sense a function of his exile: righteousness was a consolation and a
way of organizing the self for survival. The "unsettledness" of Richard
Rogers was due in part to his devious struggles with the corporate church
and its bishops; but Rogers, who remembered his Essex birthplace as a
"dunghill," was ever an outsider, and Puritanism his way of stirring up
his heart. When William Whitgift, the future archbishop, cruelly taunted
the Puritan leader Thomas Cartwright for "eating at other men's tables,"
he was perhaps suggesting an important source of Cartwright's vision of
congregational unity and holiness. Margaret Hoby's life would have been
different indeed had she been raised in a traditional country family: there
would, for example, have been dancing at her wedding, and her life
thereafter would hardly have allowed for time-consuming religious exercises. Deprived of such a life, because of her social background (and the
ideas which were part of it) or, perhaps, because of basic changes in rural
life, she willfully sought new comforts.[34] Country gentlemen like John
Winthrop and Oliver Cromwell, educated at Cambridge, knowledgeable
in London, suddenly turned upon the traditional routine of English life
as if it were actually vicious. Half in, half out of that routine, they anxiously sought a new certainty. "Oh, I lived in and loved darkness and
hated light; I was a chief, the chief of sinners," wrote Cromwell of his
seemingly ordinary and conventional life before conversion. But now, he
went on, "my soul is with the congregation of the first born, my body rests
in hope; and if here I may honor my God either by doing or by suffering,
I shall be most glad." [35]

All this suggests once again the view of Puritanism as a response of
particular men to particular experiences of confusion, change, alienation,
and exile. Now, Calvinism obviously made men extremely sensitive to
disorder in all its forms. It is more important, however, that it gave mean-

ing to the experience of disorder and provided a way out, a return to certainty. It was an active response, and not a mere reflection of social confusion, for indeed other men responded differently. There is no rigid pattern in these responses. It seems probable that members of a rising middle class most sharply experienced that alienation from old England which drove men to the exercises of sainthood. On the other hand, there were both gentlemen and citizens who certainly enjoyed the new freedoms of mobility, extravagance, individuality, and wit and eagerly sought entrance to the Renaissance court, where freedom was cultivated. And from among these men undoubtedly came many future capitalists. It would not be easy to explain in particular cases why the court held such attractions for some men, while it was vicious and iniquitous in the eyes of others. No more is it readily comprehensible why some of the newcomers to the burgeoning city of London merged into the mob or explored the exciting underworld, while others hated the wickedness of the city, and sought out virtuous brethren in the radical conventicles. What is important for the present is that Puritanism was a response to an experience which many men had; it provided one way of understanding the experience and of coping with it.

Coping with it meant being reborn as a new man, self-confident and free of worry, capable of vigorous, willful activity. The saints sometimes took new names to signify their rebirth. If alienation had made them anxious, depressed, unable to work, given to fantasies of demons, morbid introspection, or fearful daydreams such as Calvin had suggested were common among fallen men, then sainthood was indeed a transformation.[36] Cromwell's pledge to honor his God "by doing" was no idle boast: he was obviously capable of just that. Perhaps this transformation gave businessmen the confidence necessary for innovation or freed them from the necessity of feeling guilty about routine connivance, usury, extortion. Thus argue Marxists and Weberians alike. But innovation was more likely due to the recklessness of the speculator than to the self-confidence of the saint; indeed, the saints hated the "projectors" who lived in and about the court, currying favor and waiting for opportunity. The congregational discipline, as has been seen, would have established controls hardly compatible with businesslike hard dealing. Cromwell's "doing" was obviously of a different order, and Cromwell was a representative man. His life suggests that the Puritan experience produced first of all a political activist.

The Puritan new man was active not so that success might reinforce his self-esteem, but in order to transform a world in which he saw his own ever-present wickedness writ large.[37] In a sense, his was a struggle to free himself from temptation by removing all alternatives to godliness, by organizing his own life as a continuous discipline and society as a regiment. His activity was political in that it was always concerned with government

—though not only, or perhaps not most importantly, at the level of the state. Puritans often imagined the congregation as a "little commonwealth," replacing the organic imagery of Anglicans and Catholics with expressions deliberately drawn from the world of coercion and sovereignty. Thus they made manifest their own pervasive concern with *control* rather than with harmony or love.[38] Their treatment of the family was similar: they saw it as a field for the exercise of discipline by a godly father usually described as a "governor." Puritan interest in the family parallels that of Jean Bodin (though, in contrast to Robert Filmer, also a Bodinian, the saints had little to say about paternal affection and benevolence) and probably has the same source. The insistence upon the absolute sovereignty of the father and upon the family as an institution for repressing and disciplining naturally wicked, licentious, and rebellious children derives in both cases from an extraordinary fear of disorder and anarchy. Thus two Puritan preachers in a famous treatise on "family government":

> The young child which lieth in the cradle [is] both wayward and full of affections: and though his body be but small, yet he hath a great heart, and is altogether inclined to evil. . . . If this sparkle be suffered to increase, it will rage over and burn down the whole house. For we are changed and become good, not by birth, but by education. . . . Therefore parents must be wary and circumspect, that they never smile or laugh at any words or deeds of their children done lewdly . . . naughtily, wantonly . . . they must correct and sharply reprove their children for saying or doing ill. . . .[39]

The father was continually active, warily watching his children; the elders of the congregation were ever alert and vigilant, seeking out the devious paths of sin; so also the godly magistrate. "In you it is now to cleanse, to free your country of villainy," a Puritan minister told the judges of Norwich, ". . . consider your power to reform . . . if you be faithful, and God's power to revenge if you be faithless." [40] In Puritan writings, political activity was described as a form of work: it required systematic application, attention to detail, sustained interest and labor. Much that the godly magistrates undertook might be called, in Marxist terms, progressive; some of their activity, however, would clearly impede free economic activity. But description in these terms is valuable only if one seeks to understand those aspects of Puritan activity which, through a subsequent process of selection, became permanent features of the modern world. In the seventeenth century, Puritan politics obviously had an interest rather different from that suggested by the term *progress*. Its immediate purpose was to regain control of a changing world; hence the great concern with method, discipline, and order and the frequent uneasiness with novelty. When the saints spoke of reform, they meant first of all an overcoming of social instability and all its moral and intellectual concomitants. Godly magistracy was a bold effort to seize control of society, much as sainthood had been an effort to control and organize the self. And the first of these followed from the second: in this way did Puritanism produce revolutionaries. In much the same way, it may be suggested, did the Jacobin man of virtue become an *active citizen,* and the hardened and "steeled" Bolshevik first a *professional* revolutionary and then, in Lenin's words, a "leader," "manager," and "controller." [41]

These revolutionary men do not simply attack and transform the old order—as in the Marxist story. The old order is only a part, and often not the most important part, of their experience. They live much of their lives amidst the breakdown of that order, or in hiding or exile from it. And much of their rebellion is directed against the very "unsettledness" that they know best. The analogy with the Bolsheviks is worth pursuing. Lenin's diatribes against "slovenliness . . . carelessness, untidiness, unpunctuality, nervous haste, the inclination to substitute discussion for action, talk for work, the inclination to undertake everything under the sun without finishing anything" were intended first of all as attacks upon his fellow exiles—whatever their value as descriptions of the "primitive" Russia he hated so much.[42] The first triumph of Bolshevism, as of Puritanism, was over the impulse toward "disorganization" in its own midst: here, so to speak, was Satan at work where he is ever most active—in the ranks of the godly. And it must be said that this triumph was also over the first impulses toward freedom. Thus the Puritans vigorously attacked Renaissance experimentation in dress and in all the arts of self-decoration and hated the free-wheeling vagabonds who "crowd into cities [and] boroughs . . . roll up and down from one lodging to another," never organizing themselves into families and congregations.[43] Similarly, the Jacobin leader Robespierre attacked the economic egotism of the new bourgeoisie and spitefully connected the radical free thought of the Enlightenment with antirevolutionary conspiracy. Atheism, he declared, is aristocratic.[44] And again Lenin, preaching with all the energy of a secular Calvinist against free love: "Dissoluteness in sexual life is bourgeois, [it] is a phenomenon of decay. The proletariat is a rising class. . . . It needs clarity, clarity and again clarity. And so, I repeat, no weakening, no waste, no destruction of forces." [45]

In fact, Lenin's morality had little to do with the proletariat, and the "dissoluteness" he attacked had little to do with the bourgeoisie. He might as well have talked of saints and worldlings as the Puritans did. The contrast he was getting at was between those men who had succumbed to (or taken advantage of!) the disorder of their time—speculators in philosophy, vagabonds in their sexual life, economic Don Juans—and those men who had somehow pulled themselves out of "unsettledness," organized their lives, and regained control. The first group were the damned and the second the saved. The difference between them was not social but ideological.

Puritans, Jacobins, and Bolsheviks did tend to come from the same social strata—that is, from the educated middle classes, preachers, lawyers, journalists, teachers, professional men of all sorts. But this is not because such men are representatives of larger social groups whose interests they defend. It has already been shown that the connection between Puritan theory and bourgeois interests is at best a difficult one, which is in no sense implicit in the theory, but is rather worked out later in a long process of corruption, selection, and forgetting. Men like the godly ministers speak first of all for themselves: they record most sensitively the experience of "unsettledness" and respond to it most vigorously. For reasons which require further investigation, such men seem less integrated into their society—even in the most stable periods—and more available, as it were, for alienation than are farmers or businessmen. This is not, of course, to reduce their moral discipline (or their radical politics) to the psychological therapy of alienated intellectuals. The alienation which John Knox or Richard Rogers experienced, with all its attendant fearfulness and enthusiasm, sometimes disfiguring and sometimes ennobling, was only a heightened form of the feelings of other men—in a sense, of all men, for ultimately the sociological range of the Puritan response was very wide.

But the historian must also record that "unsettledness" was not a permanent condition and that sainthood was only a temporary role. For men always seek and find not some tense and demanding discipline, but some new routine. The saints failed in their effort to establish a Holy Commonwealth and, in one way or another, their more recent counterparts have also failed. What this suggests is not that the Holy Commonwealth was an impractical dream, the program of muddled, unrealistic men. In fact, Puritan ministers and elders (and fathers!) had considerable political experience and the Holy Commonwealth was in a sense achieved, at least among those men who most needed holiness. Nor is it correct to argue from the failure of the saints that Puritanism in its revolutionary form represents only a temporary triumph of "ideas" over "interest," a momentary burst of enthusiasm.[46] For such moments have their histories, and what needs to be explained is why groups of men, over a fairly long span of time, acquired such an intense interest in ideas like predestination and holiness. Puritan ideology was a response to real experience, therefore a practical effort to cope with personal and social problems. The inability of the saints to establish and maintain their Holy Commonwealth suggests only that these problems were limited in time to the period of breakdown and psychic and political reconstruction. When men stopped being afraid, or became less afraid, then Puritanism was suddenly irrelevant. Particular elements in the Puritan system were transformed to fit the new routine, and other elements were forgotten. And only then did the saint become a man of "good behavior," cautious, respectable, calm, ready to participate in a Lockian society.

V

The argument of the preceding section may now be concluded: Puritanism was not a revolutionary ideology in the Marxist sense, reflecting the interests of a rising class. Such interests are in the seventeenth century better represented by parliamentarians and common lawyers who had their own ideology. The faith of the saints was rather a peculiarly intense response to the experience of social change itself, an experience which, in one way or another, set groups of men outside the established order. It should be obvious that this may be the result of either "rising" or "falling" in economic terms; mobility itself is the key, especially if the old social order is traditionalist, dependent for its stability upon popular passivity. The Puritan response produced revolutionaries, that is, saints, godly magistrates, men already disciplined (before the revolution begins) for the strenuous work of transforming all society and all men in the image of their own salvation. Such men, narrow, fanatical, enthusiastic, committed to their "work," have little to contribute to the development of either liberalism or capitalism. To expect freedom from their hands is to invite disappointment. Their great achievement is what is known in the sociology of revolution as the *terror*, the effort to create a Holy Commonwealth and to force men to be godly.

The contribution of these men to the future is the destruction of the old order. Alienated from its conventions and routines—from its comforts —they feel no nostalgia as they watch its slow decay. They are capable not only of establishing, underground, an alternative system but also of making a frontal assault upon the old order itself—in the case of the Puritans, upon hierarchy and patriarchy, the central principles of traditional government. Their extraordinary self-confidence, won at some cost, as has been seen, makes them capable finally of killing the king. Here Weber's analysis is undoubtedly closer to the truth than that of the Marxists: the saints are entrepreneurs indeed, but in politics rather than in economics. They ruthlessly (and anxiously) pursue not wealth or even individual power—never rely on great men, warned a Puritan preacher—but *collective control* of themselves, of each other, of all England.

The Puritan struggle for collective control is not unique in history. The illustrations already drawn from Jacobin and Bolshevik experience suggests at least the possibility of a comparative study of revolutionary ideology. To "set up" such a comparison has been one of the purposes of the foregoing argument. It remains only to defend its usefulness: it is useful primarily, of course, because the encounter with sainthood is a part of our own experience.

On the level of ideology, of perception and response, comparisons of the

Calvinist elect with the Jacobin men of virtue and the Bolshevik vanguard would not provide any test of the hypothetical description of Puritanism as a response to breakdown, disorder, and social change. They
would demonstrate only that the hypothesis can be extended to cover
other cases: other men have also lived through the experience of exile and
alienation and have shaped their characters in opposition to their environment. Other men have won a self-assurance akin to that of the saints,
and it has permitted them similar forms of activity—radical, ruthless, experimental. This extension of the range of analysis is useful even if it does
not permit scientific testing of the hypothesis. Comparison always brings
new insight: the additional examples often require elaboration and correction of the original hypothesis, and at the same time the discovery of
significant differences in similar cases defines its limits. Working back and
forth between, say, Puritans and Bolsheviks may also avoid some of the
dangers of anachronistic judgment which are probably inherent in a commitment to a single progress—to English history, for example, with its
solemn advance from precedent to precedent. For if the foregoing argument is at all correct, then the saints are likely to be similar, not to the
men who came before or after them in English history, but to other men
in other countries who lived through a similar time and shared some of
the same experiences.

The conditions of these experiences obviously may be compared in a
more systematic fashion. Measurements of social mobility of various sorts
and careful studies of economic change both might be useful here, though
it must be said again that recording such measurements or carrying out
such studies does not bring one face to face with "real life." Mobility, for
example, is a different experience for different men. Nevertheless, it can
surely be argued that urbanization under more or less similar conditions
—which can be investigated and the details quarreled over—makes a limited number of ideological responses likely, the appearance of a limited
variety of new men probable. All these men may not be present in every
case, but on a broad enough national scale and over a sufficient span of
time, they are all likely to appear: the lost worldling whom the Puritans
called damned, the exciting (and often creative) speculator in freedom,
the fearful man who desperately seeks authority, and the saint himself.

But it is probably not possible in any particular place, at any moment
in time, to predict the appearance of the last of these men—though it can
be suggested, on the basis of the argument outlined above, that he will
not be absent in a time of full-scale revolution. The ideas which shape his
character are not automatic products of some objective development—indeed, very little is yet known about their production—and it is not easy to
guess when they will take hold or what their precise nature will be. And
here comparative work can only serve to increase the sensitivity of the

student. If a science is not possible, then one must resort to an older form of knowledge, to that intuition which comes, above all, from the practice of history.

NOTES

1. A classic example of this argument is to be found in A. D. Lindsay, *The Modern Democratic State* (Oxford, 1943), pp. 115–121; also G. P. Gooch, *English Democratic Ideas in the Seventeenth Century* (New York, 1959). The argument appears in a more sophisticated form in the introduction of A. S. P. Woodhouse's edition of the army debates, *Puritanism and Liberty* (London, 1951).

2. That ideas are merely "clothed" in religious fashion for convenience, out of force of habit, or because other clothing was somehow not available is, of course, a Marxist argument. See Perez Zagorin, *A History of Political Thought in the English Revolution* (London, 1954). It presupposes a very awkward theory of expression according to which content and form have little intrinsic connection.

3. Max Weber, *The Protestant Ethic and the Spirit of Capitalism*, tr. Talcott Parsons (New York, 1958), especially pp. 26–27, 53. When Herbert Marcuse analyzes Soviet Marxism, he discovers a "protestant ethic"—but this is clearly a rationalist ethic and not an acquisitive one; *Soviet Marxism: A Critical Analysis* (New York, 1961), pp. 217, 222–223.

4. This view is most clearly argued by Christopher Hill, *Puritanism and Revolution* (London, 1958), especially Chs. I and 7; compare this with Hill's earlier pamphlet, *The English Revolution: 1640* (London, 1940).

5. See Perry Miller, *Orthodoxy in Massachusetts, 1630–1650* (Boston, 1959), Ch. 1; C. H. and Katherine George, *The Protestant Mind of the English Reformation, 1570–1640* (Princeton, N.J., 1961), Ch. 6; Richard Schlatter, *Richard Baxter and Puritan Politics* (New Brunswick, 1957), Introduction.

6. Quoted in Horton Davies, *The Worship of the English Puritans* (Westminster, 1948), p. 235.

7. Richard Baxter, *Reliquiae Baxterianae*, ed. M. Sylvester (London, 1696), p. 87.

8. The term "natural political virtue" is that of Locke's latest editor; see Peter Laslett's edition of John Locke's *Two Treatises of Government* (Cambridge, Eng., 1960), pp. 108 f. The extraordinary difficulty with which self-control is learned is best described—that is, described with some sensitivity to human pain—by Nietzsche in *The Genealogy of Morals*. He is writing of a very early period in human history, but his insights have some relevance to the sixteenth and seventeenth centuries. How free Locke was from any sense of the dangers of *uncontrolled* men is evident in his "Letter on Toleration." Compare his description there of voluntary association in religious matters with Jean Bodin's demand a century earlier for a strict moral discipline enforced by elders. *The Six Books of the Republic*, tr. M. J. Tooley (Oxford, n.d.), pp. 184–185. On this point, as on many others, Bodin is very close to the Calvinists.

9. Weber's most recent critic, Kurt Samuelsson, hardly discusses the idea of rationalization which is so central to his argument; *Religion and Economic Action*, tr. E. G. French (Stockholm, 1961).

10. For a detailed criticism of Weber on these points, see George, *op. cit.*, Chs. 2 and 3; also Samuelsson, *op. cit.*, especially pp. 27 ff. Samuelsson's first chapter discusses the men who have accepted or been significantly influenced by this aspect of Weber's

argument; these are the men who are called "Weberians" in this essay. It should be said that Weber himself—if not always his followers—was very conscious of the savage repression which Calvinism sponsored; the question of why bourgeois men should accept such discipline is central to his book (*ibid.*, p. 37). Nevertheless, the particular forms of repression and control described above are not considered in *The Protestant Ethic.*

11. The restrictionist attitudes of Mably and Morelli are discussed in J. L. Talmon, *The Origins of Totalitarian Democracy* (New York, 1960), pp. 58 ff.

12. The difficulties of describing Christian's pilgrimage and yet maintaining his class character are illustrated by Jack Lindsay, *John Bunyan, Maker of Myths* (London, 1937), p. 5: "He is a writer of the transition, proletarian in that he writes from the viewpoint of the dispossessed, pre-industrialist in that he still clings to a medieval concept of reconciliation, petty bourgeois in that he is tied down to an individualistic ethic."

13. See H. B. Acton, *The Illusion of the Epoch: Marxism-Leninism as a Philosophical Creed* (London, 1955), pp. 141 ff.

14. By the end of the nineteenth century, of course, novelists were discussing precisely the problem of character: see the discussion of the social novel and its decline in Irving Howe, *Politics and the Novel* (New York, 1957), pp. 18, 19.

15. Weber, *op. cit.*, p. 119. See also the interesting, occasionally exasperating, book by Zevedei Barbu, *Problems of Historical Psychology* (New York, 1960), Chs. 5 and 6.

16. *Navaho Witchcraft* (Cambridge, Mass., 1944), especially pp. 50 ff. and 64–66.

17. Wallace Notestein, *A History of Witchcraft in England from 1558 to 1718* (Washington, 1911), pp. 14–15, 195 ff.

18. Much of the argument of this essay was first suggested by Erich Fromm's book *Escape from Freedom* (New York, 1941), but the author cannot accept Fromm's easy distinction between two aspects of modern freedom: freedom *from,* which by itself leads to anxiety and the search for authority; and freedom *to,* which presumably is realized in a sense of dignity and a creative life. That the two are not distinct in history—that is, not always embodied in different people—Fromm clearly recognizes. He seems, however, to believe that their manifestations can be readily distinguished and judged. Thus, for example, he writes that the Puritans, when fighting against the old order, were expressing positive freedom ("strength and dignity of self," *ibid.*, p. 122). Since that fight involved an effort to establish the repressive Holy Commonwealth, this seems rather dubious.

19. On the growth of London, see the figures in F. P. Wilson, *The Plague in Shakespeare's London* (Oxford, 1927), Appendix. That members of Puritan conventicles were often newcomers to the city is suggested by the court records reprinted in Champlin Burrage, *The Early English Dissenters in the Light of Recent Research 1550–1641* (Cambridge, Eng., 1912), Vol. II.

20. *Institutes of the Christian Religion* (Allen translation), Bk. I, Ch. 17, p. x.

21. *Ibid.*, p. xi.

22. Alfred Harbage has pointed out that Puritans objected more to the audience at the theaters than to the plays: see his *Shakespeare's Audience* (New York, 1951).

23. Ben Jonson, *Bartholomew Fair;* see also his characterizations of two Puritans in *The Alchemist.*

24. Robert Bolton, *Two Sermons* (London, 1635), I, 10. The passage is a curious one since it opens with a paraphrase of Hooker, *Ecclesiastical Polity*, I, iii, 2; but Hooker says nothing about the effects of disobedience *among men,* which is the Puritan writer's chief concern.

25. John Whitgift, *Works*, I, 21.

26. The report to Walsingham is quoted in Hill, *Puritanism and Revolution*, p. 234. John Penry, *An Humble Motion with Submission* (Edinburgh, 1590), p. 72.

27. The views of the moralists are described in L. C. Knights, *Drama and Society in the Age of Jonson* (London, 1937).

28. *Two Elizabethan Diaries,* ed. M. M. Knappen (Chicago, 1933), p. 69.

29. They wrote about more than these themes, of course, and even here described more than their own experience, for the outsider is an archetypal figure realized with especial force in Christian thought. The Puritans still lived within a cultural tradition which shaped their expression as it undoubtedly still shaped their experience. On the dangers of reductionism, see F. R. Leavis, *The Common Pursuit* (London, 1953), pp. 208–210.

30. *Diary of Lady Margaret Hoby, 1599–1605,* ed. D. M. Meads (London, 1930), p. 97.

31. See the comments of William Haller on Puritan wayfaring: *The Rise of Puritanism* (New York, 1957), pp. 147 ff.

32. William Perkins, *Works* (London, 1616), III, 539; the passage is quoted in Hill, *op. cit.,* p. 228.

33. Richard Greenham, *Works* (London, 1605), p. 645; Perkins, *op. cit.,* I, 398.

34. *Two Elizabethan Diaries,* p. 17; A. F. Scott-Pearson, *Thomas Cartwright and Elizabethan Puritanism* (Cambridge, Eng., 1925), p. 66; *Diary of Margaret Hoby,* p. 32— at their wedding, the Hobys sought "only to please the beholders with a sermon and a dinner."

35. *Cromwell's Letters and Speeches,* ed. Thomas Carlyle (London, 1893), I, 79–80. On Winthrop see E. S. Morgan, *The Puritan Dilemna: The Story of John Winthrop* (Boston, 1958).

36. Indeed, Calvin thought that commercial competition, with its attendant anxiety, was an aspect of the life of *fallen* man; he pictured him nervously murmuring to himself: "I must use such a mean. I must practise such a feat. I must look into such a business, or otherwise I shall be behindhand in all things. I shall but pine away, I shall not get half my living, if I proceed not in this manner." *Sermons upon the Fifth Book of Moses* (London, 1583), p. 821. Presumably the saint would be free from such anxiety.

37. Most of the calls for activity in Puritan sermons are put in terms of the struggle against social disorder; activity is rarely described as a way of overcoming the fear of damnation. The clear emphasis of the preachers is on the social effects of hard work, and not, as Weber thought, on success as a spiritual sign. See, for example, the discussion of work in Robert Cleaver and John Dod, *A Godly Form of Household Government* (London, 1621), Sig. P 6 and 7.

38. See Walter Travers, *A Full and Plain Declaration of Ecclesiastical Discipline out of the Word of God* (n.p., 1574).

39. Cleaver and Dod, *op. cit.,* Sig. S 8; Bodin, *op. cit.,* pp. 9–13.

40. Thomas Reed, *Moses Old Square for Judges* (London, 1632), pp. 98–99.

41. Lenin, *The Immediate Tasks of the Soviet Government* (1918), in *Selected Works* (New York, 1935–1937), VII, 332–333.

42. *How to Organize Competition* (1917, reprinted Moscow, 1951), p. 63; also see *Letters,* tr. and ed. Elizabeth Hill and Doris Mudie (New York, 1937), p. 161.

43. Henry Crosse, *Virtue's Commonwealth* (London, 1603), Sig. L4 *vers.;* Perkins, *op. cit.,* III, 191.

44. Quoted in A. Aulard, *Christianity and the French Revolution* (Boston, 1927), p. 113.

45. Quoted in Klara Zetkin, "Reminiscences of Lenin," in *The Family in the U.S.S.R.,* ed. Rudolf Schlesinger (London, 1949), p. 78. It should be said that in all the revolutions discussed above, there were men who did not follow the Puritan saints or the vanguard Bolsheviks in their attacks upon human freedom. These men—radical sectarians, secularists, anarchists, libertarians of many sorts—were the products of the

same society and the same experience which produced the others. They rarely made good revolutionaries, however, precisely because they never felt the intense need to yield to an organization and a discipline.

46. This is the view of revolutionary enthusiasm suggested in Crane Brinton's book on the French Revolution, *Decade of Revolution* (New York, 1934), and again in his *Anatomy of Revolution* (New York, 1938). The analogy with religion argued in both books is, however, a very suggestive one.

6

CALVINISM, CAPITALISM, AND THE MIDDLE CLASSES: SOME AFTERTHOUGHTS ON AN OLD PROBLEM

Sidney A. Burrell

Among the widely accepted conventions of modern historiography few have been more tenaciously held or more strongly criticized than the assumption that Protestantism, particularly in its Calvinist form, emerged in the sixteenth century as the ideology of a "rising middle class." Like most well-established, conventionalized forms of thought this one has been difficult to displace in recent historical thinking because it has for long been supported by the researches of a number of eminent and able scholars whose conclusions are reinforced and seemingly confirmed by the verisimilitude of an observable historical connection. Calvinism, after all, did have its beginnings in the city-state of Geneva; and as it spread across northern and western Europe during the sixteenth and seventeenth centuries it seemed to grow best in those areas where commercial activity and urban life were most flourishing. Nothing has seemed more natural, therefore, than to assume that there must have been a close, nexuslike affinity between Calvinism and commerce or, more broadly, between Calvinism and that expanding capitalism which has always been regarded as the peculiar economic attribute of the European bourgeoisie.

The nature of this relationship has been for so long the subject of warm controversy that it seems almost impossible that anything new might be said about it either pro or con. The most recent stage of the argument has been reached in the debate between R. H. Tawney[1] and H. R. Trevor-

Reprinted from Journal of Modern History, *XXXII (1960), 129–141. Copyright © 1960 by The University of Chicago Press.*

Roper[2] over the role of the English gentry as the *primum mobile* of the English civil wars, in which J. H. Hexter[3] has played the part of an *amicus curiae* whose neutrality is somewhat weighted in Trevor-Roper's favor. A summing up of the evidence by three such scholars might appear to preclude any further discussion of the matter; and yet it seems that there are two aspects of the question which have not been dealt with by anyone concerned, though Hexter has touched upon one of them. The first of these has to do with the historiographical development of the idea that Calvinism and capitalism are linked and endemic characteristics of the rising middle class. When we survey the historical elaboration of this belief, we can see quite clearly why it has been so widely accepted and strongly defended by a great many historians. A second aspect of the question which has seldom been considered or properly understood when it has been considered is the role of seventeenth-century Scotland in this controversy. Scotland, though one of the smaller states of Europe, was, after all, a kind of archetypical Calvinist society which had a great deal to do with the revolution that overturned Charles I. For this reason it deserves a far more careful examination than it has received from either side in this argument.

Let us begin by looking briefly at the historiographical development of the idea that Calvinism is the ideology of the capitalistic middle classes. Curiously enough, the origin of this belief actually goes back to the sixteenth century when it first took form in the argument between Anglicans and Presbyterians over church government. In response to the claims of the Elizabethan Presbyterians, who asserted that rule by presbyteries rather than by bishops was proper for Christ's church, Anglican defenders of the Elizabethan establishment like Archbishop John Whitgift countered with the assertion that, while elderships and presbyteries were well suited to the life of city-states and towns, episcopacy was the only useful and proper ecclesiastical polity for large kingdoms.[4] During the next sixty years this assertion proved so useful to the Anglican cause that Presbyterians were driven to make the highest *jure divino* claims for their system. It was not, they declared, "a Lesbian rule answerable to any form of civil polity" but that ecclesiastical government truly intended for the salvation of all mankind because it was "best warranted by the Word of God."[5] In its most extreme form this latter claim was put forth by the supporters of the Scottish Covenant whose revolt against Charles I, which began in 1637, took on the aspect of a vast Presbyterian crusade whose aim was to establish, first, a kind of British theocracy and, ultimately, a universal, presbyterianized Christian church. With stubborn insistence, however, their opponents, unimpressed by the exalted nature of these claims, continued to assert that the Calvinist-Presbyterian system was a religion better suited to "mercantile republicks and cantoned towns rather than to great kingdoms."[6]

Despite the vehemence of their protestations, the verdict of later historiography went against the Scottish Covenanters and other Calvinists who shared their views. During the eighteenth century, when religious fervor had somewhat cooled, another generation of thinkers swayed by different influences looked back to the civil wars of the preceding century and saw them not as struggles for the restoration of Christ's earthly kingdom nor even as great contests for the liberties of the subject but as power conflicts rooted in economic and class enmity. The reason for this transformation is not far too seek. After 1750, with the rise in prestige of that new tool of social analysis known as "political economy," an ever larger number of persons sought to test it against historical fact. By a kind of ironic twist, it was Calvinist Scotland which produced two of these early historical sociologists, James Steuart of Coltness, better known for his economic treatises, and John Millar, an academic colleague of Adam Smith at the University of Glasgow. Like Smith, both men saw deep significance in certain economic developments of the preceding hundred years. It has been suggested that Millar, in particular, was actually a forerunner of the nineteenth-century school of Marxian sociology.[7] This claim is exaggerated, for much of his thought derived from the premises of a rather conventional eighteenth-century rationalism, but the assertion does have a measure of truth. By implication at least, both men seemed to argue that economic change preceded and caused political change. In the view of Steuart of Coltness, for example, the downfall of the feudal aristocracy throughout Europe was a result of fundamental shifts in the economic relations which had controlled European life for centuries.

> In countries [he wrote] where the government is vested in the hands of the great lords, as is the case in all aristocracies, as was the case under the feudal government, and as it still is the case in many countries of Europe, where trade, however, and industry are daily gaining ground; the statesman who sets the new system of political economy on foot, may depend upon it, either his attempt will fail, or the constitution of the government will change. If he destroys all arbitrary dependence between individuals, the wealth of the industrious will share, if not totally root out the power of the grandees.[8]

In this and in one or two other respects it must be admitted that there were latent in the thought of Steuart ideas which Marx was to develop more fully toward somewhat different conclusions in the century following. Steuart believed not only that men were motivated and controlled to a large extent by economic necessity but that the possession of wealth automatically brought with it political power. Like Marx, Steuart also concluded that changes in the methods of production altered existing social relationships and aroused class hostilities, though he did not regard this eventuality as an inevitable law of history.[9]

Steuart's thought, though important for its contribution to the general climate of European opinion, was by no means unique; nor was it quite so explicitly pointed in the direction of later Marxian thought as that of Millar whose views seem to foreshadow Marx's own contribution to nineteenth-century historical and sociological theory. Millar formulated a fairly well thought-out proto-Marxian interpretation of history in which he called attention to the prime importance of class distinctions and antagonisms. It is to Millar, for example, that we owe what may be the first attempt to explain the English civil wars as class struggles. His explanation of the reasons for division between the supporters of the king and those of Parliament is one which a number of historians would find acceptable today. As he saw it:

> The adherents of the king were chiefly composed of the nobility and higher gentry, men who, by their wealth and station had much to lose; and who, in the annihilation of monarchy, and in the anarchy that was likely to follow, foresaw the ruin of their consideration and influence. The middling and inferior gentry, together with the inhabitants of the towns; those who entertained a jealousy of the nobles, and of the king, or who, by the changes in the state of society, had lately been raised to independence, became, on the other hand the great supporters of parliament, and formed the chief part of the armies levied by that assembly.[10]

While it is uncertain how much Marx, Engels, or other members of the Marxian school may have read of the writing of Steuart or Millar, we do know that Marx himself was led to the conviction that the class struggle was the central theme of history by persons whom he described as "bourgeois historians."[11] Marx, however, did make an important original contribution to the development of modern historiography and historical sociology by explicitly calling attention to the relationship between social conditions and the nonmaterial manifestations of human activity in the form of beliefs and ideas for which Karl Mannheim has credited him with the discovery of the "sociology of knowledge." His conclusion as set forth in the introduction to his *Critique of Political Economy* that the "mode of production in material life determines the general character of the social, political, spiritual processes of life" can thus be said to have closed out a revolution in historiography and social theory which had its beginnings in the eighteenth century.

What is probably most significant about Marx's thought, however, is that he brought together two distinct and previously unrelated concepts that had a far-reaching influence on nineteenth-century historical theorizing. By linking the theory that all history was the history of class struggles with the theory that the conditions of the material environment gave rise to specific institutional and ideological forms, he established a pattern of thought congenial to the nineteenth-century climate of opinion. Whether men were willing to accept his political conclusions or not, few would have denied that he seemed to be moving in the right direction; for it was the century's great hope (as it still is among behavorial scientists) that a coherent, scientifically based, sociological synthesis could be found which would clear away the rubble of uncertainty concerning man and his social relationships. In one way or another the faith that this synthesis could be found—indeed, that it was all but formulated—dominated the thinking of persons as diverse in viewpoint as J. S. Mill, Auguste Comte, and Henry Maine. Lesser men, intellectual journalizers like Leslie Stephen, for one example, gave this confident hope an almost popular currency among the reading classes of the late nineteenth century.

Almost inevitably, however, it was German scholarship that worked most diligently in this direction and sought by massive industry to arrive at a final coherence. For this there were probably two reasons: first, because of the continuing influence of the Hegelian-Marxian intellectual tradition in German academic circles; and, second, because a number of the more influential historical writers, among whom was Werner Sombart, were sympathetic to socialism and almost unconsciously tried to preserve the general outlines of Marxian theory against criticism by broadening its historical scope. It was clear, for example, that if all European history since the end of the Middle Ages was to be interpreted as a series of class struggles, then Marx's view that the bourgeoisie came into its own during the course of the eighteenth century was simply not comprehensive enough. If the French Revolution marked the emergence of a militant bourgeoisie in France, then what of earlier revolutions? [12] What of the Protestant Reformation, that great sixteenth-century overturn which had ended the sway of the medieval church and its "feudal ideology" in many parts of Europe? Surely these could not be excluded from a theory which claimed universal comprehensiveness in its interpretation of European history? In order to fill the gap there had to be some connection between Protestantism and the capitalist mode of production. Who it was that first remedied this deficiency we cannot be sure. Sombart has been given credit for it, but in the first edition of his *Der moderne Kapitalismus* (Leipzig, 1902) he inferred that the connection was a "well known fact," seemingly proved by the researches of other scholars. There was little doubt in his mind but that Protestantism, particularly in its Calvinist and Quaker varieties, was, according to the established Marxian formula, an ideological manifestation of the economic change brought on by the nascent capitalism of the sixteenth century.[13]

The first serious criticism of this widely circulated assumption came from Max Weber. In this connection it is well to emphasize that Weber was a critic and not a supporter of Marx's and Sombart's views, for this fact is sometimes forgotten. He rejected the idea that religious ideas were only ideological manifestations of particular social conditions. Ideas for him were, at least in part, autonomous entities with a power to affect social changes. As proof, he cited what seemed to him clear historical evidence that capitalism was a result rather than a cause of the Reformation. He believed that Calvinist theology, in particular, contained certain elements which were peculiarly conducive to rationalized, individualistic economic activity undertaken for profit: not simply for the purpose of enjoying the fruits thereof but rather as a duty, as part, indeed, of a new sense of ethical obligation.[14] Unfortunately, the storm of controversy which followed on the appearance of this suggestion had an effect which Weber could not foresee. By suggesting that the rise of capitalism was influenced by Calvinist thought he helped to strengthen the assumption, already strong in some scholarly and intellectual circles, that the two were somehow necessarily and intimately linked together.

In the more than half-century since Weber's hypothesis was first put forward there has scarcely been an end to controversy. Because his view still presupposed an intimate connection between Protestantism or, more specifically, Calvinism and capitalism, some of Weber's critics have overlooked the fact that he was actually trying to reverse the Marxian formula and have gone on to conclude that he was only restating it in a slightly different way. It has even been charged that his theories provided the ammunition for later attacks on Calvinism and other branches of religion by writers who sought to link religious belief with the "unpopularity of Capitalism in the twentieth century." [15] Other opponents, of whom the best known and the friendliest is Tawney, have criticized Weber's views from a totally different position. With impressive scholarship, Tawney has argued in the two most famous of his writings on the subject, *The Agrarian Revolution of the Sixteenth Century* (London, 1912) and *Religion and the Rise of Capitalism* (London, 1926), that economic change was ultimately responsible for the transformation of the Christian ethic from the sixteenth century onward. In so doing, he has not gone the whole way and asked us to accept the historiographical stereotype which links the middle classes and Calvinism. What he has attempted to demonstrate is that Calvinism, like most other religious movements stemming from the Reformation, was changed under pressure of economic forces into something that Calvin did not necessarily intend it to become. In so arguing, however, Tawney has taken a position very close to that of Marx while eschewing Marx's original terminology. Moreover, his later writings on the rise of the English gentry during the sixteenth and seventeenth centuries confirm this impression very strongly, since they clearly attempt to account for one of the peculiarities of English history which for long had seemed to put England outside the framework of Marxian theory. He was aware that the country gentlemen and not the merchants had played a decisive role in England's political and social life before the nineteenth century and that the former were to a large extent responsible for the great rebellion against Charles I. By examining various aspects of English social history in the century preceding 1640, he found what seemed to him to be conclusive evidence that the merchants and squires were far more closely linked in terms of interest and outlook than anyone had previously thought. This linkage, as he saw it, was discernible in the process of economic change which had steadily expanded commercial wealth and made it possible for the merchant to acquire land and, ultimately, the status of a country gentleman. Simultaneously, this expansion transformed the whole body of the English gentry into a class of capitalist entrepreneurs with all the acquisitive habits and economic aspirations peculiar to such a class. As the economic strength of the gentry increased, that of the older-established aristocracy declined until the time came when the gentry simply foreclosed the older landowning classes by the violent method of revolution. Thus Tawney was able to explain away the anomalies of the English civil wars that did not fit into the Marxian pattern. Pym, Hampden, Cromwell, all the gentlemen of England who took up arms against the king, became English analogues of the bourgeoisie, and Marx was right after all.

With this transfiguration, as Hexter has termed it,[16] there ensued a new and sharper controversy which has very much enlivened English historical scholarship for more than a decade. The ablest and the sharpest criticism has come from Trevor-Roper who may be said to have reversed the Tawney formula by arguing that it was not the "rising" but the "declining" gentry who, angered at their loss of public wealth and influence, provided the revolutionary impetus that overturned the king.[17] Other scholars, with less conscious critical intent, have called attention to the incontrovertible fact that Tawney's hypothesis does not hold when we examine in depth the various individual choices of those who became supporters of king or parliament, since it seems plain that men did not choose sides according to any conscious or unconscious pattern of class interest.[18]

It is not my purpose here to attempt an assessment of these various positions but rather to call attention to a fact of supreme importance which is usually left out of calculation whenever questions are raised about the connection between Calvinism and the "middle classes" or about the causes of civil war in England. That fact is that while the civil wars may or may not have been caused by a newly risen social class ideologically linked with Calvinism or its English Puritan manifestations, it was not Englishmen—gentry, merchants, or otherwise—who first took up arms against Charles I. The curiously forgotten truth is, as Cicely V. Wedgwood has recently and rightly pointed out to a generation of scholars who seem to have let it slip from memory,[19] that the English revolutions began in Scotland. Even more curious, however, is the strange oversight that has left the Scottish example out of consideration in all recent hypotheses linking Calvinism to the "rising middle class." [20] Scotland, as we have noted, was a kind of Calvinist society par excellence. In that remote corner of northwestern Europe the Genevan influence, despite all the efforts of the crown to control it, had created a Presbyterian system of church government which made it possible for Scotsmen to boast that theirs was the "best reformit kirk in Christendom." There was more than bombast in such an assertion. Nowhere was the Calvinist-Presbyterian system more strongly rooted in popular feeling or more pervasive in its influence; nowhere were the theology and liturgy of the Reformed tradition more widely accepted. In such an environment we should surely expect to find all those historical concomitants of Calvinism which are presupposed in the various hypotheses under consideration.

First of all, we should expect to find, if these hypotheses are valid, that seventeenth-century Scotland was a country with a high rate of economic growth. In the second place, it should be plain that Calvinism was a religion peculiarly associated with the "middle class" and that it was this class which took the lead in rebellion. Moreover, we should also expect to discover that the feudal aristocracy of the kingdom was opposed to rebellion and to the religious "ideology" of the revolutionary class. Let us begin by taking up the question of Scottish economic expansion. Here the evidence against any conclusion that the rate of economic growth was either equal to or greater than that of neighboring areas in western Europe is overwhelming. Scotland, on the basis of every contemporary account given by persons in a position to compare Scottish living standards with those of the Low Countries, France, or England, lagged far behind its wealthier, more industrious neighbors. Foreign travelers, even when predisposed to a favorable view of the country, continually remarked the sharp contrasts between the economic amenities and the subsistence level of this small northern kingdom and those of regions with which they were more familiar.[21] Exaggerated and biased as some of these accounts were, they were corroborated, almost without exception, by Scottish writers who simply accepted the fact that theirs was a poorer country than most others in western Europe.[22] Such evidence, quite obviously, does not rule out the possibility that the Scottish economy was accumulating capital surplus in the period before 1637 or the fact that such wealth as the nation possessed may have been concentrated in the hands of a few. Relative subsistence standards, as we know from recent historical experience, never tell us all about the rates of capital growth in an economic system, but they do tell us a great deal when we are able to compare them at various social levels. Actually, there is a great deal of scattered evidence to show that the possessing classes were much less well off than their counterparts in richer nearby kingdoms.[23]

Furthermore, the very nature of the economy prevented any large-scale capital accumulation or growth. The major economic activity of the kingdom was agriculture; and though Scotland was not unique in this respect —since even the wealthiest European states were still largely agrarian in the early decades of the seventeenth century—the level of Scottish agricultural technique and production was extremely low. Only some few areas of the country, concentrated mainly in the Lothians and Fife, could be adjudged good arable land in the English sense, and even there the full productive capacity of the soil was often limited by the primitive methods of tillage and the traditional forms of estate organization. Most farming was undertaken for subsistence, and the recurring visitations of famine indicate how precarious a subsistence it was until the eighteenth century was well advanced.[24] Rents were paid in kind to landlords whose relations with their tenants were governed by a hodgepodge of conflicting customary forms and any kind of leasehold was virtually unknown. Few, if any, landowners exhibited the entrepreneurial characteristics of the English gentry as described by Tawney. These were men for whom land was a source not simply of wealth but of a semifeudalized power: a tenant, in other words, was more than just a renter; he was also an armed retainer pledged, if and when the need arose, to support his lord against all enemies. As a consequence, seventeenth-century Scotland remained untouched by the economic ferment that had begun to transform the English countryside as far back as the fifteenth century. Enclosures, to the surprise of more than one English visitor, were almost completely unknown before 1700;[25] and the whole aspect of rural life was one which left southern observers with the impression that here was a people "generally affected with slothe, and a lazy vagrance." [26]

And yet, despite its relative backwardness, the Scottish countryside was the backbone of the nation's economic system. Agriculture was the only area of the economy capable of producing any sort of surplus either for purposes of investment or for foreign trade; and since this surplus was usually small and consisted mainly of raw agricultural products or commodities provided by crude rural industries, the trade, manufacturing, and finance of the kingdom were primitive almost to the point of nonexistence.[27] Capital, even in the simple form of specie, was continually in such short supply that it was frequently impossible to finance the simplest mercantile transactions.[28] Native coin could not be kept in circulation but generally had to be used to balance payments for imports from abroad, since the balance of trade continually ran against Scotland throughout the seventeenth century.[29] In most cases, foreign specie, when available, circulated at a higher value than that of domestic mintage. The shortage of coin alone was such a serious problem in the years before 1637 that it was the subject of petitions from the Scottish Parliament to the king and on at least two occasions all but forced the state to suspend its extremely limited functions because of an empty treasury.[30]

As a result, the commercial life of the "free" or royal burghs, among whom were numbered the largest towns of the kingdom and who alone had the right to engage in foreign trade, was quite limited in scope and afforded a means of livelihood to a narrow oligarchy of merchants. In the main, these latter were simply purveyors rather than processors of the goods they handled, and the towns themselves were only entrepôts for rural trade.[31] Over several generations the merchants of the royal burghs had built up a tightly knit, corporately controlled monopoly which, while it assured those who participated in it of a modest share in the nation's limited foreign commerce, had the further effect of adding another barrier to economic expansion.[32] The Scottish merchant, with some few exceptions, was a dealer in "small fardels" who eked out an often precarious living by selling his country's small produce when and where he could in foreign markets where the competition usually worked heavily against him.

In circumstances so extremely adverse, the growth of commercial capital was not only slow but kept the merchant community of Scotland from expanding into a large and diversified class of capitalist entrepreneurs. Few merchants became independently wealthy in trade alone—though there were, of course, some notable exceptions—and the towns had neither wealth nor population sufficient to prevent continual intervention in their affairs either by the nobles or the king. Edinburgh, for example, right down to the beginning of the Covenanting rebellion was so completely under the crown's domination that its corporation was unable to choose its own officers or to prevent Charles from pushing the city to the edge of bankruptcy in order to meet the king's various financial demands.[33] The leading merchants of the city were members of the court faction who depended for a large part of their wealth upon privileges granted by the king and who dared not risk, either for their own sakes or for the sake of the city as a whole, the withdrawal of royal government from the capital.[34]

Without going into further detail, it is plain that seventeenth-century Scotland did not actually contain a class of capital possessors large enough to constitute a serious menace to the existing status quo. Neither the merchants nor the lairds were in a position to transform the "means of subsistence" or to wage class war in their own interests; and these alone were the two classes who most nearly satisfy the criteria by which a "middle" class is defined. In fact, the very nature of the uprising against the king, which began with rioting in Edinburgh on Sunday, July 23, 1637, indicates clearly that this was a rebellion of another kind. Its immediate cause was the attempted introduction into the Scottish church of a new service book containing liturgical forms more nearly in conformity with those of the Church of England. Important as the cause of religion was to large numbers of Scotsmen, the king's action in this particular instance symbolized something more in their eyes than just a desire on his part to enforce religious conformity throughout his dominions. This was the culmination of a whole series of impolitic acts which had aroused discontent in many quarters and which, in the climax, convinced a significant number of persons of all classes that Charles and his advisers, in their efforts to transform the Scottish church and state, were attempting to Anglicize the small northern kingdom and convert it into an English province. To loyal Presbyterians the king's motives were plain in his efforts to subvert a church which, in their eyes, was not only the best reformed in all Europe but a particular manifestation of divine blessing upon the kingdom of Scotland.[35] Charles's intentions to destroy Scottish national identity and independence seemed plain to nobles and lairds who had halfheartedly submitted to the king's attempts at reform of central and local government, to his confiscatory scheme which was intended to deprive them of secularized church lands and tithe rights, and to his seeming denigration of their privileges and status by his overfondness for English advisers and court favorites.[36] The result was a fusion of discontents which united Scots of every significant social class in a corporate enterprise for the defense of kirk and kingdom. A king, whose long residence in England had made him alien to his own people, thus found himself facing not a class rebellion but a "revolt of the ephors," who represented the traditional leadership of the realm and who acted in the name of the traditional *communitas*.

Like many another revolution, this Scottish overturn was not the result of careful planning or avowed intention, even though an anticourt faction had existed among the local nobility for some years previous to the outbreak. Charles and his supporters afterward claimed that the antiservice-book rioting was the culmination of a carefully arranged plot hatched months before rebellion began.[37] That some sort of public protest against the book may have been projected beforehand is not impossible, but that the plotters intended to initiate revolution is difficult to believe. Indeed, our knowledge of the events that transpired during the early months of the rebellion makes it clear that neither the king nor those who later led the movement against him knew quite how to handle the situation with which they were confronted when rioting broke out in Edinburgh.[38]

Not until autumn did the lines of division begin to form, and by then it was evident that the leadership of the uprising was not to be found in the city merchant classes but among a section of the nobility backed by some hundreds of lairds and gentlemen. They, with their bands of armed followers, made up a formidable part of the ancient feudal array of the kingdom; and they alone had the power to resist royal authority. Once the landowning classes had determined to act, the reluctance and fear of other classes and groups was speedily overcome. By mid-October 1637 the power of the court faction which controlled the Edinburgh corporation was broken and leading members of the merchant oligarchy that controlled the city found themselves faced with a choice of flight or cooperation with the rebels.[39] At the same time, the great body of the Scottish clergy, many of whose members had watched the turn of events in trepidation and uncertainty despite the strong Presbyterian sympathies of many, were suddenly presented with a petition drawn up by leading nobles and gentlemen which called for the complete abolition of episcopacy. The account of one eyewitness, himself a minister of the Scottish church, indicates plainly that some even among the clergy were not yet prepared to go the whole way to open rebellion against the king. "When I heard the piece [that is, the antiepiscopal petition]," wrote Robert Baillie, "I was putt in great doubts what to doe; some hard passages were in it; it had neither been reasoned nor voted, but only read, and after all the nobles and gentries subscriptions, presented to our hands." [40] Baillie, like many another on that day, chose prudence over valor and added his name to the long list of hundreds appended to the document.[41]

By November of the same year the rebels had organized themselves into a revolutionary government directed by a Committee of Four Tables representing the traditional estates of the realm and the ministers of the church. Once the Tables had come into existence, the rebellion was rapidly transformed into an antiepiscopal movement disguised as a crusade against "popery" whose symbol was soon to become the ambiguously worded National Covenant of 1638 and whose revolutionary purposes were to be attained at the Glasgow Assembly held during November and December of the same year. With the successful restoration of the Presbyterian polity and liturgy, a train was laid that led straight to explosion in England. From the end of 1638 onward rebellious Scotland drove the king from necessity to necessity until Charles had no recourse left but to ask for aid from his English Parliament. Two years to the month after the Scottish Covenanters had accomplished their revolution at Glasgow the Long Parliament assembled at Westminster. As its members took their seats the enthusiasts among them fully acknowledged that Scotland was the "saviour of our liberties" and that Scottish rebels had done what Englishmen had not dared.

From this very brief description of the Scottish Covenanting rebellion there are two very obvious and extremely significant inferences to be drawn. First, and perhaps more important, is the fact that here was a society which, though formally and extensively Calvinist, did not conform in its economic and social manifestations to the commonly accepted view of such a society. Scotland was not a country with a thriving, bustling "middle class" made up of merchants or capitalist squires but an economic backwater in contrast with its wealthier western European neighbors. One might perhaps make some kind of case to prove that the nobles and lairds who took the lead in this rebellion were newly risen men in terms of wealth and status, as some of them inevitably were. A great many of them, however, represented ancient families and estates held for generations. Or it might conceivably be argued that a Scottish laird was the exact counterpart of an English squire, which he, unfortunately, was not, except by rather remote analogy. The laird, like the nobles who made up the greater aristocracy of the kingdom, was a landholder whose status and power were not determined solely by the money value of his rent rolls, which, as we have seen, were often scanty, but also by the strength he could muster when he and his ragged tenantry took the field. His place in the complex network of Scottish social relations was defined by custom, by blood relationship, or by the bonds of that peculiarly Scottish contractual arrangement known as "manrent." [42] For him, as for others at every level of Scottish society, the religion of the kirk was not a class ideology but the religion of a significant part of the nation which had to be preserved against the innovations of a king, who seemed bent on leading the country back to Rome by way of Canterbury. He and those associated with him in rebellion believed that they were thus defending not simply their material interests but what a later generation would call a "way of life." In this respect, the revolt took on certain of the characteristics familiar to observers of twentieth-century underdeveloped societies where revolutionary movements have seldom conformed to the classic Marxian pattern.

The second inference to be drawn from this Scottish rebellion is one that seems immediately obvious when we consider the chronology of the British revolutions against Charles I. However much the matter may be disputed, one cannot avoid the fact that rebellion against the king did not begin in England but in Scotland. A great deal of evidence can be adduced to show that the English uprising against Charles might probably have come without the antecedent example of Scotland. Undoubtedly, English discontent with the king's policies was serious and widespread. That point may not be argued. Whether rebellion would have come in England if Scotsmen had not set an example and, in so doing, revealed the king's weakness is impossible for us to know with ultimate certainty. What we do know, beyond question, is that Scotland, far less highly developed politically and economically than England, was the first to challenge the king's policy of Thorough.

In the end, then, the questions we must raise about the various hypotheses of Marx, Weber, and Tawney are simple enough. Can we safely assume, in view of the foregoing, that the civil wars of the seventeenth century in Britain were actually caused by the resistless and virtually inevitable push for power on the part of a rising capitalist class? Or can we continue to believe that Calvinism must somehow be linked either as cause or effect to the rise of a particular class or a particular kind of economic activity?

In answer to the first of these questions, let it be said that there is no doubt but that many of the Scottish rebels had material as well as other motives for rebellion. Nobles and lairds alike bitterly resented the king's attempts from 1625 onward to deprive them of proprietary rights in ecclesiastical lands and revenues; they joined with others in resisting or evading the increased weight of royal taxation. But these are not resentments peculiar to a single class; nor do they prove the validity of any particular hypothesis except perhaps that men do not like to part with material possessions when they can avoid it.[43] The second question we may answer by asking why it is impossible to think of the Calvinist-Presbyterian system of theology and church government as something incompatible with an agrarian or even a feudalized society. The Scottish kirk in the days of its power functioned in ways very like those of the medieval church. Furthermore, it offered to the laity a means of participating in its functions which the medieval church did not, and this in itself was one of the important reasons why the aristocracy and gentry of the kingdom wished to see the Presbyterian system restored once they came to realize that the episcopalian hierarchy as revived by the Stuarts might become dangerous to themselves.[44] In sum, it seems clear that the incompatibility of Calvinism with any particular social organization was political rather than economic. The presbyterianized Scottish church, like any other powerful, autonomous ecclesiastical institution, challenged the undiffused authority of the centralized state. In this respect, the assertion made by one of its defenders that the Presbyterian system was an "enemy to all unwarrantable power of kings" came very close to the truth.

What may we then conclude about the various hypotheses under consideration? Only that they are hypotheses and nothing more? Unquestionably, each in its way has served a useful analytical purpose by calling attention to certain broad social phenomena. Marx was correct in asserting that what men believe is conditioned by the circumstances in which they find themselves. Without question, too, class interests have decisively influenced history at particular moments. That the material environment has always and everywhere determined the precise form of class interest, or that the response of a particular class to the stimulus of environment must always be the same, is a highly questionable assumption whose proof lies in the sphere of metahistory. Even when we attempt to apply the canons of strict environmental determinism to historical phenomena, we are still confronted by the fact that the human environment is so vast and complex as to defy any attempt to analyze it into its significant component influences. If we assume with Weber that man's environment consists of something more than his material surroundings and must include his beliefs and values, the difficulty is enormously compounded. Beyond this is always the massive imponderable of man the individual. The attributes which govern human responses vary greatly from person to person:

some men are more intelligent, more learned, shrewder, more selfish, more ambitious, or more idealistic than others. Most studies of the divisions within any great revolutionary movement demonstrate, as those of D. Brunton and D. H. Pennington or Mrs. Mary Frear Keeler have recently done for the English civil wars,[45] that the patterns of interest and choice are far less clear than they seem on the basis of prima-facie assumption. Here perhaps the psychologist and the geneticist have something to tell us, but even they have not yet advanced their knowledge to a point where we can more than guess at the effects of psychological conditioning or genetic influences. This is not to suggest that the hope of a final, coherent, historical synthesis may be vain, but only that the imponderables which stand in the way of its formulation are far greater than we sometimes realize.

One final question must also be raised before concluding. In putting it forward I am aware that it may seem to reflect unfairly upon the intentions of men whose services to historical scholarship have been widely and rightly admired. It must nonetheless be asked. Are the various hypotheses we have been considering intended as objective analyses of historical phenomena, or do they have a deeper purpose? At the root of controversy there seems to lie a desire, on the one hand, to preserve and to adapt Marxian theory in such a way as to make it appear that the political success of modern socialism is guaranteed by inexorable historical law. Conversely, is it unjust to suggest that some part, at least, of the vehement criticism directed against this effort may result, consciously or unconsciously, from opposing political views? In either case, scholarship becomes the masked weapon of ideological controversy.

NOTES

1. For a summary of Tawney's views, see "The Rise of the Gentry," *Economic History Review,* Vol. XI (1941).

2. H. R. Trevor-Roper, "The Gentry, 1540–1640," *Economic History Review,* Supplement (1953), and "The Social Origins of the Great Rebellion," *History Today,* Vol. V, No. 6 (June 1955).

3. J. H. Hexter, "Storm over the Gentry," *Encounter* (May 1958).

4. John Ayre (ed.), *The Works of John Whitgift* (London, 1851–1853), III, 280.

5. Cf. Robert Baillie, *The Unlawfulness and Danger of Limited Prelacie* (London, 1641), p. 13.

6. William Drummond of Hawthornden, "SKIAMAXIA: Or a Defence of a Petition Tendered to the Lords of the Council in Scotland," *Works* (London, 1711), p. 195; for a similar view, see Pierre du Moulin, *A Letter of a French Protestant to a Scotishman of the Covenant* (London, 1640), pp. 5–6. Examples of the Scottish Covenanters' position may be found in Robert Baillie, "The Unloading of Issachars Burden," pp. 64–65, in *An Historicall Vindication of the Church of Scotland* (London, 1646); Alexander Hender-

son, *Reformation of Church-Government in Scotland* (London, 1644), p. 10; Samuel Rutherford, *Lex Rex: The Law and the Prince* (London, 1644), p. 8.

7. See R. L. Meek, "The Scottish Contribution to Marxian Sociology" in John Saville (ed.), *Democracy and the Labour Movement* (London, 1954); W. C. Lehmann, "John Millar, Historical Sociologist," *British Journal of Sociology*, Vol. III, No. 1 (1952); Roy Pascal, "Property and Society: The Scottish Historical School of the Eighteenth Century," *Modern Quarterly*, Vol. I, No. 2 (1938).

8. James Steuart of Coltness, *Works, Political, Metaphisical, and Chronological* (London, 1805), I, 327.

9. "From reason it is plain that industry must give wealth, and wealth *will* give power, if he who possesses it be left the master to employ it as he pleases. . . . It was consequently very natural of the nobility to be jealous of the wealthy merchants, and of every one who became easy and independent by means of his own industry; experience proved how exactly this principle regulated their administration." *Ibid.*, 326.

10. John Millar, *An Historical View of the English Government* (London, 1812), III, 295.

11. See Marx's acknowledgment in an oft-quoted letter to Weydemeyer, March 5, 1852, contained in Dona Torr (ed.), *Karl Marx and Friedrich Engels, Correspondence, 1846–1895* (New York, 1934), p. 57.

12. As Marx explained in the *Communist Manifesto*, the English revolution of the seventeenth century was a "bourgeois revolution" but an incomplete one which had occurred under "less advanced conditions of civilization."

13. Werner Sombart, *Der moderne Kapitalismus* (Leipzig, 1902), I, 380–381. For various estimates of Sombart's views in this matter, see the reviews of his writings contained in *Vierteljahrschrift für Social- und Wirtschaftsgeschichte*, XI (1913), 637–640; XIII (1916), 316–319; and XV (1919–1921), 111–118.

14. It is not possible to go into all the ramifications of the debate about what Weber meant to prove. His original views may be found in *Gesammelte Aufsätze zur Religionssoziologie*, 3 vols. (Tübingen, 1922–1923). Volume I includes the work translated into English by Talcott Parsons as *The Protestant Ethic and the Spirit of Capitalism* (reprint, New York, 1952), in which Ch. 4 contains what has always seemed to me to be the essence of Weber's argument. Parsons has commented astutely on Weber and so too has Tawney, particularly in the Preface to the 1937 edition of his *Religion and the Rise of Capitalism*. Other commentaries on his work are too numerous to mention here. In brief, however, it appears to me that Weber's views may be summarized thus: While he seems to have been neither a rationalist nor an idealist, as those terms are precisely defined by academic philosophers, he did believe that men's thoughts, ideals, and standards of value had a power to affect human conduct and the human environment. Moreover, it should be remembered that Weber was not concerned with the effects of religious ideas solely in economic terms. He was attempting to find the reasons for the unique development of Western civilization as manifested in science, technology, and industry. In his opinion the latter could best be explained by the Christian religious tradition which seemed to offer a rational explanation for the relationship between the natural and the supernatural. Within the Christian tradition, Protestantism and, again, particularly Calvinism seemed more conducive to the rise of scientific rationalism and thus provided a better intellectual climate for the growth of science. Compare the opinions in his *Religion of China* (Glencoe, Ill., 1951). Weber's suggestions in this connection have been followed by a number of scholars who have collected evidence to show that most of the work done in the scientific field during the sixteenth and seventeenth centuries and later was accomplished by Protestants. R. K. Merton, "Science, Technology, and Theology in Seventeenth Century England," *Osiris.*

Vol. IV, No. 2 (1938). For a very good general discussion of this controversial topic, see Bernard Barber, *Science and the Social Order* (Glencoe, Ill., 1952), pp. 56–59.

15. H. M. Robertson, *Aspects of the Rise of Economic Individualism* (Cambridge, Eng., 1933), p. xi.

16. Hexter, *op. cit.,* p. 31.

17. See note 2.

18. D. Brunton and D. H. Pennington, *Members of the Long Parliament* (Cambridge, Mass., 1954); and Mary F. Keeler, *The Long Parliament: A Biographical Study of Its Members* (Philadelphia, 1954).

19. Cicely V. Wedgwood, *The King's Peace, 1637–1641* (New York, 1955), Bk. II.

20. Sombart, however, in his *Der Bourgeois* (Munich, 1913), pp. 296–299, cited Scotland as a kind of classic example of a society where capital growth and Calvinism went hand in hand. H. M. Robertson, *op. cit.,* p. 88, rightly called attention to the fact that Scotland's emergence as an industrial country occurred only after it had been Calvinist for generations, indeed, for more than two hundred years.

21. Compare the diary of John Aston (1639) in J. C. Hodgson (ed.), *Six North Country Diaries* (Durham, 1910), p. 32; and C. Lowther, "Our Journal into Scotland A.D. 1629, 5th of November, from Lowther," contained in Lonsdale Mss., *Hist. Mss. Commission Reports,* XIII (1893), Appendix, Pt. VII, 74–88. In 1658–1659 a report to Richard Cromwell's Parliament on the finances of the three British kingdoms listed their total revenues as follows: England, £1,517,274; Ireland, £207,790; Scotland, £146,652. Scotland's fiscal deficit for the year preceding was, £163,619, while that of Ireland was £136,690. J. D. Marwick (ed.), *Scottish Burgh Records* (Edinburgh, 1881), XIII (Miscellany), xxiii. In the mid-seventeenth century, despite the chaos caused by protracted civil war and large-scale land confiscations, Ireland was regarded as a much richer country than Scotland.

22. See the statements made in this connection by Sir Thomas Craig of Riccartoun, the famous Scottish legist of the early seventeenth century, in C. S. Terry (ed.), *Sir Thomas Craig's "De unione regnorum Britanniae tractatus"* (Edinburgh, 1909), p. 413. Even in the eighteenth century Adam Smith felt that the differences were so obvious as to be plain even to a casual observer. "The country [Scotland] is not only much poorer," he wrote, "but the steps by which it advances to a better condition, for it is evidently advancing, seem to be much slower and more tardy." E. Cannan (ed.), *Adam Smith's "Wealth of Nations,"* 6th ed. (London, 1950), p. 92.

23. The Earl of Clarendon remarked the poverty of the Scottish nobles on the eve of the civil wars and concluded that the debts incurred by many of them in attempting to foot the costs of entertainment at the time of Charles I's coronation visit to Scotland in 1633 had much to do with their growing hostility toward the king's policies. W. D. Macray (ed.), *Clarendon's "History of the Rebellion"* (Oxford, 1888), I, 108. In 1634 the English traveler Sir William Brereton noted that "earl's and lord's houses here in Edenburgh [are] as mean buildings as gentlemen's and knight's in London and England." E. Hawkins (ed.), *Sir William Brereton's "Travels in Holland, the United Provinces, England, Scotland, and Ireland, 1634–1635"* (Manchester, 1844), p. 108.

24. H. H. Graham, *The Social Life of Scotland in the Eighteenth Century* (2nd ed., London, 1900), I, 146–152.

25. "We seldom meet with enclosures," wrote another English visitor, the Rev. Thomas Morer, in 1689, "either because being a corn country, they would be injured as little as may be by birds which harbour in the hedges; or being without those long and kind leases the tenants of England have, they are not encouraged by their lords in that and some other improvements." P. H. Brown (ed.), *Early Travellers in Scotland*

(Edinburgh, 1891), p. 267. Leases on the English model, with a fixed term of years and at a fixed annual rent, were not introduced until the last decade of the seventeenth century and do not appear to have become common until about 1760. Graham, *op. cit.*, I, 166 n., 201 n. The first Scottish enclosure act was not passed by the Scottish Parliament until 1695.

26. Thomas Tucker, "Report upon the Settlement of the Revenue and Customs in Scotland, A.D. MDCLVI" in Marwick, *op. cit.*, XIII (Miscellany), 16. Tucker was a commissioner of the Cromwellian government in Scotland and was responsible for the collection of public revenues during the Interregnum.

27. See the list of Scottish exports for the year 1614 in P. H. Brown, *Scotland in the Time of Queen Mary* (London, 1904), p. 226.

28. See the proclamation of the Scottish Privy Council on September 12, 1636, calling for reform of the coinage in *Register of the Privy Council of Scotland*, second series, VI, 322–324. For other evidences of Scottish capital shortage see R. Chambers, *Domestic Annals of Scotland* (London, 1861), III, 332, and P. H. Brown, *Early Travellers*, p. 277.

29. I. F. Grant, *Economic History of Scotland* (London, 1934), p. 189.

30. *Register of the Privy Council of Scotland*, second series, I, lxxxviii; II, 227. In 1638, when the English Privy Council, with a view toward incorporating the monetary systems of the two kingdoms, asked the officers of the English mint to assay samples of Scottish coinage, the council was told that these Scottish "moneys, had they been coined in England, must have been broken as unlawful moneys." For a general discussion of the Scottish monetary problem during this period see R. W. Cochran-Patrick, *Records of the Coinage of Scotland* (Edinburgh, 1876), I, clxiv–cci.

31. Thomas Tucker, the Cromwellian commissioner of customs, reported that only a few royal burghs could be called towns at all; the others, in his opinion, were little more than villages. Tucker, *op. cit.*, p. 18. Edinburgh, the capital and by far the largest city of the kingdom, had, in 1635, about 1,500 dwellings owned or leased by about 5,000 persons. C. B. B. Watson, "List of Owners of Property in Edinburgh, 1635," *The Book of the Old Edinburgh Club*, XIII (1924), 93–145.

32. John Davidson and Alexander Gray, *The Scottish Staple at Veere* (London, 1909), pp. 17–18; Theodora K. Pagan, *The Convention of the Royal Burghs of Scotland* (Glasgow, 1926), pp. 150, 166–167.

33. R. K. Hannay and G. P. H. Watson, "The Building of the Parliament House," in *The Book of the Old Edinburgh Club*, XIII (1924), 1–78.

34. The docility of Edinburgh was owing largely to the fact that, while the crown made exorbitant financial demands upon the city, the city, in turn, could not support itself without the revenues derived from the presence there of certain government bodies like the Privy Council and the Court of Session. The mere threat to withdraw them was usually sufficient to bring the town council into line. See Marguerite Wood (ed.), *Extracts from the Records of the Burgh of Edinburgh, 1626–1641* (Edinburgh, 1936), p. xvii.

35. Cf. David Calderwood, *The Speach of the Kirk of Scotland to Her Beloved Children* (n.p., 1620), p. 5, and *The Altar of Damascus or the Paterns of the English Hierarchie, and Church-Policie Obtruded upon the Church of Scotland* (n.p., 1621), *passim*, as well as George Gillespie, *A Dispute against the English-popish Ceremonies Obtruded upon the Church of Scotland* (Edinburgh, 1637), Introduction.

36. A policy intended to limit the nobles' power had been initiated by James VI and I long before his accession to the English throne in 1603. See Maurice Lee, Jr., *John Maitland of Thirlestane and the Foundations of the Stewart Despotism in Scotland* (Princeton, N.J., 1959), pp. 295–298. Charles I simply carried on this policy with greater intensity after his father's death. Unfortunately for him, his lack of Scottish

political experience led him to alieniate the lairds and gentry whom James had tried to make into supporters of royal policy. See the petition entitled "Grievances of the Gentry" submitted to the convention of the Scottish estates on July 29, 1630, in *Acts of the Parliaments of Scotland*, V, 219.

37. These charges were first put forward in a booklet issued in the king's name and entitled *A Large Declaration Concerning the Late Tumults in Scotland* (London, 1639), pp. 6–10. Its author was Walter Balcanquhall, dean of Durham. The accusation was repeated in *Memoirs of Henry Guthry, Late Bishop of Dunkeld* (London, 1702), p. 20, and John Spalding, *The History of the Troubles and Memorable Transactions in Scotland and England, from 1624 to 1645* (Edinburgh, 1828), pp. 46–47.

38. Macray, *op. cit.*, I, 145. For an account of the Scottish Privy Council's actions during this period, see its *Register*, second series, VI, ix–xi.

39. The provost (mayor) and Town Council of Edinburgh had to be coerced into joining the antiservice-book faction. Their first efforts were directed toward suppressing the riots and carrying out the king's orders. *Register*, second series, VI, 513–516; J. Robertson and G. Grub (eds.), *J. Gordon's "History of Scots Affairs from 1637 to 1641"* (Aberdeen, 1841), I, 10. This, as the Earl of Rothes, a leading Covenanting noble, afterward pointed out, "made all to cry out and except against Edinburgh; distraction begane to increase in that citie, becaus the Magistrats had never shewne their dislyke of that book, as the rest of the countrie." J. Nairne and D. Laing (eds.), *John Leslie, Earl of Rothes, "A Relation of the Proceedings Concerning the Affairs of the Kirk of Scotland from August 1637 to July 1638"* (Edinburgh, 1830), p. 11. In the end, Sir John Hay, the provost and a leading member of the king's faction, fled the city "swearing never to come amongst them again." *Ibid.*, p. 21.

40. David Laing (ed.), *The Letters and Journals of Robert Baillie* (Edinburgh, 1841), I, 35. The ministers of Edinburgh had been particularly slow and reluctant to join in opposition against the king. See Thomas Craufurd, *History of the University of Edinburgh, from 1580 to 1616* (Edinburgh, 1808), p. 131; and Robertson and Grub, *op. cit.*, I, 17 n.

41. A list of names headed by those of leading nobles is contained in J. D. Ogilvie (ed.), *The National Petition, October 18, 1637* (Edinburgh, 1925). The various signatures provide us with an excellent sampling of the revolutionary leadership in its earlier stages.

42. The "bond" or "band" of manrent was an agreement entered into usually between lesser men and their great landholding neighbors for mutual protection in a society where the police power of the state was almost nonexistent. It should not be confused with the older feudal contract. See J. K. Hewison, " 'Bands' or Covenants in Scotland with a List of Extant Copies of the Scottish Covenants," *Proceedings of the Society of Antiquaries of Scotland*, fourth series, VI (1907–1908), 166–167; and Cosmo Innes (ed.), *The Black Book of Taymouth* (Edinburgh, 1855), pp. 162–172.

43. An Act of Revocation, passed in October 1625, had recalled to royal ownership all lands granted away by the crown during the two preceding reigns. Most of these were holdings in church property. This procedure was nothing new in Scottish history, since every sovereign upon his accession or upon reaching his majority usually did so. What was unusual in this case, however, was, first, the extensiveness of the measure, which reached back to 1542 and, second, the fact that Charles clearly intended to retain as much as he could of these holdings for the benefit of the church and the royal treasury. The result might have been a social revolution had the king not given way to public outcry in 1629 and permitted the repurchase of lands and tithe rights by their former owners. Even so, he aroused fear among all those affected; and these included lords, gentry, townsmen, and even the clergy. In other words, the important issue of church lands was one that touched the interests, not of a single entrepreneurial

class, but of all classes in various ways. The best account of this affair may be found in A. A. Cormack, *Teinds and Agriculture* (Oxford, 1930), pp. 99–121.

44. One of the first steps taken by the revolutionary Glasgow Assembly in 1638 was to restore the office of "ruling" or "lay" elder, which had fallen into disuse in the church. In this way, despite the opposition of some among the Scottish clergy who feared the intrusion of lay influences, the nobility and gentry assured themselves of some control in ecclesiastical affairs. See G. D. Henderson, *The Scottish Ruling Elder* (London, 1935), pp. 161–162, and Robertson and Grub, *op. cit.*, I, 121. Robert Baillie has left us a record of the bitter opposition offered by at least one Covenanting minister to the reintroduction of the office of ruling elder into the church. Laing, *op. cit.*, I, 104.

45. See note 18.

7

PROTESTANTISM AND CAPITALISM IN PRE-REVOLUTIONARY ENGLAND

Charles and Katherine George

It has become a truism of historical thought that some degree or kind of positive relationship exists between the ideology of Protestantism and the psychology of early capitalists.[1] Statements of the nature of this relationship have varied, however, and have been often based upon inadequate sampling of the relevant literature or inexact analysis of Protestant social theory.

The purpose of this paper is to survey the compatibility, or the lack of it, between an important segment of Protestant opinion and the practices and ideas of nascent capitalism. The material in question consists of the writings and preachments produced by English Protestant divines in the seven decades between 1570 and 1640. Within these temporal limitations the literature has been intensively analyzed and has been constantly considered in the differing perspectives of Roman Catholic thought and the teachings of the other Protestant schools.

Because so much emphasis has been placed in this area of speculation upon the presumed distinction in spirit between Lutheran Protestantism and Calvinist Protestantism, the former being said to have maintained for the most part the framework of a traditionalist social theory while the latter alone afforded a suitable ethic for early capitalism, it should be noted at the outset that, theologically speaking, the literature of English Protestantism in this period is overwhelmingly Calvinist. Differing degrees may be no doubt detected in the intensity of this Calvinism, and the so-called Puritans may be perhaps defined as a group of particularly consistent and dedicated adherents of Calvinist theology, but those individ-

Reprinted from Church History, *XXVII* (December 1958), 351–372.

ual English Protestants who in the years involved can be cited as non- or anti-Calvinist constitute an extreme minority of the whole. Hence whatever the nature of the social ethic which emerges from these writings, it is assuredly a Calvinist rather than a Lutheran social ethic.

The theological context of the problem we are pursuing—the problem of the relationship in English life and thought between capitalism and Protestantism—is a very broad and historically deep one: it is no less than that primary tendency in the sophisticated religions to assume that the twin objects of human anxiety and entreaty—salvation in terms of immortal life on the one hand, and success in terms of mortal life on the other—are altogether mutually exclusive or that at least a state of permanent tension or antagonism exists between them. In the formulation of this dichotomy one would appear to be dealing with a well-nigh universal ingredient of the religious mentality which encompasses the whole mechanism of sacrifice and which, even in the historical phases of its development, exhibits no simple dependence upon time, place, or social circumstance. Both Buddha, the prince, and Christ, the carpenter, reject the pomp and circumstance and the vanity of the world. Because of the nature of its social origins, however, Gospel Christianity does afford an especially pointed statement of the concept which, with reference to the glory of eternity, penalizes the rich and powerful in the world of time and rewards the poor and humble—there is, in short, the initial assertion at the least of a straightforwardly subversive doctrine that the first in the City of Man shall be last in the City of God. And throughout the history of Christianity a basic element in its theory tends to be this assumption of the existence of a negative correlation between social triumph in the one realm and spiritual triumph in the other.

Yet this is only one side of the story, for compromises with the human drive for worldly success have assuredly been effected in Christianity. Concessions to material viewpoints and worldly desires are evident, indeed, from the miracles of Christ (whose principal focus is the preservation of bodily life and health) through the long history (charted by Troeltsch and others) of doctrinal adjustment to the social *status quo* and to the demands of European ruling groups for religious support and confirmation. Thus there is no area in Christianity to which one can turn where both these conceptual elements—both the rejection of worldly goals and the acceptance and defense of them—are not present in some combination of relative rank and emphasis. Despite their evident opposition, neither pole of the antithesis is ever completely eliminated.

The Roman Catholic solution to this ideological tension in Christianity has been the construction of a double standard of morality by means of which the two emphases are separated to a large extent and placed in hierarchical relationship to each other: one emphasis becomes part of the way of life of the saint—the saintly cleric typically—who is indubitably heaven-bound; while the other becomes part of the way of life of the ordinary Christian who, if he does eventually reach heaven, will probably do so only after a further period of purgatorial trial and training. Those few who endeavor to follow the classic course set by the upper level of Roman Catholic morality are expected to abandon material ambitions in a thoroughgoing fashion—to the extreme limit ideally of which human nature is capable. The triple monastic vow of poverty, obedience, and chastity signalized this wholesale turning from worldly wealth and power which is felt to be essential for the truly dedicated soul. In the Roman Catholic drama of sanctity, world rejection and self-abnegation are primary and absolute essentials. The traditions of asceticism venture to attack, indeed, that ultimate desideratum of the individual—the comfort and soundness of the body, and even its survival. Thus the saint is left at last, and barely left, with but one tiny corner of the world to stand upon —his life. The greatest part of his interest and joy has presumably already moved to heaven.

No such extreme otherworldliness was possible, however, for the vast majority of Christians, if the work of the world were to be done and if society and even the church itself were to continue. And for them therefore another regimen was established which was much more relaxed and lenient in regard to material interests. The standards of the lower level of Roman Catholic morality occasionally become such, indeed, as almost to approximate to those of some primitive cult, the principal business of whose deity is to protect the health, support the battles, and promote the economic and social advancement of its adherents. But even where the lapse from spirituality was not so profound as this, great concessions were made on all fronts to the material desires of men for worldly success.[2]

Practices of physical asceticism were not expected, marriage was permitted, and the accouterments of worldly status which the society viewed as legitimate were religiously sanctioned. There was more than moral allowance; there was active, positive spiritual hallowing of worldly success. The quality of excess was taken from wealth, the quality of presumption from power, if certain minimum religiously sponsored rules regarding acquisition and use were observed. What this second level of morality amounted to in practice then was that the way of the worldly—in terms, that is, of the proprieties of worldliness at the time—was made acceptable, though not in any sense ideal, as a Christian way of life through acknowledgment by the worldly of the institutional supremacy and spiritual leadership of the visible church.

The theoretical latitude for Roman Catholicism's support of worldly institutions is, therefore, very wide. There are historical reasons, but there is no logical reason, for example, why Roman Catholicism could not have provided as stanch a defense for the ideology and practices of a capitalistic and bourgeois society as it did in fact provide for the ideology and practices of a feudal and aristocratic one. But the double standard was so profoundly rooted in Roman Catholic doctrine that any life in the world, whatever its nature or function, was bound to be viewed as of second quality in comparison to the life of church and cloister. The irony of the situation was, moreover, that sanctity, rather than being, as a consequence of the scorn of worldly circumstance, more readily available, in the Gospel pattern, to the poor and humble in society, came rather to be, in the centuries of Roman Catholic dominance at least, a virtual monopoly of those fortunately born few who could afford to reject the world and desert its responsibilities.[3]

Protestantism initially, consistently, and in all its forms undertook as a primary task the demolition of this Roman Catholic barrier between the two levels of morality. Thus the English Protestant of the period we are considering finds himself to be part of a general stream of Protestantism in his constant contention that there are not two ways to go to God but only one and that this one must lead directly from earth to heaven. The English Protestant, again like Protestants as a whole, endeavors to solve the tension between Christian spirituality and materialism by cutting off both of the extremes of the double solution characteristic of Roman Catholicism and then proceeding to occupy a single intermediate position. Relative to Roman Catholicism, there is both a materializing of the spiritual and a spiritualizing of the material. Physical asceticism in all its forms is abandoned. More important, the ordinary domiciles and the usual occupations of the world are not to be fled or eschewed in the effort to achieve the utmost reaches of spiritual fulfillment. The intensest forms of religious experience, instead of being isolated in monastic cells, are to be brought into the housewife's kitchen, the carpenter's shop, the merchant's countinghouse, and the magistrate's palace.

I

Instead of distinguishing, as did the Roman Catholic, between two levels of living in the world, one which rejects and the other which accepts it and its limitations, the typical English Protestant distinguishes between the two aspects in which the world may be viewed: its natural soundness on the one hand, and its corruption (in a sense "unnatural") on the other. Thus Perkins, the greatest theologian English Protestantism produced, asks:

> . . . if every man . . . must shewe himselfe to be a pilgrime and stranger in this world . . . is it not a good state of life, for a man to contemne the world, and all things in it, and to betake himself to perpetuall beggarie, and voluntarie poverty?

And he answers:

The world in Scripture is taken divers ways: first, for the corruptions and sinnes in the world: and these must be contemned by all meanes possible. . . . Secondly, for temporall blessings, as money, Lands, wealth, sustenance, and such like outward things, as concerne the necessarie or convenient maintenance of this naturall life. And in this sense, the world is not to be contemned, for in themselves, these earthly things are the good gifts of God, which no man can simply contemne, without injurie to God's disposing hand and providence, who both ordained them for natural life.[4]

There are many similar and some even more emphatic passages in this literature, in which the believer is enjoined to look upon the world in terms of its temporal blessings as essentially good and apt for the service of the most Christian man, provided, of course, that he uses it aright. John Dod remarks that "all manner of goods and possessions are for the service of life, either to be for the necessary use, and reliefe thereof, or as ornaments and delights unto it, to make it the more comfortable." [5] "Of gifts temporal," Lancelot Andrewes states, "the heathen have doubted whether they were good, to wit, riches, honour, etc., but the Christians are resolved that they are good." [6] Even the sins and corruptions of the world are not in the world as such, the English Protestant asserts, but arise instead from man's wrongful use of the world. Richard Sibbes makes this point:

. . . wee must know it is not the *world* simply that draws our heart from God and goodnesse, but the *love* of the world; worldly things are good in themselves and given to sweeten our passage to Heaven; they sweeten the profession of Religion; therefore bring not a false report upon the world, it is thy falseness that makes it hurtfull, in loving it so much. Use it as a servant all thy dayes, and not as a Master, and thou maiest have comfort therein.[7]

Not the world, then, but man's misuse of it is the evil to be feared. English Protestantism, however, was fully as pessimistic as any branch of Christianity regarding the sinfulness of man and his consequent inability to use the world as God meant it to be used or to avoid immoderate love of worldly things. The initial presumption of the goodness of the world, in that it is the creation of a good God, becomes nonetheless in this literature therefore the basis for a far greater proportional emphasis on the danger of too much involvement in or too much dependence on it. The same Sibbes who has spoken above of worldly things as being "good in themselves and given to sweeten our passage to Heaven" also enjoins the Christian to labor "to know the world, that thou maiest detest it . . . the more we know the vanities of the world, and the excellence of grace, the more we will love the one, and hate the other." [8]

The term "world" is undoubtedly more often employed by English
Protestant divines in the negative rather than the positive sense; that is, it
is more often, even in the absence of modifying adjectives or phrases, a
word which stands for inordinate love of the world or for those who are
afflicted with such love and whose condemnation is symbolized thereby
than a word which refers merely to the temporal blessings whose essential
goodness is assumed. Sibbes again explains this negative usage:

> . . . the ungodly . . . are called the world because they swagger in
> the world, as if they were upon their owne dunghill there. . . .
> they have their name from that they love. . . . Now carnall men
> are in love with the things of the world. . . . This world must be
> condemned.[9]

In another treatise Sibbes states succinctly that "wicked men are called
the world because they love it; and holy men are called heavenly because
they are carried in their affections and wills to heavenly things." [10]

There is certainly no complete escape in English Protestant literature,
therefore, from the ancient Christian tension between the pursuit of
worldly and of heavenly goals. One might even argue, indeed, that in the
analysis of the problem which these English Protestant spokesmen present, a solution is achieved which is very similar in basic logic to that
offered in Roman Catholic thought. For the distinction which is made in
English Protestantism between the world as evil and the world as good
depends in the long run upon the manner of man's life in the world, and
thus here likewise two levels of life may be said to exist: one of the saints
who use the world as a highroad to salvation and the other of the damned
who misuse the world that they may compound with committed sins their
original reprobation. Yet even when this elementary continuum between
the Roman Catholic and the English Protestant argument is acknowledged, there is still a difference, and, historically speaking at least, a very
significant difference in emphasis and interpretation between the two. For
the English Protestant saint, whatever the peculiar qualities of his approach to the world may be, is not in any way institutionally isolated
from it but lives his entire life finally and entirely in its midst. And assuredly also by the very fact that the English Protestant saint can be or,
rather, must be a saint while living in the world and being busy in its
tasks, that world and its activities acquire an additional guarantee and
advertisement of their positive qualities which Roman Catholic ideology
does not afford.

No more than Roman Catholic permissive acceptance does the positive
English Protestant sponsorship of the life of the world logically entail,
however, allegiance to or support of any specific political or economic
regime. One possesses at this point of the discussion only the possibility in
the newer as compared with the older theology of fuller and more inti-

mate integration between the interests and goals of faith and the interests and goals of whatever social system was recognized as legitimate in the time and place. The English Protestant divine of the period under survey intended this integration to mean, of course, the energetic penetration of the secular realm with what he considered to be Christian standards of conduct, yet, unconscious though he himself might be of the fact, the way was also opened more widely to the working of an opposite process: the adjustment instead of Christian standards to fit the standards of the world. It is the relatively greater flexibility of the English Protestant position which strikes one here as its particular characteristic. Since, unlike Roman Catholicism, English Protestant theology preserves no ecclesiastical or monastic area of fixed practice and idea, the faith is thrown, unreservedly, as it were, into the stream of time and change.

Despite the shifting quality of the logical ground they stood upon, the creators of the literature being analyzed did not hesitate to make pronouncements concerning specific social issues and policies, and, when they spoke, moreover, they did so always as if extracting their censures and commendations from God's own storehouse of eternal verities and from a clear conception on their part of the constitution of the good society. They wrote often and at length of wealth, for instance. Yet when one attempts to sum up what they had to say about wealth, its proper function in society or its place in the life of the Christian, one finds oneself confronted with contradictions, and, while certainty and absolutism characterize the manner of presentation, the term *flexibility* comes again to mind as most suited to the substance of the viewpoint which is presented. The English Protestant accepted wealth as the essence of worldly success, the foundation of honor and high place. Adams writes:

> Observe that Salomon in the donation of the left hand couples together Riches and Honour: as if these two were for the most part inseparable companions. . . . First Riches, and then Honour: for it is lightly found, so much Riches so much Honour; and reputation is measured by the Acre. . . . Riches are the staires whereby men climbe up into the height of dignitie; the fortification that defends it; the food it lives upon. . . .[11]

The English Protestant, then, recognized and had adjusted to the realities of his age—an age whose elite had come to be defined more by place and possession than by blood and military exploit.

In regard to the attitude toward wealth, the break between English Protestantism and the Roman Catholic tradition is partly here in the very acknowledgment of a changed society (though there is little consciousness that society in fact had changed). It is also to be found in English Protestantism's explicit acceptance of wealth, as of all other worldly conditions, as a feasible setting for the most strenuous spiritual life. "Now we tell you from him, whose title is Rich in mercy," Hall declares, "that ye may be at once rich and holy. . . . It is a true word of the sonne of Sirach which I would have you carie home with you, and write it as a fit Motto, in your counting-house. . . . Substance doth well in the hand, if there be not evill in the heart." [12] Andrewes, having observed that the blessed Abraham was "rich in cattell, in silver, and gold," assures the wealthy Christian that "one may be so rich and so use his riches together as they . . . no waies hinder but helpe forward his accompt with God. . . ." [13] John Downame likewise comments:

> . . . prosperitie is good when it is enjoyed by a faithful man, who being in Christ, hath recovered that right in all Gods blessings which we lost in Adam. . . . it is good when as it is used . . . for the advancement of Gods glorie . . . and the furthering of our owne salvation. And if any such enjoy prosperity and thus use it . . . it is to be accounted unto them Gods singular blessings, and as a temporall pledge of eternall happinesse.[14]

Passages of this sort do occur in the literature (though they are not numerous) which establish the point that it is possible for the child of God to be at once wealthy and saintly and which, taken by themselves, might appear even to affirm the existence of some positive correlation between prosperity and godliness. The least acquaintance with the intricacies of the English Protestant viewpoint, however, completely eliminates interpretation of it in such simple and materialistic terms. The blessings of the world, far from being seen as a reliable indicator of divine favor or the soundness of one's spiritual state, are universally asserted to be distributed indiscriminately by God to both the good and bad. There is, indeed, a very strong current of opinion (particularly strong in the so-called Puritan and hence most emphatically Calvinist segment thereof) which contends that by far the best for quality and the most for quantity of the gifts of the world fall to the share of the wicked rather than the virtuous. "For all outward happiness," Robert Bolton remarks, "are for speciall reasons, and by particular indulgence more often, and very plentifully in this world vouchsafed to the wicked and prophane." [15] Downame states the same:

> . . . doth not common experience teach us, that worldly prosperity is a step-mother to vertue, those being most destitute of it, who most abound in worldly things, and they most rich in spirituall grace, who are most wanting in them? [16]

The argument readily moves on from here, and wealth, so often linked with the wicked, becomes almost a wicked and certainly a dangerous entity itself, a web of temptation in which all but the spiritually strong are bound to be snared. And how few are spiritually strong! "Who seeth not,"

Adams writes, "that prosperitie encreaseth iniquitie; and where is more want, there is lesse wantonnesse?" [17]

Insofar as capitalism is defined as involving the conscious, rational, and continuous pursuit of wealth—and for whatever purpose—the English Protestantism of this period cannot therefore be other than unreservedly anticapitalistic.[18] A great deal of commentary in this literature, moreover, is specifically directed against those economic practices in late sixteenth- and early seventeenth-century England which embodied important elements in the development of modern capitalism. English Protestantism takes a decisive stand, for instance, against interest on money, or usury, and a chorus of complaint arises against "cruell inclosures," engrossing and monopoly practices in general, forestalling, high prices, high rents, rigged markets, secret contracts, "binding poore men to unreasonable covenants," taking of high fees, and against the loss of church livings to impropriators.[19] When English Protestant divines invoke that classic theologian's theme—the evil of the times—as frequently they do, their primary emphasis tends to be upon the presumed wealth-centered interest of their age. "Men can well endure to sit telling and taking money," Thomas Gataker observes, "and it were all day long . . . but to heare the word, but an houre . . . the most can hardly endure." [20] Such competition for wealth is altogether incompatible with competition for godliness and the life of grace.[21] Bolton thunders the warning:

> A Christian dare not . . . gaine by any unwarrantable meanes . . . and therefore in this griping and greedy age, in the highest noontide iniquitie . . . he doth not commonly come to that excesse . . . of temporall things, which many times worldlings with wider consciences easily and immeasurably engrosse.[22]

Yet inveigh against wealth and particularly against the pursuit of wealth though he may, the English Protestant divine never enshrines its opposite, poverty, in the Roman Catholic manner. Rather than seeing poverty as a social condition to be accepted and even cherished, for the sake of the opportunities for charity it may afford, the English Protestant tends to consider it as an evil to be questioned or even as a problem to be solved.[23] Where he finds social policies—he frequently cites some of the practices of nascent capitalism as being such—which unconscionably increase the numbers of the poor, he condemns them. Where he discovers "sturdy beggars" choosing poverty rather than the self-supporting labor they might obtain, he advocates punishment. In the case of the "truly poor," of course—widows, orphans, the handicapped, the sick, the aged—he urges, nay he commands, charity, but more as a duty which the community must perform than as an exercise in godliness for the heaven-striving soul. From the standpoint of the individual's search for salvation, furthermore, poverty, like wealth, is thought to be a state beset with hazards. "Both poverty and riches . . . have their temptations," John Robinson declares,[24] and all English Protestants agree that neither is properly to be sought by the Christian. English Protestantism's rejection of poverty as an ideal of life for the Christian is made particularly explicit in the course of its energetic repudiation of the total pattern of monasticism.

From the analysis of wealth and poverty as dangerous extremes one seems logically to emerge with a commendation for some status of economic moderation in between. And indeed Downame does observe that "the meane estate . . . preserveth us from forgetfulnesse of God, irreligion and profaneness, which accompanieth prosperity . . . and from impatiency, murmuring and repining against God, to which we are tempted in poverty and adversitie." [25] The usual assumption of English Protestantism is that the good Christian will occupy this "meane estate," in the sense at least that he may legitimately seek and will probably possess a suitable competence in this life: "God allwaies giveth for sustentation, though not for satietie," comments Arthur Dent.[26] Gouge assures the believer that "if thou get heavenly blessings, temporall things, so farre as they are needfull for thee, shall be cast in." [27] What constitutes this competence, however, is subject to a variety of interpretations. Hall explains:

> It is true there can be no certain proportion of our either having or desiring the goods of this world since the conditions of men are in a vast difference . . . and it is but just and lawfull for every man to affect so much as may be sufficient, not only for the necessity of his person, but for the decency of his estate.[28]

Any effort to state precisely at what economic point a man may or must consider his particular sufficiency to have been achieved is further discouraged by such observations as this from Robinson's writings upon the relativity of wealth and poverty:

> . . . he is a rich man, who wants no outward means, wherewith to maintain himself, and his, plentifully, in that state of life in which God hath set him, whether high, or low: and he poor on the contrary, to whom the proportion is wanting. And hence it comes to pass, that there are poor kings and rich cobblers. . . .[29]

The flexibility of thought, evident in these last passages, which makes possible for the English Protestant divine a relatively receptive attitude toward the possession of wealth in the world, is, in the last analysis, merely another corollary of the conviction that all worldly conditions have been determined and assigned by God's will and Providence and that it is the Christian's duty to live contentedly in the place in which he finds himself. The whole resistance to the ascetic tradition is rooted in this doctrine, after all, which emphasizes the absolute supremacy of the divine over the human will. He flies in the face of Providence and sins therefore who seeks the cross which is not given him, as equally he does who strives for the prosperity which God has not seen fit through Providence to bestow. The injunction to dependence on God's design for every man, significant though it is as a thesis in the English Protestantism we are considering, never becomes complete quietism, to be sure; yet on the other hand, it does serve effectively to spoil characterization of this literature in terms of activist sponsorship of institutions or practices in the world except as they are merely the established proprieties of the time. The Christian is encouraged by the great weight of the argument we have thus far surveyed to accept the universe, both in its personal and its social character, and not to change it.

The first general statement which can be made therefore about the connection between capitalism and the social theory of English Protestantism before 1640 is simply that English divines had accepted, in their own religious terms, of course, the new orientation toward worldliness and the one life in the world, which was also an aspect of the humanism of the Renaissance, and that they felt reasonably at home in a society in which wealth (still for the most part landed wealth) was becoming the acknowledged basis of power and prestige. They had, in short, decisively cut their moorings from the social bias and the dominant feudal and clerical philosophy of the Middle Ages. Likewise capitalism, whether as a system of ideas or a set of economic practices, participated in the same broad movement away from one and toward another pattern of thought and living. Protestantism and modern capitalism shared thus the same heritage of discontents and the same age of birth. Inevitably there were links, some of which have been noted in the process of this discussion. But on the basis of the analysis up to this point the association can hardly be stated in other than these tentative, general, and, from the standpoint of the religious ideology, relatively passive terms.

II

There is, however, a more aggressive aspect of English Protestant social theory to which adequate attention must be paid before attempting to sum up the exact nature of the relationship between capitalism and this body of religious literature. For it is in the doctrine of the calling that English Protestantism, like Protestantism in general, made its most significant contribution to a new view of society and of man's place in society. The doctrine in question concerns the particular rather than the general calling. Robert Sanderson makes the distinction:

> The Scriptures speak of two kinds of Vocations or Callings: the one
> . . . the General, and the other the Particular Calling. . . . the
> General Calling, is that wherewith God calleth us . . . to the faith.
> . . . Here is no difference in regard of Persons: but one Lord, one

Faith, one Baptism. . . . Our Particular Calling is that wherewith
God enableth us, and directeth us . . . on to some special course
and condition of life, wherein to employ our selves, and to exercise
the gifts he hath bestowed upon us. . . . the thing whereunto men
are thus called, is not one and the same to all, but differenced with
much variety according to the quality of particular persons. . . .[30]

Perkins, who wrote an entire treatise on vocations,[31] makes a further two-
fold distinction among particular callings. He marks out, on the one
hand, a category of personal callings, "such as be of the essence and foundation of any societie, without which, the societie cannot be"—in a family, the callings of husband and wife, parent and child, master and servant; in a commonwealth, the callings of magistrate and subject; and in
the church, the calling of the minister—and, on the other hand, those
callings "such as serve onely to the good . . . estate of a society"—the callings of husbandman, merchant, physician, lawyer, carpenter, or mason.[32]
Commentary on this second type of "particular callings" by English Protestant divines is abundant, lengthy, and very detailed and carries treatment of the subject well beyond anything attempted by either Luther or
Calvin as individual theologians.

The English Protestant divine assumes and proclaims the necessity of a
particular calling for every particular man, whether saint or reprobate. A
man's proper calling is determined by the Providence of God and is
matched by the possession of natural gifts appropriate to the tasks involved. Sanderson declares:

> . . . that is every man's Proper and right Calling, whereunto God
> calleth him. . . . When therefore we speak of the Choice of a Call-
> ing, you are not so to understand it, as if it were left free for us ever,
> to make our Choice where, and as we list. The Choice that is left
> us, is nothing but a conscionable Enquiry, which way God calleth
> us, and a conscionable Care to take that way.[33]

In addition to matching the talents of the individual who follows it, a
calling, to be suitable and legitimate, whether from the standpoint of natural or Christian law, must be socially approved as well. "A vocation or
calling," Perkins asserts, "is a certain kind of life, ordained and imposed
on man by God, for the common good." The whole moral, as distinct
from the spiritual, function of the calling is summed up, indeed, in this
fact of its social utility. Connecting and binding the members of society
together through an intricate network of interweaving services, the calling assures that the maintenance of each shall be dependent on work
oriented toward the benefit of all. With some emotion Sibbes invokes the
fruitful quality of the calling:

Let us then strive . . . to be fruitfull in our Places and Calling: for it is the greatest honour in this world, for God to dignifie us with such a condition, as to make us fruitfull. We must not bring forth fruit to our selves. . . . Honour, Riches, and the like, are but secondary things, arbitrary at Gods pleasure to cast in: but, to have an active heart fruitfull from this ground, that God hath planted us for this purpose, that we may doe good to mankind, this is an excellent consideration not to profane our calling.[34]

Since the whole moral function of the calling consists in its social utility, to pursue through the calling a nonsocial or a narrowly individual goal is to live immorally. English Protestant divines warn against the endeavor to gain personal profit or advantage by means of the calling. "And that common saying, *Every man for himselfe, and God for us all,*" Perkins remarks, "is wicked, and is directed against the end of every calling, or honest kind of life." [35] "They profane their lives and callings," the same theologian continues, "that imploy them to get honours, pleasures, profits, worldly commodities etc. for thus we live to another end than God hath appointed, and thus we serve our selves, and consequently neither God, nor man." [36] The man who wishes to live virtuously in his calling is specifically enjoined to avoid ambition, "a vice whereby any man thinking better of himselfe, then there is cause hee should, becomes malcontent with his particular calling and seekes for himselfe an higher place, and a better estate." [37] Hence constancy in the calling is assumed to be the only righteous course for most men in most circumstances, and change is allowed only when, because of a previous error in choice, a man's calling is clearly inappropriate to his capacities and greater service to society would result from a readjustment.[38]

While provisions regarding the moral function of the calling apply to all men, the spiritual function of the calling concerns, of course, only those few truly Christian and predestinate souls among them, since for them alone does the calling serve as a worldly arena for the demonstration of grace received and the proof of salvation promised. It is with these predestinate souls primarily in their view that our English Protestant sermonizers develop the calling as an aspect of the Christian life and assert its importance as the chief embodiment of a Christian's worldly, as distinct from his purely religious, duty. The religious duty and the duty of the calling are seen, in fact, to be inextricably intertwined. The calling becomes a kind, and an absolutely essential kind, of Christian worship. Perkins writes that "if a man be zealous for Christ, he must be zealous within the compasse of his calling; and not be zealous first, and then looke for a calling, but first looke for a calling, and then be zealous." [39] "Religion is no vocall profession," Sibbes asserts; "every man must have some calling or other, and in his generation, he must doe good. . . . We must serve God . . . in our life." [40]

In the voluminous literature of English Protestantism, made up, as it is, of contributions from so many individual minds, the full revolutionary character of the Protestant doctrine of the calling emerges with particular clarity and impact. It is not so much that any really new ingredient is added to the formulas originated by the great pioneers of Protestantism as that potentialities are more completely realized in the vast variety of English sermons. The extent of the break from the outlook of Roman Catholicism can hardly be overstated. To begin with, the English Protestant doctrine of the calling presents a concrete embodiment of the general Protestant rejection of the Roman Catholic double standard of morality. It does more than this, however, for it goes on to establish so strong an affirmation of the world and of the value of life in the world that the concepts of asceticism, deep-rooted though they are in the Christian tradition, cease almost entirely, in this area of English Protestant thought, to have any valid relevance.

Weber has summed up the Protestant (and particularly the Calvinistic Protestant) doctrine of the calling in terms of a concept of worldly asceticism. As we moved through the discussion of the calling in the literature under scrutiny, the Weberian interpretation came to appear less and less appropriate to the data we encountered. Much depends, to be sure, in these matters of historical analysis, upon the standpoint from which one makes one's judgments. Weber looked back on sixteenth- and seventeenth-century Protestantism from the standpoint of his own time—a time in which standards of life enjoyment had become established against the background of which these early Protestant ideas appeared dour and self-denying. But the much more suitable procedure, historically speaking, is to attempt first to see an idea in the context of its own time and secondly against the background of the past from which it emerged. When the English Protestant doctrine of the calling is viewed thus, its essentially affirmative and nonascetic nature becomes apparent.

There is a definite shift in this literature, for example, from the Roman Catholic emphasis on the penal quality of labor, and especially of manual labor, to a contrary emphasis on its positive, creative, and enjoyable aspects. Occasional references to the penal function of work are found in English Protestant writings, of course, and God's judgment on Adam in his fall is seen to provide the basis for the painfulness of toil. Yet the primary sanction for human labor as such is found, not in the fact that Adam sinned, but in the prior fact that he tended a garden in Paradise. Hall observes:

> Paradise served not onely to feed his Adam's senses, but to exercise his hands. If happiness consisted in doing nothing, man had not

beene employed; All his delights could not have made him happy in an idle life. Man therefore is no sooner made, than he is set to worke: neither greatnesse, nor perfection can priviledge a folded hand; he must labor, because he was happy; how much more wee that wee may be? [41]

In addition, though the Christian is warned of the iniquity of using the calling as a means for securing material reward, he is nonetheless assured that in connection with, if not as a consequence of, the diligent and God-fearing conduct of a proper calling, material reward may be confidently expected. The Christian, as we have previously noted, is urged to be confident of the provision by God of a sufficiency to meet his worldly needs, and he is expected to obtain this sufficiency through following his calling. "In every honest vocation," Dod declares, "wherein a man shall diligently and faithfully imploy himselfe there is aboundance." [42] "If a man," Preston concurs, "would be content . . . to use those talents that God hath given him, not for his owne, but for his Masters advantage; I say, if he would doe this, he shoulde finde God All-Sufficient." [43]

The comfortableness of this English Protestant doctrine of the calling is further enhanced by the fact that relaxation, rest, and recreation are thought to be essential parts of the Christian's regimen of life. The Sabbath, incidentally, though it is seen as a day of rest, is never positively asserted in these writings to be part of the recreational allowance. What is meant by recreation is other periods of time in the regular workday week which are devoted to approved kinds of relaxation of mind and body. Moderation is urged in the enjoyment of lawful recreation, and there is an expected subordination of means to ends in the entire doctrine: just as the calling is a means subordinated to the end of total godly living, so recreation is a means subordinated to the end of the calling. "And therefore . . . hee God admitteth lawful recreation," Perkins notes, "because it is a necessarie meanes to refresh either bodie or minde, that wee the better doe the duties which pertaine unto us." [44] That the antiascetic temper of English Protestantism is central to the support of recreation is evident, however, in this passage from the works of Adams:

They are too rigid and austere, that forbid lawfull delights: let no Teacher make the way to heaven more thorny, than God himselfe made it, and meant it. . . . I cannot beleeve, that God will ever give a Papist thankes for whipping himselfe. Our lawfull pleasures are his pleasures. . . . That is a superstitious worship which makes the worshippers miserable. God delights not in our blood, but when the witnesse of his glory calles for it. The world hath wages enough to vex us, we need not to be our owne tormentors. It is no credit to a man's holinesse that he condemns all recreation. Let me looke to please God, and then know that he hath made the world to serve me.[45]

There is a second general aspect of the English Protestant doctrine of the calling which involves a sharp departure from Roman Catholic social theory, in its Thomistic formulation particularly.[46] We are referring here to the considerable modification by English Protestant divines of the social hierarchy of callings accepted and confirmed in the earlier creed and to their absolute denial of the existence of any spiritual hierarchy whatever. In regard to the first point—the social hierarchy of callings—the philosophy of Thomistic Catholicism had perpetuated the invidious distinction between mental and manual toil or the liberal and servile arts which the idealist philosophies of antiquity had championed. Aristotle and St. Thomas Aquinas had joined in the common concept which glorified the intellectual and contemplative way of life (and secondarily the governing or administrative role, whether in state or church) and assumed that the ordinary productive labors of the world would be performed by inferior natures. It is an extremely significant fact therefore that in this English Protestant literature the calling is linked so frequently to labor with the hands or, more accurately perhaps, that mental and manual toil are so frequently—indeed, so consistently—equated in the common dignity of the calling. The metaphors, the examples, the images, employed in English Protestant discussion of the necessity of work are drawn almost entirely from the terms and tasks associated with labor with the hands. The sheep to be watched, the vineyard or the garden to be cared for, the sweat that drops from the diligent worker's brow—these are the references which one meets repeatedly. "We must then," Robinson typically asserts, "mingle our own sweat with faith to make a sweet odour withal to God." [47]

The English Protestant minister exhibits little tendency to deny or even seriously to modify the social hierarchy of callings as his time conceived it; he is not, in the period we are studying at least, a leveler in any overt sense. But what he does maintain (as neither Aristotle nor St. Thomas Aquinas maintains it) is the moral equivalence of all legitimate callings in that all, in being necessary to society, are in a basic sense equally necessary and that all, in serving a utilitarian function in society, are in a basic sense equally useful. "God hath so distributed the variety of his gifts with singular wisdom," Sanderson observes, "that there is no man so mean, but his service may be useful to the greatest: nor any man so eminent but he may sometimes stand in need of the meanest of his brethren. . . ." [48] Employing the typical metaphor of the husbandman, Adams likewise reduces the differences of rank and function in society to this same essential equality of service:

> Every one thinkes himselfe Gods sonne: then heare this voyce, Goe my sonne. You have all your Vineyards to goe to. Magistrates Goe to the bench to execute judgement and justice. Ministers Goe to the Temple, to preach, to pray, to doe the workes of Evangelists. People Goe to your callings, that you may eate the labours of your owne hands. . . . every man to his profession, according to that station, wherein God hath disposed us. . . . The Incitation gives way to the Injunction, Worke.[49]

This equality of callings in regard to their moral aspect is perhaps more a matter of implication than of direct statement in these writings and, in justice to the full complexity of the argument, should probably be defined as a relative departure from the classical and medieval viewpoint rather than as an absolute position in itself. The equality of callings in regard to their spiritual aspect, however—their relationship, that is, to the salvation of the soul—is stated so often and so emphatically by English Protestant divines that it emerges from their sermons as one in a small company of entirely unequivocal concepts. The linkage to fundamental Protestantism is close, of course, since we are dealing here with a particular application of the general Protestant insistence that salvation, whose mark is inward, cannot be limited or affected by any external condition of life or livelihood. To equate this viewpoint with complete denial of the value of works in the pursuit of salvation is, however, greatly to misrepresent the issue. Perkins specifically states that there will surely be at the Day of Judgment a "giving and rendring to every man according to his workes" and that not the least of these works are those of a man's calling.[50] What the spokesmen of English Protestantism do assert again and yet again is that this evaluation of the work of the calling depends not at all upon the kind of calling involved but altogether instead upon the manner in which its duties, whatever they may be, are conducted and fulfilled. Thus Perkins declares:

> Now the works of every calling, when they are performed in an holy manner, are done in faith and obedience and serve notably for Gods glory, be the calling never so base. . . . The meannesse of the calling, doth not abase the goodnesse of the worke: for God looketh not at the excellence of the worke, but at the heart of the worker. And the action of a sheepheard in keeping sheep, performed as I have said, in his kind, is as good a worke before God, as is the action of a Judge, in giving sentence, or of a Magistrate in ruling, or a Minister in preaching.[51]

Perkins hammers the viewpoint home with an even more dramatic illustration:

Now if we compare worke to worke, there is a difference betwixt washing of dishes, and preaching the word of God; but as touching to please God none at all: For neither that nor this pleaseth God, but as farre forth as God hath chosen a Man, and hath put his spirit in him, and purified his heart by faith and trust in Christ. As the scriptures call him carnall which is not renewed by the spirit and borne againe in Christs flesh, and all his workes likewise . . . whatsoever hee doth, though they seem spirituall and after the law of God never so much: So contrariwise he is spirituall which is renewed in Christ, and al his workes which spring from faith seeme they never so grosse . . . yea deedes of matrimonie are pure and spirituall . . . and whatsoever is done within the lawes of God though it bee wrought by the body, as the wipings of shoes and such like, howsoever grosse they appear outwardly, yet are they sanctified.[52]

Hall has much the same to say:

The homeliest service that we doe in an honest calling, though it be but to plow, or digge, if done in obedience, and conscience of God's Comandement, is crowned with an ample reward; whereas the best workes for their kinde (preaching, praying, offering Evangelicall sacrifices) if without respect of Gods injunction and glory, are loaded with curses. God loveth adverbs; and cares not how good, but how well.[53]

Since the validity of the parable of the widow's mite is never entirely ignored and never denied in any Christian doctrine concerning the spiritual value of works, it can perhaps be argued that this English Protestant emphasis on the inward rather than the outward quality of a task is present, by implication at least, in Thomistic Catholicism too. But to argue thus is merely to state that all forms of Christianity are alike Christian in that they all contain the fundamental elements of Christianity, self-contradictory though these elements may often be. It is certainly true that from one standpoint Roman Catholicism and Protestantism may both be seen as being joined in a common continuum of Christian ideas, but it is equally true that from another standpoint significant differences of approach and interpretation may be observed. One of the most important and sharply defined of these differences, moreover, is clearly existent here in the contrast between the English Protestant and the Thomistic Catholic position on the spiritual value of works. On the one side we have the resolute assertion of the spiritual equality of all works qua works, and on the other side the tendency to divide works into categories of more or less meritorious, first on the basis of the hierarchy of the double standard of morality as more or less ascetic, and secondly on the basis of the hierarchy of a feudal world, as more or less worthy, dignified, or involved with the rule of others, some of the merit for whose virtuous actions accrues, in this often highly mathematical system, to the original source of guidance. Thus, while in the writings of St. Thomas Aquinas we have found no single passage to match those most recently quoted above from Perkins and Hall, which proclaim the total indifference in regard to good works of all external considerations of dignity or kind, neither have we found in the writings of English Protestantism a statement to match the Angelic Doctor's declaration, contained in his *De Regimine Principum,* that the king who rules well over his subjects deserves and will receive a higher reward in heaven than any subject who simply lives well under his king.[54]

In relationship to the doctrinal past from which he emerges, therefore, the English Protestant divine can confidently be said to celebrate work in the calling, as an aspect of Christian life, in a peculiarly wholesale and emphatic manner. His viewpoint is not wholly new, of course. Elements of it occur in the Gospels especially, in the moralizings of sectarian preachers on the fringes of medieval Roman Catholic thought, and even in the rules of established monasticism. What is original in English Protestantism, however, is the intensity and frequency of the sermons on the worth of work and the unhesitating application of these ideals to all social levels and all occupational groupings in English society. It is one thing to commend with condescension the godly labor of the serf or poor monk whose efforts keep alive the organic whole, feeding the higher organs of mind and might for their tasks of leadership and rectitude, or to advocate labor as a penance for the spirit of the proud; it is quite another thing to make work in a calling the *summum bonum* of the human spirit's striving for fulfillment in the world: the "categorical imperative" of priest or preacher as well as congregation, of ruler as well as ruled, of rich as well as poor.

Recognizing the significance in Protestant social theory of the doctrine of the calling, Weber has assigned to it the principal role in establishing a mutually sustaining connection between the Protestant ethos and the spirit of capitalism. Though our findings certainly coincide with the Weberian hypothesis in its emphasis on the importance of the doctrine of the calling, they do not support any interpretation of this doctrine as capitalistic in nature or direction. Weber himself defines the spirit of capitalism as consisting essentially in the rational pursuit of profit. What is farthest from the English Protestant doctrine of the calling, what is specifically contrary to it, in fact, is this very rational pursuit of profit. The Christian pursues nothing in the calling except, through the proper performance of the duties it involves, the service of God and his fellow man. Even the Christian's simple maintenance (which surely is to be socially and economically distinguished from profit, that excess of reward beyond maintenance or immediate expense)—even the Christian's simple maintenance is to be seen as an incidental consequence of diligence in the calling rather than as an object of endeavor. Profit entails enriching, furthermore—an increase of wealth in the hands of the person undertaking the profitable enterprise. The English Protestant divine, as we have seen, attacks from many angles any orientation of life toward the increase of wealth. Through exhortations to constancy in the calling and other related arguments, he encourages and sponsors, just as does his Roman Catholic forebear, a stable rather than a mobile society. And the mobility which he does allow to individuals finds its basis, not in the rational pursuit of profit by these individuals, but in the occasional readjustments attendant upon society's need for the most efficient service from all its members.

That we have found little in the English Protestant doctrine of the calling which justifies the application of the label "capitalistic" to it is not to deny or diminish the extent of the break which this doctrine represents from the social theory of medieval Roman Catholicism. In this doctrine of the calling, which is in its essence broadly Protestant, as much Lutheran as Calvinist, we find as in no other single concept perhaps the ideological watershed between the ancient medieval and the modern mind. To link it particularly to capitalism, which is merely one aspect of modernity, is to limit and weaken rather than to strengthen its real potentiality. In the face of certain social pressures, in the hands of certain groups, this doctrine was capable no doubt of acquiring a capitalistic coloration, but as we meet it here in these English Protestant pronouncements in the late sixteenth and early seventeenth centuries, its scope is much greater and its reach is socially much more profound—as a viewpoint whose primary focus is not business activity but productive toil, it is not so much a bourgeois as an antifeudal, not so much a capitalistic as an industrial, ethic.

NOTES

1. For an introduction to the problems involved see especially Ernst Troeltsch, *The Social Teaching of the Christian Churches*, 2 vols. (New York, 1931); Max Weber, *The Protestant Ethic and the Spirit of Capitalism* (London, 1930); Lujo Brentano, *Die Anfänge des modernen Kapitalismus* (Munich, 1916); R. H. Tawney, *Religion and the Rise of Capitalism* (London and New York, 1926); the essays of Talcott Parsons, for which see the bibliography in *Essays in Sociological Theory*, rev. ed. (Glencoe, Ill. 1954); W. S. Hudson, "Puritanism and the Spirit of Capitalism," *Church History*, XVIII (1949); H. G. Wood, "Puritanism and Capitalism," *The Congregational Quarterly* (April 1951); and the bibliographical essay by Tawney in *The Times Literary Supplement*, January 6, 1956.

2. See Sylvia L. Thrupp, *The Merchant Class of Medieval London* (Chicago, 1948), *passim*, for an insight into the extraordinarily independent spheres of religious and secular life in medieval London, which left the parish clergy almost completely isolated from the merchant and artisan classes. In the view of the fifteenth-century London merchant, the clergy existed to operate the traditional mechanisms of the religious es-

tablishment; they were not expected to preach against unethical practices or to supervise right conduct in the business community (even though the merchants were probably aware that in the Thomistic scheme of things their total way of life was to some degree spiritually suspect). This is an important aspect of the "double standard" of Roman Catholic morality. The function of the clergy vis-à-vis the business community in fifteenth-century London more nearly resembles that of nineteenth-century London than it does that of Reformation London. For in Reformation London perhaps the most remarkable feature of merchant and artisan life was its penetration by the ideals of the Protestant pulpit. It is this hold on the city (and country) elite which is the great —if temporary—triumph of Protestant ideology.

3. See Katherine and C. H. George, "Roman Catholic Sainthood and Social Status," *The Journal of Religion* (April 1955).

4. William Perkins, *The Workes*, 3 vols. (London, 1612–1613), III, 102–103.

5. John Dod, *A Plaine and Familiar Exposition . . . of the Proverbs of Salomon* (London, 1609), p. 20.

6. Lancelot Andrewes, *Works*, 11 vols. (Oxford, 1841–1854), VIII, 314–315.

7. Richard Sibbes, *The Saints Cordials* (London, 1637), pp. 187–188.

8. *Ibid.*, pp. 188–189.

9. *Ibid.*, pp. 100–101.

10. Sibbes, *Beames of Divine Light* (London, 1639), p. 15.

11. Thomas Adams, *The Works* (London, 1629), pp. 872–873.

12. Joseph Hall, *The Works*, 4 vols. (Oxford, 1863), I, 716.

13. Andrewes, *XCVI Sermons* (London, 1629), p. 315.

14. John Downame, *The Christian Warfare* (London, 1633), p. 369.

15. Robert Bolton, *The Workes*, 4 vols. (London, 1631–1644), IV, 56.

16. Downame, *op. cit.*, pp. 557–558.

17. Adams, *The Works*, p. 1147.

18. See C. H. George, "English Calvinist Opinion on Usury, 1600–1640," *Journal of the History of Ideas*, XVIII, No. 4 (October 1957).

19. See John Donne, "LXXX Sermons," in *The Works*, 6 vols. (London, 1839), III, 217; Hall, *Works*, I, 717; IV, 786–790; Arthur Dent, *The Plaine Mans Path-way to Heaven . . .* (London, 1601), pp. 200–205; and Christopher Hill, *Economic Problems of the Church* (Oxford, 1956), for a definitive discussion of the complicated economic abuses relating to the church.

20. Thomas Gataker, *Certaine Sermons . . .* (London, 1937), p. 144.

21. *Ibid.*, pp. 141–147.

22. Bolton, *Workes*, IV, 283–284.

23. Cf. Christopher Hill, "Puritans and the Poor," *Past and Present* (November 1952), and V. Kiernan on the same subject, *Past and Present* (February 1953).

24. John Robinson, *Works*, 3 vols. (London, 1851), I, 125.

25. Downame, *op. cit.*, pp. 375–376.

26. Dent, *op. cit.*, p. 116.

27. William Gouge, *A Guide to Goe to God . . .* (London, 1626), p. 30.

28. Hall, *Works*, IV, 17.

29. Robinson, *op. cit.*, I, 122.

30. Robert Sanderson, *XXXVI Sermons* (London, 1689), p. 205.

31. Perkins, *op. cit.*, Vol. I.

32. Perkins, *op. cit.*, Dedicatory Preface.

33. Sanderson, *op. cit.*, p. 215.

34. Sibbes, *Bowels Opened . . .* (London, 1639), pp. 17–18.

35. Perkins, *Works*, I, 750.

36. *Ibid.*, p. 757.

37. *Ibid.,* p. 773.

38. Bolton, *op. cit.,* p. 48.

39. Perkins, *Workes,* I, 194.

40. Sibbes, *Beames of Divine Light,* p. 184.

41. Hall, *Works,* II, 836.

42. Dod, *op. cit.,* p. 122.

43. John Preston, *The New Covenant* . . . (London, 1630), p. 178.

44. Perkins, *Workes,* I, 774.

45. Adams, *op. cit.,* p. 1130.

46. St. Thomas Aquinas has served throughout this study as the particular point of reference for our summations of the social theory of medieval Roman Catholicism. In the rich literature of controversy and commentary surrounding the Angelic Doctor, viewpoints undoubtedly exist which differ from his and which in some instances may approach more nearly to the viewpoints of the Protestant writers we are analyzing. But in the light of Roman Catholicism's own long and often avowed acknowledgment of the pre-eminence in the Church of St. Thomas and the structure of doctrine he erected, one is surely justified in employing him as the spokesman par excellence of the Roman Catholic position for the period with which we are concerned. It is in his works, moreover, that one finds most fully developed that tension between Christian philosophy and an idealized feudal society which constitutes the basis, and, in one sense, the whole essence of the difference between Roman Catholic and Protestant social theory.

47. Robinson, *op. cit.,* I, 116.

48. Sanderson, *op. cit.,* p. 56.

49. Adams, *op. cit.,* p. 419.

50. Perkins, *op. cit.,* I, 777.

51. *Ibid.,* p. 758.

52. *Ibid.,* p. 391.

53. Joseph Hall, *Holy Observations* (London, 1607), p. 137.

54. See Katherine Archibald (George), "The Concept of Social Hierarchy in the Writings of St. Thomas Aquinas," *Historian,* XII (1949), 50.

8

CALVINISM AND LAW

David Little

Max Weber was fascinated by the problem of order. That problem stimulated him to investigate not only the various ways in which societies structured their institutions and designed centers of authority. He also examined the process by which a pattern of social order became "significant" or "legitimate" in the hearts and minds of "whole groups of men." Accordingly, Weber was unwilling to dissociate normative patterns of belief and action from the actual elaboration of institutional arrangements. For him the problem of order was at once a matter or religious-moral commitment and a matter of organizing political, familial, and economic relations.

More particularly, Weber wished to understand the process by which modern capitalism developed into a way of life, into a pattern of order that commanded *moral* loyalty. Assuming, as he did, that institutional developments are never self-authenticating, but always rely on "higher" religious justifications, Weber set out to show that the leading characteristics of rational capitalism found religious warrant in English Puritanism. Correspondingly, he claimed that "traditionalistic" social patterns (whether "patrimonial" or otherwise) were deeply opposed to rational capitalism and thus rested on religious-moral foundations quite contrary to those of Puritanism. Weber, of course, thought of Anglicanism and its aristocratic social bias in just these terms.

In other words, Weber's argument in *The Protestant Ethic and the Spirit of Capitalism* depends on three propositions being true:

1. "Rational capitalism" constitutes a recognizable "way of life," with its own inherent institutional and normative characteristics—a way of life that conflicts with the equally recognizable patterns of "traditionalism";

2. England of the seventeenth century was the setting for at least the beginnings of a struggle between these two types of social order;

From *David Little,* The New Order and Old England (*New York: Harper & Row, 1967*).

3. Puritanism and Anglicanism can be shown to polarize meaningfully along the lines of this conflict and to have legitimated respectively the two types of order on the basis of distinctive religious presuppositions.

So far as the first two propositions are concerned, we have argued in this study that a part of the radical social tensions of late sixteenth- and early seventeenth-century England involves a conflict between rudimentary "rational capitalism" and "traditionalistic" economic organization. Throughout, we have taken the category of *differentiation* to be central. According to Weber, rational capitalism is distinguished, above all, by modes of calculation and behavior that are specifically and systematically "oriented, by deliberate planning, to economic ends." This means that the market becomes relatively free of outside control. Rational economic activity, in becoming more autonomous, encourages private or voluntary enterprise on the universalistic basis of "salable services" or functional capabilities. Preferential treatment, whether as the result of political favoritism or customary privilege, is minimized. In fact, severe limitations are placed upon the opportunities for economic interference permitted the political-legal agencies. In Rheinstein's words, "Modern capitalism requires a legal system which guarantees . . . freedom from arbitrary, unpredictable government interference."

Naturally we have here and there emphasized what Weber knew very well: that rational capitalism did not come into its own in any unmistakable way until the nineteenth century. However, our analysis of certain early seventeenth-century decisions in corporation law—decisions like *Davenant* v. *Hurdis, Darcy* v. *Allen, Tailors of Ipswich*—revealed a remarkable foreshadowing of the characteristics of rational capitalism. Not only did Coke and his colleagues greatly circumscribe the economic power of the crown (*Prince's Case* and *Darcy* v. *Allen;* even more significantly they overturned long-standing forms of industrial regulation, such as guild monopolies (*Davenport* v. *Hurdis* and *Tailors of Ipswich*) and statutory regulations (*Telley's Case*). Indeed, the Statute of Monopolies of 1624 boldly instituted Coke's unhistorical judgment that "monopolies in times past were ever without law, but never without friends."

All of this innovation contributed to the emancipation of industrial activity from the fetters of tradition and to the development of a few "rational" legal categories as general ground rules for business practice. The law of contract, the law of patents (contained within the 1624 Statute), as well, of course, as the law *against* all monopolies not specially provided for, are examples of these general ground rules. Of most interest to us is the set of appeals made—to "free voluntarism" in trade, to the opportunity for *anyone* to practice a trade, and so on.

At least against the background of the Middle Ages and the Age of the Tudors, what Coke determined in the field of industrial activity amounted to a pronounced departure from tradition. The foundations were laid here—however incomplete they might be—for the emergence of a "free-market economy" some two centuries later.

There are grounds, then, for identifying the late sixteenth and early seventeenth centuries as the setting for an important break-through in the elaboration of economic institutions—a break-through of the sort Weber was after. There are also grounds for contrasting these inclinations toward rational capitalism with a configuration of patterns appropriately called "traditionalism."

Whether we are considering the "pure traditionalism" of the lawyers or the "patrimonial traditionalism" of the Tudors and Stuarts, it should be clear that neither one represents a type of order conducive to economic differentiation. The kind of general position Coke developed on corporations *only in spite of itself* encouraged independent business action. The judgments of the *City of London Case* and the *Chamberlain of London's Case,* both of which tolerated customary town monopolies, do not harmonize with the antimonopoly decisions. We noted a similar discrepancy in the Statute of Monopolies.

As a matter of fact, legal traditionalism in itself could never be relied upon to provide anything more than arbitrary and sporadic restrictions against market interference. To take the patterns of the ancient realm as the final standard was to open the door for all kinds of "irrational" controls such as were allowed in decisions like the *City of London Case.* It does not take much wit to appreciate that the ancient realm consisted of a system of very extensive town, guild, and patent monopolies. Even Coke would have a hard time ignoring them completely. Certainly, without the introduction of some "new ideas"—ideas that substantially undercut the patterns of the old order—the antimonopoly decisions could never have been determined in the way they were. Thorne is right: "it is not the past but the future" that is implied in many of Coke's legal judgments.

Patrimonialism, like unaided legal traditionalism, does not possess the requisites for economic differentiation. The tendency of the Tudors and early Stuarts to encourage "court-bound capitalism" in direct opposition to a free market is abundantly obvious. Political absolutism is no more suited to rational capitalism than are the patterns of medieval industrial life.

What is especially interesting about the struggle between the lawyers and the crown in our period is that it comes to more than a simple conflict between customary law and royal prerogative. Indeed, that is one of the major conclusions of a study of the cases on corporation. Had the lawyers been concerned *only* to assert traditional rights and privileges over against the crown, a decision like *Darcy* v. *Allen* would have turned out quite differently. It is clear that a persuasive case could have been made for the "ancient rights" of London as opposed to the "arbitrary" and "recent" patent which Elizabeth had dispensed. Were that argument adopted by the courts, it would merely have been one form of market regulation against another. That kind of contest would have been understandable in terms of the ancient law.

But the conclusion of *Darcy* v. *Allen*—that all monopolies are void—is a decision not only against the crown but also (unconsciously) against established law. The conclusion places the discussion over industrial activity in a new context revealing that the tensions of prerevolutionary England do not by any means exhaust themselves in the conflict between legal and patrimonial traditionalism. At least at the point of *Darcy* v. *Allen, Tailors of Ipswich, Davenant* v. *Hurdis,* and so on, the struggle is between the two types of traditionalism, on the one side, and the beginnings of rational capitalism, on the other.

We have established, we believe, the general relevance of Weber's typology of order to late sixteenth- and early seventeenth-century England. The tensions of society, as reflected in the legal decisions, constitute the social institutional setting within which we have examined the third of Weber's propositions: that Puritanism and Anglicanism can be shown to be wrestling in religious terms with this very conflict of order.

In dealing with Weber's conclusions both as to the independence of a religious-moral system and as to the connection between religious-moral commitment and a conception of social life, we think it is fruitful to analyze religious language in terms of the ingredients of "order." Different religious systems will have a different symbolic understanding of the source and nature of "order" (the "command" and "structural" dimensions), as well as of the demands of "obedience" and the character of "disobedience" and "disorder." Religious systems will respond in some coherent way to all of the essential implicates of "order," and the kind of response will lead to a particular conception of social order. Indeed, the fact that religious language handles the problem of order provides a theoretical basis for pursuing connections between theological assertions and social institutional arrangements, such as Weber did.

With respect, first, to Puritanism, we have taken issue with all the critics of Weber who declare the *impossibility* of a positive association between Puritanism and the "spirit" of rational capitalism. According to our analysis, the heart and soul of Calvinism and late sixteenth-century Puritanism is the idea of a *differentiated new order.* The ethical implications of the new order correspond strikingly with Weber's characteristics of rational capitalism. Above all, the principle of the new order institutionalized an independent sphere of behavior, one that devalues political authority and established social patterns. It emphasizes voluntary, consensual participation on the basis of universalistic criteria, and it gives special place to self-initiated economic behavior as an aspect of one's religious calling.

Through an investigation of Calvin, Cartwright and Perkins, one can demonstrate the fundamentally common theological-moral "pattern of order" they all share. In other words, the degree can be made clear to which theological continuities existed between Calvin and the Elizabethan Puritans, with all the particular discontinuities and differences it would be possible to indicate. Given the understanding Weber had of the spirit of rational capitalism, it is simply not impossible that for very good theological reasons the Calvinist-Puritan system could be associated with it.

It may be, however, that Weber's own conclusion about the association between Puritanism and rational capitalism as stated in *The Protestant Ethic* is, after all, oversimple. It should be understandable that Calvinist Puritanism has its own inner dynamics; just as it does not lead automatically to a "free church," neither does it lead automatically to a "free economy." While Calvinism is noticeably distinct from either Anglicanism or Lutheranism in elaborating a theological basis for differentiated order, it possesses countervailing tendencies as well. It has on its hands the "dilemma of earthly power," and under certain circumstances it inclines to *de*-differentiate the new order from the old. Geneva, colonial New England, Scotland, even Cromwellian England, are examples of this important aspect of Puritanism. In these instances, it could hardly be argued that either the church or the economy institutionalized in any very radical way the characteristics of independence, voluntarism, and so forth.

Still, with all that, the characteristics of ascetic Protestantism are never eliminated entirely, for the reason that they are inherent in the fundamental theological and ecclesiological affirmations of Calvinism. They are, so to speak, carried with Calvinism wherever it goes. Some time spent on Calvin's own thought demonstrates precisely how the ingredients of ascetic Protestantism could emerge from the theological position of one who is not in any obvious sense a "free churchman" or a "free enterpriser."

At various points, the historical picture is more complex than some of Weber's judgments imply. It is possible to get the impression from *The Protestant Ethic* that ascetic Protestantism more or less inevitably "homes" toward the characteristics of a differentiated, rational capitalist economy and that once Puritanism appears, an ever expanding open market cannot be far behind. Of course, such was not the case in the early American colonies nor, for that matter, in Puritan England. A method is needed for the study of Calvinist Puritanism that does full justice to the *tensions* within the system; we must be able to show how the inclinations toward social, religious, and economic "regimentation" (so obvious in colonial New England, for example) can and did live side by side with inclinations in the opposite direction—toward vigorous, voluntary action in church and world to the glory of God.

Given the sort of method we have developed, *the association between*

Calvinist Puritanism and the modern capitalist spirit remains always a live possibility, but never a necessity. It remains a possibility for critically important theological, ecclesiological, and ethical reasons within its pattern of order. We can agree with Weber's conclusions in *The Protestant Ethic* up to a point. When Puritanism appears, the moral pressure will be on for voluntary, self-initiated economic behavior.

At the same time, the association is never a necessary or inevitable one, both on account of historical contingencies and on account of the "countervailing tendencies" within Calvinist Puritanism. The notion of the new order very readily generates a religious elite which seeks, to a degree at least, to subordinate the old order to its perceptions of righteousness. When that happens, a fully rational economy is not exactly around the corner.

Nevertheless, while we feel impelled to introduce a number of qualifications regarding Weber's understanding of Puritanism, we would certainly not agree with Kolko so far as the English experience is concerned. Kolko asserts that Weber misunderstood "the nature of Puritanism" and sharply exaggerated "its differences with Anglicanism as a means of social control and economic stimulus." If our investigations have established anything, it is that there is nothing in the official Anglican position to even begin to legitimate a differentiated pattern of order or any of Weber's marks of a rational society. Our judgment here can be quite categorical. If Anglicans ever did come to favor a free market, independent of political and traditional regulation, if they ever came to side with voluntarism in ecclesiastical and social affairs, they did not "get that" out of Anglicanism (just as Coke did not "get" his attitudes toward monopolies out of Anglicanism or out of the ancient realm). So far as these things are concerned, there simply is no ambiguity in Whitgift and Hooker. Their views on social control and economic stimulus are almost diametrically opposed to the views of Cartwright and Perkins.

There is, of course, one notable point of ambiguity within the Anglican position—a point of utmost relevance to our examination of the tensions between legal and patrimonial traditionalism. Both Whitgift and Hooker straddle the fence on the question of royal authority versus the authority of the old order. Both make room for the discretion of the crown in the church and society; yet both come very close to a kind of "Cokian" theory of fundamental law. Both affirmed with Bracton that the king rules *sub Deo et lege*. What is important is that prior to the turn of the seventeenth century a serious conflict between crown and law was not anticipated. The old order was seen to be a harmonious, integrated whole, with all the parts complementing one another. The discretion of the crown was understood as part of the ancient pattern (as it most assuredly was!).

My own impression is that the early seventeenth-century struggle between the two types of traditionalism did pose questions of social order for which no ready answers could be found in the ancient realm or the Anglican tradition. Obviously, the crown and the courts could not get on with each other forever so long as each was making the kind of claims to authority it was. A solution had to be worked out, but it would have to come from sources other than the old English order. In one sense it was a struggle that should not be taking place at all. The deep-seated tensions of early seventeenth-century English society had to be solved by some rather novel rearrangements of the political and legal institutions. However, dreaming up novel rearrangements never was the strong suit of the Anglican Establishment.

We have been considering the question whether, in roughly sixty years, Max Weber has been dispensed with or whether there are suggestions in his method that can be of service for the study of religion and society. There should be no mistaking our answer. Weber made an abiding contribution not only to the systematic study of society but to the investigation of religious phenomena as well. The key concept of order which we, drawing on Weber, have elaborated in our own way provides a useful bridge for relating religious-moral language to issues or social organization. It is hoped that our effort has both helped to underscore the significance of Weber and to supplement and revise his work in an appropriate way.

9

CULTURE CHANGE AND THE RISE OF PROTESTANTISM IN BRAZIL AND CHILE

Emilio Willems

INTRODUCTION

The present study concerns the forms of Protestantism that can be traced back to proselytic beginnings in Brazil and Chile. In both countries Protestant proselytism has been connected with the systematic efforts of foreign missionaries, especially North Americans representing North American versions of Protestantism. In their religious convictions and methods of operation these missions resembled those that had conquered the American West in the second half of the nineteenth century. One could consider the efforts to infiltrate Latin America as an extension of earlier efforts to rechristianize the American frontier.

The basic values which these missionaries tried to spread in Brazil and Chile beginning in about 1860 can be briefly summarized in the following way:

1. There is an unflagging belief in the Holy Scriptures as the revealed Word of God and thus the ultimate and only source of authority in all matters concerning religious creed and practice.

2. Complete freedom of conscience or "soul liberty" enables the individual to seek the truth and to make his own choice and decisions with regard to the supernatural. This includes not only free choice among existing religious bodies and doctrines but also the right to dissent. The logical result of this principle is the acceptance of a "pluralistic" society and mutual toleration of divergent creeds.

This chapter is a revised version of the author's "Protestantismus und Kulturwandel in Brasilien und Chile," Kölner Zeitschrift für Soziologie und Sozialpsychologie, Sonderheft 7 (1963).

3. The belief in the priesthood of all faithful and the consequent tendency to minimize distinctions between laity and clergy. From a mere believer and recipient of sacramental benefits, the layman came to be a dynamic factor in the propagation of the faith. In frequent meetings he gained considerable experience in public speech and in conducting assemblies. The Sunday School pattern was particularly apt to impart self-confidence to the layman. Ignorant he might be, but this really did not matter as long as God's spirit was guiding his teachings.[1]

4. There is relatively little interest in "professional scientific theology." American Protestantism is "weak in theology, but strong in action." [2] Lack of emphasis on theological training probably contributed to improve the chances of the laity for active participation in church work.

5. The revival pattern, the basic traits of which were shaped by the "Great Awakening" of the eighteenth century. It emphasized religion as a personal experience with strong emotional accents, designed to purify the individual and to establish communion with the deity.

6. Strong emphasis on moral discipline and righteousness. Closely related to Puritanism and other forms of Dissent, these values gained in scope and practical relevance during the rechristianization of the American frontier. "Frontier Baptist, Methodist, and Presbyterian churches disciplined members not only for personal lapses, such as drunkenness and immorality, but also brought them to look for fraudulent business dealings, such as selling unsound horses, removing boundary stones, or cutting down corner trees." [3] Insistence on moral discipline seems related to the revival pattern; and both play a conspicuous role in the struggle for the soul of the frontier settler.

English Dissent and its American derivatives were symbolic expressions of class differences. Here, as in England, a fundamentalist and revivalist Protestantism became the religion of the common man who strove for social status and saw in the social ethics and structure of his denomination a symbolic protest against the existing social order. This aspect is especially important because it plays a crucial role in the diffusion of Protestantism in Latin America.

The almost revolutionary content of Protestantism organized in the way described above becomes apparent when compared to the traditional structure of Latin American society. In Protestant communities (1) all members, regardless of wealth, education, and occupation, are considered ethically equal; (2) all members have the intellectual and moral ability to solve mutual problems in a responsible manner; (3) the leaders should not restrict the freedom of opinions and decision making of the members nor stand in the way of individual initiative.

These principles were given expression in the belief that the local congregation was to have considerable if not complete autonomy and a constitution which would grant fullest participation of all members in the selection of church functionaries and in the conduct of current affairs. As conceived by the missionary, the life of the congregation was implicitly dependent on the assumption of individual responsibility by its members. The missionary's role was to be of a *primus inter pares* whose presence should encourage rather than stifle expression of individual judgment and participation in church proceedings. The only model available to the missionary was that of American congregations, and regardless of the obstacles he might have expected to meet, eventual success meant the formation of a congregation with an associational and institutional life similar to that of a Presbyterian, Methodist, or Baptist congregation in the United States. The existence of these models in the mind of the early missionary may be inferred from their actual projections, which bear indeed a remarkable resemblance to American congregations, not as they are now, but as they were half a century ago.

SOCIOCULTURAL CONTRASTS

If one asks what traditional structural conditions of Latin American society, as represented by Brazil and Chile, are likely to make the social and ethical characteristics of Protestantism appear as revolutionary, one may be inclined to think first of the Roman Catholic church as it was by the turn of the last century. The rigid, inner hierarchy of the church tended to mirror the rigidity of the class structure. The church was perceived as a class-bound institution concerned with preserving the economic and political *status quo,* in alliance with the conservative landholders. The upper classes did not regard the lower strata as ethically equal or as able to solve their own problems in a responsible way. The lower classes had to be protected from their own irresponsibilities and political inexperience with a firm paternalistic hand. Active political participation, especially at the municipal level, was not very common and is even today rather restricted, at least in Chile.

Protest against the existing social order gained momentum after the turn of the century and expressed itself in various ways. One of several alternatives open to the lower classes to project their protest was adherence to a Protestant denomination.

The importance attributed to the individual and the granting of individual rights and responsibilities in a community of believers had a strong appeal. However, the dictates of puritan ethics were in strong contrast to certain behavior patterns and attitudes of Latin American culture. The missionaries assumed that "man and God have to work together in order to build a better world; no situation is so bad that man cannot change it with God's help." [4] The concept of sin which these missionaries tried to instill into their Chilean and Brazilian churches was either new or had never received more than lip service. Most converts found it strange that otiosity, irregular and undisciplined working methods, and leisure should be attacked as sinful. Equally strange were the demands made on the individual's sense of economic responsibility, especially in his relation to family members, employers, customers, business partners, and employees. These new commandments even included gambling and buying lottery tickets—all matters about which one had never lost any sleep but which were suddenly presented as sinful. Even stranger was the missionaries' notion that the commandment of chastity applied not only to women, within and outside marriage, but also to men.

The proselytism of the Protestant missionaries brought culture contact. It meant transmitting normative behavior patterns and ideologies by forming a religious community which would be able to embody these norms and furnish structural support to put them into practice. The introduction of Protestantism into Brazil and Chile will be described below as a process of cultural transmission. These countries were chosen because both have a long and successful history of Protestantism. Furthermore, if there were significant differences in the reaction to Protestantism, they would probably show up in a comparison between the response of Portuguese America and that of a Spanish American country.

HYPOTHESES

While our initial observations generated a series of hypotheses referring to culture change "produced" by Protestantism, a closer scrutiny of all available data suggested that the diffusion of Protestantism itself might be tied in with major sociocultural changes whose origin and dynamics were apparently unrelated to any religious movement. Thus in a second set of hypotheses Protestantism appeared as a possible "effect" or, perhaps, a function of certain cultural changes.

The short history of Protestantism in either country abounds with evidence (1) of numerous schismatic movements within different Protestant bodies and (2) of considerable differentials in the appeal which competing Protestant churches and sects seemed to hold for the people. These facts were hypothetically interpreted as attempts to adapt Protestantism to existing or emerging culture patterns, either by changing it or by selecting its most adjustable versions, to the detriment of less adjustable ones.

Finally, our previous reference to cultural changes produced by Protestantism involves the following hypotheses:

1. Acceptance of the ethical components of Protestantism modifies particular values and their corresponding attitudes in the recipient society.

2. The practice of a Protestant code of behavior tends to redefine the social relationships Protestants maintain among themselves and with non-Protestants.

3. Since the aforementioned redefinitions are primarily concerned with obligations or responsibilities inherent in these relationships, the changes

they produce tend to affect the socialization of the child, economic behavior, political behavior, the class structure, family structure, and the patterns of voluntary association.

PROTESTANTISM AS A FUNCTION OF CULTURAL CHANGE

The early history of the different Protestant denominations shows that Brazilian and Chilean society of the nineteenth century was not particularly favorable to the religious and ethical reforms intended by the Protestant missionaries. The Brazilian Baptist church, for example, which eventually became the most successful of the historical churches, was founded in 1882.[5] After seven years of considerable missionary effort, it had nine local churches with a total membership of 312.[6] Ten years later there were only 784 Baptists in the entire country.[7] In 1862 the first Presbyterian congregation was established in Rio de Janeiro. By 1869 there were six churches with a total membership of 279. After forty-three years of incessant proselytism and a major schism, there were 14,000 Presbyterians in Brazil.[8] In the same year (1905) the Methodist church, which had been established in 1872,[9] reported a membership of 6,000.

Although very few reliable figures are available, the Protestant missions seemingly encountered even greater difficulties in Chile. At the turn of the nineteenth century, the Presbyterian church had approximately 500 members "in full communion." By 1954 the total membership was 2,078, certainly not a very impressive growth for half a century of evangelical endeavor.[10] The Methodist church in Chile never fully recovered from the schism of 1909, which carried away most of its followers, including one of its most respected leaders. The minutes of the fifty-eighth Annual Conference of the Methodist Church, in 1958, reported a total of 4,581 communicant members "or slightly less" than the official figure of 1957. More successful than either Methodists or Presbyterians, the Baptists counted 7,205 members in 1958.[11] During the first decades very few people were converted to the new creed. By 1920, six years after the Foreign Mission Board of the Southern Baptist Convention of the United States had decided to subsidize the Chilean Baptists, these merely consisted of a "few scattered congregations mostly around Temuco, with little training, no institutional work, not a single church house, school or pastor's home."[12] Even if Moore's estimate of a Baptist constituency of 50,000 seems too high, there is no doubt that many more Chileans were attracted by the Baptists than by the other historical churches. What appears to be more relevant in the present context, however, is the fact that *growth on a large scale began only after 1920*, when the rate of social change picked up momentum and the traditional culture began to crack up under the strain of the great depression, industrialization, and population increase.

The assumption of a functional relationship between sociocultural change and the growth of Protestantism seems even more viable with regard to the development of the Pentecostal sects. In Chile, Pentecostalism emerged from a schism in the Methodist church which took place in 1909. In Brazil it was a Swedish missionary who in 1910 founded the Assembly of God, and in the same year an Italian missionary who had been a member of the Presbyterian church in Chicago established the Christian Congregation of Brazil. As the Pentecostals have shown a biblical reluctance in counting their followers, almost no figures are available on early developments, but for about two decades their proselytic effort seems to have caused little concern to the historical churches. A survey on Brazil, published in 1932, stated that only 9.5 per cent of the Brazilian Protestants, excluding the communities of German origin, belonged to Pentecostal bodies.[13] It seems that after 1930 the Pentecostal movement gained momentum, both in Brazil and Chile. According to the Evangelical Federation of Brazil, the Christian Congregation had, in 1958, a total of 500,000 members, including minors.[14] At the same time, the total membership of the Assembly of God was reported to be 1,000,000. In other words, out of a total of 2,697,273 Brazilian Protestants, 1,500,000, or 55 per cent, belonged to the two principal Pentecostal bodies.

The growth of the three largest historical churches gained momentum after 1930. In 1935 the Brazilian Baptist Convention reported 43,306 members,[15] and in 1958 the total membership had climbed to 163,859.[16] The Presbyterian church of Brazil has maintained the second place so far as membership growth is concerned. From 55,468 communicants in 1946 it grew to 88,154 in 1954. The total membership, including minors, was then 158,179. The Methodist church of Brazil has grown at a considerably slower rate. Its membership of 6,000 in 1905 climbed to 30,060 in 1941[17] and reached 44,453 or, if minors are added, 65,685 in 1958.

Official census data on religious affiliation were sporadic in the past, but beginning in 1940 they have been consistently included in the national censuses. The first count of Protestants, which was carried out in 1890, reported a total of 143,743, or 1 per cent of the entire population of Brazil. In view of the relatively slow development of the proselytic churches, one may assume that the overwhelming majority of these Protestants were composed of members of the German Evangelical churches. After a gap of half a century, the census of 1940 reported 1,074,857 Protestants, representing 2.61 per cent of the Brazilian people. Ten years later, according to the census of 1950, there were 1,741,430 Evangelicals in Brazil, and the percentage of the total population had grown to 3.35.[18] The Evangelical Confederation of Brazil reported a total of 2,697,273 Protestants for 1958. If we assume that the population of Brazil had grown to 62,000,000 in the same year—a figure which corresponds to the estimates of the Brazilian Institute for Geography and Statistics—then 4.3 per cent of all Brazilians were affiliated with some Protestant church.

Statistical data on the expansion of Pentecostalism in Chile are unavailable or perhaps nonexistent. In 1957 Strachau estimated that 500,000 Chileans were members of Pentecostal sects. Other estimates are higher.[19] Whatever the actual figures may be, one may safely assume that the increase gained considerable momentum during the last two decades. The first Chilean census to report on religious affiliation was the one of 1907. According to its findings, 1 per cent of the country's total population was Protestant, a figure which confirms our previous statement that the early development of the Evangelical churches was considerably slower in Chile than in Brazil, where the same percentage had already been reported in 1890. In 1920 the proportion of Chilean Protestants reached 1.4 per cent of the total population. In 1940 the percentage was 2.4, and in 1952 it came to be 4.1, thus surpassing the growth rate of Brazilian Protestantism.[20] In 1955 a Catholic priest estimated that 681,770, or 11.36 per cent, of the total population of Chile were Protestants.[21]

The marked increase in growth rates of Protestantism runs parallel with the rhythm of change in the traditional social structure of both countries. This change consists primarily of a slow disintegration of the feudalistic agrarian structure, the settlement of new agricultural lands, the urbanization and industrialization of some regions, as well as the development of a new class structure.

If there really is a functional relationship between cultural change and Protestantism, one would expect to find the largest Protestant concentrations in those regions which have shown the highest rate of culture change, while the smallest percentage of Protestants would be located in the most tradition-bound areas. Table 9–1 shows the distribution of Protestants in relation to the population, broken down by the six main cultural regions of Brazil.

TABLE 9–1

Distribution of Protestants by Regions (1960)

Region	Population*	Per cent of total population	Number of Protestants†	Per cent of total number of Protestants
North	2,601,519	3.7	50,913	2.7
Northeast	15,677,995	22.1	174,727	9.2
East	24,832,611	35.0	459,373	24.2
South	24,848,194	35.0	1,167,484	61.5
Center West	3,006,866	4.2	45,164	2.4
Brazil	70,967,185	100.0	1,897,661	100.0

* I.B.G.E. Anuário Estatístico, 1962.
† I.B.G.E. Estatística do Culto Protestante, 1960.

There is a marked contrast between the Northeast, which contains 22.1 per cent of the total population but only 9.2 per cent of the Protestants, and the South, which holds 35 per cent of the population but 61.5 per cent of all Protestants. There is not the slightest doubt that the South has undergone the greatest cultural changes in the last decades, and it is just as certain that the Northeast of Brazil evidences the strongest ties with the agrarian structure of the past. However, to make comparisons between these two regions more meaningful, one must regroup the states. The states of Rio Grande do Sul and Santa Catarina are eliminated because the nonproselytic Protestants of German extraction are very strongly represented here. No connection between German Brazilian Protestantism and recent culture changes can be assumed, for most German immigrants settled in the South several decades before the changes began to take place.

The states of the East, a statistical rather than a cultural unit, can be assigned partly to the South, partly to the Northeast. In the following we define the South as including the states of Paraná, São Paulo, Minas Gerais, Guanabara, Rio de Janeiro, and Espírito Santo. This area had 35,334,195 inhabitants in 1960, or 44.4 per cent of the total population. Of these, 936,902 were Protestants, amounting to 49.4 per cent of the total Brazilian Protestant population.

Baía and Sergipe, the two other states of the East, are included here as part of the Northeast because of their cultural affinity with this area. This entire region had 22,428,893 inhabitants in 1960, or 31.6 per cent of the total population. The 221,480 Protestants of this area constitute only 11.6 per cent of the Protestant population of Brazil.

A similar comparison can be made for the state of São Paulo. Each of the twenty-three ecological areas of this state has a distinct settlement pattern and exploits the environment differently (Table 9–2). The social structure of each area is closely tied to the economic system, which in turn shows different degrees of receptivity to the changes of the last decades. Of all these areas, none has been more exposed to the effects of industrialization and urbanization than Zona Industrial which consists of São Paulo City surrounded by a fringe of satellite towns. According to the national census of 1960, 233,175, or 58.1 per cent, of all Protestants of the state live in that area. In eight other ecological areas (16–23), all settled within the last fifty years, another 21.5 per cent of São Paulo's Protestants were located. These eight areas are, or recently were, typical agricultural frontiers the social structure of which contained radical deviations from the traditional social order.

In Chile the strongest concentrations of Protestants are also found in areas whose social structure has been most affected by industrialization and urbanization since 1930. The province of Santiago, with the nation's capital and the largest industrial complex of the country, had 60,974 Protestants in 1952, or 25.3 per cent of the country's entire Protestant population. The 754,954 inhabitants of the province, however, represented only 15.2 per cent of Chile's population. The most strongly industrialized and urbanized provinces, Santiago, Valparaiso, and Concepción, had 111,187 Protestants in 1952, or 45.28 per cent of the total. The share of total population was 40.13 per cent.[22]

Cautín is the area of the second largest Protestant concentration, but it is mainly rural. At the turn of the century Cautín was a frontier society.

TABLE 9–2

Distribution of Population and Protestants by Ecological Areas in the State of São Paulo, 1960*

Area	Population	Per cent of total population	Protestants	Per cent of Protestant population
1—Vale do Paraíba	465,424	3.6	9,405	2.3
2—Serra do Mar	115,864	1.0	1,862	.5
3—Litoral	560,720	4.3	15,796	3.9
4—Paranapiacaba	178,993	1.4	4,652	1.2
5—Zona Industrial	5,975,260	46.0	233,175	58.1
6—Mantiqueira	443,231	3.4	6,953	1.7
7—Campos Gerais	258,366	2.0	9,678	2.4
8—Campos Cerrados	217,398	1.7	3,432	0.9
9—Terras Roxas de Ourinhos	187,906	1.4	6,668	1.7
10—Invernadas de Botucatú	158,462	1.2	4,464	1.1
11—Pastagens de São Carlos	127,434	.9	2,413	.6
12—Terras Roxas de Ribeirão Preto	495,758	3.8	6,679	1.7
13—Alta Mogiana	185,044	1.4	3,554	.8
14—Baixa Araraquarense	194,470	1.5	4,329	1.6
15—Douradense	215,688	1.7	1,967	.5
16—Noroeste & Alta Paulista	379,415	3.0	12,023	3.0
17—Alta Araraquarense	445,799	3.4	11,971	3.0
18—Invernadas de Barretos	270,775	2.1	4,159	1.0
19—Alta Sorocabana (Assis)	236,236	1.8	7,586	1.9
20—Alta Sorocabana (Pres. Prudente)	240,780	1.9	6,669	1.7
21—Alta Noroeste e Alta Paulista	781,060	6.0	17,559	4.4
22—Sertão da Alta Sorocabana	238,376	1.8	4,250	1.1
23—Sertão da Alta Noroeste e Alta Ararquarense	602,240	4.7	21,692	5.4
Total	12,974,699	100.0	400,936	100.0

* *I.B.G.E. VII Recenseamento Geral do Brasil, 1960.*
Estado de São Paulo. Sinopse Preliminar do Censo Demográfico.
I.B.G.E Estatística do Culto Protestante, 1960.

Settlement began as the feudalistic agrarian structure north of the Bío-Bío showed the first signs of change. Cautín has many small and medium farms which cover about one third of the agricultural land.[23] Cautín is somewhat comparable with the newly settled areas of São Paulo.

In traditional provinces of Chile, Protestantism has found relatively few followers. Coquimbo, for example, had 5.4 per cent of the total population in 1952 but only 1.1 per cent of Chile's Protestants.

Our data thus indicate that the recent rapid expansion of Protestantism accompanies, in time and space, current cultural transformations. Change provides the "climate" necessary for the development of the various Protestant denominations, particularly the Pentecostal sects. Under the old social order it was especially the kinship group and the conservative landowners which prevented Protestant expansion. In our interviews with Protestant missionaries, we were repeatedly told how difficult it is to gain a foothold in communities where potential converts fear the mockery and disapproval of numerous relatives and compadres. Since most potential converts belong to the lower classes, economic dependency on the extremely conservative, paternalistic upper classes is to be added as a further barrier. Migration to big cities or to new lands frees the individual from these traditional forms of social control and facilitates his joining groups whose structure and ideology deviate from tradition.

On the other hand the individual, thus freed from kinship ties and the control of feudal landowners, finds himself cast into an improvised society in which it is difficult to orient himself and to replace lost values with new ones. The individual and his family miss the institutional protection of the "personal community," that is, the group of people on whom one can count for recognition and approval.[24] Emotional isolation and economic insecurity are intensified by the social problems of slum living to which hundreds of thousands are exposed. No wonder that under such conditions religious or political proselytism of all types can be very successful. One should not forget that Protestant churches and sects are only a few among many alternatives from which the individual may choose. Radical political groups, spiritualistic organizations, African cult groups, and the Catholic church itself all compete with Protestant missionaries and denominations. A significant proportion of this uprooted population fluctuates here and there among all these alternatives. The individual motives for conversion can be ascertained from many life histories which we collected. Almost all of these confirm our expectation that conversion is seen as the solution of personal problems, which are in turn reflections of a social order in transition.

SELECTION, ADAPTATION, AND REINTERPRETATION: THE EMERGENCE OF THE NATIONAL CHURCHES

Our second hypothesis is based on the well-known fact that cultural transfer usually brings about changes in the traits transmitted. The concepts of adaptation and reinterpretation cover this phase of culture change.

The irreconcilability of certain aspects of Protestantism with Latin American value orientation is expressed in schismatic movements leading to new churches and sects. This is clearly evident, for example, in the schism of 1903 which split the Brazilian Presbyterians over the *questão de maçonaria* (question of freemasonry). Americans see no contradiction between freemasonry and Christianity, and members of the clergy may be members of Masonic lodges. However, this is inconceivable to Brazilians, who perceive freemasonry to be the archenemy of Christianity. Furthermore, there was a basic difference between "North American Pragmatism" and "Latin American Humanism" which brought American missionaries and their Brazilian colleagues into conflict. "In general, the young and intellectually strong Latin churches were disappointed in American pragmatism and the theological weakness of certain American clergy; they reacted with an intellectual superiority complex against something they considered as an ethnic superiority complex of the missionaries." [25] It is not surprising that nationalistic feelings of the local congregations and their native clergy intruded in such conflicts. The words *national, independent, free,* appear with great regularity in the names of newly founded Protestant groups in Chile as well as in Brazil. A favorite argument of nationalistic dissenter groups concerns the supposed lack of understanding on the part of foreign missionaries of Latin American culture and the need to adapt religious teachings to its peculiarities.

The numerous schisms experienced by most Protestant churches can be divided into organizational and dogmatic movements. The former led simply to the formation of independent church bodies whose religious teachings were hardly distinct from those of the mother church. Dogmatic schisms, however, constitute radical deviations and usually lead to the formation of true sects. An example is the schism in the Chilean Methodist Church of 1909 which generated the Iglesia Metodista Pentecostal de Chile. "Possession by the Holy Ghost" and its numerous manifestations were regarded by traditional Methodists merely as hallucinations, mental aberrations, or epileptic seizures,[26] whereas the new sect members made them the central part of the cult. The split also provided opportunity to adopt new organizational forms reflecting the Latin American pattern of "rebellion against constituted authority." Repeated schisms and splits became an institutionalized pattern in Chilean Pentecostalism. Schism is interpreted by Pentecostals today as a normal growth process comparable to physiological growth through cell division. Schisms are usually based on the individual initiative of ambitious religious leaders, and the pattern of *caudillismo* serves as a clearly recognizable model.

If the rise of Protestantism in Brazil and Chile is really a symbolic protest against the traditional social order, one would expect the relative success of a new religion or sect to be the greater the more its structure and ideology deviate from those of the traditional social order. A comparison of different Protestant groups confirms this expectation. The phenomenal success of Pentecostal sects seems to be related to the following characteristics:

1. Organization of the sect is democratic. All members are "brothers" and "sisters." Hierarchical structures are completely rejected. The ministers have no theological training. Success as a preacher and missionary, which is interpreted as a special grace of the Holy Ghost, constitutes the sole criterion for a clerical career. The Christian Congregation of Brazil, the second largest sect in the country, does not even have clergy. The priesthood of the laity is taken literally. In some sects there is a contradiction between the *caudillismo* of the leader and the supposedly democratic structure of the sect. This contradiction is frequently to be interpreted as a sign of impending schism. The new sect claims to be more democratic than its predecessor. The egalitarian constitution of the sect stands in strong contrast to Latin American class structure, but especially to the hierarchical structure of the Catholic church.

2. The structural principle of centralization which is characteristic of both the political and the religious constitutions of Latin America stands in contrast to the congregationalism and absolute autonomy of the local Pentecostal church. The laymen elect their own pastor and functionaries. Each individual has an opportunity to participate in church affairs. Each member of the Pentecostal sects is a missionary who often sacrifices his occupational interests and spends all his free time in proselytic activities.

3. The Pentecostal sects are oriented toward the lower classes in ideology, religious teachings, ritual, and organization. Intellectual demands on the individual are restricted to reading the Bible and religious tracts. Beyond this all learning is considered dangerous to the faith. The doctrine of salvation not only concerns itself with the future promises of a supernatural world but insists on an immediate form of salvation in the form of the Holy Spirit who comes to each person individually, speaks and acts through him, and cures him of physical and mental ills. Being possessed leads to an ecstatic euphoria which undoubtedly compensates for the misery of daily life. Being filled with the Holy Ghost lends a feeling of power which stands in sharp contrast to the political and economic impotence of the lower classes. Equally important are the opportunities afforded to the individual to co-operate in the development of the sect. In the extremely close solidarity of the group he finds the lost personal community. In other words, the sect provides what social reality denies him.

Many of these characteristics are found not only among the Pentecostals but also among the historical versions of Protestantism. Among the three competing major churches, Baptists, Presbyterians, and Methodists, the Baptists are the most successful. The fundamentalist position of the Baptists, their congregational setup, their rejection of any kind of ecclesiastical hierarchy, their complete local autonomy, as well as direct and fullest participation of the church members, stand in contrast to the traditional social structure. According to the Evangelical Federation of Brazil, the Brazilian Baptist Convention had 183,768 members in 1957, and various smaller associations bring the total to about 200,000. The Chilean Baptist Convention had about 7,000 members in 1959, but the total of all Chilean Baptists amounted to 50,000, according to Moore.[27]

The two Brazilian Presbyterian churches had 217,314 members. Neither one has bishops or any kind of hierarchy, and the Igreja Presbiteriana do Brazil considers itself as an "association of local congregations." [28] Each member takes part in the election of pastor and functionaries.

In both countries Methodism lags behind, in spite of the fact that in the United States it is the largest Protestant church and certainly no less active in missionary work than the other major churches. Brazil had 67,703 Methodists in 1957; Chile, between 5,000 and 6,000. Although other variables may be related to the differential diffusion of the three main churches, the episcopal and hierarchical structure of Methodism seems to make it less appealing and therefore less successful than the congregational structure of the other denominations.[29]

Comparing the historical development of the different churches and sects in the last four decades, it is rather obvious that their relative success depends on the capacity of each denomination to adapt its internal structure, its teaching and cult, to the needs, expectations, and ambitions of the lower classes.

PROTESTANTISM AS A FACTOR OF CULTURAL CHANGE

The initiatives of the foreign, mainly North American, churches have had a profound impact on technology, political and economic behavior, education, and family structure. This may not mean, of course, that Protestantism has been the only cause of cultural change or even its main cause. Furthermore, the forms of culture change that solely affected the Protestant congregation must be distinguished from those which affected Brazilian and Chilean society at large.

The following description of patterns of behavior is not by implication a comparison with the Catholic population. No more than 20 per cent of all Brazilians and Chileans may safely be considered as practicing Catholics. Our comparison is only between Protestants and "non-Protestants."

Changes in Economic Behavior

Our field data indicate that in many communities Protestants have gained the reputation among non-Protestants of being especially reliable, conscientious, and industrious. Numerous interviews with employers left no doubt that Protestant workers are especially sought after and even given advantages. There was, however, a difference between Pentecostal and historical church members. The former were regarded as incapable of making independent decisions and therefore useless for positions of more than ordinary responsibility. Pastors are often asked by non-Protestants to suggest members of their congregations for jobs or services. A sample of thirty-six Presbyterian ministers in São Paulo and surrounding areas revealed that twenty-one, or 58.3 per cent, of them had at some time or other recommended parishioners for jobs or professional services. Some recalled from twenty to forty such inquiries; similar conditions were encountered in Chile, particularly in Santiago.

Numerous Protestants assured us that their conversion, regularly described as "rebirth," had led to economic improvement. The reason given was that prior to conversion they had spent a great deal of money on alcohol, lottery tickets, gambling, tobacco, cosmetics, movies, and prostitution. Once they gave up these "sins," substantial amounts of money were available for permissible and necessary things. Industriousness, pride, and thrift were often mentioned subjectively to explain improved economic conditions. The knowledge that conversion and the observance of a puritanic morality results in economic compensations is so widely diffused that one may speak of a "success folklore" which finds expression in the oral and written tradition of the churches.

This attitude is especially significant within the context of a changing culture. In view of an increasing participation in the emerging industrial civilization based on mass production, mass consumption, and social mobility, it makes sense to forgo "sinful" pleasures and to replace them with the satisfaction of permissible wants. It is hardly surprising that Protestant families living by the code of a puritanic ethic have better housing, clothes, more sewing machines, bicycles, radios, and so on than do non-Protestants of comparable social status. In contrast to the economic hopelessness of the lower classes in traditional Latin American society, the development of industrial society opens avenues of social mobility of which the Protestant population avails itself to a greater extent than non-Protestants. This applies to the historical rather than to the Pentecostal denominations, whose worldly interests are not strong enough to motivate the individual beyond a very moderate degree of economic betterment.

Empirical studies of the economic behavior of Protestant groups were carried out in a suburb of Santiago and three rural communities of the state of São Paulo. Los Nogales, a shantytown of the Chilean capital, is homogeneous insofar as its population is composed exclusively of lower-class families. Each inhabitant builds his own "house" and seeks to improve it if and when his economic position permits. Housing conditions may thus be considered as an index of economic advancement. We used data of a survey which divided the housing conditions of the respondents into bad, medium, good. A comparison of the 563 Protestants of Los Nogales with a random sample of 563 non-Protestants produced the following results.

TABLE 9-3

Housing Conditions in Los Nogales

Quality	Protestants		Non-Protestants	
	Number	*Per cent*	*Number*	*Per cent*
Bad	93	16.5	193	34.3
Medium	362	64.3	298	52.9
Good	108	19.2	72	12.8
Total	563	100	563	100

No detailed account of the three community studies can be included here. May it suffice to state that among the Protestants of all three we detected significant differences in technological and economic behavior as compared with that of non-Protestants, and in each case such behavior had resulted in a significant measure of economic advancement.

Economic change which seems so closely related to the expansion of historical Protestantism in Brazil and Chile may be ascribed to a considerable extent to the initiative of the churches. Methodists, Presbyterians, Baptists, and some others may indeed be considered as pioneers of planned cultural change. The pragmatism of the American missionaries led, according to Émile Léonard, to the founding of institutions for "indirect propaganda" intended to generate a "Christian civilization" or even the "Kingdom of God on Earth" which was "more or less consciously equated with the American economic system." [30] It was education, and especially vocational instruction, which concerned these missionaries at the turn of the century. Illiteracy was combated because a believer must be able to read at least the Bible and religious tracts. These efforts accompanied missionary activity, so that there are today very few illiterates among Protestants. A sample of 35 parishes in São Paulo revealed an illiteracy rate of 3.5 per cent, which contrasted sharply with an over-all illiteracy rate of 34.6 per cent in 1950 for the entire state's population.

Many educational institutions founded by American missions soon became very popular among the middle and upper classes. This was especially due to the fact that the American educational system contained many elements whose absence in Latin American schools was felt to be serious in the more progressive sectors. In contrast to the authoritarian, humanistic-encyclopedic system, based on vote learning, improvised teachers, and unsuccessful copying of European education, the Protestant schools tried to instill critical thinking into their students. More emphasis was put on science and its application to the immediate environment. Coeducation and emphasis on sports stood also in marked contrast to the traditional school system.

Originally these institutions were intended to educate Protestants and to carry on religious proselytism. However, the growing attraction which the new educational methods and subjects had on the non-Protestant population led these institutions away from their original goals. Rarely were the students or their families interested in Protestantism as such. They expected a "modern" education, and Protestant schools became pioneers of progressive education which won them friends and protectors in politically influential circles. These schools helped to consolidate Protestantism in Brazil and Chile without practicing much proselytism.

Similar effects were generated by the purely technical schools founded by American missionaries. For example, the model farm and the agricultural college of El Vergel in Chile, run by the Methodists, contributed substantially to the modernization of Chilean agriculture at a time when there were no other institutions to meet such a task.

The development of public education, general as well as technical, during the last three decades has considerably reduced the distance between the national educational systems and Protestant education. At the same time, restrictive legislation has forced private institutions, particularly in Brazil, to adapt their organization to the official pattern; on the other hand, the non-Protestant school system, public as well as private, has made considerable progress, especially in the field of scientific and technical education. This may have contributed to certain directional changes of Protestant initiatives. In Northeastern Brazil, for example, the Presbyterian mission participates in development projects which are intended to bring about technical and economic changes among the rural population without the benefit of formal education.

Political Behavior

The political forces which controlled Brazil and Chile in the second half of the nineteenth century were either openly hostile or indifferent to the emerging Protestant churches. The union between the Catholic church and the state imposed constitutional restrictions upon any form of heterodoxy, particularly upon practices interfering with the monopoly of the Catholic church. To the average Protestant, politics mostly meant defense of the *status quo,* and thus participation in party politics would have been equivalent to self-destruction.

This attitude, however, has changed during the last three decades, at least within the historical churches, while the position of the Pentecostal sects has been determined by a number of contradictory factors which make generalizations difficult. These changes are roughly concomitant with the gradual democratization of the political process in Brazil and Chile, especially with the development of opportunities for minority groups to protect themselves more effectively against discrimination. In view of the structural differences between the two countries, it is not surprising that the political activation of the Protestant bodies should have begun at different times and proceeded in different fashions and with widely varying intensity.

All things considered it would seem that the Brazilian situation offered chances for an earlier and more massive participation of Protestants than the political situation in Chile. Since ideological commitments were rarely involved, Brazilian Protestant voters felt free to pick candidates deemed personally "dependable," while the regional character of most parties made nationwide commitments dispensable. Since 1946 the growing Protestant contingent in the general electorate has reflected not only increasing participation but also a growing church membership. In most parts of Brazil, Protestants are now recognized as a political force to reckon with, and most candidates running for office carefully avoid commitments which could alienate the Protestant electorate.

The extent to which Protestants are now encouraged to participate in political activities is reflected by the attitudes of thirty-six pastors of the Presbyterian church of Brazil. Asked whether Protestants should protect their civil rights, especially freedom of religion, through some kind of political action, twenty-seven answered affirmatively. In fact, all pastors except one declared that they had encouraged the members of their church to participate in political elections.

The same thirty-six ministers were asked whether they knew cases of Protestants having been elected to municipal or city councils. Since official records do not show the religious affiliation of the members of municipal and state legislatures, we attempted to gather as much information as possible in personal interviews. The answers cover five states, but as most interviewed ministers came from localities situated in the state of São Paulo, the latter is of course overrepresented. The answers reported a total of thirty-four legislative bodies with one or more Protestant members. Almost all pastors referred to localities in which they were residing then or had resided at some time in the past.

Asked whether in their opinion the political record of the Protestant members of legislative bodies was in any sense different from that of non-Protestants, all pastors except one replied that indeed there were differences, which they proceeded to formulate. Thirty-five pastors virtually agreed that Protestant legislators

did "not defend personal interests";
were "not sectarian" in the exercise of their mandate;
defended "freedom of conscience";
had "more respect for human rights";
were willing to assume "more moral responsibilities";
worked for "honest administration";
"worked more";
were "more interested in solving social problems";
showed "greater strength of conviction";
had "more idealism";
had "moralizing influence upon municipal council";
showed "more responsibility in spending taxpayers' money";
showed "more interest in public welfare";
had "more moral courage";
were "more progressive";
were "more democratic."

In 1960 four members of the national Chamber of Deputies were Protestants representing four different political parties. All four were members of a Committee for Education and Culture. According to one of our non-Protestant informants, member of parliament himself, three of these Protestant congressmen, one Baptist and two Presbyterians, always act like a "monolithic block" whenever a proposal of interest comes up for discussion.

In contrast to the historical churches, the principal Pentecostal sects maintain an attitude of aloofness or even hostility toward political participation. There is no known case of a sect member committing the votes of his followers to any particular party. The charter of the Christian Congregation "does not admit political parties of any description in the congregation," but recognizes the legal obligation of its members to cast their votes in political elections. So far as election to political office is concerned the charter is quite explicit: "No brother who has been called to serve the Ministry of the Word of God, or holds any kind of office in the work of God, is allowed to accept political positions.

"Even for other brethren who, without holding office (in the sect), wish to serve God with a tranquil conscience it is advisable not to accept political office."

While it is possible to distinguish a sense of moral proselytism in the way Brazilian Protestants participate in politics, the predominant motive inducing Chilean Protestants to play an active role in political elections seems to be the felt need to protect the late victory of complete religious freedom against restrictive schemes attributed to certain ultramontane groups.

Family Structure

Latin American society has frequently been called "androcentric." In fact, the male does enjoy jealously guarded privileges which are reflected in the occupational, legal, and family system. There is a double standard of sex morals which judges the behavior of the sexes by two different sets of criteria. This double standard plays an extremely important role in the traditional family structure, particularly in the middle and upper classes.[31]

There is no need to insist upon the incompatibility of the double standard of sex morals with the model of the Protestant family. The double standard is a survival of a patriarchal-agrarian past, obviously out of step with the emerging industrial society of Latin America. The fact that the Protestant congregations have been relatively successful in eradicating among their membership the customary male privilege of committing adultery with impunity should be weighed against the changing role of the women in the economic structure. Widespread and growing female competition in the labor market suggests that at least the economic determinant of female submissiveness is losing its former effectiveness.

Our data indicate that membership in a Protestant church indeed reinforces the position of the married woman vis-à-vis a husband relapsing into customary sex behavior. Saunders writes:

> The woman whose husband is a "crente" is able to protest effectively against his sexual irregularities, and very often does so by bringing the situation to the attention of group leaders who then take the necessary corrective steps, in the form of a committee that first admonishes the member against his behavior, then asks for a resignation, and finally, if necessary, engineers the formal expulsion of the individual from the group. Because of loss of face, severance of group relationships, possible fear of supernatural sanctions, and the fact that it is nearly impossible to keep secret extra-marital sexual relations over a long period of time, this has proved to be an effective means of social control.[32]

Unwillingness on the part of Protestant women passively to accept the age-old pattern of marital infidelity and the willingness of the sinning husband to submit the accusation of the spouse to the decision of ecclesiastical authority indicates a second major change referring to the relative position of the family within the general social structure. Neither the protest of an offended wife nor the husband's acceptance of suprafamily authority adjudicating such intimate matters as sexual misbehavior would have been conceivable in the old social order. Traditionally, the husband was the supreme arbiter of his own sexual behavior. To surrender that authority to "outsiders" would have meant to jeopardize not only his status within the family but the status of the family within the community as well. As a highly self-centered unit, it was expected to settle its internal disputes without external interference, and for centuries it jealously defended that privilege against communal, judicial, and ecclesiastical encroachments.[33]

Protestantism and Class Structure

The differentiation of Protestantism into numerous sects can be traced back, according to H. Richard Niebuhr, to its efforts to cater to the needs and problems of the lower classes. Under the influence of religious discipline such communities gain a certain bourgeois respectability which sooner or later leads to the neglect of the lower social strata and thus to the emergence of new sects. "This pattern recurs with marked regularity in the history of Christianity. Anabaptists, Quakers, Methodists, Salvation Army and more recent sects of like type illustrate this rise and progress of the churches of the disinherited." [34]

The early Protestant missionaries in Brazil and Chile approached their work very much in the revivalistic spirit with which the American West had been evangelized. Their message was featured to reach the "common man," and due to the peculiarities of the existing social structure it happened that the common man was essentially uncommitted to the value system of the upper strata and consequently "available." Although the common man was, roughly speaking, synonymous with the lower classes, some qualifications are necessary. By the time the first Methodist and Presbyterian missionaries set foot on South American soil there was of course a class of people who by occupation, education, and level of living differed from the vast rural proletariat. There were the small landowners and tenant farmers, the owners of small stores which could be set up with very little capital, the artisans and low-level employees of business establishments, banks, railroads, and factories, and finally the lower echelons of the government bureaucracy. It seems a matter of semantics whether these categories are to be considered as "upper lower" or "lower middle" class. Either classification could be justified, but in order not to suggest parallels with the American class structure, we prefer to call this rather heterogeneous conglomerate the *transitional class.*

The chronic instability of the transitional class and the middle class made it virtually impossible to erect boundary-maintaining mechanisms at these levels, a condition which has probably added to the chances of Protestantism as a factor of social mobility. At any rate, it seems that the transitional class contributed about as many converts to the first Protestant nuclei as the lower classes. Of course the number of faithful was small, and if a local congregation were to survive, at least some of its members would have to be in a position to make contributions to the construction and maintenance of a church.[35] One may assume that there was a deliberate effort on the part of the first missionaries to establish a foothold in the transitional class.

The middle class proved to be more accessible in Brazil than in Chile, and toward the end of the nineteenth century Protestantism had already established a solid bridgehead in the Brazilian bourgeoisie. Unlike the Chilean "aristocracy," the upper class of Brazil was not entirely unreceptive to the preachings of the early missionaries. In 1878, "seven ladies of the highest Brazilian aristocracy" (to use the words of the historian) joined the Presbyterian Church of São Paulo,[36] and Léonard mentions further examples of upper-class people who joined the Presbyterian church.[37] Around the turn of the century the Brazilian Presbyterian church had an intellectual elite whose reputation extended beyond religious circles and contributed substantially to the social standing of Protestantism. In answer to our questions, we were repeatedly told that in Brazil members of the upper and middle classes were concentrated in the Presbyterian churches and least common in the Baptist church, while the Methodists occupied a middle ground.

What effects did the social ascent of the historical churches have upon their structure? Have they absorbed middle-class culture to the point of losing contact with the lower classes? In other words: Have they become churches of the rising middle class? To answer these questions the social composition of a number of congregations was examined. Since we had to rely on informants and interviewers, no attempt was made to go beyond the conventional tripartite division—lower, middle, upper—with which all our co-workers appeared to be familiar. "Lower class" denotes, within the cultural context of either country, mostly unskilled or semiskilled menial workers, complete dependence on wages, poor housing, and a high illiteracy rate. The "upper class," according to current local definitions, is composed of the liberal professions, owners of haciendas, well-to-do merchants, industrials, real estate owners, and individuals in high managerial or civil service positions. The "middle class" is defined as a residual category composed of independent artisans, small merchants and entrepreneurs, small landowners, white-collar workers, and civil servants in subordinate positions. Due to its heterogeneous composition and somewhat amorphous characteristics, we prefer, as already indicated, the designation *transitional class*.

There is some ambiguity about the concept of the upper class. By small-town criteria, the individuals identified as members of the upper class actually belong to the highest stratum of the *local* community. By metropolitan and national standards, however, they would undoubtedly be considered as middle class. Since none of the Protestant congregations under scrutiny appeared to have any members belonging to the *national* upper class, the term was dropped altogether and the designation *middle class* was chosen instead.

In a random sample of sixty-seven Protestant families in two Chilean cities (Concepción and Temuco) the three social classes were distributed as follows:

Lower	53.0%
Transitional	9.1%
Middle	37.9%

In a Chilean Methodist parish (Santiago) 60 per cent of the members belonged to the lower classes, 30 per cent to the transitional class, and 10 per cent to the middle class. Out of 104 families affiliated with the Seventh-Day Adventist church of a Chilean city (Concepción), 47.5 per cent belonged to the lower class, 37 per cent to the transitional class, and 15.5 per cent to the middle class.

The analysis of thirty-four Presbyterian congregations in São Paulo and neighboring states yielded the following class distribution:

Lower	59.4%
Transitional	34.0%
Middle	6.6%

These congregations, however, appeared to be so heterogeneous that a more detailed scrutiny seems to be in order.

TABLE 9-4

Class Distribution in 34 Presbyterian Congregations
(São Paulo and neighboring states)

Percentage of membership	Lower	Transitional	Middle
0	1	2	12
1–10	3	4	17
11–20	2	10	3
21–30	3	4	2
31–40	1	4	0
41–50	2	0	0
51–60	4	3	0
61–70	4	3	0
71–80	10	1	0
81–90	0	2	0
91–100	4	1	0
Total	34	34	34

Thus in 22 out of 34 parishes people of lower-class extraction represent more than half of the total membership, and only one congregation appeared to have no lower-class members at all.

In order to obtain a sample of class distribution in a metropolitan area, three congregations from widely differing residential districts of Rio de Janeiro were selected. Methodist I is located in a predominantly proletarian suburb; Methodist II lies in a district where transitional- and middle-class people are predominant; and the Presbyterian Cathedral, as it proudly calls itself, is located in a *bairro chique,* a predominantly middle- and upper-class residential district.

TABLE 9–5

Class Distribution in Three Protestant Parishes in Rio de Janeiro

Class	Methodist I	Methodist II	Presbyterian Cathedral
Lower	86.7%	54%	25.2%
Transitional	9.8%	25%	33.9%
Middle	3.5%	21%	40.9%

The class extraction of the clergy constitutes another criterion of the extent to which the historical churches have maintained contact with the lower classes. The following table shows the class origin of three distinct groups: 36 Presbyterian pastors, 74 students of a Presbyterian seminary, and 43 students of a Methodist seminary in Southern Brazil.

TABLE 9–6

Class Origin of Three Clerical Groups
(Brazil)

Class	Presbyterian pastors	Presbyterian seminarists	Methodist seminarists
Lower	30.6%	39.2%	37.2%
Transitional	47.2%	32.4%	16.3%
Middle	22.2%	28.4%	46.5%

At least two conclusions may be drawn from these tables: (1) The social ascent of the historical Protestant churches is a fact. The average proportion of transitional- and middle-class membership in a total of forty congregations amounts to 43.7 per cent. (2) The historical Protestant churches did not lose contact with the lower classes. Quite the contrary, the average proportion of lower-class membership in these congregations represents 56.3 per cent of the total.

The Brazilian Presbyterian church is of course overrepresented in our sample, and on the other hand there are no figures at all on class distribution in the Baptist churches. Virtually all our informants agreed that of the three main church bodies the Baptists appeal more strongly to the lower class than either the Methodist or Presbyterian church. Thus if Baptist congregations were included in our sample, the figure referring to lower-class membership would probably be higher.

The social stratification within the historical churches in Brazil and

Chile rules out the hypothesis that the acquisition of "new cultural respectability," to use Niebuhr's terms, has led to the neglect of the "new
poor." If a larger proportion of new converts joins the sects rather than
the churches, this does not mean that the sects simply succeeded the
churches by taking over their lower-class members; they rather compete
with them for such membership, and their relative success appears understandable in the light of certain ideological and structural peculiarities of
the sect.

In order to explain the competitive advantages of the sects we need not
repeat what has been said about the functional compatibility between
Pentecostalism and lower-class culture. Our own findings confirm what
John L. Gillin wrote about these affinities in 1910: "Sects originate generally in the lower classes which have been shut out from any part in the
socializing process." The lower classes, he continues, "are not represented in the state as it exists, consequently they organize themselves so as
to be able to deal as classes with the upper classes." [38] The Pentecostal
sects of Chile and Brazil are class organizations; the historical churches
are not. Like most sects, the Pentecostalists refuse to accept the traditional
symbols, because these are symbols of the upper classes. As pointed out
before, the Pentecostal sects, to a much higher degree than the historical
churches, are protest movements against the existing class structure. The
historical churches attempt to reconcile class tensions and antagonisms in
their own structures. Their accommodative attitude makes them less attractive to those who seek redemption from the evils of a social order
which is felt to be unjust.

The aggressiveness of the sects is further reflected in their approach to
the organized diffusion of the Gospel. The sects thrive on proselytism;
every active member is not just a churchgoer but a missionary who does
not recoil from the ridicule and contempt which the public may heap
upon him. In the cities of Chile the historical churches have virtually
withdrawn from street-corner evangelism, which is held to be incompatible with the dignity and respectability of their constituency. The Brazilian churches are more aggressive, but in both countries the boundless
missionary zeal of earlier times has given way to a more cautious attitude
which in many local congregations has resulted in complete abstention
from any missionary effort whatsoever. In its stead one hears nowadays
much talk about "consolidation." "The leaders of our church believe,"
one Chilean critic remarked, "that the mission field lies in Africa, Korea,
India, or China, but not in Santiago or any other part of Chile. When I
criticized the lack of missionary zeal in our church, I was told that I was
stepping out of line."

A further advantage of the Pentecostal missionaries is to be seen in
their class origin associated with the lack of formal training. They are not
given opportunity to develop status aspirations in an institution of higher

learning. Their "low" level of living enables them to work anywhere and under any conditions. As Davis has accurately stated, "Such humble leaders can live upon an economic level which would be impossible for highly trained men." [39]

However, it would be unrealistic to describe the relationship between the Pentecostal sects and the class structure solely in negative terms of abstention and protest. The sects do not live in Utopia; their members cannot and do not withdraw from the dynamics of sociocultural change, and more often than not they are engulfed by it. True enough, as a rule they do not cultivate the ideals of economic and professional advancement; their attitude toward educational achievements is that of indifference or antagonism. Mere literacy is deemed sufficient, but even this modest level of aspiration is not incompatible with a measure of bourgeois respectability. The practice of asceticism never fails to be of some help in attaining at least a modest degree of economic security. The rigidity of the class structure and the lack of economic opportunities in Chilean society make such changes very difficult. Consequently, the Chilean sects are socially much more homogeneous than their Brazilian counterparts. Especially in São Paulo, it is not unusual for white-collar workers and small businessmen to belong to the Christian Congregation or to the Assembly of God. In the most urbanized areas of São Paulo, perhaps one-fifth of the Pentecostalists belong to the transitional class, and a few have been able to accumulate considerable wealth.

Assuming that further economic development and increased social mobility will change the class composition of the Pentecostal movement, a change from "otherworldliness" to a "worldlier" value orientation, from protest to increasing conformity, may be expected. At least this seems to be a viable hypothesis for future studies of this sort.

The Protestant churches have served the function of furthering upward mobility by capitalizing on the virtues of Christian asceticism, but they are also being victims of the process they have helped to develop. Equipped with the educational resources for further social advancement, second-generation Protestants may find it more advantageous to drift away from active church membership to nonparticipation. No longer do they want "to be associated with obscure groups of *crentes*"; they are not motivated by the evangelical ardor of the parent generation; and Christian asceticism seems singularly unrewarding once professional and financial success is deemed obtainable merely by secular effort. Writing in 1943, Davis already reported a considerable loss of younger church members. In fact many congregations were losing from 20 to 70 per cent of their youth to the value orientation of a highly secularized society. Thus the old cultural conflict which the parent generation seemed to have overcome crops up anew among the second-generation Protestants. Meanwhile many urban congregations at least have relaxed their puritanical strictness, often to the scandal of their rural brethren.

Loss of younger members was also reported by Chilean pastors. Pious Protestant parents often make great efforts to provide a college education for their children. Families living in the provinces have to send their sons to Santiago, where they tend to become estranged from the church. A Baptist churchman in southern Chile estimated that there were approximately 30,000 persons in Chile who at one time or another had been baptized in the church, while the official membership of the Chilean Baptist Convention (for 1957) was 7,957. By the end of 1958 the number was down to 7,205, mostly due to exclusion and resignations.[40]

It may be argued that further secularization accompanying upward mobility will gradually reduce and eventually extinguish the role of the historical churches as factors of culture change. There is enough evidence at hand to make this a promising avenue for further research.

NOTES

1. T. C. Hall, *The Religious Background of American Culture* (Boston, 1930), p. 243.

2. W. W. Sweet, *The American Churches* (New York and Nashville, 1947), p. 110.

3. *Ibid.*, p. 50.

4. *Ibid.*, p. 48.

5. A. P. Crabtree, *História dos Baptistas do Brasil* (Rio de Janeiro, 1927), p. 54.

6. *Ibid.*, p. 82.

7. *Ibid.*, p. 119.

8. J. A. Ferreira, *História da Igreja Presbiteriana do Brasil*, 2 vols. (São Paulo, 1959), II, 92.

9. P. E. Buyers, *História do Metodismo* (São Paulo, 1945), p. 412.

10. J. H. McLean, *Historia de la Iglesia Presbiteriana en Chile* (Santiago de Chile, 1954), pp. 72–73.

11. *La Voz Bautista*, LI, No. 6 (1959), 12.

12. R. C. Moore, "These Other Americans to the South," manuscript, pp. 16–17.

13. Erasmo Braga and K. G. Grubb, *The Republic of Brazil: A Survey of the Religious Situation* (London, New York, Toronto, 1932), p. 71.

14. *Brazil Evangélico* (1959), p. 4.

15. A. N. de Mesquita, *História dos Batistas do Brasil* (Rio de Janeiro, 1940), p. 349.

16. Conselho Nacional de Estatística, *Anuário Estatístico do Brasil* (1960), No. 1.

17. Buyers, *op. cit.*, p. 435.

18. Conselho Nacional de Estatística, *Anuário Estatístico do Brasil* (1953), No. 1.

19. H. P. van Dusen, "The Challenge of the Sects," *Christianity and Crisis*, XVIII, No. 13 (1958), 104.

20. República de Chile, *XII Censo General de Población ye de Vivienda* (Santiago de Chile, 1952), I, 199.

21. Ignacio Vergara, "Es Chile un Pais Catolico?", *Mensaje* (1955), No. 41.

22. República de Chile, *op. cit.*

23. L. P. Stagno, "La Propiedad Agrícola y su Extensión," *Seminario de Investiga-*

ciones sobre el Desarrollo de la Provincia de Cautín (Santíago de Chile, 1956), p. 114.

24. Jules Henry, "The Personal Community and Its Invariant Properties," *American Anthropologist*, LX (1958), No. 5, 827.

25. Émile Léonard, "O Protestantismo Brasileiro," *Revista de História*, Ano II, No. 7 (1951), p. 180.

26. *El Heraldo Evangelico*, Ano XXXVIII, No. 1526 (1909).

27. Moore, *op. cit.*, p. 17.

28. *Manual Presbiteriano* (São Paulo, 1960), p. 8.

29. Émile Léonard, "O Protestantismo Brasileiro," *Revista de História*, Ano III, Nos. 10, 11 (1952), pp. 145–146.

30. Léonard (1951), p. 180.

31. Emilio Willems, "The Structure of the Brazilian Family," *Social Forces*, Vol. XXXI (1950).

32. J. van D. Saunders, "The Social Organization of a Protestant Congregation in the Federal District, Brazil," unpublished M.A. dissertation, Vanderbilt University, Nashville, pp. 160–161.

33. L. A. Costa Pinto, *Lutas de Famílias no Brasil* (São Paulo, 1949), pp. 186 ff.

34. H. Richard Niebuhr, *The Social Sources of Denominationalism* (New York, 1929), p. 28.

35. G. F. Arms, *El Origen del Metodismo y su Implantación en la Costa de Sud-America* (Santiago de Chile, 1923), pp. 30, 40, 46–47.

36. Ferreira, *op. cit.*, I, 195–196.

37. Léonard (1952), pp. 450–451.

38. J. L. Gillin, "A Contribution to the Sociology of Sects," *American Journal of Sociology*, XVI (1910), 239.

39. J. M. Davis, *How the Church Grows in Brazil* (New York and London, 1943), p. 85.

40. *La Voz Bautista*, Vol. LI, No. 6 (1959), 12.

10

SCIENCE AND REFORMATION

R. Hooykaas

Statistical research has established that among the *foreign members* of the Royal Society (in 1829 and in 1869) and the Académie des Sciences (from 1666 to 1883) the Protestants far outnumbered the Roman Catholics.[1] Likewise it has been found that although in the sixteenth century the Protestants in the southern Netherlands formed but a very small part of the population, their scientific production in quantity and quality surpassed that of Roman Catholic authors, whereas after their expulsion science in Belgium had some difficulties and in the eighteenth century was practically nonexistent.[2] It has also been pointed out that among the group of ten scientists who during the English Commonwealth formed the nucleus that would afterward grow into the Royal Society, seven were decidedly Puritan, whereas on the list of members of the Royal Society of 1663, 62 per cent (42 of the 68 for whom the religious affiliation is known) *were clearly Puritan*, a percentage still more striking because Puritans constituted a minority of the population.[3]

Efforts have been made to explain this predilection for observational and experimental sciences by the economic ideals of the class to which those Protestants (mainly Calvinists) belonged. Indeed, the utilitarian interest in applied science often bore relation to the fact that the investigators belonged to the rising middle class.

The flourishing of exact sciences and technology in Holland about 1600 may be attributed to the expansion of the trade, industry, and navigation of that province, which had no clergy in the proper sense (a Reformed minister is not a priest) and almost no nobility. But at the same time there was a great interest in the study of languages (classical and orien-

This essay was prepared for the International Commission for a History of the Scientific and Cultural Development of Mankind and was originally published in Journal of World History, *III, No. 1 (1956). Subsequently reprinted in Guy S. Métraux and François Crouzet (eds.),* The Evolution of Science *(New York: Mentor Books, 1963).*

tal), botany, and zoology, which are not directly "useful." Probably it will always remain impossible to decide whether their economic interests or their religion was first in urging the scientists of England and Holland to research; in any case the religious share in the rapid growth of science is easily underestimated by those modern historians who cannot imagine that religion was the paramount interest of large groups of the population in the sixteenth and seventeenth centuries and who, consequently, do not take seriously the evidences of religious convictions in the works of the great scientists.

For an age in which the religious sanction was necessary to make anything socially acceptable, it made a great difference whether science was condemned, merely tolerated, or positively encouraged by religion.

There is nothing in the dogmas of the three main divisions of Western Christianity—Roman Catholicism, Lutheranism, and Calvinism—to discourage scientific research; great scientists will be found among all three. Yet, they do not all three encourage scientific research to the same degree. Max Weber's idea that a special form of the doctrine of election (*Bewährungsglaube,* that is, the belief that performance of "works" is a sign of election)[4] led to a special attitude in economic and consequently in scientific endeavor among the Calvinists has found little favor with experts on Calvinism. Apart from this explanation, however, which indeed seems to oversimplify matters, the work of Weber and especially that of Merton have established the fact that the Reformed (Calvinists, Zwinglians), because of their *innerweltliche Askese* (an intramundane asceticism), were very much inclined toward science. Here a general attitude, an ethical conception of the human task on earth, rather than a special dogma seems to have been the main incentive.

In the present chapter we shall try to expound how the religious attitude of so-called "ascetic" Protestantism, which more or less stood under Calvin's influence, furthered the development of science.

LOVE OF NATURE

All three confessions held that contemplation of nature may lead the mind to God, the Maker of all things; on the other hand, there was also a general warning that the study of nature may turn the mind away from God, as it will become absorbed in visible things and in secondary, natural causes, forgetting the invisible things and the great Primary Cause. Both views could be corroborated by biblical quotations, and it is evident that a thoroughgoing scientific investigation was liable to be regarded from the latter point of view. When the Middle Ages sought edification in nature, it was for the purpose of illustrating spiritual truths, not of conducting scientific study. In cases where a scientific study of nature was recommended as useful to religion (Thomas Aquinas), it was natural philosophy in the Aristotelian sense and not observational, experimental science that was intended.[5]

The new, humanistic movement showed little inclination to appreciate nature for its own sake. In the works of the humanists "we do not hear the whisper of the winds nor the song of the birds," and Petrarch, who was in this respect an exception in spite of his aesthetic appreciation of nature, spoke scornfully about scientific research.[6] The overgreat admiration for the ancients led to attempts to reconstruct science on the data borrowed from the oldest sources. In many cases the authority of Aristotle was replaced by other authorities, preferably the most ancient (Hippocrates instead of Galen; Galen instead of Avicenna; the genuine Aristotle instead of his medieval interpreters; Plato, Democritus, or "Pythagoras" instead of Aristotle).

A really positive evaluation of nature and of the scientific investigation of nature was furthered by the Reformation. The number of sixteenth-century botanists in central and northern Europe who were of the Reformed faith is indeed remarkable.[7] The "German Fathers of Botany," Otto Brunfels (d. 1534), Jerome Bock (1498–1554), and Leonhard Fuchs (1501–1566), were zealous Protestants; Clusius (1526–1609), Dodoens (1517–1585), Jean and Gaspard Bauhin (1560–1624), de Lobel (1538–1616), belonged to the Reformed Church; William Turner (1520–1568), "the true pioneer of natural history in England,"[8] had a share in the introduction of Calvinism into England. The same independence of thought which led many botanists to throw in their lot with the spiritual reformers of their day also led them to discard many of the superstitious beliefs connected with plants (astrology, signatures), though they were not quite free from it.[9] Many of the early Protestant botanists and zoologists (Clusius, de Lobel, Pierre Pena, Jean Bauhin, Felix Platter, Volcher Coiter) were for some time pupils of the great naturalist Guillaume Rondelet (1507–1566), one of the leaders of the Reformed in southern France.[10] Some of them stood in immediate contact with the Reformers: Platter with Calvin,[11] Konrad von Gesner, the great Zürich naturalist, with Bullinger, Clusius with Melanchthon, Turner with Hugh Latimer, Johannes a Lasco, and Thomas Cranmer.[12] All these authors show a wholehearted acceptance of nature in which they recognize the work of God's hands. Volcher Coiter (1534–1576), one of the founders of embryology and comparative anatomy, "the most religious anatomist of the 16th century," never tired of praising God on account of the wonderful adaptation of animal structure,[13] and Clusius testified that botanical discoveries gave him as much joy as if he had found a prodigious treasure.[14] Bernard Palissy (1509–1589), the famous Huguenot potter, reveals throughout his works a sympathetic love for the earth and the trees, often maltreated by the laborers; he passionately admired the plants "even the most despised." [15] These early Protestants shared the deep love and admiration of animals and plants of which the Psalms, the Book of Job, and the Gospels give testimony and which is also evident in the works of Luther and Calvin.[16]

But love of nature does not necessarily include love of the science of nature, and from this latter does not necessarily ensue appreciation of the experimental and observational method of scientific research. Therefore we have to consider *why* the Reformers believed that science ought to be cultivated (viz., *to the glory of God* and *to the benefit of mankind*) and *how* this should be done, according to them (viz., *in an empirical way, in spite of human authorities,* and *by using our hands*).

I

THE GLORY OF GOD

The predilection for scientific research in Protestant circles may be largely explained by the great emphasis laid by Reformed theology upon the central theme: "the glory of God." This has been beautifully worded by Kepler (1571–1630), when he said that, being priests of God to the book of nature, the astronomers ought to have in their minds not the glory of their own intellect, but above anything else the glory of God (1598).[17]

The Reform confessions emphasize that God reveals Himself in Scripture and in nature, "which is before our eyes as a beautiful book, in which all created things, large and small, are like letters, showing the invisible things of God." [18] Recommendation of pious contemplation, however, does not necessarily imply an urge to scientific research. The latter was often regarded as a real danger to religion, not only by medieval asceticism but also by some spiritualistic sects of the sixteenth century (Anabaptists). Reformed theology maintained an opposition to this belief that the duty of glorifying God on account of His works should be performed by all faculties, not only by the eyes but also by the intellect. Calvin deemed those who neglect the study of nature as guilty as those who, when investigating God's works, forget the Creator. He sharply reproved "phantastic" opponents of science, as being only fit to make men proud and not as leading to a "knowledge of God and the conduct of ordinary life." [19] Again and again he testified his positive appreciation of scientific research as penetrating deeper into the wonders of nature than mere contemplation. And he does not mean the speculative "physics" of his time, but the real sciences (in the modern sense) of that epoch: astronomy and anatomy, which revealed the secrets of the macrocosm and the microcosm.[20]

His followers, even the most conservative among them (like G. Voetius), were enthusiastic supporters of science and learning. Reformed theology not only tolerated scientific research (this had also been done by Roman Catholic and Lutheran theology) but even demanded it.[21]

The duty of scientific investigation of nature was not regarded as a hard law; it was enjoyed as a duty of love, as is clearly shown in the works of Robert Recorde (c. 1510–1558), L. Fuchs, Thomas Digges (1545–1595), B. Palissy, J. Kepler, and Philips van Lansbergen (1561–1632). Sometimes it was even exaggerated: perhaps as a consequence of a growing but as yet unconscious rationalism, it was often propounded in the sixteenth century that rational scientific investigation is a higher fulfillment of the divine command than mere contemplation. Thomas Browne[22] and Robert Boyle[23] believed that the scientist performs the duty of glorifying God better than anyone else: a "learned admiration," a "philosophical worship," is the highest act of religion. They were not aware of the fact that thus they were conceiving a new separate priesthood, to wit, the priests to the book of nature, for they sincerely believed that the cultivation of science does not require much special training and talent: "Here is enough business for minds of all sizes." [24] Yet earlier investigators, while recognizing with Calvin that the scientist looks deeper into God's work, did not conclude that, consequently, he better accomplishes his duty of glorifying God. They considered the question from the standpoint of the parable of the talents, which played an important role in their ethics (for example, Palissy; van Lansbergen). He who has the talent and the occasion for doing research has the duty to exploit his talent.[25] Consequently, Kepler was of the opinion that the unlearned who praises God only for what is seen by the eyes does not do Him less honor than the astronomer to whom God gave also the eye of reason to see more clearly (1609).[26]

THE GENERAL PRIESTHOOD OF BELIEVERS

On the other hand, the conception that everybody ought to glorify God by discovering His wisdom, power, and glory in creation according to his *talents* meant that the competency and right to do scientific work did not belong exclusively to a certain class of people.

The Protestant doctrine of the priesthood of all believers proclaimed not only the *right* but even the *duty* of everybody (who was able to do so) to read the book of Scripture for himself. As a consequence, likewise the right and duty to read the book of nature, without regard to the authority of the fathers of natural philosophy—Aristotle, Pliny, Ptolemy, Galen— was put forward. While fully acknowledging the value of specialized biblical scholarship, the Reformers had nevertheless maintained that the meaning of Scripture is self-evident on essential points and, accordingly, that nobody can be excused by delegating the responsibility for reading Scripture to the hierarchy. In the same way everybody, in principle and according to his capacities, might be a priest to the book of creation, in defiance sometimes of the ancient authorities. When Palissy was derided because of his ignorance of the classical languages and hence of the scientific books written therein, he proudly answered that he had obtained his knowledge through the anatomy of nature and not through reading books, for "I have had no book but heaven and earth and it is given to everyman to know and read this beautiful book." [27] The belief that everyone should read the book of nature according to his capacities supported the defenders of the "new" science when they called upon the unlearned to contribute to the knowledge of natural history, geography, and physics by communicating their observations on birds and flowers, on ebb and flood tide, on celestial phenomena and the inclination of the magnetic needle. Travelers and mariners especially were invited to do so.[28] Because of the experimental character of the "new philosophy" the manual workers were invited to contribute their skill and knowledge, for it was a "philosophy of hands" more than a "philosophy of words and notions."

The general priesthood of believers is perhaps the only specifically Protestant doctrine that was sometimes consciously, sometimes unconsciously, used to back up science. In any case this doctrine had a large share in framing Protestant thought.

THE BENEFIT OF MANKIND

The glory of God and the benefit of mankind are as closely connected in Christian theology as the two tables of the Law, summarized by Christ as the duty of love for God and our neighbors. Therefore the insistence of Reformed theology on the benefit that may come to mankind from useful inventions in medicine and technique is not a manifestation of the capitalistic mentality of a rising merchant class that hides its mammonistic intentions behind a pious pretense. Here again genuine love for God and one's fellow beings is the main driving force. Even Francis Bacon (1561–1626), often represented as the patron of utilitarianism, was largely inspired by religious motives. He refused to mix up science and theology, but his Calvinistic religion[29] shines out on the pages of his nontheological works. He cited St. Paul in order to proclaim that knowledge without love is vain and that the scientist demonstrates love through the production of works,[30] which are not done for mental satisfaction alone. "La science pour la science" is totally opposed to Reformed ethics; the glory of God and the invention of useful things to lessen the burdens of human life are the final aims of science. Pierre La Ramée (Petrus Ramus, 1515–1572) defined each science by its application: "geometry is the art of measuring well," and so on. Not the knowledge of things but their useful application is, according to him, the aim of science, and Kepler afterward nicknamed him a "usuarius." His influence on Puritanism was very great: it was especially felt in Cambridge and Harvard.[31] Milton, Ames, and Rudolf Snellius belonged to his followers. It seems, however, that the utilitarian tendencies of Puritan science were not *caused* by the philosophies of their heroes Ramus and Bacon, but that these scholars only gave an able expression of feelings that were already widespread independently of them.

In Holland, during the Eighty Years' War, Reformed ministers, inspired by religious and social motives, furthered scientific schemes, especially those of value for the development of industry (windmills) and navigation. These were necessary to continue the war against Spain, the success of which was closely linked with the economic and naval power of the Netherlands. Dr. Isaac Beeckman (1588–1637) in Dordrecht founded the first meteorological station in Europe with the help of the town magistrate. There he made observations with the minister Colvius. The minister Philips van Lansbergen spent his time on astronomy, generously supported by the Estates of Zeeland; the minister Plancius (1552–1622) at Amsterdam, one of the ablest geographers of his time, delivered lectures on astronomy and cartography from the pulpit of the Zeedijk Chapel and was the driving force behind the efforts of the Hollanders to find a new way to the Indies.

In England, Leonard Digges (c. 1530–1563) and his son Thomas, both zealous Protestants, wrote in the vernacular to further astronomy, geodesy, and so on.[32] Thomas Digges even abandoned pure mathematics; in order to employ them in the service of prince and country, he reduced the "sciences mathematicall from demonstrative contemplations to experimentall actions." [33] In 1588 Thomas Hood delivered lectures in London on geometry and astronomy for soldiers, artisans, and mariners. At Gresham College, founded in London in 1597, lectures on divinity, music, geometry, and astronomy were to be delivered in English and Latin. In Rotterdam, Beeckman, together with a physician, a mill builder, and a mathematician, founded a "Collegium Mechanicum" in order to give gratuitous advice to the town magistrates on the emendation of the harbor, shipbuilding, mill building, and drainage, and he planned lectures on mechanical problems in the vernacular "for the benefit of carpenters, masons, skippers, and other burghers." [34]

II

EMPIRICISM

The Reformers wanted to keep exclusively to the record of divine revelation as written down in the Bible. They wished to abolish what they considered rationalistic, superfluous additions to the biblical revelation and to return to the pure source. A parallel attitude was assumed toward the book of creation. In the interpretation of nature the same sense of responsibility prevailed as in the exegesis of Scripture: they were anxious not to deviate from the true meaning of the Bible, so they felt religiously bound to nature. Here also they considered themselves to be on holy ground, confronted with a book of God that had to be accepted even when not completely understood. It was sacrilege to make it conformable to human reason, which, after the Fall, is always prone to blur and distort the facts in order to satisfy its own pride. This faithfulness to a reality, that may even be incomprehensible, becomes evident in Francis Bacon's opinion that being tied to facts prevents the divagations of human reason and fantasy: "The understanding left to itself ought always to be suspected." "The wit and mind of man, if it work upon matter, which is the contemplation of the creatures of God, worketh according to the stuff and is limited thereby, but if it works upon itself, as a spider worketh his web, then it is endless, and brings forth indeed cobwebs of learning." [35] The same attitude was prevalent in William Gilbert (1540–1603), who founded his science primarily upon observation and experiment because "it is easy for men of acute intellect, apart from experiments and practice, to err." [36] Christian religion, they believed, is a religion of facts; it bears a historical character. In the same way, natural science is founded upon facts, however much they may transcend human understanding. In their antirationalism the spirit of the Reformation and the spirit of experimental science show a close affinity. In accordance with biblical theology, Bacon ascribed rationalistic aspirations to the *hubris* that lies at the bottom of all revolt against God; by following the dictates of our own reason and imposing our ideas upon nature instead of religiously seeking to discover how it pleased God to make things, we have lost our dominion over nature.[37] There was a distrust of general systems, excogitated by the human brain, and consequently investigation of particular things was encouraged.

Protestant theology was perfectly aware of this resemblance between its own spirit and that of experimental science, and it often regarded the latter as an aid to religion. The Puritan army chaplain John Webster considered it an advantage of the experimental "science of facts" above the old "speculative science of notions and words," that the students "may not grow proud with the brood of their own brains," [38] and Thomas Sprat compared the qualities of a good Christian to those of a good experimental philosopher: both doubt their own thoughts and acknowledge their own ignorance.[39]

The religious submission to facts sometimes led to quite unexpected results. Kepler was thoroughly imbued with Platonism and, accordingly, he was a priori convinced of the truth of the dogma of the circular and uniform movement of the celestial bodies. Yet, after a heavy inner struggle, he abandoned this prejudice, which had never before been doubted, not even by Copernicus and Galileo, because of a small difference of eight minutes, and propounded nonuniform motion in elliptic orbits. This was the birth of really modern astronomy (Copernicus was only restoring the "very ancient," so-called Pythagorean, tradition instead of the younger Aristotelian one). Without exaggeration he could state that "these eight minutes paved the way for a reformation of the whole of astronomy." [40]

Angelo Sala (1576–1637), an Italian Reformed refugee who was physician to the Stadthouder of Holland and to the Duke of Mecklenburg, had less difficulty in abandoning old prejudices, as he was first of all an experimenter with little inclination to speculation. He analyzed and synthesized copper vitriol and demonstrated the identity of artificial and natural vitriol (*Anatomia vitrioli*, 1617). In this way he overthrew the general prejudice, deeply imbedded in medieval and ancient science, that the products of nature cannot be made by art.[41] Sala rejected the speculative chemistry of his days, "for chemistry occupies itself only with things that may be touched by human hands and it consists only in concrete proofs."

Palissy, the Huguenot martyr, repeated throughout his works, "I was there," "I saw that"; he promised to satisfy the senses of sight and touch to everyone who might visit his collection, where within two hours more might be learned by contemplation of the displayed objects than by fifty years of study of the theories and opinions of the ancient philosophers.[42]

In the same way Gilbert pretended that his philosophy was proved by "real demonstrations and by experiments manifestly apparent to the senses," and Bacon's main objection to the Greeks was that they relied more upon reason than upon immediate observation of nature (their philosophy is "talkative," not "generative"; it bears contention instead of fruit); truth ought not to be sought in the mind, but in the world.[43] Palissy praised experiences as being prior to theory; it has the first and the last word: "Practice brought forth theory"; "by practice I find . . . the theory of many philosophers, even of the most ancient and the most renowned, to be false."[44] Another artisan, the instrument maker Robert Norman (1581), promised to base his arguments on magnetism not upon conjectures and imagination, but only upon experience, reason, and demonstration; according to him, experiments are "Reason's finger," pointing to truth.[45]

This empiricism led the experimental scientists to a mild skepticism, even toward their own theories. The geographical discoveries had exploded all philosophical reasoning about the division of land and water and about the inhabitated parts of the earth. Here bare facts overthrew all clever theories. The unexpected discovery of countries with human inhabitants, animals, and plants never dreamt of proved the possibility of the seemingly marvelous and corroborated the religious acknowledgment of God's infinite power. As William Watts remarked: the *thoughts* of the philosophers were contradicted by the *unexpected observations* of the navigators.[46] As age-old prejudices crumbled down, a remarkable freedom of thought and openness toward new inventions and discoveries was created. The seventeenth-century scientists liked to say that there are no "columns of Hercules," no *ne plus ultra* in philosophy. This led them, especially the followers of Bacon (who very often were Puritans or, like Bacon himself, were influenced by Puritanism), to propound audacious hypotheses. Precisely the fact that hypotheses were regarded as only provisory, and that consequently a suspension of judgment was indispensable until experience had confirmed a supposition, caused this freedom of theorizing.

Isaac Beeckman, the Calvinist rector of the Latin School at Dort, accepted the Copernican hypothesis as probable, but did not consider it an established truth. The Puritan clergyman Henry Gellibrand (well known for his magnetical experiments) assumed the same attitude; he sees no escape from Copernicanism, however much it contradicts everything considered as "rational" up to his time; it easily leads us "to the consideration of the imbecillity of Man's apprehension, as not able rightly to conceive of this admirable opifice of God or frame of the world, without falling foule on so great an absurdity." [47] The Puritan divine John Wilkins, a bold thinker, said that not everything marvelous should be considered beforehand as supernatural; it is one of the tasks of natural science to reduce the apparently supernatural to the natural. As Beeckman had put it before him: theology goes from nonwonder to wonder, science from wonder to nonwonder.[48] Antirationalism on a religious basis evidently did not mean gullibility toward supernatural. This aloofness was perhaps the very consequence of the fact that these intensively religious people satisfied their religious demands by means of scriptural revelation and did not want a substitute for it in systems of natural philosophy. This becomes evident in Beeckman. He was one of the first defenders of atomism (both Descartes and Gassendi were influenced by him), but this atomism did not have a quasi-religious significance for him. It was only a physical hypothesis more satisfactory than scholasticism, but in his opinion it did not even answer every physical question, let alone metaphysical ones.[49] The same critical attitude toward his own theories prevailed with the "sceptical chymist" Robert Boyle, whose free thought and mild skepticism were closely connected with his religious faith. This attitude was extremely favorable for the development of natural science, but it destroyed the magnificent illusions of the Middle Ages as well as those of the seventeenth century (Cartesianism). A conservative theologian, Alexander Ross, rightly complained that the new philosophers had left the old and known path and had reduced Aristotle's "comely order" into the old chaos.[50] The new philosophy could not be better characterized: an adventurous quest for truth, even when harmonious illusions were destroyed by it.

It should be pointed out that an *empiricism* founded upon a theological basis was not new. It had been anticipated by those defenders of Augustinian theology who, like Bishop Tempier in 1277 and Nicole Oresme in 1377, maintained the possibility of marvelous natural phenomena which seemed impossible to scholastic rationalism.[51] The theological background of the Reformed scientists had much in common with theirs; the difference was only that science had progressed since then and that the appreciation of scientific research had grown immensely.

The empiristic tendency was perhaps strongest among the Puritans of the Commonwealth, many of whom, though Calvinistic in theology, in many respects deviated from continental Calvinists and from early Puritans by their bolder conceptions of political and ecclesiastical freedom and in their stronger bias toward science and even against the humanities. John Webster demanded "laboratories as well as libraries" in behalf of the academic youth, in order that "they may not be idly trained up in notions, speculations, and verbal disputes, but may learn to inure their hands to labour." [52] John Hall, in his proposal for reform of the universities, rejected "formal logick" as leading to vain disputes and metaphysics as "abstrusely abstract" and thus far remote from use. He felt more sympathy with mathematics and natural philosophy, but his knowledge of the latter was derived not from books but from "experiences." [53] Evidently Ramus had influenced him. Ramus was against deductive logic, rhetoric, and so on; he wanted to start from actual practice and to state the rules observed therein. In the same way John Webster opposed the teaching of formal grammar, because grammar may be learned much better from reading and conversation, and Jean Drury wished that logic should be taught not in an abstract way but "by examples of every kind and in concreto."

The Puritan educationists particularly stressed the value of concrete examples, phenomena, material aspects. Their passionate desire to substitute truth for imagination could easily lead to a rejection of the literary aspects of education as "vanities," when the counterbalancing influence of their biblical background, which with them was still all-pervading, gradually grew weaker. But at first any excessive enthusiasm for scientific education was opposed by such moderate Puritans as John Wilkins. Seth Ward recognized that "verbal exercises" should be replaced by observations and experiments and that more attention should be given to chemistry, agriculture, and such, but the academies he regarded as having a more general character which made it necessary for them to give assistance to those who wanted to study theology and languages and literature.[54] This moderate attitude prevailed in England even during the Commonwealth, and certainly also in New England. It was recognized that experimental science should have a more prominent place, but that humanistic studies also are important. On the Continent (and here the Netherlands, where the Reformed Church—ruled on Presbyterian principles—was the only one officially recognized, offer the best example) this same attitude was prevalent. The position of science here never was such a bone of contention as in England, but neither was it so much a matter of popular and theological emotion as in England. Yet the interest in science was so great in Holland that it was put up as an example to his countrymen by the English apologist of science Thomas Sprat.

It seems, however, that there was no country where the fate of the scientific movement was so closely and so generally connected with religion as in England, and undoubtedly the most ardent apologists of freedom of science on religious motives were amongst the English Puritans. Science formed an integral part of their idea of a *civitas Dei*.

The Reformed were criticized by their Lutheran brethren because of their "this-worldliness" and because of their zest for "works." Indeed, they wanted to animate every department of life by the ferment of Christian religion. They did not believe that the kingdom of God could be founded on earth; their real fatherland was in heaven. And yet they considered this life as a preparatory stage for the life to come—a stage in which they had to act *as if* the kingdom could already be realized. They went to New England "to found the perfect society . . . and never expected it to be perfect, but only the best that fallible men could make." [55] This comprehensive view of life, so characteristic of Calvinism, was never more consciously conceived than by the English Puritans, and when they founded their Commonwealth many of them forgot all theological reserve and genuinely believed that the *kingdom of God on earth* was nearer than ever before. Milton belonged to these optimists; John Hall was another one. All good things having been accomplished, only the establishment of "learned piety" [56] was still lacking. He wrote to Parliament: "If you will now make good our hopes in this one thing, you will put an end to all our wishes, and settle us in a condition which will somewhat resemble that eternall fruition which we all breath after, a time of prayses." [57] The difficulties of the time should not dissuade Parliament from this work of peace, for there is the illustrious example of Holland, which, while struggling with a sad war and not yet wholly free from a "perfidious and horrid Tyrant," showed "prodigal magnificence for learning." [58] The "discovery of a new world full of knowledge" seemed quite near. "God surely . . . begins a fuller manifestation of himselfe" and that manifestation was largely by means of scientific discovery.

The Puritan enterprise of establishing a commonwealth wherein Christianity would not be a matter of Sunday worship alone but should penetrate social ethics, economics, politics as well as science, was shipwrecked. Yet some remnants were saved and used to construct the edifice of post-Restoration England with its firmly established experimental science.

"ENTHUSIASM" AND SCIENCE

When Calvin wrote against those "phantastic people" who decry all sciences because they would only make man arrogant and lead him away from God, he was thinking of spiritualists like the Anabaptists. In the upheaval of the English Civil War such spiritualistic sects came to the fore and in 1653 Parliament even considered the suppression of universities as heathenish and unnecessary. However, the majority "gave a stop to their frenzy." [59] In 1657 Cromwell had to protect Oxford against Anabaptist hostility. The members of the spiritualistic sects like the Quakers in England and the Labadists and the Mennonites in Holland were not very friendly toward human learning in general. Their aversion to school theology was of the same nature as that of some otherwise very culturally inclined Puritans (like Webster); their dislike of metaphysical philosophy they shared with all opponents of rationalism; their indifference to science took its origin in a type of asceticism which approached monastic *ausserweltliche Askese*. But the Mennonites had already ceased their opposition to learning before 1620,[60] whereas the Quakers soon took an active interest in applied science.

On the other hand, many conservative clergymen, supported by political reactionaries, were more afraid of science than most sectarians. They regarded it as a danger to the established church, and after the Restoration of the Stuarts, Joseph Glanvill, Robert Boyle, and Thomas Sprat did much to refute their arguments, especially as the charge of Puritanism ("enthusiasm" or "fanaticism") as well as that of deism and atheism was made against the "virtuosi." Now, it has already been made evident that those who were most radical in their return to "Scripture alone" in theology (to wit, the Reformed, Zwinglians, and Calvinists or, in general, the puritanically minded) were also most radical in their support of a direct inquiry into nature by experiment and observation, which was the ideal of the Royal Society, which was founded shortly after the Restoration. Consequently it is small wonder that after 1660 "fanaticism" and "new learning" were decried as cognate vices by High Church divines (like Robert South) and by the playwrights and "wits" who vied with each other in hatred of the Puritans. At the beginning of the republican period it had been just the reverse: the Puritans then were accused by the High Church party of destroying all learning; they were called "Goths and Vandals." They were then all deliberately identified with some left-wing extremists. The Puritan government, however, furthered scientific investigations in the Baconian sense, as is evident from the fact that some of the most important founders of the Royal Society had been appointed at Oxford during the Commonwealth (Wilkins, 1648; Wallis, 1649; Goddard, 1651; Petty, 1651).[61] In 1653 Parliament appointed a committee "for the advancement of learning" (of which the Puritan physicians Sydenham and Goddard were members). The Protector Richard (1658) also had the intention to advance "useful learning," and in New England the Puritan clergy were foremost in their promotion of new astronomy and science.[62] Thus it was impossible to maintain that the Puritans hated every kind of learning, and therefore after the Restoration the charge was reversed and they were accused of loving science too much.

It is tragicomical that on this occasion the *defenders* of science identified "puritanism" with the "enthusiasts," the zealots of 1650, in order to demonstrate that science was quite fashionable and had nothing to do

with Puritanism. Sprat, who took up the cause of science against its de-
tractors, did his best to prove that "enthusiasm" was obnoxious to science
but that the true Church of England doctrine alone could and should
foster it. People like Sprat, often "trimmers" (ex-Puritans) themselves,
knew perfectly well that most Puritans had as violent a dislike of "enthusiasm" as their High Church antagonists. "Solid learning," secular as well
as sacred, was dear to them.

III

AUTHORITY IN SCIENCE

Experience versus reason was the background of empiricism. This includes also experience versus the reason of the ancients, experience versus
authority. The opposition to human authority appealed very strongly to
the Reformed. Their minds had been trained to the idea that one has to
find out the truth for oneself and that there ought to be independence of
human authority in order that the submission to divine authority be the
more complete. The general laicization must have influenced also their
scientific attitude. New ideas could easily get hold of them and were at
least not rejected because of their nonconformity to traditional beliefs.[63]
No ecclesiastical censure on books and scientific ideas was officially applied by a central body of discipline, and scholastic philosophy was not
officially connected with theology. When, for example, the great Dutch
theologian Gisbertus Voetius (1588–1676) defended the Aristotelian philosophy as a necessary support of orthodox Protestant theology, his opponents of the Cocceian party either divorced philosophy from theology or
inclined to Cartesianism. When Voetius regarded the geocentric world
picture as the only one compatible with Scripture, the no less orthodox
Cocceians freely adhered to Copernicanism without interference of synods
or church consistories.

In spite of their reverence for the Fathers of the Church, the Reformers
never forsook a critical and free attitude toward them. Likewise the Protestant scientists liked to point out against their Romish opponents, who
recognized "Tradition" as well as Scripture as a source of revelation, how
many mistakes the Church Fathers and the popes had made in scientific
matters. The Reformation might signify to some of its adherents a return
to the church of the first centuries, but to the majority it was a return to
Scripture. In the same way many naturalists were not content with rejecting medieval commentators but also wished to be free from classical antiquity, as they wanted to return to Nature herself. Of course this led to
exaggeration, but on the whole this iconoclasm was healthy for the development of science. It was necessary that criticism of the ancients and consciousness of the value of the present age should replace the adoration of
the past.

Many Protestants could not wholly free themselves from the spirit of humanism; it was difficult for them to purify their thoughts of the influence of their university education. Beza and Melanchthon, the immediate successors of the two great Reformers, even returned to *scholasticism*. Perhaps it may be said that the scientists often were more thoroughly Protestant than the theologians. Kepler, who profoundly admired Plato, obeyed "divine revelation" rather than the "divine philosopher," not only in metaphysical questions but also when accepting elliptic orbits. He was a devoted Lutheran, but Luther's authority did not move him to accept the Lutheran doctrine of Holy Supper. This same freedom he maintained in scientific questions: "Holy Lactantius, who denied that the earth is spherical; holy Augustine who acknowledged the sphericity of the earth, but denied the existence of antipodes; holy the Officium that recognized the antipodes, but rejects the motion of the earth . . . but holier yet is to me Truth, which reveals that the earth is a small sphere, that antipodes exist, and that the earth is moving." [64]

Palissy, the founder of paleontology and agricultural science, declared "the Ancients were as human as the moderns, and they may have erred like us." [65] The same opposition to the authority of the ancients is evident in the works of Norman, Gilbert, Wilkins, and many other English writers. Especially the "Philosophia Libera" (1621) of the clergyman Nathaniel Carpenter (a protégé of the Calvinist Archbishop Usher) was a plea for liberty of scientific research and freedom from authority.

THE REFORMATION OF SCIENCE

The adherents of new philosophy and those of new theology were both accused of forsaking ancient traditions and rashly accepting dangerous novelties. On the other hand, the scientists of the period themselves were keenly aware of the fact that there was a connection between the liberation of theology from ecclesiastical and philosophical tradition by the Reformation and the liberation of science from ancient authority through the New Learning. Both were considered a return to the original and truly ancient and authentic source of knowledge. When speaking of Paracelsus the physician Richard Bostocke (1585) said: "He was not the author and inventour of this arte as the followers of the Ethnickes phisicke doe imagine . . . no more then Wicklife, Luther, Oecolampadius, Swinglius, Calvin, etc. were the Author and inventors of the Gospell and religion in Christes Church, when they restored it to his puritie, according to Gods word," and he made the same comparison with Copernicus.[66]

Bostocke compared the cause of true religion, which was oppressed because only interpretations in accordance with Scotus and Aquinas were allowed, with the cause of true chemistry, agreeing with experience, which was eclipsed by the "sophisticall stuffe" of Aristotle, Galen, and Avicenna.[67]

Aristotle, often considered as the common enemy to Reformed theology and the new science, was called a "pope in philosophy," and the "new philosophers" warned against the custom of quoting his texts as if they had Scriptural authority.

Thomas Culpepper (1655) gathered in a few sentences some typical aspects of the Reformation and their parallels in the new science, to wit, the antiauthoritarian character of both and the collegiate character of their activities in synods and scientific societies.[68] And John Hall, like Noah Biggs, was of the opinion that after ecclesiastical and political reform "this last piece of reformation" ought to be the "reformation of learning." [69]

After the Reformation the Latitudinarians in the Anglican Church went on to compare the Reformation with the New Learning; according to Sprat, they have much in common, both of them "passing by the corrupt copies, and referring themselves to the perfect originals for their instruction; the one to the Scripture, the other to the large volumes of the creatures." [70]

PURITANS AND AUTHORITY IN SCIENCE

The Puritans of the sixteenth century as well as their opponents (until about 1630) of the "Anglican" type generally were Calvinist in doctrine. However, in their desire to abolish episcopacy and to keep the Sabbath very strictly, they went further than Calvin, who did not think it necessary to impose the Genevan form of church government on churches abroad and who adhered to more liberal views on Sabbatical rest. Gradually many Puritans, by the persecution they underwent, were driven into a certain extremism, so that the Puritanism which shook off the yoke of Charles I and Archbishop William Laud contained sections which were more radical than the Presbyterian or moderately Episcopalian Puritans who started the movement. In these groups laicization, so important for natural science, had progressed furthest, and the dislike of authorities in theology and science was strongest. As uncompromisingly as some Puritans combated the introduction of alien elements in biblical theology, they withstood the adulteration of science by speculative ingredients. They were the most intrepid defenders of scientific freedom, which they regarded as a necessary supplement to theological freedom. Both should be liberated from Aristotle and scholasticism. Noah Biggs (1651) asked for an "Academy of Philosophick freedom," [71] and Webster remembered those "valiant champions who have stood up to maintain truth against the impetuous torrent of Antiquity, authority, and universality of opinion" and demanded a "philosophical liberty to be bound to the authority of none, but truth it self." [72]

The Puritans when dealing with theological and ethical issues were inclined to reject anything not sanctioned by the Bible; especially scholasticism seemed to them popish and half-heathenish. One step further and Aristotelian natural philosophy was also condemned because of its heathen origin. This could be a strong argument to the Protestant mind, especially to people like Biggs, Webster, and William Dell. The disciples of Paracelsus made liberal use of it; the title of Bostocke's work is a whole program: "the difference between the auncient Physicke, first taught by the godly forefathers, consisting in unitie peace and concords and the latter Phisicke proceeding from Idolaters, Ethnickes, and Heathen: as Gallen, and such other consisting in dualitie, discorde, and contrarietie." The fact that Biggs and Webster, like Bostocke seventy years earlier, were apologists not only of experimental, Baconian learning but also of Paracelsus, proves that they had a tendency to mysticism of a kind not congenial to Calvinism. This becomes evident in their attitude to "learned divinity." Continuing a venerable tradition from the Middle Ages to Luther and Calvin, they opposed the blending of biblical doctrine with pagan philosophy, but they went much farther in that they joined the "spiritualists" in their rejection of a "learned ministry." On the other hand, the conservatives seemed to forget the danger, both to science and theology, that was hidden in the connection with Aristotelian philosophy. The Netherlands Reformed theologian Voetius was too much in need of the help of scholastic philosophy in his combat against Cartesianism, atomism, and Copernicanism to bother about its pagan or "Romish" origin.[73] And, like Alexander Ross, he was of the opinion that the very cause of science and religion demanded unswerving loyalty to Aristotle.

In general, however, the *via media* was chosen. What was acceptable in the ancients was accepted, and at the same time it was felt that contemporary science was at least equal and in many respects superior to that of antiquity. The doctrine of "common grace," which plays such an important role in Calvin's theology, may have been influential in warning Protestants against a rigorous and wholesale rejection of the ancients on religious grounds. According to Calvin the Fall had done most damage to mankind in religious and ethical respects (here only a very faint glimmer of light has been left in "natural" man), but the intellectual faculties were comparatively little impaired. He was too realistic to extend the situation of religion to all departments of life only for analogy's sake; he believed that outside the sphere of the Church, truth had been revealed in a general way in degrees differing according to the subject. He was of the opinion that we owe much to the heathen in the arts and sciences, and on the grounds of the Bible and of common experience he refused to consider this contribution worthless. According to Calvin the light of truth often shines clearly in the heathen and "if we hold the Spirit of God to be the only source of Truth, we will neither reject, nor despise this truth wherever it may reveal itself, provided we do not wish to offend the Spirit of God." [74] In this moderate attitude most Reformed scholars persisted, though deviations to one or the other side occurred. They shook off the yoke of systems and selected from the pagan or Roman Catholic past everything that, according to them, could stand the test of Scripture and "reality." As the Calvinist poet Johan de Brune (1657) put it: "Wheresoever Truth may be, were it in a Turk or Tatar, it must be cherished. . . . Let us seek the honeycomb even within the lion's mouth." [75]

MANUAL LABOR

The love for experimental science and the technological interest of the Reformed were closely interwoven with their ethical evaluation of manual labor. Experimentation often derives the choice as well as the solution of its problems from the crafts, and now that the speculative occupations were to a certain extent devaluated, there was, even among the learned, less disrespect for manual labor. In principle manual labor had never been slighted by Jewish and Christian ethics as it had been in late antiquity and, perhaps under the influence thereof, by the humanists.

In a beautiful poem the sixteenth-century clergyman George Herbert expressed the Christian attitude to labor. "For Thy sake" is the tincture that makes the meanest labor bright; this clause "makes drudgery divine," even the sweeping of a room.[76]

The Reformed matrimonial service of the Netherlands calls upon the husband to "labour faithfully and diligently in his Divine calling," and this was certainly more than a pious phrase. Isaac Beeckman, although a theologian and a medical doctor, did not deem it below his dignity to be a chandler and manufacturer of water conduits. He found therein abundant occasions for experiments in mechanics, hydrostatics, and hydrodynamics and he only abandoned this profession when the headmastership of a Latin school seemed to offer more leisure for pursuing scientific investigations. Esteem for manual labor and diligence in "industries" were regarded as the main causes for the increased wealth of the Hollanders and the improvement of their minds; they "not only disgraced, but terrified their neighbours by their industry." [77]

Agriculture also was extolled by this ethical conception. Palissy was proud of being an artisan, and he urged the sons of the rural nobility to spend their energy on agricultural inventions instead of idling away their time, for agriculture is "a right labour, worthy of being honoured." [78] Of all manual labor, that of the peasant was held in the greatest contempt; Palissy gave it a scientific background (he is now regarded as one of the founders of agricultural chemistry), as he was of the opinion that "there is no occupation for which more science is required." [79] Bacon stigmatized the opinion that the dignity of the mind should be impaired through occupation with material things; he stressed the importance of the mechanical arts, like chemistry and agriculture.[80]

The conservatives, on the other hand, thought they could not better disqualify new ideas than by pointing out that they were accepted only by artisans. William Barlowe declared that arguments for the rotation of the earth, like those of Mark Ridley, "may goe current in a mechanicall Trades-man shop, yet they are very insufficient to bee allowed for good by men of learning." [81] The Roman Catholic canon Libertus Fromondus (of Antwerp) emphasized that the Copernican theory was especially favored by the heretics of Holland and Zeeland (and not by the Catholics of Spain and Portugal) and that amongst them only the seafarers, not the really learned, upheld it.[82] That manual labor was little appreciated by the conservatives is demonstrated by their using this argument (which was not entirely just).

The experimental and empirical character of the new science made the co-operation of the craftsmen indispensable. More than the philosophers, they were confronted with hard facts. Confidence in wrong theories on ebb and flood tide or on the magnetic needle could cause a disastrous end of a sailor's life. Therefore, the advocates of "new philosophy" mocked their opponents for shunning manual operations and extolled the simple artisan as being nearer the truth. And did not the craftsmen have every reason for their growing self-esteem? Had not the first effective blow to traditional science been delivered by the seafarers who crossed the torrid zone, discovered the inhabitants of the Southern Hemisphere (against the opinion of Greek philosophers as well as that of Christian Church Fathers), and found a new world with plants and animals unheard of in the books of Greek and medieval naturalists? Not a new theory but simple *facts,* discovered by simple people, overthrew the old philosophy. The same was true of experimentation: "Simple workmen were capable of convicting of error all great men who are called philosophers" (Pascal).[83]

The artificers were not reluctant in proving their claims; sometimes they were even rather provocative. Palissy lamented the fact that he did not know Latin, because this prevented him from detecting the errors of the philosophical works that had not been translated, and he warned his readers against the "crooked theories of vain philosophies." Robert Norman (1581) was hardly less defiant. Some learned people had written that mechanics and mariners should not meddle with scientific questions, and Norman replied that the scholars in their studies amongst their books can imagine far-fetched theories, "yet there are in this land diverse Mechanicians, that in their severall faculties and professions, have the use of those arts at their fingers ends, and can applie them to their severall purposes, as effectuallie, and more readilie, than those that would most condemne them." [84]

The new philosophy needed the co-operation of the "learned" (mathematicians) with the artificers, and very often this was indeed accomplished. John Dee, Robert Recorde, Thomas Digges, Petrus Plancius, Isaac Beeckman—all men who had university training—entered into friendly collaboration with artificers who wrote on experimental science, like John

Blagrave (instrument maker), William Bourne (writer on navigation),
William Borough and Robert Norman (writers on magnetism), Willem
Janszcon Blaeu (cartographer), and others. In some cases the trained
mathematicians came from the class of artificers (for example, Beeckman)
or they were in an intermediate position: engineers without university education (Simon Stevin). But whether they belonged to that class or not,
they shared its ideals on the emancipation of the manual workers, and this
could only be beneficial to the new science. Bacon's ideal was an England
in which wealth rested in the hands of "merchants, burghers, tradesmen,
freeholders, farmers in the country"; an evident example was found "in
our neighbours of the Low Countries, who could never have endured and
continued so inestimable and insupportable charges . . . by their mechanical industry, were it not that their wealth was dispersed in many
hands" of people of "inferior conditions." [85] He wanted, however, not
only material goods, but also intellectual goods more equally divided, as
the sixteenth-century scientists mentioned above had already advocated.

It was felt that the manual workers ought to have some scientific training, but also that people of the higher classes should not shun manual
work. Just as Palissy wanted the young noblemen to invent tools for agriculture, William Petty (1648) wanted children of the highest rank to be
taught some manual occupation to enable them to make experiments and
become patrons of science. Even the Restoration could not wholly subdue
this "democratic" spirit of the new science. According to the optimistic
Sprat, "Philosophy will then attain to perfection, when either the Me-
chanic Labourers shall have philosophical heads, or the Philosophers
shall have Mechanical Hands." [86] In the Royal Society "the tradesman,
the merchant, the scholar" represented a "union of Men's Hands and
Reasons" and preferred "Works before Words." [87] The Society realized an
ideal much alive since Bacon, and that Gresham College was its meeting
place was significant of the old union of Puritanism and science. Since its
foundation in 1597 Gresham College had been a meeting place of the
learned artificers, astronomers, and physicists of London—a true center of
the "new philosophy" but also of Puritanism: two of its professors, Samuel Foster and Henry Gellibrand, were in trouble during the Laudian
persecution of Puritanism.

IV

THE SOURCE OF NATURAL SCIENCE

To the modern reader it seems self-evident that the science of nature
should be founded upon the observation of nature, the stellar universe,
the earth, the plants and animals. Yet other possibilities presented themselves in the sixteenth century, namely (1) the writings of the ancients,
(2) immediate enlightenment, (3) rational reflection, and (4) Holy Scripture. Therefore further consideration is needed to explain why the Re-

formed in general had chosen the book of creation as the fifth possibility.

1. The Reformed were sometimes enticed by the writings of the ancients. Bookish people were attracted by the parallel between the return to the oldest documents of Christian religion and the oldest documents of human science. In general, however, this humanistic attitude did not prevail.

2. As to the second possibility, just as some people founded their religion largely upon divine illumination by the Spirit (Anabaptists, Quakers), there were theosophists who expected scientific enlightenment from an immediate insight into the hidden workings of nature. Renaissance mysticism (Neo-Pythagoreanism, hermetism, alchemy) furthered the idea that man (microcosm) by a sympathetic feeling could immediately grasp the inner essence of the universe (macrocosm). Kepler's rejection of the scientific esotericism of the Rosicrucian Robert Fludd [88] was paralleled by the attitude of the Reformers toward the "enthusiasts" and theosophists.

3. The third way to science, that of logical deduction from innate ideas, had little attraction for people who attributed small value to "natural theology" because of their distrust of "unaided" reason. Bacon's violent opposition to logic-spinning in science was a reflection of the Puritan attitude and consequently was much appreciated by the Puritans.

Sometimes, however, the dislike of Aristotelianism was so great that Cartesianism was welcomed as an ally against it (Webster, Hall). However, those, like Boyle, who really carried on scientific research were less enthusiastic, as they were afraid that a heavier yoke would be laid upon them by this liberator. They accepted mechanical explanations in general but recognized that Descartes' physical explanations were "chimerical" (Christian Huygens). This opinion prevailed since the triumph of Newton, who was, in principle, a Baconian. The preface to the second edition of the *Principia,* written by the Rev. Roger Cotes (1713) with Newton's approval, could have been written by any Puritan scientist of the school of Bacon. According to Cotes, the business of true philosophy is to seek after those laws actually chosen by God to form the world, not those He might have chosen, had He so pleased.[89] He opposed Descartes, who was "presumptuous enough to think that he can find the true principles of physics and the laws of natural things by the force alone of his own mind, and the internal light of his reason." [90]

4. The fourth possibility presented the greatest temptation to the Reformed. Because of their principle of founding theology and ethics (and often politics also) upon Scripture, it was easy to draw the parallel of founding science too upon scriptural data. Scientific research, then, only served to elaborate and to detail a discipline of which the principles were already known by the exegesis of the Bible.

In the first centuries of the Christian era some of the Fathers, in their reaction to pagan philosophy, wanted natural philosophy to be based upon the Bible, whereas others tried to demonstrate that the Greek world picture indeed was in the Bible. Both lines were followed by Protestants. Protestant scholasticism (L. Daneau, 1576; G. Voetius, 1636) clung to Bible texts in order to refute the theories concerning the movement of the earth; Protestant antischolasticism quoted Bible texts in evidence of a peculiar doctrine of elements. Scripture thus proved to be a two-edged sword when drawn into scientific controversies.

The tendency to build up a "Mosaic" science—that is, a science founded mainly on texts from Genesis—was particularly strong among the alchemists and the Paracelsists. The charge that Paracelsus was an innovator was answered by the countercharge that scholastic philosophy was heathenish whereas Paracelus founded his doctrine upon Scripture, a more reliable and also more ancient foundation. Paracelsus put forward the definition: "What generates is an element" (*Als ist das ein Element das da gebieret*),[91] evidently an allusion to Genesis 1:11, 21, 24. The Huguenot physician Joseph du Chesne (1593; 1605) consequently excluded air and fire from the elements because they are not mentioned in Genesis as "bringing forth" things, and "we prefer to follow the divine Seer rather than the heathen philosopher." [92] Richard Bostocke (1585), Thomas Tymme (1612),[93] and Noah Biggs (1653)[94] also stressed the biblical character of Paracelsism as a contrast with the heathenish character of scholasticism. Sometimes, reference to Bible texts seemed advantageous even to Copernican astronomers, as in the case of the Calvinist astronomer John Bainbridge (1618) who (with reference to the text that the heavens will wax old as doth a garment) explained the natural origin of comets in the heavens. On this occasion the heathenism of Greek and scholastic philosophy was also used as an argument.[95]

On the other hand, the Copernican system could easily be rejected by referring to passages in the Bible (Joshua 20:12–13; Ps. 19:6–7; Ps. 104–5; Eccles. 1:4–5). Therefore, to prevent theological opposition, the Lutheran Pastor Andreas Osiander inserted a preface to Copernicus' *De Revolutionibus* (1543) in which the Copernican theory was represented as a merely mathematical hypothesis with no pretensions to any physical truth. Luther and Melanchthon were against the Copernican system as not being in accordance with the Bible; Melanchthon's rejection was also inspired by his scholasticism. Yet there was no violent hostility. Rheticus, the first disciple of Copernicus, was professor of astronomy at Wittenberg; Michael Mästlin, who initiated Kepler into the secrets of the Copernican system, taught at Tübingen. The Danish astronomer Tycho Brahe, in order to agree with the Bible, propounded an intermediate system (a geocentric universe with the sun and the moon revolving about the earth and the five planets about the sun). After the condemnation of the doctrine of the motion of the earth by Rome (in 1616) and the trial of Galileo (1633) because of its conflict with the biblical text, Roman Catholic authors often accepted the Tychonian system. Many Protestants followed Gilbert and Origanus, who modified this latter system by admitting the daily rotation of the earth (Edward Wright, Fr. Godwin, M. Ridley, N. Carpenter). It could be expected that those Protestants with whom biblicism was the strongest, that is, the Puritans, would be the stanchest opponents of the motion of the earth. Yet the reverse is true. In England Thomas Digges (1573), John Bainbridge (1618), Henry Gellibrand (1643), John Wallis, and John Wilkins (1640) were Puritan supporters of the Copernican system, and this openmindedness to new and bold ideas went even further. In 1576 Digges put forward the theory that the fixed stars are at varying distances beyond the orb of Saturn, thereby breaking through the closed, spherical universe which Copernicus had not abandoned and which Kepler and Galileo would adhere to. Not the Italian freethinker Giordano Bruno, but Thomas Digges was the first to propound this audacious hypothesis.[96] Wilkins also accepted the idea of an infinite universe; he ascribed the opposition of Copernicus to servility to the ancients and to the fear of deviation from the exegesis of Scripture phrases as given by "the supposed infallible Church." [97]

CALVINISM AND COPERNICANISM

The main reason for the open attitude of so many Reformed authors toward the movement of the earth seems to be that their biblicism was related only to religious (historical, ethical, ecclesiastical) aspects, not to scientific topics. As a rule they gave little room to "Mosaic" science and sought indeed the data of science in the book of creation. One of the reasons for this must have been the example set by Calvin, their greatest theological teacher. First of all, it is important that Calvin, notwithstanding his severe critique on Greek philosophers, did not reject everything that originated with the heathen, but carefully tested each of their ideas on its own merits. In principle, the same was done by those conservative theologians (Roman Catholic as well as Protestant) who put the Aristotelian world system to the test of Scripture and were of the opinion that there was perfect agreement. Calvin, however, saw more clearly than any of his contemporaries that the world picture of the Bible conflicted with the Aristotelian system. He remarked that Genesis speaks of one expanse, whereas the Aristotelian astronomers make a distinction of spheres. He pointed out that Genesis calls the sun and moon the "great lights," whereas the astronomers prove by conclusive reasons that the little star of Saturn is greater than the moon.[98] Yet Calvin did not reject the current astronomical system. As a layman in astronomy he accepted the almost unanimous beliefs of the astronomers. The cause of the difference between "Moses" and astronomy is, according to him, that Moses wrote in a popular style; he only described what all ordinary persons endowed with common sense are able to understand, whereas the astronomers investigate whatever the sagacity of the human mind can comprehend. Thus Calvin's manner of exegesis of "scientific" texts in the Bible is closely connected with the generally accepted Protestant doctrine that the biblical revelation is accessible to everyone. According to him, the Holy Spirit opens a common school for the learned and the unlearned and therefore chooses what is intelligible to all. If Moses had spoken in a scientific way, the uneducated might have pleaded in excuse that such subjects were beyond their capacity. Therefore Moses adapted his writing to common use. "He who would learn astronomy and other recondite arts, let him go elsewhere." [99]

Consequently, it is to Calvin's great credit that he recognized the discrepancy between the scientific world system of his days and the biblical text and, secondly, that he did not repudiate the results of scientific research on that account. It is quite irrelevant that Calvin did not know the Copernican system.[100] If the Aristotelian system is not in the Bible and yet may be true, the scriptural argument for the rejection of every other astronomical system is without value; from the religious point of view the old system henceforth loses its advantages over the Copernican system.

Calvin's influence is evident in the preface to Gilbert's *De Magnete* (1600) by Edward Wright. Kepler defended the Copernican system with almost the same arguments[101] as did the reformed pastor Philips van Lansbergen (1619; 1629)[102] and his son, Jacob van Lansbergen (1632).[103] P. van Lansbergen's work was published with the support of the strongly Calvinistic Estates of Zeeland; it was applauded by the poet and "Pensionaris" Jacob Cats, the poet Johann de Brune, and the secretary to the Synod of Dort, Daniel Heinsius. Simon Stevin and Isaac Beeckman were Copernicans, and the most influential Reformed theologian of the first half of the seventeeth century, André Rivet, did not deem the Copernican system contrary to Scripture.

This sufficiently demonstrates that when Calvinism in Holland was in its heyday, it did nothing to prevent Copernicanism.[104] During the Cartesian controversy which raged in Holland in the middle of the seventeenth century, the Voetian party tried to discredit Cartesianism and Copernicanism by connecting them with Arminianism and libertinism. This fact may perhaps have helped to establish the now prevailing opinion that Arminians and libertines showed more inclination toward the new hypothesis than the orthodox Reformed—an opinion, however, that is not confirmed by the facts.

It should, however, be stressed that by no means did all Reformed writers on theology agree with Calvin's method of exegesis. Many of them adhered to scholastic philosophy, and for that reason were prompted to a traditional exegesis (Zanchi, Daneau, du Bartas, Voetius). The famous Independent theologian John Owen was against the Copernican system on purely biblical grounds.

G. Voetius, the first rector of the University of Utrecht, deemed scholastic philosophy the only philosophy conformable to Scripture. Moreover, he was of the opinion that "Holy Scripture teaches not only what is necessary to salvation, but also lays down the . . . principles of all other good sciences and arts";[105] the Copernican system is in flat contradiction with the text and the intention of the Bible. If the Holy Spirit accommodated Himself to the ordinary people, He would tell a lie on behalf of the common people.[106] When recommending commentators on Genesis, Voetius especially mentioned Pereira S. J.[107] On the other hand, his opponents within the Reformed Church, the Cocceians, had a predilection for Calvin's accommodation theory and were, in general, Copernicans. Calvin was, according to Dean Farrar, "one of the greatest interpreters of Scripture who ever lived." [108] Not only was his exegesis scholarly and remarkably free from prejudice, but he was also very careful not to arrive too soon at an apodictical conclusion. Therefore, John Donne preferred him to Melanchthon because "Calvin will say. It seems to be thus, Melanchthon, It can be no otherwise but thus. But the best men are but problematical, only the Holy Ghost seals with infallibility." [109] This is also the highest praise one could bestow on a scientist. Possibly Calvin by his manner of exegesis of Scripture indirectly influenced his followers who devoted themselves to the exegesis of nature.

There is a tendency to contrast the presumably milder and more cultural attitude of High Church Anglicanism and Roman Catholicism with a conventional caricature of Puritanism and Calvinism as a cold, unemotional, static orthodoxy. "Calvinism has usually been discussed in an atmosphere of controversy and has often been judged, even by academicians, with slender reference to the evidence." [110]

The myth of the Puritan hatred of music and art has been exploded by P. A. Scholes; that Calvin and Puritanism had a stimulating influence upon science has been made evident by several recent studies. "Puritanism was an important factor . . . in promoting the type of thinking that helped to arouse interest in science" (Stimson). "Calvinism or puritanism or ascetic protestantism generally . . . played no small part in arousing a sustained interest in science." "The happy marriage of these two movements was based on an intrinsic compatibility" (Merton). The religion of the Reformed neither regarded grace as an addition to nature nor as an antithesis to it, but closely intertwined them. Consequently, a radical renewal of every department of life—church and state, individual and society, morals and science—was their aim. It seems evident that they achieved considerable success with respect to science.

NOTES

1. A. de Candolle, *Histoire des sciences et des savants,* 2nd ed. (Geneva and Basel, 1885), pp. 329-331.

2. J. Pelseneer, *L'origine protestante de la science moderne* (Lychnos, 1947), p. 246; "La réforme et le progrès des sciences en Belgique au XVIᵉ siècle," in *Science, Medicine, and History* (Oxford, 1953), p. 281; *Les persécutions contre les savants en Belgique* (Le Flambeau, 1954), p. 636.

3. Dorothy Stimson, "Puritanism and the New Philosophy in Seventeenth-Century England," *Bulletin of the Institute of the History of Medicine,* III (1935), 321-334; Robert K. Merton, "Science, Technology and Society in Seventeenth Century England," *Osiris,* IV, No. 2 (1938), 474.

4. Max Weber, *Gesammelte Aufsätze zur Religionssoziologie,* 3 vols. (Tübingen, 1920), I, 83, 120, 124, 163.

5. Cf. R. Hooykaas, "Science and Theology in the Middle Ages," *Free University Quarterly,* III, 142.

6. J. H. Waszink, *Bloesemtij der Letteren* (Arnhem, 1951), pp. 45, 49.

7. Agnes Arber, *Herbals,* 2nd ed. (Cambridge, Eng., 1953), p. 266.

8. C. E. Raven, *English Naturalists from Nockam to Ray* (Cambridge, Eng., 1947), p. 127.

9. Arber, *op. cit.,* p. 266.

10. *Ibid.,* p. 85.

11. R. Herrlinger, *Volcker Coiter* (Nuremberg, 1952), p. 23.

12. Raven, *op. cit.,* pp. 54, 91, 96.

13. Herrlinger, *op. cit.,* pp. 42, 68.

14. Arber, *op. cit.,* p. 88.

15. Bernard Palissy, *Œuvres,* ed. A. France (Paris, 1880), pp. 35, 114.

16. Calvin's preface to the New Testament, 1535; cf. J. T. McNeill, *The History and Character of Calvinism* (New York, 1954), p. 232.

17. J. Kepler, *Gesammelte Werke,* ed. Caspar (Munich, 1945), XIII, 193.

18. Confessio Belgica, art. II.

19. Calvin, *Commentary on I Corinthians,* VIII, I.

20. Calvin, *Institutes,* I, V, 2.

21. Merton, *op. cit.,* p. 446.

22. Thomas Browne, *Religio medici* (1643), Pt. I.

23. Cf. R. Hooykaas, *Robert Boyle, Een studie over natuurwetenschap en christendom* (Loosduinen, n.d.), pp. 65-66.

24. Thomas Sprat, *The History of the Royal Society of London,* 4th ed. (London, 1734), p. 435.

25. Cf. Calvin's *Commentary on Genesis I:16,* where he says that "they who have leisure and ability" ought not to neglect astronomical research.

26. Kepler, *Werke* (Munich, 1937), III, 33.

27. Palissy, *op. cit.,* p. 321.

28. For example, in W(illiam) B(orough), *A Discourse of the Variation of the Compasse* (London, 1614), Preface dated 1581.

29. Cf. *Works,* XII, 219-226.

30. Cf. Benjamin Farrington, *Francis Bacon* (New York, 1949), p. 148.

31. Cf. Perry Miller, *The New England Mind* (New York, 1939), pp. 116 ff., 493 ff.

32. D. Diggers, *A Booke Named Tectonicon* (1556). Ed. London, 1952, "To the Reader."

33. Thomas Digges, *An Arithmeticall Militare Treatise, Named Stratioticos* (London, 1579), Preface.

34. Isaac Beeckman, *Journal*, ed. de Waard, II, 455; cf. R. Hooykaas, "Science and Religion in the Seventeenth Century," *Free University Quarterly*, I, 169–183.

35. Francis Bacon, *Works*, ed. Spedding, and Heath, Ellis (London, 1858–1859), I, 453.

36. *De Magnete* (1600), cit. by R. F. Jones, *Ancients and Moderns* (Washington, 1936), p. 19.

37. Bacon, *op. cit.*, V, 132.

38. John Webster, *Academiarum Examen, etc.* (London, 1654), p. 106.

39. Sprat, *op. cit.*

40. Kepler, *Werke*, III, 178.

41. Cf. R. Hooykaas, "The Discrimination between 'Natural' and 'Artificial' Substances and the Development of Corpuscular Theory," *Arch. Intern. Hist. Sc.* (1948), pp. 640–651; R. Hooykaas, *Het Begrip Element* (Utrecht, 1933), pp. 143–159.

42. Palissy, *op cit.*, p. 166.

43. Bacon, *op. cit.*, IV, 21.

44. Palissy, *op. cit.*, p. 166.

45. R. Norman, *The New Attractive* (London, 1613), "To the Reader"; Ch. II, B 32.

46. "An Advise Concerning the Philosophy of These Late Discoveryes," Appendix to *The Strange and Dangerous Voyage of Captain Thomas James* (London, 1633).

47. Henry Gellibrand, *A Discourse Mathematical on the Variation of the Magneticall Needle* (London, 1635), p. 20.

48. Beeckman, *op. cit.*, II, 375.

49. Cf. R. Hooykaas, "Science and Religion in the Seventeenth Century," pp. 178–180.

50. Cf. Jones, *op. cit.*, p. 127.

51. Cf. R. Hooykaas, "Science and Theology in the Middle Ages," pp. 77–163.

52. Webster, *op. cit.*, p. 106.

53. John Hall, *An Humble Motion to the Parliament of England Concerning the Advancement of Learning and Reformation of the Universities* (London, 1649), pp. 38–42.

54. *Vindiciae Academiarum* (Oxford, 1654), p. 50.

55. Perry Miller and T. H. Johnson, *The Puritans*, 2 vols. (London, 1938), p. 61.

56. Hall, *op. cit.*, p. 44.

57. *Ibid.*, p. 33.

58. *Ibid.*, p. 23.

59. Jones, *op. cit.*, p. 119.

60. According to Gisbertus Voetius, *Sermoen van de nuttigheydt der academien, etc.* (Utrecht, 1636), p. 134.

61. Cf. Jones, *op. cit.*, p. 122.

62. Merton, *op. cit.*, p. 480.

63. Except, of course, Protestant scholasticism (see below under "Copernicanism").

64. Kepler, *op. cit.*, III, 33.

65. Palissy, *op. cit.*, p. 74.

66. Richard Bostocke, *The Difference between the Auncient Physicke . . . and the Latter Phisicke, etc.* (London, 1585), Ch. 19.

67. *Ibid.*, Ch. 9.

68. Thomas Culpeper, *Morall Discourses and Essays . . .* (London, 1655), p. 63.

69. Hall, *op. cit.*, p. 21.

70. Sprat, *op. cit.*, p. 370.

71. Noah Biggs, *Mataeotechnia . . .* (London, 1651), "To the Parliament."

72. Webster, *op. cit.*, p. 110.

73. Voetius, *Disputationes selectae*, Ultrajecti (1648), Pars I, pp. 177–881.

74. Calvin, *Institutes*, III, 2, No. 15.

75. Cf. P. J. Meertens, *Letterkundig leven in Zeeland in de 16ᵉ en de eerste helft der 17ᵉ eeuw* (Amsterdam, 1943), p. 308.

76. Cf. Farrington, *op. cit.*, p. 29.

77. Sprat, *op. cit.*, p. 423.

78. Palissy, *op. cit.*, pp. 116, 120.

79. *Ibid.*, p. 24.

80. Bacon, *op. cit.*, IV, 81, 257.

81. William Barlowe, *A Breife Discovery* . . . (London, 1618), p. 9.

82. Libertus Fromondus, *Vesta . . . Antverpiae* (1634), p. 13.

83. Cf. R. Hooykaas, "Pascal, His Science and His Religion," *Free University Quarterly*, II, 119.

84. Norman, *op. cit.*, "To the Reader."

85. Bacon, *op. cit.*, VII, 60.

86. Sprat, *op. cit.*, p. 397.

87. *Ibid.*, p. 434.

88. J. Kepler, *op. cit.*, VI, 374, 377, 385, 387, 399, 451; cf. R. Hooykaas, "Het hypothesebegrip van Kepler," *Orgaan chr. vereen. nat. geneesk.* (1939), pp. 38–60.

89. *Newton's Mathematical Principles*, ed. Cajori (Berkeley, 1947), p. xxvii.

90. *Ibid.*, p. xxxii.

91. Cf. R. Hookyaas, "Die Elementenlehre des Paracelsus," *Janus, Arch. Intern. Hist. Med.*, XXXIX (1935), 181.

92. Cf. R. Hooykaas, "Die Elementenlehre der Iatrochemiker," *Janus*, XLI (1937), 15, 27.

93. Thomas Tymme, *A Dialogue Philosophicall* . . . (London, 1612), pp. 31–38.

94. Biggs, *op. cit.*, p. 88.

95. John Bainbridge, *An Astronomicall Description of the Late Comet* . . . (London, 1619), p. 24.

96. Fr. R. Johnson, *Astronomical Thought in Renaissance England* (Baltimore, 1937), pp. 163–169.

97. Cf. Johnson, *op. cit.*, p. 279.

98. Calvin, *Commentaries upon the First Book of Moses, Called Genesis*, trl. J. King, (Edinburgh, 1874), Vol. I, Ch. 1:16.

99. *Ibid.*, Ch. 1:6.

100. The quotations attributed to him by A. D. White, *A History of the Warfare of Science with Theology* (London, 1896), p. 127 (between quotation marks!), which are repeated by many authors on Calvinism, offer one more example to show that many historians pass judgment on Calvin without having a serious knowledge of his works. Moreover, an equitable judgment on Calvin is not possible without comparing his ideas with those of his contemporaries and predecessors. "Many would be glad to damn and dismiss Calvin by a reference to Servetus; but no man ought to be judged solely by his worst acts. The advocates of tolerance do not always exercise that virtue . . . even toward the intolerant of the past, to whom 19th century liberalism was a thing wholly unknown." "Calvin's intolerance has usually been exaggerated and the range of his tolerance has been overlooked." (McNeill, *op. cit.*, pp. 228–229.) The execution of Servet was approved by the Catholics, by the mild Bullinger (Zwinglian), and the gentle Melanchthon (Lutheran).

101. Kepler, *op. cit.*, III, 28–34; IV, 161, 196.

102. *Progymnasmata astronomiae restitutae* (Middleburg, 1628), p. 106; *Bedenckingen*

op den dagelijckschen ende Iaerlijckschen loop van den Aerdt-kloot (Middelburg, 1650), pp. 17–22.

103. J. Lansbergius, *Apologia pro Commentationibus Philippi Lansbergii* (Middelburg, 1633), pp. 49–55.

104. A. D. White's verdict that "the Calvinistic Church" in Holland was at first strongly against the whole new system but that "Calvinism even in its stronghold was powerless against it" is based on ignorance of the real situation. The Reformed Church did not meddle with the Copernican question. Cf. White, *op. cit.*, p. 150.

105. Voetius, *Sermoen*, pp. 35–36.

106. Voetius, *Thersites heautontimorumenos*, Ultrajecti (1635), pp. 266, 281, 283.

107. *Ibid.*, p. 256; *Disputationes selectae*, I, 552.

108. F. W. Farrar, *History of Interpretation* (London, 1886), p. 343.

109. Cf. C. M. Coffin, *John Donne and the New Philosophy* (New York, 1937), p. 252.

110. McNeill, *op. cit.*, p. vii; R. H. Tawney, *Religion and the Rise of Capitalism* (London, 1938, Pelican ed.), accuses Puritans of mourning a lost paradise, whereas Anglicans and Catholics saw the earth in a heavenly light (p. 228). Thus Tawney commits the same error of generalizing too much—an error of which he accuses Weber (pp. xi, 313). He charges Puritans with a lack of social solidarity (p. 270) and also condemns the Calvinist defense of the poor as being "without compassion" (p. 139). Cf. McNeill, *op. cit.*, p. 419, "this judgment could have been reached only by ignoring a great body of evidence."

III

THE APPLICATION OF THE PROTESTANT ETHIC THESIS OUTSIDE OF EUROPE

11

REFLECTIONS ON THE PROTESTANT ETHIC ANALOGY IN ASIA

Robert N. Bellah

The work of Max Weber, especially the so-called Protestant ethic hypothesis, continues to exercise an impressive influence on current research in the social sciences.[1] The great bulk of this research is concerned with refining the Weberian thesis about the differential effects of Protestant compared with Catholic religious orientations in the sphere of economic activity. In recent years, however, there have been increasing though still scattered attempts to apply Weber's argument to material drawn from various parts of Asia. I shall not undertake here to review these attempts with any completeness. Rather this essay will be devoted to a selective consideration of several different approaches to the problem with a view to determining some of their possibilities and limitations.

Perhaps the commonest approach has been to interpret the Weber hypothesis in terms of the economists' emphasis on the importance of entrepreneurship in the process of economic development. Weber's "Protestant ethic" is seen as an ideological orientation tending to lead those who hold it into an entrepreneurial role where they then contribute to economic growth. We shall consider shortly how serious this oversimplification of Weber's view distorts his intention. At any rate those who have taken this interpretation have proceeded to analyze various Asian religious groups to see whether examples of this-worldly asceticism, the religious significance of work in a calling, and so forth have been associated with successful economic activity. Cases in which the association has been claimed include in Japan Jodo and Zen Buddhists, the Hōtoku and Shingaku movements; in Java the Santri Moslems; in India the Jains, Parsis, and

Reprinted from Journal of Social Issues, *XIX, No. 1 (January 1963),* 52–60.

various business or merchant castes and so forth.[2] David C. McClelland has subsumed a number of such examples under the general rubric of "Positive Mysticism" within which he finds Weber's Protestant example to be merely a special case.[3]

Whether or not the claim to have discovered a religious ethic analogous to Weber's type case can be substantiated in all these Asian examples, this general approach has much to recommend it. For one thing, it calls attention to the motivational factor which historians, economists, and sociologists have often overlooked. For another, it calls attention to subtle and nonobvious connections between cultural and religious beliefs and behavioral outcomes. This latter point is one which some readers of Weber have consistently failed to understand, Kurt Samuelsson being merely one of the more recent examples. The latter claims in refutation of Weber that since the Puritan fathers did not espouse a materialistic dog-eat-dog capitalism their theology could not possibly have led to its development.[4] Milton Singer, on the other hand, proves himself a more discerning pupil of Weber when he argues that economic development is not supported merely by "materialistic" values but may be advanced by an "ethic of austerity" based perhaps in the case of India on the tradition of religious asceticism.[5]

But the application of the "entrepreneurship model" or motivational approach to Weber's thesis has, I believe, certain grave limitations. Some of the difficulty lies in the original essay itself when it is not grasped in its proper relation to the whole of Weber's work. One of the most serious of these limitations is emphasis on the importance of the motivational factor at the expense of the historical and institutional setting.

However important motivational factors may be, they have proven time and again to be highly sensitive to shifts in institutional arrangements. The consequences for economic development depend as much on the institutional channeling of motivation as on the presence or absence of certain kinds of motivation. For example, the entrepreneurial potential of the Japanese samurai, who from at least the sixteenth century comprised what most observers would agree was the most achievement-oriented group in Japan, could not be realized until the Meiji period when legal restraints on their entering trade were abolished and their political responsibilities eliminated. Chinese merchants who made an indifferent showing within the institutional limitations of imperial China turned into a vigorous capitalist class under more favorable conditions in Southeast Asia. Clifford Geertz has shown how the Moslem Santri group in Java, characterized by a long merchant tradition and a favorable religious ethic, began to burgeon into entrepreneurship under favorable economic conditions early in this century only to wither on the vine when economic conditions worsened markedly during the great depression.[6] Gustav Papanek has indicated how several relatively small "communities" (quasi castes) of traditional traders were able to spearhead Pakistan's remarkable industrial growth in recent years by taking advantage of highly favorable economic conditions which had not previously existed.[7] On the basis of such examples one might argue that there exists in most Asian countries a small but significant minority which has the motivation necessary for entrepreneurial activity. If this is the case, then, it would be advisable to consider motivation in close connection with institutional structure and its historical development.

In *The Protestant Ethic and the Spirit of Capitalism,* Weber himself seems to lean rather heavily on the motivational variable, and this may be what has led some of his readers astray. In the later comparative studies in the sociology of religion, however, we get a much more balanced view and an implicit correction of emphasis in the earlier work. Following Weber's comparative studies, a number of students have undertaken what might be called an "institutional approach," attempting to discern institutional factors favorable or unfavorable to economic development. Examples of this kind of study are Albert Feuerwerker's monograph *China's Early Industrialization,*[8] my *Tokugawa Religion,* about the inadequacies of which I shall speak in a moment, Joseph Elder's dissertation on India,[9] and perhaps the most comprehensive in scope and historical coverage, Clifford Geertz's work on Java contained in a number of published and unpublished writings.[10] In all these studies Weber's emphasis on the religious ethic continues to receive a central focus. It is seen, however, not simply in relation to personal motivation but also as embodied in or related to a wide range of institutional structures. Feuerwerker writes, ". . . one institutional breakthrough is worth a dozen textile mills or shipping companies established within the framework of the traditional society and its system of values." [11] And Geertz says in a similar vein:

> The extent and excellence of a nation's resources, the size and skill of its labor force, the scope and complexity of its productive "plant," and the distribution and value of entrepreneurial abilities among its population are only one element in the assessment of its capacity for economic growth; the institutional arrangements by means of which these various factors can be brought to bear on any particular economic goal is another. . . . It is for this reason that economic development in "underdeveloped" areas implies much more than capital transfers, technical aid, and ideological exhortation: it demands a deep going transformation of the basic structure of society and, beyond that, perhaps even in the underlying value-system in terms of which that structure operates.[12]

My study of Tokugawa Japan, taking a somewhat more optimistic approach to traditional society, stressed the extent to which traditional Japanese institutions were or could under certain circumstances be made to be favorable to economic development. In so doing I drew a number of parallels between certain aspects of "rationalization" in Japan and the rationalization Weber was talking about in the West. It was precisely on this point that Maruyama Masao's review in the April 1958 issue of *Kokka Gakkai Zasshi* was sharply critical.[13] Without denying that a number of the mechanisms I discussed, for example the concentration of loyalty in the emperor, may have been effective in bringing about certain social changes contributing to economic growth, he points out that they were far from rational in Weber's sense and indeed had profoundly irrational consequences in subsequent Japanese development, not the least of which were important economic inefficiencies.

With Maruyama's strictures in mind one is perhaps better able to deal with some remarks of Milton Singer near the end of his sensitive and illuminating review article on Weber's *Religion of India:*

> To evaluate Weber's conclusions is not easy. In view of the complexity of Hinduism, and of Asian religions generally, any characterization of them or any comparison of them with Western religion is going to involve large simplifications. Certainly Weber has brilliantly constructed a characterization based on an impressive knowledge of both textual and contextual studies. But one may wonder whether the construction does justice to elements of Asian religions. Some of these are: a strand of this-worldly asceticism; the economic rationality of merchants, craftsmen, and peasants; the logically-consistent system of impersonal determinism in Vedānta and Buddhism, with direct consequences for a secular ethic; the development of "rational empirical" science; religious individualism; and personal monotheism. Weber is certainly aware of all these elements and discusses them in his study. . . . But in the construction of the "Spirit" he does not give very much weight to these elements. With the evidence today before us of politically independent Asian states actively planning their social, economic, and scientific and technical development, we would attach a good deal more importance to these elements and see less conflict between them and the religious "spirit." [14]

For Maruyama the mere *presence* of rational elements for which I argued in the Japanese case along lines quite parallel to those of Singer is simply not enough if they exist passively side by side with irrational elements (as they do in both Japanese and Indian cases) and are not pushed through "methodically and systematically" to their conclusion as they were in Weber's paradigmatic case of Protestantism. If Maruyama is right, and I am coming increasingly to believe that he is, then it becomes necessary to press beyond both the motivational and the institutional approaches and

to view matters in an even broader perspective, as the above quotation
from Geertz already hinted.

Concretely, this means that we are forced to take seriously Weber's argument for the special significance of Protestantism. The search through
Asia for religious movements which here and there have motivational or
institutional components analogous to the Protestant ethic ultimately
proves inadequate. The Protestant Reformation is not after all some mere
special case of a more general category. It stands in Weber's whole work,
not in the *Protestant Ethic* essay alone, as the symbolic representation of a
fundamental change in social and cultural structure with the most radical
and far-reaching consequences. The proper analogy in Asia then turns
out to be, not this or that motivational or institutional component, but
reformation itself. What we need to discern is the "transformation of the
basic structure of society" and its "underlying value-system," to use
Geertz's language. Before trying to discover some examples of this structural approach to the Protestant ethic analogy in Asia, it is necessary to
note briefly that we see here an example of what must occur in any really
serious confrontation with Asian examples: we are forced back to a recon-
sideration of the European case which provides us so many of the conscious and unconscious categories of our investigation.

The first consideration is that the development in Europe is neither
even nor uniform. Developments in different countries and at different
times have very different significance. As Reinhard Bendix has so clearly
indicated, it was Weber's growing discernment of the failure of structural
transformation in important sectors of German society which led him to
the Protestant ethic problem.[15] As every reader of the famous essay knows,
the material is derived from England primarily, and not from Germany,
where the Reformation remained abortive in important respects and its
structural consequences stunted. This is indeed the background for Weber's profound cultural pessimism. Interestingly enough, one of the first
Japanese to penetrate deeply into the structure of Western culture, Uchimura Kanzō, made a similar diagnosis. Writing in 1898, he said:

> One of the many foolish and deplorable mistakes which the Sat-
> suma-Chōshū Government have committed is their having selected
> Germany as the example to be followed in their administrative pol-
> icy. Because its military organization is well-nigh perfect, and its
> imperialism a gift of its army, therefore they thought that it ought
> to be taken as the pattern of our own Empire. . . .
>
> Germany certainly is a great nation, but it is not the greatest,
> neither is it the most advanced. It is often said that Art, Science, and
> Philosophy have their homes in Germany, that Thought has its
> primal spring there. But it is not in Germany that Thought is real-

ized to the fullest extent. Thought may originate in Germany, but it is actualized somewhere else. The Lutheran Reformation bore its best fruit in England and America.[16]

These suggestions about European developments, which must in the present brief paper remain without adequate elaboration, have a further important implication. Germany is certainly one of the most economically developed nations in the world, yet it lagged, according to Weber, in some of the structural transformations which he discovered to be crucial in the development of modern society. Once the crucial break-throughs have been accomplished, it becomes possible for other nations to take some of them over piecemeal without the total structure's being transformed—possible, but at great cost, as the German case indicates.

These considerations bring us back to Maruyama's criticism of my work and the criticism of a number of Japanese intellectuals of American analyses of Japan in general.[17] Japan, too, comparatively speaking, is one of the world's most economically advanced nations. Looking at economic growth as our sole criterion, we are inclined to consider Japan as a rather unambiguous success story. But to Japanese intellectuals who feel as acutely as Weber did the failure of modern Japan to carry through certain critical structural transformations which are associated with modern society, the evaluation of Japan's modern history is much more problematic. It would be convenient for social scientists and policy makers if economic growth were an automatic index to successful structural transformation. This does not, however, seem to be the case. Indeed, where economic growth is rapid and structural change is blocked, or as in the Communist cases distorted, social instabilities result which under present world conditions are serious enough to have potentially fatal consequences for us all. A broader perspective than has often been taken would seem then to be in order.

As examples of the structural approach, which I believe to be the most adequate application of the Weberian problem to Asia, I may cite again the work of Clifford Geertz on Indonesia and especially a very suggestive recent article on Bali,[18] together with a highly interesting study of recent religious and social developments in Ceylon by Michael Ames.[19] In the Balinese case only the beginnings of the questioning of traditional assumptions are evident and the degree to which rationalization at the value level will have social consequence is not yet clear. In Ceylon, Ames documents the existence of movements of religious reform which have gone far in changing some of the most fundamental assumptions of traditional Buddhism and replacing them with orientations supporting social reform. The degree to which the structural reform itself has gotten under way is not as yet clear. In Japan a century of ideological ferment has given rise to a number of tendencies and potentialities which need much more clarification, a problem on which the writer is currently working.[20]

There are indications from a number of Asian countries that traditional elements are being reformulated as part of new nationalist ideologies. Joseph Elder has presented some evidence that the Indian caste ethic is being transformed into a universalistic ethic of occupational responsibility detached from its earlier anchorage in the hereditary caste structure.[21] Such examples would seem to support Singer's argument as quoted above, as indeed in a sense they do. But it should not be forgotten that these reformulations have occurred under Western impact (not infrequently under Protestant Christian impact, as Ames shows in Ceylon) and involve fundamental alterations in pattern even when based on traditional material, making them often formally similar to Western paradigms. This is not to imply that Asian cultures are inherently imitative but rather that modern Western societies are not fortuitous cultural sports. Since they represent the earliest versions of a specific structural type of society, it is inevitable that Asian societies should in some patterned way come to resemble them as they shift toward that type. Another set of problems arising from the structural approach have to do with the extent to which nationalism or Communism can supply the ideological underpinning, the cultural Reformation if you like, for the necessary structural transformations. It is not possible to review here all the work done on these topics, some of which is certainly relevant to the present problem concern.

In conclusion let me say that the whole range of problems having to do with social change in Asia would be greatly illuminated if we had a comprehensive social taxonomy based on evolutionary principles of the sort that Durkheim called for in 1895.[22] Among recent sociologists I can think only of S. N. Eisenstadt as having made significant contributions to this end.[23] With such a taxonomy in hand we would be in a much stronger position to interpret the meaning of the results obtained by those currently concentrating on motivational and institutional research. We might also be in a better position to clear up profound problems both of science and policy which hover around the definition of the concept of modernization.

NOTES

1. For example, the April 1962 issue of the *American Sociological Review* contains two articles explicitly claiming to shed light on "the Weberian hypothesis." Among some important books in which the influence of Weber's work is very evident are Gerhard Lenski's *The Religious Factor* (New York, 1961) and D. C. McClelland's *The*

Achieving Society (Princeton, N.J., 1961). One might also mention Kurt Samuelsson's scurrilous attack, *Religion and Economic Action* (New York, 1961). That Weber can at this date generate such irrational hostility is in itself a kind of indication of his importance.

2. The influence of Jodo Buddhism and the Hōtoku and Shingaku movements in Japan was discussed by R. N. Bellah in *Tokugawa Religion* (Glencoe, Ill., 1957), Ch. 5. The Zen case in Japan was discussed by McClelland, *op. cit.*, pp. 369–370, under the mistaken impression that the samurai in the Meiji period were devotees of Zen Buddhism. The Santri Moslems of Java were treated by Clifford Geertz in *The Religion of Java* (Glencoe, Ill., 1960) and more especially in terms of the present context in "Religious Belief and Economic Behavior in a Central Javanese Town," see Ch. 16 below. McClelland has discussed the Jains and the Parsis in *op. cit.*, pp. 368–369, and Milton Singer has discussed several Indian examples in "Cultural Values in India's Economic Development," *The Annals*, CCCV (May 1956), 81–91. The latter article received further comment from John Goheen, M. N. Srinivas, D. G. Karve, and Milton Singer in "India's Cultural Values and Economic Development: A Discussion," *Economic Development and Cultural Change*, VII, No. 1 (1958), 1–12. Hajime Nakamura, in a brief article entitled "The Vitality of Religion in Asia" which appeared in *Cultural Freedom in Asia*, ed. Herbert Passin (Rutland, Vt., 1956), pp. 53–66, argued for the positive influence of a number of Asian religious currents on economic development. In his more comprehensive *The Ways of Thinking of Eastern Peoples* (Tokyo, 1959) (an inadequate and partial translation of *Tōyōjin no Shii Hōhō*, 2 vols. [Tokyo, 1949]), Nakamura takes a position very close to that of Weber. The types of argument put forward in the above very partial listing of work on this problem are quite various. In particular Clifford Geertz was careful to point out that the Santri religious ethic seemed suited to a specifically precapitalist small-trader mentality which Weber argued was very different from the spirit of capitalism. This distinction could perhaps be usefully applied to many of the above cases of traditional merchant groups which seem to have some special religious orientation supporting their occupational motivations.

3. *Op. cit.*, pp. 367–373, 391.

4. *Op. cit.*, pp. 27–48.

5. Goheen *et al.*, *op. cit.*, p. 12.

6. "The Social Context of Economic Change: An Indonesian Case Study," Center for International Studies, MIT (mimeo 1956), pp. 94–119.

7. "The Development of Entrepreneurship," *American Economic Review*, Vol. LII, No. 2 (May 1962).

8. Albert Feuerwerker, *China's Early Industrialization* (Cambridge, Mass., 1958).

9. Joseph Elder, "Industrialism in Hindu Society: A Case Study in Social Change," unpublished Ph.D dissertation, Harvard University, 1959.

10. In addition to writings already cited, see especially "The Development of the Javanese Economy: A Socio-Cultural Approach," Center for International Studies, MIT (mimeo 1956).

11. *Op. cit.*, p. 242.

12. "The Development of the Javanese Economy . . . ," pp. 105–106.

13. *Kokka Gakkai Zasshi* (The Journal of the Association of Political and Social Sciences), Vol. LXXII, No. 4 (April 1958), Tokyo.

14. *American Anthropologist*, LXIII, No. 1 (1961), p. 150.

15. *Max Weber: An Intellectual Portrait* (New York, 1960), Ch. 2.

16. *Uchimura Kanzō Zenshū* (Tokyo, 1933), XVI, 361–362.

17. Some illuminating remarks on this topic are to be found in J. W. Hall's "Japan and the Concept of Modernization: Hakone and Aftermath" (mimeo 1962).

18. "'Internal Conversion' in Contemporary Bali," in J. Bastian and Roelot Rool-vink, *Malayan and Indonesian Studies* (London, 1964).

19. "An Outline of Recent Social and Religious Changes in Ceylon," *Human Organization* (forthcoming).

20. "Ienaga Saburo and the Search for Meaning in Modern Japan" (mimeo 1962) is the first study concerned with this problem which the writer has completed.

21. *Op. cit.*

22. *The Rules of Sociological Method* (Glencoe, Ill., 1950), Ch. 4.

23. See his *From Generation to Generation* (Glencoe, Ill., 1956) and especially *The Political Systems of Empires* (Glencoe, Ill., 1963).

12

ECONOMIC DEVELOPMENT AND ULTRAMUNDANEITY

Ralph Pieris

This note is concerned with the economic implications of the dichotomy between spiritual and temporal, as conceived by people professing certain Oriental religions, particularly Hinduism and Buddhism. Durkheim points out that this bifurcation of the world into two categories, sacred and profane, is common to all religions, but in some the division is absolute, and the two domains are conceived of as hostile and jealous rivals. "Since men cannot fully belong to one except on condition of leaving the other completely, they are exhorted to withdraw themselves completely from the profane world, in order to lead an exclusively religious life." [1] The practical man, the trader and farmer, do invoke the assistance of functional deities through offerings and prayers, but that extratemporal intervention in mundane affairs in no wise imparts any religious quality to secular activity, which is an autonomous domain of endeavor which neither confers merit nor brings salvation. The root of our problem then is, what secular activities are considered to be compatible with the attainment of a desired afterlife?

The religious texts of both Hindus and Buddhists contain innumerable prescriptions and restrictions. The dharmasutras were concerned with the entire gamut of social relations and enmeshed the round of daily activities in a network of ritualistic and ceremonial regulations which the average man found impossible to observe in the workaday world. The way of salvation or liberation is the abolition of the illusory self, freeing oneself from the wheel of karma. The ideal can be reached in stages, the penultimate period of preparation was one of isolated asceticism in a forest (vanaprastha), the final stage the life of the *sannyasin* who renounces the world. These are exacting demands. Even at the "lower" stage, the house-

Reprinted from Archives de Sociologie des Religions, *VIII, No. 15 (1963), 95-100.*

holder's life is ascetically regulated; in particular he is enjoined to avoid profitable economic pursuits such as trade and usury.

It is not with the religious texts, however, that we are concerned, but rather with the interpretations of the average believer. Indeed, the scriptures being written in a language unintelligible to the common man, other forms of communication brought home to him the basic religious values. In Ceylon the Jataka stories provide a popular literature for the edification of the laity. These birth stories are concerned with general moral values and the inexorable law of karma, as illustrated in the previous births of the Buddha,[2] and are vividly illustrated in Sinhalese temple murals. Again, sermons (*bana*) preached by monks on *poya* days (the four lunar phases), particularly on full-moon nights, communicate the Buddhist virtues to the busy householder.

Monastic life is regulated by the exacting *vinaya* rules (*vi-nayati*—"to lead away" from evil, "to discipline")[3] which commit the initiate to poverty, celibacy, and inoffensiveness. The monk is enjoined to cultivate abstraction, lest attention to detail kindle sensuous desires. He must always keep his eyes downcast, gazing fixedly ahead "at the distance of a yoke." [4] A fan is usually held before his face so as to avoid distracting sights which might cause impure thoughts.[5] The decision to be ordained as a Buddhist monk is not irrevocable. To abjure the monastic life, though rare, is not considered a dishonor, merely a confession of weakness which, if sincere, is creditable.[6] The following observations in a seventeenth-century account of the Sinhalese are applicable even today:

> They do much extol and commend Chastity, Temperance, and Truth in words and actions; and confess that it is out of weakness and infirmity, that they cannot practice the same, acknowledging that the contrary vices are to be abhorred. . . . They do love and delight in those Men that are most Devout and Precise in their Matters.[7]

The life of the world renouncer is the ideal which the man in the world strives to approximate. The minimal discipline expected of the layman is the regular observance of the Five Precepts (*pan sil*) involving abstention from taking life, stealing, sensuous misconduct, false speech, and intoxicants that tend to cloud the mind. To attain nirvana, however, a break with society is essential, and the laity can, at least, withdraw from the profane world for brief periods by observing five further precepts (viz., abstaining from eating at forbidden times;[8] dancing, singing, music, and stage plays; the use of garlands, scents, unguents, and ornaments; the use of high or broad beds; and the handling of money). The devout villager who observes three (*ata-sil*) or five (*dasa-sil*) of these additional precepts on each of the four sacramental days of the month is known as an *upasaka,* who places himself outside society temporarily.

The reconciliation of this-worldly and otherworldly philosophies is therefore foreign to the Buddhist, for whom real salvation lies outside the things of this world, an outlook which is aptly symbolized in the Burmese *shinbyu* ceremony and its Thai counterpart. Every Burmese boy is initiated as a novice (*koyin*), and the *shinbyu* ceremony involves ordination, taking the vows of abstinence, and the assumption of the yellow robes. The boy thereafter enters a monastery for a period, after which he opts either to return home or to remain a monk. The ceremony symbolically reenacts Buddha's Great Renunciation. The legend depicts the Buddha as a prince living in luxury, without contact with the world of sorrow. Satiated with pleasure, he became oversensitive to the unpleasant. The crisis came one night, after the usual pleasures, when he was dramatically made aware of the reality of death, disease, and decay and chose the path of homelessness, of world renunciation. In the Burmese *shinbyu* ceremony the initiate is first adorned in princely finery. After the ceremony this resplendent attire is removed, the initiate washed and shaved bald, and the monastic robes worn. The ritual is redolent of the cultural value attached to the life of the mendicant who seeks to realize nirvana through meditation and withdrawal from the cravings and temptations of mundane affairs.[9] The ceremony also underlines the Buddhistic idea that religious and secular activity are poles apart.

The utterances of a charismatic leader who by his life and teachings inspires significant groups may point to sociologically significant aspects of a religion or sect. Thus Weber sought to analyze the content and implications of the writings of New England Puritans such as Benjamin Franklin. There is no better example of a charismatic leader in India than Mahatma Gandhi. In the course of his celebrated "experiments with truth" Gandhi was squarely confronted with the inexorable dichotomy between religion and mundane affairs. Having resolved to make "morality the basis of all things,"[10] the code of conduct which he imposed on himself and advocated for others involved a puritanical denunciation of sensuous pleasure. "Lustful love" and "carnal lust," even within marriage, is condemned along with prostitution. Moreover, gambling, alcoholism, and even smoking and enjoyment of indecent jokes are considered morally reprehensible.[11] "My life, according to the Mahatma, is based on disciplinary resolutions."[12]

The scrupulous adherence to moral ideals is not incompatible with economic activity. Indeed, throughout his life Gandhi castigated immorality in the pursuit of worldly undertakings. He was revolted by the sight of "cunning shopkeepers" who infested the precincts of the Kashi Vishvanatha temple at Banaras.[13] A speech to Indians in Pretoria as early as 1893 concerned truthfulness in business,[14] while thirty-four years later he dwelt on the same subject and urged Indian businessmen in Ceylon to use correct weights and measures and to be scrupulous in their business dealings.

This long preoccupation with business ethics is surely remarkable. But it is understandable that, coming as he did from the Gujrati Banya or merchant caste, the sharp practices of merchants of his community must have left a deep impression on him at an early age. Hence his determination to demonstrate that his moral ideals were consonant with the rational conduct of business, in his management of the finances of the Natal Indian Congress. He had receipt books printed although donors did not care to have receipts:

> Such economy is essential for any organization, and yet I know it is not always exercised. . . . Every *pie* was thus clearly accounted for. . . . Carefully kept accounts are a *sine qua non* for any organization. Without them it falls into disrepute. *Without properly kept accounts it is impossible to maintain truth in its pristine purity.*[15]

But it can hardly be claimed that Gandhi's views penetrated the market place of life. He lamented that:

> Even today there are merchant friends who contend that truth is inconsistent with business. . . . They argue that practical affairs are one thing while religion is quite another.[16]

In the West, in contrast, Tawney explains:

> The emergence of the idea that "business is business," and that the world of commercial transactions is a closed compartment with laws of its own, if more ancient than is often supposed, did not win so painless a triumph as is sometimes suggested. Puritan as well as Catholic accepted without demur the view which set all human interests and activities within the compass of religion.[17]

A corpus of Protestant literature has been unearthed by Weber and Tawney which aimed at eliminating any dualism which segregates the secular and the religious aspects of life.

Despite his exhortations regarding morality in business, Gandhi himself never imputed any religious quality to secular activity.[18] Indeed according to Hindu doctrines profitable economic activity is an impediment to liberation. Gandhi's own career clearly underlines this inexorable dichotomy between religion and life which the devout Hindu accepts. During the grueling marches connected with his *Satyagraha* campaign in Johannesburg, he had already realized that he "must relinquish the desire for children and wealth and live the life of a vanaprastha—of one retired from household cares." Again, "a perfect observance of *bramacharya* (celibacy) means realization of *brahman*." The dichotomy between asceticism and worldliness is absolute, and only the world renouncer can attain the ideal of immunity from passion which enables him to control the senses in thought, word, and deed;

There should be a clear line between the life of a *brahmachari* and of one who is not. The resemblance that there is between the two is only apparent. Both use their eyesight, but whereas the *brahmachari* uses it to see the glories of God, the other uses it to see the frivolity around him. Both use their ears, but whereas one hears nothing but praises of God, the other feasts his ears upon ribaldry. Both often keep late hours, but whereas the one devotes them to prayer, the other fritters them away in wild and wasteful mirth. Both feed the inner man, but the one only to keep the temple of God in repair, while the other gorges himself and makes the sacred vessel a stinking gutter. *Thus both live as poles apart,* and the distance between them will grow and not diminish with the passage of time.[19]

Gandhi's institution of an ashrama is in accord with the Hindu view that moksha can only be achieved by a self-discipline which requires a withdrawal from the temporal world.

In contrast, in the practice of the Protestant ethic there was a persistent tendency to secularize mystical contemplation, to follow a methodically rationalized code of conduct. The religious conception of conduct strode, as Weber says, into the market place of life, producing a middle-class morality which placed a premium on continuous, systematic, conscientious activity. In the ordinary business of life sobriety, punctuality, frugality, and, above all, honesty were extolled, while vain ostentation, lust, and unbridled enjoyment of undisciplined impulses were roundly condemned. The honest earning of money was considered an expression of rational proficiency in a calling. Subsequently, the pursuit of wealth was apparently severed from its original religious base, and capitalism no longer needed that support for its success.[20]

In a social order which rigidly demarcates the sacred from the profane, rational economic activity is, by definition, at variance with religious practice. The secular morality associated with Calvinism is less likely to take root where the religious life is insulated from the temporal, where moksha or nirvana, liberation or salvation, can be realized only by withdrawal from the temptations of the world. Consequently the highly irrational world of magic intrudes into everyday economics without imparting any sanctity to worldly activity. Herein lies the antinomy between religion and magic. The latter seeks mundane technical and utilitarian ends rather than mystical contemplation by withdrawal from society. Moreover, as Durkheim puts it, "magic takes a sort of professional pleasure in profaning holy things." [21]

The significance of the dominant belief in, and practice of, magic was that it was not conducive to a rational ethic of worldly behavior. In China, "in the magic garden of heterodox doctrine (Taoism), a rational economy and technology of modern occidental character was simply out of the question." [22] Elsewhere the trader and farmer both invoke the assistance of functional deities through gifts and prayers, and this indeed is a regular device by which the mass of the people seek to master their environment. In Ceylon "officials and businessmen often take astrological advice before making important decisions." [23] Prominent among worshipers at the Kali temple in Calcutta on Bengali New Year's day are businessmen who place their account books before the image of the deity. On payment of a few of 33 *naya paisas* (d. o.o7) the zealous worshiper has a representation of Ganesha, the God of success, stamped in vermillion in his ledger. Such instances of invocation of supernatural powers can be adduced from all Asian countries. The point in common is that desire for worldly success with divine assistance does not impart any religious quality to secular activity, the latter being an autonomous domain which neither bestows merit nor brings ultimate salvation.[24] The drive for gain is ever present but

> was lacking in precisely that which was decisive for the economics of the Occident: the refraction and rational immersion of the divine character of economic striving and its accompaniments in a system of rational, inner-worldly ethic of behaviour, e.g. the "inner-worldly asceticism" of Protestantism in the West.[25]

In Japan alone the philosophy of nonattachment preached by Theravada (Hinayana) Buddhism did not find favor. According to the Mahayana Buddhist doctrine which appealed to the Japanese, absolute truth could be attained within secular life. The interpretations of certain commentators are curiously reminiscent of Calvinist attitudes. Shosan (1579–1655), for example, exhorted merchants to "discard pleasures and pursue profits single-heartedly. But do not enjoy the profits; instead work for the good of others." [26] Among oriental peoples the successful secularization of religion was as unique to Japan as was her phenomenal economic development, and the achievement may be attributed in part at least to this emphasis on practical activities within the human nexus.[27] An unmistakable ideological stress on an ethic of hard work may be discerned. The "beautiful custom" of workers' loyalty to employers facilitates recruitment of factory labor,[28] while the Lotus Sutra, the most important of scriptures in Japan, which provides a theoretical basis for a work ethic, has been described as "the Scripture of Labour." [29]

An intense religious revival, such as the recent revival of Buddhism in Ceylon, can have an inhibitive effect on economic development, particularly if the movement underlines the general orientation of the religion to ultramundaneity.[30]

NOTES

1. Émile Durkheim, *Elementary Forms of the Religious Life* (London, 1917), p. 33.
2. Conze, *Buddhism* (Oxford, 1951), p. 87.
3. *Ibid.*, p. 54.
4. Saint-Hilaire, *The Buddha and His Religion* (London, 1914), p. 335.
5. *Ibid.*, p. 356.
6. *Ibid.*, p. 329. In Hinduism, the sannyasi who returns to the life of householder, and his children, despite performance of penances, are treated as untouchables. Dumont, "World Renunciation in Indian Religions," *Contributions to Indian Sociology,* IV (1960), 44.
7. Knox, *An Historical Relation of Ceylon* (1681).
8. That is, after midday.
9. In Ceylon the calling of a monk is usually a lifetime commitment, and the Burmese practice of withdrawal and return on the part of youths is absent. There is, however, the withdrawal on the four sacramental days, symbolized in taking *sil,* particularly on full-moon days, the chief of which are now public holidays.
10. M. K. Gandhi, *An Autobiography* (Ahmedabad, 1927), p. 25.
11. Gandhi, *Self-Restraint vs. Self-Indulgence* (Ahmedabad, 1947), and *Drink, Drugs and Gambling* (Ahmedabad, 1952), *passim.*
12. Gandhi, *Autobiography,* p. 287.
13. *Ibid.*, p. 177.
14. *Ibid.*, p. 91.
15. M. Desai, *With Gandhiji in Ceylon* (Madras, 1928).
16. Gandhi, *Autobiography,* p. 109.
17. R. H. Tawney, *Religion and the Rise of Capitalism* (London, 1938, Pelican ed.), p. 203.
18. Gandhi: *Autobiography,* pp. 150, 151.
19. *Ibid.*, p. 153.
20. This is a bare statement of the argument in Weber, *The Protestant Ethic and the Spirit of Capitalism* (London, 1930).
21. Durkheim, *op. cit.*, 43.
22. Max Weber, *The Religion of China* (Glencoe, Ill., 1951), p. 227.
23. T. Morgan, "The Economic Development of Ceylon," *Annals of the American Academy of Political and Social Science,* Vol. CCCV (1954).
24. Failure to take note of this schism accounts for conflicting interpretations of the "influence" of a given cultural factor. Thus B. F. Hoselitz, "Non-Economic Barriers to Economic Change," *Economic Development and Cultural Change,* Vol. I (1952), argues that Theravada Buddhism hampers economic activity in Burma, while Manning Nash, "Some social and cultural aspects of economic development," *Economic Development and Cultural Change,* Vol. VII, No. 2 (1959), asserts that the same doctrine in the same country "is not in conflict with success in the world, and the twelvefold path has many roads which may lead to development." But worldly success is one thing, religious salvation quite another.
25. Max Weber, *The Religion of India* (Glencoe, Ill., 1958), 337.
26. H. Nakamura, "The Vitality of Religion in Asia," in *Cultural Freedom in Asia* (Tokyo, 1956).
27. *Ibid.*
28. Nash, "Some Notes on Village Industrialization in South and South East Asia," *Economic Development and Cultural Change,* Vol. III, No. 3 (1955).
29. Nakamura, *op. cit.*
30. Dumont, *op. cit.*, p. 46, rightly contends that a break with society is necessary to attain salvation in Buddhism.

13

RELIGION, BUREAUCRACY, AND ECONOMIC GROWTH

W. F. Wertheim

In Max Weber's otherwise so lucid studies on the Protestant ethic and the spirit of capitalism, the relationship between these elements during the Golden Age of the Dutch United Republic remains in a hazy twilight.

On the one hand, Weber stresses that contemporary foreign observers ascribed the tremendous growth of the Dutch economy in the first half of the seventeenth century to Dutch Calvinism.[1] On the other hand, he appears to have been aware that many of the patrician merchants of Holland were by no means Calvinists but members or sympathizers of a more liberal branch of Protestantism: the so-called Arminians, followers of Arminius, Professor of Theology in Leiden. Even after the Arminians were ousted from the official church in 1619, liberal orientations remained strong among the richer merchants. Weber notes that the Arminians rejected the orthodox doctrine of predestination and had no part in the inner-worldly asceticism considered by him one of the psychological roots of the rise of modern capitalism. Surprisingly enough, as appears from one of his footnotes, Weber considered this aspect, in connection with his thesis, "without interest" or even of "negative interest." [2]

In another footnote[3]—one has quite often to look for Weber's main arguments in his footnotes—he elaborates his view of the Dutch case more explicitly. He acknowledges that Dutch Puritanism showed less expansive power than its British counterpart. But his argument seems to be that the Calvinist ethic and the ascetic spirit, which had called forward the rising of the Dutch against the Spanish king in the second half of the sixteenth century, began to weaken in Holland as early as the beginning of the

Reprinted from Transactions of the Fifth World Congress of Sociology, *Washington, D.C., September 2–8, 1962 (Louvain, Belgium: International Sociological Association, 1964), III, 73–86.*

seventeenth century. Evidently, in his view, the rapid rise of Dutch economic power was still related to the Protestant ethic, but its force had
been somewhat impaired by the ascension to power of the patrician regents, whom Weber calls "a class of *rentiers*." [4]

The inadequacy of Weber's theory for a clarification of the Dutch case
has been pointed out by his manifold critics more than once.[5] Tawney
has argued that the rise of a positive attitude to economic growth was a
comparatively late development within Calvinism.[6] Hyma has shown the
role of other denominations and spiritual currents in the process of economic development within the Dutch Republic, and more in particular
the specific contribution provided by the Arminians,[7] generally called
"Remonstrants" in Holland, a term derived from the *Remonstrance* presented in 1610 by the statesman John of Oldenbarnevelt.[8] Robertson has
called attention to the importance of the rise of the Renaissance state and
to the ascension of merchants to a position of influence in the state.[9]

Whereas Weber, in his assessment of the role of Calvinism within
Dutch society, appears to perceive a declining influence of this creed in
the first half of the seventeenth century, according to the view held by
Dutch historians the actual development was rather the other way round.
At the end of the sixteenth century a rather small percentage of the population of the Netherlands could be called Calvinist, and the adherents of
this creed were not to be counted among the people in the forefront of
economic growth, as prosperous merchants were rare among them at that
time. In the course of the seventeenth century, however, their number
and their power increased; and though, after the short period of persecution of the Remonstrants by Stadholder Maurice, Prince of Orange, culminating in the execution of his rival Oldenbarnevelt (1619) and lasting
until his death (1625), his successor and younger brother Frederick Henry
(1625–1647) pursued a more liberal policy toward Arminian trends, the
second quarter of the seventeenth century is still generally viewed as a
period of an increasing impact of Calvinism upon social life in the Netherlands.[10] According to the thorough investigation undertaken by Beins,
however, even at that time the economic tenets of Dutch Calvinism could
hardly be called conducive to the growth of a capitalist spirit.[11]

Therefore, it is beyond doubt that the economic growth of the Dutch
Republic during its Golden Age was largely due to forces other than the
Protestant ethic as defined by Max Weber. And the inapplicability of
Weber's thesis to the Dutch case has been of some help to those concerned
with European religious history in bringing about a more balanced ap-
preciation of the ultimate value of his brilliant conception.

One is tempted to ask to what extent the Dutch case might do more
than serve a negative goal only: the disproving of part of Weber's thesis.
In view of the fact that an important part of the present discussion regarding Weber's thesis is centered on the problem of its applicability in

the modern Asian setting, I have set about to inquire whether a more thorough analysis of Dutch economic growth might contribute toward a better understanding of the relationship between religion and economic development in the Far East. It would appear that recent investigations in that field have carried the problem to a point where such a comparison may be fertile.

In his study of *The Origin of Modern Capitalism in Eastern Asia,* Norman Jacobs has attempted to draw a comparison between two great Far Eastern countries and societies—China and Japan. Jacobs states his central problem in this way: "Why did modern industrial capitalism arise in one East Asian society (Japan), and not in another (China)?" [12] In accordance with Weber's concept, Jacobs endeavors to detect religious forces comparable with the Protestant ethic, but he is not able to find any: "there is no positive logical link between Japanese religion and the rising capitalist forces as such." [13] Still, he clings to the belief that "Japan developed capitalism spontaneously." [14] Thus Jacobs arrives at the conclusion that in Japan, "although no force arose positively to support the cause of modern capitalism," [15] there was at least no dominant ideology opposing its rise. On the other hand, the dominant Confucian ideology in China was definitely inimical to the development of capitalism. Jacobs even goes so far as to label China, in accordance with K. A. Wittfogel's view, as an example of an "Oriental Society" apparently incapable of independent economic growth.[16]

Much more enlightening is Robert N. Bellah's attempt to clarify the interdependence between religious values and economic growth in his brilliant work *Tokugawa Religion.* Jacobs does not attempt to draw any conclusions from the fact that, as he admits, "the religious values of Japan in the mid-nineteenth century, if they can be related to non-religious behaviour at all, were concerned with the problem of the establishment of a modern centralized state." [17] Bellah, on the other hand, uses this striking phenomenon as a starting point for a searching analysis. Japan remains a riddle only to those who view world history from the usual platform occupied by Western observers, to whom there exists but one road to economic progress: the way of private capitalism. To those who share this view, there remains an aura of mystery about the question to what extent capitalism in Japan might be seen as a product of "spontaneous" growth, in view of the powerful state intervention during the Meiji period.

To Bellah, Japan is not a case apart; it only "takes on special significance when compared with other non-Western societies." [18] Whereas industrialization in the West has been the product of a slow process of accumulation, industrialization in the East "has been government-controlled or government-sponsored, because only the government has been able to marshal the requisite capital." [19]

Therefore, Bellah is not at all put out of countenance when he finds that religious values in Tokugawa Japan were not as positively correlated with the growth of private capitalism as would be required in order to justify an interpretation of Japanese economic history in Weberian terms. Nor does he feel any need to reverse Weber's basic thesis by stating, as Jacobs does, that the "absence" of impeding ideological factors would be enough to produce a "spontaneous" growth of capitalism out of a society with a "feudal" structure. What Bellah tries to establish is that "Tokugawa Religion" contained several elements conducive to an ideology which during the Meiji period could bring about a profound government-sponsored economic change. It was the samurai class of aristocratic officials, not the merchants, who were the bearers of the new economic spirit. Principles of samurai ethics, as applied to the modern industrialized setting, are listed by Bellah as follows:

> Art. 1. Do not be preoccupied with small matters but aim at the management of large enterprises.
> Art. 2. Once you start an enterprise be sure to succeed in it.
> Art. 3. Do not engage in speculative enterprises.
> Art. 4. Operate all enterprises with the national interest in mind.
> Art. 5. Never forget the pure spirit of public service and *makoto*.
> Art. 6. Be hard-working and frugal, and thoughtful to others.
> Art. 7. Utilize proper personnel.
> Art. 8. Treat your employees well.
> Art. 9. Be bold in starting an enterprise but meticulous in its prosecution.[20]

In Bellah's view, then, the correlation between religion and bureaucracy was decisive in Japanese history. Whereas according to Jacobs, apparently, the correlation between bureaucracy and economic growth can only be negative, to Bellah it is precisely "a strong polity" which has accounted for the astounding growth of the Japanese economy.

Moreover, in Bellah's view there is no basic contrast between the Japanese case and the Chinese. Bellah, who is much more realistic in his assessment of what is happening in China and the Soviet Union, apparently rejects the "Oriental Society" approach advocated by Wittfogel. "China . . . since its shift from the traditional integrative values to the Communist political values has shown a marked spurt in industrialization and can be expected to join Japan and Russia as the third great non-Western society to industrialize." And Bellah concludes with the observation that "political values and a strong polity would seem to be a great advantage and perhaps even a prerequisite for industrialization in the 'backward' areas of today's world." [21]

Bellah's lucid analysis inspires us to inquire into its wider implications. If economic growth in the present world may be due to factors which can hardly be considered as "capitalistic" in the traditional sense, one is easily tempted to reconsider Weber's thesis in the light of recent developments outside Europe. Just as Weber's theory was developed by comparing the Protestant ethic with religious values in the Asian world, recent experiences in the same part of the world may provide an indication of which direction we should look for a revision of Weber's concept.

To put our new problem briefly: if state intervention is a decisive element in producing economic growth in the world of today, it may well be that past developments in the Western world were much less occasioned by "private" capitalism than has been generally assumed by Western observers grown up in a world which considered private initiative the decisive key to economic growth. In his analysis of the impact of different religious values Max Weber, too, started from the assumption that it was the attitudes of private capitalists that mattered. In this connection he hardly paid any attention to the spirit of bureaucracy, to other aspects of which he devoted some of the best chapters of his magnum opus, *Wirtschaft und Gesellschaft*. To quote Bellah, who also has detected this weak spot in the accepted approach to Western economic history:

> The orthodox view of European economic history has generally considered the "interference" of the state in the economy as inimical to economic development, though specific policies were often viewed as favorable. A general consideration of the relation of the polity and political values to economic development in the West might significantly alter the traditional view.[22]

As far as I am aware, Dr. Bellah has never elaborated this point.

It appears to me that the Dutch case, as expounded above, might provide a clue for further inquiry in this direction.

In Max Weber's opinion, mercantilism should be viewed as a transfer of the capitalistic ways of profit seeking to the sphere of government. "The state is treated as if it consisted exclusively of capitalist entrepreneurs."[23] In Weber's system, therefore, mercantilism was a phenomenon which could arise only after capitalism as a mode of production had attained its full growth. To Weber, mercantilism was born in Britain, as an alliance between capitalist interests and the state.[24] The British mercantilist policy was primarily directed against Dutch trade. On the other hand, in Weber's time it was still a fashion among German students of economic history to consider the Netherlands of the first half of the seventeenth century as a country cherishing the principle of free trade; Laspeyres had written that in no other country were economic attitudes as far distant from the theories which Adam Smith characterized as "mercantilistic" as they were in the Netherlands.[25]

A different view is held by Albert Hyma. He recalls that even early in the seventeenth century Walter Raleigh had observed "that the Dutch

government was vitally interested in promoting the welfare of its merchants wherever they might be engaged in commerce." [26] In Raleigh's
view "the government was exceedingly efficient in supervising all imports
and exports, and in negotiating with foreign governments who had mo-
lested the Dutch merchants." According to Robertson, these remarks are
wrongly attributed to Sir Walter Raleigh, since they were actually made
by John Keymor.[27] The French archbishop Huet had also remarked that
the States General "omitted nothing all that time to increase their trade
where it was already established, or to establish it where they never had
established it before." Hyma goes on to discuss several instances of state
intervention on behalf of Dutch trade in greater detail, such as, for example, stimulation of the importing of vast amounts of raw materials and
the assistance provided to the exporting of manufactured goods. He also
mentions the measures taken in order to prevent the imposition of any
new customs or imposts on the navigation of the five great rivers of Germany and concludes that the Dutch "perfectly understood the good
points of mercantilism." [28] Moreover, the influence which the statesman
Oldenbarnevelt brought to bear to call into life the United East India
Company as a monopolistic commercial body (1602) is an outstanding
example of official intervention in private capitalistic enterprise.

Who were those officials who played such an active part in the economic
growth of the young Republic? They were the very "regents" whom Max
Weber, in the few lines devoted to the Netherlands in his *Protestant
Ethic,* dismissed as mere *rentiers!* That is what these patricians became at
a much later stage, when the Republic was past its peak. But in the period generally considered decisive for the rise of the Republic, in the first
decades of the seventeenth century, they were for the most part vigorous
and efficient administrators who were at the same time wealthy merchants
actively interested in trade. And even after many of them had retired
from active trade and had developed a more aristocratic style of life, in
the second quarter of the seventeenth century, they remained enterprising
gentlemen actively engaged in such pursuits as the reclamation of land.

The great majority of those people who led the young Republic during
its flowering were different indeed from the Puritan type considered by
Weber as characteristic of the capitalist pioneer. Some of them were Calvinists, as for example the burgomaster of Amsterdam, Reynier Pauw,
Oldenbarnevelt's great adversary, though the two of them had together
played a prominent part in the foundation of the United East India
Company. But the large majority of the regents and wealthy merchants
belonged to a different type, as Weber himself acknowledges. Except for a
short period after Prince Maurice had switched his allegiance to the Calvinist faction, the moderates and those sympathizing with Arminian
trends formed a majority among the leading regents of Amsterdam. The

Dutch historian Johan E. Elias, who has written a standard work on the history of the City Fathers of Amsterdam, notes twenty regents, among them six future burgomasters, in a list of those who in 1628 signed a petition to the city council of Amsterdam in behalf of the Remonstrants; most of the other signatures were from prosperous and prominent people as well. The same year Calvinist citizens sent a petition to the States of Holland complaining of the slack attitude of the Amsterdam authorities toward the Remonstrants. There was only one regent among the signatories; most of the others were shopkeepers.[29]

Apparently, during the flowering of the Republic the majority of those who were most active in developing large-scale capitalistic enterprise either belonged to the Arminian Remonstrants or were more or less indifferent in religious matters. An outstanding example of this type of administrator was the burgomaster of Amsterdam, Andries Bicker, who in the second quarter of the seventeenth century equaled or even surpassed Prince Frederick Henry in political power and was once ridiculed in a satirical poem as aspiring to become the "sovereign" of the Netherlands. For example, it was he who brought about Dutch intervention in the war between Sweden and Denmark in behalf of the former, in order to enforce free passage through the Sound (1645).

The question arises to what extent the enterprising spirit of the Remonstrant merchants and regents could be attributed to their religious convictions in a positive way similar to the relationship between the Protestant ethic and the spirit of capitalism as elaborated by Weber. Should we attribute the sober and restrained way of life of the Dutch merchants in the early decades of the Golden Age, admittedly one of the prerequisites for capitalistic enterprise, at least to a certain extent, to their religious convictions? Or is it more probable that this way of life can largely be accounted for by the bourgeois origin of this patrician class, the members of which had not yet learnt to enjoy the fruits of their toil in opulence, as more matured aristocracies are accustomed to do?

At first sight, it might appear that the flowering of Dutch enterprise should rather be attributed to the absence of an all-pervasive conditioning of human actions by religious motivations than to the positive qualities of the dominant religion: several contemporary foreign observers have attributed the prosperity of the Dutch Republic to the liberal attitude toward alien religions. Tawney[30] quotes William Temple, William Petty, and de la Court as having attributed the prosperity of the Dutch to the fact that every man could practice whatever religion he pleased. If this were true, it would be indifference or moderation in religious matters that would account for economic growth, rather than the positive content or spirit of a specific religion. In that case, economic growth should by and large be attributed to the general spirit of humanism prevalent since the Renaissance, to the inquisitiveness of the adventurous human mind open to new discoveries, and to the absence of inhibitions rooted in religious dogma.[31]

But upon closer scrutiny it appears possible that the positive ideology of the Remonstrants fulfilled a more active role in the young Republic. Whereas the original concept of the *Remonstrance*, drafted by the Arminian theologians after the death of Professor Arminius of Leiden, had the character of a religious credo and of a justification of Arminian exegetics, the final text, as amended by Oldenbarnevelt and presented by him in 1610 on behalf of the "Remonstrants" to the States of Holland, is said to have had a different character.[32] It had become a political document invoking the intervention of the state to guarantee freedom of worship to the Arminians. Thus, the relationship between state and church was brought into play, and there are even indications that Oldenbarnevelt, whose personal convictions may have been nearer to the Calvinists than to the Arminians, was induced to make this move mainly in order to strengthen the position of the state. He represented in essence the regent class who could not bear the interference of dogmatic and narrow-minded clergymen in their worldly affairs. And Grotius, Oldenbarnevelt's famous companion in the struggle between the Remonstrants and the Calvinist Contraremonstrants, even went so far as to advocate the imposition of the Arminian religious doctrine as an official theology to be proclaimed by the state. On the other hand, it was also for political reasons that Prince Maurice sided with the fanatical Contraremonstrants, in order to defeat his adversary Oldenbarnevelt. There is a story—its authenticity is not beyond doubt—that before taking his dramatic decision, Maurice said that he really did not know whether predestination was green or blue.[33]

Weber maintains that the dogma of predestination contributed to the Calvinists' determination in worldly affairs. But at the time of the struggle between the Remonstrants and the Contraremonstrants it was precisely the former who, in rejecting predestination, based their position on a belief in the ability of man to improve his ways by exerting himself. In this case, such a rejection may have functioned as a stimulus to an energetic pursuit of the tasks with which the Dutch administrators were burdened.

A closer study of the Remonstrant movement and its relation to the bureaucratic ethic still needs to be undertaken. It is evident that there is an enormous distance between the appeal for religious tolerance supported by Oldenbarnevelt on behalf of the Arminian "libertines" (as they were called by their adversaries) and state Shintoism as developed in Imperial Japan during the Meiji period. Still, as far as the interplay between religious beliefs and bureaucratic proficiency is concerned, a further inquiry into parallel phenomena might appear to be worth while.

Such a study should include the further role of state intervention in the process of development of modern capitalism. In the nineteenth century, fierce competition from British interests made it impossible for German industry to flourish without strong support from governmental institutions. Werner Sombart has clearly demonstrated the role played by the Deutsche Reichsbank in promoting German industrial development.[34] Though the shares of the Reichsbank were in private hands, the directors of the bank were officials nominated by the Kaiser. Sombart calls the bank a crossbreeding of capitalist entrepreneurship and "old-Prussian correctness." [35] This expression may provide an indication that a further inquiry into the ideology and religious beliefs of Prussian bureaucrats would contribute to a better insight into the ideological components of economic growth.[36] The influence of other governmental measures, such as restrictive tariffs upon the expansion of German modern industry throughout the nineteenth century, should also be thoroughly reconsidered without any preconceptions about the benefits of economic liberalism.

The present analysis may throw fresh light upon the parallelism between the role of religious reform in western Europe and in Far Eastern countries. Last year in a paper on "Religious Reform Movements in South- and Southeast Asia," [37] I attempted to distinguish several stages in the development of religious attitudes toward emergent capitalism. I pointed out that, whereas the first reaction of reformists vis-à-vis capitalist developments may be one of rejection, a new trend develops after the self-reliant bourgeois has begun to yearn for an optimistic ideology which would affirm the possibility of increasing the productive forces of mankind. "The prosperous merchants, modern administrators and those engaged in liberal professions asked from their religion only a sanctification of their endeavours to expand their enterprises and radius of action, and to exist easily, comforted by their own enlightened views." Within Christianity, I mentioned the Dutch Remonstrants as an early example of a reformist movement of this type and then continued with an enumeration of several parallels in the more recent history of Asia. Further, I pointed to a third stage in the development of these religious movements: the stage when they tend to lose their liberal character and become more rigid, after science and rationality have taken root amongst the petty bourgeoisie. Here I had in view the Protestant ethic, as conceived by Weber, which praises strenuous effort in commerce or manufacture as in itself pious. Those who looked for Weberian parallels in modern Asia were generally concerned most of all with a study of such groups of reformist traders of the latter "Puritan" type as the most probable agents of future economic growth. For example, Clifford Geertz, who has made a penetrating study of a region in East Java (Indonesia),[38] apparently looks primarily to the stern and pious Moslems, the *santris,* who represent predominantly a petty urban business class of the bazaar type, for the future agents of economic growth in Java.[39] It is a group of shopkeeping traders among whom Islamic reformism has firmly taken root. Geertz thus envisages present developments in an Asian country from a Western point of view that might be less appropriate for countries outside the West.

As I pointed out in my paper quoted above, it would appear improbable that in modern Asia the bearers of an ideology appropriate for a petty trading class might be granted sufficient time to imitate the role played by a more rigid Protestantism in western Europe. The foregoing analysis makes it more likely that the builders of a modern economy should be looked for among efficient administrators taking over some of the qualities and conceptions developed in previous times by the Dutch Remonstrants, and latterly by their aristocratic and bureaucratic counterparts in modern Asia. Still, as economic growth ultimately presupposes a propensity to save, the desire "to exist easily," as shown by such social groups, should not predominate; the general way of life has to be sober and restrained, lest the effort to raise production be offset by increasing consumption.

In the case of Javanese society, for example, this might mean that in looking for the most propitious breeding ground for modern industrial growth, one should turn to tendencies manifesting themselves outside the class of petty traders representing a pious *santri* civilization. It may well be that the *santri* have no future under present world conditions and will be overwhelmed by groups with a different outlook. I would suggest that an ideology conducive to modern industrial growth in Java is much more likely to be developed, in the long run, among the modern representatives of the aristocratic *priyayi* class, which is more or less comparable with the regent class in the Dutch Republic, and among leaders emerging from the Javanese common people, the so-called *abangan,* whose general attitude toward life Geertz apparently considers incompatible with economic growth because of their collectivism rooted in Javanese rural tradition. In my opinion, this tolerant and syncretistic *abangan* collectivism, combined with the administrative qualities fostered among a modernized *priyayi* class, might well provide a basis for the creation of a bureaucratic apparatus and of modern organizational forms, such as co-operatives and unions, institutions which are, in the contemporary setting, much more conducive to industrial growth than old-style capitalism based on individual profit making.

Max Weber's basic problem was to explain why the modern industrial world was born in the West and nowhere else. As he could not conceive of a way other than the capitalist, he searched for psychological causes operating in the West which might account for the birth of a capitalist spirit, exclusive to this part of the world, out of comparable social and economic conditions—and these he found in religious values distinguishing the West from all types of oriental societies.

Since our experience goes beyond that of Weber, we have to shift to a different problem: why is it that the East has tended to follow a way to modern development different from the West? To what extent should our account of what happened in the Western world be revised on the basis of more recent experience in Asia?

To all appearances, the argument I have developed here runs counter to Weber's way of reasoning and, indeed, implies a reversal of his thesis, since the Protestant ethic combined with the spirit of capitalism as main agents of economic progress is replaced, in my hypothesis, by a sober and restrained humanism combined with loyalty to the state. But in its essentials Weber's approach may still have the fecundity to stimulate a more penetrating analysis of the problem. Over against the theoretical Marxists who sustained the thesis that religious ideologies were nothing but the reflections of economic conditions, Weber posited the autonomous significance of the spiritual forces dormant in religion. It may well be that in the relationship between ideology and bureaucracy as elaborated above, spiritual forces retain their autonomous role. Over against those who would pretend that the spirit of those administrators who foster economic growth is nothing but a reflection of the existing economic forces, I hazard to put forward the thesis that the practice in countries under Marxist domination has demonstrated the spiritual strength dormant in an ideology. Without their Spartan sobriety and their strict devotion to their cause, the builders of modern industrial states in the East would never have been able to build a counterpart of the imposing edifice of British eighteenth-century industrial society, which, according to Max Weber, was based on the Protestant ethic.

NOTES

1. Max Weber, *The Protestant Ethic and the Spirit of Capitalism*, tr. Talcott Parsons, 5th ed. (1956), p. 43.

2. *Ibid.*, p. 217.

3. *Ibid.*, p. 273.

4. *Ibid.*, p. 169.

5. One of the best surveys of earlier critical studies of Weber's thesis has been published in Dutch by R. F. Beerling, *Protestantisme en Kapitalisme. Max Weber in de Critiek* (Groningen-Batavia, 1946).

6. R. H. Tawney, *Religion and the Rise of Capitalism* (London, 1938, Pelican ed.).

7. Albert Hyma, *The Dutch in the Far East* (1942), pp. 10 ff., and *Christianity, Capitalism and Communism* (Ann Arbor, Mich., 1937), p. 144.

8. J. L. Motley, *Life and Death of John of Barneveld* (1874), I, 384-385.

9. H. M. Robertson, *Aspects of the Rise of Economic Individualism* (Cambridge, Eng., 1933), pp. 56 ff., and more in particular pp. 86–87.

10. See, for example, C. B. Huet, *Het land van Rembrand*, 5th ed. (1920), II, 105; Pieter Geyl, *The Netherlands in the Seventeenth Century*, 2nd ed. (London, 1961), I, 77 ff.

11. E. Beins, "Die Wirtschaftsethik der Calvinistischen Kirche der Niederlande 1565–1650," *Nederlandsch Archief voor Kerkgeschiedenis*, new series, XXIV (1931), 81 ff.

12. Norman Jacobs, *The Origin of Modern Capitalism in Eastern Asia* (Hong Kong, 1958), Preface, p. ix.

13. *Ibid.*, p. 214.

14. *Ibid.*, p. 216.

15. *Ibid.*, p. 211.

16. *Ibid.*, p. 217.

17. *Ibid.*, p. 214.

18. R. N. Bellah, *Tokugawa Religion—The Values of Pre-Industrial Japan* (Glencoe, Ill., 1957), p. 192.

19. *Ibid.*, p. 193.

20. *Ibid.*, p. 187.

21. *Ibid.*, p. 193.

22. *Ibid.*, p. 192.

23. Max Weber, *Wirtschaftsgeschichte* (Munich, 1924), p. 296. (The English translation published in 1927 and 1951 under the title *General Economic History* was not available to me.)

24. *Ibid.*, p. 298.

25. E. Laspeyres, *Geschichte der volkswirtschaftlichen Anschauungen der Niederländer* (1863), p. 134.

26. Hyma, *The Dutch in the Far East*, pp. 14 ff.

27. See Robertson, *op. cit.*, p. 66.

28. Hyma, *op. cit.*, p. 18.

29. J. E. Elias, *De vroedschap van Amsterdam 1578–1795* (1903), I, lii, note 5.

30. Tawney, *op. cit.*, p. 187.

31. Jan and Annie Romein, *De lage landen bij de zee*, 4th ed. (Phoenix Pocket) (1961), II, 133–134.

32. H. Y. Groenewegen, "Arminius en de Remonstrantie," in G. J. Heering (ed.), *De Remonstranten* (1919), pp. 68 ff.

33. Romein, *op. cit.*, II, 38.

34. Werner Sombart, *Die deutsche Volkswirtschaft im 19. Jahrhundert und im Anfang des 20. Jahrhunderts*, 4th ed. (1919), pp. 171 ff.

35. *Ibid.*, p. 175.

36. See also *ibid.*, p. 64, for the role played by the Prussian bureaucracy in promoting economic growth before the nineteenth century.

37. *Archives de Sociologie des Religions*, No. 12 (1961), pp. 53 ff.

38. Clifford Geertz, *The Religion of Java* (Glencoe, Ill., 1960).

39. See, for example, Geertz's mimeographed comparative study of two Indonesian towns, *Social Change and Economic Modernization in Two Indonesian Towns* (mimeo 1959), Ch. 3, p. 25. His view of economic leadership in Bali is, however, different insofar as the author stresses the importance of aristocratic elements as a dominant entrepreneurial group.

14

IDEOLOGICAL AND SOCIAL CHANGE IN CEYLON

Michael Ames

The Buddhism of Ceylon, known as Theravada or Hinayana in contrast
to the Mahayana of China, Japan, and other northern countries, was according to tradition first introduced to the island 2,300 years ago by King
Asoka of India. It was adopted by the Sinhalese-speaking inhabitants as
their national and state religion. Despite periodic invasions, civil wars,
conflict with heretical faiths, and a series of monastic scandals, the Sinhalese have managed to maintain a continuity of religious tradition until
the present time. But now, perhaps for the first time in its long history,
Sinhalese Buddhism appears to be facing a fundamental transformation
or "reformation." [1]

In this essay I wish to discuss some of the dynamics behind, and implications of, this impending change both in doctrine and in practice.
Changes are still occurring; in many cases they are vague, uncertain, and
various. It is too soon to assess their importance for the future of Sinhalese
religion, and there is no doubt that allegiance to traditional values is still
widespread.[2] But even if their ultimate consequences cannot be gauged,
it is possible to outline at least in general terms the dominant characteristics and directions of these changes. That is my intention here: to describe
how the more general process of religious resurgence, enthusiasm, or revitalization has operated among the six million Sinhalese-speaking Buddhists who comprise about 65 per cent of the island's population. First, I
will briefly characterize the traditional religious system, then mention the
different status groups most concerned with religious change and the special interests which appear to motivate them. Finally, an outline will be
given of some of the ideological reinterpretations and reformist activities

Reprinted from Human Organization, *XXII, No. 1 (1963), 45–53.*

promoted by these groups. In passing, it will be possible to comment on several generalizations about social change.

THE TRADITIONAL RELIGION

Sinhalese or Theravada Buddhism was organized hierarchically somewhat like a pyramid. A few hermit monks (*āranyavāsika bhikkhū*) practicing systematic meditation (*bhāvanā*) stood at the apex of the system, followed by less specialized village monks (*gramāvasika bhikkū*) and elderly lay apostles (*upāsakā*). Ordinary laymen or householders (*gihi*), who tended to their worldly pursuits and performed, or observed, the occasional Buddhist ritual (*pinkama*), made up the wide base of this pyramid. It was the orthodox view[3] that because a specialized theology of meditation promoted by the literati monks could not meet the needs of all people, nor for that matter could all people meet its demands, a secondary "religion of the masses" should be allowed to flourish beneath the official doctrine. On the one hand there were the merit-earning rituals of village Buddhism (*pinkama*), and on the other hand a complex and relatively unrationalized system of profane magical-animism (*bhuta vidyāva*), or science of spirit-manipulation.[4]

But magical-animism is not simply a religion of the masses, for all social strata—both literati monks and illiterate peasants—participate in magic. In Ceylon, Buddhism and magical-animism have always remained quite distinct from each other, forming two separate but complementary subsystems of a more general religious system which may be termed "Sinhalese Religion." Each performs the special functions of worship and therapy respectively:[5] Buddhism is concerned with sin, rebirth, and the fate of the soul; magical-animism is solely concerned with well-being in this life itself. By handling everyday misfortunes and frustrations, magic actually facilitates the more demanding activity of Buddhist worship.

This functional complementarity between Buddhism and magical-animism—that is, the contrast between religious worship and religious therapy—and the hierarchical structure of Buddhism reflect the traditional Buddhist view of the world. Such a view assumes the spiritual and mental inequality of man, the prevalence of ignorance and superstition in the world, the overriding importance of mental development through arduous contemplation, and the high status of monastic life. This model of Sinhalese religion (hierarchy and complementary functions) also enables us to evaluate the nature of recent religious changes. In anticipation of a later section of this essay, two major trends of religious development may be briefly mentioned here. On the one hand, the hierarchy of religious pursuits is being less emphasized in favor of a more universalistic approach to religious worship. Modern reformers encourage everyone to strive for religious virtuosity in this life itself. Ignorance is no longer excusable. The second major religious change is in the form of an expansion of religious function. Magical-animism is not becoming more rationalized or systematized like Buddhism, nor synthesized with it. What is happening is that reformers interpret Buddhism in more worldly terms so that it appears to take over therapeutic functions traditionally performed by magic. But before discussing in greater detail the nature of these developments, it would be useful to outline some of the structural changes which preceded them.

RECENT SOCIAL AND RELIGIOUS CHANGES

Several historians have suggested that Sinhalese Buddhism has undergone a steady decline since the twelfth century. Whether that is true or not, Buddhism certainly suffered a series of setbacks during the successive occupation of Ceylon from 1505 onward by the Portuguese, Dutch, and British. During this period, change was unequal and varied; but several events stand out. The coastal areas of the island have been under continuous domination by Western powers since 1505; the interior Kandyan region was not subjugated until the British united the entire island under one administration in 1815, some three hundred years later. The most important religious change was begun by the Portuguese along the coast and completed by the British when they took over the entire island. The specific sequence of events can be found in any one of a number of publications.[6] Briefly, what happened was that the colonial powers disestablished the Buddhist church by secularizing the state. Several important consequences followed from this:

1. When, by the 1800's, the ecclesiastical courts lost the state backing which they had traditionally depended upon, there was no formal way of checking monastic corruption and schism. In 1800 there was one monastic fraternity; today there are thirty. No longer able to settle their disputes before ecclesiastical judges, monks began taking their personal disagreements to public courts. In the view of modern Buddhists, both the schismatic tendencies and the broadcast of personal squabbles only served to weaken the prestige or charismatic appeal of the monks.[7]

2. The traditional service-tenure system was restricted in the interior and practically abolished along the coast. As a result, monks in many cases lost direct control over the tenants who occupied the vast monastic estates and performed essential services and rituals for the monks. In some cases monks lost their estates altogether.[8]

3. With the spread of government and Christian mission schools which followed colonial expansion, the monks also lost their absolute control over the educational system. As a result of this, and for the first time in 2,800 years, a new status group of nonmonastic-educated intellectual elite threatened to supersede the literati monks and thereby threatened as well the structural foundation of Buddhism. This, perhaps, has been the most critical change in the entire history of Sinhalese religion.[9]

During the past one hundred years nonmonastic-educated lay Buddhists have taken an increasingly active part in religious affairs.

Following these and related developments there was a widespread growth of resentment and dissatisfaction among Buddhists concerning the state of their religion. How long such feelings lay dormant it is not possible to say. But by the early 1800's there were signs of organized religious movements which in one form or another have continued unabated until present times.

Broadly speaking, there were two types of people concerned with this religious resurgence. On the one hand there were those who wished to restore or to retain certain privileges which were threatened. This group would include the monastic elite in Kandy, who had already suffered a considerable loss of prestige and influence. If restoration of the precolonial order was no longer possible, at least they could try to retain the few remaining privileges they held. During the colonial period, for example, a number of the monastic elite bargained with the British for titled statuses, in return for which they gave support to British policies; just prior to independence in 1947, when a number of coastal monks passed a resolution calling for immediate freedom, the Kandyan monks publicly reaffirmed their allegiance to the British crown.[10] Kandyan monks also protested against what they felt was a growing influence of Buddhist laymen. In a memorial to Edward VII in 1904, the chief monks of the Kandyan fraternity (*Siam Nikāya*) strongly opposed the British policy of making lay trustees of temple properties independent of monastic control. It was argued in the memorial that:

> The religion of the Buddha consists of only the three elements of the Buddha, the *Dhamma* (doctrine) and the *Sangha* (monkhood), and nothing more, by the laws of the Buddha the laity form no part of religion, they have no proprietary rights in the temples, or in the religious endowments. They are never allowed to interfere in either the internal discipline of the *sangha* or in the management of its temporalities.[11]

The same Kandyan-controlled fraternity objected again in 1959 when the Buddha Sasana Commission Report (see the subsection on Buddhist Commissions below) recommended that the government frame new laws to control the fraternities. Monastic reform must come from the monks themselves, the Kandyan prelates argued; no lay institution should interfere.

The feudal aristocracy, vernacular schoolteachers, and Ayurvedic or native medicine men were also anxious to win back what they considered to be their traditional rights, which in many ways were once closely identified with religion. The position of the landholding gentry, for example, was effectively buttressed by the traditional religiosity of the peasants. The landed wealth of the aristocracy also gave it some influence with the British; but the vernacular teachers and Ayurvedic physicians were less fortunate in this respect, and they did not receive their due until a Sinhalese nationalist party gained parliamentary control in 1956.

A second kind of people active in the Buddhist resurgence were those who were attempting to secure privileges newly won because of the changing times. These were primarily the new, nonmonastic-educated intelligentsia who were emerging from the coastal regions of Ceylon. The interests of such people frequently obliged them to oppose the traditional groups, at times quite bitterly. In contrast to the Kandyan monks, for instance, they strongly favored government-sponsored monastic reforms. It was mentioned earlier how the coast has been under direct Western influence since 1505, long enough for Western administration, Christian churches and schools, and commerce and trade to become well established there. It has been suggested before that when man is influenced by changes in political status, class, occupation, and new realms of social experience, he develops a need for, or an interest in, a religion different from that which his culture provides. The new Sinhalese intelligentsia were certainly more interested in religious reform or revitalization than in restoration; it is they who concern me in this article. The impending religious transformation is largely due to their efforts to reconcile traditional beliefs to modern circumstances.

Among this new intelligentsia were those with political ambitions who, after universal franchise was granted in 1931, switched from Christianity to Buddhism for opportunistic reasons. They became known as "political" or "Donoughmore Buddhists." On the whole it was natural for them to favor a new, revitalized form of Buddhism more suitable to their own status interests. Not having been educated by the literati monks, but in Christian schools, they felt less committed to, and knowledgeable about, the traditional system. In any case, they were not interested in promoting a Buddhist church which supported the traditional Kandyan aristocracy with whom they competed for political power.

The coastal milieu also produced enthusiastic Buddhist devotees motivated by pious religious sentiments. The fact that they were educated in Christian schools only served to sharpen their interest in Buddhism; they appeared deeply concerned about the future of their own religion. Such a concern is indicated in Buddhist newspapers and pamphlets of the late nineteenth and early twentieth centuries.

The political Buddhists and these devotees frequently joined forces with low-country monks who were disgruntled over being excluded from monastic privileges by the Kandyan hierarchy.[12] From these three types of people came practically all the major Buddhist reform movements of the past 150 years. As most of them lived in the Westernized coastal areas, they had political and economic advantages which steadily increased as Ceylon modernized.

The new intelligentsia were active in systematizing religious action and in promoting new religious organizations, including lay piety groups, Buddhist schools, political action groups, monastic fraternities, and suprafraternity councils. They promoted religious literacy, not only through Buddhist schools but also by sponsoring various publications and newspapers and the translating of Pali scriptures into colloquial Sinhalese. They were also responsible for encouraging, perhaps more than they realized, a reinterpretation of Buddhist doctrine to suit present conditions in Ceylon and above all else their own condition as a modern intelligentsia.

In addition to these local interest groups, there were several events of a more international nature which greatly contributed to the Buddhist resurgence. In the 1880's a number of Western theosophists spirited by the American Colonel H. S. Olcott came to the East in search of a new religion. While in Ceylon, Olcott practically started a Buddhist renaissance on his own; he organized local Buddhists and acted as their representative in dealing with the British. In 1947, relics of Buddha's two close disciples, Mogallana and Sariputta, were taken through various Buddhist countries, including Ceylon, and consequently gave rise to scenes of great enthusiasm and piety. In 1954, Burma convened a meeting of all Asian Buddhist leaders for the Sixth Great Council held since the Buddha's death. This again stimulated interest in Buddhist affairs. And finally, in 1956, Ceylon held a gigantic celebration in honor of the 2500th anniversary of the Buddha's attainment of salvation, a date which the Sinhalese claim coincides with the Aryan colonization of Ceylon. All over the island tremendous preparations were made; to many it marked the return of the Golden Age of Buddhism and Sinhalese nationalism.

DOCTRINAL REINTERPRETATIONS

It is possible to outline some of the general characteristics of the ideological "reinterpretations" stimulated by these enthusiastic movements. But it should be understood that Buddhist reformers never presented a unified front or a consistent ideology. To the contrary, they represented numerous small interest groups which often worked at cross purposes. It was rare even for an individual to be solely concerned with reform without also wishing to restore certain traditional elements. Everyone expressed a mixture of sentiments reflecting a variety of personal interests, even though one kind might predominate. The influence of some reformers did not extend far beyond their own groups. But despite this over-all empirical complexity, it is still possible to talk about certain common features and a certain directionality of change at a more general or analytical level. Reformers tend to emphasize aspects of doctrine which traditionalists usually ignore, and on the other hand, they ignore arguments which traditionalists tend to emphasize.

The general pattern of events in Ceylon closely parallels developments which took place during the Christian Reformation. Pre-Reformation Christianity, like Sinhalese Buddhism, was also based on a dualism between monks who followed a religious vocation and laymen who pursued worldly occupations. But through the course of the Reformation and accompanying social changes, in many Christian communities the monastic vocation became more worldly while the laity grew more ascetic. As ethics were universalized, the distinction between monk and layman became less important or ceased to exist at all.

No Sinhalese advocates abolition of the monkhood, but some ascetic-minded intellectuals are taking ethics, traditionally the concern of a few virtuoso hermit monks, and generalizing or universalizing them to apply to all people, both lay and cleric.

According to these reformers one need not necessarily renounce the world for a hermitage (āranya) to practice the Buddha's teaching and to attain salvation. One may work for salvation "here and now" even while pursuing an ordinary family life.[13] Traditionally, and in rural areas today, salvation (nirvana, nibbana) was considered hundreds of births away; it was a long path to travel even for the virtuous. But reformers see it as being closer. This is reflected in the increasing popularity of public meditation centers in urban areas and of meditation rooms in private households. This is the most important doctrinal change: that is, the belief in the possibility of a more immediate and direct contact with the divine, which in the Buddhist case is a self-induced mystical experience. Such a change is characteristic of enthusiastic and sectarian movements everywhere.[14] In fact, it provides the justification for enthusiasm, and for the Sinhalese it is the principle which substitutes for the charisma of the Buddha himself.

As more is expected of the layman, so the role of the monk is reinterpreted. Rather than work out his own salvation in secluded meditation, the monk is now expected by some people to become a social worker who devotes his whole life for the "good and happiness of the many."

In addition to the universalization of higher ethics, there are a number of other closely related ideological developments, several of which may be cited as examples. It appears, for instance, that a greater emphasis is being placed on a pragmatic and rational interpretation of tradition. Reformers frequently cite the Kalama Sermon in which the Buddha advised people not to give blind obedience to traditional authority but to search out the truth for oneself. Today it is claimed not only in regard to strictly theological concerns but in other matters as well that neither tradition nor traditional authority should be respected for themselves, but only if it is efficient and practical to do so. The emphasis is placed upon reasoning and a cognitive rather than an emotional attitude toward the world. Modern reformers identify Buddhism with science and the scientific method:[15] both are said to be based on research and experiment, the one introspective or subjective and the other objective. It is even suggested that Buddhism made many scientific discoveries long before Western science did.

One also gets the impression, not unexpectedly, that modern Buddhists are more achievement-oriented than are their rural counterparts. Because salvation is felt to be closer or more immediate, reformers feel less need to pay attention to the round of rebirths and the many Buddhist *pinkama* rituals concerned with improving one's rebirth chances. It is how one performs here and now, in this life itself, that really counts. Among villagers and in popular ritual the Buddha is described as being the savior of the world, the "god above the gods" (*dēvātidēva*); members of the new intelligentsia point out that he was an individual who attained Enlightenment through hard and very human striving. The Buddha is seen by them as a person to be emulated more than adored.[16]

Closely related to this is a fourth major emphasis of the doctrinal reformers, which is in the form of a protest against the excessive ritualism and idolatry of the traditional monks and unsophisticated villagers.[17] The Buddhist way for all people is held to be the simple and rational path of meditation (*bhāvanā*) that leads directly to salvation. There is no need for ritual of any kind, Buddhist or magical. The Buddha, after all, reacted against priestly ceremonialism; so why should people not do so again today? Ritual and magic are denounced, not because they are considered false, but because they are unnecessary for a pious Buddhist. Rational ascetic virtue will provide its own protection just as it provides its own reward.

REFORM MOVEMENTS

A description of several reform movements will illustrate various combinations of these doctrinal arguments. In a general way it is possible to correlate the radical nature of a movement with the degree of emphasis it places upon the four points listed above (universalism, pragmatism, achievement, and antiritualism). The greater the emphasis, the more radical are the proposals for institutional reform. A large number of movements have emerged during the past 150 years. Only four will be discussed here in order to illustrate their variety: these are (1) new fraternities, (2) meditation centers, (3) Buddhist commissions, and (4) the *Vinaya Vardhana,* the "Anabaptists" of Buddhism. (Most of the information concerning these movements was gathered from informants and from Ceylonese publications similar to those already cited. Scattered references can also be found in recent histories of Ceylon.)

New Monastic Fraternities

In 1750 there was only one monastic fraternity in Ceylon, called the *Siam Nikāya* after the monks who brought higher ordination back from Siam. This group eventually restricted ordination to the high-caste Goyigama or "cultivators" and restricted fraternity leadership to the elite Goyigama of the Kandyan district. As it was the only order of monks for a number of years, the *Siam Nikāya* naturally assumed control over all sacred centers, relics, and temple lands and therefore became the direct successor to the ancient tradition. But with the increased wealth, political power, education, and mobility of the coastal Sinhalese, many of whom were non-Goyigama and hence excluded from monastic privileges, a protest movement soon developed. Within a span of about 150 years, beginning in 1802, over thirty new fraternities were established in the coastal areas in opposition to the one controlled by the Kandyans. Higher ordination was brought back from Burma on five different occasions for this purpose, practically equal to the number of times it was reintroduced from abroad during the whole previous 2,200 years.

According to a Sinhalese observer writing in 1845, the Burmese and the Siamese-ordained monks were bitter antagonists:

> They deny *nirvana* to each other; and as much animosity is to be seen among them as it is to be found between two sects of any other religion. Their animosity is so great that they do not salute each other when they meet, and call each other *dusilayas,* or priests without sanctity. The object of the (Burmese monks) is to bring back the doctrines of Buddhism to its pristine purity, by disentangling them from caste, polytheism, and other corruptions to which it has been subject for ages; and these priests, how difficult soever the task may be, have made a considerable progress in this reformation in the low countries.[18]

The Burmese monks, as they were called, ordained people from all the major castes (although not from the lowest castes), preached against the excessive ritualism and secular preoccupations of the Kandyan monks, and also called into question the sanctity or legitimacy of many monastic traditions.

As a postscript to this, it might be mentioned that originally only four fraternities were established in the coastal areas. But they quickly splintered into many more. By 1870, there were almost ten independent monastic fraternities, and today there are about thirty. The *Siam Nikāya* was itself at one time subdivided into six factions. The coastal fraternities fragmented first on the basis of caste—each of the major caste groups sponsored its own order of monks—and then further subdivided over arguments concerning rights of ownership to temples and lands and succession to titled statuses.[19] With few exceptions, most of these new fraternities eventually adopted practices very similar to those objected to over a hundred years ago. There are references in chronicles and legends to the existence of several fraternities during ancient times, but apparently there were never more than three or four at any one time.

Meditation Centers

There are several movements devoted almost entirely to the promotion and popularization of meditation (*bhāvanā*) both among the monks and laity. According to a number of informants several of the better known monastic hermitages (*āranya*) were not inhabited as recently as fifty years ago. On several occasions I met wealthy and pious laymen who were constructing secluded hermitages or retreats where fellow laymen could spend week ends or holidays. This appears to be completely an innovation, for there is no evidence of lay hermitages in Ceylon during the past 2,300 years.

But more dramatic than either of these two developments is the growth of meditation centers in the major urban areas. In the middle of Colombo's wealthy district, Cinnomen Gardens, for example, a grand new hall was recently constructed and dedicated to lay meditation. Several worldly-wise monks are kept in attendance to instruct a middle-class lay clientele. Several other monks tour urban centers on the island and hold group meditation classes for the laity. A number of middle-class Colombo people have constructed secluded meditation rooms in their own houses, a striking contrast to village houses which have shrine rooms dedicated to the Buddha and to the various deities of the Sinhalese pantheon.

Corresponding to the growth of institutions for meditation is a growing body of literature on the subject, expounding the technique and extolling its virtues. Not gods but one's own mental development brings health and happiness. One who diligently practices the "way of mindfulness" (*satispatthāna*) is, in the words of one monk, "clad in invincible armour and equipped with an all-conquering sword." [20] Both learned monks and laymen busily write devotional articles and translate scriptures into colloquial Sinhalese. Especially active in these respects are the *Vajirārāma* temple in a Colombo suburb and the Forest Hermitage near Kandy. A number of the leading *Vajirārāma* monks were professional men who in their adult years converted from Christianity to Buddhism and joined the monastic order (village monks, on the other hand, have usually entered the order before attaining puberty). And almost all the *Vajirārāma* monks are from non-Goyigama castes of the low country (except for one who was an Englishman). The Forest Hermitage is directed by a German monk and acts as a clearinghouse for many of the devotional publications in English and in Sinhalese. A number of these are written by the *Vajirārāma* monks.

Buddhist Commissions

During the past few years a number of interested urban Buddhists have organized investigations into the state of the Buddhist church. They published polemical articles in a variety of local journals, and they also issued two reports on Buddhism. One of these, known in English by the title "Betrayal of Buddhism," was published immediately prior to the 1956 parliamentary elections and assisted in the election of a new Sinhalese Buddhist nationalist government. The report claimed that Buddhism had been betrayed by the British and by the English-educated local gentry who succeeded them. It called for a government which would protect Buddhist interests. The second report, known as the *Sāsana* or "Church Report," was sponsored by the new nationalist government and published in Sinhalese in 1959.[21] Because both reports demanded that the state should intervene in religious affairs, they have been likened to the ancient royal proclamations of the Sinhalese kings who acted as patrons of Buddhism. But in most other respects these reports are quite different from the ancient proclamations.

To begin with, unlike the traditional investigations which were sponsored and executed by Sinhalese kings on behalf of the monastic hierarchy, these reports were instigated and largely composed by pious laymen (again, mostly from coastal areas). The ancient royal proclamations accepted the world in Buddhist fashion as a place of misery; there was little attempt to reform society but only the individual wayward monk, for the ultimate object was to withdraw from the world rather than to correct it. The new reports, on the other hand, do not attempt to explain the decline of Buddhism or other events as due to previous karma, they do not emphasize the impermanence of life, nor do they advocate withdrawal from the world to put an end to rebirth. Rather, they want to change the world; they take human progress for granted; they trace events not to former actions but to economic and political causes. Where the royal proclamations dealt with corruption and schism within the monkhood, these reports are in addition concerned with reforming the laity and the government. People are even admonished to rise early in the morning, work hard, save their money, and abstain from drinking and gambling. The government is advised as to how it might bring about monastic reforms. The reports assume, in fact, that if Sinhalese Buddhism is to survive it must have a rebirth and reformation. In the words of a young Colombo lawyer who worked on the reports, Buddhism "must leave the monastery and take its place in the social world outside or it will perish." It was felt that the government should aid in this transformation.

Vinaya Vardhana

This means "protection of the Buddhist discipline" and refers to a lay movement by that name started twenty-three years ago by a Sinhalese scholar. Unlike most other reform movements, the *Vinaya Vardhana* appears to obtain much of its following from rural people and Sinhalese-educated intellectuals. Today there are said to be 150 branches, containing a few active members each, distributed over the island. It is also the most radical of all reform movements for, Anabaptistlike, it denies the purity or validity or apostolic succession or monastic ordination (*upasampadā*) which is the source of charisma for the monks. *Vinaya Vardhana* spokesmen claim all ordained monks are corrupt and heretical and that they have corrupted the doctrine and the laity as well. Monastic landlordism, elaborate temple rituals, the "useless" propitiation of spirits within temple precincts, and the worship of Buddha images are cited as examples of this degradation. Buddhists should return to the pristine purity of the primitive gospels of the Buddha, which are complete and sufficient in themselves.

About seven years ago the *Vardhana* people aligned with a small group of ascetics or *tapasas,* a sect of unordained monks who live in a very secluded hermitage[22] and whom the *Vardhana* people call *anagārika Yogis* or "recluses who practice meditation." (These ascetics may be the remnants of a *tapasa* movement which appeared in 1954. At that time, apparently a number of uneducated men made robes from discarded rags and wandered the countryside making a great show of pious asceticism by eating simple meals and sleeping in graveyards. For a short while these *tapasas* received a wide following among the rural villagers, but within a year or so they disappeared. They caused the ordained monks a great deal of embarrassment, however, and they are still talked about today.)

In contrast to other reformers who advocate utilitarian functions for the monks, such as social welfare work, teaching, and scholarship, the *Vinaya Vardhana* wish to restrict all monks to isolated hermitages like their own *anagārikas* or *tapasas.* Both the *Vinaya Vardhana* and other reform groups want to eliminate monastic corruption; but whereas others believe this could be done by making monks more responsible to society, the *Vardhana* people believe the proper solution is to remove monks from society altogether. Laymen should become like ascetic monks who yet remain in the midst of social life. Extreme virtue is the only way to happiness. As one informant explained it, "The Buddhist layman is a warrior who must perform his worldly duties with nonattachment." Pious and learned laymen would also take over the duties of village monks, that is, preaching, leading devotional services, and reciting sacred scriptures (*pirit*) at funerals. The only duty for a monk is to lead the life of a homeless one and to meditate.

Due to its radical nature, the *Vinaya Vardhana* has been frequently censured by other groups, especially by the established monastic orders. But *Vardhana* members are nevertheless respected for their piety, and many people sympathize with their complaints about monastic corruption. They perhaps would have had a greater impact were they not restricted by their own piety. They believe the world should be purified and converted through providing a living example, not through force or popular persuasion. And because they consider that all other groups, except their own *tapasas,* are tainted by corruption and heresy, they have so far refused to join forces with other groups no matter how pious the others' intentions.

The *Vinaya Vardhana* evaluation of Buddhism suggests a second way of determining the radical nature of a group, that is, by correlating it with the distance it must go back through history and myth to find the Golden Age. *Vardhana* spokesmen claim the only Golden Age was right at the beginning, the age of the Buddha and the primitive gospels. All later church traditions and scriptures are degenerate and invalid. The more moderate reformers, on the other hand, see the more recent ages of Sinhalese kings as constituting times of glory. Some refer to the ancient kingdom of Anuradhapura, which flourished around the beginning of the Christian era; others point to the Polonnaruva kingdom of the Middle Ages; still more moderate reformers and some restorationists suggest the Kandyan kingdom of the eighteenth century represented a golden mean.

SUMMARY AND CONCLUSIONS

In summary it would appear, as Max Weber has said,[23] that a change in the socially decisive strata of a religion can be of profound importance. Due to a certain pattern of social change in Ceylon, the consequent decline in status of literati monks, and the emergence of a new group of intellectuals, religious ideology was subjected to reinterpretation. Some of the new Sinhalese intelligentsia tended to generalize or universalize higher Buddhist ethics so that they applied to all people, not just to a few religious professionals. Because they believed that by active striving almost anyone could become a religious virtuoso in this life itself, these reformers felt no need for the less sophisticated "religion of the masses," which they therefore rejected.

Finally, in the way of a conclusion, I want to make several qualifying statements. Regarding the process of Westernization, it has been suggested that when in prolonged contact, an indigenous population tends to adopt Western or Christian values and institutions. The actual process appears to be more complicated than that. Sinhalese reformers were certainly influenced by Christian values, but they seldom consciously adopted them. A greater influence of Christianity, and of the West in general, was in the way they stimulated a reaction on the part of the

Sinhalese intelligentsia. In self-defense against Christian missionizing and criticism, modern Buddhists sought in their own heritage proof that their way of life was superior. Enthusiasts and reformers cited ancient Buddhist texts to show that the Buddha was a better Protestant even than Calvin and that, in fact, Buddhism has an ethical system superior to Christianity and extremely adaptable to the needs of a modern world. In defense against the pressure group known as the Catholic Union, Buddhists organized their own action groups. Other Buddhists suggested monks should be as disciplined as Catholic priests. In response to Christian newspapers and devotional literature, Buddhists began their own publication societies. They established Buddhist schools to compete with mission schools. A Young Men's Buddhist Association, patterned after the Y.M.C.A., was established. A Buddhist Aid to Travellers was located at the harbor. Monks began holding Sunday School classes.

The second qualification concerns the processes of urbanization and industrialization. It is usually suggested that such developments foster a secular attitude, and as a result magic and religion give way to progress. Ceylon has certainly progressed both politically and economically; but religion has not declined. There is no simple correlation between modernization, increased secularization, and decrease in magic. The stress of social change adds to the popularity of certain rituals while de-emphasizing others, as, of course, we know from the study of nativistic movements. And the Sinhalese peasant, whatever the influence of Western rationalism, frequently continues to treat Western medicine as just another, perhaps somewhat more efficacious and wondrous, system of magical remedies.

Where there has been a significant decline in religious behavior it was not due to secularization but, paradoxically, to an increased feeling of religiosity. Magic and the more stereotyped Buddhist rituals are being displaced by the growth of an intensely pious and all-encompassing form of Buddhist enthusiasm. This enthusiasm, like the secular attitude, is a response to modern development. It was precisely in the more Westernized coastal areas of Ceylon that Buddhist enthusiasm reached its highest fervor since the Middle Ages and where religious movements have been most active.

In these coastal areas it was the devout and pious Buddhist—the kind of person who saw the divine or the sacred as closer or more immediate or more penetrating—who felt in less need of traditional rituals (the religion of the masses, in other words) and who was more active in denouncing or rejecting them. The nonenthusiast, no matter how Westernized or secularized, would nevertheless resort to magic when placed under stress. For the enthusiast, however, Buddhism is no longer abstract and otherworldly. It has come back into the world, and it is becoming intimately concerned with the day-to-day stresses and strains of a worldly life. Problems which formerly were handled by an elaborate, but profane, system of magic are now faced by a confident attitude of enthusiastic pietism and ethical asceticism. Revitalization movements, which are an expression of this pietistic fervor, function like socialization mechanisms in that they facilitate the individual's learning of and adjustment to a new way of life. Doctrinal changes illustrate the cognitive process of attempting to interpret disturbing social changes in a more meaningful way.

It is in this general fashion that religious reform may have important social repercussions. Religion is not necessarily static, nor does it always impede change. It may actually facilitate a transformation. The great achievement of ethical religions, especially certain forms of Protestantism, was to shatter the fetters of kinship and to establish the superior community of faith and a common ethical way of life in opposition to the community of blood and privilege. In traditional Buddhism this ethical universalism was restricted to the monastic order. Society, and secular life in general, remained unchanged. But if the systematization of religious action and proselytizing by modern Sinhalese intelligentsia are continued and successful, then they may very well serve to extend the Buddha's ethical revolution into the midst of secular life. This would allow both for a more universal expression of enthusiasm free of sectarian and routinizing tendencies and perhaps for far-reaching, and radical, social changes.

NOTES

1. As there is space here only for a minimum of descriptive material, frequent references will be made to published sources. Nevertheless, most statements concerning contemporary Sinhalese religion are based on my own interview material and documents gathered while in the field. See my "A Structural Analysis of Sinhalese Religion," *Proceedings of the Seminar on Indian Religions* (Berkeley) (August 1961). For authoritative histories of Buddhism in Ceylon, see W. Rahula, *History of Buddhism in Ceylon* (Colombo, 1956); W. Geiger, *Culture of Ceylon in Mediaeval Times* (Wiesbaden, 1960); V. Panditha, "Buddhism during the Polonnaruva Period," in "The Polonnaruva Period," a special issue of *The Ceylon Historical Journal*, IV (July–October 1954 and April 1955), 113–129; D. T. Devendra, "Buddhism in Ceylon," in René de Berval (ed.), "Présence du Bouddhisme," *France-Asie*, XVI (February–June 1959), 861–878. For an extensive, annotated bibliography, see R. A. Gard, *A Bibliography for the Study of Buddhism in Ceylon in Western Languages*, 2nd ed. (San Francisco, 1957).

2. Bryce Ryan, "Status, Achievement and Education in Ceylon, an Historical Perspective," *Journal of Asian Studies*, XX (August 1961), 463–476.

3. Descriptions of Sinhalese Buddhism may be found in references cited above and in A. Maitreya, "Buddhism in Theravada Countries," in K. W. Morgan (ed.), *The Path of the Buddha* (New York, 1956), pp. 113–152; R. S. Copleston, *Buddhism Primitive and Present in Magadha and in Ceylon*, 2nd ed. (London, 1908, W. Rahula, *What the Buddha Taught* (Bedford, 1959).

4. For descriptions of Sinhalese magical-animism, see especially E. R. Sarachandra,

The Sinhalese Folk Play (Colombo, 1953), Chs. 1–2; P. Wirz, *Exorcism and the Art of Healing in Ceylon* (Leiden, 1954); D. deS. Goonerante, "On Demonology and Witchcraft in Ceylon," *Journal (Ceylon Branch) Royal Asiatic Society*, IV (1865–1866), 1–117; N. Yalman, "The Structure of Sinhalese Healing Rituals," in *Proceedings of the Seminar on Indian Religions* (Berkeley) (August 1961); Edmund Leach, "Pulleyar and the Lord Buddha: An Aspect of Religious Syncretism in Ceylon" (manuscript). A description of *pinkama* rituals may be found in my "Popular Ideology and Village Rites of the Sinhalese Buddhists," *Proceedings of the Buddhist Studies Conference,* University of Wisconsin.

5. For discussion of the worship and therapy subsystems of religion, see R. N. Bellah, "Some Suggestions for the Systematic Study of Religion" (manuscripts, Harvard University).

6. A brief but penetrating introduction to Ceylon history is provided by G. C. Mendis, *Ceylon Today and Yesterday: Main Currents of Ceylon History* (Colombo, 1957). An exhaustive survey of the recent period and of all the relevant literature is given by W. H. Wriggens, *Ceylon: Dilemmas of a New Nation* (Princeton, N.J., 1960).

7. Some idea of the state of Buddhist monasticism during the British period can be learned from the following: G. W. Woodhouse, " 'Sissiyānu Sissia Paramparāva' and Other Laws Relating to Buddhist Priests in Ceylon," *Ceylon Antiquary and Literary Register*, III (1917–1918), 174–186 (see especially note 7, p. 183); F. H. Hayley, *A Treatise on the Laws and Customs of the Sinhalese* (Colombo, 1923); R. S. Hardy, *Eastern Monachism* (London, 1860). An interesting picture of more recent ecclesiastical disputes can be obtained from law cases reported in K. Balasingham (ed.), *New Law Reports* (Colombo). See especially 14 *NLR* (1910), p. 400; 20 *NLR* (1919), pp. 385–404; 22 *NLR* (1921), pp. 236, 323; 59 *NLR* (1958), pp. 79, 121.

8. Bowles, Daly, *et al.*, "Reports of Buddhist Temporalities," *Ceylon Sessional Papers* (Colombo), especially Sessional Papers 17 of 1876; 23, 33 of 1904; 4 of 1907; and 23 of 1910; E. A. L. Wijeyewardene *et al.*, "Report of the Commission on Tenure of Lands of Viharagam, Dewalagam and Nindagam," *Ceylon Sessional Paper* 1–1956 (Colombo 1956).

9. For the role of Christian education in modern Ceylon, see the following: The Buddhist point of view: Buddhist Committee of Inquiry, *The Betrayal of Buddhism* (Balangoda, 1956); J. M. Peebles (ed.), *Buddhism and Christianity: Being an Oral Debate Held at Panadura between a Buddhist Priest and a Wesleyan Clergyman* (Colombo, n.d.) (a republication of an earlier book by the same author). The Catholic view: The Catholic Union of Ceylon, *Companion to the Buddhist Commission Report* (1957), pp. 1–76.

For the findings of several recent surveys, see: Ryan, *op. cit.;* D. D. de Saram, "Social Class Differences in Education under the Central School Commission," *University Ceylon Review*, XVII (July–October 1959), 99–105; W. I. Jennings, "Race, Religion and Economic Opportunity in the University of Ceylon," *University Ceylon Review*, II (October 1944), 1–13. For a comparable situation in Christian history, where monastic elite were superseded by a new intelligentsia, see N. F. Cantor, "The Crises of Western Monasticism, 1050–1130," *American Historical Review*, LXVI (1960), 46–67.

10. These and other incidents concerning monks and the British are reported in W. Rahula, *Bhikkuvage Urumaya* (Colombo 1946), pp. 73–85. Buddhist Committee of Inquiry, *op. cit.*, alludes to such practices.

11. For the 1904 Memorial, see "Memorial of the Siam Nikaya (Malwatta and Asgiri) to Edward VII, 29 December, 1904," in "Correspondence Relating to the Buddhist Temporalities Ordinance," *Ceylon Sessional Papers*, 4–1907. The 1959 complaint, made in the form of a letter to the Prime Minister of Ceylon, is reported in "Divergent Views on Sasana Report," *World Buddhism*, VIII (January 1960), 10–11.

12. M. D. Raghavan, *The Karāva of Ceylon* (Colombo 1961), pp. 136–137; Bryce Ryan, *Caste in Modern Ceylon* (New Brunswick, N.J., 1953), pp. 39–43.

13. There are numerous devotional publications in English and Sinhalese which express this and other themes to be mentioned in the paper. See Gard, *op. cit.;* issues of *The Buddhist* (monthly publication of the Young Men's Buddhist Association, Colombo); *World Buddhism* (a Colombo monthly); *The Bosat* (a Colombo monthly); *University Buddhist* (annual magazine of the University Buddhist Brotherhood, Colombo); various *Vesak Annuals* published in Colombo.

The Buddhist Publication Society, Forest Hermitage, Kandy, is the most active publishing house. Virtually all its tracts are in English, and almost half are written by European Buddhists. Translations of canonical sermons are reprinted as well as devotional articles. The following listing of titles will give some idea of the selections: "Influence of Buddhism on People," "Self-Mastery," "A Teaching for Our Time," "The Case for Rebirth," "Everyman's Ethics," "Buddhism and Christianity," "Buddhism and Worship." "The Buddhist Concept of Mind," "The Kālāma Sutta," "Kamma and Rebirth," "Anattā Nibbāna."

By June 1960 the Buddhist Publication Society had published 150,000 copies of 32 different booklets and pamphlets which were sent to 1,270 subscribers in Ceylon and 56 foreign countries (information based on the Society's annual report). In addition, copies of several booklets are on sale in bookstores throughout the island. The Society began in 1960 to issue Sinhalese-language pamphlets, two for that year and two for 1961; both devotional articles and translations from Pali scriptures were included.

14. R. A. Knox, *Enthusiasm: A Chapter in the History of Religion* (New York, 1950); L. Berger, "The Sociological Study of Sectarianism," *Social Research*, XXI (1954), 467–485. Comparable developments are evident, for instance, in Hindu reform movements, especially in the Westernized Bengal area: see D. S. Sarma, *Hinduism through the Ages* (Bombay, 1956), pp. 61–278; S. Kulandran, *Resurgent Religions* (London, 1957), pp. 7–15.

15. K. N. Jayatilleke, R. F. Spencer, and Wu Shu, "Buddhism and Science," *The Wheel*, No. 3 (Kandy, 1958); Jean Filliozat, "The Psychological Discoveries of Buddhism," *University Ceylon Review*, XIII (1955), 69–82.

16. W. S. Karunaratne, "Buddhism as a Form of Activity," *University Buddhist* (Colombo, 1959), pp. 4–5; R. Abeyasekera, "The Master's Quest for Light," *Bodhi Leaves No. 7* (Kandy, n.d.).

17. S. F. de Silva, "The Dhamma and the World Today," *Vesak Sirisara* (Panadura, 1960), pp. 58–62; Ben Jayawardene, *Ceylon's Uplift* (Through Buddhism) (Colombo, n.d.); A. de Silva, "Undue Emphasis on Pujas and Ceremonies," *World Buddhism*, VIII (May 1960), 3–4; A. Nimalasuria (ed.), "Buddha the Healer," *The Wheel*, No. 22 (Kandy, n.d.).

18. A. de Silva, *Ceylon Friend* (September 1845). I was unable to locate the original source, however. De Silva is quoted in Hardy, *op. cit.*, pp. 328–329, from which the above is excerpted.

19. A. L. Green, "Sangha and King: The Structure of Authority in Medieval Ceylon," paper presented at the Tenth Pacific Science Congress, August 1961. The problem of recent monastic schisms is scarcely mentioned in the literature, excepting Hardy, *op. cit.;* Copleston, *op. cit.*, Ch. 27; Raghavan, *op. cit.*, pp. 136–140; Ryan, *Caste*, pp. 39–43, 270–271.

20. Bhikkhu Soma, *The Way of Mindfulness (Satipatthāna Sutta)* (Colombo 1949), p. vii.

21. Buddhist Committee of Inquiry, *op. cit.;* K. Pannasekera *et al.*, "Buddha Sasana Commission Report" (typescript draft of English-language translation of the Report). I am indebted to the Ministry of Cultural Affairs, Government of Ceylon, for making

the typescript available. The Report was published in Sinhalese in 1959; as of yet there is no authorized English-language version. A detailed summary of the Commission's recommendations may be found in "Sasana Commission Wants Reform of the Sangha," *World Buddhism*, VIII (December 1960), 1–2, 11–12.

For analyses of the 1956 Report, see Mendis, *op. cit.*, Ch. 12; Catholic Union of Ceylon, *op. cit.*; Wriggens, *op. cit.*, pp. 193–210.

22. N. Yalman, "The Ascetic Buddhist Monks of Ceylon," *Bulletin of the London School of Oriental and African Studies*. The *tapasas* appear to be a modern version of the ancient *Pamsukūlikas* who wore rag-robes and emphasized strict observance of monastic regulations; see Rahula, *History of Buddhism*, pp. 108, 212; Geiger, *op. cit.*, p. 202.

23. H. H. Gerth and C. W. Mills, *From Max Weber: Essays in Sociology* (New York 1953), p. 270.

15

SANCTITY, PURITANISM, SECULARIZATION, AND NATIONALISM IN NORTH AFRICA

Ernest Gellner

The most characteristic social institution of North African religious life is the saint, the holy personage. As Islam does not enjoin celibacy, saints proliferate and form lineages and dynasties. "Nepotism" would be a misnomer, as the North African saint does not need to bequeath his spiritual power to a nephew, for there is no reason why he should not have or should not admit to having a son. Moreover, no condemnation attaches to such a family succession, for spiritual merit and role are expected to be passed on in the family line. But such genetic-spiritual lineages, so to speak, are not the only possible bond between successive generations of holy personages: there are also spiritual-spiritual lineages, in which the links are formed not by father–son relationships but by teacher–disciple ones. Thus living saints and dead enshrined ones are connected by a complex net of two kinds of "kinship."

The saints are not all of one kind, of course. One interesting spectrum is that between rural and urban ones, the former operating in tribal contexts, the latter amongst city populations. It is still possible—though it will not be possible for much longer—to study the functioning of rural saints by observation. I studied one saintly lineage intermittently during the 1950's. By way of contrast, it would also have been interesting to see something of the working of their urban counterparts, but by the middle of this century whatever was left of this phenomenon—and no doubt something remained—was extremely difficult or impossible to study. In

Reprinted from Archives de Sociologie des Religions, *VIII, No. 15 (1963), 71–86.*

any case, such attempts as I made in this direction soon discouraged me.

Fortunately, a book appeared recently which assembled a good deal of documentation concerning one urban saint.[1] The book is written from the viewpoint of interest in religion as such rather than religion as a social form. The present essay is an attempt to interpret the material sociologically and to place it against a general picture of the role of religion in North Africa, traditionally and in transition.

In religion, the southern, Moslem shore of the Mediterranean is a kind of mirror-image of the northern shore of Europe. Europe is, or was, Christendom. Within Western Christianity, one has become habituated to the opposition between the central tradition and the deviant splinter churches and sects which, even when relatively large, remain small in comparison with *the* Church. The central tradition has certain marked features: it has a hierarchy, it makes use of personal mediation between the ordinary believer and the deity, it verges on a cult of personality or personalities, it has a strong rural appeal, it stresses and uses ritual a good deal, it incorporates or is tolerant of a good deal of rural superstition or rites, it possesses an organization economically dependent, at least in part, on the donations of the faithful, it satisfies the emotional needs of its believers. By contrast, the deviant splinter groups tend to dispense with personal mediation, with ritual, with emotional and sensuous accompaniments of faith, with hierarchy; they tend to be puritanical, stress *the Book* and hence literacy rather than mediators and ritual, and so forth.

In North Africa, all this is reversed. It is the central tradition which has the "protestant" characteristics—a tradition without clergy in the full sense (but rich in lawyer-theologians) or personal mediation; based on trading towns, stressing literacy and learning, sometimes hostile to shrines and popular cults. It is the deviant cults which are hierarchical, employ personal mediation with the deity, indulge in greater ritual richness, personal cults, and so forth.

Moreover, in Europe with its strong states and long-established freedom from tribalism, *the* Church is or was a kind of disembodied (and not always disembodied) state. In North Africa, where states were weak and tribalism strong, the deviant religious organizations were a species of disembodied (and not always disembodied) tribes.

This is the reality under the apparent religious homogeneity of North Africa. Statistically, disregarding the European and Jewish minorities, virtually all North Africans are Sunni Moslems of the Maliki rite. (The only significant exception is the Ibadi minority, with such strong "protestant" features as have been described as "the Calvinists of Islam" and who, thanks to trade, manage to wrest a living from their desert base in Mzab and their island base in Djerba. This group still awaits its Max Weber.) But this appearance of homogeneity is only superficial. Underneath, there is, or was, a rich and varied world of religious associations, of living traditions of sanctity, perpetuated and reproduced by both physical and spiritual lineages of saints. The saints whom one can find on the map of Europe from, say, St. Andrews to St. Tropez no longer represent a living social form. The map of North Africa is richer in Sidis than the map of Europe is in saints, but the type of personage commemorated by place and shrine is still to be found in life.

But here some qualification is required. In very recent years, even in North Africa there has been a decline in this form of popular religious life. Uprooting and industrialization, a new wave of Moslem Reformism and purification, and finally nationalism have all significantly diminished the extent and importance of these religious manifestations. In this respect, there is a striking contrast with West Africa. There, Europeans were identified with Christianity, and so all forms of Moslem religious life could continue to flourish, whether orthodox or not: none were tainted by association with colonial powers. In North Africa, Christian proselytism was not significant: insofar as the colonial power worked on the indigenous masses through religion, it did so not through Christianity but through the more archaic and segmented religious traditions. Partly for this reason, national revival also meant a decline of the saints and special cults. Today they are on the way out: the day is probably near when a "Sidi" on the North African map will, like a "St." on a European one, merely be an echo of a past form of life.

Except for the occupying French and Spaniards, Europeans have on the whole not had much contact with this sanctity—at least for some time. (Outside Tangier there is a shrine of a saint who became such for fighting the English when they held the town—and of course a far greater number became sanctified for fighting the Portuguese.) In the twentieth century, more Europeans in Europe have probably been in contact with these forms of North African religious life unwittingly, *in the circus,* than in any other way: southern Morocco exports circus acrobats, and it is not generally recognized that these form something between a clan and a guild and attribute their skill to the saintliness (transmitted charisma) of their patron saint.

The literature on this subject in English is scanty (the most important item is probably the book by an Englishwoman who married into one of the saintly lineages—Emily Shareefa, of Wazan, and one sociological masterpiece—Professor E. Evans-Prichard's study of the Sanusi Order), and Martin Lings's book is a most welcome addition to it. Lings is interested in religion and mysticism as such, rather than specifically in the social manifestations of it. But this in a way makes the sociological material all the more valuable: it is assembled quite unself-consciously.

Sheikh Ahmad al-'Alawi was born in Mostaganem in western Algeria in 1869 and died in 1934. He was an extremely interesting example of the living tradition of sanctity as it is conceived in North Africa. Lings remarks that he remains wholly unknown "outside the precincts of Islamic mysticism." Within those precincts he did however acquire enough fame to attract the interest of French scholars concerned with Sufism, notably of A. Berque and of Massignon. The former of these published an article about him two years after his death, entitled *Un Mystique Moderniste*. This article curiously reproduces as fact an emergent legend about the Sheikh's supposed travels in the East, including India. A legend is a fabrication or, as Lings more charitably puts it, these ten years in the East were no more real than a dream, . . . (but correspond) to what the Sheikh would have chosen for himself if his destiny had allowed it." Lings's charity suggests that there is something like a Mystic's License which permits some vagueness in differentiating between real and imaginary travels. In my own experience, North African saints are indeed addicted to mystical travels to the holy places of Hejaz—travels frequently unaided by normal means of transportation (though sometimes aided by sprouting wings for the purpose) and extremely speedy. As Lings remarks in another context, Sufis (Moslem mystics) visit Medina in spirit every morning and evening; and, it appears, the distinction between spiritual and material peregrinations is sometimes blurred.

Lings polemicizes with A. Berque's earlier study, but not so much on account of such insufficiently critical use of material: just as the imaginary journey becomes validated qua "dream," so Berque's contention that the Sheikh hypnotized his disciples is accepted, but reinterpreted by the assertion that the disciple's passivity, as that of "a corpse in the hands of the washer of the dead," really presupposed "an undercurrent of extreme spiritual activity" and led in the end to independent spiritual perception on the part of the disciple. Lings's real disagreement with Berque concerns the fact that the latter describes the Sheikh as a *moderniste*. In Lings's views, he was, on the contrary, "essentially very conservative." He goes on to remark that the Sheikh's "so-called 'modernism' appears to have been nothing other than the great breadth of his spiritual interests."

This brings us to what, from the outside, is really the most interesting thing about the Sheikh: his position on the range of alternative possible religious positions. Sociologically, it is this range, the nature of the alternatives, oppositions, and affinities in it, which is of the greatest interest. The span of the Sheikh's life corresponds roughly to the period when the French domination of North Africa was at its height, the period when the *Pax Gallica* was most securely superimposed on Moslem life. The pre-French period of Maghribi life, so to speak, when saints were leaders against the infidel, was almost over: the year of the Sheikh's death was also the year in which the last tribal, Marabout-led dissidence against the French in North Africa came to an end. The new form, so to speak, in which Moslem puritanism provided the basis for a modern nationalism had begun in his lifetime, but its nationalist and political aspects were hardly prominent at the time when he was most active. In view of the passivity or co-operation of the saints, the Marabouts, vis-à-vis the French, it is curious to reflect that their historical origin lies not only in Sufism and in Berber tribal practices but equally in military orders fighting Christian invaders, in a kind of Moslem equivalent of Crusaders, Knights of Malta, and the like. But in the Sheikh's own life and times, the militant aspects of both the past and the future were in abeyance.

It is difficult to agree with Lings's own characterization of the Sheikh's position (as "essentially very conservative"), at any rate sociologically, for it too has, so to speak, primarily a spiritual significance and validity. Lings agrees with certain characteristically Sufi claims, notably that Sufism is not really a later development within Islam but that, properly understood, it is there to be found in the Prophet's own pronouncements; and furthermore, he has much sympathy with a kind of panmystic eclecticism, in which he goes a good deal further than the subject of his study, the Sheikh himself. Lings's own attitude is a kind of "Mystics of all religions, unite" approach. He quotes with approval a statement of Pope Pius XI to the effect that Moslems are eligible for salvation, he recommends a reinterpretation of Jesus' words "None cometh to the Father but by Me" to include Hindu avatars, Buddha, and others in the "Me" [2] (whilst allowing that the apparent and exclusive meaning is providentially useful in being adapted to the ethnocentric attitudes of Europeans and Semites, "incapable of following seriously a religion unless they believe it to be the only one or to be exceptionally privileged"), and he compares the Sheikh to Indian, Red Indian, and Chinese mystics. Lings makes some interesting observations on the relative merits, from his standpoint, of Christianity and Islam: it is "one of the excellencies of Christianity that it has a definitely constituted spiritual authority consisting of a small minority of men"—but unfortunately this minority is pushed "further and further into a remote corner of the community from which it can barely function and from which it sometimes seeks to emerge by pandering to mundane triviality." It is, on the other hand, "one of the excellencies of Islam that there is no laity and every Moslem is in a sense a priest"—but the corresponding disadvantage is "the existence of a large number of very limited individuals who imagine that the whole religion is within their grasp."

Precisely: the fundamental issue is the equality of believers. The central tradition of Christianity denies it, and the deviants affirm it. The central tradition of Islam affirms it, and the deviants deny it. The saintly Sheikh, like his very numerous North African fellow saints, was in this sense a deviant in Islam. This conclusion of course neither he nor Lings would accept, despite the fact that Lings does provide the crucial premises for it. From the viewpoint of Lings, the Sheikh was not a deviant: neither in virtue of being a Sufi (for he holds Sufism to have been present in Islam from the start) nor in virtue of the tolerant breadth of his spiritual

interests (for truth is present in many religions, and their exclusive protestations are only a sugar-coating for the benefit of ethnocentric Europeans and Semites). The Sheikh's own eclecticism, one should add, is of
course not nearly so sweeping, open, and daring as Lings's: we are told
(p. 82), for instance, that "as an extremely subtle and penetrating meta-
physician, he was able to reconcile plurality with unity in the Trinitarian
conception . . . (but) he rejected it none the less, (though) his understanding of it made some people (his enemies) think that he adhered to
it." It is interesting to have so striking a refutation of a widespread view
—that doctrines of such difficulty have to be believed to be understood.

The kind of religious eclecticism openly advocated by Lings and much
more cautiously flirted with by the Sheikh is of course generally inspired
by most admirable motives, by the desire to avoid exclusiveness and intolerance whilst not cutting oneself off from the intensity and richness of
specific religious traditions. Or, to put it in another way, it is an attempt
to combine the symmetrical, tolerant, from-the-outside view of religions,
inherent in the present pluralistic one-world society, with the exclusive
claims which, alas, at least seem to be part of some religions when seen
from the inside. Such syncretism is an interesting phenomenon in its own
right: it underlies movements such as the Ahamdiya, and academic versions of it are not unknown. Whether such syntheses can be made logically acceptable to those who do not share to the full the Sheikh's metaphysical penetration and subtlety, I am not sure. In any case, granted the
premises, the Sheikh was not, at a spiritual level, either an innovator in
virtue of being a mystic or in virtue of his breadth of interests.

But on a sociological rather than a spiritual level, one must also take
him as he appeared to his contemporaries, however misguided. From their
own premises, he did sometimes seem to be a deviant (and even from his
own later viewpoint, he was such earlier in his spiritual career), and he
did not repudiate their premises, for he polemicized with them in print
on their own terms. Fortunately from the viewpoint of those interested in
the mundane and social aspects of the saint's life, the book does contain a
wealth of illuminating information about it. This is contained not so
much in Lings's commentary or in the saint's reproduced devotional
poems, but in the saint's quite long autobiography, most of which is reproduced. This document was found amongst his papers after his death. It
has an absolutely authentic ring and constitutes for me the most fascinating part of the book.

A devotional work by one of the Sheikh's disciples tells us that prior to
his conception, his mother had a vision of the Prophet in her sleep. The
Sheikh's own recollection begins with a memory of having had no school-
ing whatever other than being taught the Koran by his father, and he
states that his handwriting remained ever unproficient. Economic pressure forced him to give up Koranic scholarship when he reached the Surat

ar-Rahman. (He modestly omits to say that this entails that he knew nine-tenths of the Book by heart. Those familiar with the Book must tumble to this at once. For those who are not, Lings makes the point explicit.) The pressures which prevented him learning the remaining tenth led him to become a cobbler. This eased the family's situation. The Sheikh tells us that previously they did not have enough to live on, but that his father was too proud to betray the fact to outsiders. (Again, a footnote by Lings tells us that the Sheikh's grandfather was one of the notables of Mosta-ganem. The name "Alawi" would lead one to suppose that he was of Sher-ifian descent, that is, descended from the Prophet, and in the same wider family as the Moroccan royal house. The book does not confirm that this indeed was one of the Sheikh's claims. One should add that the number of people making such claims, and having them accepted, is extremely large in North Africa, so that there would be nothing unusual in it.)

He lost his father at the age of sixteen. He remained a cobbler for some years and then took up trade. The precise nature of the trade is not speci-fied. He soon acquired the habit of attending devotional religious meet-ings and lessons at night. At first, this involved conflict with his mother—who survived until he was forty-six—but later she gave in to his religious tendencies. Not so his wife: she complained of his nocturnal studies and habit of bringing a teacher home, and claimed her divorce. (We are told of this episode, but not of the preceding marriage.)

At the time he composed the autobiography, he clearly did not think much of what he learned in these early studies: he valued them only for giving him some mental discipline and enabling him at least to grasp "some points" of doctrine. (The mystical insights he later valued he refers to as *the* doctrine.)

His first contact with esoteric religious fraternities was with what is perhaps the most exotic and notorious of all North African "ways," the 'Isawi Tarika. Amongst the followers of this "way," snake charming, fire eating, and other practices are extensively used. The Sheikh himself be-came a proficient snake charmer. However, one day God willed that his eyes should alight on a saying traced back to the Prophet—the Sheikh does not say which—which made him realize the error of his ways: he gave up these practices, for the time being, except snake charming (no reason is given for making this exception). There appear to have been two stages in his dissociation from the 'Isawi followers, though he does not so say in so many words: for he says that at first he avoided the practices by making "excuses to my brethren" but also that he wished to take the entire broth-erhood away from them too. Evasion by excuses and attempted conversion of his fellows presumably followed each other.

Thus we see the Sheikh, already in the early parts of his story, oscillat-ing between the two poles of Moslem religious life, between the specialist-esoteric on the one hand, and the egalitarian-orthodox on the other. His

evaluation of his early instruction places him clearly on the side of esoteric understanding, but his rejection of the extreme and specialized
'Isawi practices, and the reason given for this rejection, imply the opposite
premises.

It is after telling us about his involvement with the ritual extremists of
the 'Isawi order that he comes to speak of his meeting with his true
Teacher. He had already heard of him in connection with a successful cure
of an illness in his childhood, effected by means of an amulet obtained
from this Sheikh. Now he met him again, apparently by accident, together
with his own (our Sheikh's) business partner and friend. Gradually he
came under his influence and received instruction and encouragement,
including predictions of future spiritual eminence, from the Teacher.
The Teacher dissuaded him from continuing with his remaining 'Isawi
practice, snake charming, with the help of a parable (the snake in one's
own body, that is, one's soul, is far more venomous and worth charming),
though apparently he had no disrespect for the founder of the 'Isawi order
—insofar as the prediction of spiritual eminence for the disciple had the
form of saying that one day he will become like that founder.

The instruction appears to have consisted mainly in the training in
reciting litanies and the Divine Name. The Sheikh records no regret at
giving up snake charming, but he did go through a struggle when asked
by the Teacher to give up attending lessons in scholastic theology. "No
order he ever gave me was so hard to obey as this." (There are other
remarks which throw light on the authoritarian relationship between
teacher and disciple, as later between the disciple-become-Sheikh and his
disciples.) The Teacher had a low opinion of the hairsplitting courses.
The disciple had four consolations—perhaps the mystical knowledge was
superior to that which he was now missing; the prohibition was only temporary; he had just taken an oath of obedience; and perhaps he was just
being put on trial, as apparently was the custom of Teachers. But these
consolations or arguments "did not stop the ache of sorrow" he felt within
him.

Instead of scholastic, intellectual theology, he was given mystical training. The main technique employed was "the invocation of the single
Name with distinct visualization of its letters until they were written in
(the disciple's) imagination. Then he would tell him to spread them out
and enlarge them until they filled all the horizon. The *dhikr* would continue in this form until the letters became like light." After this, the subsequent stages apparently escape the possibility of verbal description. He
would reach ultimate illumination, and having attained it would be allowed to return to the ordinary world, though one now transformed by
the preceding insight.

Having successfully passed through the mystical training, the Sheikh
was allowed to return to formal theology by his Teacher, and when he did

so, he says, "I found myself quite different from what I had been before as regards understanding. I now understood things in advance before the Sheikh who was teaching us had finished expounding them. Another result of the invocation was that I understood more than the literal sense of the text."

The subsequent quoted part of the autobiography contains a digression concerning the development of the Sheikh's Teacher himself—his travels in Morocco, his affiliation to *his* (in turn) teacher, placing him within one of the orders and its spiritual genealogy. (As North African tribes are organized around genealogies, so the fraternities are organized along spiritual genealogies. These, like the tribal, physical ones, tend to be "segmentary," that is, possess a treelike pattern: but spiritual genealogies can occasionally, unlike unilineal physical ones, flow together. There is fusion as well as fission on the ancestral map: a man may have more than one spiritual father.) There are also interesting allusions to the dangers and difficulties of such mystical affiliation and proselytism: at various crucial times in his career, the Teacher, in view of opposition and hostility or on the other hand of opportunity, had to vary his strategy from proselytism to restrained silence and back again. Each of these changes in the dialectical line, as it were, were heralded and guided by the appearance to him in his sleep of the Prophet or a prominent spiritually ancestral saint, the latter accompanied in the dream, perhaps by way of introduction and guarantee, by one of the Teacher's real ancestors.

The Sheikh was by now initiated into the Teacher's order and qualified to receive and instruct novices. So was his business partner and friend, though he appears to have concentrated more on keeping the business going: the Sheikh gratefully remarks that but for him, the business would have been altogether ruined. His own activities made "our shop more like a *zawiya* (religious lodge) than anything else."

The major crisis in the Sheikh's life came, after fifteen years in the service of his Teacher, when the Teacher died. The Sheikh tells us that prior to the Teacher's death, God had put in his, the Sheikh's, heart the desire to emigrate. He gives no motive for this desire to emigrate. He gives no motive for this desire more specific than the moral corruption of his country. Thus he found himself torn between the desire to move and his obligation to stay with the ailing Teacher. He did, however, even before the Teacher's death, liquidate his property and so on. But even the Teacher's death did not resolve the conflict: difficulties arose with permits from (the French) authorities and through the illness and death of the Sheikh's then wife. The major difficulty now was however through the need of the local segment of the order to find a successor to the Teacher.

The Teacher had not nominated a successor. The Sheikh himself, either because he was busy at his wife's deathbed and/or because he remained determined to emigrate, and also because, as he says, he was willing to accept the verdict of the other followers, did not take part in the deliberations about succession. These discussions proved inconclusive and "somewhat argumentative." The Sheikh hints that this was because the members knew that he was determined to go away (that is, no other candidate appeared generally acceptable). His old friend and business partner, who did take part in the deliberations, then proposed that the decision be postponed, in the hope that some of the brethren might in the meantime have a guiding vision. And in due course and before the day appointed for decision a good number of visions were had, and all of them—or at any rate all of them that were subsequently recorded when our saint was the Sheikh of the order—pointed to one conclusion, namely, that he should be the successor. The Teacher who, when he was still alive, had refused to name a successor (perhaps on the Parkinsonian principle that subordinates are kept in order by fear of their rivals' promotion and hope of their own) and declared that such matters had to remain in God's hands, made up for his indecision in life by proffering ample and clear guidance after death. The Teacher appeared in visions to many disciples to notify them of the right succession: it appears that the theological objections he felt during his life to usurping this function no longer obtained after death. These visions, incidentally, apart from having great clarity and freshness, are, it appears, followed by "a state of entire vigilance without any intermediary process of waking up": so Lings was informed by the one disciple of the Sheikh with whom he had direct contact. Thus, succession was determined in favor of our Sheikh.

If one were to suspect that political motives may have been present in the Sheikh's plans for emigration, two possibilities suggest themselves: one, that a threat of emigration was a means of putting pressure on the brethren to come to reach agreement; and two, that the plan provided an alternative in case of defeat. (Fraternities of this kind invariably tend to proliferate and consist of a number of dispersed centers: the Sheikh may have preferred to be No. 1 in a spiritual colony rather than hold a lower rank in the founding center.) But whether or not these motives operated, the Sheikh also appeared to be possessed by a genuine and independent wanderlust. All appeared to go well after his accession to leadership: the followers took their oath of allegiance to him (he later introduced a new style of doing so), and members of affiliated centers in other places also came in due course to accept him as leader. All the members of the order thus came to be united, "except two or three." This union was, as he says, "counted by us as a miraculous Grace from God, for I had no outward means of bringing within my scope individuals from so many different places."

Nevertheless, in due course he set off on travels. He hesitated between his duty as "remembrancer" to his followers and his desire to travel, but after a time the latter prevailed. The actual travels are described as occurring with an apparent inconsequentiality: they begin by a desire to visit some nearby brethren with a view to curing an affliction. He then, with a companion, decides to visit some others farther off: and then to proceed to Algiers with a view to finding a publisher for one of his manuscripts. (One assumes that the possibility of such a trip may have been present in his mind from the start, for he appears to have had the required manuscript with him.) He failed in this purpose in Algiers, so he and his companion decide to proceed farther, to Tunis, where "the whole thing would be quite simple." In fact, he did make some progress toward publication in Tunis: he also made some converts to his order and was constantly visited by "theologians, canonists and other eminent men."

He was tempted by the thought of making the pilgrimage (to Mecca), but desisted in view of the fact that it was forbidden that year by the French because of an epidemic in Arabia.[3] So, instead he went to Tripoli, to visit his cousins who had emigrated there. He found them well and prosperous. He comments that the country was "a good place to emigrate to, since its people (are) as like as possible to those of our country both in speech and ways." (This is an odd reason in view of the motive given earlier for wishing to emigrate—namely, the moral corruption of his own country. It may be relevant that the western parts of North Africa have for considerable time been exporting saints to Tripolitania and Cyrenaica, where their superior skill is recognized. Why this should be so is not clear.)

A Turkish Sheikh who was also a government official (in the department of maritime revenue) invited him to settle and offered him a *zawiya* "and all the out-buildings that go with it." Our Sheikh agreed—but there is no further follow-up of this offer and episode in the narrative. Instead, he reports hearing the town crier advertising cheap tickets to Istanbul— and after a terrible crossing he reached it. Whatever his plans there, he concluded that the times were not propitious for them. Here occur the only comments on general politics which are to be found in the saint's autobiography. His visit to Istanbul was shortly after the deposition of Abdul-Hamid, but this was no source of joy to him. On the contrary, he makes bitter remarks about the Young Turks and the degradation which was to reach its culmination under the Kemalists, and he decided that this was no place for him. Indeed, by now he "had no peace of soul until the day when (he) set foot on Algerian soil, and . . . praised God for the ways of (his) people and their remaining in the faith of their fathers and grandfathers and following in the footsteps of the pious." Here the autobiography ends. If, following Berque's epithet, the Sheikh was a modernist, he clearly was not an extreme one. One wonders what he would have thought of the F.L.N.

There are some important aspects of the Sheikh's religious career which are not discussed in his autobiography. One of them concerns his hiving off from the system of Darqawi *zawiya's*. Lings reports, plausibly, that the greatest jealousy the Sheikh had to face was from the heads of neighboring Darqawi lodges, who were jealous of his success and influence, and that this was brought to a head when "after about five years" (that is, presumably five years after his succession) he made himself independent of the central Darqawi *zawiya* (in Morocco). This must have meant repudiating, or at least no longer observing, the kind of oath of allegiance which, as reported, he himself exacted from followers and heads of dependent sublodges of his own. The motive given for this declaration of independence was an innovation in mystical technique. (North African religious fraternities generally differentiate themselves from each other by the "way"— that is, to God—which they employ.) The Sheikh's innovation was to introduce the practice of *khalwah*—this being a cell in which a novice is put after swearing not to leave it for forty days if need be, and in which he must do nothing but repeat ceaselessly, day and night, the Divine Name, drawing out each time the syllable *ah* until he has no more breath left.

Lings observes that the declaration of spiritual independence caused violent ill feeling and that he lost some of the disciples he had inherited, so to speak, from the Teacher. But new disciples came, and it appears there were even cases of whole *zawiya's* affiliating to him en bloc, leader and followers together. A major triumph for the Sheikh was to gain as a follower a descendant, a great-grandson, of the very founder of the order from which the Sheikh had seceded. This grandson had, it seems, been of no great significance in his own ancestral order, for he remarks (in a letter quoted by Lings), "until (meeting the Sheikh) I had simply been an initiate of the order and nothing more." The Sheikh opened his inward eye and led him to direct knowledge of God, as the cited letter observes. Of course, choosing freedom in this manner, so to speak, could not but cause indignation among his own betrayed relatives: but the great-grandson in question says he "paid no attention to those of my family who blamed me for following (the Sheikh)."

In Lings's view the hostility of the rival lodges was short-lived, except for that of "one or two hereditary Marabouts who were in danger of losing their influence altogether." But if in due course he escaped the hostility of his rivals on the right, so to speak—of the Isawis whom he had deserted early, of the Darqawis from whom he seceded with a whole lodgeful of followers, and from the hereditary Marabouts—he had in due course to face hostility from the left, as it were, from the newer and more puritanical, rigoristic, anti-Sufi forms of Islam. This battle was fought in a rather modern form, by means of pamphleteering. The Sheikh answered an attack on mysticism by a teacher at the Religious College in Tunis—an attack which sounded the war cry by its very title, *A Mirror to Show up Errors*.

Lings's sympathies are clearly with the mystics, and he finds the arguments of the Tunisian religious teacher "petty and childish" and manifests regretful surprise that the Sheikh should have bothered to reply at all. He excuses him by observing that the Sheikh must have realized that this attack had a significance going beyond that of their immediate author, being a crystallization of a general hostility which could not be ignored. If the Sheikh did realize this he was quite right. The future—if not the very distant future—lay with these puritanical, more Protestant, so to speak, religious teachers: they lay the foundations of the modern North African national consciousness in their struggle against the religious particularism of those such as the Sheikh. (The generation of nationalists formed by these thinkers has since been replaced by another, whose thoughts wander to Peking or Belgrade rather than Mecca. But that is another story.)

The essence of the critic's argument is simple: "Islam is nothing other than the Book of God and the Wont of His Messenger." In other words: the ritual and other excrescences of the mystics are to be condemned. The Sheikh's answer was to claim that there was in the Book a wealth of hidden meanings which is beyond most men's attainment—in other words, that he was merely making explicit what is hidden (and must remain hidden for the majority) in the Book. He did not dispute the premise that the Book and the Prophet's custom exhaust Islam: but there was more in these than could meet the uninitiated eye.

An interesting issue between the puritans and the mystics concerns *dancing*. The Sufi mystics generally make use of dancing on ritual contexts: the puritans forbid it and claim that the Prophet forbade it. Opinions differ on this point, as Lings observes: he himself, sympathizing as ever with the mystics, finds it difficult not to believe that the Companions (of the Prophet) did not make some spontaneous rhythmic movements of the body when reciting their various litanies. Lings also goes on to remark, much more convincingly, that these practices incorporate "traditional local dances which . . . as it were in the blood of (the) disciples . . . had . . . a more immediate appeal for them." In the region of central Morocco where I worked, at about the same time as the Sheikh was practicing in Algeria, two tribes (in the literal kinship and territorial sense) of saints went to war on this issue of the permissibility of dancing, and it took their lay clients a long time to bring them to peace again. Those who were against dancing were closer to towns—that is, to urban learned men who were more frequently of the "reformist," or puritan, persuasion. The prodancing group were deeper in the recesses of the hills, where the local dances were more firmly embedded in custom.

The critic, the author of the *Mirror,* bluntly affirms that "anyone who considers dancing to be legal is an infidel": the cautious Sheikh does not deny his position outright. He argues: "Do you imagine that the Sufis hold dancing to be absolutely lawful, just as you hold it to be absolutely unlawful? . . . It behoves the learned man not to pass any judgment about it until he knows what is the motive behind it, lest he forbid what God has allowed."

This seems extremely sound: unfortunately it leaves the believer without guidance between two risks, either to commit what may be forbidden or to forbid what God has allowed. The safest course would seem to be not to dance but not to forbid it to others either. Curiously, this is precisely what neither side to the dispute has done: some do dance, and some forbid it.

Another issue arising between the mystics and the puritans concerns the use of rosaries. Their use is indeed very widespread and so characteristic of the religious fraternities that one can refer to a fraternity, or its distinguishing spiritual technique, as a *werd* (rosary). For the puritans, the crucial fact is that rosaries were not used by the Prophet and his Companion. The Sheikh, replying to the *Mirror,* points out that the Companions did count with the help of date stones and pebbles. He also argued from a tradition reporting the use of a knotted cord. From pebbles and knotted cords together, the argument by analogy to rosaries is surely powerful!

Another objection of the puritans to the rosary was that it is shaped like a cross. Here the Sheikh can hardly contain himself: "By all that is marvellous, what has the form of a rosary to do with the cross? However, 'The eye of hatred ferrets out faults.' " Triumphantly, the Sheikh points out that the human shape has more resemblance to a cross than has a rosary, so that the critic would consistently have to put an end to his own existence, or at least take care never to see himself.

The critic had castigated as hypocrites "all those who use rosaries," that is, the religious orders. The content and tone of antiorder criticism is very similar to anti-Popery criticism in Europe. The critic concentrates on the alleged hypocrisy, profit motive, scripturally unwarranted and sensuous innovations and additions in ritual, use of shrines, use of music (and dancing) and religious aids. Concerning shrines, the Sheikh defends his followers against the imputation that they believe that the dead sheikhs in shrines have powers to give or withhold: they merely believe, the Sheikh maintains, that they are intermediaries between the believer and God. Most interestingly, the Sheikh concedes that in a higher spiritual state "all mediation is abolished," and defends the use of intermediaries only for those who have not reached this fuller state.

Thus we see him implicitly conceding the "protestant" religious ideal and defending mediation by saints and shrines as merely a second best. We also see that he is by no means a mystic *only,* but that in dialectical self-defense he is willing to employ, with skill and vigor, scholastic arguments from analogy and so on.

In his struggle against the puritans of this Salafiyyah reform movement, the Sheikh also in 1922 started publishing a religious weekly newspaper, which in 1926 was replaced by another with a wider scope. Both were published in Algiers. The journal was used to rebut puritan charges at length. Even the sympathetic Lings finds the treatment of the rival position unmerciful. Nevertheless, when the editors of the two rival papers and protagonists of two religious attitudes came to meet in 1931, the meeting was cordial and was reported as such in the puritans' paper. The report is worth quoting, to show that from the cells-of-solitary-confinement-with-the-Divine-Name aspect, the Sheikh's life also had its more homely, Pooterish side:

> "A supper was given by Shaikh Sidi Ahmad Bin-'Aliwah and it was attended by some of the leading men of Mostaganem, together with about one hundred of the Shaikh's pupils. The Shaikh himself was exceedingly cordial and gracious to the point of serving some of the guests with his own hands. . . . After supper verses from the Koran were recited, and then Shaikh's pupils began to chant . . . The pleasure of the evening was further enhanced in between the singing by literary discussions . . . ; and among the many examples of courtesy shown us by our host the Shaikh, I was particularly struck by the fact that he never once touched on any point of disagreement between us."

It is difficult not to suspect that the style of this report has been influenced, not only by the mystic or puritan traditions, but also by the manner of reporting of social events in the nearby French provincial press.

The autobiography and the other documents assembled by Lings give us an excellent, if not wholly complete, picture of an Algerian religious personage of a given period, of the alternatives, opportunities, dangers facing it: the Sheikh was located somewhere in the middle of the spectrum ranging from the extreme "right," so to speak—hereditary Marabouts, practices such as snake charming—and the extreme "left," puritanical, rigorously devoted to the Word, to strict observance, denial of superstition, and equality of believers. He fought on both fronts; he had in his youth been further to the right, and in his age, merciless journalistic polemics notwithstanding, he took trouble to maintain at least courteous, if not cordial, relations with the "left." The religious spectrum had not yet acquired the political significance which it was due to have some decades later: though it is worth noting that a year prior to the dinner party reported above the puritans in Fez had laid the foundation stone of modern Moroccan nationalism by organizing a protest movement against French support of heterodox tribal practices. . . . The various aspects of religious life illuminated by his career are worth specifying individually.

Organization: there is a clear hierachy of Sheikh–*moqadem*–disciple.

Discipleship varies in kind: the rural converts were not generally expected to become mystical initiates: " . . . when the Shaikh stayed for a few days in the country, it sometimes happened that almost the whole countryside would come to him for initiation. If they did not aspire to follow the path, they came for the 'initiation of blessing.' "

Within the hierarchy there was some division of labor. We have seen how, under the old Teacher, both the Sheikh and his business associates reached a high rank, but the associate continued to look after the business whilst the Sheikh neglected it for religion.

The hierarchy did not end with the status of Sheikh. The Sheikh is validated, as it were, by a spiritual lineage, which at the same time affiliates him to other centers—*zawiya's*—which perpetuate the same lineage and which are, spiritually and physically, descended from figures higher up on the Sheikh's spiritual lineage. Such affiliation implies subservience if the other center is somehow on a "straighter" line from the spiritual center—if it is the original founding center, from which the mystical practices radiated by conversion and initiation, and/or if it is led by a (literal) descendant of the founder. We have seen our Sheikh declaring his independence from such a system, giving as his reason an innovation in mystical technique. There can be no doubt but that some advantages are connected both with being independent and with having dependent centers. It is a striking feature of these systems of spiritual allegiance that they are territorially discontinuous and comprise units within quite different social structures—for example, urban clubs and rural communities.

The "totems," as it were, of these spiritual lineages—that is, their differentiating marks—are ritual and mystical specialisms. There can be no doubt about the "esotericism" of these organizations: there is only an apparent contradiction between the appeal of specialized initiation by strenuous practices and the desire to maximize the number of followers. In modern terms, this is the difference between party "militants" and mere supporters. Nevertheless, there are theoretical difficulties about the claims to privileged access and special ways to God in Islam, and the claims are made cautiously and with some ambivalence.

The loyalties and solidarity of these hierarchical but voluntary organizations are reinforced by oaths of allegiance and obedience. The manner in which this oath is taken (for example, whether by mouth or by handclasp) is itself one of the ritual differentiations of orders. These oaths do not appear to be totally effective: we have seen how the Sheikh lost, and acquired, disciples and that on occasion whole lodges went over to his allegiance en bloc. One should add that in traditional North Africa, affiliation to some fraternity or other, at some degree of initiation, must have covered a very large part, if not virtually the whole, population, so that conversion to a more or less exclusive brotherhood could on the whole be only at the expense of another one. We have also seen the fissions, fusion, and ambiguities of succession, which provide the raw material for the formal rules of these associations.

The texts assembled by Lings in connection with the Sheikh do not explicitly tell us much about the economics of the movement, but they do tell us a certain amount. How much wealth flows along the devotional lines? Enough, evidently, to allow a successful Sheikh to dispense with other forms of income. In his late years, the Sheikh does not seem to have carried on with trade, and even in his earlier years he could afford to neglect it. The land of his *zawiya* had been bought for him by a group of devotees, and the labor supplied free by volunteers, specialists and laborers, drawn from a wide area including tribesmen from the Rif. (This is described in a report by Dr. Marcel Carret, a Frenchman who attended to the Sheikh and became his friend.) There are allusions to rules made by the Sheikh for his lieutenants and representatives, not to accept more in the way of entertainment on their wanderings than is absolutely necessary; allusions to the failure on the part of devotees sometimes to perceive his material needs; and to the extent to which travel is facilitated by the existence of devotees in the area which is being covered. In brief, there clearly is a flow of good and services upward compensating for the spiritual flow downward: but as with regard to esotericism and special practices, the spiritual recipient of the material flow is aware of the possibility of puritan criticism and adjusts himself to it and guards against abuses.

For classificatory purposes, one could arrange the phenomena exemplified or touched on by the Sheikh's life along a number of loosely correlated spectra:

1. Kinship/voluntary association. There are hereditary Marabouts, and within some of the voluntary orders (for example, the one from which the Sheikh seceded) there is a kind of kinship backbone of a dominant family, descendants of the founder, surrounded by voluntary converts. At the other extreme there are lodges of a newly prominent Sheikh, recruited voluntarily.

2. Urban/rural centers. This opposition clearly has an intimate connection with the preceding one, insofar as in rural areas both saintly personages and their devotees come as it were in kin parcels. (Although there are numerous intertribal religious festivals, and so forth, nevertheless these festivals, pilgrimages, and such are attended by groups rather than by individuals. There is no room for persisting religious associations cutting across kin lines.) Similarly, urban life, with its mobility and relative lack of kin groupings, is suited to genuine associations. Nevertheless, this correlation is subject to some qualifications: as we have seen, within one associated set of centers, the Sheikh's, there is room both for village grouping and for the central urban one. This is, I believe, a very typical

situation. Secondly, rural or even nonrural hereditary saints may be found, and remain the nucleus of, a genuine order (that is, one recruited by individual conversion).

3. Puritanism/others. I deliberately oppose puritanism by a residual notion ("other") rather than mystics of Sufis, for the following reason: at least two things are opposed to proper, rigorous Islam. One is mysticism, with its esotericism, extra ritual richness, mediation, and so on. The other is rural, tribal heterodoxy, conscious or not. The notion of a North African saint has embraced the two: it covers mystics, specialists in ecstatic techniques, *and* specialized lineages within tribal structures, magicians-arbitrators. Historically, it seems obvious that North African sanctity derives from *both*. (Historically, there is also a third root—warriors in the holy war against infidels on the coast, especially Portuguese.) As Lings rightly remarks, the dancing of the Sufis is both a mystic aid and something rooted in local customs. The saints arise to satisfy (at least) two needs—the need for an emotionally richer religion, and the requirements of tribal social structure. Leaving historical origins aside, the two forms now coexist, barely distinguished conceptually, often within the same order. But the difference is still visible: on the whole, tribesmen come to saints for political leadership rather than mystical exercises, and towns-folk for spiritual rather than political reasons.

This distinction, between the puritans and the others, correlates with the preceding ones to some extent. Only urban life provides a good base for the puritans—for their rigorism requires literacy. The converse does not hold: for the mystics and sometimes their (literal) lineages are also found in towns.

There is also a temporal consideration which is relevant here; the puritans have gained in importance very considerably in recent times as a result of the Salafiyya movement. And although town-based, they do make their impact on the countryside. (Consider the little war, mentioned earlier, which took place about the turn of the century, about *dancing*, in the tribal recesses of the Atlas mountains.)

It is a corollary of the puritans' objection to esotericism and mediation that they are opposed to the role of lineages and privileges (other than based on piety and learning) in religious life, and to this extent the puritan/others dichotomy correlates with the kin groups/associations distinction.

Insofar as sanctity is partly rooted in tribal requirements (arbitrators, mediators), one should not suppose that in characteristic life histories of saintly "ways" or movements a tribal episode necessarily comes in the beginning. I believe that the various religious movements do have characteristic life histories—that is, they generally do undergo structural transformation while maintaining nominal continuity. For instance, a movement may begin as a missionary one, devoted to spreading knowledge of pure

Islam among tribes. Success may lead it to acquire such interests within the tribes, and such importance in the running of tribal affairs, that with time the original missionary impetus and function are lost: the movement becomes a kin group and segment within the tribes. The reverse story, of course, is just as liable to occur: a mountain lineage of hereditary saints may produce one who, starting with his local prestige, succeeds in founding a genuine and territorially discontinuous order. (This has occurred to the mountain saints whom I studied, intermittently, from 1954 till 1961.) More complex variants of such life histories are of course possible and indeed likely. One might perhaps classify them in terms of their beginnings—whether they started as purifiers and missionaries, or as purveyors of mystical specialisms, as Holy Warriors, or as specialized tribal segments. In the nature of things, success must modify them, by altering the milieu in which they operate. And this is, of course, a corollary of the point made earlier, namely that different parts of the same order may also follow differing paths of development.

It would be difficult to offer any simple generalization about the political role, in a wider sense, of the saints. Among their historical antecedents, as indicated, are the leaders in wars against the infidel. As long as there were tribes engaged in such wars, in the old sense, saints were found among them as their leaders. Modern, national opposition to European colonization, on the other hand, was inspired by the puritans rather than the saints. Abd-el-Krim, who stands somewhere half way between a traditional and a modern national resistance to Europeans, opposed the orders and Marabouts on his territory. (Without definitive success, evidently: for Dr. Carret reports, in his account of the Sheikh with whom we were concerned, that among the volunteers-builders of the Sheikh's *zawiya* "the most humble of them all" were Rif mountaineers. To urban dwellers, whose judgment Dr. Carret is presumably echoing, hill tribesmen would seem "the humblest," if not worse: this is significant, for the contempt in which tribesmen, especially Berbers, are often held by townsfolk constitutes one stumbling block in their acceptance of purer, urban Islam. The saints are less fastidious socially, as it were.)

In the modern national struggle, the saints generally found themselves on the side of the French, or at any rate objects of hostility of the nationalists. The explanations of this normally offered are: the fact that the nationalists were formed by the reform movement, the Salfiyya (though this only pushes the question one step further back); and the fact that the saints found a place under the French system, the French often worked through them, and, in nationalist eyes, encouraged obscurantism in the subject population. These factors no doubt operated, but one is tempted to seek a more fundamental sociological cause. Certainly, there were more prospects for the orders and saints among a subject population which, as our Sheikh put it, stayed in "the faith of their fathers and grandfathers and (followed) in the footsteps of the pious" than in a free national and modernist state which is the aspiration of the nationalists. (We saw the distaste of our Sheikh for the Young Turks and Kemalism.) But his explanation too assumes they were acting from long-term rational political foresight. The real clue is, I suspect, that the orders and systems of saintly allegiance were essentially far too segmented and particularistic to serve as bases or even vehicles for national feeling. They really were spiritual tribes, not spiritual nations. It is curious to reflect that both in Europe and in North Africa there seems to be a connection between nationalism and a "protestant," that is, antisaintly or antireligious-specialism and antiritual-richness movement: but in Europe the connection lay through Protestantism breaking up the unity of a spiritual superstate, whereas in North Africa it was through its overcoming segmented, minuscule spiritual tribes, or substates.

NOTES

1. Martin Lings, *A Moslem Saint of the Twentieth Century* (London, 1961).

2. One is reminded of Kant's conviction that when Christ recommended love, He meant not what He said but a kind of abridgement of the *critique of Practical Reason*.

3. The year was 1909. Lings appears to have made a slip in the footnote referring to this episode, when remarking that there was an epidemic in Saudi Arabia—meaning, presumably, in the territories which only became parts of Saudi Arabia much later.

16

RELIGIOUS BELIEF AND ECONOMIC BEHAVIOR IN A CENTRAL JAVANESE TOWN

Clifford Geertz

Since Max Weber's *Religionsociologie,* interest in the relationships between religious commitment and economic behavior has been an important theme both in economic history and in the sociology of religion. The broad relationship he postulated between certain kinds of religious ethic and certain types of economic practice has proved as stimulating as it has proved elusive, and the grand over-all approach which Weber used, the correlation of social structures and religious systems for whole civilizations over the entire course of their history, has left many contemporary students with a conviction that Weber's basic insight was at least in part valid, that there was "something in it," and that it was nevertheless extremely difficult to tell in a particular situation what it meant, to "pin it down" in terms of specific times and places and to account for the embarrassing number of mixed and marginal cases with which it seemed unable to deal.

As a result there has been a tendency, particularly in the United States, to turn to more specific analyses, to deal with smaller social units, less generally considered religious systems, and shorter periods of time, to see whether one might elucidate the relationships involved more precisely. With the postwar appearance of the problem of economic development in the so-called "underdeveloped" countries as a major practical and theoretical concern, interest in more explicit statements of functional interdependence between economic and noneconomic aspects of social behavior has become even more intense. At the same time, it is coming to be real-

Reprinted from Economic Development and Cultural Change, *IV, No. 1 (1956), 134–158. Copyright 1956 by The University of Chicago Press.*

ized that the industrial revolution as it takes place in these countries, with their varying resource patterns, population sizes, and geographical locations, may not simply replicate the pattern that the revolution took in Europe, especially since the underdeveloped countries, unlike the forerunners of European industrialization, exist in a world already partially "developed." The simple application of European experience to such new situations is unlikely to prove adequate, and much of the *Protestant Ethic and the Spirit of Capitalism* theory may have to be not so much discarded as refined and reformulated.

It is in such a context that this essay is presented: it is an attempt to lay the groundwork for a full analysis of religious belief and economic behavior in a given town in East Java, Indonesia. It is preliminary, heuristic, and not intended as a thorough analysis of the situation: it is intended to provide a model for such a thorough analysis and to indicate, if but dimly, some of the results such an analysis might produce.

I

Modjokuto (a fictitious name), a small town in east-central Java studied by the writer in 1953–1954, lies at the extreme eastern edge of a great irrigated rice plain through which a rambling, circular swinging river flows northward toward the Java Sea. A half-day's drive from Surabaja, the Republic of Indonesia's second city and best port, Modjokuto marks the point at which the flat, fertile countryside begins to tilt upward toward the cluster of active volcanoes which tower over it to the east and whose periodic eruptions provide much of its fertility.

A commercial, educational, and administrative center for eighteen surrounding villages, the town has a population of almost twenty thousand, of whom about eighteen thousand are Javanese, eighteen hundred Chinese, and the remainder a handful of Arabs, Indians, or other minorities. Its spatial form is determined by the juncture of three poorly paved secondary roads: from Surabaja, the provincial capital; from the regional capital fifteen miles to the west; and from a large inland city on the other side of the eastern mountains:

The town is surrounded on three sides by thousands of small mud-walled rice fields, most of them not more than twenty-five yards square. Flooded in the rainy season by means of an age-old irrigation system of gullies, springs, and water traps, improved by Dutch-introduced cement dams and steel sluice gates, these fields are cultivated almost entirely in rice for six months of every year. In the dry season, which is pronounced in East Java, the land does not lie fallow but is planted in maize, soybean, peanuts, onions, peppers, or yams—usually two or three of these in turn. Almost all landholdings are small—under three acres—and although there is, particularly near the town, considerable share-crop tenancy, neither are the landlords involved absentee nor are their holdings any larger,

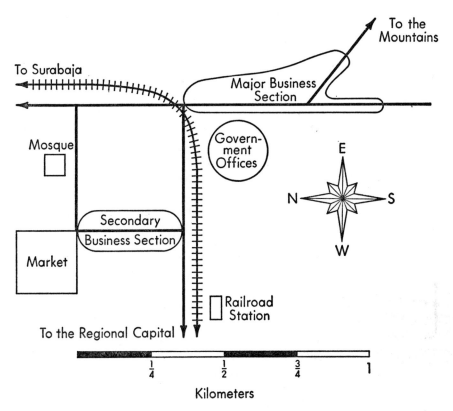

To the Mountains

To Surabaja

Major Business Section

Mosque

Government Offices

E

N — S

W

Secondary Business Section

Market

Railroad Station

To the Regional Capital

¼ ½ ¾ 1

Kilometers

with one or two not very dramatic exceptions, than those of the peasants themselves.

On the fourth side of Modjokuto, the southwest, lies either forest or dry, broken, largely unirrigable land, on which, in the early part of this century, an extensive plantation system, in coffee, rubber, and sugar, was built up. Dutch-owned, Dutch-managed, and Javanese-worked, this network of plantations and sugar mills had a heavy impact on Modjokuto's economy before the war. As the town was only founded toward the latter half of the nineteenth century, the interaction between the small-scale, intensive, wet-rice farming system practiced by the independent Javanese peasant and the large-scale, extensive, cash-crop estate agriculture of the Dutch has shaped the region's economic history almost since the beginning.

The Dutch are gone from Modjokuto now, their estate and factory system shaken by the depression and shattered by the war and revolution. What remains is a peasantry very used to both money and foreign goods, tremendous underemployment, both rural and urban, and an overcomplex economic system in which the Chinese minority controls the main streams of trade. The Chinese form the heart of Modjokuto's economic circulatory system, pressing goods, many of them imported, down through its arteries, pulling back goods, the greater part of them agricultural, through its veins, and passing them on to the large urban centers for further distribution; Javanese commercial activity becomes relevant only between the ends of the two channels—where they braid out into a complex network of tiny, doubled-over, and marvelously interwound economic capillaries reaching into the small crevices of native life.

Both business districts are lined with small, open-front, wooden stores, almost all of them Chinese-run. Inside the stores one finds hardware, home furnishings, various types of food, jewelry, false teeth, automobile and bicycle parts, building materials, textiles, drugs from sulfa to such promising herbs as crocodile tongue and cat's beard. Even more important in terms of economic power, the Chinese control the trade in dry-season crops grown in Javanese fields, and their mills process the rice from those fields (although for the past few years a great part of the actual buying has been done under government contract and, nominally, under government control). They own almost all the trucking, almost all the string-and-bailing-wire jitneys which carry a great proportion (with the busses and the train) of interlocal travel, and almost all the bicycle rickshaws which, Javanese-pedaled, provide the bulk of passenger transport within the town. The larger small-scale factories in town and outside it—rice, lumber, soda pop, bread, charcoal—are, with a few notable exceptions, in their hands. They own the movie, the theater where the Javanese plays are given, and they manage the carnival when it comes to town. They are prevented from total domination of the economy by only one restriction: they are forbidden, by a Dutch law continued into the Republican period, to hold farm land.

The Javanese stores, almost all of them marginal, number about a dozen, most of them in the secondary business section. But the core of native-run commercial life is the market, where each day hundreds of professional or semiprofessional Javanese salesmen and speculators, both male and female, bargain vigorously in a desperate attempt to earn a living or part of a living out of small-scale person-to-person trade. Textiles, daily food supplies, and dry-season crops probably form the bulk of the business, but buttons, dried fish, mats, baskets, perfumes, religious books, cooked food and hot coffee, chairs and tables, nails, ready-made clothing, meat, patent medicines, leather goods, parasols, pots and pans—in fact, almost everything portable—are each day passed from hand to hand to someone's (usually small) profit.

In the market you can have your hair cut, your bicycle fixed, and your pants mended while you wait. For an Indonesian quarter you can rent a spot under a tree or a wooden shed and sell cigarettes for a penny more than you just paid for them in a Chinese store across the street. You can buy a basket of corn in the morning and sell it at noon, never leaving the market—getting your profit out of the slight rise in price which every day takes place as the market day wears on (if you are a friend or a paying acquaintance of the man who runs the scales, you may make something out of the greater weight the corn has when you sell it than when you bought it). Or, for two rupia a day (and a few hundred capital) you can become one of the aristocrats of the market with a three-meter stall of your own, selling imported and domestic textiles for as much more than they are worth as you can wheedle an unwary peasant into paying. For the Modjokuto Javanese, buyer or seller, the market is the very model of commercial life, the source of nearly all his ideas of the possible and proper in economic behavior.

Aside from petty commerce, three other nonagricultural activities play an important part in the Javanese sector of the economy: simple manual labor, independent craft and repair work, and white-collar office work. The manual laborers, if they find work at all, may be employed by the Chinese in their rice factories, lumberyards, or other enterprises, by the government fixing roads, building irrigation dams, or sweeping streets, or by one of the scattered here-today gone-tomorrow Javanese cottage industries. A great many are employed by the narrow-gauge railroad which runs four short passenger trains a day from the regional capital through Modjokuto to the main Surabaja line fifteen miles northward. Many too are servants for their richer townsmen, though the departure of the Dutch has markedly reduced job opportunities in this field. The independent artisans—carpenters, chauffeurs, bricklayers, blacksmiths, watchmakers, barbers, tailors—are spread unevenly throughout the town, for they mostly work in their own homes, accepting jobs as they come fitfully to them, and drifting uneasily into unskilled occupations if forced to by economic pressure.

The white-collar clerks, teachers, and government officials form the intellectual and social elite of Modjokuto, inheritors of a political tradition in which the ability to read and write was confined to a hereditary court class, born to rule and venerated for doing so. Many of the old caste marks of the literati are nearly gone now—the variously colored parasols symbolizing rank, the deep bow of the inferior to touch the knee of the standing superior, the proclamation of pedigree through the use of court title, the tongue-tied shame of the peasant in the presence of the government official—but the general attitude of respect and subservience on the part of the uneducated toward the educated remains.

The number of the educated has been rather rapidly increasing of late with the postrevolutionary expansion of the school system. In Modjokuto there are a half-dozen six-grade government elementary schools, a government technical school at the junior-high level, three private junior high schools, a government school for elementary teachers, and scattered other private schools including Chinese and Catholic elementary schools. Further, each of the surrounding villages has a school of its own, and there are still a number of old-style religious schools in the area, recently semi-modernized. The result of this sudden florescence of educational activity is that teachers, on the one hand, and advanced students, on the other, form two of the most clearly defined and dynamic social groups within the society—perhaps the two groups least closely bound to the Indonesian past and whose relationships with the rest of the society are the most ambiguous.

There are two major government offices in Modjokuto, for it is both a district and a subdistrict capital. The subdistrict, the lowest level to which the wholly appointive national bureaucracy reaches, administers eighteen villages all lying within ten miles of the town. The district administers four contiguous subdistricts, including that of Modjokuto itself, and is in turn subordinate to the regional government. In addition, the regional headquarters of the central government police force is in Modjokuto, as are the government pawnshop and the government hospital for the area. Offices concerned with the repair of roadways, the building and maintenance of irrigation systems, the improvement of agriculture, and the administration of the market further swell the total of white-collar workers employed or underemployed by the government, as do the post office and the office of the local representative of the Ministry of Religion.

These five major occupational types—farmer, petty trader, independent artisan, manual laborer, and white-collar clerk, teacher, or administrator—represent the Javanese population of Modjokuto, grouped according to their economic activity. The crystallized typology of work patterns reflects the underlying organization of the economic system of the town of which it is an outcome. Similarly, the same population grouped according to their world outlook—according to their religious beliefs, ethical preferences, and political ideologies—yields three main cultural types which reflect the moral organization of Javanese culture as it is manifested in Modjokuto, the general ideas of order in terms of which the Javanese farmer, laborer, artisan, trader, or clerk shapes his behavior in all areas of life. These types, being so essentially Javanese, need Javanese terms to name them—terms the Javanese themselves apply: *abangan, santri, priyayi.*

II

The great majority of Modjokuto Javanese pronounce themselves to be Moslems. Within this more general category, however, they make a clear distinction between the *santri,* the pious Moslem who takes his Islam seriously and attempts to keep it free of local adulterations, and the *abangan,* whose main adherence is to what is often miscalled "the Javanese religion" (*agama djawa*). To understand this "Javanese religion," one must understand its history, for *abangan* beliefs are the outcome of a centuries-long synthesis of animistic, Brahman-Buddhist and Islamic belief within the strictly organized, comparatively self-sufficient agricultural village of pretwentieth-century Java. They are a symbolic reflection of the demands of simple rural living, a balanced mixture of native conceptions and foreign suggestions, nicely adjusted to perpetuate a relatively undifferentiated social system without serious change and without widespread individual dissatisfaction within an environment unmarked by sharp variation in economic conditions.

The *abangan* world outlook views the individual human being as but a small part of a wider natural-social world, and social prescription is felt to flow directly from metaphysical necessity. The order of social life is fixed because it is a part of a general order of nature, which, mysterious as it may appear in some of its aspects, is ultimately regular and invariant. For the fully adult Javanese peasant, man, his society, and his natural environment strike a harmony almost mathematical; children, madmen, simpletons, foreigners, and rebels are "not yet human" because "not yet Javanese." To "be human" is to be Javanese, to submit to an unusually precise system of social and linguistic etiquette which constrains individual behavior into patterns emphasizing interfamilial co-operation, emotional restraint, orderliness, and self-effacement. These are the values religious ritual and belief dramatize and those which control everyday behavior in each area of the common life. For the most part, Javanese village life tends to be co-operative, quiet, predictable, and colorless.

The religious elaboration of the *abangan* outlook includes agricultural ceremonies, folk tales, curing practices and a theory of disease, witchcraft, numerical divination systems, rites of passage, and a belief in spirits; but the central ceremony in the traditional Javanese religious system is the communal feast, the *slametan*. The *slametan* and the beliefs surrounding it not only draw together all these separate strands of *abangan* religion but provide both a clear picture of the way in which Indian and Islamic elements are blended with local concepts in traditional Javanese ceremonial and an example of the manner in which this ceremonial strengthens the central values of village society.

Slametans are given on almost every occasion which has ritual significance for the Javanese: pregnancy, birth, circumcision, marriage, and death; calendrical Moslem holidays such as Lebaran and the Prophet's birthday; to prevent illness, witchcraft, or theft; as harvest ceremonies; when one is to go on a journey, change one's residence, or begin a new enterprise; and, annually and communally, to pacify the village guardian spirit. But although the details vary—the foods served, the words chanted, the associated symbolic acts and objects—the general form and purpose of the *slametan* is invariant. It is a sacred communal feast of close neighbors designed to insure the general well-being (*slamet*) of all those who participate, most particularly of the host.

Slamet, being untranslatable, has been variously translated: well-being, safety, health, prosperity. What it actually indicates is a state of stasis, a state in which, literally, "nothing happens" to one (*gak ana apa-apa*). To be *slamet* is to be safe, in the sense of unbothered by either natural difficulties or supernatural annoyances. It indicates a kind of abstract well-being marked only negatively by being free of extraneous and disturbing influences from this world or the next. In the *slametan,* the Javanese asks not for joy, for an increase in wealth, for excellent health, but merely that nothing should happen to upset or sadden him, to impoverish him, or to make him ill. He does not request the spirits to do anything for him, but merely pleads with them that they do nothing to him—he seeks a tranquil independence of natural and supernatural contingency. When I left Modjokuto, the mother of the Javanese family with whom I had lived did not wish me a pleasant, comfortable journey and great success in my future life, but said she hoped I would get home without disaster and urged me to repeat *slamet, slamet, slamet,* over and over again during the whole trip so that nothing would happen to me.

If a man wishes, for whatever reason, to give a *slametan,* he will usually hold it in the evening just after sunset. He will call in all the male neighbors in the houses immediately surrounding his own, notifying them of the event only a few minutes before it is to take place. They assemble immediately, squatting in formal Javanese fashion on the floor along the edges of the main living room. In the center of the room is the food which the women of the house, now concealed in the kitchen, have spent the whole day preparing. The food is much more elaborate than the daily fare—rice pyramids, cooked meal dishes, various special kinds of vegetables, meats, fishes, most of them bearing some symbolic significance.

After all are gathered, the host (or some aged man appointed by the host) makes a very formal speech in high Javanese. He states the reason he is giving the feast, requests God, the spirits, and some Hindu deities thinly disguised as Moslem saints not to "bother" him or his family, describes the meaning of the various foods and the purport of the ceremony, and thanks his neighbors for coming, begging their pardon if anything is lacking in his preparations or if he has been in any way impolite. Then either he himself if he is able, but more usually one of the guests who has been to a religious school, recites a prayer in Arabic which neither he nor his auditors understand. This person chants for a few minutes, while the assembled guests hold their hands out, palms upward, in Islamic supplication and murmur "amen" at appropriate points. When the prayer is complete, the food is dished out by one or two of the guests. Some of each type of food is put into banana-leaf dishes and handed to each individual, with the exception of the host, who does not eat out of politeness' sake. The host bids them eat, and they each take four or five small handfuls, gulping the food in the quiet, hurried, embarrassed manner typical of the

Javanese. Within five minutes they excuse themselves, wrap up the remainder of the food, and take it home to share with their families. With this the *slametan* ends, and the incense which has been burning since its beginning may be extinguished. What has happened is that the spirits have eaten the odor of the food, the humans merely its substance. Hopefully, both are satisfied.

This brief, undramatic, formal, and almost furtive little ceremony is but a micromodel of the wider social order, a religiously distilled essence of the ethical "oughts" with which, in the secular life, the Javanese attempt to coerce both inner needs and environmental pressures into human patterns. In the *slametan* the dependence of neighboring individuals upon one another and upon the crops of their fields is symbolized, and the necessity for interfamilial co-operation, behavioral predictability, and de-emphasis of individual peculiarities are underlined. What food the group has is shared equally, whatever deep-going emotions the participants feel are carefully concealed under a bland exterior, and everyone is committed to a politely genteel behavior which can provide no surprises for anyone else. All are united in the fervent wish that the environment, personified in spirits and gods, will provide no surprises either—that all will be regular and that "nothing will happen."

As in any society, these ideal patterns of behavior, religiously consecrated or not, do not always get applied to actual behavior with undeviating firmness: Javanese, too, are often stingy or quick-tempered, and they have been known to forget their manners on occasion. In the traditional village it seems likely that this happened rather less often than it does in either the present-day village or, most particularly, in a semiurban community such as Modjokuto. These ideal patterns are the result of a constant adjustment of ethical prescription, social organization, and technical development to one another over a long period in which change on all sides was slow and undramatic, and so the fit between them and actual practice probably grew rather close and precise by the middle of the nineteenth century. However that may be, the marked and rapid economic and social change in Java in this century has thrown them rather suddenly into a social environment to which they seem to be much less suited.

The results have been various: cultural backsliding on a wide scale, what has come to be called anomie; the development of new types of ethic based either on adoption of culture patterns external to the system or on differentiated parts of the traditional system reorganized to function more adequately in the new context; or, finally, a more or less compulsive clinging to the older patterns with only minimal adjustments to changed circumstances. It is this last result that the *abangan* pattern in Modjokuto represents, and its economic implications are discernible in all the main aspects of economic life in present-day Modjokuto—in agriculture, in petty trade and craftwork, and in what scattered small-scale industrial organizations Javanese entrepreneurs have been able to set up in and around the town.

III

The traditional Javanese agricultural system was one in which the chief technical problem to be faced was that of labor organization. With a relatively small population (at least up until the time of the Dutch forced-culture system in the midnineteenth century, a period from which nearly all rapid economic change in rural Java can be dated), a remarkably fertile volcanic soil, and an adequate water supply, neither access to land nor questions of the differential employment of capital were serious issues. The central issue was how to organize the comparatively large rural labor force needed to work wet rice in irrigated terraces.

To meet this problem, there came to be built up a set of land and work distribution mechanisms by means of which intensive labor could be brought to bear on particular fields at the necessary points in time, as well as mechanisms of communal distribution of the harvests from these fields, which would be able to maintain individual subsistence in periods of low labor demand. Complex landownership rotation systems, communal work requirements, elaborate reciprocal labor-lending customs among both kith and kin, sharply defined rights to work on lands of one's relatives, and specifically outlined payments in kind for specific contributions of labor made possible an agricultural system demanding periodic applications of intensive labor from a relatively small and immobile population.

The *abangan* village came to be comprised of a group of approximately equal-status subsistence farmers, each with more or less identical political, social, economic, and religious rights and duties, all locked together in an intricate system of mutual aid and assistance in order to make efficient wet rice agriculture possible. The remarkable characteristic of traditional village agriculture in Java—aside from the double growing season—was (and is) the narrow margin between overpopulation and underpopulation. With the given techniques (of which a good example is the method of harvesting rice stalk by stalk with a knife the size of a razor), the number of people required to open a new wet rice field and work it adequately nearly equaled the number who could subsist from its output at a level the peasant would accept as decent, and both numbers were rather large.

In such a situation the tendency will be to provide for small increments in population by increasing the intensity of the cultivation rather than by extending cultivation to new lands, thus slowly narrowing the gap between over- and underpopulation still further. In any case, the possibilities of absorbing a larger population through bringing more land into wet rice cultivation was limited in Java from the beginning because tropical land untreated with volcanic ash is rather infertile, and much of the southern part of the island is porous limestone. In addition, the peculiar form in which the Dutch cast their economic impact upon Javanese rural society further stimulated both population growth and the tendency to absorb that growth through increasingly intensive farming. By attempting to force Javanese peasants into producing export crops on their own lands in their own manner, rather than introducing a self-contained plantation system complete with imported labor (as the British did, for example, in Malaya), the Dutch both sharply stimulated Javanese population growth and provided the agricultural means, through introduction of new plants and growing methods from their own intensive farming background, for greater intensification of traditional Javanese farming.

But intensification, too, has its limits, and so the Javanese village has come into this century with a rapidly increasing population, now clearly too great for its agricultural foundation, a set of values which commit those who hold them to a communalistic rather than an individualistic approach to economic problems, and methods of farming no longer able to increase output significantly. Unable either emotionally or technologically to reorganize agriculture on an extensive plantation basis, and unable too to increase output through further intensification, the *abangan* has been forced to solve his population problem by lowering his standards concerning what he will accept as a decent level of living for one of a set of equally privileged peasants. Rather than the rapid concentration of wealth and the formation of an impoverished, alienated rural proletariat, as one finds in so many other "underdeveloped" areas, we have had in East and Central Java a process of near-equal fractionization of landholdings and of the wealth which they represent. Thus the farmer has been able, by and large, to maintain his religious, political, social, and economic equality with his fellows, since the level of living of all concerned has sunk.

This general pattern of response to a worsening economic situation through a division of the economic pie into smaller and smaller pieces might well be called "shared poverty." The *abanga*, committed to world outlook which emphasizes a close interdependence among separate families in the same village, tends to share food equally when he has it and share its absence equally when he doesn't have it, not out of a general commitment to humanitarianism or to co-operation as such, but out of a traditionalized mode of solving problems. Java's twentieth-century impoverishment lacks some of the tense drama and spectacular injustice of countries with great wealth differences and large-scale landholdings, but the impoverishment is just as real, and so, ultimately, is the injustice; it is merely that Javanese do all things quietly, subtly, politely, and communally—even starve.

IV

The effect of this "shared poverty" pattern is clearly evident in Modjo-kuto. In the village at the edge of town in which I lived, somewhat more than half of the peasants were nominally landless; yet even with the relatively heavy urbanization and the long contact with foreign influences, both Dutch and Chinese, not more than 10 per cent of the land was held by individuals nonresident in the village itself, and there was only one landholding which could be called at all large, and it ran only to about thirty acres. Almost all the rest of the holdings were between one and three acres, and yet a large proportion of these small holdings were share-cropped on a half-half basis.

Actually, the relationships between nominal ownership of the land and working of the land were enormously more complicated; both sides of the equation were usually further fractionated. The owner might rent the land to one man. This man would then find a tenant to work it for him on a half-half basis (actually, the system of tenant payment was rather complicated and varied according to location and type of land, responsibility for various capital equipment—most particularly seed—length of time tenant and landlord had been associated, and the like; but the half-half arrangement was both the norm and the mode). The tenant in turn would then subcontract out blocks of the work on either a cash payment or a further share arrangement. A man and his womenfolk might be found to plant, weed, and harvest for $\frac{1}{5}$ the crop; a man and his oxen might be hired to plow for 150 rupia, and the harvest was always accomplished by a mass of people, each receiving $\frac{1}{10}$ of what they harvested as a share. Thus the fractionization of output of these small pieces of land grows to rather fabulous proportions, with a whole series of people making a poor living rather than one or two making a good one.

Further, there is a strong moral obligation on a man, particularly if he has a job in town or if he has more than two acres or so, not to work his own land but to hire a tenant. The one large landholding is split into small holdings and tenanted out, even though the owner admitted that a foreman-worker system would have been far more efficient. The reason given was that if a labor system were used the tenants in their revenge would destroy the harvests or steal them, as they had on a number of other occasions when land was worked on a foreman system. The tenant too was obligated to farm out certain blocks of the work, particularly to relatives, and even if he paid wages in cash, the amount of the wages was tied directly to the amount of rice it would buy so that there was, in many cases, explicit and conscious, an attempt to maintain a "fair shares" relationship in terms of the output of the land in kind between the various claimants to that output. In short, the land-tenancy system is, in part, an attempt to replicate rural village patterns in a more urban situation and is supported by the same ethic which had supported those patterns in the simpler past.

Even in the wholly urban, nonagricultural context of the market, the same replication occurs. To understand the Javanese market, one must see it not merely as a specific geographic location at which daily trading takes place but as a patterned type of economic activity, with its own peculiar formal characteristics—a pattern of economic activity only partly localized in the market proper. Javanese sell things to other Javanese on street corners, in homes, at sidewalk stands, in stores, over a cup of restaurant coffee, on village roads, in fact, everywhere. The market is merely the concentrated center and the visible model of a trading institution much wider than itself, and so when one says "market," one refers to the whole range of Javanese small trading activities.

The goods flow into this "market" from various sources, but very few of them have not at one point or another passed through Chinese hands, and the local products—almost entirely agricultural—come to them in the end as well. Not in all cases, however, are the Chinese involved locally. Much of the cloth is bought in Surabaja by the Javanese directly, from Chinese stores there; a few larger-scale native traders sell crops directly to urban wholesalers; and Chinese from the cities and larger towns come often to Modjokuto (or send agents) to trade with the Javanese market people.

Once the goods enter the wholly Javanese market complex they do not go directly to the ultimate consumer, but circulate among the professional traders, each transaction nibbling away at the profit margin; the economic return for passing the goods from the large Chinese distributors to the ultimate consumers, small enough in the first place, gets divided among several people. Further, most of the capital these petty traders employ is in the form of credit extended by the Chinese wholesaler, the latter being unwilling to lend cash now that the Dutch are no longer present to enforce contracts. The Javanese trader keeps a running debt balance with the Chinese trader, a balance carefully managed on both sides not to grow so large as to encourage flight on the part of the Javanese and not to shrink so small as to leave the Javanese without any control over the Chinese. In sum, the complexity of economic structure for a fairly simple economic function is surprisingly great.

In a sense the same subcontracting pattern which fractionates the returns from land operates here to fractionate the return from retail distribution. The main Javanese traders are those who have debt balances with the Chinese: the larger the balance the Chinese allows, the larger is the scope of the trader's activities. But it is only in the exceptional case that the goods derived from this relation to the Chinese go directly into consumer hands. Almost always they go into the hands of other Javanese traders who hold a smaller debt balance with the larger trader. And so it goes all the way down the line. The goods pass from hand to hand, their course regulated by debt manipulations, leaving only a very small profit behind at any point along that course. Again, the moral obligation upon the Javanese trader to cut others in on a good deal shows that this response is not wholly rational, wholly economic, but is supported by a motivational pattern rather deeply ingrained in many Javanese individuals. It is, in fact, the commercial interpretation of an ethic originally created as a response to purely agricultural demands.

Finally, the "industrial" sector of the Modjokuto economy is a very thin reed indeed, but even here one can see the power of the *abangan* ethic. One of my informants set up a cigarette factory in a shed behind his house. He began with two workers—girls—rolling the cigarettes by hand, in corn sheathes provided by the workers themselves. The factory grew to employ a work force of twenty girls, the number being determined not by economic considerations but by the entrepreneur's and the girls' notions of the "correct" number which should be employed, given the amount of work involved. The result was an extremely uneconomically operated factory. Unable to accumulate enough capital to provide sufficient tobacco to keep twenty girls working even six hours a day at full capacity, the entrepreneur merely apportioned out regulated quantities of the available tobacco to each girl each day, and the girls worked at a very slow speed, producing only 1,000 cigarettes in a working day where they might easily have produced 1,500 to 2,000.

Instead of trimming his work force to fit the dimensions of his industry, my informant, the entrepreneur, decided—quite consciously—that twenty workers was a "fair" number to employ. If he employed less than this number, the girls would always be demanding he hire a relative or friend of theirs; as soon as the number of workers was "high enough" in the girls' eyes, he could refuse such demands without fear of criticism. He thus increased his overhead and cut his profits (and his workers' wages, as they were paid piece rate). The outcome was typical: twenty workers and an entrepreneur made a semiadequate living, and no one made a good one, with the added consideration in this case that this economically inefficient operation reduced even further the opportunities for the entrepreneur to amass enough capital to increase output and hire more workers. As a matter of fact, the business failed after a while, and the Javanese entrepreneur fled his Chinese creditors.

So it is that the *abangan* ethic affects the whole range of economic activity in Modjokuto. In agriculture, in trade, and in manufacturing, it emphasizes and legitimizes a pattern of economic behavior derived from past experience in a different setting; it organizes new experiences in old forms and meets new challenges with old responses. But it is not the only ethic extant in Modjokuto, for not all village Javanese projected rudely into the twentieth century have clung unreservedly to old beliefs, nor, as Java has been civilized since shortly after the time of Christ, has the back-ground of all Javanese been wholly rural. The *santri* world view reflects an attempt to readjust and reinterpret the village ethic in terms of con-siderations derived both from foreign religious influence and from a longer experience in trade, and the *priyayi* world view has grown up in an urban environment focused on the great Hinduized court centers of east and central Java.

V

Islam, it has been said, lies on Java like a veil, concealing little and shap-ing nothing; where Hinduism brought a civilization, Islam brought but a religion. The degree to which this aphorism has become pregressively un-true over the past fifty years is a measure of the degree to which one can speak of a *santri*, as opposed to an *abangan*, world outlook in Javanese society. The self-conscious, religiously sophisticated, exclusivist Moslem is a child of this century, although Indonesia has been nominally Islamic since the sixteenth.

Until the latter part of the nineteenth century, the religious system of Java struck a balance between Islamic, Hinduistic, and animistic ele-ments, in which the man who had memorized a little Arabic, or did his prayers somewhat more regularly, or went blindly and uncomprehend-ingly on the pilgrimage to Mecca, was but a slightly differentiated special-ist, useful to chant at a *slametan* or a death, or to organize the local version of the annual religious tax, or perhaps to provide a particularly exotic and efficacious remedy picked up in some crowded Meccan dormi-tory. Slightly more well-to-do perhaps, somewhat more serious religiously, maybe, a little more powerful magically, quite probably, his interest in Islam was but a personal interpretation of the general village beliefs. As his less interested neighbors, his religious concern was both mystical and cabalistic and magical and materialistic; of the Moslem law, theology, and ethics he knew little and cared less. He was but another *abangan*, going more regularly to *slametans* than to mosques.

In time, this all changed, but the process by which the present-day *santri* group has come to be rather sharply set off from the non-*santri* groups has not been a wholly rural one, but rather has found a basis in both the rural and urban sectors of the society. The recent history of Islam in Java has been one of the appearance of a still embryonic rural yeomanry on the one hand and of a small class of free urban traders on the other, and their increasing interrelationship legitimized in terms of a common religious bond. Since about 1910 both these groups, the rural and the urban, have been progressively influenced by reformist ideologies streaming out of the great Islamic centers of learning in the Middle East, and so there has arrived upon the Javanese social scene a still small, pre-carious, and fragile middle class of slightly wealthy peasants, small shopkeepers, and weak independent entrepreneurs, largely comprised of rather pious, self-conscious, aggressive, and often quite religiously sophisticated Moslem modernists.

The rural part of this development owes its existence to the fact that the problems connected with Western-stimulated economic change were not always met in the villages by a simple reassertion of traditional values. In many cases they were met, instead, by increasing emphasis on the more Islamic elements of the traditional religious system at the expense of the other elements in the system, together with an attempt to justify a new social and economic ethic in terms of this altered religious emphasis. Two particular Moslem institutions—the system of rural religious education and the pilgrimage to Mecca—played an especially important role in this process. A shift to increased concern with things Islamic as opposed to things more generally Javanese led to a greater interest in the teaching of a more purely Islamic tradition, and the provision of content for such teaching naturally depended upon increased contact with the center of the Moslem world. In turn, the necessity for accumulating wealth to go on the pilgrimage led to economic and social consequences which further strengthened the preference for things Islamic in the group to which they accrued.

Speaking concretely, the financial demands of the ever more attractive pilgrimage induced into the *santri* family a distinct emphasis on a value the Javanese call *gemi. Gemi,* which means obsessive thrift, was if anything disvalued by the *abangan,* who usually despised the *santri* as a solemn miser hoarding his money merely to gain useless prestige from having completed a fool's errand, but for the *santri* it was a central concern. For him it was a source of pride to work hard, dress simply, eat sparingly, and to avoid large ceremonial and festival expenditures. A man who by such means saved enough money to go to Mecca for a year or so at the age of fifty or sixty was immensely respected by the rural Moslem community.

Upon his return, the hadji (as Meccan pilgrims are called) became the center for a kind of local cult, for not only was he more holy for his trip but he was more learned in correct Islamic practice as defined in the capital of Islamic civilization. A local Moslem school (*pondok*) was likely to form about him as a teacher, in which each morning and evening youths aged six to twenty-five chanted books in an Arabic they did not understand—books brought back to them by the returned hadji who as often did not understand Arabic either. These *pondok* varied in size from small one-room bamboo shacks, where boys came only in the evenings to chant for an hour or so, to large stone buildings built on land deeded officially to God, in which the students lived continuously, chanting up to five and six hours a day. In time there would grow up a kind of religious complex of mosque, school, teacher, and students, the latter—many of them come from goodly distances—living ascetically, doing their own housework and earning their way by working in the surrounding fields, either those of the hadji himself or of other well-to-do supporters of the school.

Now, there have been religious schools of this general sort scattered throughout the Javanese countryside for centuries. In nearly every village there was an old man who considered himself learned in some mystical or magical art, nominally Islamic, who had set himself up as a teacher to his neighbors, and it was out of this general tradition, originally Buddhist, that the *santri* community elaborated the explicitly Moslem *pondok*. In an effort to distinguish it sharply from other types of religious schools, which they came to hold as *kaffir* (a concept of religious exclusiveness rather foreign to traditional Javanese "theology," which, if not always tolerant in practice, was usually relativistic in theory), they created a sub-culture around the *pondok* which took on a definitely Near Eastern cast. Arabic music, dances, and religious dramatic performances were intro-duced and Hindu-Javanese art forms rejected; imitation of Arabian clothing and some types of Arabian food became popular; and the young *santris* developed the kind of cult of body development, strength display-ing, and masochistic endurance testing which is so often associated with semisecret fraternities around the world. The *abangans* called them Arabs—whom they didn't like either—and said that like their Near East-ern cousins they were interested more in getting rich than religious.

However that may be, this valuation of individual effort, thrift, and simplicity—combined with a tendency to avoid land fractionization and easy accessibility to a labor pool of nonlandowning students—did yield the hadji and his supporters a larger personal fortune than was possible for the general run of peasant. The rich hadji, surrounded by a group of satellite landholders and young laborer-students, could build up a system of agricultural production (often with home industry attached) which took the form of a kind of small-scale plantation. For the most part these small plantations, if that is what they should be called, did not grow very large, nor did the hadji and his followers become very rich, at least in the Modjokuto area. But the system had enough of an impact to create a fairly sharp economic distinction between *abangan* and *santri* which supported and strengthened the cultural distinction. Almost all the more wealthy peasants around Modjokuto today are *santris* or sons of *santris*, and "rich man" and "hadji" are nearly synonymous terms.

The urban side of the *santri* development may be dealt with more briefly. In the large cities, that part of the distributive trade which was not in Chinese hands tended for a number of reasons to fall into Moslem ones. In the first place, most aristocratic, non-Moslem urban Javanese managed to attach themselves in one form or another to the Hinduized courts and to the colonial bureaucracy, becoming civil servants rather than businessmen. Secondly, up until World War II the immigrant Arab community played an important role in non-Chinese petty urban trade and consequently had a rather strong ideological impact on the Javanese traders. And lastly, the tradition of Moslem trading, which, in a sense, formed the basis of the Islamization of the archipelago in the first place, never completely died out or got wholly absorbed into the predominantly agricultural Javanese economy. Particularly along the north coast, in such Islamic enclaves as Cheribon-Indramajoe in West Java, Semarang-Demak-Kudus in Central Java, and Bondjo-negoro-Gresik in Eastern Java, there continued to exist a native commercial tradition associated with an explicit Islamism.

The relations between the peasant Moslems and the urban ones grew more intimate as time passed because of their common ideology, because the Moslem peasants were from the urbanites' point of view more significant economically than the poorer *abangans,* and because, in an attempt to avoid the fractionization of landholding entailed by an equal-division inheritance system, some hadjis sent their younger sons into business. In this way, part of the urban *santri* trade came to be capitalized with rural wealth, and the mutual dependence between the groups increased.

But the gulf remained, nevertheless, quite wide. The urbanites, in closer touch both with the local Arab community and with influences from the Middle East generally, had a far more accurate idea of the actual requirements of Islam than was possible for the more isolated peasants and so tended to look on the latter as at best only half Moslem. Also, the new economic pressures introduced, or at least intensified, by the twentieth century played more directly, at first, upon the trading population than the agricultural, driving their interests apart.

So, while Islam in the countryside remained focused in relatively isolated, independent, and often mutually antagonistic mosque school complexes, a demand arose in the cities and towns for a wider and more closely knit religious movement which could harmonize new economic and political interests with an unadulterated Islamic tradition. The traders found the rationale for such a movement in the doctrines of the Islamic reformers who wrote, taught, and preached in Cairo and Mecca during the latter part of the nineteenth and early part of the twentieth centuries, impulses of whose thought began to reach Indonesia through returning hadjis and immigrant Arabs around 1910. By 1920 a surprisingly large-scale "back to the Koran" movement was under way in the larger Javanese cities—a movement demanding economic protection against Chinese competition and political freedom from colonial rule in the same breath with fundamental religious reform.

The reformers centered their attack, insofar as it was religious, not upon *abangan* beliefs as such, but rather upon the series of compromises with that system which rural and uneducated *santris* had come to accept as a legitimate halfway covenant. Not only did the modernists attack the modified form of the *slametan* spirit-pacifying cult these *santris* had decided was sufficiently orthodox for everyday purposes, but they went so far as to criticize the rural religious-school system itself as perpetuating a merely formal worship at the expense of fundamental religious enlightenment. They rejected not only the clearly heterodox Indian mysticism but the nominally Islamic Near Eastern as well. The nearly exclusive reliance upon the secondary religious commentaries of Arabic scholastics and upon the most conservative of the Moslem law traditions, the *shafiites,* they pronounced mere medievalism. Revealing themselves as the true puritans they in fact were, the reformers demanded that all compromises with traditionalized sin and sanctified heterodoxy be abandoned; that a true understanding of the meaning of the Glorious Koran and the Traditions of the Prophet (Hadith)—rather than local habit or medieval Islamic theory—form the basis for Indonesian Islam.

For the *slametans* at birth, circumcision, marriage, and death, they would substitute simple prayer and contributions to religious foundations and mission work to the poor. For mysticism they could substitute the clear perception of the otherness of God in all his Middle Eastern majesty, power, and glory and the necessity for absolute submission to and trust in the purity of his will, reflected in the individual experience as predestination. For the *pondok* and its meaningless chanting they would substitute modern schools where religious subjects (including the translation of Arabic) would be taught side by side with natural science, economics, and history and where the content of Islam would be transmitted as well as the form. And for the medieval lawbook they would substitute a flexible use of the whole of the Islamic tradition—of all four lawbooks and most essentially of the Koran and Hadith unadorned with scholastic fretwork—in an attempt to adjust Islam to the modern world, to make it relevant to contemporary social problems, and to build in Indonesia's green and tropical land a true Islamic state—the kingdom of God on earth.

The attack of the reformers was therefore inward; it was directed primarily against the rural and more backward part of the *santri* community itself rather than against the *abangan,* who could be expected to regard it with indifference. It was a genuine attempt at internal reform, at self-purification and the building of a unified *santri* community, and the initial reaction of the rural *santris,* attacked as they were at their most sensitive point—their religious orthodoxy—was violently antagonistic. From about 1915 to the Japanese occupation in 1942, a sharp ideological struggle took place between a modernist urban group of reformist Moslems, best symbolized by the well-known religious welfare organization *Muhammadiyah,* and a traditionalist rural group of orthodox Moslems, organized into the powerful league of religious teachers, the *Nahadatul Ulama.*

But the modernists had time, the direction of social change, and organizational proficiency on their side. The traditionalists were forced more and more to copy modernist forms of organization in order to compete effectively. To articulate their own orthodox message, they had increasing recourse to such modernist innovations as the Friday sermon in the mosque, small evening prayer meetings at which religious points are discussed and explicated, traveling lecturers, the translated Koran, and schools organized on more Western lines to provide capable leadership. And so, insofar as the organizational side is concerned, the modernists have achieved a near-total victory: even conservative Moslem leaders in Modjokuto today support Western educational forms, socioreligious organizations, and active involvement in everyday affairs by the pious. On the ideological side the victory is less unambiguous; much of rural Islamic reorganization is old wine in new bottles. But, in general, the postwar gap between the urban-centered modernists and rural-centered traditionalists is much less than it was before the war. If the two groups still do not always see eye to eye on the theological legitimacy of certain details of religious practice and belief, they have grown sufficiently close organizationally to be able to submerge these differences in the interests of a general defense against the increasingly sharp antagonisms of the rest of the Javanese community. The battle more or less won inwardly, the *santris* have turned outwardly toward the wider society with their message and have found there an even sharper antagonism.

VI

In the twenties and the thirties the Modjokuto countryside was dotted with *pondoks*. Ranging in size from ten to three hundred students, many of these little monasterylike institutions formed small independent agricultural enterprises in which religion and rice growing were but part of a single activity often supplemented by small-scale home industry, such as cloth dyeing or brickmaking.

The perpetuation of this pattern of semiextensive agriculture was further stimulated and strengthened by the manner in which the Dutch sugar-growing system impinged upon the village economy. Rather than planting cane in fields bought outright from native landholders, the sugar factories rented irrigated land from the peasants on a contract basis. Each village was obliged to rent one-third of its ricelands each year to the factory, the actual owner of the land being paid in money for giving up the use of it. Sugar matures, conveniently enough, in a year, and so each year a different third of the village land was rented out and the two-thirds planted by the peasant in his regular crops. The factories worked the land extensively with a seasonal labor force organized under foremen, although parts of the job, particularly in harvesting and transportation of cane to the factory, might be subcontracted to peasants who could organize, capitalize, and manage the labor force required. The result of this rather intricate and unusual system was rapid monetization of the peasant economy, enforced diversification of agriculture, increasing entanglement of the peasant economy with the Western, a proletarianization of much of the peasantry, and differential economic growth of that part of the population which had a degree of familiarity with money, a strong motivation to accumulate it, and access to pools of labor and the skill and capital to organize them. To an extent, although not a very great one, the somewhat rich got somewhat richer and the slightly poor got slightly poorer. And—for the most part—the somewhat rich were the *santris*.

So, many members of the rural *santri* community in the years before the depression were able to maintain an increasing prosperity in a generally declining village economy because they were equipped with the rudiments of a social and economic organization capable of taking advantage of the enforced contact with Western forms of agricultural enterprise. In addition, the most famous Javanese *pondok* of the time led by the most famous religious teacher of the period was in the same general area as Modjokuto at Tebu Ireng. It was at Tebu Ireng that *Nahadatul Ulama,* the organizational reply to the modernists, was founded in 1915, and so the Modjokuto area was plunged into the orthodox-reformist conflict from the beginning. The battle raged hot and heavy for a while but, as nearly everywhere, the modernists at length won, so far as methods are concerned, and today the emphasis in the area has shifted away from the *pondok* system toward the Western-type school. A number of *pondoks* still remain, two of them quite large with about 150 and 300 students, respectively, but the students bring their tuition from home and the work-study system has decreased nearly to the vanishing point.

Why, then, supported both by Dutch economic intrusion and by local ideological stimulation, did not the *santri* pattern of agriculture grow even stronger? Why did the *santris* not develop into great plantation landlords employing—or exploiting—large masses of proletarianized peasants? In the first place, the Dutch colonial government, reacting against the excesses of the culture system, hemmed the sugar concerns in by a series of uneconomic welfare regulations which were designed to minimize the impact of those concerns upon the peasant economy and protect the forms of traditional village society from disruption. Secondly, the world-wide collapse of commodity prices in the thirties removed even this blunted stimulus from the Javanese scene. Thirdly, nationalism, war, and revolution have turned Indonesian interests away from the economic field toward the political, and economic means for achieving ideal ends have been replaced by largely political ones; for the moment almost all the energies of the society are engaged in a simple struggle for political power on the assumption, as one religious teacher and political leader told me, that "if your party gets elected, the rest is easy."

But perhaps the most important factor which has limited the growth of *santri* economic power is that the *santris,* particularly the rural ones, are, after all, Javanese. If they have turned away from the *abangan* ethic, they have not turned very far. The appeal of the old values of interfamilial co-operation, of restraint of individual aggressiveness, and of the minimization of open acquisitiveness is still quite strong for the *santri.* The average *santri* has been unable to bring himself to disinherit his younger sons by explicitly adopting a primogeniture pattern in place of the time-honored equal-inheritance system; he has proved insufficiently hard-shelled to resist kith and kin demands for economic aid or to reject totally the traditional festival obligations; and he has proved unwilling to exploit the available labor without regard for the traditional norms and prescriptions regulating its employment and remuneration. The rural *santri* has not had the heart—nor perhaps the skill—to become a real landlord.

Turning to the urban side of the picture, the *santri* community within the town of Modjokuto was originally made up, not of local peasants forced off the land, but almost entirely of migrant traders from larger urban centers, men whose families had been in small trade for at least two or three generations. They came to Modjokuto in the first place as young men, traveling out as agents of their father, their uncle, or their cousin, who had an established business back in Demak or Gresik or Kudus. Actually, they were not true agents, but small independent traders, for the *santri* method of introducing young relatives into the business, even sons, was neither to take them in as junior partners, nor to provide them with an initial lump of capital sufficiently large to start a going business, nor to employ them as commission or salary salesmen; rather they presented them with a half-dozen pieces of cloth (pairs of shoes, cartons of cigarettes), marked them down on the books for a debt corresponding to an only slightly preferential version of the local retail price of the merchandise, and then sent them out to sell the goods for as much as the market would bear. In time, the capital got returned and the boy began to buy his own cloth, shoes, or cigarettes out of his minuscule profits. It is the hard-knocks school of business education, a sink-or-swim method, and whatever its shortcomings, it inured the apprentice to living perpetually on the economic margin; it equipped him with the psychology necessary to survive in a petty capitalist society.

But with six pieces of cloth bought at retail a young man could not survive among the old hands in Kudus. The apprentice traders were driven out to the more marginal towns and small cities toward the south and east where distance from commercial centers and ports, low intensity of competition, and local ignorance combined to permit a higher profit margin. Traveling light, they learned the ropes from older traders and from their coreligionists, the Arabs. "They used to say we were just like Arabs," one old *santri* trader said gleefully. "We dressed in rags, ate one meal a day of rice and corn with no trimmings, and walked for miles peddling our stuff every place we had a chance. We weren't liked much, but we all got rich." Fiercely independent, they moved back and forth between their home base and Modjokuto less and less frequently and in time tended to settle permanently in Modjokuto, perhaps marry a local girl (usually from a rural *santri* family), and go off only now and then on buying trips to the larger centers. Often partly specialized according to origin (Kudus men sold cigarettes, Gresik men sold fish, and Bawean men sold cloth), the urban *santris* formed a rather tight in-group, set off (residentially as well as socially) from both the peasants and the government clerks and progressively disliked by both.

Stimulated by the market the Dutch factories and plantations provided, this little group flourished until the depression. In the twenties there were nearly a dozen native stores in town, some of them rivaling the Chinese in the size and diversity of their inventories—almost all *santri*-run. The *santris* controlled the cigarette, cheap cloth, and small hardware businesses, and, except for luxury textiles, they dominated the fairly extensive trading that went on among the various local markets in the area. They built restaurants, started repair shops, tailored clothes, and cobbled shoes, and some even owned a truck or two. Some of the larger stores were able to apply, in part, more "rational" pricing mechanisms than those provided by bargaining over each individual item, to employ salesmen to go out into the countryside and sell the peasants in their homes, and to keep written books. Economic development and religious reform went hand in hand: by 1930 Islamic modernism with its attendant economic and political ideologies was well rooted in the *santri* community. Each of the various phases of the national movement (as well as of the counter-movement) found its counterpart in Modjokuto, where there occurred a remarkable efflorescence of association life—among all groups, as a matter of fact—which has continued on into the present day.

The depression and the consequent departure of Dutch capital stunted this development half-grown; a number of the stores and restaurants failed, the Chinese muscled in on the cigarette trade, and a flood of landless *abangans*, released from jobs as Dutch servants and seasonal agricultural workers, pushed into the town to engage in commercial activities previously in largely *santri* hands. The pattern of economic life changed somewhat from one of sharp competition between aggressive and independent entrepreneurs running businesses with a certain degree of elaborated economic organization toward one of mutually interdependent impermanent traders set directly in the general all-over market complex without any mediating structure at all.

But the *santri* element, built for survival, has remained rather strong, considering the circumstances. There are today perhaps seven Javanese establishments worthy of the name "store" left in Modjokuto; six are *santri*-owned. Much of the cheap textile business is still in Islamic hands, but on a rather smaller scale. And not only are there a number of *santri* free craftsmen—shoemakers, tailors, barbers, bike repairmen—but a certain amount of small sweatshop industry continues to flourish under strictly Moslem management. In fact, in Modjokuto town today one can find a continuum of types of Javanese retail trading activity ranging from the "market complex" type to what might be called the "store complex" type, and this continuum correlates remarkably well with variations in religious belief from an *abangan* to a *santri* pole. As one moves toward the store complex, *santri* domination of economic activity grows steadily greater, although, as in any society, many of the cases are mixed ones and embarrassing exceptions occur.

The market is, of course, patronized by everyone, but most particularly it is oriented to rural and to lower-class town trade; the informality, the bargaining, the generally cheaper quality of goods sold, all are directed ultimately toward bit selling to a generally poor clientele. On the other hand, the best Javanese stores (they sell shoes and textiles mostly), situated among the Chinese in the main business section, are generally directed toward the upper-class town populace or toward the few rural rich. Their formality, their tendency toward fixed prices, their fancy glassed-in display cases, and their more expensive line of goods are adjustments to a clientele beginning to feel slightly superior to the jostling commonness of the market. In the secondary business section, particularly along the outside of the market in shops rented from the government, there are a few "transitional" stores which try to combine selling to both publics, the rural and the upper-class urban, but which are still in large part inside the market complex.

Within the market, the poorer *santris* do engage in the small-scale moment-to-moment hawking of hardware, food, cigarettes, and the like already identified as an *abangan* pattern, but, given *santri* preferences, it is a rather lowering thing to do, and most of them tend to avoid it for small craftwork, if at all possible. Most significant *santri* activity in the market is concentrated in the cheap textile trade—which they almost completely dominate—in the buying, selling, and processing of the so-called *kain kasar* which forms the staple Javanese dress. These cloth salesmen sell not only cheap bulk cloth but ready-made underwear, trousers, shirts, coats, and sometimes fancier cloth as well (although luxury textiles have had a rather special commercial history in Java which, until recently, has kept them, in part, out of *santri* hands).

As a result, the market stalls these salesmen operate are often merely the largely wholesale distributing outlet for a wider enterprise which includes a small garment factory and a "transitional" store outside the market as well as numerous *abangan* satellite sellers within the market proper and out in the villages. Against the relatively homogeneous background of *abangan* market trading, one can see a development of differentiated economic structure ranging from cheap cloth trading and processing in the market, to transitional stores which, while connected more or less directly with the market, try also to attract some of the urban nonmarket business, to fully developed "pure" stores wholly adjusted to the tastes of a small group of highly urbanized clerks and teachers. And one can see also that at each point this development is almost wholly owned, managed, and capitalized by men explicitly adhering to a revivified Islamic ethic.

In the area of small industry one also finds a sharp contrast between *santri* and *abangan* patterns—contrasts evident in what is perhaps Modjokuto's largest wholly Javanese-run industry: garment making. Most of the well-to-do urban population have their clothes made to order by one of the dozens of independent tailors (almost all of them *santris*) who work their own machines in their own homes. But to serve the rural and lower-class market, there exists a number of independent cottage industries in which from two to fifteen tailors are organized into a small garment factory producing ready-made clothes of the cheapest variety: hats, coats, shirts, women's blouses and brassières, trousers, underwear, socks, and even head shawls for Moslem ladies. Almost entirely *santri*-owned, managed, and staffed, these small garment factories are not organized on the make-work pattern of *abangan* industry, but are rationalized according to the structure of the work task, carefully budgeted in terms of shrewd estimates of future market conditions, and operated at costs minimized by means of careful planning, close overseeing, and sweatshop exploitation of the labor force.

The father of one of my informants ran such a factory. Originally from Kudus, this man employs from two to five tailors, according to the season (the market for clothing being dependent upon the agricultural cycle and to a degree upon the ceremonial calendar), and sells their production in the market. The entrepreneur, as is usual in such factories, does all the designing himself. About four or five o'clock each morning he cuts the cloth according to pattern, lays it out for the tailors, and then leaves for the market with the previous day's output. The tailors work through the day at his home on machines he owns; in the afternoon he returns to check what they have done and arrange his accounts.

In rush seasons, the tailors may specialize on types of clothing for greater efficiency and sometimes may even divide the work of the more complicated jobs in production-line fashion, but in the off-time there is no division of labor and they merely work at whatever is next to be done. They work from 8 A.M. until 1 P.M., from 2:30 until 5:30, and from 7 until 10 P.M., a common pattern generally, particularly in the peak period. They are paid piece rate, laid off when there is no work, and, unlike workers in *abangan*-run enterprises, they are given no extras such as food and cigarettes.

This particular entrepreneur does not pay his workers their wages as they earn them. Rather, he pays them a steady five rupia a day (barely a living wage; low wages and long hours combine to give Javanese tailors a reputation for a short life expectancy), irrespective of how much work they have done, and keeps records as to the amount he owes them according to their output and the amount he has so far paid them in "salary." As their output is almost always more than five rupia (in the rush season it may reach fifteen for an excellent tailor), he is usually in slight debt to each of them. This enables him to have greater leverage over his labor force as well as greater control over their spending habits; the system is also designed to prevent the tailors from attempting to borrow money from the entrepreneur in difficult times.

On the distributive side, the entrepreneur has three itinerant sellers who travel as far as twenty miles to sell his clothing to the plantation-area people. These sellers are in constant debt to him—reversing the tailor arrangement—according to a rather complicated system which maintains the indebtedness of about one-half of the seller's daily turnover. On the other hand, the entrepreneur buys his cloth from a Chinese who comes to Modjokuto two or three times a week from the regional capital, and is in fairly heavy debt to him. In the market, most of the entrepreneur's selling is to other smaller sellers—also on credit—though both his wife and his daughter maintain stalls selling directly to the public (his family also cooperates to make buttonholes for him in the evening). Obviously, this man is the center of a fairly complicated set of financial arrangements and productive and distributive facilities. It is little wonder that he works twelve to fifteen hours a day, is rather disliked by his sons, is well-to-do, and is secretary-treasurer of the oldest modernist Islamic organization in Modjokuto.

VII

Priyayi in the narrow sense signifies someone who can trace his ancestry to kings and who consequently is permitted to write his name with a title before it, but it has come to be applied more generally to government officials, clerks, and, to an extent, to teachers—in short, to the whole of the literati. This little group, originally comprised of relatives and retainers of the Hindu-Javanese sultans, was the chief native agency of colonial government, the chosen instrument of indirect foreign rule, and so has been deeply affected both by the mystical aesthetics of pre-Islamic court culture and by the functional prerequisites of the hierarchical, paternal, bureaucratic, and remarkably efficient political administration introduced by the Dutch. The progeny of this ideological miscegenation turned out to be a carefully ranked caste of obsessively polite literate administrators and educators combining an inward-looking pantheistic imagination with a status-worried bureaucratic conscience.

The *priyayi* ethic ties together a series of moral preferences consecrating the kind of world outlook such a caste requires. The preferences involved are for the intense cultivation of the inner man and the intense formalization of the outer; for a highly refined sense for the nuances of status and a polished skill in expressing them in external behavior; for an interest in purity of descent and a concern for the well-made marriage; for a highly sophisticated formal art with mystical overtones and allegorical interpretations; for an attitude of paternalistic support; reserved distance, and amused condescension toward the uneducated masses; for an education system emphasizing literature, music, and philosophy at the expense of economics and technics; and for making one's living, insofar as it is necessary to work for it, in white-collar occupations rather than in either farming or business. Literati, gentry, patricians, brahmans, aristocrats—whatever you wish to call them—the *priyayi* are the Javanese version of a social type seemingly universal in nonindustrial civilizations: the men who are able to write.

Religiously, the *priyayi* have been particularly interested in neither *slametans* nor the Koran. Rather, they have been concerned with a search for ultimate mystical enlightenment, with elaborate philosophical and mythological speculation upon the nature of man and the basis of his spiritual life, and with secret systems of mystically supported prophecy and moral exhortation. Phenomenalists all, their religious patterns have been more intellectual than ritualistic, more psychological than physicalistic, more private than public. With neither the fixed forms of collective ritual behavior of the *abangans* nor the logically articulated dogmatic beliefs of the *santris*, *priyayi* religious belief and behavior shows a wider internal variation than that of either of the two other groups. But this greater range allowed for individual interpretation is merely a surface phenomenon: at base the *priyayi* religious orientation is as well defined as the *santri* and *abangan* and at least as carefully adjusted as the underlying moral commitments it is supposed to legitimize.

The core of *priyayi* religious belief is individual affective experience. Largely uninterested either in the movements of the stars in their courses or in the vagaries of the natural environment, the *priyayi* pays rather strict attention to the state of what he calls his "heart," by which he means the general tone of his emotional life. For the metaphysical astrology of so many of the world's religions he has substituted an allegorical psychology, and for their naturistic omen reading he has substituted systems of mathematical divination based upon mystical insight. Mystical insight—itself an indescribable emotional experience—is, in fact, the core within the core of his religion, and, like power, prestige, and beauty of character, it flows from the top of the social and bureaucratic hierarchy down to the bottom. It is not cleanliness but high office which is close to godliness.

This, at least in the past, was nearly literally true. The belief in the divine king, a belief widespread in Southeast Asia, formed a fitting capstone to religious theory which held that access to God through mystical experience was directly correlated with one's rank at the court and later in the colonial administration. An ascending scale of purity of heart and excellence of character found its climax in the concept of a king who was not merely an exalted servant of God, but, in some vague sense, *was* God. Around the king clustered the great philosophers, poets, musicians, and dancers—accomplished mystics all—who provided the content for the religion of a whole caste out of the fuzzy intuitions of prolonged spiritual meditation. This content, as well as the music, the dance, and the poetry, flowed outward and downward from the court centers to the *priyayi* manning the lesser outposts of government, roughening and coarsening as it went. The lower the man, the more partial his own religious experience of God must inevitably be and the less capable he must be of understanding that of others higher than himself, either in pure form or clothed in a spiritualized art. The Javanese have two words to indicate the two poles of this cultural continuum which are crucial in understanding the *priyayi* world outlook: *alus* and *kasar.*

Alus means pure, refined, polished, polite, exquisite, ethereal, subtle, civilized, smooth, and then again it doesn't. A man who speaks flawless high Javanese is *alus,* a piece of cloth with intricate, subtle designs painted onto it is *alus,* an exquisitely played piece of music or a beautifully controlled dance step is *alus;* so is a smooth stone, a dog with his hair petted down, a farfetched joke, or a clever poetic conceit. God is, of course, *alus* (as are all invisible spirits) and so is the experience of him; one's own soul and character are *alus* insofar as one emotionally comprehends the ultimate structure of existence, and one's behavior and actions are *alus* insofar as they are regulated by the intricacies of the complex court-practiced etiquette. *Kasar* is merely the opposite: impolite, rough, uncivilized; a badly played piece of music, a stupid joke, a cheap piece of cloth. Between these two poles the *priyayi* arranges everyone from peasant to king.

Priyayi religious organization is part of the same general pattern. It consists of a series of independent sects, sometimes merely local in occurrence, sometimes more widely spread throughout Java, but with little over-all organization. Each local sect is headed by a teacher who transmits a set of concrete religious beliefs, usually concerned with the metaphysical implications of individual emotional experience and almost always accompanied by specific (but rather simple) yogalike techniques for the achievement of oneness with the One. The original center of such a concrete set of religious beliefs and practices is almost always some famous king or high-rank scholar at the king's court who evolved them out of his inner consciousness by means of years of quiet meditation, usually in the woods or at the top of a volcano. Both the techniques and the true knowledge achieved by them were then taught by this original teacher to disciples, who in turn taught them to lower disciples, and so on down the line. The sects are often secret, the teachers usually favored with gifts, and the students ranked according to their mystical abilities. It is always well understood that approximation to the mystical success of the original teacher, and often even to that of the local teacher, is not to be expected. These things are high and difficult and take time as well as a certain amount of breeding. For those who believe in it, reincarnation offers some hope for long-range improvement of a significant sort, but for many merely a certain small increase in spiritual understanding is possible.

The content of these various self-contained religious movements varies widely. Some are concerned with allegorical interpretations of traditional mythological material, with reading between the lines of classical Javanese poems, or with psychological glosses on the ever-popular puppet plays. Others have described various stages of mystical advancement and developed meditation techniques appropriate to each. Still others have worked out physiological theories based on phenomenological considerations and derived curing practices from these, and yet others are concerned with such problems as the nature of the self, the validity of mental ideas, and the transempirical sources of human unhappiness. But their general outlook is identical: all are pantheistic, all are mystical, and nearly all draw explicit moral conclusions from their metaphysical assumptions—conclusions which celebrate the *alus* over the *kasar*.

There are in present-day Modjokuto about six major sects of this sort and a number of unaffiliated people with independent "religions" of their own, derived from the works of one scholar or another or studied originally in some other town. Of the major sects, four have their sources in the great inland culture capitals of Central Java, one is a Javanese version of the international theosophy movement of Annie Besant and also has its headquarters in one of these court centers, and the last had its origin in West Java and has turned into a Communist-dominated politicoreligious party directed more toward *abangans* than *priyayis*. The membership of these sects, with the exception of the last, is mostly *priyayi*, but some are more completely so than others. Particularly since the revolution, but even before it, some of the court-evolved religious systems have filtered vaguely down to the *abangans*, being rather corrupted as they went into magical recipes and ritualistic spirit cults. The sect movement, while predominantly a *priyayi* affair, has not been entirely so. With the weakening of the nearly absolute prewar caste barrier between *priyayi* and non-*priyayi* and the growing solidarity of all non-*santris* in the face of what they conceive to be the Moslem menace, the penetration of sophisticated *priyayi* philosophical systems into *abangan* society has increased.

VIII

In considering the *priyayi* economic position within the Javanese society generally, one immediately comes to wonder why they are so unlanded an aristocracy, relatively speaking. Their economic base lies, even today, almost wholly in the government bureaucracy. A few have accumulated a little land, a small number may have fairly extensive holdings, and the king has always had his estate, but by and large, Java's traditional ruling class has not been able to build up a truly feudal relationship to the peasant masses. In Modjokuto, although some *priyayi* have managed to buy a dozen acres or so as an economic cushion, there is almost no tendency for the urban clerk to develop serious property interests in the rural hamlet. Now, as in the past, the relations between the village and the town are almost wholly administrative and commercial.

The reasons for this situation are to be found wholly in history—a history still insufficiently clarified. The degree of political development reached by native Javanese "states"—if any such there were—prior to the coming of the Hindus; the form the contact with the Hindus took— whether the immigrants were mainly traders or priests, whether they settled mainly on the coasts or moved quickly inland, whether they were many or few; and the degree to which the early courts were integrated into the society generally are still all moot questions. But it seems clear that at no point have the ties between the courts and the people been well defined and stable ones. Whatever bonds have existed between the villagers and the nobles have been brittle and opportunistic rather than permanent and traditionalized. As the courts rose and fell the villagers shifted allegiance from one kingdom to the next, giving temporary allegiance to the one at the moment most able to provide maximum protection in return for taxes paid or services rendered.

With some exceptions, then, true feudalism was never able to get off the ground in Java. The *priyayi* have been almost entirely an urban class, and a permanent rural gentry living on the land has never appeared. Instead the tie between town and country has been a loose one in which temporary occupants of the lower ranks of the urban bureaucracy negotiated with relatively self-contained rural village units for support in exchange for protection, and it was this system the Dutch rationalized by eliminating the competition between bureaucracies. Even today the distinction between local and national regional government is very strong in peasant minds, and the crucially difficult link in government is that between the lowest rank of the centrally appointed and wholly urban bureaucracy and the elected leaders of the various village governments. Now, as in the past, the central government and the *priyayi* outlook which justifies it sits uneasily in the general social context of Javanese peasant society, with much less actual control over the behavior of the villager than it would seem at first glance to have. Without the intricate ties between the urban and rural gentry one finds, for example, in China, or without the deeply rooted, clearly defined, land-rights-linked social code of reciprocal obligations of feudal Europe, the *priyayi* has always found outward submission, exaggerated respect, and placating excuses easier to obtain from the *abangan* than actual obedience.

At any rate, and for whatever reasons, the *priyayi* are not today a class of large landholders, and their economic base lies almost entirely in the governmental bureaucracy. To this general statement one not very important exception must be made. The court culture, with its emphasis on art and on dress, gave rise to a native textile craft now known the world over as batik. Produced by drawing designs slowly and carefully in wax onto a piece of muslin and then dyeing the cloth—and repeating this process several times with different designs and different-color dyes—batik was originally worn almost entirely by *priyayi*. Batik making became, as a result, a rather important home industry in the great court centers. Often these industries were run by wives of lower-echelon court attendants and officials whose underpaid husbands were occupied with their obligations to king and country, and so a somewhat peculiar pattern of female-dominated textile industry grew up.

With the development of simpler and faster methods of production and the expansion of the market for batik beyond the court, the *santris* more and more pushed their way into the industry, until today many of the largest concerns are *santri*-run; but the low-level *priyayi,* somewhat accidentally in on the ground floor, managed to hold on to a certain part of the business. Before the war, in Modjokuto batik was sold almost entirely by a few *priyayi* women who bought the material from central Javanese cities; now, batik is sold mainly by *santris* and *abangans* in the market, though for the finest work one has to go to the homes of somewhat more upper-class women who still supplement their husband's meager salaries with a little genteel batik trading.

Thus, *priyayi* activity in both the rural agricultural, and urban small-trade sectors of the Javanese economy has been rather marginal at best. But with the coming of the twentieth century this group benefited almost exclusively, from greater educational opportunities, from the expanded demand for clerks and technical help induced by the Dutch plantation-factory enterprises, and from the ever-expanding role of the government in the country's economic life. The *priyayi* became the doctors, lawyers, and engineers as well as the accountants, personal secretaries, and sugar chemists, and when the revolution finally came they became also the civil servant inheritors of a governmental structure which had come to play a leading part in the organization of economic activities in the society in general and in the cities in particular. If the *santris* were the vanguard of petty capitalism in Java, the *priyayis* became, more or less accidentally and passively, the group most readily identifiable with the form of large-scale corporation-centered administered capitalism which has marked the Western industrial countries in this century.

Not, of course, that the economic structure typical of western Europe and the United States has appeared to any great degree in Java, or most particularly in Modjokuto, or that the *priyayi* represent a class of managers in the Western sense. But industrialization of any significant scope occurring today in the Javanese sector of the Indonesian economy is almost inevitably under the aegis of the central government, for the government is the only social institution capable of mobilizing the capital and, perhaps, of providing the directive personnel, and, as a result, larger enterprises are almost always directly or indirectly capitalized by the government and organized along lines similar to those of the civil bureaucracy, from whose ranks their managers are most often recruited.

In Modjokuto, there are two Javanese-owned factories whose scale of operation is noticeably greater than that of petty cottage industry; one is a large rice and sugar mill and one a beer-crate manufacturing concern. Both are somewhat mechanized, the first with diesel and electrically driven milling machines for both sugar and rice, the latter with electrically run power saws imported from West Germany, and both employ more than fifty workers. The first industry is owned and run by a man who is at once head of the regional chapter of the Nationalist political party (a largely *priyayi* organization), a representative on the executive board of the regional governing council, and a man with a marked *priyayi* outlook on life; his chief technical assistant is a former *priyayi* employee of a Dutch sugar factory. The second industry is run by a former official of the very forestry department upon whose decisions the fate and prosperity of his enterprise depends, as it is his ability to obtain wood—almost all of it government-owned—at economic prices which enables him to survive.

In addition, both industries were government-subsidized in part. Clearly a familiarity with the methods of the government bureaucracy as well as an ability to manipulate it both in its own terms and by means of personal contacts is a rather more important skill for a would-be Javanese entrepreneur than those one learns in small-scale, self-capitalized trade and cottage production.

The entrance of non-*priyayi* groups onto the political stage and the growth of a universal educational system since the revolution may serve to moderate this process somewhat, but with a near monopoly of what little advanced technical training the Dutch provided the Javanese, with the highest-developed skills of bureaucratic manipulation, and with a majority of the posts in the civil service in their hands, the *priyayi* are almost bound to play a major role in economic development in a country where the private sector of the economy is not likely to prove able to finance large-scale enterprises. If so, the pattern of industrial organization in Java, if ever it appears at all, may take a form consonant with the over-all rank-conscious *priyayi* ethic as previously defined, and the group of inward-looking mystic bureaucrats seemingly so unsuited to either agricultural or petty-capitalist forms of economic organization may find the more complex phases of economic development more congenial. Or perhaps they will merely suffocate them.

IX

The *abangan, santri,* and *priyayi* world outlooks are the major cultural orientations present in contemporary Modjokuto. Not only economic practices and occupational types, but political parties, social organizations, women's groups, residential areas, and familial relations tend to be organized and grouped according to these general rubrics. But it must be understood that these orientations are not hermetically sealed ideological systems, perfectly logical, perfectly articulated, and perfectly realized from which the social, economic, and political structures of Modjokuto are mere deductions. No more than the Westerner's is the Javanese individual's social behavior but the outcome of his ethical preferences and metaphysical assumptions; as the Westerner's, his actions are always and everywhere the complex result of ideological, religious, economic, political, familial, and wholly individualistic considerations.

In the foregoing analysis I have tried to present a picture of a series of social structural forms—occupational role types, forms of agricultural, commercial, and industrial organization—intersecting differentially with a series of religiously justified social ethics and to indicate the resultant patterns of behavior this intersection has produced. In the broader sense, the whole social organization on Modjokuto may be seen this way: it is a tenuous balance of forces, some ideological, some environmental, some organizational, in which the various factors so far outlined act in practice to produce a series of conflicts, compromises, and pure cases, as well as a number of exceptions to the rule; it is, as Max Weber once remarked, only because things are so very confused in practice that we must make our distinctions clear in theory.

It is also well to remember, though it cannot possibly be demonstrated here, that the three major cultural groups described above are neither wholly discontinuous, one with the next, nor does Javanese social organization take the form of three isolated subgroups united by mere geographical contiguity. Not only is there a common system of values, a deeper pan-Javanese world view underlying all three of the separate orientations described, but a town such as Modjokuto displays a genuine integration of each of them into a social structure wider than any of them. In a sense, the *priyayi* world view is but an intellectualization of the *abangan,* and the *abangan* a corruption of the *priyayi;* the *santri* ethic, for all its Near

Eastern pretentions, is still but a slightly differentiated interpretation of both *abangan* and *priyayi* conceptions. And the actual social relationships between individuals holding these slightly separate ethics within such a concrete community as Modjokuto is the most crucial study of all, for it can demonstrate the manner in which both social and cultural change occurs and depict the clash of value and power that forms the content of the historical process.

But even the relatively simple analysis presented here suggests interesting questions for social and cultural theory. What are the crucial factors determining the degree to which a given set of moral commitments finds adherents within a given society? To what degree is a religious system a dynamic factor in economic change and to what degree a mere outcome and reflection of it? What are the formal elements of various world outlooks which make them particularly conducive to certain patterns of economic organization? What is the nature of the motivational link between religious behavior and economic behavior? And is there a tendency toward sequential order in the development of either types of world view or forms of economic organization—is there such a thing as cultural drift and social evolution, and if there is what are its typical stages and what are the selective mechanisms producing it? Such questions are easier asked than answered; but in the microscopic investigation of concrete communities undergoing rapid social change—communities such as Modjokuto —some vague outlines of the replies we may eventually be able to give may be dimly discerned.

17

SECULARIZATION, MODERNIZATION, AND ECONOMIC DEVELOPMENT

Gino Germani

SOCIAL PROCESSES OF MODERNIZATION AND ECONOMIC PROCESSES OF DEVELOPMENT

A preindustrial society is transformed into a "developed" society through a series of very complex processes involving total change. To simplify, we can distinguish two main series of processes, each series including a complex of partial processes: the *economic* process of *development* and the *social* process of *modernization*. The two series may be correlated but at the same time are characterized by a certain degree of independence because the *sequence* of their successive stages can vary considerably with historical circumstances and internal (national) conditions, as well as external (international) ones. This same relative independence must be assumed of the partial processes that constitute each of the two main series.

We are dealing of course in gross simplifications. One must realize that the distinction between the two series is at least partly a question of analytic convenience. The differential synchronization of the total and partial processes also has a geographic aspect in the sense that an important distinction must be made in all cases between *central* areas (modern and developed) and *peripheral* ones (more archaic and less developed). The form taken by this relationship between the central and peripheral areas has important implications for the internal life of each nation, as well as for its position (that is, central or peripheral) within the international system. Those problems related to the synchronization of the different

This chapter is a revised version of an essay published in Resistência a Mudança *(Rio de Janeiro, 1960).*

processes of change would require a more detailed treatment than this discussion can afford.

Within each of the two series of processes we can distinguish two types of partial processes: (1) *primary* processes and (2) *secondary* processes of modernization and economic development, respectively. The former are the changes required to initiate the transition, that is, its necessary preconditions; the latter may be roughly defined as including (1) the extension of the primary processes to other institutions and social groups and other areas (that is from the central to the peripheral areas), (2) the intensification of such primary processes in the same institutions, groups, or areas where they first occurred, and (3) all the other effects, consequences, and changes induced by them in other parts of the social structure. It is important to note that secondary processes may occur in a given geographical area, as a result of primary processes occurring elsewhere (within the same national society, or originating from abroad).

This analysis is devoted to those processes of modernization (both primary and secondary) which are sometimes indicated by the name of *secularization*. While secularization is only a part of the total process of modernization, it is certainly one of its basic components. It refers to the more universal and necessary conditions required for the existence of a modern industrial society. At this point the existence of a variety of possible types of industrial societies as well as of forms of transition must be taken into account. It is legitimate and necessary to identify the universal and necessary characteristics of the transition, as well as the constant elements in industrial society (that is, those conditions characterizing *industrial society as such*). Such analysis, however, is only an initial approach to the problem, and although necessary as a first step, it can by no means be considered sufficient for the study of concrete historical processes. The usual dichotomic typology ("traditional" versus "industrial" society) is a convenient or perhaps a necessary point of departure. But any further analysis would require a typology of the various and divergent forms of transition and of industrial societies as well. Unfortunately, while it seems possible to delineate the general characteristics of industrial society, the construction of a valid typology of industrial societies and forms of transition is still lacking. The main reasons for the variety of industrial societies and types of transition should be sought not only in the difference among the various possible "starting points" (types of traditional societies), and historical circumstances characterizing the transition, but also in the variation in the possible types of sequences among the many partial primary and secondary processes.

A DEFINITION OF SECULARIZATION

Secularization is conceived here as a complex process including three basic modifications of the social structure: (1) type of social action: from *prescriptive to elective action;* (2) acceptance of change: from *institutionalization of tradition* to *institutionalization of change;* (3) institutional specialization: from a *relatively undifferentiated* complex of institutions to a higher degree of *institutional differentiation and specialization.*[1]

These changes occur at different levels. At the psychosocial level they affect attitudes and behavior, while at the normative level they affect institutions, values, statuses, roles, and other norms. But they do not necessarily involve all the members of a society, all types or areas of behavior and attitudes, all institutions and values. Secularization usually begins in relatively small groups (involving either the transformation of pre-existing minority sectors or the emergence of new groups), while the great majority of the population remains relatively unchanged. Also, from the point of view of geographic diffusion, these ruptures are localized in determined territorial areas (in some cities), while the rest may remain relatively unaffected during the first steps of the transition. The emergence of groups bearing new attitudes and values, or the transformation of pre-existing groups, is an expression of modifications produced in the society. They constitute a reaction to the fact that certain institutions of the pre-existent social system no longer function as normatively expected. I am referring here to the active response (the "mobilization") of groups *made available* by such disintegration who generate innovations in both attitudes and behavior.[2] We are speaking of minority or elite groups (in a broad sense, to distinguish them from the masses), for even when the process of dislocation has affected large parts of the population, the active response begins to arise from small sectors, either because the impact is particularly great on pre-existent elites or because new elite emerge from the interior of those sectors made "available." The active response, the "mobilization" of large segments of the population, also constitutes an essential aspect of modernization—but this is a "secondary" process, that is, a process that does *not necessarily precede* the first stages of the transition.

Among the three basic modifications mentioned above, the change in the type of social action is the more general requirement for the existence of modern industrial society, in the sense that institutionalization of change and institutional differentiation and specialization may be considered to a large extent consequences of the predominance of "elective action." For this reason, in describing the three modifications a more detailed analysis will be devoted to the topic.

FROM "PRESCRIPTIVE" TO "ELECTIVE" ACTION

Growth in rationality (especially instrumental rationality) is usually considered one of the main traits of secularization. In this sense it is maintained that "rational action" (or at least some type of rational action) tends to replace "traditional" action in many areas of behavior. While not denying the validity of this approach, in the present discussion "rational" action will be considered as a particular type of action within the category of "elective action." Not all elective actions are rational actions, and while secularization certainly involves a strong trend toward increased rationality, its more general trait is the exercise of *individual choices*—even if such choices are not always "rational." [3]

Elective and prescriptive actions occur within different types of normative frameworks which may be considered as "pure" types, or opposite poles of a continuum along which it should be possible to classify "mixed" (empirical) types. Prescriptive action takes place within a basically rigid normative system that limits the margin of possible variation by the actor. In the case of elective action, the normative framework not only is less rigid but *actually operates differently*. In the first case, a specific course of action is normatively imposed (and subjectively internalized) for each specific situation. In elective action, the normative system still regulates ends, means, and the relation between them, but it is characterized by the imposition of a certain degree of choice on the actor, rather than by the prescription of a fixed course of action. We may take as an example situations arising from a comparative analysis of industrial and nonindustrial societies. In the latter, status is more frequently ascribed than acquired. The son inherits the position of the father; the choice of profession does not imply a real decision, as there is a prescribed response to the problem of occupation. Furthermore, the actor has internalized a series of patterns that motivate him to occupy the position of his father and is socialized to develop the proper attitudes. The problem of the economic activity of the subject is thus resolved by society. On the other hand, what is the norm in industrial society? Here the prescription is that of *choosing a profession*. But does there exist absolute liberty to do so? Here also we find a series of conditions that the actor *must* (in the normative sense) take into consideration: his vocation, his aptitudes, his money, his social connections. Furthermore, the required choice must be made in accordance with certain criteria—the choice of an occupation is criticized if made in an "unrealistic" manner, for example, if one decides to be a pianist without considering the relevant aptitudes. The demand that *one must choose* an occupation is a *norm* that *must* be respected. The man who allows his parents to choose his occupation for him will be considered too dependent. A person who selects his father's occupation simply because it is his father's demonstrates an "abnormal" affective dependency on his father. It is hoped always that each person will choose an occupation in accordance with his vocation, and the choice is judged on such criteria. But it is essential to note that the criteria for this choice are prescribed. In this type of action, then, a normative system exists, but it is different from that system typical of prescriptive action. In one case, simply the assignment of a determined occupation is prescribed. In the other, the *choice* is prescribed, and also certain criteria for making it. In the type that we have called "prescriptive" one does not lack a certain latitude in his interpretation of the norm. It is possible as well that concrete situations may vary in a certain degree from the "typical" situations envisaged by the norm; here arises the necessity of "interpretation" to determine whether it is suitable to apply the norm. Thus, there arises a series of possible vacillations and deviations with respect to that which is socially prescribed. But this whole margin of variation does not change the nature of the prescriptive action which is characterized by its assignment of a determined response before a given situation (also "culturally defined"). Although it admits or tolerates a certain margin of variation (that can become fairly broad), it is not based, as is elective action, on a *prescription to choose*, an *affirmation of individual liberty* (and the *responsibility for the exercise of this liberty*), as a *value sustained by the culture* ("individualism"). It is rather *tolerance* rooted in the absence of sanctions against deviations that arise in the concrete application of a norm, either as the result of chance in this application or as the product of a certain imprecision in the circumstances which accompany each concrete situation and which make the socially established norm more or less applicable to each.

The *individual* character of decisions taken within the system of elective action contrasts as well with another characteristic that can be assigned to the prescriptive ideal type; in the latter, any decision that is taken within its fairly rigid and narrow limits tends to be a decision of the *collective order*, that is, taken by the group as such, considering its own interests, which may be above, and at times in conflict, with those of its present members. Not only is the choice of a spouse (and also divorce in some cases) based on an interpretation of relevant traditional rules, but also this very interpretation is charged to the familial group and not to the individuals directly affected. It is obvious that all action is action by single individuals, but in prescriptive action the individual acts as the carrier of group norms, values, and interests rather than his own or individual ones.

Collective choice in a system of elective action is based on very different norms and assumptions. This can be illustrated by the ideology of public opinion as expressed in liberal rationalist thought: here the decision of the group is assumed to be reached through the accommodation of individual wills, each individual supposedly deliberating and deciding *as such*.

It is important to distinguish the elective normative framework from the situation of *anomie*. *Structural* anomie has often been confused with the situation that arises in a type of society in which elective action predominates. Historically, the very development of the concept of anomie is partly linked to the formulation of the concept of elective action; for example, both are found in Durkheim (compare his two types of "egoistic" suicide). Durkheim also gives indications of the origin of this phenomenon, interpreting it as a result of rapid change from one type of society (rural, tradition, with a mechanical solidarity) to another (urban, industrial, with an organic solidarity). But it is clear that his origin is only one of a number of possible ones and that anomie can develop as much in predominantly prescriptive structures as in those characterized by elective action, although historically it has been in the latter that it has been observed most frequently.

Rational action may now be defined as a type of elective action in which the criteria of choice are based on some type of rationality (usually instrumental rationality), and this is the case of actions to be carried on in many areas of behavior in industrial society. But there are also elective actions based on nonrational criteria or which combine rational with other criteria. This occurs for instance when the individual is required in his choice genuinely to express his own personality, such as the "vocational" component in the choice of an occupation, or the emotional component in the choice of a mate. The more general and essential trait which distinguishes this type of action from traditional behavior is the existence of genuine individual choice, even if such choice is normatively expected to be based on nonrational criteria.

Most social actions in every society, traditional or modern, are based on habit. If a type of action is defined by its normative system, the fact that certain actions are empirically performed without reflection or deliberation is not relevant when judging the elective or prescriptive normative nature of the action. Although it would seem obvious that all traditional action is at the same time habitual, it is possible to show that these are two analytically distinct categories. Habitual action lacks any explicit reflection over all or part of the moments that integrate the course of the action. This takes place partially or totally below the level of consciousness or at least, if there is a *consciousness of execution,* there is still no *explicit reflection* as to the opportunity for undertaking the action, the means employed, the ends chosen, and the conditions considered. All of this is kept at an implicit level, when not totally below the threshold of consciousness, and action responds more or less automatically to a given situation. Now a *prescriptive* action is not necessarily automatic or based on habit. It may require reflection and even deliberation. Thus a *nonhabitual prescriptive* action supposedly elevates to the conscious level the internalized norms, to identify the situation, to determine if it corresponds to that foreseen by the norms, and eventually to resolve the problems of interpretations and adaptation of the norms themselves to concrete situations. As mentioned earlier, the prescriptive character of a normative system does not eliminate a margin of variation, indeterminacy, and indecision. Certainly many prescriptive actions are performed by habit: phenomenologically they seem to be automatic or almost automatic reactions to given situations. But, this does not mean that *all* habitual actions correspond to a prescriptive framework. The important point to be stressed here is that "habit" may correspond to an elective framework. The case of an elective action that is taken in whole or in part below the conscious level, without a reflection or deliberative phase, may seem a contradiction (an "elective action," or an action "by choice," without "choice"); but the paradox is resolved by the fact that the habitual aspect of the action is set in the context of an elective normative system. An elective action that has been repeated many times becomes almost habitual, and the whole elective and deliberative process becomes permanently implicit. This pattern can be seen in many economic actions taken in industrial society.[4] In this type of structure, the normative system is of the elective type, demanding instrumental rationality. However, many economic actions take place in a routine and habitual manner without a deliberative process of rational choice of means. This is certainly the case in much action by consumers who become used to spending their income in a routine or almost automatic manner, and it is true of numerous actions taken by managers or entrepreneurs.

With respect to habitual action by consumers, one may object that they are following prescriptive norms defining the "proper" level of living of each social group. Although this cannot be denied, it must be remembered that in an industrial society, the "ascriptive" (or traditional) character of these norms is gradually diminished by the stimulus toward greater consumption. An impulse for higher levels of aspiration—an impulse at the same time institutionalized—introduces strong elements of choice into the consumption pattern. For example, according to some research on consumer behavior, its character (habitual or not) depends on the importance of the purchase and whether or not it is repetitive. The case of habitual action by a manager reveals most clearly the relation between habit and choice. Take the example of certain expenditures, as those for advertising; often they are made entirely automatically, based on decisions taken once and never or seldom opened for re-examination. The same is true of many other managerial decisions (pricing, calculation of costs, restocking, and so on). Many political actions in stable democracies have this habitual character as well, in spite of the expressly elective nature of their normative systems.[5] It is obvious that the habitual character of these actions does not mean that they are prescriptive; they are instead actions of an elective type (corresponding to an elective normative system), but they are performed as habitual actions. Quantitatively, habitual actions represent a great majority, corresponding to the functional process whereby behavior that was once conscious passes to an automatic, unconscious, repetitive level. A very large part of culture is not manifest, but intervenes in behavior patterns under the form of habitual action. Furthermore, to the degree to which we can differentiate the various normative systems, we are also able to distinguish their elective or prescriptive character (in the sense here defined).

We must clarify the notion of "habit" as used here, for it refers only to behavior that is *learned* and that, in some way, has reference to a system of norms; that is, applies to *regulated* conduct. It is possible that this may become completely automatic (at the conscious level) or may have been so since learned, if the process of internalization took place very early in the life of the individual; but even in these cases, the observer can infer the existence of a normative system that molds the apparently automatic behavior.

Finally, we must mention one last possibility. Although historically one can observe a tendency toward the successive extension of the elective normative system, in all societies (including the urban, industrial, "developed" ones) there are important areas organized within a prescriptive framework. In spite of this, it is possible that "traditions" may be redeveloped in areas characterized previously by choice. In this case, the rise of a prescriptive system is the result of a process linked to changes that include a sphere of values and norms of a wider significance than the specific area in which the changes themselves can be verified. Given the significance of this process, the mere fact of habit is not sufficient to accomplish such a transformation in the normative system (not solely because an action is repeated does it become a tradition); however, it is very possible that the passage from an elective to a prescriptive system is *accompanied* often by habit.

FROM THE INSTITUTIONALIZATION OF TRADITION TO THE INSTITUTIONALIZATION OF CHANGE

Traditional society is rooted in the past, rejecting all that is new while reaffirming the repetition of pre-established patterns. All change, in this type of society, is seen as profoundly abnormal and as *always constituting a violation of the norms.* In industrial society, on the other hand, *change becomes a normal phenomenon,* one anticipated and institutionalized by the norms themselves.[6] These set what we might call the rules of change. The most illustrative example, other than that of the economy, may be found in science, where assertions are *always* provisional. They can *always* be replaced by others, but *always* according to the established methodological canons. These canons, therefore, constitute the normative system of change itself.

The institutionalization of change and elective action seems somewhat of a paradox in view of the essential function that forms of integration, based on a prescriptive framework, perform for the maintenance of stability. Here one may find a structural source of tension which may induce further elements of change.

INSTITUTIONAL DIFFERENTIATION AND SPECIALIZATION

Preindustrial society—especially the preliterate type—has a relatively undifferentiated structure for the performance of functions. In industrial society, each function tends to be specialized, thus spawning a series of structures each increasingly specific and limited to determined and clearly fixed tasks. This, again, can be seen especially in the realm of economic activities which, in preindustrial societies, does not possess clearly differentiated institutions. On the contrary, it is the family which, in this aspect as in others, assumes the central role. The family, the local community, and the religion are all tightly linked and embrace the greater part of the gamut of human activity. With industrial society comes an increasingly accentuated differentiation of function. The economy assumes particular importance and creates its own organization. The same occurs with education, political activity, recreational or expressive activity, and so forth. It is essential here to observe that old institutions are also transformed and specialized.

All society involves differentiation and relative structural complexity; in this respect one should establish a clear distinction between the labels applied to "primitive" cultures, preliterate ones, and "historical" nonindustrial societies, in which the degree of differentiation and specialization is undoubtedly much above that of the former. But in modern societies the process continues to the extreme of modifying the type of structure. Thus it is also legitimate to distinguish this type of society from the "historical" nonindustrial ones.

It should also be pointed out that the increasing specialization and differentiation of corresponding normative spheres tends to give rise as well to a plurality of value systems (insofar as they are also adaptable to institutional specialization). Each institutional sphere tends to acquire *autonomy of values*. This in no way affects the hypothesis of the interdependence or interrelation of all the parts of the social structure, integrated to varying degrees around central and common values. It is obvious, however, that with respect to this last type of integration, secularized societies are characterized by much less "valorative congruence," although this does not eliminate the possibility of the existence of certain underlying common values.

From the point of view of economic institutions, change thus presupposes the emergence of a specific normative system, governing both economic values and attitudes, with its correlates at the level of motivation and personality type.

THE LIMITS OF SECULARIZATION

One of the more intriguing problems of the social sciences is the definition of the minimum universal conditions for the functioning of an industrial structure. In the past century England could be taken as the paradigm answering this question. Everyone knows now that there are various models for industrial society and various types of transition, and basic features reviewed above seem very general (although colored by the Western experience). But from here questions arise; (1) to what point must the process of secularization proceed and (2) which are necessary and which are accidental consequences of this process (considering their extension to different sectors of society as well as their degree of intensity)? We can postulate the existence of a limit, as a universally functional necessity. If this is so, in all industrial society the secularization process itself will have to develop within a normative framework that assures a minimum base of integration. This opens the question as to whether, for the functioning of industrial society, a certain degree of secularization must be extended to all sectors of society, or whether this is only necessary in those spheres most closely linked to economic development. Finally we should also answer the question of whether it is possible to limit secularization to a certain level and restrict it to determined sectors, or if, on the contrary, we are dealing with a process endowed with an internal autonomy that, once begun, reaches a maximum of intensity and extension beyond control.

Discussions of these themes have occupied a considerable part of sociology, as much in the last century as in the present. And a good part of the ideological controversies of our day take the form of distinct and opposite positions on this very problem. The difficulty in keeping the discussion on a purely scientific plane, free from valorative and ideological connotations, is obvious here and does not require special commentary. As is known, formulations in functional terms often mask ideological positions. Limiting the discussion to purely economic concerns (as in many discussions of the conditions of economic development) does not eliminate these connotations. It simply eliminates them from the realm of possible discussion, turning them into inexplicit premises of tacit assumptions behind positions that, on the surface, appear to be purely technical or economic.

It will be difficult to avoid all these valorative connotations in the discussion that follows. The criterion to be used in describing the scope of secularization, in both its extension and its intensity, will be that of the minimal conditions for the functioning of a type of social organization compatible with the basic requirements of economic development. We shall now attempt at least partially to answer these questions.

SECULARIZATION AND INTEGRATION

All society presupposes—as a universal functional requirement—the existence of a minimal level of normative integration. This term indicates the existence of an underlying nucleus of norms shared by all the members of the society. Adopting a sufficiently broad definition of norms, this means that the common nucleus would have to include cognitive elements, as well as valorative and regulative ones. "Sacred" or nonsecularized societies accord this requisite considerable preponderance: the three features previously pointed out (the prescriptive character of the action, the perpetuation of the tradition, and finally the undifferentiated character of the institutions) produce as a consequence the very high degree of homogeneity and stability that all typologies attribute to this type of society. Nevertheless, as our discussion of elective action and the institutionalization of change demonstrates, societies characterized by a high level of secularization also rely on a certain degree of normative integration, the very minimum necessary to assure the existence of the *criteria* of choice and change.

An appropriate illustration can be found in modern science. This is composed of a series of propositions (for each discipline) of a provisional character; that is, potentially, at least, each proposition can be substituted for the other. Permanent change, however, takes place within a fixed system, based on criteria governing the acceptance or rejection of propositions. Only in this way is it possible to speak of a "science" relatively integrated with respect to both substantive contents and the human group bearing and believing in those contents: the scientists. The society —the social group of scientists—will exist as such only as long as its members continue to participate within the common normative framework, that of the criteria for accepting and rejecting scientific propositions. The so-called crisis of science, since the end of the past century until the present, seems to be precisely a discussion of the validity and universality of this normative framework itself (as, for example, the debate about the criteria of truth). But since this debate has been limited to the philosophical sphere, without disturbing the concrete labor of the scientists relying on the essentials of this normative framework, it has not dislocated nor disintegrated science as an institution or human group. (This latter could occur, however, with the disappearance of normative consensus.)

MINIMUM AREAS OF SECULARIZATION IN INDUSTRIAL SOCIETY

Secularization in the field of science, technology, and economy is certainly a minimum universal requirement for the existence of industrial society. A degree of secularization in the three areas is also a precondition (that is, a primary process as defined earlier), but the degree of the primary process at the beginning of the transition and the nature of secondary processes of secularization in the same area will vary a great deal according to the social setting and historical circumstances of the transition.

Modern science as well as technology is distinguished by the three aspects of secularization: "electivity," "institutionalization of change," and "increasing specialization." Science should be distinguished from all other intellectual activities or forms of knowledge (as for example theology and philosophy)—a distinction affecting not only the content of science but also its material and social organization in teaching and research. The principle of its functional autonomy should be dominant without limitations. In the field of natural knowledge secularization is certainly a primary process, but its extension to the social sciences takes the form of a secondary process, varying, again, with the various cultural settings and historical conditions.

In the *economy* the process of secularization signifies, first, the differentiation of *specifically economic institutions*—that is, those organized on the basis of norms and values free from connotations of religion, morality, aesthetics, or prestige, and generally oriented toward the demand of efficiency—incorporating instrumental rationality as a basic principle of action and the institutionalization of change. Whatever the variance of political or economic organization in industrial society, all the basic aspects of the economy are transformed.

Economic activity will probably be concentrated in a type of specific organization that—whatever its legal system (private, collective, "mixed," state-sponsored)—should be characterized basically by *rationality* and all its consequences (bureaucratic organization and so forth).

Forms of property, exchange, division of labor and its organization, distribution and the allocation of human and material resources to different sectors of the population, should be oriented toward the principles of efficiency and change. A phenomenon of "mobility" should be produced in all those aspects as they acquire their own dynamism, unhampered or minimally hampered by the sociocultural structures pertaining to the other sectors of the society.

Historically this secularization of the economy has taken place in various forms. In countries of earlier modernization this assumed the economic and political form broadly termed "liberal." But in those countries in which the process occurred later on, or is now going on, there have appeared a great variety of other forms that generally can be called "nonliberal." Furthermore, in these same countries significant transformations have been experienced that have distinctly removed them from primitive structures. Although it is difficult to arrive at a conclusion on this point, which belongs to the realm of ideological controversy, it is now obvious that the rise of industrial society can be accompanied by either "liberal" or "nonliberal" forms, as long as both result in secularization in the three spheres of science, technology, and the economy. This mere affirmation, however, leaves unanswered some of the major questions related to the conditions that determine the appearance of one form or the other, the stability of each one, the comparative cost of the various forms of development, and their consequences for the other aspects of society.

In each of the sectors indicated (science, technology, economy) the process of secularization should be extended to all levels: the normative level in the larger sense and the motivational level (or that of personality). In other words, the attitudes corresponding to the new normative framework of the secularized society must be internalized, and the new personality types suited to this type of structure must arise. This condition has often been pointed out as, for example, in the emergence of *managerial* attitudes and, in more advanced stages, "general" motivations adapted to industrial work and to the capacity of responding to the particular incentives of this work, and so on. As these conditions have been described numerous times, there is no need to dwell on them here.

SECULARIZATION AND SOCIAL STRATIFICATION

The development of an advanced economy imposes at least two requirements essential to the stratification system. In the first place, just as the division of labor is subjected to the principle of efficiency, traditional types of stratification also undergo substantial change. A great number of obsolete offices and occupations disappear, while a growing number of new activities arise. In the second place, the assignment of people to different tasks, which in most underdeveloped societies tends to follow the system of *ascription,* must now be transformed substantially to that of achievement. In other words, it must assure a greater social and ecological mobility so that the recruitment of personnel for different positions in the occupational structure is governed by the principle of efficiency, rather than other considerations like family, religion, ethnicity, and such. It is for this reason that a *relatively open class structure* (or some equivalent) must be considered one of its requirements or a basic condition for its functioning. It is known that the degree of social and ecological mobility in developed society—although usually greater than that in traditional stratification structures—is still very far from the theoretically possible maximum of a strict equality of opportunity and access to all positions according to the principle of efficiency. Certain obstacles, existing in all known societies, tend to limit the full functioning of this requirement of maximum social mobility, that is, the principle of maximum instrumental rationality in the assignment of people to different functions and tasks. It is a debatable question whether such obstacles represent a universal characteristic of all society or are merely features observed in all historical societies up to the present but are not necessarily linked to all types of social structure and may disappear in some future type. In any case, the

present existence of such obstacles indicates a limit to the process of secularization in the sector of social stratification. It has been noted that this
limitation is bound up with other functional requirements, for example,
the necessity of maintaining familial institutions.[7]

In spite of these limitations, however, and regardless of the economic
and political forms assumed in the modernization process, societies reaching a certain level are preoccupied with establishing normative mechanisms
that, without modifying the stratification system, tend to compensate
partially for those obstacles limiting the rational selection of personnel,
especially for scientific and technical tasks. Thus in the early phases
of developing societies the need for universal primary education was proclaimed, followed by its extension to the secondary level and by the establishment of other educational reforms capable of rationalizing the recruitment system. It is important to observe that, if on the one hand this
was the result of the greater cultural and political participation of the
popular classes, it also was and is (often expressly) a response to the need
for a maximum use of human resources. This tendency, however, could
coexist with a contradictory phenomenon: the growing numerical limitation and inaccessibility of the highest levels of the class structure (especially in the so-called "power elite"). In this case, greater mobility and a
rational distribution of personnel would take place solely in the lower
and middle levels, while an opposite tendency would appear at the top.

Extensive secularization of the stratification system must be considered
a secondary process. In fact, according to some widely known theories,
what is needed (at least as a necessary if not a sufficient condition) to
initiate the process of modernization is some kind of partially blocked
upward or downward mobility, some type of status deprivation.[8] This
may be considered as a form of mobility not fully accepted or not fully
legitimized in terms of the still predominant values and norms of the society, that is, *noninstitutionalized* or *de facto mobility*. Such a situation is
likely to cause the displacement of a group, to mobilize it against the *status
quo,* and eventually to transform it into a modernizing elite. In contrast
with this process of noninstitutionalized nobility, the mobility required for
the smooth functioning of a mature industrial society must be fully institutionalized. A certain degree of complete mobility (mobility on all dimensions of a stratification system) should be normatively expected (within
the structural limits indicated in the previous discussion). Such institutionalized mobility is then a requirement for the stability of any industrial social system, even if the various types of industrial society offer
different solutions for this general requirement.[9] A related secondary
process is the rising aspirations of the lower strata who everywhere tend to
achieve in practice the equalitarian principles somewhat implicit in industrial society. Along with other aspects this process gives rise on the one
hand to the protest movements characteristic of industrialization, while

on the other it becomes a powerful factor for further change in the social structure. In one way or another it leads to actual increase in the participation of the traditionally excluded sectors.

The sequences between these primary and secondary processes of change as well as their respective rates may vary a great deal in different societies and under different historical conditions. Taking as a reference the Western experience, it may be said that in these presently advanced countries both structural and psychosocial changes tended to follow the more mature stages of economic development. The spread of rising aspirations among the great majority of the individuals belonging to the lower strata was more gradual and tended to keep pace with the actual structural transformation of the stratification system, especially with changes in its profile (as with the expansion of the middle strata) and the institutionalization of mobility. In presently developing countries other types of sequences may occur. In the more common case attitudinal changes—the so-called "revolution of rising expectations"—is taking place at a much less advanced stage of economic development, and the rate of the mobilization process is much higher than in the Western case. This means that new attitudes are created without counterparts in the occupational structure, the stratification system, the actual rate of mobility (and most often its legitimation), the level of consumption and other forms of participation into the modern type of life. As is well known, this situation turns the "rising expectations" into "rising frustrations." In the Western experience widespread social unrest and deep social conflict accompanied the extension of participation (in its various forms), but the integration of the emerging sectors of the population could take place through gradual reform because the structural changes produced by economic development permitted a relatively easier absorption of the conflicts. It must be noted that not all differences can be imputed to the higher rate of mobilization of the larger strata and the ensuing social pressure "from below." Other significant and no less important factors intervene to use such potential pressure and turn it into a powerful means for drastic social change: the type of available elites and their attitudes, the type of predominant ideologies, the existence of various and contrasting models for development, and the peripheral and often subordinated position of the developing countries.

A different type of sequence, less common than the one described, involves structural changes in the stratification system very similar to those which have occurred in advanced societies, but based on a less developed economic structure. This is possible in relatively rich countries with a medium level of per capita income and where the rate of urbanization, the degree of bureaucratization, and the growth of a modern service sector —especially education—has been higher than the rate of industrial growth proper and took place at less advanced stages of economic development (as compared with the Western model). The considerable expansion of the urban middle strata is likely to cause sociological and psychosocial consequences very similar to those observed in fully advanced societies. However, lacking the corresponding economic structure, this type of "premature" modernization of the stratification system has given rise to serious obstacles to further development. This is the case of some of the relatively developed but stagnant Latin American countries, such as Argentina and Uruguay.

SECULARIZATION AND POLITICAL ORGANIZATION

Only two aspects of this complex question have been selected for the present discussion. The first refers to the *rational organization* of the state as one of the necessary conditions of development. This is well known, having been formulated long ago by Max Weber and others. The experience of recent decades suggests the possibility, however, of certain significant variations in the forms in which rationalization takes place. In the countries most advanced in the process, the type of administrative and political organization tended to be rationalized to the maximum. At the same time, the type of authority assumed—within certain limits—this same form, with traditional and charismatic components diminishing considerably. In countries where change was initiated much later, however, the organization of the state acquired a rationalized form, but the type of authority, particularly on the highest levels, assumed nonrational forms.

It is possible that this phenomenon is related to the particular necessities of normative integration found in countries undergoing a very rapid rhythm of secularization: in these cases, the loyalty to the national state and its symbolic personification reach the required intensity only if accompanied by forms of charismatic authority.

It is probable, moreover, that this phenomenon is related to the general tendency toward centralization. Those countries would pass thus almost without transition from what we can call traditional centralization to the newest forms of concentration of power, linked to advanced forms of technical and economic development.

The second aspect regards the degree of participation of the popular strata in political institutions. Although here there are also striking differences between advanced and developing countries, in both the degree of participation indicated above is very much higher than that more commonly observed in traditional society. It is difficult to distinguish whether this experience in participation constitutes a necessary condition of development or whether it is an implication (an inevitable consequence) of this. At any rate, whatever the political form assumed—and even when such participation turns out to be merely illusory—the position of the popular strata in developed societies varies substantially with secularization, as it has been defined here. This increase in participation is undoubtedly a result of changes in social stratification, but it is also part of the rupture of the limits of the local community and the transfer of loyalties to the national community. The extension of political participation is a secondary process, and here again one may observe that it is taking place at a different rate and in a different sequence with regard to the stages of economic development in presently developing countries, as compared to the past experience of more advanced ones. The pattern is the same as was noted with regard to the stratification system: an acceleration of the growth of political participation involving an inversion of the sequence between economic development and this partial process of social modernization.

SECULARIZATION AND THE FAMILY

Some degree of secularization in familial relations constitutes a necessary condition of development. As is well known, the scope of primary relations (like those that characterize the family) should be kept to a minimum to allow for the secondary type of relations required by the institutions peculiar to a developed society. The first, as opposed to the latter, consists of relations that are diffuse, affectively charged, particularistic, and governed by ascription. The latter condition, however, requires relations that are specific, affectively neutral, universalistic, and based on achievement. Solely by accentuating this second type of relation will it be possible to achieve an extreme specialization of functions and institutions and, at the same time, the optimum allocation of personnel on the basis of efficiency. Consequently, the sphere for the application of kinship relations is reduced to the minimum, as are all types of extended family relations. It has been pointed out that this is a source of tension implicit in the very nature of industrial society and perhaps a possible intrinsic limit to secularization. Indeed, the permanence of primary type groups (and especially of an institution like the family) is often considered a functional and universal requirement, at least in historically observed societies, in the sense that it discharges functions that can only be accomplished in structures of this type (as the socialization of the child and the creation of an intimate group for the sustenance of the adult personality). The whole of the social structure, especially the stratification system, is affected by this limitation. The impersonal milieu created by the predominance of secondary relations emphasizes the necessity of the continuous formation of primary groups; thus, for example, small groups defined by secondary relations (as work groups and such) tend to become transformed into primary ones if the interaction is prolonged. The kinship group itself, extended beyond the bounds of the nuclear family, never disappears. On the contrary, it tends to remain at least as a preferred field of recruitment for spontaneous primary groups.

Up to now, we have dealt with the necessary reduction in the operative limits of primary relations to the isolated nuclear family and spontaneous primary groups. As another necessary consequence, substantial modifications occur in many aspects of the primary relations themselves. Without losing their primary character, they acquire different characteristics than those they held or were given in traditional society. In particular, interpersonal relations within the nuclear family tend to be more egalitarian, as there is greater participation by all members in the different activities of the group, as well as greater access to the decisions of the group, and as the stability of the group itself becomes based more on volition than on mechanically applied normative prescriptions. One of the most important phenomena of this whole process—one that can be taken as a general measurement of levels of secularization—is birth control, that is, the introduction of deliberate instrumental rationality into one of the most intimate spheres of human life. It appears fairly clear that all these results are nothing but an extension of the principle of elective action to larger areas of behavior. This process is characterized by its emphasis on new *values,* particularly in the affirmation of the individual and his full development. This is a field dominated by ideological controversies, as it is here that the most resistance arises. It is also a question open to scientific debate as to whether these results are rigidly determined by changes in social organization required by development, or whether there exist certain structural alternatives that, on the one hand, assure the minimal conditions of development and, on the other, maintain traditional forms in these sectors of behavior.

Various authors have criticized the hypothesis, generally accepted until now, of a closer correlation between the type of industrial structure and the predominance of the nuclear family. While, on the one hand, a functional alternative for this type of family may exist in developing societies, on the other hand, there are examples of nonindustrial societies with nuclear families of the Western type.[10] Following this line of reasoning, the hypothesis has been suggested of a great degree of indeterminacy between the family structure and other parts of the social structure, especially of a wider range of compatibility between the industrial structure and family type. Accordingly, the diffusion of the nuclear family in Western developed societies would be rather a historical coincidence: those countries were characterized *before* the transition by such a family type, rather than developing it as a consequence of the transition itself.

This historical coincidence, moreover, can also be interpreted in another sense. Inverting the causal relation between the industrial structure and the nuclear family, we could consider the existence of this type of family as one of the preconditions facilitating the rise of industrial society (emphasizing the value of the individual, diminishing the scope of ascriptive relations, and so on).[11]

These and other criticisms of the hypothesis of a close functional relation between the isolated nuclear family and the industrial structure are, of course, of great importance and should be remembered: however, they do not seem to support the contrary hypothesis of an almost complete indeterminacy or absence of correlation between the two. Rather, in many cases, the facts can be interpreted in accordance with the hypothesis. Japan is a good illustration, often cited as the classic case of the permanence of the traditional family despite its advanced level of technical-economic development. In that country, the divorce rate appears to diminish instead of increase with the advance of industrialization; at the same time, the divorce rate in rural areas is higher than that in urban areas. Thus, we find in Japan correlations exactly the opposite of those established in Western countries. But rather than negating the hypothesis of the interdependence between the nuclear family and the industrial structure—as it would appear superficially—this could be interpreted, on the basis of a more detailed examination of the data, as a confirmation of it. Such is the conclusion of some of those conducting research on this topic.[12] The "starting point" in the case of Japan "was a society in which lineage and not matrimony was sacred." Divorce was permitted and rates were high. But it was a very different kind of divorce from that of the West: it was rather a "traditional" type of divorce, determined by the familial group and exercised essentially in favor of this group and its continuity (as with the repudiation of a sterile woman). Industrialization and urbanization weakened exactly this type of family and the ideas that sustained it. The individual began to emerge from the kinship group, and marriage began to be seen as an individual affair. Consequently, the decline of the divorce rate should be interpreted as a symptom of the weakening of the traditional structure. On the other hand, the authors could distinguish another type of divorce, of a Western variety, based on the individual decisions of the partners. This type of divorce, precisely an expression of the nuclear family that was emerging in the transition toward a more advanced industrial structure, was, on the contrary, increasing. In other words, the total divorce rate represented a balance between two opposing tendencies: a decrease in "traditional" divorce and increase in "modern" divorce. Concomitant with this process an inversion was observed in later years in the differences between urban and rural divorce, that is, a higher rate of divorce in urban areas.

The Japanese example is sufficiently illustrative of the type of modifications (or, better, specifications) that should be introduced in the generic hypothesis of correlation between "modern" family type and industrial structure. The basic characteristic is the introduction of a normative system of the elective type in relations previously of a prescriptive nature. But the particular forms of the transition depend on the pre-existent traditional structure, and it is probable that the family type that emerges is considerably influenced by such a structure. In particular, it is possible that the rapidity of the transition, as much as the degree of the extension of election in the field of familial relations, can vary widely.

SECULARIZATION IN OTHER ASPECTS OF THE SOCIAL STRUCTURE

It has already been noted that education tends to spread to the whole population and that it becomes necessary to reduce the differences in educational opportunities caused by stratification. Another essential condition is the change in educational content: a very great increment in technical and scientific instruction is required, and, as is known, this requirement usually clashed with prestige values that are assigned in traditional societies to nontechnical forms of knowledge. This applies particularly to the humanistic form of upper-class education, but also to other attitudes and values, especially religious ones. The problem that must be resolved here is that of defining the limits of this transformation of educational content and of determining to what degree it is possible to integrate the two types of education. This question is tightly bound up with the extension of secularization to other objects of knowledge besides those referred to as "natural." If indeed the rise of a natural *science* is a condition immediately linked to economic development, the extension of this type of knowledge to the sphere of human actions is probably another necessary condition, determined, however, more by the transformation of the social organization and interpersonal relations than by economic development directly. The less direct character of this link and the fact that this sphere of knowledge is more impinged upon by the values of the traditional society can explain the greater resistances to the secularization of knowledge in the social sciences. At any rate, historically this process of secularization strictly accompanies economic development, and the advances in scientific sociology in particular in all countries in recent years has been universally recognized as an expression of this process.

According to the general principle of institutional specialization, those structures that in the past tended to encompass the whole society must now be circumscribed by well-defined specific functions. We have already seen that this is the case with respect to family organization and kinship groups; another illustration is religion. The importance of religion, especially in the first stages of development (as much in a positive as a negative sense), is well known and will not be dealt with here. We wish to point out, however, that as an essential condition of development, religion also acquires a specific sphere, that is, it must be transformed into a specialized institution. This has a series of consequences on the other results (implications) of development, for example, on changes in the family, the position of women, education, science, individual values, and so on.

The present discussion does not attempt to cover all the aspects of secularization, but has been limited to a few selected for their importance or as appropriate illustrations of the process.

OBSTACLES AND RESISTANCES TO SECULARIZATION AND DEVELOPMENT

Obstacles to changes connected with the process of secularization can arise in any of the areas discussed and generally do in all of them, although with different degrees of intensity; these differences are due to the particular historical and cultural circumstances in which development itself takes place. Following the scheme presented up to here, we can classify these obstacles into different groups.

1. Obstacles based on tensions implicit in the very structure of industrial society. We have seen at least three aspects of these possible "functional contradictions" to the impulse toward the expansion of secularization: (1) the necessity of maintaining a minimal base of normative integration, (2) the necessity of maintaining structures oriented toward "primary" relations, and (3) other contradictions arising about the stratification system.

2. Obstacles originating in the pre-existing structures. These, in turn, can be classified into three groups: (1) those rooted in each one of the structures subjected to modification (secularization), (2) those which originate in the coexistence of secularized structures with others still persisting from previous stages, and (3) obstacles arising from the disorganization provoked by the transition from one system to another (for example, the destruction of the traditional structures and the imperfect of nonexistent reorganization of the new "secular" structures).

3. Obstacles originating in particular forms of transition and especially in the nature of the sequences between the various partial processes.

While the obstacles classified in the first group must be considered, on the basis of accepted hypotheses, of a *permanent character* and a source of permanent tension (and change) in industrial societies, the other two groups are typical of *transition*. It is also important to observe that, while the first are independent of the cultural type and historical circumstances of each country, the second and the third are tied much more closely to national peculiarities, so that the latter determine not only the importance of the obstacles but also the specific form assumed by development and by the limits of secularization.

It is obvious that the distinctions formulated above, although helpful in understanding the nature of the obstacles and the varying limits of secularization in each case, will only furnish this help when employed as a method of investigation, not as simple criteria of classification.

Empirically, the majority of obstacles arise as conflicts among groups and, in a good many cases (not in all, of course), assume an ideological expression. In this respect, it is convenient to distinguish "total" from "partial" obstacles to development:

1. *Total* resistance to the development and, in particular, to the adoption of the necessary attitudes in the spheres of natural science, technology, and economic activity (in the strict sense). This type of obstacle has received most attention from economists, sociologists, and anthropologists. Here the resistance to secularization arises directly from the persistence of internalized traditional patterns; for example, the prestige of certain traditional occupations, of certain forms of propriety, and so forth; the absence of motivation for industrial work and the lack of "entrepreneurial" or "managerial" attitudes and the like. These obstacles do not always assume an ideological form, although they tend to do so when they become open group conflict. To the degree to which they are a direct expression of a "social character," incapable of accomplishing the types of actions required by development, they are conducive to "disorganization," lack of adaptation, and so on. At other times they do assume an ideological character, while there are many forms that have both characteristics. For example, the first "protest movements" of workers faced with industrial work could be interpreted as ideological resistance based on attitudes rooted in a "traditional social character" inadequate for this type of activity. This type of resistance tends to reject the entire process and to cling to the existing situation in its preindustrial stage. This resistance can be more or less "blind" (that is, more or less conscious of its real situation), but it should be distinguished from the types of resistance that accept in principle the necessity of economic development while rejecting part of its conditions and implications or results.

2. *Partial* resistance to development and/or some of its consequences, especially that of the secularization of determined aspects of social organization. This type of resistance generally assumes ideological form and tends to rise from or be directed by groups at least partially secularized. Among the principal areas in which we encounter this type of resistance are the following:

—Social stratification: resistance to the modification of the system of closed strata.

—Political organization: resistance to the extension of the level of political participation.

—Familial organization: resistance to the acceptance of the degree of secularization of the family implied in development and the tendency to maintain traditional forms inadequate to the new structure.

—Scientific knowledge: resistance to the extension of the type of natural scientific knowledge to the disciplines of social science.

—Education: resistance to the extension of education to all social strata; resistance to the acknowledgment of the importance of scientific and technical education.

—Central social values: resistance to the acceptance of some value changes implicit (or supposedly implicit) in development (rational individualism and the like).

Many of the problems that are the source of conflict revolve around the consequences of development whose ties to it have been under discussion and which can be interpreted as "unnecessary." As stated previously, these conflicts express, in part, implicit contradictions in all industrial society. The possibility of transcending the ideological level of the conflict depends, therefore, on a more penetrating investigation of that society.

NOTES

1. This essay has been greatly influenced by W. E. Moore, especially his "The Social Framework of Economic Development with Reference to Latin America," UNESCO International Office on Social Implications of Technological Change (mimeo, 1956).

2. The concepts of availability, mobilization, integration as used here are analyzed in Gino Germani, "Mobilization and Social Tension," in L. I. Horowitz (ed.), *The New Sociology* (New York, 1964).

3. An important antecedent of the distinction presented here concerning social action is the formulation by David Riesman, in turn inspired by Erich Fromm and others, treating the three types of social character: "traditional," "inner-directed," "outer-directed." The first could be considered the character structure corresponding to the framework of "prescriptive" action, the second to that of "elective" action. The "outer-directed" type is better seen as a variant also corresponding to the "elective" framework: here there is still individual choice (it is normatively expected), but the "criteria" for choice are defined differently than in the case of the "inner-directed" character. Cf. David Riesman *et al.*, *The Lonely Crowd* (New Haven, Conn., 1950), Ch. 1; Erich Fromm, *The Fear of Freedom* (London, 1945), Ch. 3.

4. Examples of *habit* in "elective" actions, presumably of a *rational* (instrumental) type—as economic actions—can be found in George Katona, *Psychological Analysis of Economic Behavior* (New York, 1951), pp. 231–232 on price setting, pp. 50–52 on other "routine" activities, pp. 67 and following on routine consumer behavior.

5. The importance of "family tradition" in voting decisions, pointed out by many studies in the United States and also France, is a good example of this possible resurgence of prescriptive action in a sphere characterized for a certain time by an "elective" framework. Cf. H. H. Hyman, *Political Socialization* (Glencoe, Ill., 1958), Ch. 4; S. M. Lipset *et al.*, "The Psychology of Voting," in Gardner Lindzey, *Handbook of Social Psychology*, 2 vols. (Cambridge, Mass., 1954), Vol. II.

6. Talcott Parsons, *The Social System* (Glencoe, Ill., 1951), pp. 58 and following; Parsons *el al.*, *Toward a General Theory of Action* (Cambridge, Mass., 1952), pp. 80 and following; M. J. Levy, *The Structure of Society* (Princeton, N.J., 1952), p. 108.

7. See, for example, Parsons, *The Social System*.

8. M. J. Levy, "Contrasting Factors in the Modernization of China and Japan," in Simon Kuznets, W. E. Moore, and J. J. Spengler (eds.), *Economic Growth: Brazil,*

India, Japan (Durham, N.C., 1955); E. E. Hagen, *On the Theory of Social Change* (Homewood, Ill., 1962).

9. A more detailed analysis of the relation between types of mobility, consensus, and stability of the social system may be found in Germani, "The Social Consequences of Mobility," in S. M. Lipset and N. J. Smelser (eds.), *Social Stratification and Economic Development* (in press).

10. S. M. Greenfield, "Industrialization and the Family in Sociological Theory," *American Journal of Sociology*, LXVII (1961), 312–322; W. J. Goode, "Industrialization and Family Change," in W. E. Moore and B. F. Hoselitz (eds.), *Industrialization and Society* (Paris, 1962).

11. Goode, *op. cit.*

12. T. Kawashima and K. Steiner, "Modernization and Divorce Rate Trends in Japan," *Economic Development and Cultural Change,* IX (1960), 213–239.

18

CALVINISM, EQUALITY, AND INCLUSION: THE CASE OF AFRIKANER CALVINISM

Jan J. Loubser

The significance of ascetic Protestantism for the development of the values of modern society and its central institutional complexes is generally recognized. Weber's thesis about the importance of ascetic Protestantism for the development of industrial capitalism is the classical example. Recently it has been argued that this thesis could be generalized to other characteristic features of modern industrial societies, especially to civil, political, and social-rights institutions.[1]

Even with respect to Weber's main thesis, however, there is still considerable difference of opinion. It is by no means only Marxian scholars who reject it as unproven. But efforts to disprove the thesis have increasingly taken the form of attempting to show that it is incompatible with or cannot account for the facts of certain concrete cases. Weber's argument is usually taken at its face value while the issue is argued on the basis of the presence or absence of a correlation between the two phenomena in the thesis: either industrial capitalism appeared in situations where ascetic Protestantism was absent, or the former failed to appear where the latter was present.[2]

If this type of argument was not meaningless from the outset, it has now largely become so in the light of our current theoretical understanding of these problems. Weber's own formulation certainly is not unambiguous, but it is careful enough to cast serious doubt on the simple assumption that the thesis implies significant correlations in every empirical situation, regardless of the other variables that may be operative. Apart from any qualifications we might find necessary to introduce into Weber's original formulation, we must also go beyond him and study the interdependen-

cies among these phenomena systematically as they relate to other variables in every situation. From this point of view the cases where there is no
significant correlation are crucial for our understanding of the relationship involved since they provide an opportunity to explore the various
alternative outcomes of the interdependencies. The important problem
relevant to the Weber thesis is not whether a correlation is observed or
not, but whether the specific outcome can be meaningfully related to and
interpreted in terms of the main direction of the causal relationship as
influenced by other variables in the system. Theoretically there is no reason why in a particular empirical situation the correlation might not be
absent or negative. Such cases might, but do not necessarily and *ipso
facto,* disprove the thesis; they must be analyzed carefully and systematically before inferences for the thesis can be drawn legitimately.

One important methodological point is to distinguish the initial impact
of ascetic Protestantism from those consequences that worked out later. A
developmental perspective is indispensable for an adequate understanding of the problem. If the institutional impact of Protestantism in the
direction of modernization varied in different situations, it is mainly the
initial consequences that were almost everywhere in the opposite direction.[3] This is particularly true of the early stages of Calvinism. While in
some situations it provided a powerful impetus for the development of
modern values such as equality, in others it proved a formidable obstacle
to the process.

There are at least three factors that are obviously related to this variance in some form or another. First, the Calvinistic conceptions of man
and of order introduce a two-class distinction between the elect and the
damned, the order of grace and the order of nature. Although all men are
created in the image of God and are equally sinful as a result of the Fall,
the elect has a special position of responsibility to implement the will of
God in the world. In the order of nature God ordained that some should
rule and some obey, and so on, and the order of grace never violates the
order of nature.[4] These conceptions obviously provide justification for
inequality and the limitation of equality strictly to the community of the
elect in situations where such arrangements are deemed necessary or desirable.

Related to this is, secondly, the problem of the development of Calvinism as a religious system. The two-class conceptions of man and order
were central aspects of the Calvinist belief system only in its early stages.
Although Calvinism initially represented a dedifferentiation or retrogression of the cultural system of Western Christianity, it constituted a new
logic of order that contained the internal impetus for its own evolution,
as well as the patterns of modern institutions.[5] There seems to be a close
interdependence between the capacity of Calvinism to supersede its two-

class stage and the development of modern institutions, such as equality, in Calvinist societies.

There is, thirdly, a particular type of situational exigency that constituted a serious obstacle to the development of both Calvinism and modern institutions. In situations where Calvinists were confronted with a large population of different cultural background, defined as less civilized, there was a strong tendency to categorize these people as belonging to the lower class of the Calvinist two-class system, that is, to the nonelect. Where this definition of the situation prevailed, development was markedly inhibited, especially in situations where color differences were involved.[6]

Although these problems can be settled only by the comparative analysis of all the historical cases, I shall confine myself to the analysis of the case of Afrikaner Calvinism in South Africa. I shall consider two phenomena calling for explanation: the survival of orthodox Calvinism, and the failure of equality to become institutionalized on an inconclusive basis in South African society. However close their interdependence might be, it is not sufficient to explain the one in terms of the other. I shall argue that both must be systematically related to the conditions under which Afrikaner Calvinism existed in the South African situation and to the consequences of these conditions for the social-action system as a whole. This case is of crucial significance for our understanding of the historical role of ascetic Protestantism precisely because superficially it violates our expectations based on the main direction of this role.

RELIGION AND EXISTENTIAL ANXIETY

Before embarking on the analysis of the empirical case it may be useful to make explicit a few of the primitive concepts and assumptions I shall employ. If we define religion as that aspect of action relating to problems of the ultimate meaning of existence, it is desirable to specify as concisely as possible what these problems are in any situation. The appropriate level of generality seems to be the existential conditions of man as a symbol-using animal. We may then specify certain dimensions of meaning within which symbols take on more concrete, situation-specific meanings. I shall use four dimensions of meaning: *Being*, which derives from the condition of man as a symbol-using animal who can create meaning by the use of symbols and can pose the question of the meaning of his own being. The existential anxiety that might arise in this dimension is *meaninglessness*, or the threat of nonbeing. Its exact nature depends on the symbol system in terms of which meaning is defined. The aspect of religious action giving meaning to being in the face of ultimate meaninglessness is *faith*. Faith, in this sense, whatever its content, is a religious phenomenon.

The dimension of *belonging* derives from the condition of man as a symbol-*sharing* animal. I assume that ultimately no symbol can have meaning for an actor unless it is shared by some significant social object. Belonging is a condition of being and as such an existential problem. In this dimension he may experience a threat of loneliness, which may give rise to existential anxiety about *loneliness*. The aspect of religious action relating most directly to this dimension is the type of communal ritual characteristic of worship activities; I shall call it simply *worship*.

A third dimension of meaning has to do with the fact that the human animal is not born with a ready set of symbols but has to acquire them through a long process of learning in which he is in a more or less dependent position. However much societies vary in the extent to which they emphasize this dependence, it is a safe assumption that there is no society in which this hierarchical principle is completely eliminated. In this dimension it is the meaning of *doing* as an aspect of existence that is problematical insofar as there is always a discrepancy between actual performance on the one hand, conceptions of what one ought to do, and rewards on the other hand. Discrepancies may give rise to guilt feelings which under certain conditions may amount to a generalized anxiety about *guilt*. The aspect of religious action relating to guilt is ethical or moral action in the service of some religious purpose. This I shall call *mission*.

The final dimension distinguished here arises from the fact that man as a symbol-using animal is ultimately dependent on the condition of life as an organism. But the existential problem of *living* derives from the combination of the relatively short span of the individual and the cross-generational valence of culture or civilization in society. In this dimension *death,* want, and suffering, all forms of deprivation, ultimately constitute threats to life and may give rise to anxiety about *survival,* individually or collectively. The aspect of religious action relevant to this problem may be called *therapy*. Where the anxiety is collective, what Durkheim called representative or commemorative rituals may affirm continuity with the past and commitment to posterity. Therapy promises gratification in the face of deprivations or threats of deprivation of the ultimate means of life.[7]

Where these existential problems are not solved in a meaningful manner, the development of a high level of anxiety in some or all dimensions of meaning is likely. In many situations and for a wide range of analytical purposes it is not necessary to assume that these anxieties rise above a "normal" level; they can be treated as random. In other situations this assumption is clearly not justified, as, for example, where people are transplanted into a hostile environment, culturally uprooted, and deprived of the resources, symbolic and otherwise, with which they formerly coped with these problems. In these cases high levels of existential anxiety must be treated as possible independent variables in the patterning of meaning and action. Such a situation, I submit, existed in South Africa; the peculiar characteristics of Afrikaner Calvinism, its failure to develop in a liberal direction, and its special relation to the problems of equality and inclusion in South Africa cannot be adequately explained without this assumption.

MEANINGLESSNESS AND FAITH

The characteristic tenets of the orthodox Calvinistic faith are well known: a belief in the sovereign God, sole creator and ruler through his Providence of the universe; the inborn sinfulness of both man and the world as a result of the Fall; the election by predestination of the few through grace to glorify God in building his kingdom on earth; and the damnation of the rest of mankind, also to the glory of God. The radical supernaturalism of this faith lies in the ultimate meaning that it imputes to all existence: the glory of the totally other, inscrutable God, well expressed in the Calvinist motto: *Soli Deo Gloria.*[8] Those who settled at the Cape of Good Hope between 1652 and 1707 when immigration was terminated were almost exclusively Calvinists of this stamp.[9]

Another equally significant characteristic of Calvinism is the central place which it gives to the Bible. For all Calvinists—with the possible exception of the well educated—this meant a thoroughgoing fundamentalism, a literal interpretation of the Bible, not only as the revealed Word but also as the final source of all knowledge. It is, therefore, not surprising that for more than two centuries the Bible, the Heidelberg Catechism, and the Psalm Book were virtually the only sources of information and cultural symbolism of the Afrikaner people as they forged their identity in Africa. In the new situation the identity symbols of their societal communities in Europe very soon became meaningless as Dutch, German, and French settlers were thrown together in frontier communities. Under frontier conditions the symbolic resources of their religious system were reduced to the bare essentials given in the Bible. There was no educational system beyond the most rudimentary beginnings, with almost no differentiations in the cultural content.

As a result the Afrikaners' definition of their situation, their conceptions of themselves, of others, and of the world, were derived from the symbolism and mythology of the Bible, especially the Old Testament. The meaning of their being in the new land found expression in the symbols of the Chosen People, the Promised Land, the Children of Ham, and the Philistines. They were called and led by Jehovah, their King, Ruler, and Judge, to glorify him by establishing his kingdom on the dark continent among the heathen. The Calvinist doctrines of predestination and election provided justification of their position as defined by these constitutive symbols.

The persistence of antihumanistic supernaturalism, anti-intellectualistic dogmatism, and literalistic fundamentalism in Afrikaner Calvinism and its failure to develop in a liberal direction may be understood against this background. The traumatic experience of prolonged deprivation of their more differentiated symbolic resources in a completely new situation gave rise to so much anxiety about meaninglessness that they regressed to a primitive, totalistic dependence on the Bible. It also involved a reaction formation against the liberal-rational tensions in the Calvinistic faith system, the repression of these tensions, and their projection on negatively affected objects such as liberals, Communists, and the like. The compulsive adherence to their own dogmatism and equally compulsive rejection of the liberal ideas of the modern Christian community, especially those of the universal fatherhood of God and brotherhood of man, are aspects of the same syndrome. As a result Afrikaner culture was not significantly influenced by the rationalism and naturalism of the Enlightenment nor by modern liberalism.[10]

In terms of this faith system the desirable type of society for the Afrikaner had to be a religious society ordered according to divine prescriptions. No distinctions of rank should be recognized; a strong commitment to equality among themselves has always characterized Afrikaner societal values. However, the identity, solidarity, destiny, and survival of the "volk" as an organic collective entity are given primacy in the Afrikaner ideology of Christian Nationalism. The values emphasizing a collectivistic orientation and particularism and quality as criteria of inclusion in the society are the basis of legitimation of apartheid and inequality as mechanisms for maintaining the exclusive identity of the volk. The Calvinistic two-class conceptions of man and of order, interpreted in terms of the symbol system outlined above, provided justification for these societal values.

GUILT AND MISSION

In the dimension of doing, the Calvinistic faith infused action with an activistic meaning. Man, in relation to both nature and society, stands under the command of God to implement God's will in creating a new order on the divine pattern. Man has a mission to master nature and to mold society according to the divine plan. This dimension was explored thoroughly by Weber and Troeltsch. If Weber's focus was somewhat exclusively on the implications for mastery over nature, Troeltsch provided the necessary complement by stressing the Calvinist sense of mission to shape society on the pattern of the Holy Community.[11] An adequate understanding of the orientational implications of Calvinism can dispense with neither of these; both are valid and both are central. In the logic of Calvinism the saint and the Holy Community were united, equally bound by the command of God under his covenant to create his new order in the world to his glory.[12] The psychological mechanism creating tension to implement the perceived mission is guilt.[13] When this active thrust, triggered by the logic of order of Calvinism, is frustrated by conditional or other factors the incidence of anxiety about guilt is extremely likely.

In Afrikaner Calvinism this meaning of mission remained essentially the same. The only crucial new element was injected by the distortion of the faith system where Afrikaner identity symbols were taken directly out of the Old Testament in a peculiar "fallacy of misplaced concreteness." [14] Consequently the Calvinistic mission was particularized as the Holy Community became identified with the Afrikaner volk and its mission with the destiny of the volk in their specific situation in Africa. This element thus increased the likelihood of high anxiety about guilt under the prevailing conditions.

The most important condition was the inevitable dispersion of Afrikaner pastoral life that made it almost impossible to relate the simple everyday tasks of a seminomadic existence to a collective mission, strongly affirmed in daily religious practice. Even more significant are the consequences of these conditions for the social structure which was almost reduced to the extended family of the farmer. The farther frontiersmen moved into the interior, the less affected were they by the rudimentary market, the limited political, legal, educational, and religious organization of the settlement around Cape Town, and the more self-reliant and self-sufficient they became. The family was the only socializing agency. In extended form it remained the most significant larger collectivity throughout adult life. Even after the social structure became more complex, the family retained its central position as the most permanent and immediate collective context of action to the Afrikaner.

A high level of anxiety about guilt may be predicated on the fact that the patriarchal family was also the unit of religious action in which the faith and mission outlined above were expressed and reaffirmed daily. The family used to gather in the morning and evening "around the home altar," as it is expressed in Afrikaans, where the father would officiate in Bible reading and prayer. It is hardly possible to imagine a structural setting for socialization that would maximize more the development of the superego over other components of the personality.[15] The religious role of the patriarchal father as the manipulator and dispenser of the commands of the Calvinist God, when internalized, could not but become the source of much anxiety about guilt, especially in a situation where the conditions did not permit the active carrying out of the inculcated religious mission.

Under these circumstances it is not surprising that the Calvinist concern with the mission aspect of religious action became compulsive and reactionary. The collectivity orientation of Afrikaner societal values provided added justification for attempts to institute their conception of the Calvinist divine order in society, to create an Afrikaner religious Utopia. Much of the motivation for the founding of the Afrikaner Republics of the nineteenth century—as well as the present one—was aimed at gaining control of the polity to institute the divine order in society as a whole. The two-class system of the elect and the reprobate was applied in this context as that of the responsible and the irresponsible, those who are and those who are not committed to the religious values of the volk. However, the conception of a religious elite was early associated with the highly reliable criterion of skin color, hence providing justification for white supremacy and political oligarchy. Legitimation for the utopian schemes of apartheid is derived from the identity symbols of a chosen people with the mission to preserve the light of Christianity and Western civilization in Dark Africa.[16] Collective consciousness of and commitment to this mission are reflected in the concept of trusteeship which is a central component of the ideology of apartheid, in the policies that flow from it, and in political and religious oratory.[17]

The nonwhites of South Africa constitute the hostile environment of this society. It is imperative by divine command to gain and maintain control over them by force if necessary to keep them in lower-class position in the interest of creating the Utopia. The African in particular has been an object of justified—in their terms—aggression in a contact situation characterized by internecine conflict. Repressed aggressiveness to the strong Afrikaner authority figures could be displaced and projected on the African. At the same time submissiveness to these authorities was reinforced by the removal of much of the ambivalence toward them. As the nonwhite in South Africa becomes increasingly the symbol of continental black nationalism, determined to eliminate the white man from Africa, the polarization of identities and destinies is driven to its schizoid extreme.[18]

The other historically significant social object for the Afrikaners was the British since 1806. Their presence soon became a symbolic defense against the very forces for liberalization they represented. To the frontier Afrikaner the British reform measures of the early nineteenth century were malicious attempts to break down the established social order by extending equality before the law to nonwhites. This interpretation was confirmed by the humanitarian and philanthropic zeal of the missionaries of the London Society in behalf of the nonwhites in the "Black Circuit" and similar actions.[19] The implications of the mixture of piety and rationalism, romanticism and liberalism, of these heirs of the Enlightenment were not only deeply disturbing to the frontier society but also diametrically counter to their religious conception of order. These confrontations provided the negative symbolism that up to the present has formed an insurmountable barrier against political liberalization.[20]

The United Nations and other critics and advocates of change increasingly share this symbolic significance. These forces representing strain toward the extension of equality to nonwhites are deflected by the limit images of the rigid symbol system. The more they resort to this reaction-formation and projection, the more fervent they become in their devotion to the mission that provides legitimation for inequality and apartheid.[21]

Monopolization of political control by the whites could perhaps be explained simply in terms of their vested interests. But the resolute persistence with which the Afrikaner nationalists have done this long after its rationality as a means has disappeared obviously cannot be so explained except as sheer ignorance and error on their part in defining their own interests. The foregoing analysis of the sources of a high level of anxiety about guilt, their consequent strong sense of mission and political destiny, and their determination to carry out their utopian schemes provides a more plausible interpretation of the nonrationality of their political action.

THE PROBLEM OF SURVIVAL

In the Afrikaner's subsistence economy, droughts, locusts, and storms were common hazards beyond his control, while the hostilities of the indigenous people and wild animals often threatened livelihood as well as life.[22] In such a situation, where control over the environment is ineffective and a fair degree of public safety and security cannot be taken for granted, anxiety about death is bound to increase. Where there is a strong collectivity orientation, it may also take the form of anxiety about survival, about the continuity of existence of both the individual and the group.

The therapeutic aspect of religious action relates in a special way to the problem of the meaning of death and suffering. Here again we may venture the proposition that the greater the anxiety about this problem, the greater the probability that religious action to cope with it will become unbalanced. Calvinist asceticism radically relativizes the existential problem of death in relation to the ultimate purpose of life: the glory of God. However, this is meaningful only in situations where Calvinism can be on the offensive, where it is possible to rationalize all action systematically toward the ultimate end. In a seminomadic pastoral existence under conditions where the Afrikaner found himself most of the time on the defensive against threats to life and livelihood, it was not possible.

Under these circumstances the ascetic ethic of Calvinism was slanted in the direction of a compulsive sexual asceticism and total devaluation of expressive symbolism. The patterning of sexual activities in society is an aspect of the dependence of action systems on their base in living organisms relating to the problem of survival and continuity through reproduction. Anxiety about this problem is likely to be manifested in this context. The alleged racial inferiority of the African and the tendency to deny his membership in the human species are relevant symptoms of the perceived strains.

Connubial and commensal rituals became especially important boundary-setting mechanisms insuring the ethnic survival and continuity of the volk. Sexual relations with nonwhites are regarded as sinful, especially for an Afrikaner, while a strong sentiment against intermarriage is firmly institutionalized. Since both lead to miscegenation, they constitute threats to the survival and continuity of the Afrikaner volk. "White womanhood," as sacred as in the southern United States, is primarily a symbol for Afrikaner *motherhood* which shows its relation to these problems.[23]

The fact that the first issue in the racial segregation of the church was objections against sharing Holy Communion with nonwhite members is equally significant.[24] Apartheid and the denial of equality in the same society to the nonwhite derive much of their meaning from being barriers against the possible erosive effects that mixing at such ritual occasions might have on the symbols of the volk.

This concern with the survival of the volk is also evident in a syncretistic growth of nativism on the asceticism of Calvinism. Commemorative and representative ritual occasions are marked by a nativistic glorification of the Afrikaner volk, its history, its heroes, and its sufferings. Two outstanding yearly occasions for such nativistic rituals are Hero's Day and Covenant Day,[25] but others like Van Riebeeck Day and Republic Day also serve the purpose. Sermons are often devoted to these themes. On these occasions leaders, past and present, are often hailed as prophets sent by God to lead his people, while divine intervention in the history of the people, especially in leading them to victory over the indigenous peoples, is often proclaimed. This nativism is legitimized and supported by the "chosen people" symbolism and religious utopianism.[26]

Finally, the growth of nativism has meant a deflection of the rationalizing implications of the Calvinistic ethic for economic action. Not only was their pastoral life not conducive to such rationalization but the tension in this direction in their religious ethic was drained by the nativism.[27] It is only in the last generation that the Afrikaner has started to play a significant role in the industrialized economy. Even then motivation was provided mainly by the collective nationalistic purpose of gaining political control of the society. Under urban and industrial conditions the implications of the religious ethic for the motivation and patterning of economic action are becoming more evident and important.

It is, however, quite significant that the ascetic ethic is internalized strongly enough that the Afrikaner finds it necessary to project his own failure to implement it on the nonwhite who, like the Negro American, is a symbol of the values opposite to diligence, thrift, hard work, self-discipline, and so on. In terms of this projection the nonwhite lacks conspicuously in the signs of grace and is therefore to be avoided by the Calvinist.

It also provides justification for the denial of equality of opportunity and the maintenance of a two-class economic system in which the nonwhite would be permanently in a lower-class position in the white society. The implications of the Calvinist ethic fostering an impersonal, instrumental orientation to other men, especially the nonelect, as means for the attainment of individual and collective ends in the service of God strengthens this justification.[28]

EXTREME LONELINESS

For more than two centuries the isolation of the frontier, where families were dispersed on scattered farms without any contact or communication with outsiders for weeks and even months, constituted the conditions of existence of the Afrikaner. The assumption of anxiety about loneliness under these conditions is further justified by the fact that we often find the theme of loneliness expressed and symbolized in Afrikaans culture.[29] The regularity with which families worshiped together in isolation for generations relates closely to this anxiety. Worship was emphasized more and performed more often than other types of religious action since it dispelled loneliness by affirming the belonging or solidarity of the members of the worshiping unit with each other and their God.[30] The role of the family as a unit of worship had highly significant consequences for its structure and function in Afrikaner society. We have already noted the consequences for the societal values and political orientation.

In the normative system it increased legalism. Rules of conduct took the form of particularistic prescriptions and expectations of meticulous conformity by stern authoritarian parental figures. Hence compulsive conformity marked orientation to all norms of behavior which were firmly internalized and infused with religious meaning. External sanctions were very strong in a family that was almost a total institution. As the church later added its surveillance, strict conformity to the norms of society became widely sanctioned. Legalism is also evident in the tendency to legislate every aspect of life, private or public, that is seen as slipping from the control of these agencies.

Another aspect of the structure of the situation is of crucial importance here: the family usually was not entirely alone on the farm. There were servants, nonwhite families, who squatted on the farm and could become meaningful objects in the dimension of belonging. However, the master–servant relation did not and could not fit into any of the general categories of relations constituting the family.[31] Hence it was primarily a relation between two collective units, the master family and the servant family.

Servants were usually excluded from daily family worship. When they were invited or ordered to attend they sat aside on the floor. At these occasions it was therefore not their solidarity with the farmer's family that was affirmed but their servant status in relation to the master family. One of the grievances leading to the Great Trek was that the British administration and laws broke down the proper relation between master and servant to which the *Voortrekkers* were committed as part of the divine order of their society. This structural setting of worship institutionalized firmly inequality between white and nonwhite and insured a compulsive concern with conformity. By the middle of the nineteenth century, worship in the Dutch Reformed Church, formerly somewhat integrated, was segregated, leading to separate churches for nonwhites by the eighteen-eighties.[32]

In such a society there is no room for nonconformity. Especially with respect to the central norm of inequality, nonconformity is invariably defined as disloyalty and treason, particularly when committed by Afrikaners. Although excommunication from the church is rare, ostracism is widely applied as a sanction against nonconformity and deviation. This mechanism is patently a denial of belonging, a ban on association, and intended to impose loneliness.

Although urbanization and industrialization have changed conditions radically, for the majority of Afrikaners it is only their first or second generation of urban life. For recent migrants to the city its anonymity and impersonality are likely to pose the same problem of loneliness and to sustain anxiety and dependence on the old defense mechanisms before becoming a more meaningful social situation. Since they are in more direct competition with the nonwhite in the urban labor market, they also welcome the protection of inequality and apartheid.[33]

CONCLUSION

I have attempted to analyze the ultimate conditions and ultimate reality of the Afrikaner action system and to relate them to its peculiar characteristics. I have argued that a combination of the ultimate conditions and the ultimate symbols of reality resulted in existential anxiety in several of the dimensions of meaning. These anxieties led to unbalanced outcomes in the Calvinistic religious system, which in turn had specified consequences for certain aspects of the structure and function of the rest of the action system. These consequences were then related to the patterning of the relations of the Afrikaners to nonwhites on the basis of inequality and apartheid.

The characteristics of Afrikaner Calvinism relate meaningfully to the ultimate conditions indicated. In the faith system, attempts to cope with the high anxiety of meaninglessness resulted in an extraordinary degree of literalistic fundamentalism and anti-intellectualistic dogmatism. Anxiety of loneliness gave worship a very special significance in relation to solidarity so that the worship system became exclusive and restricted to those who belonged in contexts extraneous to the religious system. In the mission system, high anxiety about guilt increased collective religious utopianism, while in the therapy system anxiety about death and suffering introduced a strong strain of nativism. The combined effect on orthodox Calvinism was partly to reinforce tendencies inherent in it in these directions, especially in its faith and mission aspects, and partly to introduce emphases, especially in its worship and therapy aspects, which tended to inhibit its internal capacities and tendencies to supersede its two-class conceptions of man and of order. The survival of orthodox Calvinism in South Africa can, therefore, be related to the peculiar nature of the ultimate conditions in the situation.

The responses of the Calvinistic religious system determined to a significant degree the characteristic features of Afrikaner society. The fundamentalistic faith system provided biblical identity symbols and a concept of the desirable type of society that was religious in content, constituted on particularistic and quality criteria, and collectivistic in orientation. Its active concern with exclusive worship reinforced the ethnocentric solidarity of the society and compulsive conformity to its legalistic norms, especially inequality between whites and nonwhites. The this-worldly religious utopianism legitimized political oligarchy to fulfill the destiny of the Afrikaner people in Africa, justifying political control over the nonwhite human environment who did not share this mission and on whom aggression could be projected and displaced. Finally, the nativistic therapy system provided the means for drawing the boundaries of the society vis-à-vis its human environment in the interest of its own survival and security, setting up rules against miscegenation and ritual crossings of the boundary as well as for the monopolistic control of economic resources.

Inequality and apartheid are mechanisms that Afrikaner society applies to maintain its own identity, solidarity, destiny, and security. In all four areas Afrikaner symbols constitute insuperable barriers to the inclusion of the nonwhite population in the society and to extending equality to them. In a cybernetic sense, the limit images of this society are so programed that it cannot make a realistic assessment of its situation, whatever information it is fed. The failure of Afrikaner—and white—society to survive in South Africa will be largely a result of the ossification of these barriers of insulation that impair its generalized adaptive capacity to such an extent that it cannot cope with the exigencies of its environment.[34]

Finally, with respect to the general problem of the relation of Calvinism to equality and inclusion, this analysis suggests that in this case the failure of orthodox Calvinism to develop and to promote the development of equality in a more inclusive social system must be related to the ultimate conditions conducive to high levels of existential anxiety. The special significance of the presence of a large population of nonwhites derives from the extent to which it is perceived as constituting a threat and hence to increase existential anxiety in any of the dimensions of meaning.

Calvinist symbolism seems to structure meaning, especially in the dimensions of being and doing, in such a way that adherents are peculiarly vulnerable to perceiving a situation such as the South African as threatening to their identity and as a challenge of destiny. This may mean not only a certain incapacity on the part of Calvinism as a religious system to cope with existential anxieties in these dimensions but also a tendency to resort to reaction-formation against the demands for higher levels of performance, regressing to and fixing on the earlier, more primitive solutions provided by its two-class conceptions, which then further contributes to this incapacity.

We may then conclude that, however strong the legitimation for internal equality in Calvinism, and whatever its significance for the development of this value of modern society has been in other situations, it is not likely to foster the extension of equality to a more inclusive system in situations such as South Africa. Yet the commitment to equality and other modern values, especially economic development, within the exclusive system may provide a very important impetus for development once the exclusive system has been broken up.

This interpretation is consistent with Weber's thesis; the case of Afrikaner Calvinism does not disprove the general hypothesis about the main direction of the role of ascetic Protestantism in the modernization of Western institutions.

NOTES

1. See especially Herbert Lüthy, Ch. 4 above; Talcott Parsons, "Christianity and Modern Industrial Society" in E. A. Tiryakian (ed.), *Sociological Theory, Values, and Sociocultural Change* (Glencoe, Ill., 1963), pp. 33–70; R. K. Merton, *Social Theory and Social Structure*, rev. ed. (Glencoe, Ill., 1957), pp. 574–606; also Perry Miller, *The New England Mind*, 2 vols. (Boston, 1961); A. C. McLaughlin, *Foundations of American Constitutionalism* (New York, 1961).

2. The outstanding recent example remains Kurt Samuelsson, *Religion and Economic Action*, tr. E. G. French (New York, 1961).

3. S. N. Eisenstadt, "Transformation of Social, Political, and Cultural Orders in Modernization," *American Sociological Review*, XXX, No. 5 (October 1965), 659–673, especially pp. 670–673.

4. J. T. McNeill, *The History and Character of Calvinism* (New York, 1954); Ernst Troeltsch, *The Social Teaching of the Christian Churches* (New York, 1960), pp. 576–691; Max Weber, *The Protestant Ethic and the Spirit of Capitalism*, tr. Talcott Parsons (New York 1958), pp. 98–128.

5. David Little, *The Logic of Order—An Examination of the Sources of Puritan-Anglican Controversy and Their Relation to Prevailing Legal Conceptions of Corpora-*

tion in the Late Sixteenth and Early Seventeenth Century in England; J. J. Loubser, "Puritanism and Religious Liberty: An Analysis of Normative Change in Massachusetts, 1630–1850," unpublished Ph.D. dissertation, Harvard University, 1964.

6. The southern United States and Prussia seem to be two relevant cases besides South Africa. Cf. K. K. Bailey, *Southern White Protestantism in the Twentieth Century* (New York, 1964); Christine R. Kayser, "Calvinism and German Political Life," unpublished Ph. D. dissertation, Radcliffe College, 1961.

7. This section is especially indebted to R. N. Bellah, "Some Suggestions for the Systematic Study of Religion," manuscript, Harvard University; Paul Tillich, *The Courage to Be* (New Haven, Conn., 1952), especially Chs. 2–4; and Kenneth Burke, *The Rhetoric of Religion* (Boston, 1961).

8. Troeltsch, *op. cit.*, pp. 579–587; McNeill, *op. cit.*; John Calvin, *Institutes of the Christian Religion*, tr. Henry Beveridge (Edinburgh, 1875), II, 677–689.

9. See Sheila Patterson, *The Last Trek* (London, 1957), Ch. 1; A. Walker, *A History of Southern Africa* (London, 1957), pp. 24–46. For the rest of this section see E. A. Walker, *The Frontier Tradition in South Africa* (London, 1930); G. B. A. Gerdener, "Die Kultuurhistoriese Bydrae van die Nederduits Gereformeerde Kerk in Suid-Afrika," in C. M. van den Heever and P. de V. Pienaar (eds.), *Kultuurgeskiedenis van die Afrikaner,* Deel 11 (Kaapstad, 1947), pp. 249–292.

10. See G. D. Scholtz, *Die Geskiedenis van die Nederduitse Herformde of Gereformeerde Kerk van Suid Afrika, 1842–1885* (Kaapstad, 1956), pp. 252–254; C. Spoelstra, *Het Kerkelyk en Godsdienstig Leven der Boeren na den Grooten Trek* (Kampen, 1915), pp. 222 ff.; A. H. Murray, "Die Afrikaner se Wysgerige Denke," in Van den Heever and Pienaar, *op. cit.*, pp. 164–187; see also D. F. du Toit Malherbe, *Afrikaner Volkseenheid* (Bloemfontein, 1942); F. A. van Jaarsveld, *Die Ontwaking van die Afrikaanse Nasionale Bewussyn—1868–1881* (Johannesburg, 1957); Patterson, *op. cit.*, pp. 176–215.

11. See Troeltsch, *op. cit.*, pp. 587–592, 602–625; Weber, *op. cit.* and "The Protestant Sects and the Spirit of Capitalism," in H. H. Gerth and C. W. Mills, *From Max Weber: Essays in Sociology* (New York, 1958), pp. 302–322.

12. See especially Little, *op. cit.*, and J. L. Adams, "Max Weber and Talcott Parsons as Interpreters of Western Religious and Social Development," paper read in New York, October 1965; also C. J. Friedrich, Introduction to *Politica Methodice Digesta of Johannes Althusius* (Cambridge, Mass., 1932), especially pp. lxxvii–lxxix; E. S. Morgan, *The Puritan Dilemma* (New York, 1958). See Burke, *op. cit.*, pp. 172–272, for a logological analysis of some of the capitalized terms.

13. Sigmund Freud, *The Ego and the Id*, tr. Joan Riviere (London, 1950); Karen Horvey, *The Neurotic Personality of Our Time* (New York, 1964), pp. 230–258.

14. The phenomenon of reification is not confined to science just as scientists often succumb to methodological fundamentalism. These are two sides of the same coin.

15. See Talcott Parsons, *Social Structure and Personality* (New York, 1965), Pt. I; Patterson, *op. cit.*, pp. 239–255.

16. The Constitution of the old South African Republic (now the province of Transvaal) contained a clause barring persons with mixed blood to the *tenth* generation from any of their assemblies and proscribed equality between white and colored in both church and state.

17. Cronje, G., *Regverdige Rasse-Apartheid* (Stellenbosch, 1947); H. J. C. Snyders, "Die Taak van die Kerk ten opsigte van Rasseverhoudinge in Suid-Afrika," *Tydskrif vir Rasseaangeleenthede* (July 1958). Political leaders increasingly claim their authority directly from God since "the voice of the people," sometime in the past taken as "the voice of God," might disastrously be taken to mean the voice of all people in South Africa. The attempt on Verwoerd's life increased their charisma enormously.

18. See Gregory Bateson, *Naven* (Cambridge, 1936), pp. 175–186. In Bateson's terms

there has been a shift from complementary to symmetrical schismogenesis. See also P. L. van den Berghe, *South Africa: A Study in Conflict* (Middletown, Conn., 1965).

19. Walker, *A History of Southern Africa*, pp. 139–233. The Great Trek was primarily a flight from these revolutionary measures and a rebellion against British authority.

20. Relations with the British during the nineteenth century culminating in the Anglo-Boer War reinforced this meaning. See *ibid.*, Chs. 9–13; Patterson, *op. cit.*

21. The events in Rhodesia and the role of Smith and his party indicate how conducive the situation is to symbolism of this type.

22. The following statement of the nineteenth-century traveler Barrow applies to the situation in general: "An inhabitant of the Sneewberg not only lives under constant apprehension of losing his property, but is perpetually exposed to the danger of being put to death. If he has occasion to go to the distance of five hundred yards from his house, he is under the necessity of carrying a musket. He can neither plough, nor sow, nor reap without being under arms. . . . To endure such a life of constant dread and anxiety, a man must be accustomed to it from his infancy and unacquainted with one that is better." Quoted in Patterson, *op. cit.*, p. 10, also p. 244.

23. *Ibid.* pp. 240–243.

24. See Scholtz, *op. cit.*, pp. 15 ff., and B. J. Marais, *Color—Unsolved Problem of the the West* (Cape Town, 1952), pp. 291–292.

25. Covenant Day celebrates the victory of a few hundred Voortrekkers over thousands of Zulus in the battle of Blood River, prior to which the Trekkers made a covenant with God that they would always celebrate this day as a Sabbath if he gave them victory over the enemy.

26. For an example that can hardly be matched in vulgarity, see the collection of speeches of a Dutch Reformed minister who is one of the most eminent and influential Afrikaners in the Transvaal: G. J. J. Boshoff, *U Volk is my Volk* (Johannesburg, 1959).

27. Max Weber, *The Sociology of Religion* (Boston, 1963), Chs. 6 and 7, and "The Social Psychology of World Religions," in Gerth and Mills, *op. cit.*, pp. 267–301.

28. See Weber, *The Protestant Ethic*, pp. 121–123, and Talcott Parsons, *The Structure of Social Action* (Glencoe, Ill., 1949), pp. 54–55. For the mechanism of stereotype projections, see Bruno Bettelheim and Morris Janowitz, *Social Change and Prejudice* (New York, 1964).

29. The psychopathological consequences of prolonged isolation and solitary confinement are indicative of the dynamic relations I have in mind. It is poetic irony that the only book that recent political detainees of the Nationalist regime were allowed to read in solitary confinement was the Bible.

30. See Bellah, *op. cit.* The Afrikaans term for loneliness can be broken down into words literally meaning one-together-ness, which is often done in sermons and pastoral literature to affirm that loneliness really means togetherness with the One.

31. The structure of the family along the dimensions of generation and sex provides channels of socialization into adult roles and collectivities and society itself. The servant role and collectivity, when they are highly visible and set apart by a criterion like color, do not constitute such a channel. The child can *never* become a member of the servant collectivity. For an analysis of the family, see Talcott Parsons and R. F. Bales, *Family, Socialization and Interaction Process* (Glencoe, Ill., 1955).

32. See Scholtz, *op. cit.*, pp. 281–282.

33. It was a pact with the Labor Party that first brought the Nationalists to power in 1924. White labor has always supported and demanded the extensive work reservation legislation.

34. See Talcott Parsons, "Evolutionary Universals in Society," *American Sociological*

Review, XXIX, No. 3 (June 1964), 339–357; R. N. Bellah (ed.), *Religion and Progress in Modern Asia* (Glencoe, Ill., 1965), Epilogue, especially pp. 168–194. For a journalistic but perceptive report providing many observations substantiating or confirming this analysis, see Joseph Lelyveld, "The Afrikaner Feels Lonely in the World," *The New York Times Magazine,* February 6, 1966.

BIBLIOGRAPHY

I. MAX WEBER'S MAJOR WRITINGS ON THE PROTESTANT ETHIC, CAPITALISM, AND THE SOCIOLOGY OF RELIGION

"Die protestantische Ethik und der Geist des Kapitalismus," *Archiv für Sozialwissenschaft und Sozialpolitik* (1904–1905); reprinted in his *Gesammelte Aufsätze zur Religionssoziologie* (Tübingen, 1920–21; 4th ed., 1947).

The Protestant Ethic and the Spirit of Capitalism, tr. Talcott Parsons (New York, 1930).

"Antikritisches zum Geist des Kapitalismus," *Archiv für Sozialwissenschaft und Sozialpolitik*, Vol. XXX (1910).

"Antikritisches Schlusswort zum Geist des Kapitalismus," *Archiv für Sozialwissenschaft und Sozialpolitik*, XXXI (1910), 554 ff.

Wirtschaft und Gesellschaft (Tübingen, 1922).

Gesammelte Aufsätze zur Religionssoziologie, 3 vols. (Tübingen, 1920–21). (Parts translated into English.)

The Religion of China, tr. and ed. H. H. Gerth (Glencoe, Ill., 1951; new ed., with an introduction by C. K. Yang, New York, 1964).

Ancient Judaism, tr. and ed. H. H. Gerth and D. Martindale (Glencoe, Ill., 1952).

The Religion of India, tr. and ed. H. H. Gerth and D. Martindale (Glencoe, Ill., 1958).

The Sociology of Religion, tr. Ephraim Fischoff (Boston, 1963).

Wirtschaftsgeschichte (Munich, 1924).

General Economic History, tr. F. H. Knight (Glencoe, Ill., 1927).

II. MAJOR EXPOSITIONS OF WEBER'S GENERAL THEORIES WITH SPECIAL BEARING ON THE PROTESTANT ETHIC THESIS

ANDRESKI, STANISLAV. "Method and Substantive Theory in Max Weber," *British Journal of Sociology*, XV, No. 1 (March 1964), 1–18. (Included in this book.)

BENDIX, REINHARD. *Max Weber: An Intellectual Portrait* (New York, 1960).

———. "Max Webers Religionssoziologie," in R. König and J. Winckelman (eds.), "Max Weber zum Gedächtnis," *Kölner Zeitschrift für Soziologie und Sozialpsychologie*, Sonderheft 7 (1963), 273–294.

———. "Max Weber's Sociology Today," *International Social Science Journal*, XVII, No. 1 (1965), 9–22.

GOLDSCHMIDT, D. (chairman). "Die Aktualität Max Webers in der modernen

Religionssoziologie," in *Max Weber und die Soziologie heute,* Verhandlungen des fünfzehnten deutschen Soziologentages (Tübingen, 1965), 221–246.

HERBERG, W. *Protestant, Catholic, Jew* (New York, 1956).

HINTZE, OTTO. "Max Webers Religionssoziologie (1922)," in Otto Hintze, *Soziologie und Geschichte* (Göttingen, 1964), II, 126–134.

KOLKO, GABRIEL. "A Critique of Max Weber's Philosophy of History," *Ethics,* LXX, No. 1 (October 1959), 21–35.

MOMMSEN, WOLFGANG. "Max Weber's Political Sociology and His Philosophy of World History," *International Social Science Journal,* XVII, No. 1 (1965), 23–45.

PARSONS, TALCOTT. " 'Capitalism' in Recent German Literature: Sombart and Weber," *Journal of Political Economy,* XXXVI (1928), 641–661; XXXVII (1929), 31–51.

————. "The Theoretical Development of the Sociology of Religion," *Journal of the History of Ideas,* V (1944), 176–190.

————. "Max Weber's Sociological Analysis of Capitalism and Modern Institutions," in H. E. Barnes (ed.), *An Introduction to the History of Sociology* (Chicago, 1948).

————. *The Structure of Social Action* (Glencoe, Ill., 1949), 500–579.

————. "Christianity and Modern Industrial Society," in E. A. Tiryakian (ed.), *Sociological Theory, Values, and Sociocultural Change: Essays in Honor of Pitirim A. Sorokim* (Glencoe, Ill., 1963), 33–70.

————. "Introduction," in Max Weber, *The Sociology of Religion* (Boston, 1963).

————. "Die Aktualität Max Webers in der modernen Religionssoziologie," discussion, in O. Stammer (ed.), *Max Weber und die Soziologie heute,* Verhandlungen des fünfzehnten deutschen Soziologentages (Tübingen, 1965), 234–241.

SCHELTING, ALEXANDER VON. *Max Webers Wissenschaftslehre* (Tübingen, 1932).

VAN DER SPRENKEL, O. B. "Max Weber on China," *Theory and History,* III (1964), 348–370.

III. LANDMARKS IN THE PROTESTANT ETHIC CONTROVERSY

BEERLING, R. F. *Protestantisme en Kapitalisme. Max Weber in de Critiek,* Publicaties van het Sociologisch Instituit, Groningen (Groningen-Batavia, 1946).

EDMOND, MICHEL-PIERRE. "L'éthique catholique médiévale en matière économique," *Preuves,* XIV, No. 166 (December 1964), 88–91.

FANFANI, AMINTORE. *Cattolicismo e protestantesimo nella formazione etica del capitalismo* (Milan, 1934); English tr. *Catholicism, Protestantism and Capitalism* (London, 1935; New York, 1938).

FISCHOFF, EPHRAIM. "The Protestant Ethic and the Spirit of Capitalism: The History of a Controversy," *Social Research,* XI (1944), 53–77. (Included in this book.)

FREUND, JULIEN. "Controverse sur Max Weber," *Preuves,* No. 163 (September 1964), 85–92.

GREEN, R. W. (ed.). *Protestantism and Capitalism. The Weber Thesis and Its Critics* (Boston, 1959).

HANSEN, N. M. "Weber and Veden on Economic Development," *Kyklos,* XVII (1964), 447–469.

HOLL, KARL. *Gesammelte Aufsätze zur Kirchengeschichte* (Tübingen, 1927), Vols. I, II.

———. *The Cultural Significance of the Reformation* (New York, 1959).

HUDSON, W. S. "The Weber Thesis Re-examined," *Church History*, XXX (1961), 88–99.

LÜTHY, HERBERT. *La banque protestante en France de la Révocation de l'Édit de Nantes à la Révolution* (Paris, 1959–1961), Vol. I, Ch. 1, and Vol. II, 749–786.

———. "Once Again: Calvinism and Capitalism," *Encounter*, XXII, No. 1 (January 1964), 26–38. (Included in this book.)

———. *Le passé présent* (Monaco and Paris, 1965), Pt. I, 13–99.

MCCLELLAND, DAVID. *The Achieving Society* (Princeton, N.J., 1961).

NELSON, BENJAMIN. "In Defence of Max Weber," *Encounter*, XXIII, No. 2 (1964), 94–95.

PARSONS, TALCOTT. "H. M. Robertson on Max Weber and His School," *Journal of Political Economy*, XLIII, (1935), 688–696.

RACHFAHL, FELIX. "Calvinismus und Kapitalismus," *Internationale Wochenschrift für Wissenschaft, Kunst und Technik*, III, No. 39 (1909), 1217–1238; No. 40, 1249–1268; No. 41, 1287–1300; No. 42, 1319–1334; No. 43, 1347–1366.

———. "Nochmals Calvinismus und Kapitalismus," *Internationale Wochenschrift für Wissenschaft, Kunst und Technik*, IV, Nos. 22–25 (1910).

ROBERTSON, H. M. *Aspects of the Rise of Economic Individualism* (Cambridge, Eng., 1933).

SAMUELSSON, KURT. *Religion and Economic Action*, tr. E. G. French (London, 1961).

TAWNEY, R. H. *Religion and the Rise of Capitalism* (London and New York, 1926).

———. "Religion and Economic Life," *The Times Literary Supplement*, January 1956.

TROELTSCH, ERNST. *The Social Teaching of the Christian Churches*, 2 vols. (New York and London, 1931).

———. *Protestantism and Progress* (Boston, 1958).

IV. GENERAL ANALYSIS OF THE RELATIONS BETWEEN THE DEVELOPMENT OF CAPITALISM AND THE REFORMATION, INFLUENCED BY OR RELEVANT TO WEBER'S THESIS

BIRNBAUM, NORMAN. "Conflicting Interpretations of the Rise of Capitalism: Marx and Weber," *The British Journal of Sociology*, IV (1953), 125–141.

BOUMAN, P. J. "Eenige beschonwingen over de historische betrekkingen tusschen godsdienst en kapitalisme," *De Economist* (Haarlem, 1932), 181–198.

BURRELL, S. A. "Calvinism, Capitalism, and the Middle Classes: Some Afterthoughts on an Old Problem," *The Journal of Modern History*, XXXII (1960), 129–141. Reprinted in S. A. Burrell (ed.), *The Role of Religion in Modern European History* (New York, 1964), 37–43. (Included in this book.)

DROOGLEEVER FORTUIJN, A. B. "Kapitalisme en Protestantisme," *Sociologisch Cahier*, Vol. II (September 1964 and November 1964).

FEBVRE, L. "Capitalisme et réforme," *Foi et Vie* (1934).

FULLERTON, KEMPER. "Calvinism and Capitalism," *The Harvard Theological*

Review, Vol. XXI (1928). Reprinted in R. W. Green (ed.), *Protestantism and Capitalism* (Boston, 1959), 6–20.

GUNSTEREN, W. F. VAN. *Calvinismus und Kapitalismus* (Amsterdam, 1934).

HAUSER, HENRI. *Les débuts du capitalisme* (Paris, 1927), a chapter on "Les idées économiques de Calvin." This chapter is reprinted in his *La modernité du XVIe siècle,* Cahiers des Annales, No. 21 (Paris, 1963), 105–133.

HILL, CHRISTOPHER. "Protestantism and the Rise of Capitalism," in F. J. Fischer (ed.), *Economic and Social History of Tudor and Stuart England* (Cambridge, 1961), 15–39.

HUDSON, W. S. "Puritanism and the Spirit of Capitalism," *Church History,* XVIII (1949), 3–16. Reprinted in R. W. Green (ed.), *Protestantism and Capitalism* (Boston, 1959), 56–62.

HYMA, ALBERT. *Christianity, Capitalism, and Communism* (Ann Arbor, Mich., 1937), Chs. 3–4.

KNAPPEN, MARSHALL M. *Tudor Puritanism* (Chicago, 1939), pp. 478–480.

KRAUS, J. B. *Scholastik, Puritanismus und Kapitalismus* (Munich, 1930).

LEFORT, CLAUDE. "Capitalisme et religion au XVIe siècle," *Les Temps Modernes,* VII (April 1952), 1892–1906.

MACK, R. W., *et al.* "The Protestant Ethic, Level of Aspiration and Social Mobility: An Empirical Test," *American Sociological Review,* Vol. XXI (June 1956).

MÜLLER-ARMACK, ALFRED. *Religion und Wirtschaft* (Stuttgart, 1959).

NELSON, B. N. *The Idea of Usury* (Princeton, N.J., 1949).

NORWOOD, F. A. *The Reformation's Refugees as a Force* (Chicago, 1942).

ROUGIER, L. "La réforme et le capitalisme moderne," *Revue de Paris* (September–October 1928).

SÉE, HENRI. *Les origines du capitalisme moderne* (Paris, 1926).

———. *Modern Capitalism* (New York, 1928).

———. "Dans quelle mesure Puritains et Juifs ont-ils contribué aux progrès du capitalisme moderne?", *Revue Historique,* CLV (1927), 57–68. Reprinted in English in R. W. Green (ed.), *Protestantism and Capitalism* (Boston, 1959), 62–64.

THORNER, ISIDOR. "Christian Science and Ascetic Protestantism: A Study in the Sociology of Religion, Personality Type and Social Structure," unpublished thesis, Harvard University, 1951.

TREVOR-ROPER, H. R. *Religion, the Reformation and Social Change,* Historical Studies, IV (London, 1964), 18–45.

WAGNER, HELMUT. "The Protestant Ethic: A Mid-Twentieth Century View," *Sociological Analysis,* XXV, No. 1 (Spring 1964), 34–41.

WALKER, G. P. C. "Capitalism and the Reformation," *The Economic History Review,* VIII, No. 1 (1937), 1–19.

WEMYSS, A. "Calvinisme et capitalisme," *Bull. Soc. Hist. Prot. Fr.* (1956), 33–38.

WOOD, H. G. "Puritanism and Capitalism," *The Congregational Quarterly* (April 1951).

V. HISTORICAL ANALYSES OF THE REFORMATION, INFLUENCED BY AND RELEVANT TO WEBER'S THESIS

General

ELTON, G. R. *Reformation Europe* (London, 1963).

GELDER, E. VAN. *Revolutionaire Reformatie* (Amsterdam, 1943).

GRIMM, H. J. *The Reformation Era, 1550–1660* (New York, 1954).

HAUSER, HENRI. *La modernité du XVIe siècle,* Cahiers des Annales, No. 21 (Paris, 1930).

————. *La naissance du protestantisme* (Paris, 1940).

HILL, CHRISTOPHER. *The Century of Revolution: 1603–1714* (Edinburgh, 1961).

HNIK, F. N. *The Philanthropic Motive in Christianity* (Oxford, 1938).

LITTLE, DAVID. *The New Order in Old England* (New York: Harper & Row, 1967). (A portion of this is included in this book.)

PAUCK, WILLIAM. *The Heritage of the Reformation,* rev. and enl. (ed.) (Glencoe, Ill., 1961).

POUJOL, P. "Modernes interprétations de la Réforme, mouvement religieux et social," *Christianisme Social* (1959), 168–174.

RITTER, GERHARD. "Das 16. Jahrhundert als weltgeschichtliche Epoche," *Archiv für Geschichte der Reformation,* Vol. XXXV (1938), and *Die Neugestaltung Europas im 16. Jahrhundert* (Berlin, 1950), Ch. 3, especially 133–170.

ROBERTS, MICHAEL. "Queen Christina and the General Crisis of the Seventeenth Century," *Past and Present,* No. 22 (July 1962), 36–59.

TREVOR-ROPER, H. R. "The General Crisis of the Seventeenth Century," *Past and Present,* No. 16 (November 1959), 31–64.

————. "Discussion of Trevor-Roper's 'General Crisis of the Seventeenth Century,'" by *Past and Present,* No. 18 (November 1960), 8–33. Reply by H. R. Trevor-Roper, 34–42.

Some of the Major Religious Movements

LUTHERANISM

ADAM, ALFRED. "Die nationale Kirche bei Luther," *Archiv für Geschichte der Reformation,* XXXV (1938), 30–62.

BAINTON, RONALD. *Here I Stand. A Life of Martin Luther* (New York, 1955).

BIRNBAUM, N. "Luther et le Millenarisme," *Archives de Sociologie des Religions,* Vol. III, No. 5 (1958).

ELERT, W. *Morphologie des Luthertums,* Teil II: *Soziallehren und Sozialwirkungen* (1932).

FIFE, R. H. *The Revolt of Martin Luther* (New York, 1957).

CALVINISM

BARON, HANS. "Calvinist Republicanism and Its Historical Roots," *Church History,* Vol. VIII, No. 1 (1939).

BEILER, A. "La pensée économique et sociale de Calvin" (Geneva, 1959).

BOHATEC, JOSEF. *Calvins Lehre von Staat und Kirche* (Breslau, 1937).

CALVIN, JOHN. *Institution de la religion chrétienne* (new edition published by the Société Calviniste de France, 1955).

DAVIES, A. *John Calvin and the Influence of Protestantism on National Life and Character* (London, 1946).

EMERSON, E. H. "Calvin and the Covenant Theology," *Church History*, XXV (June 1956).

FOSTER, H. D. "The Political Theories of Calvinists before the Puritan Exodus to America," *American Historical Review*, Vol. XXI, No. 3 (1916).

HARKNESS, GEORGIA. *John Calvin: The Man and His Ethics* (New York, 1931).

HAUSER, HENRI. "À propos des idées économiques de Calvin," *Mélanges*, H. Pirenne, I (1926).

MCNEILL, J. T. "Thirty Years of Calvin Study," *Church History*, XVII (September 1948).

———. *The History and Character of Calvinism* (New York, 1954).

MERCIER, CH. "L'esprit de Calvin et la democratie," *Revue D'Histoire Ecclésiastique*, XXX (1934), 5–53.

SCHELVEN, A. A. VAN. *Historisch onderzoek naar den levensstiyl van het Calvinisme* (1925).

WEBER, HERMANN. *Die Theologie Calvins* (Berlin, 1930).

WENDORF, HERMANN. *Calvins Bedeutung für die protestantische Welt* (Leipzig, 1940).

WOLIN, S. S. "Calvin and Reformation," "The Political Education of Protestantism," *American Political Science Review*, Vol. LI, No. 2 (1957).

PURITANISM

BRAUER, J. C. "Puritan Mysticism and the Development of Liberalism," *Church History*, XIX (1950), 151–170.

CRAGG, G. B. *From Puritanism to the Age of Reason* (Cambridge, Eng., 1950).

HALLER, WILLIAM. *The Rise of Puritanism* (New York, 1939).

———. *Liberty and Reformation in the Puritan Revolution* (New York, 1955).

HILL, CHRISTOPHER. "Puritans and the Poor," *Past and Present*, No. 2 (November 1952), 32–47.

KRAPP, R. M. "A Note on the Puritan Calling," *The Review of Religion*, VII, No. 3 (March 1943), 242–251.

MOSSE, G. C. "Puritan Radicalism and Enlightenment," *Church History*, XXIX (1960), 424–437. Reprinted in S. A. Burrell (ed.), *The Role of Religion in Modern European History* (New York, 1964), 65–76.

TRIMTERUD, L. J. "The Origins of Puritanism," *Church History*, XX (1951), 31–57. Reprinted in S. A. Burrell (ed.), *The Role of Religion in Modern European History* (New York), 56–64.

WALZER, MICHAEL. "Puritanism as a Revolutionary Ideology," *History and Theory*, III (1964), 59–90. (Included in this book.)

———. *The Revolution of the Saints* (Cambridge, Mass., 1965).

Specific Countries

GERMANY

BIRNBAUM, NORMAN. "Social Structure and the German Reformation," unpublished thesis, Harvard University, 1958.

DRUMMOND, A. L. *German Protestantism since Luther* (London, 1951).

HASHAGEN, JUSTUS. "Kalvinismus und Kapitalismus am Rhein," *Schmollers Jahrbuch*, XLVII (1924), 49–72.

HINTZE, OTTO. "Kalvinismus und Staatsräson in Brandenburg zu Beginn des 17. Jahrhunderts," *Historische Zeitschrift*, CXLIV (1931), 229–286.

KAYSER, CHRISTINE R. "Calvinism and German Political Life," unpublished Ph.D. dissertation, Radcliffe College, 1961.

KÖLLMANN, W. "Frühe Industrialisierung und Reformation in Wuppertal," *Beitrag zur Soziologie der industriellen Gesellschaft* (1952), 25–32.

RITTER, GERHARD. "Why the Reformation Occurred in Germany," *Church History*, XXVII (1958), 99–106, reprinted in S. A. Burrell (ed.), *The Role of Religion in Modern European History* (New York, 1964), 28–36.

FRANCE

"Calvin et la Réforme en France," numéro spécial de la *Revue de théologie de la faculté de théologie d'Aix-en-Provence* (1944).

HAUSER, HENRI. "Les origines du capitalisme moderne en France," in his *La modernité du XVIᵉ siècle*, Cahiers des Annales, No. 2 (Paris, 1930), 69–104.

LÉONARD, E. G. *Problèmes et expériences du protestantisme français* (Paris, 1940).

———. "Le protestantisme français au XVIIᵉ siècle," *Revue Historique*, LXXII (October–December 1948), 153–179.

———. "Le protestantisme français de la Révocation à la Révolution." Positions de problèmes et bibliographie, *L'Information Historique* (1950), 134–140.

———. *Le protestant français* (Paris, 1953).

———. *Histoire générale du protestantisme*, 3 vols. (Paris, 1961).

NÜRNBERGER, RICHARD. *Die Politisierung des französischen Protestantismus und die Anfänge des protestantischen Radikalismus* (Tübingen, 1948).

ZOFF, O. *Die Hugenotten: Geschichte eines Glaubenskampfes* (Constance, 1948).

THE NETHERLANDS AND BELGIUM

BEINS, E. "Die Wirtschaftsethik der Calvinistischen Kirche der Niederlande, 1505–1650," *Niederlandsch Archief voor kergeschiedenis*, new series, XXIV (1931), 81–150.

FRUIN, R. "De wederopluiking van het Katholicisme in Noord-Nederland, omstreeks den aanvang der XVIIᵉ eeuw," *Verspreide geschriften*, deel 3 (Travenhage, 1901), 249–344.

GEYL, P. "De protestantisering van Noord-Nederland, 1930," in his *Noord en Zuid* (Utrecht and Antwerp, 1960), 150–162.

———. "Godsdienst en nationaliteitsgevoel tijdens Frederik Hendrik (1934)," in his *Noord en Zuid* (Utrecht and Antwerp, 1960), 162–173.

———. *The Netherlands in the Seventeenth Century*, 2nd ed. (London, 1961–1965).

HAUSER, HENRI. "Calvinism and Capitalism in the Dutch Netherlands," *Journal of Modern History*, X (1938), 321–343.

HILL, J. E. C. "The Ruling Classes in Holland in the Seventeenth Century," in J. S. Bromley and E. H. Kossmann (eds.), *Britain and the Netherlands* (Groningen, 1964), II, 109–132.

HYMA, ALBERT. "Calvinism and Capitalism in the Netherlands, 1555–1700," *Journal of Modern History*, X (1938), 321–343.

——. *The Dutch in the Far East* (Ann Arbor, Mich., 1962).

Koch, P. *Der Einfluss des Calvinismus und des Mennonitentums auf die Nieder-rheinische Textilindustrie* (Krefeld, 1928).

Kok, J. A. de. *Nederland op de brueklijn Rome-Reformatie* (Assen, 1964).

Kruijt, J. P. "Mentaliteitsverschillen in one volk in verband met gods dienstige verschillen," *Mens en Maatschappij*, jrg. 19 (Jan en Maart, 1943), 1–28, 65–83.

——. "Rooms Katholieken en Protestanten in Nederland, in het bijzonder in Friesland en Noord-Holland," *Sociologisch Bulletin*, jrg. 1, No. 1 (1947), 3–29.

Lejeune, Jean. *La formation du capitalisme moderne dans la principauté de Liège au XVIᵉ siècle* (Liège and Paris, 1939).

Nauta, D. *Het calvinisme in Nederland* (Franeker, 1949).

Rogier, L. J. *Geschiedenis van het Katholicisme in Noord-Nederland in 16ᵉ en 17ᵉ eeuw* (Amsterdam, 1945–1947).

Schöffer, I. "Protestantism in Flux during the Revolt of the Netherlands," in J. S. Bromley and E. H. Kossmann (eds.), *Britain and the Netherlands* (Groningen, 1964), II, 67–84.

——. "De Nederlandse revolutie," in Z. R. Dittrich *et al.*, *Zeven Revoluties* (Amsterdam, 1964), 9–29.

Smitskampf, H. *Calvinistisch national besef in Nederland voor het midden der XVIIᵉ eeuw* (The Hague, 1947).

Weiler, A. G., O. J. de Young, L. J. Rogier, C. W. Monnir. *Geschiedenis van de Kerk in Nederland* (Utrecht, 1962).

ENGLAND

Brauer, J. C. "Reflections of the Nature of English Puritanism," *Church History*, XXIII (June 1954).

Flynn, J. S. *The Influence of Puritanism on the Political and Religious Thought of the English* (New York, 1920).

George, C. H. "A Social Interpretation of English Puritanism," *The Journal of Modern History*, XXV, No. 4 (December 1953), 327–342.

——. "English Calvinist Opinion on Usury, 1600–1640," *Journal of the History of Ideas*, XVIII, No. 4 (October 1957), 455–476.

George, C. H. and Katherine. "Protestantism and Capitalism in Pre-Revolutionary England," *Church History*, XXVII (December 1958), 351–372. (Included in this book.)

——. *The Protestant Mind of the English Reformation, 1570–1640* (Princeton, N.J., 1961).

Hill, Christopher. *Puritanism and Revolution: Studies in Interpretation of the English Revolution of the Seventeenth Century* (London, 1958).

——. *Intellectual Origins of the English Revolution* (Oxford, 1965).

Knappen, M. M. *Tudor Puritanism* (Chicago, 1939).

Simpson, Alan. *Puritanism in Old and New England* (Chicago, 1955).

Wright, L. B. *Religion and Empire: The Alliance between Piety and Commerce in English Expansion, 1558–1625* (Chapel Hill, N.C., 1943).

Zagorin, P. "The Social Interpretation of the English Revolution," *Journal of Economic History*, XIX (1959), 376–401.

SCOTLAND

DONALDSON, G. "The Scottish Episcopate at the Reformation," *English Historical Review,* LV (1945), 349–369.

HIGHET, JOHN. "The Protestant Churches in Scotland: A Review of Membership, Evangelistic and Other Aspects," *Archives de Sociologie des Religions,* IV, No. 8 (1959), 97–104.

McROBERTS, DAVID. *Essays on the Scottish Reformation* (Glasgow, 1962).

MAITLAND, F. W. "The Anglican Settlement and the Scottish Reformation," *The Cambridge Modern History,* 2 vols. (New York, 1934), Vol. II.

TAYLOR, M. *The Conflicting Doctrine of the Scottish Reformation?,* 245–274.

TREVOR-ROPER, H. R. "Scotland and the Puritan Revolution," in H. E. Bell and R. L. Ollard (eds.), *Historical Essays, 1660–1750, Presented to David Ogg* (London, 1963), 78–130.

SWITZERLAND

BIRNBAUM, NORMAN. "The Zwinglian Reformation in Zürich," *Past and Present,* No. 15 (1959), 27–47.

HAURI, R. *Die Reformation in der Schweiz im Urteil der neueren schweizerischen Geschichtsschreibung* (Zurich, 1945).

SAYOUS, A. *Les placements de fortune à Genève depuis le XVᵉ siècle jusqu'à la fin du XVIIIᵉ siècle* (Brussels, 1935).

———. "Calvinisme et capitalisme à Genève," *Annales d'histoire économique et sociale,* VII (1935), 225 ff.

———. "Calvinisme et capitalisme: L'expérience genevoise," *Annales d'histoire économique et sociale,* VII (1935), 225–244.

———. "La banque à Genève pendant les XVIᵉ, XVIIᵉ et XVIIIᵉ siècles," *Revue économique internationale* (September 1934).

VASELLA, O. "Die Ursachen der Reformation in der deutschen Schweiz," *Zeitschrift für schweizerische Geschichte,* XXVII (1947), 401–427.

SCANDINAVIAN COUNTRIES

DUNKLEY, E. H. *The Reformation in Denmark* (London, 1949).

HAAG, TH. VAN. *Die apostolische Sukzession in Schweden* (Upsala, 1944).

HOFFMANN, J. G. H. *La réforme en Suède et la succession apostolique* (Neufchâtel and Paris, 1945).

———. *Les fondements historiques des Églises du Nord (Denmark, Islande, Norvège, Suède, Finlande)* (Geneva, n.d.).

HOLMQUIST, HJALMAR. "Kirche und Staat im evangelischen Schweden," *Festgabe für Karl Müller* (Tübingen, 1922), 209–277.

KJOER, J. C. *History of the Church in Denmark* (London, 1945).

SCHREY, HEINZ-HORST. "Geistliches und weltliches Regiment in der schwedischen Reformation," *Archiv für Reformationsgeschichte,* XLII (1951), 146–159.

THE UNITED STATES

BRUCE, P. A. *Economic History of Virginia in the Seventeenth Century* (New York, 1895).

HIRSCH, A. H. *The Huguenots of Colonial South Carolina* (Durham, N.C., 1928).

HUDSON, W. S. *American Protestantism* (Chicago, 1961).

JOHNSON, E. A. J. *American Economic Thought in the Seventeenth Century* (London, 1932).

KOLKO, GABRIEL. "Max Weber on America: Theory and Evidence," *History and Theory*, I (1961), 243–260.

LOUBSER, J. J. "Puritanism and Religious Liberty: Change in the Normative Order in Massachusetts, 1630–1850," unpublished Ph.D. dissertation, Harvard University, 1964.

MEANS, RICHARD L. "American Protestantism and Max Weber's Protestant Ethic," *Religious Education* (March–April 1965), 90–90.

———. "Weber's Thesis of the Protestant Ethic: The Ambiguities of Received Doctrine," *The Journal of Religion*, XLV, No. 1 (January 1965), 1–11.

MILLER, PERRY. *The New England Mind from Colony to Province* (Cambridge, Mass., 1953).

———. *The New England Mind: The Seventeenth Century* (Cambridge, Mass., 1954).

———. *Errand into the Wilderness* (Cambridge, Mass., 1956).

SIMPSON, ALAN. *Puritanism in Old and New England* (Chicago, 1955).

WEEDEN, W. B. *Economic and Social History of New England 1620–1789* (Boston, 1890).

WINTHROP, JOHN. "Model of Christian Charity," in Perry Miller and H. Johnson (eds.), *The Puritans*, 2 vols. (New York, 1938).

STUDIES ON THE RECENT SCENE IN THE UNITED STATES

ALLINSMITH, W. and B. "Religious Affiliation and Politico-Economic Attitude," *Public Opinion Quarterly*, XII (1948), 377–389.

GREELEY, A. M. "Influence of the 'Religious Factor' on Career Plans and Occupational Values of College Graduates," *American Journal of Sociology*, LXVIII (May 1963), 658–671.

GREELEY, ANDREW. "The Protestant Ethic: Time for a Moratoriam," *Sociological Analysis*, XXV, No. 1 (1964), 20–33.

JOHNSON, BENTON. "Ascetic Protestantism and Political Preference," *Public Opinion Quarterly*, XXVI (Spring 1962), 35–46.

———. "Ascetic Protestantism and Political Preference in the Deep South," *American Journal of Sociology*, CXIX (January 1964), 359–366.

LENSKI, GERHARD. *The Religious Factor* (New York, 1963).

MAYER, A. J., and HARRY SHARP. "Religious Preference and Worldly Success," *American Sociological Review*, XXVII (April 1962), 218–227.

The Spread of Protestantism in Catholic Countries

ITALY

CASSIN, HÉLÈNE. "Quelques facteurs historiques et sociaux de la diffusion du protestantisme en Italie méridionale," *Archives de Sociologie des Religions*, I, No. 2 (1965), 55–72.

MIEGGE, MARIO. "La diffusion du protestantisme dans les zones sous-développées de l'Italie méridionale," *Archives de Sociologie des Religions*, IV, No. 8 (1959), 81–96.

LATIN AMERICA

BASTIDE, ROGER. "Sociologie des missions protestantes," *Archives de Sociologie des Religions*, IV, No. 8 (1959), 47–52.

MÉTRAUX, ALFRED. "Fêtes religieuses et développement communautaire dans la région andine," *Archives de Sociologie des Religions*, VII, No. 13 (1962), 121–126.

PEREIRA DE QUEIROZ, M. I. "Mouvements messianiques et développement économique au Brésil," *Archives de Sociologie des Religions*, VIII, No. 16 (1963), 109–121.

WILLEMS, EMILIO. "Protestantism as a Factor of Cultural Change in Brazil," *Economic Development and Cultural Change*, III, No. 1 (1955), 321–333.

——. "Protestantismus und Klassenstruktur in Chile," *Kölner Zeitschrift für Soziologie und Sozialpsychologie*, XII (1960), 652–671.

——. "Protestantismus und Kulturwandel in Brasilien und Chile," in R. König and J. Winckelman (eds.), "Max Weber zum Gedächtnis," *Kölner Zeitschrift für Soziologie und Sozialpsychologie*, Sonderheft 7 (1963), 307–333. (Included in this book.)

The Analysis of Eastern Christianity in Weberian Terms

HOLL, KARL. *Gesammelte Aufsätze zur Kirchengeschichte* (Tübingen, 1927), Vol. III.

MÜLLER-ARMACK, ALFRED. *Religion und Wirtschaft* (Stuttgart, 1959).

SAVRAMIS, DEMOSTHENES. *Zur Soziologie des Byzantinischen Mönchtums* (Leiden/Köln, 1962).

——. "Max Webers Beitrag zum besseren Verständnis der ostkirchlichen und 'ausserweltlichen' Askese," in R. König and J. Winckelman (eds.), "Max Weber zum Gedächtnis," *Kölner Zeitschrift für Soziologie und Sozialpsychologie*, Sonderheft 7 (1963), 334–357.

VI. THE RELATION BETWEEN PROTESTANTISM AND THE RISE OF SCIENCE

BAINTON, R. H. "Comment on Hooykaas' 'Science and Reformation,'" *Journal of World History*, III, No. 3 (1956), 781–784.

BEN-DAVID, JOSEPH. "Scientific Growth: A Sociological View," *Minerva*, II, No. 4 (Summer 1964), 455–476.

——. "The Scientific Role: The Conditions of Its Establishment in Europe," *Minerva*, IV, No. 1 (Autumn 1965), 15–64.

CARROLL, J. W. "Merton's Thesis on English Science," *American Journal of Economics and Sociology*, XIII (1954), 427–432.

CARTER, C. F. "Economic Incentives and Consequences of Technical Invention," in A. C. Crombie (ed.), *Scientific Change* (Oxford, 1961), Symposium on the History of Science (London, 1963), 678–690.

CONANT, J. B. "The Advancement of Learning during the Puritan Commonwealth," *Proceedings of the Massachusetts Historical Society* (1939–1941).

ESPINASSE, M. "The Decline and Fall of Restoration Science," *Past and Present*, No. 14 (1958), 71–89.

FEUER, L. S. *The Scientific Intellectual* (New York and London, 1963).

GELDER, H. VAN. *The Two Reformations in the Sixteenth Century* (The Hague, 1961).

GRIFFITH, OLIVE. *Religion and Learning: A Study in Presbyterian Thought from 1662 to the Foundation of the Unitarian Movement* (Cambridge, Eng., 1935).

HALL, RUPERT. "The History of Science," in H. P. R. Finberg (ed.), *Approaches to History—A Symposium* (Toronto, 1962), 175–196.

HILL, CHRISTOPHER. "Debate—Puritanism, Capitalism and the Scientific Revolution," *Past and Present*, No. 29 (December 1964), 88–97.

HOOYKAAS, R. "Science and Reformation," *Journal of World History*, III, No. 1 (1956), 109–139.

———. "Answer to Dr. Bainton's Comment on 'Science and Reformation,'" *Journal of World History*, III, No. 4 (1957), 854–880.

———. *Humanisme, Science et Réforme* (Leiden, 1958).

JONES, R. F. *Ancients and Moderns: A Study of the Rise of the Scientific Movement in Seventeenth Century England* (St. Louis, 1961).

KEARNEY, H. F. Introduction in H. F. Kearney (ed.), *Origins of the Scientific Revolution* (London, 1964), x–xxi.

———. "Puritanism, Capitalism and the Scientific Revolution," *Past and Present*, No. 28 (1964), pp. 81–101.

———. "Puritanism and Science," *Past and Present*, No. 31 (1965), 104–110.

MASON, S. F. "The Scientific Revolution and the Protestant Reformation," in H. F. Kearney (ed.), *Origins of the Scientific Revolution* (London, 1964), 100–105.

MERTON, R. K. "Puritanism, Pietism and Science," *The Sociological Review*, XXVIII (1936), 1–30. Reprinted in his *Social Theory and Social Structure* (Glencoe, Ill., 1949), 329–346.

———. "Science, Technology and Society in Seventeenth Century England," *Osiris*, IV, No. 2 (1938).

———. "Science and the Economy of Seventeenth Century England," *Science and Society*, III, No. 1 (Winter 1939), 3–27. Reprinted in his *Social Theory and Social Structure* (Glencoe, Ill., 1949), 347–363.

ORSTEIN, MARTHA. *The Role of the Scientific Societies in the Seventeenth Century* (Chicago, 1938).

PLESNER, JEAN. "L'origine protestante de la science moderne," *Lychnos* (1946–1947), 246–248.

RABB, T. K. "Puritanism and the Rise of Experimental Science in England," *Journal of World History*, VII (1962), 46–67. Reprinted in L. M. Marsak (ed.), *The Rise of Science in Relation to Society* (New York and London, 1964), 54–67.

———. "Religion and the Rise of Modern Science," *Past and Present*, No. 31 (1965), 111–126.

RAISTRICH, ARTHUR. *Quakers in Science and Industry* (London, 1950).

ROSEN, G. "Left-Wing Puritanism and Science," *Bulletin of the History of Medicine*, Vol. XV (1944).

RUSSO, F. "Rôle respectif du Catholicisme et du Protestantisme dans le développment des sciences aux XVIe et XVIIe siècles," *Journal of World History*, III (1957), 854–880.

SCOVILLE, W. C. "Migrations and the Diffusion of Technology," *Journal of Economic History*, XI (1951).

———. *The Persecution of Huguenots and French Economic Development, 1680–1720* (Berkeley, Calif., 1960).

———. "The Huguenots and the Diffusion of Technology," *Journal of Political Economy*, LX (1952), 294–311. Reprinted in T. P. Hughes, *The Development of Western Technology since 1500* (New York and London, 1964), 50–60.

STIMSON, DOROTHY. "Puritanism and the New Philosophy in Seventeenth-Century England," *Bulletin of the Institute of the History of Medicine*, III (1935), 321–334.

———. "Amateurs of Science in Seventeenth Century England," *Isis*, XXXI (1939), 32–47.

STONE, LAWRENCE. "The Educational Revolution in England, 1560–1640," *Past and Present*, No. 28 (July 1964), 41–80.

SUFRET, R. H. "The Origins of the Royal Society," *Notes and Records of the Royal Society of London*, V (1948).

THORNER, ISIDOR. "Ascetic Protestantism and the Development of Science and Technology," *American Journal of Sociology*, LVIII (1952), 25–33.

WESTFALL, R. S. *Science and Religion in Seventeenth Century England* (New Haven, Conn., 1958).

VII. ATTEMPTS OF APPLICATION OF THE PROTESTANT ETHIC THESIS BEYOND EUROPE AND ITS CRITIQUES

General

BELLAH, R. N. "Reflections on the Protestant Ethic Analogy in Asia," *Journal of Social Issues*, XIX, No. 1 (January 1963), 52–61. (Included in this book.)

———. "Epilogue: Religion and Progress in Modern Asia," in his *Religion and Progress in Modern Asia* (New York, 1965), 168–229.

DESROCHE, HENRI. "Religion et développement, le thème de leurs rapports réciproques et ses vacations," *Archives de Sociologie des Religions*, VI, No. 12 (1961), 3–34.

KEDDIE, N. R. "Western Rule versus Western Values," *Diogenes*, No. 26 (1959), 71–96.

OTSUKA, H. "Max Weber's View of Asian Society," *The Developing Economies*, IV, No. 3 (1966), 275–298.

PAPANEK, GUSTAV. "The Development of Entrepreneurship," *The American Economic Review*, LII, No. 2 (May 1962), 46–58.

SOEDJATMOKO. "Cultural Motivations to Progress: The 'Exterior' and the 'Interior' Views," in R. N. Bellah (ed.), *Religion and Progress in Modern Asia* (New York, 1965), 1–14.

WERTHEIM, W. F. "Religion, Bureaucracy and Economic Growth," *Transactions of the Fifth World Congress of Sociology*, Washington, 1962 (Louvain, 1964), III, 73–86. (Included in this book.)

In Specific Countries

JUDAISM

GUTTMANN, JULIUS. "Max Weber's Soziologie des antiken Judentums," *Monatschrift für Geschichte und Wissenschaft des antiken Judentum*, LXIX (1925), 195–223.

KATZ, JACOB. *Tradition and Crisis* (New York, 1961).

SOMBART, S. *The Jews in Modern Capitalism* (Glencoe, Ill., 1951).

WIENER, M. *Jüdische Religion im Zeitalter der Emancipation* (Berlin, 1933).

SOUTHEAST ASIA

ALATAS, H. S. "The Weber Thesis and South East Asia," *Archives de Sociologie des Religions*, VIII, No. 15 (1963), 21–35.

JACOBS, NORMAN. *The Origin of Modern Capitalism in Eastern Asia* (Hong Kong, 1958).

PIERIS, R. "Economic Development and Ultramundaneity," *Archives de Sociologie des Religions*, VIII, No. 15 (1963), 95–101. (Included in this book.)

WERTHEIM, W. F. "Religious Reform Movements in South and South-East Asia," *Archives de Sociologie des Religions*, XII (1961), 53–62.

INDIA

DUBE, S. C. "Cultural Problems in the Economic Development of India," in R. N. Bellah (ed.), *Religion and Progress in Modern Asia* (New York, 1965), 43–55.

ELDER, J. W. "Industrialism in Hindu Society: A Case Study in Social Change," unpublished Ph.D. dissertation, Harvard University, 1959.

———. "Brahmans in an Industrial Setting," in W. B. Hamilton (ed.), *The Transfer of Institutions* (Durham, N.C., 1964), 139–164.

GOHEEN, JOHN, M. M. SRINIVAS, D. F. KARVE, and MILTON SINGER. "India's Cultural Values and Economic Development: A Discussion," *Economic Development and Cultural Change*, VII, No. 1 (1958), 1–12.

KAPP, LORE L. and W. K. "Hindu Culture and Economic Development," in W. K. Kapp, *Hindu Culture, Economic Development and Economic Planning in India* (New York, 1963), 3–20.

———. "The Hindu Social System," in W. K. Kapp, *Hindu Culture, Economic Development and Economic Planning in India* (New York, 1963), 21–40.

———. "The Retardation of Economic Development," in W. K. Kapp, *Hindu Culture, Economic Development and Economic Planning in India* (New York, 1963), 41–66.

KAPP, W. K. "Economic Development, National Planning and Public Administration," in W. K. Kapp, *Hindu Culture, Economic Development and Economic Planning in India* (New York, 1963), 67–95.

SARAN, A. K. "Hinduism and Economic Development in India," *Archives de Sociologie des Religions*, VIII, No. 15 (1963), 87–94.

SINGER, MILTON. "Cultural Values in India's Economic Development," *The Annals*, CCCV (May 1956), 81–91.

———. *Traditional India: Structure and Change* (Philadelphia, 1959).

———. "The Religion of India" (Max Weber), *American Anthropologist*, LXIII, No. 1 (1961), 150.

SINGER, MILTON. "Religion and Social Change in India: The Max Weber Thesis," *Economic Development and Cultural Change*, XIV, No. 4 (July 1960), 497–586.

JAPAN

BELLAH, R. N. *Tokugawa Religion—The Values of Pre-Industrial Japan* (Glencoe, Ill., 1957).

———. "Religious Aspects of Modernization in Turkey and Japan," *American Journal of Sociology*, LXIV (1958), 1–5.

———. "Values and Social Change in Modern Japan," *Asian Cultural Studies,* III (1962), 13–56.

BENDIX, R. "A Case Study in Cultural and Educational Mobility: Japan and the Protestant Ethic," in Neil J. Smelser and Seymour M. Lipset (eds.), *Social Structure and Social Mobility in Economic Development* (Chicago, 1966), pp. 280–310.

ISHIDA, T. "A Current Japanese Interpretation of Max Weber," *The Developing Economies,* IV, No. 3 (1966), 349–366.

MASAO, MARUYAMA. *Kokka Gakkai Zasshi* (The Journal of the Association of Political and Social Sciences), Vol. LXXII, No. 4 (April 1958).

———. *Thought and Behavior in Modern Japanese Politics* (London, 1963).

SANIEL, JOSEFA M. "The Modernization of Traditional Values in the Modernization of Japan," in R. N. Bellah (ed.), *Religion and Progress in Modern Asia* (New York, 1965), 124–149.

YAWATA, YASUSADA. "Religionssoziologie Untersuchungen zur Geschichte Japans," in R. König and J. Winckelman (eds.), "Max Weber zum Gedächtnis," *Kölner Zeitschrift für Soziologie und Sozialpsychologie,* Sonderheft 7 (1963), 358–406.

CEYLON

AMES, MICHAEL. "Ideological and Social Change in Ceylon," *Human Organization,* XXII, No. 1 (1963), 45–53. (Included in this book.)

SARACHANDRA, E. R. "Traditional Values and the Modernization of a Buddhist Society: The Case of Ceylon," in R. N. Bellah (ed.), *Religion and Progress in Modern Asia* (New York, 1965), 109–123.

THE PHILIPPINES

MCHALE, T. R. "Religion, Religious Change and Economic Development in the Philippines," *The Philippine Economic Journal*, Vol. I (1962).

MANGLAPUS, R. S. "Philippine Culture and Modernization," in R. N. Bellah (ed.), *Religion and Progress in Modern Asia* (New York, 1965), 30–42.

INDONESIA

GEERTZ, CLIFFORD. "The Development of the Javanese Economy, A Socio-Cultural Approach," Center for International Studies, MIT (mimeo., 1956).

———. "Religious Belief and Economic Behavior in a Central Javanese Town," *Economic Development and Cultural Change,* IV, No. 2 (1956), 134–158. (Included in this book.)

———. *The Religion of Java* (Glencoe, Ill., 1960).

———. *Peddlers and Princes* (Chicago, 1963).

———. " 'International Conversion' in Contemporary Bali," J. Bastran and Roelof Roobvink, *Malaysian and Indonesian Studies* (London, 1964), 289–332.

————. "Modernization in a Muslim Society: The Indonesian Case," in R. N. Bellah (ed.), *Religion and Progress in Modern Asia* (New York, 1965), 92–108.

KOCH, D. M. G. *In Mededulingen omtrent onderwerpen van olgemeen belang* (Wettevreden, 1920).

————. *Verantwoording: Even halve eeuw Indonesie* (The Hague, 1956).

MEILINK-ROELOFSCH, M. A. P. *Ancient Trade and the European Influence in Indonesia between 1500 and 1630* (The Hague, 1962).

SCHRIEKE, B. *Indonesian Sociological Studies, Selected Writings,* 2 vols. (The Hague, 1955–1957).

VAN LEU, J. C. *Indonesian Trade and Society: Essays in Asian Social and Economic History* (The Hague, 1955).

ISLAM AND ISLAMIC COUNTRIES

BELLAH, R. N. "Religious Aspects of Modernization in Turkey and Japan," *American Journal of Sociology,* LXIV (1958), 1–5.

COULSON, N. J. "The Concept of Progress and Islamic Law," in R. N. Bellah (ed.), *Religion and Progress in Modern Asia* (New York, 1965), 56–73.

EISTER, A. W. "Perspectives sur les fonctions de la religion dans un pays en voie de développement: l'Islam au Pakistan," *Archives de Sociologie des Religions,* VIII, No. 15 (1963), 35–42.

JACOBS, NORMAN. "La religion et le développement économique: le cas de l'Iran," *Archives de Sociologie des Religions,* VIII, No. 15 (1963), 43–48.

MARTHELOT, PIERRE. "L'Islam et le développement: essai sur quelques publications récentes," *Archives de Sociologie des Religions,* VII, No. 14 (1962), 131–138.

NORTH AFRICA (ISLAM)

GELLNER, ERNEST. "Sanctity, Puritanism, Secularization, and Nationalism in North Africa," *Archives de Sociologie des Religions,* VIII, No. 15 (1963), 71–86. (Included in this book.)

INDEX

Drury, Jean, 221
du Chesne, Joseph, 232
Durkheim, Émile, 47, 249, 252, 256, 348, 370
Dutch Reformed Church, 378
Dutch Republic, 259; *see also* Holland

Eastern Church, 6, 16, 18–20
economic development, secularization and, 343–365; ultramundaneity and, 252–257
economy, meaning of term, 105
Eisenstadt, S. N., 3–38, 249
Elder, Joseph, 245, 249
election, doctrine of, 212
elective and prescriptive action, 346–350
Elias, Johan E., 265
Elizabeth I, 179
empiricism, 217–222
Engels, Friedrich, 138
English (Puritan) Revolution, 88, 92, 101, 113, 141–143, 222
Enlightenment, 88, 127, 372, 374
entrepreneurship, 13, 73, 93, 244
equality, Calvinism and, 367–380
equity, law of, 107
Erasmus, Desiderius, 8
Evangelicalism, 171–172, 189–190
Evangelical Federation of Brazil, 189, 196
Evans-Prichard, E., 291
evil, Puritanism and, 116–124, 127–128
existential anxiety, 369–371

Fabri, Adhemar, 106
family structure, China, 26; Japan, 31; Latin America, 202; Puritanism and, 126
Fanfani, Amintore, 3, 5, 70, 87
Farrar, Dean, 235
Feuerwerker, Albert, 245
Fichte, Johann Gottlieb, 46
Filmer, Robert, 126
finance, Catholic versus Protestant, 7
Fischer, H. K., 68–69, 74, 76
Fischoff, Ephraim, 4, 67–81
Fludd, Robert, 231
Foster, Samuel, 230
Franklin, Benjamin, 88, 254
Frazer, Sir James G., 50
freedom, concept of, 114; fear of, 119
French Revolution, 92, 103, 107, 139
Freud, Sigmund, 71
Fromm, Erich, 70, 119
Fromondus, Libertus, 229
Fuchs, Leonhard, 213, 215
Fugger family, 8, 95, 98–99, 106
fundamentalism, 185, 372, 378–379
Funk, F. von, 69

Galen, 213, 215, 225, 227
Galileo Galilei, 218, 232–233
Gandhi, Mohandas K., 254–256
Gassendi, Pierre, 220
Gataker, Thomas, 163
Geertz, Clifford, 19, 244–248, 267–268, 309–342
Gellibrand, Henry, 220, 230, 233
Gellner, Ernest, 20, 289–308
George, Charles and Katherine, 4, 155–174
Germani, Gino, 343–365
Germany, Reformation in, 247
Gesner, Konrad von, 213
Gilbert, William, 218–219, 225, 233–234
Gillin, John L., 207
Glanvill, Joseph, 223
God, "glory of," 214–215; goodness and, 159; infinite power of, 219; revolt against, 218
Gouge, William, 164
grace, doctrine of, 227
Great Awakening, 185
Great Schism, 102
Greenham, Richard, 124
Grotius, Hugo, 266
Grubb, Isabel, 69
Gunsteren, W., 69

Hall, John, 221–222, 226, 231
Hall, Joseph, 162, 164, 168, 172–173
Hampden, John, 141
Hashagen, Justus, 78
Hauser, Henri, 87
Heinsius, Daniel, 234
Henry VII, 102
Herbert, George, 228
Hermelink, H., 69
Hexter, J. H., 136, 141
Hinayana Buddhism, 257, 271
Hinduism, 16, 18–19, 32–35, 53, 62–63, 246, 252, 255–256, 316, 323, 334, 338
Hippocrates, 213
Hobbes, Thomas, 120–123
Hoby, Margaret, 123–124
Hoby, Sir Thomas, 123
Hohenzollern family, 15
Holl, Karl, 5–7
Holland, Calvinism in, 77, 259; Catholicism in, 55; industry in, 97
Hood, Thomas, 217
Hooker, Richard, 182
Hooykaas, R., 211–235
Hudson, W. S., 4
Huet, C. B., 264
Hugenots, 5, 7, 94, 96, 98, 100
humanism, 91, 165, 194, 213, 225, 228, 231, 265, 269, 362
Hutten, Ulrich von, 99